Contemporary Educational Issues

The Canadian Mosaic

Contemporary Educational Issues

The Canadian Mosaic

Edited by

Leonard L. Stewin
University of Alberta
and
Stewart J.H. McCann
University College of Cape Breton

Copp Clark Pitman Ltd.
A Longman Company
Toronto

©Copp Clark Pitman Ltd. 1987

All rights reserved. No part of the material covered by this copyright may be reproduced in any form or by any means (whether electronic, mechanical, or photographic) for storage in retrieval systems, tapes, disks, or for making multiple copies without the written permission of the publisher.

Editing: Barbara Tessman, Pat Trant
Design: Julia Veenstra
Cover: serigraph entitled "Around the Pole" by Sheila Maki
© Sheila Maki 1985.
Printing and binding: D.W. Friesen & Sons Ltd.

ISBN: 0-7730-4688-7

Canadian Cataloguing in Publication Data

Main entry under title:

Contemporary educational issues

Includes bibliographical references.
ISBN 0-7730-4688-7

I. Education—Canada. I. Stewin, Leonard L.
II. McCann, Stewart J.H.

LA412.C66   1987   370'.971   C87-093283-7

Copp Clark Pitman Ltd.
495 Wellington Street West
Toronto, Ontario
M5V 1E9

Associated companies:
  Longman Group Ltd., London
  Longman Inc., New York
  Longman Cheshire Pty., Melbourne
  Longman Paul Pty., Aukland

Printed and bound in Canada.

CONTENTS

ACKNOWLEDGMENTS	viii
INTRODUCTION	1
1. HUMAN RIGHTS IN CANADIAN EDUCATION	7
Romulo F. Magsino, Teacher and Pupil Rights: Prospects for Change	9
Douglas Ray, Emerging Issues in Human Rights Education	23
Larry Eberlein, Legal Concerns for Classroom Teachers: Rights, Duties, and Responsibilities	38
Edward H. Humphreys, Conflicting Imperatives: Personal Privacy or Enhanced Educational Service Delivery?	55
2. THE IMPACT OF COMPUTERS IN CANADIAN EDUCATION	67
Steve Hunka, The Role of Computers in Canadian Education	69
Ronald G. Ragsdale, Computers in Canada: Communications and Curriculum	82
C. Paul Olson and E.V. Sullivan, Beyond the Mania: Critical Approaches to Computers in Education	95
3. STANDARDS AND STANDARDIZED TESTING IN CANADIAN EDUCATION	109
Verner Richard Nyberg, Educational Standards in Canada	110
Charles S. Ungerleider, Testing: Fine Tuning the Politics of Inequality	126
George Fitzsimmons, Advances in Achievement Testing: Some Implications for the Classroom	137
4. IMPLICATIONS OF ETHNIC DIVERSITY FOR CANADIAN EDUCATION	147
Ronald J. Samuda, Raymond T. Chodzinski, and Harry Marissen, Assessment and Placement of Ethnic Minorities in Canadian Education	149
Robert F. Mulcahy and Kofi Marfo, Assessment of Cognitive Ability and Instructional Programming with Native Canadian Children: A Cognitive Processes Perspective	157

Joseph E. Couture, What Is Fundamental to Native Education? Some Thoughts on the Relationship Between Thinking, Feeling, and Learning — 178
Jim Cummins, Immersion Programs: Current Issues and Future Directions — 192
Stephen Carey, The Francophone School–Immersion School Debate in Western Canada — 207
Bruce Bain and Agnes Yu, Issues in Second-Language Education in Canada — 215
Nick Kach and Ivan DeFaveri, What Every Teacher Should Know About Multiculturalism — 228

5. VALUE CONFLICTS IN CANADIAN EDUCATION — 239
William J. Hague, Teaching Values in Canadian Schools — 241
Bernard J. Shapiro and Brian K. Davis, The Public Funding of Private (Religious) School in Ontario: A Conflict in Values — 252
Goldwin James Emerson, The Teaching of Evolution and Creation in Publicly Supported Schools — 265

6. CANADIAN EDUCATION IN RELATION TO SOCIAL PROBLEMS AND ISSUES — 279
Donald C. Wilson, Social Issues in Canadian Schools — 282
Hilary M. Lips, Education and the Status of Women: A Challenge for Teachers — 293
John D. Friesen, Family and School: An Uneasy Partnership — 304
Alan R. Pence, Day Care: Changes in the Role of the Family and Early Childhood Education — 313
Edward Herold, Sex Education in Canadian Schools — 322
Larry Eberlein and Betty Mason Swindlehurst, Child Abuse and the Teacher — 338
Michael S. Goodstadt, Substance Abuse: The Role of the Educator — 355
John Rowland Young, Prejudice and Discrimination: Can Schools Make a Difference? — 370
Myrne Nevison, Counselling in a Society in Transition — 381
David Close, A Case for Teaching World Affairs in Canadian Schools — 392
John J. Mitchell, Comprehending the Danger of Nuclear War: The Role of Education — 403

7. EDUCATION FOR THE EXCEPTIONAL CHILD IN CANADA — 419
G.M. Kysela, F. French, and J. Johnston, Legislation and Policy Involving Special Education — 420

R.S. Gall, Developmentally-Delayed Children and Their Rights to Education in Canada: An Analysis of Major Contemporary Developments — 442

G. Patrick O'Neill, The Education of the Intellectually Gifted Student in Canada — 462

8. TEACHER TRAINING IN CANADA — 477

Daniel R. Birch and Murray Elliott, Towards a New Conception of Teacher Education — 479

David C. Smith, Teacher Selection, Preparation, Perspectives, and Mobility: Some Critical Issues in Teacher Education in Canada — 503

Larry Sackney, Teacher Training: An Exploration of Some Issues and a Direction for Model Development — 514

R.S. Patterson and E. Miklos, It's Time For Change in Teacher Education: Real Change This Time! — 522

9. CANADIAN EDUCATION IN THE FUTURE — 537

Michael A. Awender and A.S. Nease, Government Control of Education — 540

Lawrence M. Bezeau, The Financing of Canadian Education — 558

John D. Dennison, Community Colleges in Canada: Future Issues, Future Solutions — 569

Allan W. Hayduk, The Emergence of Distance Education From the Educational Mosaic — 583

D.W. Livingstone, Reforming Postsecondary Education: Policy Initiatives and Popular Sentiments — 591

Harvey Zingle and Lawrence Dick, Counselling and Counsellor Education in the Future — 604

David Pratt, The Owl, the Rose, and the Big Bang: Curriculum Options for the Twenty-First Century — 610

CONTRIBUTORS — 629

ACKNOWLEDGMENTS

Many individuals have contributed to the successful completion of this book. We would like to thank, first of all, the contributors who made this volume possible.

We would also like to thank every person at Copp Clark Pitman who contributed to the various stages of the publication process. In particular, we would like to thank Patrick Burke, former Executive Editor of the College Division, for his support and direction during the earlier stages of this endeavour; Brian Henderson, Executive Editor of the College Division, for supporting the project to its completion; and Barbara Tessman, our editor, for her extraordinary commitment to this project and her attention to detail. Her skill in co-ordinating the many aspects of the book production process helped bring this work to fruition.

Stewart McCann would like to thank Linda Keirstead, Atlantic Representative of Copp Clark, for her helpful suggestions, and Shirley DiPersio for carrying out several word processing tasks with efficiency and good humour. He is also thankful for the other forms of support provided by the University College of Cape Breton. Finally, he would like to express his appreciation to Mrs. Ethel McRoberts, one of his former teachers. He remains grateful to her for her outstanding teaching and her caring, stimulating, and understanding manner.

Leonard Stewin would like to extend his thanks and appreciation to Bob McCelland for his able assistance with the preliminary overviews and to Jennifer Kastendieck for typing manuscript and letters. Last but not least, he would like to thank Carol and Mike for their patience, understanding, and encouragement.

L.L.S.
S.J.H.M.
February 1987

INTRODUCTION

The impetus for this book grew from the challenge of developing, at the University of Alberta, a senior undergraduate educational issues course that was to have an interdisciplinary flavour and a firm focus on the Canadian educational milieu. In our opinion, a suitable text did not exist. During the last fifteen years, perhaps a half dozen books have been published that purportedly dwell on Canadian educational issues. We found that, for our purposes at least, the material was outdated, or the coverage was too limited in scope, or there was not a clear enough emphasis on Canadian concerns. We felt the need for a substantial book of original readings comprising the Canadian educational issues that are surfacing most often in professional journals, conferences, and symposia as well as those issues that are attracting a great deal of popular attention in newspapers, magazine articles, radio talk shows, and television documentaries.

Our book is especially intended for a senior undergraduate audience and we feel that it can be most profitably employed in educational foundations courses, sociology of education courses, Canadian studies courses, and interdisciplinary courses where the principal intent is to survey and discuss the most common, current, and pressing issues facing educators in Canada today and, in particular, facing those who are soon to enter the teaching field. The book may also prove to be beneficial as a convenient resource for inservice and professional development wherein practitioners may examine, under one cover and at a comfortable reading level, some of the contemporary issues.

Before discussing the structure of the book, a few words are in order about how the issues and the authors were selected. Through a multifaceted process including perusal of tables of content in relevant journals, examination of pertinent indexes of educational publication directories, general attention to popular media content that seemed to pertain to educational issues in a Canadian context, and varieties of editorial brainstorming, we managed to develop a rather broad list of issues we felt could be of importance to the project. Subsequently, some issues were pooled, some were subdivided, and some were made more specific. Some issues were rejected because their importance was on the wane, others were dropped because they were too localized, and many were discarded, not because they were not important educational issues, but because they were not deemed to be sufficiently "Canadian." Eventually, the issues were categorized under nine general themes, and these groups became the sections of the book. We just had to find suitable authors!

By searching the indexes of various directories and abstracting services, by surveying the contents of more recent educational periodicals, and by appealing through academic grapevines, we managed to locate potential authors who ostensibly could produce papers related to most of the issues left on our still rather lengthy short list. Each of the potential authors had to meet two fundamental criteria: each had to be an experienced author with prior publication in the area concerned with our selected topic, and each had to be affiliated with a Canadian institution of higher education.[1] In our initial contact with possible contributors, we provided a brief overview of the aim and structure of our book and asked the targeted author if he or she would be interested in producing an article on some aspect of an issue we had selected based on our needs and our knowledge of his or her interest area. We also specifically instructed potential writers to direct their efforts toward a fourth-year university audience and to feel free to bring in more general content than might ordinarily be allowed in most academic journals. The response to our requests for contributions was overwhelmingly positive, and we were enthusiastically encouraged to proceed with the book.

From the list of authors that appears at the back of the book it is apparent that we have drawn on a wealth of knowledge, expertise, and experience. Our book has been written by some outstanding academics throughout the country, from St. John's to Victoria. In addition to postsecondary appointments outside of Canada and elementary and secondary school postings both inside and outside the country, the authors have taught at over thirty of this nation's universities and colleges.

The articles chosen for the book are written from a range of perspectives and traditions reflective of the multiplicity of backgrounds and disciplines spanned by the authors. We provided only minimal orchestration for the contributors and relied on their proven competence and expertise to produce chapters that discussed the topics in whatever fashions they felt might be appropriate. The authors speak for themselves; occasional alterations were made in form but not in content.

We make no claim for an exhaustive selection of issues, but the ones chosen do appear to comprise the more dominant and current issues that have fundamentally Canadian implications, or at least implications that can be tailored for the Canadian context. No single volume can cover everything, but we did want the scope of the issues to be rather broad and diverse since the book is primarily intended for undergraduate courses where the main goal is the survey and discussion of contemporary problems and issues facing Canadian education.

The structure of the book evolved as we developed the list of suitable topics and as we received papers from our authors. The final order of sections in the book emerged somewhere in midstream, and the most appropriate sequence of papers within a section often only became apparent once all of the submissions for a section had been examined. In some cases, perhaps, arguments could be made for alternative organization, but we believe we have produced a rational and satisfying structure for the contributions we have included.

Several contributors demonstrate how the Charter of Rights and Freedoms has prompted a revaluation of a host of educational practices in Canada and, clearly, the full impact of this major constitutional change remains to be seen. In line with this current emphasis, authors in the first section of our volume deal specifically with human rights in Canadian education, discussing teacher and pupil rights, legal concerns for classroom teachers, the personal privacy issue in an educational context, and emerging issues in human rights education.

A second force having a tremendous impact on the nature of education is computer technology, which may have the potential to revolutionize both the philosophy and the practice of education in this country. The authors in our second section focus on numerous general and specific issues that we will have to address if we are to maximize the benefits of computers in education.

Perhaps in part as a result of more sophisticated means for data tabulation and analysis, and a more careful evaluation of our rights and responsibilities in education, we are increasingly aware of shortcomings in the educational experiences of some students, particularly in some social strata, and we are also more obligated to optimize the opportunities for all students. There appears to be a renewed search for excellence in education, and this has resulted in an increasing concern in Canadian education with academic standards and standardized testing. The authors in the third section discuss current standards in Canadian educational systems and the pros and cons of using standardized aptitude and achievement testing to reach educational decisions.

Canada is a complex multicultural society, and our fondness for the preservation of ethnic pluralism has created special problems for Canadian schooling systems. In Section 4, the authors examine issues arising from our ethnic diversity, such as the problem of placing students from different minority backgrounds into our educational systems, the inappropriateness of using standardized assessment procedures with minority pupils, the special considerations that must be given to Native students, the attempts to promote biliteracy through immersion programs in Canada, the maintenance of Francophone and immersion schools outside Quebec, the complexities of second-language acquisition in a culturally heterogeneous nation, and the morality and legality of our multicultural commitment.

Given the diversity of Canadian society, differences in religious backgrounds, a movement toward secularism, and a decline in respect for authority, it is not surprising that our values may be in serious conflict. The school has traditionally been viewed as one of the major inculcating agents, and, as such, it must cope with the brunt of the contemporary values controversy. Authors in the fifth section discuss issues arising from our confusion of values, morals, and rules and the implications for values education, the value conflicts related to the funding of religious private schools, and the continuing debate about the teaching of evolution and creation, which is essentially a dispute about the values of science and religion.

There is a growing consensus that the school must play a more active role in responding to a variety of social problems and issues that result from rapid changes and transitions that are occurring in our social fabric. The erosion of the family, the rise of feminism, dramatic advances in communication and transportation, the replacement of workers through automation, the quickening pace of modern life, the growing alienation of segments of our society, the reality of the global village, the pressing need for better relations between peoples, and the overwhelming scale of the arms race have cumulatively and concurrently led to social problems and issues that are becoming increasingly difficult for educators to downplay or ignore. In Section 6, the authors address the teaching of social issues, the changing relationship between the school and the family, the changing status of women and its implications for educators, the emerging crisis in preschool education, sex education in the schools, the responsibilities of educators with regard to child abuse, the role of the educator in coping with substance abuse, the issue of prejudice in Canadian schools, and the importance of teaching world affairs and making students aware of the threat of nuclear annihilation.

Changing legislation regarding human rights has made us even more acutely aware of our educational responsibilities to not only the "typical" child but also the "exceptional" child. Over the past fifteen years, we have become increasingly conscious of the desirability of affording all children appropriate educational opportunities regardless of their academic aptitude, and the Charter of Rights and Freedoms has spurred this movement. We appear to be increasingly more willing to modify our educational programs and criteria to accommodate differing student potentials. The authors in Section 7 discuss a number of educational and legal issues involving students at both ends of the academic ability spectrum.

Alterations resulting from human rights legislation, advances in computer technology, renewed interest in students and standardized testing, the implications of increasing ethnic diversity, the contemporary value conflicts in education, the school's expanded role in relation to social problems and issues, and the broadened services for exceptional children will, of necessity, lead to changes in teacher training in Canada. The authors in our eighth section examine many of the issues facing those involved in teacher education in Canada and, where possible, suggest directions for the future.

This whole book is essentially about change. The problems and issues discussed by our authors largely result from changes—changes in human rights policy and legislation, in information and transportation technology, in demographics and family patterns, in values, in the status of women, in economic conditions, in the balance of power. Education at all levels is undergoing a process of evaluation and redirection. The authors in our final section continue this theme of change by examining current developments that may have a marked influence on the future of education in Canada and also by speculating on possible scenarios in the hope that we may be somewhat more effective in approaching our educational goals in the 1990s and in the twenty-first century.

NOTES

1. In the final selection of primary authors, there was one exception. Dr. Michael S. Goodstadt is the Head of the Education Research Program at the Ontario Addiction Research Foundation. In the past, he too, though, has been an Assistant Professor in the Department of Psychology at the University of Western Ontario.

SECTION 1:
HUMAN RIGHTS IN CANADIAN EDUCATION

Since 1982, the Canadian Charter of Rights and Freedoms has served as a potent catalyst for the evaluation of human rights in various facets of our educational system. The contributors in this section examine several issues resulting from the impact of this renovation of our legal structure on the rights and responsibilities of educators and students.

Magsino traces the transformations in teachers' and students' rights and obligations that have taken place as a result of Supreme Court decisions in the United States. Drawing parallels between Canada and the United States, he concludes that a similar transitional process has been set in motion by our Charter. He points out that, even though few cases have been heard or are pending, to ensure the protection of individual rights and freedoms, future court decisions will undoubtedly have repercussions on educational practices. Magsino argues that the Charter will result in changes in policy and procedure in Canadian education even though federal courts have traditionally been reluctant to interfere with the administration of our educational system.

Ray, in discussing some emerging issues in human rights education, stresses the responsibility of the schools to foster critical examination of human rights and their violations, and to encourage the development of ways in which conflicts over human rights may be resolved. He emphasizes the promotion of human rights through developmental education, peace education, global education, and through the understanding and support of all minorities who are limited in the extent to which they can effect their own destiny.

Eberlein provides an informal discussion of the rights, duties, and responsibilities of the classroom teacher, particularly in regard to discipline, classroom management, unintentional torts or negligence, and affirmative duty to act. Since there is clearly a lack of teacher training centred on legal ramifications that might arise from teacher practices, this chapter, as an overview of legal concerns for the teacher, serves as a valuable springboard for future investigations of issues pertaining to the teacher's own position. The emphasis is on common sense, communication skills, and preplanning strategies in order to prevent situations with negative retroactive legal consequences.

The last chapter in this section addresses the conflict that is brewing as a result of the responsibility of educational institutions to provide appropriate educational services for each student and the necessity of protecting each student's right to personal privacy. Humphreys, in discussing the ramifications of these conflicting imperatives, notes that students and parents are at risk. They have become more vulnerable because of new technology and through revealing an increased amount of information about themselves in order to benefit more fully from the educational services that are available. According to Humphreys, what is at question is not the need for more accurate, complete, current, and pertinent data to govern sound educational decisions but rather the lack of policy and regulations guiding rights of access, of appeal, and of information control.

TEACHER AND PUPIL RIGHTS: PROSPECTS FOR CHANGE

ROMULO F. MAGSINO

THE LAW AND SOCIAL CHANGE

There is a recurrent controversy in legal history between those who believe that law should essentially follow clearly formulated social sentiment and those who believe that the law should create new social norms. In his pioneering study in the late 1950s, Friedmann[1] concluded that the latter had emerged triumphant. He also noted that there is a variety of ways by which the law could foster social change. A determined "individual or small minority group may initiate and pursue a legal change in the face of governmental or parliamentary lethargy and an indifferent public opinion."[2]

The United States, from the 1950s onward, provides a clear example of a society where attempts were made to bring about social and institutional changes by way of law. Consisting of nine politically independent jurists, the U.S. Supreme Court penned, with profound potential for wide-ranging changes, major constitutional doctrines related in particular to equality in race relations, administration of criminal justice, the operation of the political process, and school law.[3] Whatever the extent of changes, what is known as the Warren Court (after the chief justice, Earl Warren) opened the door for extensive societal reform through its constitutional decisions.[4] It is arguable that the present Court, dominated by justices with conservative leanings, might still turn towards judicial restraint and do no more than reflect societal sentiment. However, it has demonstrated how the law could initiate new directions for the body politic.

The reformist approach to American law attracted committed adherents among Canadian legal scholars. One prominent sympathizer was a former professor of law, Pierre Trudeau. He attributed Canada's serious political and cultural problems to inadequacies in our fundamental law and to lack of action in correcting these legal flaws.[5] Thus, as minister of justice in the Pearson government, he began his quest for change in Canada through legal reform by formulating the Canadian Charter of Human Rights in 1968. Then as prime minister, he pushed the idea of renovating the country's legal structure and, in 1982, succeeded in repatriating the Canadian Constitution with its Charter of Rights and Freedoms. The actual changes that will occur following the new Constitution and the Charter are a matter of speculation. One thing is certain, however. Trudeau's success in bringing to Canada a new

Constitution with the Charter has opened up possibilities for liberal or reformist justices to act as agents of societal change.

The functions of the Canadian federal courts are the same as those of the U.S. Supreme Court. They can define the meaning of constitutional rights provisions and resolve all questions related to the constitutional protection of individual rights. Yet, in contrast with their American counterparts, Canadian federal courts have shied away from breaking paths towards new societal policies. Legal scholars ascribe this at least in part to the absence, in the past, of constitutionally guaranteed individual rights. But, as Sedler put it,

> With the entrenchment of individual rights in Canada by the promulgation of the charter, the structures of constitutional governance established by the Canadian and United States constitutions have moved more into congruence. In Canada, as in the United States, there are now constitutional limitations on the exercise of governmental power designed to protect individual rights and, under the constitutional systems of both nations, the courts can provide relief against governmental action that they find to be violative of those constitutional provisions.[6]

Indeed, section 24 of the Charter specifically invites anyone whose rights or freedoms have been infringed or denied, to apply for remedy to a court of competent jurisdiction. As individuals respond to this invitation, the courts will have numerous possibilities of interpreting the Charter's vaguely stated provisions, though whether the courts will show a conservative or liberal temperament is a matter of debate.[7]

THE COURTS AND CHANGING ENTITLEMENTS IN EDUCATION: THE AMERICAN EXAMPLE

TEACHERS' RIGHTS

The role that courts play in altering societal perceptions and relationships shows in the U.S. Supreme Court's decisions affecting the rights of teachers. There is no question that, prior to the 1950s, it was common practice to regulate wide-ranging aspects of teachers' lives in a way that would appear offensive today. As absurd as it might seem, female teachers in the nineteenth-century U.S. were required, among other things, "not to fall in love", "to abstain from dancing", and "to consider themselves willing servants of the [school] board and the townspeople."[8]

Such requirements were part of regulations that educational systems have used to govern teachers' grooming, sexual conduct, non-curricular speech, and other behaviours. Local school boards derived their power to establish requirements and to discipline teachers from state legislation that either proscribed specific conduct or delegated broad regulatory and disciplinary authority to school boards.[9] This power was reinforced by a legal doctrine that public employment was a privilege to which the state could attach certain conditions. These conditions could be used to restrict the employee's freedoms and rights, subject only to the ill-defined limitation that such conditions be reasonable.[10]

Fortunately, teachers at public institutions have begun to receive increased protection against interferences by school boards and school officials in their professional and personal lives. In a 1967 case, the U.S. Supreme Court explicitly discredited the doctrine of public employment as privilege. In its ruling, the Court rejected, as an Appeals Court in the same case had done, the doctrine that public employment (which may be denied altogether) may be subjected to any condition, regardless of how unreasonable such condition might be.[11] This ruling has placed teachers on an equal footing with all public employees protected against unconstitutional conditions. Subsequently, teachers have won cases involving freedom of speech in the classroom,[12] freedom of speech outside the classroom,[13] personal sexual activities,[14] personal appearance,[15] and membership in controversial organizations.[16] There are, however, cases that teachers have lost involving similar issues. Although courts have strongly supported the right of teachers to express their beliefs freely in the schools, they have curtailed this right when certain state interests, such as the communication of fundamental values and the preservation of order in the schools, are involved.[17] Still, the burden of proof lies with school boards that are dismissing teachers in light of the Court's conclusion in the *Pickering* case: "A teacher's exercise of his right to speak on issues of public importance may not furnish the basis for his dismissal from public employment."[18]

Naturally, teachers' personal conduct and appearance have not always drawn support from the courts either. Particularly because of the strong influence that teachers exercise over their pupils at the elementary and even secondary levels, courts have tended to balance educational consideration against teachers' liberty. Still, Fischer and Schimmel have concluded that to dismiss teachers, it must be demonstrated that their private activity affects their ability to teach. They also have found that, "As long as his competence as a teacher is not affected, most courts hold that his private acts are his own business."[19] This is quite a departure from an earlier era when women teachers were required not to get engaged or secretly married.

STUDENT RIGHTS

About twenty years ago, a legal critic could complain that students were being treated worse than hardened criminals. While the latter had been enjoying due process rights (such as being informed of charges, having legal counsel, defending oneself at a fair hearing, etc.), students could be instantly suspended or expelled by school officials.

This differential treatment of students has been inevitably intertwined with their status as children. Until recently, children were regarded as chattels of the family and wards of the state, with no recognized political power and few legal rights.[20] To some degree, their situation was improved by the "child-saving" movement in the late 1800s and early 1900s. This movement secured legislation designed to protect children (e.g., laws regulating child labour or penalizing parents for abuse of their young) and to establish institutions for their education or reform (e.g., laws establishing compulsory schooling or juvenile court systems).[21] Yet, as Platt found, the movement so assumed the "natural" dependence and incompetence of the young that the institutions it helped establish were characterized by paternalism and use of force.[22]

To what degree American schools were influenced by the assumptions of the "child-saving" movement is uncertain. What is obvious, however, is that, in contrast with students' lack of rights or power, decision makers were permitted enormous discretion in enforcing established norms.[23] Whether deriving from the common-law doctrine of *in loco parentis*, which allowed educators as parental surrogates to determine students' conduct, or from state laws that delegated power to governmental bodies like school boards, school control over students was generally accepted. This acceptance was reinforced by judicial deference to educational authority as, in case after case, the courts upheld action or policies by educators.[24]

The landmark case paving the way for the recognition of the rights of young people in the United States is *In re Gault* handed down by the Supreme Court in 1967. The Court ruled that the fifteen-year-old boy committed by a juvenile court judge to an industrial school without observing due process requirements was unfairly treated. Young people like Gault, the Court declared, have the constitutional right to notice of charges, to counsel, to the privilege against self-incrimination, and to a hearing. Prophetically, it stated: "Neither the Fourteenth Amendment nor the Bill of Rights is for adults alone."[25]

Subsequently, the Court decided in *Tinker v. Des Moines* (1969) that children are persons under the U.S. Constitution, "possessed of fundamental rights which the state must respect." It held that students are entitled to freedom of expression of their views, unless schools can show valid constitutional reasons to regulate such freedom.[26] Then, in 1975, the Court applied the *Gault* pronouncement to the school situation. In *Goss v. Lopez*[27] it ruled that schools are required to set up hearing procedures before students can be suspended. Minimally, such procedures should include notification of the charges, presentation of evidence if the students request it, and the opportunity to argue their side of the conflict. *Wood v. Strickland*[28] showed the Court's seriousness when it held school officials liable for damages (by fine and/or imprisonment) if they maliciously abridged the civil rights of students.

Ten years after the *Goss* and *Wood* decisions, the Court seemingly executed a turnaround when it decided *New Jersey v. T.L.O.* (1985).[29] The Court ruled that a school official's search of a student's purse, based on a report that the student had been smoking, was not a violation of the student's constitutional rights. The Court differentiated between searches in non-school situations, which ordinarily would require probable cause to believe that a crime or violation of the law had been committed, and searches in school situations where legality simply requires reasonableness. However, to conclude, based on this decision, that the Court had turned around to deny students' constitutional right to privacy is erroneous. Here, the issue was simply the standard to be used in safeguarding this right. For the Court, the constitutional validity of the young's right to privacy was not contentious at all.

The status of teachers and students within American society has been transformed from what it was barely twenty or thirty years ago. It is difficult to imagine this transformation as successful had the American Supreme Court not led the way.

TEACHER AND STUDENT RIGHTS IN CANADA: EXPLORING PRESENT REALITIES

The issue of teachers' academic and civil rights has not seen much litigation in Canada.[30] Why this is so awaits a socio-historical study that has yet to be initiated. A possible explanation emerges, however, when we consider the analogous situation of students. Not too long ago, Sweezy critically observed that student cases seldom reached the courts due to immense discretionary power wielded by school authorities; to lack of precedents because lawyers, uncertain of litigation in this area, tended to settle out of court or to refuse handling school regulation disputes; and, more importantly, to a doubt that students could invoke constitutional rights to support their cause.[31] These factors, which militated against litigation of student cases, might equally have discouraged teachers from pursuing academic and civil rights grievances.

ACADEMIC AND CIVIL RIGHTS OF TEACHERS

As McCurdy observed, there are very few statutory provisions in Canada that distinguish the teacher from any other citizen, professional or otherwise, in the full exercise of academic and civil rights. In the absence of relevant distinctions, he advised teachers to assume and exercise such rights for themselves.[32] Still, we could doubt that teachers would have found it easy to follow this advice. The common-law tradition defining the school board-teacher relationship as a master-servant or employer-employee relationship,[33] where the latter party could be discharged if he or she turned out to be unfit, could be dissociated only with great difficulty from teachers' perceptions of their academic and civil liberties. This tradition has been reinforced by legislation passed by provincial governments exercising their constitutional powers over educational matters. This legislation—generally called the "Education Act" or "School Act"—establishes departments of education and school boards with wide-ranging authority. For example, in Newfoundland, the Education Act (1968) states that the powers, functions, and duties of the minister extend "to and include all matters relating to education generally" and then enumerates seventeen items under ministerial authority.[34] The Schools Act (1969) of the same province provides a lengthy list of powers and duties attributed to school boards, including the power to appoint and dismiss teachers and to implement the courses of study and texts prescribed by the minister.[35] When we relate such broad powers to the fact that most educational legislation in Canada allowed summary dismissals of teachers for cause or for such reasons as gross misconduct, inefficiency, immorality, insubordination, and the like,[36] we can understand teachers' hesitation to test the limits of their academic and civil rights. Add, on top of all this, the generally conservative tone of Canadian communities and the lack of civil rights guarantees in this country in the past,[37] and we end up with a psychologically insurmountable barrier against pursuit of academic and civil rights cases by teachers.

This is not to say that teachers have had no protection against the governmental agencies employing them. Appropriate legislation has specified procedures to validate and formalize school board-teacher contracts and relationships.[38] These procedures serve to prevent capricious and malicious actions by school boards. Thus, teachers facing the prospect of termination from service have been entitled to notice and reasons for dismissal and to inquiry by an investigating committee or a board of reference.

The courts have, consistently over the years, upheld sections of laws protecting teachers.[39] For example, in an early case, a Saskatchewan court insisted that the right to proper notice of termination is obligatory and that a teacher's being eligible for superannuation is no reason to act otherwise.[40] More recently, a British Columbia court ruled in favour of two teachers who were suspended without pay for not appearing before a school board's meeting to determine their involvement in staff problems in their school. The board, the court held, did not follow the procedures laid down in the relevant legislation.[41] In Alberta, a court that ruled in favour of a superintendent dismissed summarily declared that his school board was bound to act fairly and was under a duty to afford the superintendent a hearing.[42]

Finally, the role of teacher organizations in protecting their members against school boards has to be noted. As Nediger pointed out, teacher organizations, using collective bargaining as a powerful weapon, have brought about significant changes not only to school board-teacher relationships but also to the process of decision making on educational policies.[43] Increasingly, school boards have had to contend with guidelines established by the bargaining process. Insofar as these guidelines are mutually agreed upon by the board and the organization representing the teachers and insofar as the process is provided for in existing legislation, the courts may be expected to enforce such guidelines. Thus, in *Syrette v. Transcona-Springfield S.D. No. 12*, a Manitoba court decided in favour of a teacher dismissed in contravention of a collective bargaining agreement, then in force, that disallowed termination of any teacher's contract during the year.[44]

Yet, in spite of fairly heavy litigation pitting school boards against teachers, academic and civil rights cases have seldom reached Canadian courts. Seventeen years ago, McCurdy saw potential for litigation in relation to teachers' rights to select and assign controversial or "objectionable" readings in literature classes.[45] So far as can be ascertained, this potential has not been actualized,[46] although one related case has been recorded. This involved the right of a teacher to speak out publicly against her teachers' union. Urged to engage in an illegal walkout by the union, she wrote two letters to a local newspaper editor, both critical of the conduct of the meeting that resulted in the walkout. When the union's professional committee found her guilty of unbecoming conduct and recommended a reprimand, she went to court to quash the decision. The court ruled in her favour.[47]

Lately, however, one sector in the field of education seems to be gaining the dubious distinction of engaging in active pursuit of litigation involving the right of teachers to conduct their personal lives as they see fit. A substantial segment in most provinces, Catholic school systems appear to be insisting on their right to determine the qualifications of their teachers in the face of increasing libertarianism in Canadian society. This insistence received support from the court in *Re Essex County Roman Catholic Separate School Board and Porter*. This case involved two teachers discharged by the school board for having entered into civil marriages. When a board of reference ordered their reinstatement, the school board contested the order before the courts and finally received vindication from the Ontario Court of Appeal. Justice Zuber stated categorically, "... If a school board can dismiss for cause, then, in the case of a denominational school, cause must include denominational cause."[48] However, this Ontario decision was not echoed in similar, earlier Newfoundland cases in which the court did not find any need to refer to the notion of "denominational cause." In *Re Stack and the R.C. School Board for St. John's*, the court referred the case of a divorced Catholic teacher back to the arbitration board that had, in an earlier ruling, accepted the school board contention that it had the constitutional right to hire and fire for denominational reasons. The court ruled that the arbitration board had the duty, not simply to accept the school board contention, but to make a determination of the validity of the dismissal as mandated by the province's Collective Bargaining Act.[49] In a subsequent case, *Re R.C. School Board for Conception Bay North and the Newfoundland Teachers' Association*, a Catholic teacher who married an Anglican in an Anglican ceremony won her grievance against the school board that had fired her. The court found that the school board had dismissed her on the basis of an invalid by-law and in violation of an existing collective bargaining agreement between the school board and the Newfoundland Teachers' Association.[50]

Nevertheless, a recent Supreme Court (Trial Division) decision, which is being appealed, confirms the right of a denominational school board to impose its denominational requirements on its teachers. *In the Matter of NTA and Richard Walsh* involved a teacher who was hired to teach by the Roman Catholic School Board for St. John's when he was a Catholic. Subsequently, he joined the Salvation Army and got married in that church. He was fired and contested the school board action. In ruling for the school board, the court agreed with the Arbitration Board's finding that he had been employed to teach in a Roman Catholic school; that, by his own act, he eliminated his occupational qualification; and that, therefore, the school board's decision had to be upheld.[51]

The landmark judgment in recent years, however, is *Caldwell v. Stuart* in British Columbia. A Catholic teacher on a yearly contract, Caldwell married a divorced Methodist in the latter's church's ceremony. Contesting her subsequent dismissal for marriage outside of her church, Caldwell appealed to the highest court in the land. She contended that the school board action violated the non-discrimination clause (section 8) in the British Columbia Human Rights Code. The Canadian Supreme Court declined, however, to support her contention. The Court, examining the Code's section 22 (exempting non-profit religious organizations that operate primarily for the welfare of its members), reasoned as follows:

> The purpose of the section is to preserve for the Catholic members of this and other groups the right to the continuance of denominational schools. This, because of the nature of the schools, means the right to preserve the religious basis of the schools and in so doing to engage teachers who by religion and by the acceptance of the Church's rules are competent to teach within the requirements of the school. This involves and justifies a policy of preferring Roman Catholic teachers who accept and practise the teachings of the Church. In my opinion..., the dismissal of Mrs. Caldwell may not be considered as a contravention of the *Code* and the appeal must fail.[52]

Unfortunately, the import of the *Caldwell* decision is not clear for teachers in denominational schools in other provinces. How the Court would rule on a subsequent case based on an appeal to the freedoms guaranteed by the Charter remains a tantalizing question.

STUDENT RIGHTS

The interrelationship between students and educational authorities is defined by both legislation and common law, which has been articulated by the courts in the course of time. Legislation such as Education Acts, Schools Acts, and School Attendance Acts specifies student entitlements against educational systems. With respect to such legislation affecting students, the role of the courts has been to interpret contentious provisions brought to their attention through litigation. To date, fairly heavy litigation is evident concerning students' rights to attend school, to transportation, and to reasonable care and protection in school or while engaged in school-sponsored activities. Interesting litigation has also occurred concerning the right of children to refuse or receive religious instruction in schools.[53]

Apart from interpreting provisions in educational statutes, courts have also been asked to rule on cases involving student conduct that can be resolved by use of common-law principles. In Canada, the common-law concept of *in loco parentis* underlies much current practice related to the control of students. Basically, this concept involves a delegation of parental authority to teachers and includes both the power to suspend or expel from school and the authority to administer corporal punishment. Combined with the necessity for maintaining order in and about the school, *in loco parentis* has justified an educational authority's power to control the conduct of pupils, limited only by the restraints that the law and the courts place upon it. Generally, courts do not interfere with this power unless the reasonableness of the power exercised is questioned. It is in this regard, however, that most litigations occur.[54]

There has been little litigation on the civil rights of students. This does not mean that no contentious incidents involving students' civil rights have arisen. Mackay cites an incident at Forest Hill Collegiate where students were prevented by the principal from holding a debate on the rights of high school students. Following this, students satirized their principal in the student newspaper. Subsequently, the principal had the newspaper confiscated and a distributing student instantly suspended. When students protested in the school corridor, they were forced outside, and two more students were suspended. Mackay also refers to a recent case involving twenty-four Grade 10 boys at the Bev Facey Composite High School who were subjected to a strip search by the principal and vice-principal to recover a stolen watch. In both cases, a storm of protest raged. Yet no litigation was initiated.[55] Legal scholars might have criticized educational authorities for proscribing student styles of dress and grooming[56] and for banning high school political clubs,[57] but the factors cited by Sweezy[58] earlier might easily have dampened initiative on the part of the students and their parents.

At least four relevant cases appropriate to our discussion have been litigated, however. A fairly recent pre-Charter case in Quebec involved three students who were expelled by school commissioners for dealing in drugs at school. The expulsion was decided by the commissioners in the absence of the students, who were not informed of the details of the charges or given the opportunity to defend themselves. Judge Vallerand of the Superior Court of Quebec reinstated the students, overturning the commissioner's action which, he believed, violated the rules of natural justice.[59] Whether, in this judgment, Judge Vallerand was influenced by the due process cases in the United States is an interesting question.

A second, unreported case related to a student's right to wear blue jeans and a T-shirt in school. Predictably, the court held that the principal, who banned the wearing of such attire, was acting within his authority.[60]

A third case worth mentioning is *Ward v. Board of Blaine Lake School Unit No. 57.* An eleven-year-old boy was suspended for refusing to cut his hair in accordance with a school board resolution defining the maximum hair length for male students. When the boy and his mother appealed to nullify the resolution and the suspension, the court confirmed the board's authority to pass the resolution and the principal's power to suspend the pupil for defying the resolution. In handing down the judgment, the court lengthily traced the common-law statutory bases for its conclusions. This ruling did not remain unnoticed, however. In a critical article, Hunter sought to demonstrate that the court relied erroneously on a general provision of the relevant provincial education law that stated: "...*Subject to the other provisions of this Act,* [the board may]...exercise a general supervision and control over the schools of a unit."[61] Set aside was another, pertinent provision of the same act that specifically provided for procedures and valid reasons for expulsion. Hunter thus concluded that the courts had lent assistance to the increasing encroachment by the educational system on what would have been considered an individual and family decision.[62]

The fourth, recent case in British Columbia seems to indicate greater concern for just treatment of young people. In this case, a thirteen-year-old girl was suspended from October until the end of the academic year for smoking marijuana. The suspension was based on the school board's discipline policy, which allowed a school to suspend a pupil immediately for using narcotics for up to the remainder of the school year or for a minimum of five school months. The court, ruling in favour of the girl, declared the policy invalid. It pointed out that the policy's minimum of five months suspension and the absence of "due warning" requirements did not conform to the province's School Act and its regulations, which require kind and judicious discipline as well as the use of procedural fairness in disciplining students.[63]

RIGHTS IN EDUCATION: CHANGE IN THE OFFING?

That courts render judgments to support consciously or unconsciously a school system's encroachment into individual and family rights makes for a contentious claim. Yet there is no doubt, as Bargen observed, that Canadian courts have not made it their habit to interfere in the administrative affairs of educational systems. In general, they have seen fit to intrude only when these systems show lack of conformity to statutory or constitutional provisions. This judicial restraint, together with the absence of definitive declarations guaranteeing civil rights for Canadians, may partially account for a generally dim view of teachers' and students' rights.

The Charter of Rights and Freedoms may be seen as an attempt to remedy the latter situation. The declaration in section 2 guaranteeing fundamental freedoms of conscience and religion, belief and expression (including freedom of the press), peaceful assembly, and association may provide teachers and students a greater measure of autonomy in varied areas of school life. Intent on testing the boundaries of their newly declared entitlements, teachers feeling constraints in the school system may initiate action related to assigning controversial, "objectionable" materials for home study or projects; discussing and expressing their positions on sensitive topics like creationism versus evolution, sex, abortion, etc.; publicly criticizing school policies; the inclusion of "objectionable" books in classroom resource centres or in libraries, and the like.

Moreover, despite the unclear status of the right to privacy in Canada,[64] teachers may appeal (perhaps in conjunction with section 2) to section 7 of the Charter concerning their right to the personal conduct of their lives.

Students may equally see the Charter as the basis of new rights and freedoms in the classroom. As Bergen has pointed out, a substantial number of Charter provisions may relate to the liberties and protection of young people in the school.[66] Sections 2 (fundamental freedoms), 7 (life, liberty, and security of person), 8 (unreasonable search and seizure), 9 (arbitrary detention), 10 (rights of persons arrested or detained), 11 (rights of persons charged with offences), 12 (cruel and unusual treatment or punishment), 15 (equal protection and benefit without discrimination on the basis, for example, of age), 23 (minority language rights), and 28 (preservation and enhancement of the multicultural heritage of Canadians), are likely to attract test cases.

The fact remains, however, that there is no infallible way to predict how Canadian courts will interpret relevant Charter provisions where teachers' and students' rights are at issue. Because the Charter provisions are couched in general terms, their application to specific situations requires interpretation by the courts themselves, particularly the Supreme Court.

Despite some insistence that courts remain a stronghold of objective, impartial decision making, it is true that members of the judiciary are human beings who have socio-political perspectives that respond from time to time to the societal climate. As concerned participants in the educational process, educators and young people might profitably get involved in the discussion of educational and socio-political issues. The more members of the judiciary develop an appreciation of public sentiments, the closer their decisions may be to such sentiments.

The greater contribution that educators and students can give relates, however, to the task of examining present educational policies and arrangements. There is no doubt that members of the judiciary do not wish to act as superintendents of the nation. But they do not hesitate to interfere in the field of education when some participants therein are behaving in unreasonable ways. Thus educators and students must evaluate existing policies and arrangements in order to justify, modify, or replace them in conformity with acceptable standards of reasonableness. The shock and apprehension that followed judicial intervention in education in the United States during the last three decades need not be experienced in this country.

NOTES

1. W. Friedmann, *Law in a Changing Society*, abridged ed. (Harmondsworth: Penguin Books, 1964).
2. Ibid., 25.
3. Archibald Cox, *The Warren Court* (Cambridge: Harvard University Press, 1968).
4. For a critical appraisal of the Warren Court, see Alexander Bickel, *The Supreme Court and the Idea of Progress* (New York: Harper Torchbooks, 1970).
5. David Milne, *The New Canadian Constitution* (Toronto: James Lorimer, 1982), 14.
6. Robert A. Sedler, "Constitutional Protection of Individual Rights in Canada: The Impact of the New Canadian Charter of Rights and Freedoms," *Notre Dame Law Review* (forthcoming).
7. Even as arrangements are being made for the publication of this chapter in the present volume, events are already unfolding that would indicate that the Supreme Court, through its decisions on litigated cases, will be active in interpreting Charter provisions. For a good account of this development, see T.A. Sussell and M.E. Manley-Casimir, "The Supreme Court of Canada as a National School Board: The Charter and Educational Change," *Canadian Journal of Education* (forthcoming).
8. David Schimmel and Louis Fischer, "On the Cutting Edge of the Law," *School Review* 82 (Feb. 1974), 262.
9. David Schimmel and Louis Fischer, "Project. Education and the Law: State Interests and Individual Rights," *Michigan Law Review* 74 (June 1976), 1455.
10. David Schimmel and Louis Fischer, "Developments in the Law—Academic Freedom," *Harvard Law Review* 81 (March 1968), 1065.
11. *Keyishian v. Board of Regents*, 385 U.S. 589 (1967).
12. *Keefe v. Geanakos*, 418 F. 2d 359 (1969).
13. *Pickering v. Board of Education*, 391 U.S. 563 (1968).
14. *Morrison v. State Board of Education*, 1 C. 3d 214 (1969).
15. *Finot v. Pasadena City Board of Education*, 58 Col. Rptr. 520 (1967).
16. *Keyishian v. Board of Regents*.
17. Schimmel and Fischer, "Project," 1465.
18. *Pickering v. Board of Education*, 391 U.S. at 573.
19. Louis Fischer and David Schimmel, *The Rights of Students and Teachers* (New York: Harper and Row, 1982), 135.
20. Hillary Rodham, "Children Under the Law," *Harvard Educational Review* 43 (Nov. 1973), 489.
21. Margaret Rosenheim, "The Child and the Law" in *Child Development and Social Policy*, vol. 3, edited by Bettye Caldwell and Henry Riccuiti (Chicago: University of Chicago Press, 1973), 515–520.
22. Anthony Platt, *The Child Savers* (Chicago: University of Chicago Press, 1969).
23. Hillary Rodham, "Children Under the Law," 490.
24. Richard Berkman, "Students in Court: Free Speech and The Functions of

Schooling in America," *Harvard Educational Review* 40 (Nov. 1970): 567–577.
25. *In re Gault*, 387 U.S. 1 at 13 (1967).
26. *Tinker v. Des Moines Independent Community School District*, 393 U.S. 503 at 511 (1969).
27. *Goss v. Lopez*, 419 U.S. 565 (1975).
28. *Wood v. Strickland*, 420 U.S. 308 (1975).
29. *New Jersey v. T.L.O.* No notation available at time of writing. Copy from Public Information Office of the Supreme Court of the United States.
30. Sherburne McCurdy, *The Legal Status of the Canadian Teacher* (Toronto: Macmillan of Canada, 1968), 155.
31. Gilmour Sweezy, "Free Speech and the Student's Right to Govern his Personal Appearance," *Osgoode Hall Law Journal* 7 (1969): 297–299.
32. McCurdy, *Legal Status of the Canadian Teacher*, 150.
33. Ibid., 159.
34. An Act Respecting the Department of Education, S. Nfld. 1968, c. 58.
35. An Act Respecting the Operation of Schools and Colleges in the Province, S. Nfld. 1969, c. 68.
36. Fortunately these legislative provisions have been increasingly stricken out and replaced by guidelines reached through collective bargaining agreements.
37. Refer, for example, to the Supreme Court judgment in *Saumur v. City of Quebec and A.-G. Quebec* (1953), 4 D.L.R. 641 at 665–6.
38. McCurdy, *Legal Status of the Canadian Teacher*, 68–95.
39. Indication of this can be found by surveying the cases abstracted in Canadian Teachers' Federation, *Schools, Teachers and the Courts*, Fourth Draft (Ottawa: CTF, 1981).
40. *Metcalfe v. Board of Trustees of Moose Jaw District No. 1* (1938), 2 D.L.R. 726.
41. *Johnstone v. Langley School District No. 35 Board of School Trustees* (1979), 12 B.C.L.R.
42. *McCarthy v. Calgary R.C. Separate School District No. 1 Board of Trustees*, [1979] 4 W.W.R. 725.
43. W.G. Nediger, "The Impact of Collective Bargaining on Financial Gains and Management Rights in Canadian Education" (paper presented at the CSSE Annual Conference in 1981).
44. *Syrette v. Transcona—Springfield S.D. No. 12* (1976), 67 D.L.R. (3d) 568.
45. McCurdy, *Legal Status of the Canadian Teacher*, 150.
46. In his study Wayne Mackay notes that, so far, there is little case law on academic freedom issues. See Wayne Mackay, *Education Law in Canada* (n.p.: Emond-Montgomery Publications, 1984), 279.
47. *Re Busche and Nova Scotia Teachers' Union* (1975), 62 D.L.R. (3d) N.S. 330.
48. *Re Essex County Roman Catholic Separate School Board and Porter* (1977), 89 D.L.R. (3d) 445 at 447.
49. *Stack and Roman Catholic School Board for St. John's* (1979), 99 D.L.R. (3d) 278.
50. *Re Roman Catholic School Board for Conception Bay North and the Newfoundland Teachers' Association*. Supreme Court of Newfoundland, 1983.

51. *In the Matter of NTA and Richard Walsh*, Supreme Court of Newfoundland (Trial Division), January 1986 (not yet reported).

52. *Margaret Caldwell and Director, Human Rights Code of B.C. v. Ian Charles Stuart and A.G.B.C. Supreme Court of Canada*, photocopy, 32.

53. Canadian Teachers' Federation, *Schools, Teachers and the Courts*.

54. Peter Bargen, *The Legal Status of the Canadian Public School Pupil* (Toronto: Macmillan of Canada, 1961), 115.

55. A. Wayne Mackay, "The Canadian Charter of Rights and Freedoms: Implications for Students" (Paper presented at the National Educational Policy Conference in Vancouver, B.C., held 1–3 June 1983), 1–2.

56. Gilmour Sweezy, "Free Speech."

57. Robert Kerr, "Commentary on Constitutional Law—Political Rights and High School Political Clubs," *Canadian Bar Review* 50 (1972): 347–352.

58. Sweezy, "Free Speech," 294–302.

59. Judge C. Vallerand. "Expulsion of Students Went Beyond Routine Discipline," *The Gazette* (Montreal) 5 June 1980, 14.

60. *Choukalas v. St. Albert Separate School Board and Petheridge*, 1 Aug. 1962 (unreported).

61. William Hunter, "Case Comment—School Board Regulation Relating to Dress and Grooming," *Saskatchewan Law Review* 36 (1972): 479-483 at 480.

62. Ibid., 483.

63. *Taylor v. Board of School Trustees of School District No. 35*, discussed in Judith Anderson, "Board's Pupil Suspension Policy Declared Invalid," *The Canadian School Executive* (February 1985), 22.

64. Mackay, *Education Law in Canada*, 274–275.

65. Section 7 of the Charter reads: "Everyone has the right to life, liberty and security of the person and the right not to be deprived thereof except in accordance with the principles of fundamental justice."

66. John Bergen, "Rethink your Treatment of Students," *Canadian School Executive* 3 (Feb. 1984): 13–15.

EMERGING ISSUES IN HUMAN RIGHTS EDUCATION[1]

DOUGLAS RAY

This chapter examines the definition, scope, method of, and resources for human rights education in Canada. The debate about the validity of human rights education is examined from the perspective of four current philosophies underlying curricular decisions. Some legal issues are examined, including traditional human rights protections and those that may emerge as a result of appeals based on the Canadian Charter of Rights and Freedoms. Since the standards or arguments that are respected elsewhere in the world influence Canadian thinking, the chapter concludes with an examination of certain international issues that are relevant to the Canadian scene. The conclusion identifies some current research that is relevant for our thinking about human rights.

This chapter reflects data from a 1984 survey of human rights education conducted in eight provinces and the territories, and pertinent information from influential Canadian and international authors. The content of human rights education is identified, but there are notes on justifications, limitations, and methodology, and the interdisciplinary nature of resources is stressed.

Human rights education, as it has emerged in Canadian society, has a political and legal impetus deriving from the constitutional debates, several court cases based on the Charter of Rights and Freedoms, and recent discussions of the roles of provincial human rights commissions. One aspect of human rights education is to promote awareness of these key legislative and jurisdictional issues.[2]

Ministries of education, school boards, faculties of education, and teachers' federations evince a "school based" interest in human rights issues and how they may be discussed most effectively. They expect discussion of international events, problems, and approaches to result in comparisons and evaluation. They do not rely exclusively upon federal or provincial documents.

Teachers see the age or maturity of pupils to be vital in determining strategy and selecting appropriate examples.[3] Young children are rarely taught human rights as a subject, but teachers try to ensure that it is reflected in most school or social activities (e.g., it is *wrong* to discriminate on the basis of sex, race, or disability). This kind of lesson is conveyed in games and other school-controlled activities as well as in the formal curriculum. Although this "atmosphere approach" is continued into secondary schools, at this level specific subjects introduce issues calculated to involve and transform the students' perceptions.[4]

Teachers are advised to be scientific and to select appropriate examples rather than ephemeral trivia,[5] to involve students in meaningful appraisals of events,[6] to move beyond an exchange of opinions to mastery of expert advice on public policy,[7] and to introduce particular themes at the most effective moment.[8] Consequently, pre-service and in-service programs for teachers are vital to the success of human rights education.[9] Although a 1984 survey of teachers in most parts of Canada revealed that many of them were interested in training courses reflecting human rights, few had such opportunities. In 1985, only Nova Scotia had human rights as a requirement in teacher education, and only some faculties elsewhere offered optional courses.

In universities and community colleges, many disciplines offer a specialized approach to human rights education: women's studies, the rights of the accused and convicted, workers' compensation, and the right to work. The interests of the teachers in their own political and economic environment—specifically academic freedom and tenure—may result in these topics being discussed as case studies of vocational rights.

In this chapter, however, the emphasis will be on education in school because this seems to be the means by which public policy can most effectively be communicated to the population, and because none of the 1984 interviews revealed opposition or indifference to human rights education in the schools. In fact, most curriculum directors believe that their official programs promote awareness and respect for various rights, with some attention to challenges to rights in Canada or elsewhere. Protection of rights is considered to be vital civic behaviour in a democracy,[10] and such ideas have to be promoted. The most serious threats or infringements of human rights in Canada need to be examined.

Documents that list and define human rights are drawn upon as appropriate to the age of the pupils and the purposes of a particular subject. The most important international sources are the Universal Declaration of Human Rights (1948) and subsequent United Nations declarations and covenants. Certain historical documents such as Magna Carta, the American Constitution and Bill of Rights, and speeches such as "The Four Freedoms" are still vital. Canadian documents like the Charter of Rights and Freedoms, the Bill of Rights, provincial charters and codes, and certain other legislation are drawn upon for many classes. Several teachers employ sacred books and great literature for discussing human rights, because legal documents are not usually comprehensible in the original wording.

Within Canada, there are commonly acknowledged current and historical events that violated or denied certain rights to particular persons.[11] Canadians differ on remedies for these violations. One of the most important aspects of human rights education is the discussion of means for resolution of such differences of opinion. Many Canadians hold views about fairness or justice that do not correspond with the law. There are various processes by which citizens are able to change the law, and it is possible that they will receive official support for their efforts to win remedies. Human rights education, particularly in higher education, may even advise citizens how to participate effectively in selected struggles for rights: for women, children, the aged, language groups, ethnic or racial minorities, particular occupations, or the disabled.

DOUBTS CONCERNING EFFECTIVE INSTITUTIONALIZATION OF HUMAN RIGHTS

The school curriculum can transform what children know with considerable speed. What they value and how they act are not so easily changed.[12] Perhaps it is just as well. For forty years most educators have been reluctant to impose beliefs upon their students, hoping that providing knowledge and skills for addressing problems would promote independent thinking and resistance to facile ideologies. "Brain washing" and "indoctrination" seemed repulsive to the liberal educator. Several "value neutral" systems of exploring issues rather than imposing solutions were devised.[13]

But were these retreats from clearly held and perceived principles justified? Could the schools *lead* rather than merely respond to society? These questions were posed and answered convincingly by several giants of educational thought, most of whom agreed that teachers (and education as a whole) should affirm and reflect a consistent set of moral principles.[14] It is this positive affirmation that gives denominational schooling its special cachet. Perhaps unfortunately, public schools are often defined in negative terms by detractors who claim that, without religious instruction, they lack any moral conviction.[15] Supporters of public schooling take the opposite tack and propose that understanding, appreciation, or toleration are vital for Canadian society. Early attempts at publicly financed education (by Strachan and Ryerson, for example) were often efforts to impose the educator's own religious convictions, but eventually a broader perspective emerged.[16]

Human rights offer a means to make more rational the diversified public, denominational, linguistic, and ideologically based schools of Canada. If constraints were placed upon private schools (probably coupled with grants to induce them to conform), their curriculum and perhaps their teacher selection would fall under public scrutiny.[17] The most divisive aspects of their activities would be curtailed, but not necessarily their capacity to appeal to different interests.[18] The possibility that individual teachers abuse their roles *within public schools* remains: periodically episodes underline the danger to children, to society, and to the reputation of professional education.

The challenge is how to devise and operate a system of education that is flexible, responsive, and responsible; it is not acceptable to maintain complex security checks of all that transpires within individual classrooms.[19] Proposals assume the participation of pupils, professionals, parents, and the interested public. The reconciliation of different perspectives is complex, and human rights education would likely serve only as a framework within which diversity would be variously justified and promoted.

Not all Canadians are convinced that human rights are best promoted by government intervention.[20] To some, the periodic election of governments at the local, provincial, or federal level is the best protection—and almost the only one required. An alert and aroused electorate will "turf the rascals out" if they threaten traditional rights.[21] According to conservative interpretations of promoting rights, autocratic authorities or bureaucratic bunglers are a bigger threat to freedom than many direct challenges to it. By this reasoning, human rights commissions restrict the right of managers to run their businesses; equal rights or minimum wage regulations undermine competitiveness, prosperity, and, in the long run, jobs. Similarly, traditional parliamentarians argue that ordinary legislation is more appropriate than entrenched constitutions and codes that, over time, lose their congruence to the emerging situations.[22] Perhaps the most obvious example of this viewpoint has been the continuing reluctance of most provincial governments to entrench official language rights.

Although these debates among theorists and parliamentarians may not reflect the typical views of the public, this subject has not been systematically investigated.

WHO KNOWS WHAT IS BEST FOR THE CHILD?

Some balance must be found among the conflicting claims that the best interests of the child lie in:
1. freedom to develop, unrestrained by conventions;
2. firm but loving guidance from the family;
3. professional management of learning situations; or
4. respect for eternal truths devised through the ages.

Recent Canadian and international experience includes some indication why a balance among these ideals is appropriate. The period from the late 1960s to 1975 saw a return to progressivism and a brief flirtation with the "freedom promotes growth and responsibility" thesis, with mixed results. Few schools were able to demonstrate that effective, let alone maximum, learning was ensured when there was great freedom and diversity. Perhaps more attention to *demonstrating* what was learned would have helped, but the era encouraged behaviour that saddened and alarmed traditionalists. Perhaps the ideals of schools like Summerhill were unrealistically high. At any rate, the risk of perceived failure led educational systems to tighten controls, reduce the proportion of optional courses in secondary and higher education, add examinations, and require more attention to the basics.[23] Although this official recentralization dismisses the argument for more personal autonomy by the learner, there remains a degree of selection among a range of course alternatives and some freedom of study and evaluation modes. "The best interests of the child" is still officially upheld but, except for very mature students, it is likely to be identified and exercised on behalf of pupils by a parent or professional educator.

The family has traditionally been the official safeguard for the child's best interests. In fact, The Universal Declaration of Human Rights (1948) proposes that "parents have a prior right to choose the kind of education that shall be given to their children."[24] A Quebec case (*Chabot v. Les Commissaires d'Écoles de Lamorandière*) ruled that parents had the right to prevent religious exercises from being imposed upon their child, citing in natural law "the Authority of the father to guide and govern the education of his child."[25]

This is not the same as controlling, providing, or censoring of course. Censoring particular subjects or sources of information, or avoiding particular teachers may be extreme forms of parental choice, which for most situations are not practical because of restricted educational resources. Imperfect though existing opportunities may be, they are usually worthy of students' time and effort and pose no threat to the "full development of their human potential."

Neglect of children, or making choices that restrict educational opportunities, is not the worst offence committed by some parents. The Badgley study reveals that an alarming number of families offer more dangers than protection in sexual offences: "about one in two females and one in three males have been victims of unwanted sexual acts. About four in five of these incidents first happened to these persons when they were children or youths."[26] A great many of these incidents happened in the home, and the offenders were family members or trusted friends of the family. Children of single-parent families were often particularly vulnerable.

Physical abuse within the family is no longer tolerated. "A man's home is his castle," but even within that castle wife and children are theoretically protected by the possibility of legal action against abusers. Court procedures are available to remove children from families that pose dangers to their safety, development, and emotional health.[27] Increasingly, the schools plays a role in alerting authorities to risks of this kind, which is a very vital extension of human rights education.[28] Never before have teachers been named so explicitly as protectors of the child's best interests. It goes far beyond the professional or academic respect that had traditionally led parents to defer on many issues.

The right of the school authorities, especially of the principal and teachers, to manage all aspects of the learning process has now been effectively challenged. The law still gives professionals the authority to maintain discipline and teach without interference by the community,[29] but *realpolitik* has made it necessary to listen to the parents and the community.[30] Students in blue jeans or unorthodox hair cuts are no longer automatically presumed to challenge the system, so they are usually tolerated. This aspect of principals' authority, although still on the books, is eroding through disuse and through a natural reluctance to engage in political or legal arguments related to relatively minor aspects of school responsibility.[31]

The fourth justification of particular educational practices—"eternal truths" or "timeless traditions"—varies according to the group being considered. In Canada this has necessarily promoted compromise as various groups sent their children to the same schools. It is not easy to insist that the traditions of Ireland, Italy, India, Israel, and Indiana be simultaneously observed. Social relationships among the students become one means of questioning long established ways. It may even be that particular traditions are illegal in Canada.[32] The growing diversity of the Canadian population has made it less possible to insist on exclusively British traditions in any province, and even an officially French Quebec proves to be elusive.[33]

Canada has officially embraced multiculturalism for the federal jurisdiction, and many provinces have accepted a similar stance. The administration of multiculturalism requires viable ethnic or cultural groups to devise educational programs to which the government can lend support rather than ongoing state sponsorship for any particular group (even those buttressed by aboriginal status or "founding nations" credentials, which have assured funding from various sources). Although groups may be assured that their language will be taught where appropriate and their culture will be included in the social studies programs, no group will be able to exclude other languages or cultures from the curriculum. No single language or culture will be able to assimilate and dominate all others.[34] Although these interpretations of the meaning of various provincial legislation and regulations may not be upheld in every judicial decision, they seem to be the current mode. For example, the language policy proclaimed in 1984 for the Northwest Territories assures the rights of English, French, and six native languages. These types of policy go some distance in ensuring the group rights of the populations concerned. More aspects of human rights may in time become a significant part of education.

LEGAL ISSUES

The courts have always been important in interpreting grey areas of legislation and practice, such as defining the rights of parents, students, and teachers within the context of education. This was particularly true in the period before human rights codes and the Charter of Rights and Freedoms.[35] Decisions have an influence far beyond the particular criminal or civil cases that are actually litigated, for each ruling is taken as a general guide for other similar situations. Teachers' federations, trustees' associations, faculties of education, and sometimes other groups such as religious organizations ensure that judicial findings of particular importance have a wide audience. Recent findings often reveal human rights to be a vital part of school management and teachers' personal rights.

The test of fairness is a recent example. Basically, it requires that the process used to arrive at a decision that is of great importance to an individual must have been *fair*: for example, information could not be suppressed or protected from reasonable challenge, there must have been opportunity to seek advice and to weigh consequences, the plaintiff cannot also act as the judge, etc. The test does not ensure that decisions will be reversed, only that unfair procedures will be struck down, in effect guaranteeing a new trial or an automatic appeal.[36] Most schools fail to provide appeal procedures for minor student infractions, apparently leaving themselves vulnerable to the test of fairness.[37] Until recently, when the courts have ruled on teachers' or principals' supervisory decisions, they have endorsed the right of the authority to decide, rather than the correctness of particular actions. For important matters, there has always been the protection of the appeal to the school board and even to the minister of education.

The test also applies to disputes involving teachers and their boards. For example, no tenured teacher could be disciplined or dismissed for an unsubstantiated complaint. The appeal board might also rule that the case was properly proven but that the penalty was inappropriate.[38]

Schools were once operated on authoritarian lines. Teachers had authority *in loco parentis* in almost every situation as it arose. If they proved unnecessarily brutal, they could be charged with assault, but such legal actions were seldom successful.[39] Their relationships with students were occasionally exploitive, but only in extreme cases were there likely to be challenges. The schools operated very much like the traditional family, where secrets were seldom revealed. This is changing: students may successfully assert their rights against physical abuse, sexual harassment, psychological intimidation, and discrimination.

Many such disputes are heard by professional boards with quasi-judicial standing, which make neither criminal nor civil judgments. In some important criminal or civil cases (like rape, narcotics, assault, etc.), quasi-judicial boards may determine separately the professional consequences for a teacher (i.e., loss of job, removal of certificate, etc.).[40] Teachers are among the few Canadians who are thereby subject to double jeopardy—they can be punished twice for the same offence.[41]

A noteworthy example came in Alberta where the professional decisions (by the Board) to fire James Keegstra and (by the Minister) to revoke his teaching certificate preceded the decision to lay criminal charges of promoting hatred against a particular group of persons.[42] More commonly, the professional decisions follow the disposition of a criminal charge or lawsuit and will be influenced by the outcome of that trial. It would be unusual to dismiss or decertify a teacher who had received an absolute discharge or a court's finding of not guilty.

The personal life of a teacher is subject to an unusual degree of public scrutiny and potential official interference. Education acts invariably require teachers to lead respectable lives, and denominational school boards may legally require teachers to follow sectarian requirements.[43] Interpretations vary, but teachers have lost their jobs for living with persons who were not close relatives or legal spouses, whether such persons were of the same or opposite sex.[44] So far as is known, teachers no longer lose their jobs for refusing sexual favours to board members or senior administrators.[45]

Another interpretation of teachers' personal freedom is illustrated by the case of Joanne Young. Her principal declined to give her permission to participate (with loss of pay) in political demonstrations because a substitute would have been required, and Young might have been arrested for some offence. Young acted without permission, repeatedly and despite warnings to abide by her contract. She demonstrated at nuclear installations, Litton Industries, and city halls. In 1984 she was fired. She claimed that the nature of her political convictions was the reason for the principal's denials of permission and her ultimate dismissal. She also claimed that a higher duty than to her pupils required her to protest against the military-industrial establishment. An arbitrator who heard her appeal against suspension rejected her claim.[46] Other ways must be found by teachers who wish to be participants in political activities.

INTERNATIONAL ISSUES

No country can ignore events or ideas just because they occur beyond its borders. Most Canadians probably feel a sense of shame that Canada declined requests to help threatened Jewish populations of Europe before and during World War II.[47] They have been subsequently more generous with respect to refugees from Hungary, Uganda, Vietnam, and now Nicaragua. Most Canadians feel that merely offering sanctuary to survivors of a military, political, social, or economic catastrophe is inadequate, so they regularly support various efforts to avert such events. Because military intervention may be required, Canadian peacekeepers or observers frequently have been posted abroad, particularly for United Nations actions. "Intervention" may be much less obvious, such as in the diplomatic disapproval (and even certain forms of sanctions) to protest racism or other forms of discrimination in such countries as Rhodesia (now Zimbabwe) and South Africa. Financial assistance and various forms of technical aid are available in selected cases, and these forms of assistance can promote a degree of reform.

Systematic programs to reduce racism and other forms of discrimination by the United Nations, or the United States, Britain, France, Canada, and various other nations, raise vital academic, judicial, and political issues.

Because few topics are more compelling in the field of human rights education, these are mentioned in appropriate courses, discussed in current affairs, become the focal points of school projects, and occasionally influence career decisions. In several cases, the formal analyses have been supplemented and even supplanted by artistic interpretations, as novelists, musicians, painters, choreographers, and cinematographers tackled the great issues.

Relief of the distress of famine, earthquake, flood, etc., is another potential objective of human rights education. It is currently focussed upon Ethiopia, but other regions may quickly emerge. The critical aspect of this type of education is that it should not be restricted to band aids for consequences when the international behaviour of governments, the private sector, non-governmental organizations, and many individuals may be exacerbating the situation. Education that starts with human rights can quickly branch into development education, peace education, or global education. It is equally likely that educational programs that start with one of these other themes also address human rights very quickly. The categories blur and most educators address as many of them as appropriate to their audience and the particular discipline.

Canadians preoccupied with jurisdiction may be surprised to learn that all the provinces and the federal government have agreed to surrender to international agencies a degree of sovereignty in human rights. The authority for this intervention is most explicit in the optional protocol to the International Covenant on Civil and Political Rights (1966), which became binding for Canada a decade later. The implication was that victims of human rights violations in Canada could bring their cases to the attention of an international committee set up by the United Nations, which could investigate and propose remedies. A grievance against Canada has already been received and disposed of, although the response by Canada may prove to be less than satisfactory.[18]

RECENT RESEARCH AND ITS IMPLICATIONS

Social and educational research in Canada dispels many comfortable but mistaken views about the fundamental and even-handed justice of Canadian society. Translating research findings into effective political or social reforms has proven to be discouraging, however. For example, there can be no doubt that women are disadvantaged in Canadian society. They customarily receive less than men for doing the same job (see table 1).

The explanations for why women have been or should be financially disadvantaged have been challenged: women are not usually working to gain luxuries; they do not needlessly interrupt their participation in the work force; they do not court or receive special advantages because of their sex; they do not lack qualifications.

TABLE 1
CANADIAN WORKERS' ANNUAL INCOME (1976)

Occupation	Female	Male	Female Income as a Percentage of Male Income
Managerial	12 299	23 145	53.1%
Clerical	7 852	12 656	62.0%
Processing/ Machining	8 462	13 704	61.7%
Transport	8 827	14 191	62.2%

Source: Women's Bureau, Ontario Ministry of Labour, *Women in the Labour Force* Fact Sheet 2, n.d.

To dispel such myths, human rights education must be directed at a very large slice of Canadian society. The immediate solutions to the problems lie in the hands of business owners and governments, both often arguing that a competitive advantage can best be maintained by holding the line on current salaries. A preoccupation with inflation leads to general cutbacks in education and hiring, making it very difficult for women to achieve educational, economic, or social equality.

The issue of qualifications has some relevance. Research has shown that women are discouraged from taking high school courses in mathematics and sciences, which of course denies them entry into several high prestige, high income professions. This is too simple an explanation of the disadvantaged position of women in the labour force, however, for women *with qualifications* are still bypassed. Recognizing this historical discrimination, a few administrations have undertaken affirmative action programs. In 1984, Saskatchewan identified women, Native persons, and persons with disabilities for affirmative action programs. In 1985, the University of Western Ontario strengthened its "equal opportunity" policies to "affirmative action," expecting to increase the proportion of women hired. The implication for human rights education seems to be that women should not be channelled into traditional female courses and occupations; women should be encouraged to compete in traditional male occupations; and there should be attempts to compensate for the effects of class discrimination with special remedial programs wherever necessary.

Multiculturalism masks a host of oppressions. Disadvantages are faced by several other "minority groups," such as Native Canadians, racially, religiously, and linguistically distinguishable cultural minorities, persons with

TABLE 2
GRADUATE DEGREES AWARDED, 1981
SELECTED PROGRAMS IN CANADA

Field of Study	Total	Female
Education	3145	1542
Fine and Applied Arts	223	118
Humanities	1859	1030
Social Sciences	4767	1595
Science, Agricultural and Biological	609	229
Engineering and Applied Sciences	1036	88
Math/Physical Science	698	111
Medicine/Dentistry	229	87

Source: *Fall Enrolment in Universities* (Ottawa: Statistics Canada, 1981), 81: 204.

disabilities, and sometimes those defined by geography, occupation, or economic status. Elliott defined minorities not in terms of their numbers—which for women constitute slightly more than half the population—but for their capacity to affect their own destiny.[49]

Native persons, whether Indian, Inuit, or Metis, have long endured systematic deprivation. At one time, Indians were denied status as citizens. Now they are often denied the dignity of jobs, the capacity to direct the education of their own children, the right to make business decisions independently. They appear to provoke particular vigilance on the part of police and judicial authorities. Their despair is reflected in high rates of alcoholism, suicide, and family violence.[50]

No doubt many Canadians consider that the disadvantaged are the authors of their own misfortunes. They believe that persistence, pluck, talent, and virtue will inevitably triumph. The other explanation is that those born with the silver spoon in their mouths will seldom use it to feed others. Neither stereotype is entirely true. The implication for human rights education seems to be that a two-pronged approach is justified. For each disadvantaged group, a focussed systematic educational program should be mounted to deal with that group's typical shortcomings for participation: upgrading of general education or specific skills, devising human relations skill training, building self-esteem. These affirmative action programs are envisaged as an important means of lessening discrimination.[51] It is important to remember, however, that *individuals* within a group may not be best served by group programs.[52]

The second part of the strategy must address the education of other Canadians, particularly those who are in positions to decide how minorities will be treated in the community group. If citizens, employers, and policy makers continue to shun and demean minorities, if they avoid their role in offering a chance to prove competence, disadvantage will continue in Canada.[53]

NOTES

1. The author wishes to acknowledge the contribution of four colleagues who read and commented upon this paper: Maryann Ayim, David Radcliffe, Judson Purdy, and Gregory Dickinson.
2. Edwin Webking, "Using the Charter of Rights and Freedoms as a Tool for Teaching Civics" in *Teaching Human Rights*, edited by Marshall William Conley (Wolfville, N.S.: Acadia University Centre, 1984), 80–110.
3. James Brown, "Individual Development for Peace Education: A Prosocial Approach" in *Peace Education: Canadian and International Perspectives*, edited by Douglas Ray (London, Ont.: Third Eye, forthcoming), 77–91.
4. J. Kehoe, "An Examination of Alternative Approaches to Teaching the Universal Declaration of Human Rights," *International Journal of Political Education* 3 (1980): 193–204.
5. Ruth Whitehead, "Current Events for a Broader Context" in *Peace Education*, edited by Ray, 127–141.
6. John Kehoe, "Strategies for Human Rights Education" in *Human Rights in Canadian Education*, edited by Douglas Ray and Vincent D'Oyley (Dubuque, Iowa: Kendall Hunt, 1983), 53–67.
7. Webking, "Using the Charter of Rights and Freedoms as a Tool for Teaching Civics."
8. Judith Torney-Purta, "Socialization and Human Rights Research: Implications for Teachers" in *International Human Rights, Society and the Schools*, edited by Margaret Stimmann and Judith Torney-Purta (Washington: National Council for the Social Studies, 1982), 35–48.
9. J. Roby Kidd and Douglas Ray, "Life-long Education: An Emerging Human Right" in *Human Rights in Canadian Education*, edited by Ray and D'Oyley, 53–67.

10. Thomas R. Berger, *Fragile Freedoms: Human Rights and Dissent in Canada* (Toronto: Clarke Irwin, 1981).

11. See, for example, the cases discussed by Berger, ibid.

12. L. Ehman, "The American School in the Political Socialization Process," *Review of Educational Research* 50 (1980): 99–119.

13. For example, L. Kohlberg, "The Cognitive-Developmental Approach to Moral Education," *Phi Delta Kappan* (June 1975): 670–677; and Merrill Harmin et al., *Clarifying Values Through Subject Matter* (Toronto: Holt Rinehart and Winston, 1973).

14. George S. Counts, "Should the Teacher Always Be Neutral?" *Phi Delta Kappan* (Dec. 1969): 186–89; Martin Kaplan, "The Most Important Questions," *Oxford Review of Education* 3, 1 (1977): 89–94; Tom L. Beauchamp, *Ethics and Public Policy* (Englewood Cliffs, N.J.: Prentice-Hall, 1975); Edgar Faure et al., *Learning to Be: The World of Education Today and Tomorrow* (Paris: UNESCO, 1972); Joseph Lauwerys, ed., *Ideals and Ideologies* (London: Evans Brothers, 1968).

15. Neil G. McCluskey, S.J., *Public Schools and Moral Education* (New York: Columbia University Press, 1958).

16. Neville V. Scarfe, "The Aims of Education in a Free Society" in *Social Foundations of Canadian Education*, edited by Anand Malik (Scarborough, Ont.: Prentice-Hall, 1969), 7–26.

17. Bernard J. Shapiro, *The Report of the Commission on Private Schools in Ontario*, (Toronto: Office of the Commission, 1984).

18. Committee on Tolerance and Understanding, *Final Report* to the Minister of Education for Alberta (The Ghitter Report) (Edmonton: Ministry of Education, 1984), 104–18.

19. Ibid., 18–103.

20. Douglas Ray, "Human Rights in Canadian Education" in *Human Rights in Canadian Education*, edited by Ray and D'Oyley, 213–226.

21. The confidence in the protection of an aroused electorate is reflected in Section 33 of the Canadian Charter of Rights and Freedoms, which ensures that legislation enacted notwithstanding, violation of the Charter can stand for only five years, thereby giving the electorate a guaranteed opportunity to vote on that government's record.

22. This debate is reported well by Roy Romanow, "Reworking the Miracle: The Constitutional Accord of 1981," *Queen's Law Journal* 8, 1–2 (Fall-Spring 1982–83): 74–98.

23. Naomi Hersom, "The British Columbia Core Curriculum: A Case Study in Recentralization" in *Canadian and Comparative Educational Administration*, edited by R. Farquhar and I. Housego (Vancouver: University of British Columbia, Centre for Continuing Education, 1980), 107–114; Derek J. Allison, ed. *The Yellow Papers: The Recentralization of Canadian Education* (London, Ont.: Faculty of Education, University of Western Ontario, 1984); and Bernard J. Shapiro and Hugh A. Stevenson, "Teacher Education: Opportunities in the Steady State" in *The Education of Teachers in Canada* (Yearbook of the Canadian Society for the Study of Education), edited by D.A. MacIver (Edmonton: University of Alberta, 1978), 3–10.

24. The Universal Declaration of Human Rights (1948), Article 26, 3.
25. A. Wayne Mackay, *Education Law in Canada* (Toronto: Emond Montgomery Publications, 1984), 65.
26. Robin F. Badgley et al., *Sexual Offences Against Children*, 2 vols. (Ottawa: Ministry of Supply and Services, 1984), 175.
27. Ibid., 541-49; "Man is Jailed for Assaults at Group Home," *Globe and Mail* (23 Sept. 1983), 10.
28. Mackay, *Education Law in Canada*, 194-96.
29. Ibid., 279-80.
30. Anthony Burton, "The Rights of Teachers" in *Human Rights in Canadian Education*, edited by Ray and D'Oyley, 23-37.
31. Mackay, *Education Law in Canada*, 301-03.
32. John Kehoe "Strategies for Human Rights Education," 71-72.
33. Douglas Ray, "Human Rights and Multiculturalism: Education and Cultural Minorities in Canadian Schooling" in *Teaching Human Rights*, edited by Marshall Conley (Wolfville, N.S.: Acadia University Centre, 1984), 32-60.
34. J.R. Mallea, "Introduction: Cultural Diversity and Canadian Education" in *Cultural Diversity and Canadian Education: Issues and Innovations*, edited by John R. Mallea and Jonathon C. Young (Ottawa: Carleton University Press, 1984), 9-15.
35. See, for example, Peter Bargen, *The Legal Status of the Canadian Public School Pupil* (Toronto: Macmillan, 1961); Frederick Enns, *The Legal Status of the Canadian School Board* (Toronto: Macmillan, 1963); and Sherburne G. McCurdy, *The Legal Status of the Canadian School Teacher* (Toronto: Macmillan, 1968).
36. Mackay, *Education Law in Canada*, 31-33.
37. John J. Bergen, "Should Schools Provide Appeal Procedures for Disciplined Students?" *Challenge in Educational Administration* 21, 2 (Jan. 1982): 17-24.
38. The test of fairness originated for Canadian dismissal procedures in a disciplinary action against a probationary police constable who was not given a fair opportunity to defend himself. He lost the action in the subsequent "fair hearing."
39. Mackay, *Education Law in Canada*, 85-92.
40. McCurdy, *The Legal Status of the Canadian School Teacher*; Mackay, *Education Law in Canada*.
41. It should be noted that suspension, dismissal or suspension of certificate may be regarded as non-punitive but as protection for the students and society against incompetence or other hazards.
42. Mackay, *Education Law in Canada*, 279-80.
43. Ibid., 271-72.
44. Ibid., 271.
45. Ibid., 267.
46. *In the Matter of an Arbitration Between: Huron County Board of Education, and the Ontario Secondary School Teachers' Federation and Mrs. Joanne Young*, Ian A. Hunter, chairman of the board of arbitration, London, 1984.
47. Irving Abella and Harold Troper, *None is Too Many. Canada and the Jews of Europe 1933-1948* (Toronto: Lester and Orpen Dennys, 1982).
48. Sandra Lovelace, born a Malacite Indian, married a white man and thereby lost her Indian status as then stipulated in the Indian Act. Subsequent to her divorce,

she sought to re-establish her Indian status, which could then only be accomplished by marriage to an Indian. This discrimination was an injustice that was apparently beyond remedy in Canada, but when requested by the United Nations Human Rights Committee to find a solution, a new initiative was taken federally. See Walter Surma Tarnopolsky, *Discrimination and the Law in Canada* (Toronto: Richard de Boo, 1982). As a result, the Indian Act no longer strips women of their Indian status if they marry non-Indians. The status of those who previously lost their legal claim to Indian rights is now determined by band councils, which may fail to act.

49. Jean Leonard Elliott, ed., *Minority Canadians: Immigrant Groups* (Scarborough, Ont.: Prentice-Hall, 1971).

50. *Indian Conditions: A Survey* (Ottawa: Department of Indian Affairs and Northern Development, 1980); and Jean Leonard Elliott, *Two Nations, Many Cultures: Ethnic Groups in Canada* (Scarborough, Ont: Prentice-Hall, 1979).

51. Canada Act, 1981, 15.

52. Aaron Wolfgang, "Intercultural Counselling: The State of the Art" in *Multiculturalism in Canada: Social and Educational Perspectives*, edited by Ronald J. Samuda, John W. Berry, and Michael Laferrière (Toronto: Allyn and Bacon, 1984), 418–32.

53. Ray, "Human Rights and Multiculturalism," 54–55.

LEGAL CONCERNS FOR CLASSROOM TEACHERS: RIGHTS, DUTIES, AND RESPONSIBILITIES

LARRY EBERLEIN

Teachers beware—students have rights! When individual teachers infringe on these rights, they are taken to court. Few teachers concern themselves with issues of legal responsibility, but teachers do get sued for their school activities. Yet those courtroom appearances are not a topic covered in most teacher education programs or in the average textbook. One exception is Bargen[1] who made a careful analysis of school law for school administrators in relation to the rights and responsibilities of pupils. This paper will look at these issues and hopefully heighten teachers' awareness of and sensitivity to potential problem areas.

There has been a noticeable trend in recent years to recognize more rights for Canadian students. This paper will consider student rights—but in the context of the rights, duties, and responsibilities of the classroom teacher. Of particular concern will be a teacher's authority to act and the problems encountered when teachers intentionally interfere with a student's freedom. This usually happens in disciplinary and classroom management situations. Also of concern will be the unintentional torts or wrongs done to students through carelessness or negligence, a problem that occurs when a teacher causes an accident through lack of due care. In conjunction with this we will also consider a teacher's affirmative duty to act, such as in playground supervision or in a medical emergency.

There are other important legal issues that will not be discussed here because of lack of space or because they have been covered elsewhere. Some of these issues have seen extensive development in the U.S. and are of relevance to teachers. For example, the presence of discrimination in testing, ability grouping, discipline, or special education is receiving active attention.[2] Behaviour modification programs are extremely important in education and have serious and complex legal implications.[3] One such issue, informed consent, will be discussed later. When behavioural programs are experimental in nature or when there are risks to the child, special care must be used to gain this informed consent. Reward contingencies do not raise the same concerns as long as the child is not denied rights or privileges generally provided the rest of the students.

Another important contemporary issue is the teacher's role in child abuse, incest, and family violence.[4] In some provinces teachers are by law placed on the "front line" and legally expected to report suspected cases to the authorities, perhaps even by-passing the principal.

What of a student's right to privacy or to be secure against unreasonable searches? For years many courts in the U.S. have recognized that students, their school lockers or dorm rooms are not to be searched by school authorities without permission.[5] Recently the U.S. Supreme Court held that students have a constitutional right to privacy and set out the proper standard for searches conducted by public school officials.[6] At least one Canadian court has held that a school principal does not have the right of search and seizure.

In the past few years the U.S. Congress has become sensitive to the public school's invasion of a family's privacy. The Family Educational Rights and Privacy Act of 1974 requires parental consent to many teaching and counselling situations including testing and behavioural modification experiments.[7] These are of uncertain status in Canada where children until recently have not had a real right to an education.[8] Whether the new Charter of Rights and Freedoms will be interpreted to give children rights similar to those granted in the U.S. remains to be seen, but there is some hope for children's rights in this area.[9] The Supreme Court is only now hearing the first cases under the Charter.

TEACHERS' AUTHORITY

Teachers have a solid basis for their authority to act in the classroom, particularly in disciplinary situations. There are three basic sources of this authority for control of student behaviour: the common-law doctrine of *in loco parentis*, provincial school acts, and the Canadian Criminal Code.

IN LOCO PARENTIS

This is a legal concept that gains its definition from the common law. It refers to a person who has been put in a situation of a lawful parent by assuming the obligations incidental to the parental relationship, but without the formalities of a legal adoption. It embodies both the idea of an assumption of parental rights and the discharge of parental duties.[10] In usage it commonly refers to parental surrogates during a child's minority years. These include step-parents, foster parents, or the relationship of master-apprentice.[11] When applied to education the concept defines, in a limited and ambiguous way, the relationship between student and teacher.[12]

Traditionally when a parent delegated authority over a child to school personnel, the parent could restrict the actions of school officials and withdraw the authority at any time. With the advent of compulsory education this tradition is no longer recognized. Today, most public school personnel will listen to parent requests regarding their children and may even solicit their help. In actual fact the school has the final say and parental restrictions do not have to be honoured.[13]

When discussing corporal punishment, writers[14] and courts[15] assume the doctrine gives educational personnel the right to discipline and control. Hawkins[16] asks what happens when the teacher believes in striking a child but the parent does not. Under the *in loco parentis* doctrine, no striking would be permitted. Yet no court has refused permission to teachers for reasonable control and discipline, including striking the child. The doctrine does, however, restrict the degree of authority to something less than the latitude or discretion allowed a parent. This means that the teacher does not have the same authority as a parent to exercise lay judgment when dealing with treatment of injury or disease. *Guerrieri v. Tyson*[17] involved two teachers who immersed a child's infected finger in scalding water against the child's will. The court held the teachers liable for damages since the doctrine did not extend beyond the question of discipline.

PROVINCIAL SCHOOL ACTS

The real authority of school personnel stems from provincial legislation rather than from the common-law doctrine of *in loco parentis*. For example, section 368 of the pre-1970 School Act in Alberta required a certificated teacher to "maintain proper order and discipline." This section was eliminated in the 1970 revision but is probably covered in section 65 of the revised act, which authorizes a board of trustees to "make rules for the administration, management and operation of schools" and also to "settle disputes between a parent or child and a teacher or other Board employee." Section 146 permits teachers and principals to suspend pupils and the board to expel them. Section 167 makes parents, as well as students, responsible for intentional or negligent damage to school property.

Long[18] discusses the Ontario Act and regulations, which require the teacher to "teach diligently and faithfully the classes or subject assigned to him by the principal," a duty that will be covered later under the topic of teacher malpractice. Long also points out that regulations require teachers to carry out duties of supervision as assigned by the principal and "to maintain, under the direction of the principal, proper order and discipline in the classroom and while on duty in the school and on the school ground."

It should be clear from reading these few sections that parents cannot restrict rights of school personnel by simply saying, "You can't punish or suspend my child!" The rights to take action come from statutory authority and not from the delegation of parental authority. Similar statutes exist in all provinces.[19] It is for this reason that a large group of North American legal scholars, attempting to codify the common law in this regard, concluded that teachers are public officers and do not act as delegates of the parents.[20] When public officers are in charge of the education or training of a child, they have a privilege to use force or impose reasonable confinement, unrestricted by a parent's prohibitions or wishes. Teachers act for the government or school board in carrying out public policy.

CANADIAN CRIMINAL CODE

Two sections of the Criminal Code of Canada also presently provide a degree of legal authority to school personnel.

> 26. Every one who is authorized by law to use force is criminally responsible for any excess thereof according to the nature and quality of the act that constitutes the excess.
> 43. Every schoolteacher, parent or person standing in the place of a parent is justified in using force by way of correction toward a pupil or child, as the case may be, who is under his care, if the force does not exceed what is reasonable under the circumstances.[21]

These provisions, and their earlier antecedents, have long been used as the basis of the claim of privilege that is made by school officials in Canada when dealing with issues of assault and false imprisonment. No Canadian court has yet faced the issue of the *Baker* case[22] where a parent tried to prevent a school from using corporal punishment. The Court rejected the idea that the mother alone could determine whether her child could be corporally punished. Two years later, in 1977, the U.S. Supreme Court officially sanctioned the use of corporal punishment as a disciplinary measure in schools.[23] In the U.S., before administering corporal punishment, the following requirements must be met:

1. Written rules must be provided specifying the exact offences that led to corporal punishment.
2. The explicit offence must be serious enough to merit corporal punishment (nothing vague like "insubordination").
3. Except for the most serious case, another alternative must be tried first.
4. The failure of the alternative must be documented.
5. When alternatives fail, another warning must be given.
6. Punishment must be administered in front of a witness who is informed of the reason and agrees to be listed as a witness on an official document.
7. Written records must be maintained in detail.
8. Written guidelines about the severity and nature of punishment must be prepared in advance.

There is a decided trend away from corporal punishment in modern education and there is no longer as much need for such rules. The Law Reform Commission of Canada[24] is of the view that corporal punishment may violate the new Charter provisions. In any case, the Commission is proposing changes in the Criminal Code that will have the effect of eliminating corporal punishment from Canadian education.[25] Even though Canadian courts are not likely to formalize these rules, it still makes good psychological sense for students to be aware of the rules and the systems of reward and punishment that are operative in the school, whether or not corporal punishment is involved. It is also important that the system be applied consistently.

INTENTIONAL INTERFERENCE WITH STUDENTS

Like all people in our society, children and students are legally protected from the wrongful conduct of others, including parents and teachers. The recent public attention given to child abuse is but one illustration of this. Through regimentation and discipline, the freedom of students at school is more controlled than in most homes. This control often involves intentional interference with the student, including physical punishment and restrictions on freedom of movement. The most obvious acts which would raise questions had they occurred in other than a school setting are assault and false imprisonment; when unreasonable, these actions have legal consequences. As Barnes points out, "Assault may be committed by the application of unreasonable force, by improperly searching the person of a child, or by improperly subjecting a child to punishment such as standing in the corner. Unlawful detention of a child after school may constitute...false imprisonment."[26]

In addition to these acts, there are often other forms of physical contact between teacher and students. These range from a well-intentioned pat on the behind or an arm around a student to gross physical or sexual abuse. Some contact may be welcomed and acceptable in the lower grades only to become unwanted and problematic in junior or senior high school. Teachers should keep in mind that any unwanted physical touching constitutes an assault. Unless justified by consent or permitted by a teacher's legal authority referred to earlier, this action could lead to a civil lawsuit or criminal charge. In such cases, the teacher's certificate is also often suspended or revoked.

Another intentional wrong that teachers need to consider is defamation—especially when they are writing or speaking about their students. Defamation is a false statement that would cause a person to be shunned, avoided, or discredited.[27] Truth is one defence against such an action, but most teachers would find it difficult to show the truthfulness of rumours they repeat. More generally, when teachers are acting within the scope of their employment, they are protected by the doctrine of qualified privilege. This would protect them, for example, when discussing a student with the principal or counsellor.

Finally, a fairly recent addition to the legal responsibilities now recognized by courts is discussed by Linden.[28] This is the intentional infliction of mental suffering, as in a practical joke. Liability has usually been recognized when there has been extreme and outrageous conduct, even when no malice was intended. Needless to say teachers should not become involved in the hazing incidents or practical jokes that often occur in schools.

INFORMED CONSENT

With the exception of approving criminal activity, people can consent to intentional interference with their personal interests. Obvious examples are riding in an elevator or going to sporting events where one would expect to be bumped by the crowds. Hockey players agree to be checked according to the rules of the game and thus give consent to what otherwise would be an assault. But consent, to be valid, must be real consent, voluntarily given by one who understands the nature and consequences of the activity involved. Thus the hockey player does not consent to a game where players are hit over the head with a hockey stick. Also the Grade 1 student cannot give consent to an emergency appendectomy no matter how necessary.

This issue is of greatest importance in behaviour modification programs often used in conjunction with classroom management procedures.[29] Although teachers can use reasonable time-out or other punishment techniques as a one-time disciplinary control measure, to be safe, teachers should obtain the consent of both child and parent before using the techniques on an on-going basis. If not related to discipline, consent is essential. The consent should be in writing, should specify the nature of the program, contain a description of the purpose, risks, and effects of the plan, and contain a statement of the right of the child and/or the parent to terminate consent at any time.

The age of consent presents real problems, and there are differences of opinion among Canadian legal authorities about the appropriate age. For example, Linden suggests "young children cannot give a valid consent; their parents must do so on their behalf."[30] Klar suggests that the law is not this clear.[31] While agreeing that young children cannot consent, older children do regularly consent in a variety of situations in schools. Teachers regularly control or restrict a child's behaviour and other students have physical contact in the course of play activity. Klar suggests that minors probably have a greater power to consent or not consent than has been often recognized. He also suggests that there are limits to which parents may consent on behalf of the child, when physical acts to which the child objects are involved.

An allied area is the *misuse* of consent forms. For example, in preparation for a field trip, teachers may request a slip from home to absolve the school and teacher for any accidents or injuries that might occur during the trip. Such a permission is of little value other than as an acknowledgement that parents know a child is going on the trip and the probable recognition that the trip itself would not be dangerous. Should an accident occur and the teacher's behaviour be found to be negligent, however, damages would be assessed against both the teacher and the school. A parent cannot waive a child's rights and cannot authorize a teacher to use less than the degree of care that any reasonable person would have used in that situation.

DISCIPLINE

Teachers tend to get only a non-integrated smattering of information about discipline during their formal education.[32] Yet, all teachers desire a well-disciplined classroom climate conducive to optimal learning on the part of the students. New teachers particularly feel this lack and Clarke and Hunka found that discipline continues to be a major concern for Canadian schools.[33]

There are legal implications that result from classroom management practices, and teachers are subject to the general prescriptions of the criminal and civil law. In the usual case, to the extent teachers act with legitimate consent or legal authority and stay within the bounds of reasonableness, they are protected by the law from charges of wrongful conduct. Linden cites the privilege that furnishes this defence to charges of intentional interference with a student's rights:

> Although most of the cases deal with the alleged misdeeds of police officers during the course of making arrests, this privilege is also available to parents, school teachers, shipmasters, and others who forcibly discipline children or crew members under their control. Minor assaults, batteries, and detentions for disciplinary purposes are excused, if they are reasonable, but not if any excessive force is employed.[34]

In the past when criminal charges have been laid in disciplinary situations it has usually been because some type of corporal punishment had been carried too far. With corporal punishment on the decline, few teachers are involved in this type of action today. On the civil side, the two principal reasons why lawsuits are presently brought against the teacher and the school are either physical assault or teacher negligence, a subject to be considered later. When force is used, the main question is what is reasonable under the circumstances. Internal school procedures handle all but a few such incidents and these few tend to be only the most severe cases that are turned over to the legal authorities and the Crown Prosecutor.

In a criminal case only the school teacher would be charged, while in a civil lawsuit the school board would also be named as a defendant. In the event of a judgment, the school board's insurance would pay and only in an exceptional case would the board attempt to recover the damages from the teacher. While thus protected from paying monetary damages, the teacher may be seriously affected by the publicity and the psychological trauma associated with a trial and the lengthy pre-trial procedures. In the exceptional case where the damages exceed funds available from insurance or the school board (usually an action for negligence where a student is paralyzed for life), the teacher could be required to pay. Also if the teacher's actions were contrary to school rules, the board can recover compensation from the teacher.[35]

THE COURTS AND IMPROPER DISCIPLINE

In the past, many of the cases involving excessive corporal punishment have been tried in the criminal courts, usually at the instigation of a parent. A civil lawsuit for damages is available, however, and the required proof of wrongdoing is easier to establish. For example, in *Andrews v. Hopkins*[36] a father and his eleven-year-old daughter recovered civil damages for assault when the teacher negligently struck the girl's breast while strapping her hands. An opposite result was reached in *Murdock v. Richards*[37] when both the school board and the teacher were found not responsible for an alleged assault. After a full trial the judge found the facts did not prove unreasonable and excessive force. Win or lose, the teacher was still obliged to defend the lawsuit.

Bargen details many legal situations that affect the school pupil and includes a discussion on discipline. He concludes that courts must ask three questions when considering a discipline case:

> 1. Was the teacher acting within the scope of his legal authority? This question involves the statutory authority of the teacher as well as his authority *in loco parentis*.
> 2. Was there cause for punishment? In answering this question the Courts have indicated their reluctance to set aside a teacher's judgment.
> 3. Was the punishment reasonable under the circumstances? This question generally constitutes the heart of any litigation and must be answered on the basis of precedent and common law.[38]

It is usually this last question upon which reported decisions focus. One American line of decisions held that a teacher was responsible only when a pupil received permanent injury, or punishment was inflicted with malice, hate, ill will, anger, or for revenge. The Nova Scotia Supreme Court rejected this extreme view in *R. v. Gaul*.[39] The court concluded that a teacher who inflicts unreasonably severe chastisement upon a pupil is criminally responsible under the Criminal Code for the excess of force used, although the punishment resulted in no permanent injury and was inflicted without malice. Canadian courts have tended to follow this Nova Scotia decision. In *Campeau v. R.*[40] the Quebec Court of King's Bench approved this rule and held a teacher guilty of assault upon three children who attended the school in which he was teaching. The evidence showed that the defendant had punished an eight-year-old by taking the child's wrist and striking the back of his hand several times on the corner of the teacher's desk. The judges agreed that this was unreasonable. In *R. v. Wheaton* the teacher slapped the student across the face and then grabbed the student by the hair and "forcefully pushed Angell's face right into the books laying on his desk, telling him to get to work."[41] The court concluded that, "although Mr. Wheaton is not criminally liable for his conduct, his behaviour was certainly far less than a professional response to a discipline problem."[42]

THE COURTS AND NON-TEACHING PERSONNEL

It is less clear whether non-teachers can use force in disciplinary situations. In *Prendergast v. Masterson*[43] a U.S. court held a superintendent was not a teacher and thus was not privileged. The court decided in this case that the law considers the teacher to be the:

> One who for the time being is *in loco parentis* to the pupil, who, by reason of his frequent and close association with the pupil, has an opportunity to know about the traits which distinguish him from other pupils; and who, therefore, can reasonably be expected to more intelligently judge the pupil's conduct than he otherwise could, and more justly measure the punishment he deserves, if any.[44]

By contrast, two recent Canadian criminal cases accepted the defence offered in the Criminal Code, although the Code does not spell out who besides teachers should stand in the place of a parent. A Saskatchewan court held that a vice-principal was able to punish three pupils who shouted names at him on their way home from school.[45] In *R. v. Trynchy*[46] a Yukon magistrate's court extended the right of discipline or control to a school bus driver. On several occasions the driver had warned the students to behave. He was charged with assault after he had stopped the bus and picked up a seven-year-old who had been running in the aisles and hitting other students. The driver asked the boy if he was going to "smarten up" and upon receiving an "O.K." dropped him in a seat, the boy's head possibly hitting the side of the bus. The court found that when a parent sends a child to school via public transportation, the parent has given over the teaching and discipline of the child to the educational system. This extends to the bus driver charged with the safe transportation of the children. The court concluded that, although the driver could have used other means of discipline, the corrective force used was in fact not unreasonable under the circumstances.

THE UNINTENTIONAL TORT OR NEGLIGENCE

The most important field of tort liability today is negligence since this field controls our behaviour on a day-to-day basis. Negligence law compensates victims of accidents whose injuries result from someone else's faulty behaviour. Society imposes a standard of care or conduct—an expectation of certain behaviour—on all of its members. Some who have special training are held to a higher standard, but the usual test is what a reasonable person would have done under the circumstances. Negligence can be either misbehaviour or lack of appropriate behaviour. Linden notes that the Supreme Court of Canada has defined negligence thus: "Negligence consists in the doing of some act which a person of ordinary care and skill would not do under the circumstances, or omitting to do some act which a person of ordinary care and skill would do under the circumstances."[47]

The most common example of misbehaviour is an automobile accident. A driver is going too fast for the road conditions and skids into another car. This is an illustration of an unintentional *act*; the behaviour of the driver caused the accident. In a school setting, if a teacher accidentally hurts a child while conducting a science experiment, the teacher can be held responsible. When an accident happens as a result of a teacher's negligence, the school board and teacher are financially responsible. The behaviour can become the basis of a civil lawsuit.

The more common experience of negligence in schools comes from incidents in the school gym involving students who are not properly trained and/or who are inadequately supervised in using the equipment.[48] We will consider student physical well-being in more detail later. It is sufficient here to say that both action and inaction can be cause for concern to teachers.

A less usual type of negligence in education is malpractice, a topic discussed by Newell.[49] The basis of malpractice lawsuits against teachers is for failing to meet their professional obligations in the classroom. The logic of these claims against school boards and teachers follows from the concept of *in loco parentis*. The teacher is acting for the benefit of the child while she or he is under the teacher's supervision. When the teacher is negligent in the role of substitute parent and irreparable damage occurs, Newell argues that the teacher could be held responsible for damages.

This reasoning is hard for many to accept and, to date, none of the courts in which these suits have been filed (all in the United States) has been persuaded that teachers have this high a duty.[50] Over the years, courts have been adding constraints that regulate teacher behaviour. However, judges have not been ready to establish academic guidelines similar to these behavioural guidelines. At the present time a student has no recourse against a teacher who negligently denies him or her the benefits of a proper education. As David King, former Alberta Minister of Education, was reported as saying in January 1985, "Students are guaranteed a classroom and a teacher—but not an education." Nevertheless, Canadian writers are urging teachers to know and avoid the legal bases for malpractice actions.[51]

LEGAL PROOF REQUIRED

To receive damages, an injured student and his or her parent (the plaintiffs) must sue the responsible parties and prove four major factors:

1. Legal Duty. There has to be a legal duty of care between the plaintiff and defendant. Such is true between drivers of cars or between a teacher and a student, or between the school and student body. In these cases, the question is not so much whether a duty exists, but the extent of that duty. On the other hand, there is no such duty between a person who is drowning and a person who is merely walking by, even though attracted by the calls of the drowning person. Should the observer attempt to save the other, however, a duty of care then comes into play.

2. Standard of Care. There has to be a failure to meet a legal duty. The law requires a minimum level of performance regardless of capability but does not expect perfect behaviour. The reasonable person may be guilty of an error in judgment and under such circumstances there still may be no breach of the duty. The "reasonable person" test also considers, however, the education, experience, and qualifications of a professional person, such as a teacher.

3. Damages. An injury or loss must occur. If there is no damage, there would be little point in commencing a lawsuit. The court tries to restore the plaintiff, by means of monetary damages, to his or her status prior to the negligent act. The real question thus relates to the extent of loss that has occurred. Physical loss, such as destruction of an automobile, or medical bills and actual, loss of wages during hospitalization, can be quantified. On the other hand, some kinds of damages such as pain and suffering, are hard to demonstrate and little or no compensation may be awarded.

4. Causation. There must be a causal relationship between the damage to the plaintiff and the wrongful act of the defendant. The plaintiff must convince the judge that the loss was forseeable by a reasonable person. If the accident would not have occurred had the defendant not been negligent, then that behaviour is the cause of the injury. Sometimes the defendant is also held responsible for unexpected events that follow from an accident that should have been forseen, such as observers becoming ill from watching a classmate receiving a serious injury.

Despite the presence of a duty, a breach of duty, and resulting damage, a plaintiff's claim can still be defeated because of his or her own conduct. Consider a mature high school football player. If he is negligent with regard to his own safety during the game, such as by violating a rule designed to ensure player safety, he may be denied the protection of the law in whole or in part. Again since he voluntarily assumes the risk of being hurt during the game, he may not be able to recover damages if the risk is one that he could reasonably have foreseen. This is similar to the idea of informed consent discussed earlier.

The elements apply to any action for negligence, and teachers should keep them in mind as they think about their duty to the students entrusted to their care. For example, the duty implied by the doctrine of *in loco parentis* requires teachers to take action supportive of the student's physical well-being, but at the same time to recognize their limitations in providing direct assistance.

STUDENT PHYSICAL WELL-BEING

There are four main areas where the school has a duty of care. These include:

1. Provision of safe transportation to and from school and school activities.

2. Provision of a safe building and grounds.
3. Provision of safe equipment for use of students.
4. Provision of adequate supervision.

Although the individual teacher is most concerned about the last, there is a responsibility for teachers to report unsafe conditions to the principal when they cannot alleviate the situation on their own.

SUPERVISION

Teachers daily encounter situations that demand immediate decisions and immediate actions to preserve the physical well-being of students under their control. In each case, what is the extent of the teacher's legal responsibility toward the student? Elementary school teachers are often faced with issues of hall, gym, or playground injuries, students becoming ill in class, or with parental requests to medicate their child, often with regular doses of life-sustaining medication. Secondary school science, physical education, and vocational class instructors have special responsibilities in dealing with potential class, gym, and shop injuries or accidents. In addition all teachers have a responsibility when they expect homework or out of school activity:

> When an instructor has reason to believe that a student will work or play with instruments or materials off the premises which relate to his schoolwork and which might cause harm to himself or to others, the instructor must advise the student clearly of all potential dangers and of the precautions necessary to prevent injuries.[52]

Teachers have a special obligation to supervise dangerous situations and have on occasion been held legally responsible for improper or inadequate supervision when students have been injured. In most of these cases, the teacher has been found negligent for not preventing the accident. For example, in Prince George, B.C., a physical education instructor was found responsible because there had been a previous similar accident involving a different student. The court in that case said, "Once one youngster had become hurt, would not a prudent father want to know how and why his child had become hurt in order to avoid the same kind of risk to another child? The teacher should have forseen further trouble.... He should have guarded against that further trouble."[53]

Teachers are responsible for a student's physical well-being on school grounds and during school hours. For example, when a teacher sees a larger child assaulting a smaller one, the teacher has a duty to intervene. On the other hand, when a teacher temporarily leaves a classroom and a fight breaks out, American courts have tended to find no liability "unless under all the circumstances the possibility of injury is reasonably forseable".[54] There is probably no responsibility for after-school activities when no school sponsorship is involved. However, if students regularly use the school facilities with the implied consent of the school authorities, or with teaching staff present, liability may occur.

When school sponsorship occurs outside the school property, the teachers' duty to supervise continues. For example, both the school and teachers were found liable for damages when an accident occurred during the taking of class pictures in a public park on a Saturday. A high school senior wanted to be photographed on his motorcycle, but was careless and injured another student. The teachers knew the student was performing stunts on the motorcycle and should have forseen the danger to others; they failed to supervise the school outing properly.[55]

In addition, there may be serious problems when the school does not provide adequate transportation to outside functions. When the school cannot provide adequate transportation for out-of-school activities, teachers should not get involved in supplemental or unofficial transportation schemes. A common example is a field trip where cars are used. It is clear that teachers should not use their own personal vehicles for such activities. It is less clear what happens when teachers request students to make their own travel arrangements. Parents are usually responsible when they transport their own or other children to school-sponsored activities. However, if a teacher or school arranges for this type of transportation, the teacher and school also may be held responsible for a subsequent accident.[56]

PARENTAL REQUESTS FOR MEDICAL TREATMENT

There is an increasing call upon teachers to administer either prescription medication (such as Ritalin or insulin) or non-prescription medication (such as aspirin) during school hours. In Alberta, both the Alberta School Trustees Association (ASTA) and the Alberta Teachers' Association agree that teachers, unless medically competent, should not administer such medication. When facing such requests the ASTA points out to teachers and principals, "Regardless of the nature of the medication, school personnel should refrain from acceding to such requests. Suffice to say, the necessity for and the means of administering medication are not knowledges and skills ordinarily possessed by most school personnel."[57]

Nevertheless there is a duty to respond to a parental request for care while the student is in school. The teacher is obligated to identify such students and supervise the appropriate use of medication as would a reasonable and prudent parent in like circumstances. Most students requiring continuing use of medication (including insulin shots) learn to take or give the medication to themselves. Thus it might be appropriate for a teacher to provide safe storage for a drug, to remind a student when to take the drug or ascertain if it has been taken, and to provide a secure environment and the time during which the student can take the required drug.

One area that has raised considerable concern is the school health-care of allergic children. Elaborate procedures have been developed in some schools for the emergency care of such children when minutes will make the difference between life and death. Ekstrand[58] suggests the following components to a supplemental educational program for staff:

1. Knowledge of Allergens. Preparation of lists of common allergens that should be recognizable to all personnel.
2. Identification of Allergic Pupils. The maintenance of lists of allergic pupils for the purpose of screening against school events and schedules that might cause allergic reaction.
3. Recognition of Allergic Reaction in Pupils. The conduct of inservice meetings to assist teachers in the early recognition of pupils undergoing allergic reaction.
4. Limitation of Materials of Allergic Nature. The maintenance of appropriate purchasing procedures for all school and classroom materials.
5. Environmental Controls. The maintenance of procedures regarding temperature and humidity control, air purification, cleaning routines, and insecticide/pesticide spraying.

CONSENT TO MEDICAL TREATMENT

From time to time teachers will be faced with injuries that demand immediate attention beyond first aid. Teachers taking an injured child to a doctor or emergency room may well have trouble obtaining medical treatment because of the issue of the consent needed to obtain such treatment from the hospital and the docotr. Consent has been one of the more troublesome questions facing doctors in recent years and only in a medical emergency involving life and death will the doctor intervene without it. There is some trend toward giving children under the age of eighteen the right to consent to treatment where their own physical well-being is at stake. For example, some writers believe that even a young child could consent to the setting of a broken leg.[59] Even so, it is the policy of most doctors and emergency rooms not to perform any intrusive therapy with a minor child without the appropriate consent.

This requirement makes it difficult to treat a student when no parent is immediately available. In addition to school personnel, neither neighbours nor friends may give valid consent—only a legal guardian may do so. This practice puts the teacher (or other school personnel) in a very difficult position. While the teacher has responsibility for the welfare of the child and does have parental authority in disciplinary situations, this authority does not extend to providing medical treatment. In the event a teacher or principal finds a child in need of medical attention, first aid should be provided where appropriate. The following three recommendations of the ASTA should then be followed:[60]

> 1. School personnel, unless medically competent, should not administer medication to students.
> 2. When required, staff should provide emergency transport of students to a medical practitioner or hospital.
> 3. The teacher or other staff member should stay with the student until:
>   a. competent medical assistance is secured; or

b. the parents or legal guardians arrive; or
c. the staff member is relieved by other board-authorized personnel.

Since no school personnel can grant consent to the doctor or hospital to treat the student involved, the teacher usually will have to stay with the student until the parent or guardian arrives. The medical staff is unlikely to treat a non-life threatening situation or baby-sit the student; the teacher is thus left with this responsibility. Teachers have a duty of care for the physical well-being of their students. At times this obligation could be onerous if the full support of the other school staff is not available.

CONCLUSION

In the preceding pages we have discussed only a few of the many legal rights, duties, and responsibilities encountered daily by teachers. This discussion was general and should not be considered legal advice. Decisions ultimately are made by the courts when the law is applied to a specific factual situation. At times, decisions may seem to be inconsistent. However, it is not the law that changes as much as its application to a new and different set of facts. Thus, teachers having specific questions about their own situations should consult their own or their school district's solicitor.

Teachers should not be intimidated by what has been discussed. Almost all legal conflicts can be avoided by the use of common sense and the practice of good communication skills. Schools should anticipate possible dangerous situations and provide teachers with a plan of action for common emergencies, such as is done for fire drills. Teachers should act in a reasonable way in their daily contact with students. If there is also active communication with parents about what is happening in school, small difficulties will not become major problems with the potential for lawsuits. Most lawsuits can be prevented if the parties truly *understand* each other; hence the need for open and honest communication. Common sense and good will will avert most of the problems discussed in this paper.

NOTES

1. P.F. Bargen, *The Legal Status of the Canadian Public School Pupils* (Toronto: Macmillan, 1961).

2. K. Boundry, R. Jefferson, R. Pressman, and S. Schumack, "Recent Developments in Education Law," *Clearing House Review* (1985): 1019–1026.

3. L. Eberlein, "Behaviour Modification in the Classroom: Implications for Teachers" (unpublished manuscript, Department of Educational Psychology, University of Alberta, Edmonton, 1985).

4. L. Eberlein, "Should Counsellors Report Child Neglect?" *Alberta Counsellor* 8, 1 (1979): 8–16; L. Eberlein and B. Swindlehurst, "Child Abuse, the Law, and the Counsellor," *The School Guidance Worker* 345 (1979): 37–42.
5. R.E. Stevens, "Invasion of Student Privacy," *Journal of Law and Education* 9 (1980): 343–351.
6. *New Jersey v. T.L.O.*, 105 S.Ct. 733 (1985).
7. M.A. Ziskind, "Protecting the Privacy of School Children and their Families Through the Family Educational Rights and Privacy Act of 1974," *Journal of Family Law* 14 (1975): 255–279.
8. B. Swindlehurst and L. Eberlein "The Rights Fight in Canada," *Directive Teacher* 3, 1 (1981): 14–15.
9. R. Kimmins, W.J. Hunter, and A.W. Mackay, "Educational Legislation and Litigation Pertaining to the Practice of School Psychology in Canada," *Canadian Journal of School Psychology* 1 (1985): 1–16.
10. *Niewiadomski v. U.S.*, 159 F. 2d 683 (6th Cir. 1974).
11. *Powys v. Mansfield* (1836), 6 Sim 528, 58 E.R. 692; *Shitiz v. C.N.R.* (1927), 1 D.L.R. 951 (Sask. C.A.).
12. R.R. Hammes, "*In Loco Parentis*: Considerations in Teacher/Student Relationships," *Clearing House* 56 (1982): 8–11.
13. *Baker v. Owen*, 395 F. Supp. 294 (M.D.N.C.), affd mem., 423 U.S. 907 (1975).
14. S. Spitalli Jr., "Corporal Punishment," *Clearing House* 49 (1976): 418–420; E.G. Gee and D.J. Sperry, *Educational Law and the Public School: A Compendium* (Boston: Allyn and Bacon, 1978).
15. *R. v. Trynchy*, [1970] C.R.N.S. 95 (Y. Magis.Ct.).
16. V.J. Hawkins, "The Negativism of Corporal Punishment," *Clearing House* 49 (1976): 226–233.
17. *Guerrieri v. Tyson*, 147 Pa. Super. 239, 24 A. 2d 468 (1942).
18. M. Long, "Torts and the Teacher," *Comment on Education* 11, 4 (1981), 15.
19. Bargen, *The Legal Status of the Canadian Public School Pupil*.
20. *Restatement of the Law: Torts 2nd.* (St. Paul: American Law Institute, 1977).
21. The Law Reform Commission of Canada has recommended that section 43 be changed to eliminate the protection given to teachers. See Law Reform Commission of Canada, *Assault*, Working Paper 38 (Ottawa: Law Reform Commission, 1984).
22. *Baker v. Owen*, 395 F. Supp. 294 (M.D.N.C.), aff'd mem., 423 U.S. 907 (1975).
23. *Ingraham v. Wright*, 430 U.S. 651 (1977).
24. Law Reform Commission of Canada, *Assault*.
25. L. Eberlein, "Corporal Punishment to be Banned in the Criminal Code?" (unpublished manuscript, Department of Educational Psychology, University of Alberta, Edmonton, 1986).
26. J. Barnes, "Tort Liability of School Boards to Pupils" in *Studies in Canadian Tort Law*, edited by L. Klar (Toronto: Butterworths, 1977), 209.
27. J.S. Williams, *The Law of Defamation in Canada* (Toronto: Butterworths, 1976).
28. A.M. Linden, *Canadian Tort Law* (Toronto: Butterworths, 1977).
29. Eberlein, "Behaviour Modification in the Classroom: Implications for Teachers."

30. Linden, *Canadian Tort Law*, 56.
31. Personal communication from L. Klar, 4 Jan. 1979.
32. L. Eberlein, "The New Teacher and Classroom Deviances" (unpublished manuscript, Department of Educational Psychology, University of Alberta, Edmonton, 1984).
33. S.C.T. Clarke and S. Hunka, "Comparative Views of School Discipline," *Alberta Journal of Educational Research* 23 (1977): 305-316.
34. Linden, *Canadian Tort Law*, 73.
35. Barnes, "Tort Liability of School Boards to Pupils."
36. *Andrews v. Hopkins* (1932), 3 D.L.R. 459 (N.S.S.C.).
37. *Murdock v. Richards* (1954), 1 D.L.R. 766 (N.S.C.C.).
38. Bargen, *The Legal Status of the Canadian Public School Pupil*, 117.
39. *R. v. Gaul* (1904), 8 C.C.C. 178 (N.S.S.C.).
40. *Campeau v. R.* (1951), 14 C.R. 202 (Que.K.B.).
41. *R. v. Wheaton* (1982), 35 Nfld. & P.E.I. R. 520 (Nfld. Prov. Ct.) at 521.
42. Ibid., at 523.
43. *Prendergast v. Masterson*, 196 S.W. 246 (Cr. Civil Appeals, Texas, 1917) at 247.
44. Ibid., at 247.
45. *R. v. Haberstock* (1970), 1 C.C.C. (2d) 433 (Sask. C.A.).
46. *R. v. Trynchy* (1970), C.R.N.S. 95 (Y. Magis.Ct.).
47. Linden, *Canadian Tort Law*, 91.
48. D.M. Hutter, "Legal Liability in Physical Education and Athletics," *Physical Education* 35 (1978): 160-163.
49. R.C. Newell, "Teacher Malpractice," *Case and Comment* 83, 4 (1978): 3-10.
50. T.P. Collingsworth, "Applying Negligence Doctrine to the Teaching Profession," *Journal of Law and Education* 11 (1982): 479-505.
51. D.H. Rogers, "Educational Malpractice—Teachers and Standards of Care" in *Legal Issues in Canadian Education*, edited by J. Balderson and J. Kolmes (Edmonton: Canadian School Executive, 1982); A.C. Nicholls and Y.M. Martin, "Preventing Educational Malpractice Litigation," *Canadian School Executive* 4, 1 (1984): 21-23.
52. W.P. Hagenau, "Penumbras of Care Beyond the Schoolhouse Gate," *Journal of Law and Education* 9 (1980), 217.
53. Alberta School Trustees Association, *Medical Treatment of Students: A Dilemma For School Systems* (Edmonton: ASTA, 1980), 16.
54. C. Morgenstern, "Tort and Civil Rights Liability of Educators," *Ohio Northern University Law School* 10 (1983), 25.
55. Hagenau, "Penumbras of Care Beyond the Schoolhouse Gate."
56. Ibid.
57. Alberta School Trustees Association, *Medical Treatment of Students*, 5.
58. R.E. Ekstrand, "Doctor, Do You Make (School) House Calls?" *Children Today* (May-June 1982): 2-5.
59. E. Picard, *Legal Liability of Doctors and Hospitals in Canada* (Toronto: Carswell, 1978).
60. Alberta School Trustees Association, *Medical Treatment of Students*, 8.

CONFLICTING IMPERATIVES: PERSONAL PRIVACY OR ENHANCED EDUCATIONAL SERVICE DELIVERY?

EDWARD H. HUMPHREYS

Canadians have two imperatives that, given present trends, will bring educational institutions into conflict with the interests of individuals. The first is the need to protect personal integrity through the maintenance of a private personality. The second is the desire to obtain societal progress through the provision of personal services by public and private agencies. The expression of these requisites within the system of public education in Canada and the way in which they are treated is the subject of this paper.

Privacy has been expressed as a concept of international importance in the Universal Declaration of Human Rights. Article 12 states that: "No one shall be subjected to arbitrary interference with his privacy, family, name or correspondence, nor to attacks upon his honour and reputation. Everyone has the right to the protection of the law against such interference or attacks."

Even so, when significant advances are made by societies, liberty is frequently placed in jeopardy. Stafford Beer noted that: "most advances in human welfare have paid a price in infringement of personal liberty: whether that price is seen as reasonable or as a fundamental deprivation of human rights will often be a matter of interpretation."[1] Although North American society regards privacy as important, concern over its forfeit varies widely and results in conflict between the public and those who govern public institutions.

While recent rapid improvement in public and private services has been facilitated by advances in computer technology, after four decades of computerized information processing, the use and abuse of personal data have brought issues of privacy, confidentiality, and the right to know to the foreground of public concern. In the educational realm specifically, privacy of student information has become a focus of interest as schools develop more sophisticated services through the wider use of personal information and as personal data are maintained in computerized storage facilities, accessible through social insurance numbers.

While North Americans view the provision of public services such as education as one of the prime functions of government and while public institutions are expected to provide individuals with protection from abuse by those who provide services, the means that have been developed to guard against individual and institutional abuses have not kept pace with the explosive technological change in the now ubiquitous information processing industry. In 1979 the Civil Liberties Association noted that in the preceding ten years the information business had become so widespread as to have more people in its employ than were occupied in producing goods and services.[2] Yet even now, legal and policy measures for the protection of the right to privacy are still in their infancy in both Canada and the United States.

DEFINITIONS OF PRIVACY

Early attempts to define privacy were made within a legal framework. Cooley characterized privacy as "a right to be left alone"[3] while Warren and Brandeis indicated it was a protection of one's "inviolate personality."[4] Butler, Moran, and Vanderpool defined privacy as a person's right "to be free from unwarranted publicity" and "to be protected from any wrongful intrusion into his private life which would outrage or cause mental suffering, shame or humiliation to a person of ordinary sensibilities."[5] In discussing the responsibilities of research personnel to protect individual integrity, Ruebhausen and Brim stated that:

> the essence of privacy is no more, and certainly no less than the freedom of the individual to pick and choose for himself the time and the circumstances under which, and most importantly, the extent to which, his attitudes, beliefs, behaviour and opinions are to be shared with or withheld from others.[6]

While four states of privacy—solitude, intimacy, anonymity, and reserve—have been dealt with by the Supreme Court of the United States,[7] it is clear that current concerns over privacy have come to focus increasingly on a fifth aspect, the need to control personal information. With this emphasis Westin defined informational privacy as "the claim of individuals, groups and institutions to determine for themselves when, how and to what extent information about them is to be communicated to others."[8] Although Westin's definition has served as the foundation for much of the debate over informational privacy, it has been criticized by Lusky on the grounds that it "fails to distinguish between informational communications that are objectionable only because of their false or misleading character and those that, however accurate and complete, report facts that cannot be decently retailed."[9]

A NECESSARY EXCHANGE

While individuals should be able to control the provision of information about themselves, institutions may require personal information to provide services valued by the individual. That is, it may be necessary for the individual to exchange some information and personal privacy in order to receive a given service. While in this situation a person may, in fact, suffer a loss of what Parker has termed "the value of privacy,"[10] that individual may gain greater value from the service supplied. Of course, a positive value exchange depends on the ability of the institution to provide the desired service for which data are collected, which in turn depends upon the availability of data that are neither false nor misleading and that are maintained so as to ensure their quality. An institution that uses personal data should be expected to employ data management processes that result in information that does not mislead institutional decision makers. Thus, it is essential to address not only the right of an individual to control the disposition of personal data, but also the right to have only high quality data, that is, data that are accurate, complete, pertinent, and timely employed in important decision making.

It is in the joint interest of both individuals and institutions to ensure that student data upon which significant decisions are based are of high quality. Such data are best assembled through cooperative endeavour that recognizes both the individual's right to control personal data and the institution's need for data. However, it is recognized that the relations between individuals and institutions often are not conducted in ways that are in the best interest of both parties, and the law is employed to regulate those relations. While constitutional law regulates relations between individuals and the governing structures of society, common law regulates the rights and obligations of private persons to each other.[11] However, interactions between students and state institutions are not simple. These relations are confused not only by the structure of the educational system but also by the fact that the client group receiving educational services is usually not of legal age and, as a consequence, is lacking many of the rights and options of legal recourse open to adults. Furthermore, the age of the student frequently means that the power and resources necessary in society to command attention, if not respect, are not available to influence decision makers as they employ personal information in decisions that affect the future of the student. Thus, what would appear to be jointly advantageous, that is, the effective use of high quality student information in school system decision making, is often absent.

INFORMATIONAL PRIVACY: RECOGNITION OF THE PROBLEM IN CANADA

During the 1960s the proliferation of data banks and reported abuses of stored information led to the first official concern about informational privacy in Canada. Three provincial governments commissioned studies on the issue: the Royal Commission of Inquiry into the Invasion of Privacy in British Columbia, a Special Committee on Invasion of Privacy in Alberta, and the Ontario Law Reform Commission's study on the protection of privacy.

The federal government also commissioned a Task Force on Privacy and Computers. The only provinces that have thus far legislated a legal right to privacy are British Columbia,[12] Manitoba,[13] and Saskatchewan.[14] These statutes, however, do not define privacy in relation to information about people but rather deal with torts for "invasion of privacy, actionable without proof of damage."[15]

The government of Canada's Bill C-176, known as the Protection of Privacy Act, became law on 30 June 1974. This bill amended the Criminal Code of Canada, the Crown Liability Act, and the Official Secrets Act for the express purpose of creating offences relating to the interception of private communications. These amendments, however, relate to private communications and not to private information held in data banks. Furthermore, they deal with federal rather than provincial matters and thus are unlikely to have great effect on the maintenance of the integrity of student information, except possibly in its transmission.

Tort remedies for violation of privacy also are inadequate for dealing with the informational privacy problem in that the theoretical basis is questionable, making its application to informational privacy rather doubtful.[16] Furthermore, in the Commonwealth, no general legal right to privacy exists, and the term when used is taken to be "a statement of principle in support of some already recognized right or cause of action."[17] As a result, the handling of personal information by government has been, by necessity, the subject of statutes dealing with informational privacy. Concern with the increasing quantities and types of personal information collected by the private and public sectors, and the more extensive use of computers has led to the proposal and adoption of legislative measures intended to curb the perceived dangers inherent in these developments.[18]

Not until passage of the Canadian Human Rights Act in 1977 was the concept of privacy in terms of records and record keeping confirmed in Canadian federal law. Flaherty notes that Part IV of the act "concerns the protection of personal information and embodies the principle that the privacy of individuals should be protected 'to the greatest extent consistent with the public interest.'"[19] That is, this act acknowledges the principle of informational privacy and specifies the legally protected rights of individuals and, in a limited manner, the right to access records held on them in federal information banks. This recognition of the concept of informational privacy in Canada has resulted in the enactment of legislation that provides protection to individuals from actions that fall under federal authority. While this approach recognizes the necessity of statutes to deal with informational privacy in Canada, it does little to assist informational privacy within the areas of provincial jurisdiction, i.e., education.

Even so, it should be noted that recent developments at the federal level would appear to protect the right to privacy of at least one group of students in schools. The Young Offenders Act[20] imposes strict controls over the publication and retention of information concerning young persons charged with or found guilty of an offence. An obligation exists to make the records of a case available to a school system deemed to have "a valid interest in the proceedings."[21] Furthermore, information about the proceedings or other records required "for the purpose of administering or participating in the administration of a disposition"[22] may be retained by any person or organization, such as a school system, that is participating in the rehabilitation of a young offender. The long-term retention of those records is restricted however. Where the young person "(a) is acquitted, or (b) the charge is dismissed for any reason other than acquittal" or the young person "has not been charged with or found guilty" of a summary offence for two years or of an indictable offence for five years beyond the completion of all dispositions, "all records...and all copies, prints or negatives of such records shall be destroyed."[23] Such a provision would require school systems to destroy outdated records and, in order to ensure compliance with the act, to know of the existence and location of all records concerning young offenders retained by its personnel.

The Constitution Act (1981) with its Charter of Rights and Freedoms does not appear to have any application with reference to informational privacy although section 8 provides security "against unreasonable search and seizure." Upon interpretation, however, it may be found to protect privacy to some extent.

While the federal statutes may be helpful in furthering definitions of the concepts involved, except as noted earlier, the incompetence of the government of Canada to deal with matters pertaining to education makes it doubtful that federal statutes could be employed to protect the rights of students or parents insofar as school records are concerned. The enactment of provincial legislation to protect informational privacy would appear to be paramount in the protection of the right to privacy in Canadian schools.

INFORMATIONAL PRIVACY: RECOGNITION IN THE PROVINCES

Beyond the protections provided by the Young Offenders Act, it would appear that Canadian parents and students are forced to rely on provincial legislative powers to protect their rights to informational privacy in schools. Such reliance would appear to be ill placed for the majority of Canadians.

Except in the provinces of Quebec and Ontario, few references to student records appear in provincial statutes or regulations. Where references to records do appear, they generally delegate responsibility for the administration of student records to the local school system.

In 1973, a regulation to govern cumulative school records, dealing with contents and purpose, obligations of personnel, and procedures for consulting, revising, safeguarding, and transferring records, was introduced in the province of Quebec, but "as a result of expressions of concern by a number of groups, the regulation was withdrawn."[24] A more permanent solution, using a legislative approach, was taken in Ontario during this same period. Substantial amendments to the Education Act (1974) prescribed:

> the privileged status of records, the rights to access of a parent, the appeal procedure, the format to be used, the procedures to be used in dealing with inaccuracies in the records, the secrecy of record contents, and the protection for donors along with the duties of the principal regarding the record.[25]

This legislation delegated operational control of records to local authorities but specified the rights and obligations of students, teachers, and school officials. Regulations under the act defined the record, its format, required contents, and procedures for extension and transfer but left considerable latitude to local authorities for its administration.

Other provinces lacked legislation to control student records, and local systems tended to vary considerably in the care with which they maintained student information. In fact, a 1980 study of school records in Canada found that, except in large metropolitan jurisdictions, little or no policy on school records existed at the local level. It concluded that "neglect of policy statements, regulations, and guidelines at both provincial and local levels illustrates that educators and legislators have shown little concern over student information from the point of view of its possible abuse or even its effective use."[26]

Since local authorities had little interest in developing policies to govern the action of officials, provincial legislators failed to provide legal safeguards, and federal legislative powers were excluded from the governance process by constitutional prohibitions, individual rights remained unprotected. Canadian school students and their parents lacked the protection of informational privacy afforded by federal guarantees and, for the most part, were unable to rely on either provincial legislation or local policy to protect their interests.

A CHANGED IMPERATIVE

While it may be argued that the chaotic state of student information found by Humphreys in the 1980 study of Canadian schools and school systems was protection enough for student privacy, such a stand now would be inadvisable. Upgraded special education services, such as are required by Ontario's recently implemented Bill 82, amending the 1974 provincial Education Act, are likely to be extended across Canada in the near future. It is likely that to provide these new services each local jurisdiction will be forced to collect substantially more information than previously, and to develop more sophisticated student information systems to assist decision makers.

Bill 82 requires schools to provide "an appropriate education" for each student judged to need special education programs and services. It implies a greatly expanded base of information upon which special education programs may be founded. Furthermore the requirements for "early identification" of learning difficulties and for programs based on "continuous assessment" and "periodic reassessment" imply substantially more data than previously were retained by schools.

The special education amendment to Ontario's Education Act (1974) requires each school system to assess the learning abilities of every student on entry to kindergarten in order to discover any possible learning disabilities. Such an assessment may require a wide range of personal information, including the medical, psychological, social, and learning status of the child. As the student moves through the primary school years, progress must be assessed periodically and program changes instituted that reflect the findings of the assessments. A full history of school and family experiences of many of the children who are found by specialists to require learning assistance will be collected over the school life of the child. It is only possible to provide sophisticated services that are appropriate to the changing needs of the child if such data are collected and maintained over time.

A number of quasi-judicial procedures are also incorporated into the legislation. Hearings of Identification, Placement, and Review Committees (IPRC), of Special Education Appeal Boards (SEAB), and Special Education Tribunals (SET) are required to guarantee the honouring of student and parent rights to a fair decision process in accordance with natural justice.[27] Each of these hearings will require participants to provide evidence both upon the substantive case for which a decision is to be made and on the procedures that have been employed in reaching the decision. Clearly, legislation such as Bill 82 will have a profound impact on the needs for information, and on the type, amount, and intimacy of data that will be retained for educational decision making. Such increased data retention has serious implications for the management of student information in schools and school systems. The way this changed requirement is handled will have significant impact on the privacy of students and their parents.

While many jurisdictions presently collect substantial quantities of information, the pervasive nature of information that will now be required demands closer control over its collection, rentention, and use. Collection of personal information through sophisticated instrumentation and personal interview requires safeguards for privacy and careful recognition of the confidentiality of communications with both student and family. Students need to be informed of the boundaries of confidentiality. They should be aware of the degree to which professionals are able to hold conversations in confidence or to withhold information from parents, the courts, the police, and other persons in authority. Only with such awareness is a student able to judge the advisability of providing sensitive information that may have significant legal or family implications.

Retention, over extended periods, of information that is vital to the decisions that determine the educational experiences of the student makes careful maintenance of data even more important. If students and parents expect schools, and school systems, to provide highly sophisticated services, they must be prepared to provide information, frequently of a highly personal nature, upon which sound decisions can be based. However, when such information is made available, students and parents should be able to expect services that are provided to be effective, and to expect the information they furnish to be treated with the care and sensitivity that it warrants.

PRIVACY AND INFORMATION MANAGEMENT

The effectiveness of decisions about student needs or programs depends upon the quality of information that is employed for decision making. Four attributes of information need to be considered when personal information is to be collected by school systems for the purpose of making decisions about students.

The first, accuracy, refers to the fidelity between the attribute (e.g., a fact, an event, etc.) and the record of that attribute.[28] Decisions based on information that is inaccurate may mislead decision makers and result in counterproductive programs for a student. The maintenance system must be designed to ensure that all data are free of error. This may require the cross-checking of data with original documents, the examination of figures from other sources, and the carrying out of internal consistency procedures as are necessary to ensure that data accurately represent the subject.

The second attribute, completeness, refers to the sufficiency of the available data to fulfil the purposes for which they have been recorded.[29] Incomplete data may lead to inappropriate decisions since they may convey impressions that are incorrect and that would be shown to be in error by the addition of missing data. Information gathering processes must ensure that all available and necessary data are provided to the system and that those data that are not on hand are obtained as they become available. It is also important to ensure that data purging does not result in the loss of data that are critical to decisions to be made at other times. Data gathering tools should be designed so that respondents are able to provide requested information and so that formats assist respondents in providing the data necessary for a complete file.

The third attribute, timeliness, relates to the degree to which data are reflective of the current status of the subject and are available when required.[30] Many data lose their value as time passes and the maintenance system must ensure the removal of stale data that no longer reflect the status of a student. This requires the dating of all documents and records and the periodic removal and replacement of outdated records. As well, data must be available when decisions must be made. This requires a delivery system that will provide data to the right decision makers, in the right place, and at the right time. Record dating, purging of untimely data, periodic review of files, and the timely provision of data are all essential aspects of an effective data maintenance process.

Undisciplined collection frequently results in too much, and often irrelevant, data. Only data pertinent to decisions should be collected or retained. Pertinence refers to the degree to which data bear directly upon the purposes for which they were recorded.[31] Purpose should be defined prior to data collection. Even so, as time passes, students change. Data that describe the behaviour or characteristics of a child at one time lose their value for later decisions. The retention of such data, no longer appropriate for decisions about a student, may lead to decisions that are unreasonable and not in the best interest of the student. Furthermore, data held in a record for little or no purpose may prejudicially affect decisions. It is important to ensure that all data in the record are appropriate to the decisions that are to be made. The information system should require the purging of inappropriate and non-pertinent data and should institute a system for their removal.

If data are to be retained by schools in order for them to make program decisions, then the data that is kept ought to be of sufficiently high quality to ensure that decisions based upon them will be sound. Students should be able to count on effective decision making if they risk their privacy in the search for appropriate educational opportunity. The school, college, or university, in retaining student data, must accept the professional responsibility to maintain information that is accurate, complete, timely, and pertinent. It must also accept the responsibility to provide reasonable protection to the informational privacy of students who have provided the data.

As well as providing quality information, school systems must protect the privacy of both the student and the family, and see that data obtained for program or personal decisions are not misused. As was noted earlier, the essence of privacy is not that a person withholds information from other persons but that the person has the right to control personal information. Privacy is first in jeopardy when information is collected and again when it is passed from the collector to a third person. Invasion of privacy may be avoided if the subject is fully informed about conditions that apply to personal information and if consent is obtained prior to the information being collected, used, or exchanged.

A person who has a demonstrated interest in a subject has a right to know about that subject, but to exercise this right information must be available. The right to know refers to the "right to become maximally informed."[32] Administrative law consistently has supported the right, on the grounds of procedural fairness, of a person to be informed of events and data that may significantly affect her or his interests.[33] In this context, to protect a person's right to privacy, one must inform the subject before information is collected, used, or disseminated to a third party.

Furthermore, a person must not only be informed, but be able to influence events. Consenting or, conversely, withholding consent, is the instrument through which a person exercises control over informational privacy. Thus, a school or school system must establish procedures to permit this exercise of control. Consent is an act of the will of a person to permit an action after that person has been provided with sufficient information about the possible implications of the action to be able to assess its consequences.[34] To recognize a person's right to privacy, as well as the right to know, the consent of the subject should be obtained only after he or she has been informed, but prior to the collection, use, or dissemination of information.

Both informing a subject and obtaining consent would be meaningless if data were not protected against unauthorized examination, use, and dissemination. Therefore, the security system that is used to protect data must ensure that unauthorized access to data is prevented. Security systems must not only prevent access to files by unauthorized persons, they must be able to replace data that have been lost or destroyed through carelessness or malicious intent. This suggests not only that storage facilities should be secured by locks and keys and by strict supervision of storage areas, but that back-up files should be retained in separate and secure locations. It should be noted that the most effective control over loss will be provided by a staff of users aware of the implications of careless handling of personal data.

Privacy of personal information is possible if schools and school systems recognize its importance, inform students and their parents of procedures and implications of collecting and maintaining information, obtain consent prior to collecting, using, or retaining information, and provide adequate security arrangements to protect the integrity of their data files against tampering and unauthorized access and use. If a school system expects its students to provide information upon which decisions affecting their lives will be based, students should expect no less than a well maintained information system that provides adequate protection of their personal data.

CONCLUSION

Conflict exists between the individual's desire for personal privacy and the societal expectation for enhanced educational services. This creates a significant problem for the educational administrator whose responsibility it is to manage a school system. Privacy and improved service are positive values that are difficult to ignore, and both place on schools substantial pressures for improved functioning at a time when public education is experiencing reduced resources and weakened public support. Furthermore, the legal support that would impel schools to clearly recognize privacy as an imperative is at best weak, if not contradictory, and students lack the status to command attention to their interests.

Coupled with this lack of concern about personal privacy is the rapid development of an informational society that collects and stores more information on individuals than has ever been accumulated in the history of civilization. The result is a potentially dangerous situation in which the personal integrity of a student's private personality is placed in jeopardy as better services are provided in Canadian schools.

While information handling processes have developed at an exponentially accelerating pace, legislative protections have stumbled along. Federal legislation has largely ignored the problem, but is excluded from educational matters in any event. Provinces have made modest legislative efforts but have largely delegated their responsibilities to local authorities. The school systems, caught up in a plethora of operational problems concerning the provision of new services, have given scant attention to the issues involved and have neglected to develop effective policies and practices that will address concern for student privacy. Meanwhile, demands for more effective services mount. Data are collected and privacy is placed in jeopardy as outmoded processes are used to handle information.

Recognition of the interests of students with regard to both better services and more effective information practice is essential if students and their families are to be protected from the exposure of their private personalities while they seek public services of high quality. The dilemma is needless. Better quality information is necessary to ensure services that meet the needs of the student. High quality information is only possible when school systems employ information processes that are aimed at the development of such information. These same procedures recognize the importance and value of information and thereby integrate protections for the privacy and other interests of the student. Only with such an integrated approach, supported by appropriate legislative initiatives, will the interests of students and their families be protected.

NOTES

1. Stafford Beer, *Platform for Change* (London: Wiley, 1975), 227.
2. Civil Liberties Association, National Capital Region, *Privacy and You: An Introduction* (Ottawa: Civil Liberties Association, 1979), 2.
3. Thomas M. Cooley, *Torts*, 2nd ed. (Boston: Little, Brown, 1895), 188.
4. S. Warren and Louis D. Brandeis, "The Right to Privacy," *Harvard Law Review* 4 (1890), 205.
5. Henry E. Butler, K.D. Moran, Floyd A. Vanderpool Jr., *Aspects of Student Records* (Topeka, Kans.: National Organization on Legal Problems of Education, 1972), 6.
6. Oscar M. Ruebhausen and Orville G. Brim Jr., "Privacy and Behavioral Research," *Columbia Law Review* 55 (1965), 1189.
7. Alan F. Westin, *Privacy and Freedom* (New York: Atheneum, 1967), 356.
8. Ibid., 7.

9. Peter Burns, "The Law and Privacy: The Canadian Experience," *Canadian Bar Review* 54 (1976), 7.
10. Ibid., 9.
11. Hannah A. Levin and Fred Askin, "Privacy in the Courts: Law and Social Reality," *Journal of Social Issues* 33 (1977), 139.
12. Privacy Act, S.B.C. 1968, c.39.
13. Privacy Act, S.M. 1970, c.74.
14. Privacy Act, S.S. 1974, c.80.
15. Michael Brown, Brenda Billingsley, and Rebecca Shamai, *Privacy and Personal Data Protection*. A Report on Personal Record Keeping by the Ministries and Agencies of the Ontario Government, Research Publication 15 (Toronto: Commission on Freedom of Information and Individual Privacy, 1980), 11.
16. Ibid., 98.
17. Burns, "The Law and Privacy," 12.
18. Brown, Billingsley, and Shamai, *Privacy and Personal Data Protection*, 105.
19. David H. Flaherty, *Privacy and Government Data Banks: An International Perspective* (London: Mansell, 1979), 231.
20. S.C. 1982, c.110.
21. Ibid., s.40(e).
22. Ibid. 43(2) (b).
23. Ibid., ss.45(1) and (2).
24. Edward H. Humphreys, *Privacy in Jeopardy: Student Records in Canada* (Toronto: Ontario Institute for Studies in Education, 1980), 39.
25. Ibid.
26. Ibid., 48.
27. E.H. Humphreys, I.F. Davidson, J.D. Feeney, L.S. Weintraub, and P.A. Manuel, *The Adequacy of the Ontario Student Record in Accommodating the Record-Keeping Ramifications of Bill 82* (Toronto: Department of Educational Administration, Ontario Institute for Studies in Education, 1984), 148.
28. Ibid., 51.
29. Ibid.
30. Ibid., 52.
31. Ibid.
32. Butler, Moran, and Vanderpool, *Aspects of Student Records*, 6.
33. R.W. Cosman, "Ontario's Legal System and Special Education Appeals" (paper presented to the O.C.L.E.A. workshop Bill 82: The Legal Adgenda, Toronto, 1982).
34. Humphreys, et al., *Adequacy of Ontario Student Record*, 53.

SECTION 2:
THE IMPACT OF COMPUTERS IN CANADIAN EDUCATION

Computer technology has the demonstrated capacity to revolutionize most aspects of our society, including education. Compared to the impact of computers on other areas such as communication, transportation, manufacturing, and business, however, the widespread impact on education perhaps still remains more of a potential than a realization. Numerous issues regarding the role of computers in Canadian education are outlined by the authors in this section.

Hunka presents a brief historical overview of the development of computer-assisted instruction in the United States and Canada and describes the current use of computers in Canadian schools, colleges, and universities. He brings into focus more than thirty general and specific issues resulting from the use of computers in instruction and evaluation.

Ragsdale notes the extreme points of view that are often adhered to concerning the role of computers in education, from those who perceive the computer as a "fad" to those who envision it as the future base for most educational endeavours. He advocates a cautionary position and discusses issues revolving around our inability to predict the future in education, our inability to clearly stipulate our educational goals, the problems that arise in attaining our educational goals even if we know what we want, and ways of guiding the development of computers in education so that the benefits for students are maximized. Ragsdale cautions against the incorporation of changes simply for the sake of change and promotes a needs-assessment approach to the use of computers in education, with constant reminders to reexamine the goals and values upon which these changes are founded. The incorporation of computers must be based on the needs of the current and future curriculum, not on the attributes of the evolving technology.

Olson and Sullivan present a more guarded and pessimistic view of the future of computers in Canadian education than does Ragsdale. Will the computer simplify and accentuate power inequalities within our society? Will the computer separate students according to class structure? Will the computer create a new division between those who are "skilled" and those who are "deskilled"? Will the computer serve to centralize or decentralize education? According to Olson and Sullivan, these and other related questions have not met with close enough scrutiny. Given the promotional campaigns of computer companies, the proper perspective for guiding educational computer use may be missed. Olson and Sullivan stress the need for a critical evaluation of our educational needs and how the computer may be of service in meeting these needs.

THE ROLE OF COMPUTERS IN CANADIAN EDUCATION
STEVE HUNKA

BACKGROUND DEVELOPMENTS IN CANADA

In the late 1950s the National Research Council (NRC) recognized that Canadian universities required substantial support for upgrading their computing facilities in order to maintain an effective research program in the physical sciences. This recognition led to a program of block financial grants to major university computing centres. These grants were made to the institution in lieu of researchers including computing costs in their research grant proposals submitted to NRC. Although this financial support was motivated by the desire to upgrade facilities for the physical sciences, it indirectly assisted the social sciences, including faculties of education, to also make use of more modern computing equipment.

Up to this time, most schools in Canada had no computing equipment. An exception was the province of Ontario, which encouraged schools to install small computers under the federal government's program of financial support for purchase of capital equipment for technical and vocational education programs. Although some of these computers were designated by schools for use in business education courses, their use was expanded to include computer programming in other subject areas. Other provinces more frequently used the same source of funds for purchase of traditional equipment associated with the teaching of business education and shop courses.

Although NRC has traditionally been a government-supported agency for research and development in the physical sciences, a small team of researchers at NRC recognized the potential contribution that computers could make to instruction. This team, housed within the Radio and Electrical Engineering Division of NRC, recognized the importance of the need for specialized hardware and software requirements for computer-assisted instruction (CAI) and gave support, through grants to industry and through their own efforts, to developments for both needs. Special devices to be used in support of computer-based instruction, such as a touch sensitive screen, audio disk system, and film projection devices were prototyped at the NRC laboratory. In addition, the NRC laboratory established a CAI computing facility, which was made available to researchers across Canada, although the cost of telecommunications to the facility detracted from all but more local researchers making use of the service. Further support was provided for the development of CAI through the establishment of the Associate Committee for Educational Technology, a committee composed of members from universities, industry, and, on some occasions, from school systems. This committee not only provided advice to the NRC laboratory concerning important needs, it also provided a forum in which colleagues from across Canada could meet and exchange problems, developments, and experiences. NRC was also instrumental in establishing some standards with respect to the development and use of CAI. Specifications were drawn up for a CAI authoring language, which, it was hoped, would provide for easy exchange of courseware across Canada. These specifications were used as the basis for the development of Canada's NATAL-74 CAI authoring language.[1] Other standards developed through the efforts of NRC included documentation standards for CAI programs, and the use of the French character fonts on computer terminals.

At the time NRC became involved in developing their laboratory, three post-secondary institutions almost independently began to establish computer facilities for instructional purposes. The Ontario Institute for Studies in Education (OISE), the University of Calgary, and the University of Alberta, each with slightly differing emphases and goals, entered the field of CAI as part of their university responsibilities, supporting educational programs and faculty research. OISE and the University of Calgary established small computing systems based on commercial equipment from the Digital Equipment Corporation (DEC), while the University of Alberta in 1968 acquired one of twenty-five IBM 1500 CAI systems,[2] which were slight variations of the system used by Patrick Suppes at Brentwood School in California.

It is interesting to note that early developments in Canada of the application of computers for instructional purposes began first at NRC as a spin-off of research support of the physical sciences, and at the university level by educators who had a primary interest in educational psychology or measurement. Although NRC maintained a general interest in CAI, at the university level each institution took on a direction that differed to some extent. OISE developed software systems such as an authoring language to suit its needs, as well as courseware of interest to local colleges; the University of Calgary was involved with the needs of the mentally handicapped; the University of Alberta developed courseware that formed the primary source of instruction for students in the Faculty of Education and the Faculty of Medicine.

ASSOCIATED DEVELOPMENTS IN THE UNITED STATES

During the time the use of computers for educational functions was becoming of interest to educators, there was no indigenous computing industry in Canada. Almost all computers and their associated software were developed in the United States. An important breakthrough required to apply computers to instructional problems came about through an increase in computational speed, which allowed one computer to serve many users (time sharing) with sufficient efficiency that each user appeared to have sole access to the machine. This development, plus the increased financial support to educational programs provided by the Kennedy administration following the launching of Sputnik, set the stage for commercial interest in the development of computer-assisted instruction.

A major investment was made by IBM in the development of a specialized computing system for instruction (IBM 1500 system) in association with Patrick Suppes at Stanford University, while Control Data Corporation (CDC) associated itself with the development of the Plato CAI system at the University of Illinois. (The University of Illinois had established considerable expertise in computing through the development of the Illiac I numerical computer during the mid-1950s.) During the late 1960s and early 1970s, these two CAI systems competed for the interest of educational researchers.

The IBM 1500 system contained very specialized equipment designed specifically for instructional functions. A usual configuration of equipment for this system included a black and white television display screen and keyboard (terminal), a "light pen," which could be used for a pointing response by the student, an audio tape system from which messages could be played to the student under the control of the instructional strategies programmed, and a film projection system. In addition, drawings could be displayed on the screen as well as many different character fonts with superscripts and subscripts. In support of this equipment, the Coursewriter authoring language was developed for course authors. This type of computer system was a major advance over the teletype equipment used by most researchers.

The development of the Plato system at the University of Illinois was spearheaded by Donald Bitzer and was closely associated with electrical engineering. A major development at Illinois was the plasma plate display, a substitute for the television screen. This display device consisted of a grid of 525 by 525 minute cells of gas, sandwiched between two plates of glass, which could be made to glow under computer control. By causing a number of these to glow in a specific configuration, characters and drawings could be displayed. (Some of these display screens are used in automatic bank tellers in Canada.) Other developments at Illinois included the development of an audio system. In support of course development, the Tutor authoring language was developed for use by course authors.[3]

In both developments, at IBM and the University of Illinois, recognition was given to the importance of a number of factors related to instruction: a) the student must get a reasonable, fast reply from the computer; b) a volatile display surface was required rather than a printed output on paper; c) to approximate instructional activities of the classroom, the computing system had to be capable of displaying many different character fonts, drawings, and pictures; and d) audio was important to the instructional process. In addition, a CAI system had to provide the teacher with the capability (an authoring language) for creating courseware that would allow use of a wide variety of instructional strategies and styles, support and monitoring systems, and procedures for analysing a student's response.

Initially, the IBM 1500 system received a greater distribution than the Plato system because of its lower costs and complement of components designed specifically for instruction. It also appeared in a larger variety of educational institutions: Gauledet College used the system for instruction with deaf students; Rochester Institute of Technology used the system for upgrading of deaf students in the area of mathematics; Pennsylvania State University used the system for the development of a number of courses in special education and even used a mobile van to deliver the courses to rural areas. The U.S. Army at Fort Monmoth used the IBM 1500 system for instruction in electrical theory, while the U.S. Navy at San Diego used it for training personnel in handling specialized equipment. Florida State's use of the system was closely tied to research of factors affecting learning and effectiveness of CAI. In addition to institutional use of the system, IBM established a system for research and development at Science Research Associates (SRA), a subsidiary of IBM in Chicago. It was likely planned that SRA would become the distributing agency for IBM courseware.

During this period of time two IBM 1500 systems were exported to Canada; the first came to the University of Alberta, remaining there from 1968 to 1980, while the second went to the Department of Education in Quebec, and only remained for about two years. In addition to the developments in the United States of the IBM 1500 CAI system and the Plato system by CDC, three other projects were taking shape. Patrick Suppes at Stanford University, who had been using a prototype of the IBM 1500 system, had been working on the development of drill and practice strategies in the reading and arithmetic areas. A large amount of content was developed but could not be delivered to many students with a system such as the IBM 1500 because it had no good capability for connection to remote terminals using regular telephone lines. A commercial firm was established, the Computer Curriculum Corporation, to make a commercial application of Suppes' developments at Stanford, and continues to operate successfully today. The Computer Curriculum Corporation delivers, on a daily basis through its equipment, thousands of student-hours of drill and practice lessons in arithmetic and language arts.[4]

In Chicago, the drill and practice material developed by Suppes was converted to run on a large-scale computer system handling 1000 terminals simultaneously in local elementary schools. This material was made available to elementary school students who were identified as being behind their appropriate grade level in arithmetic, language arts, and reading. Since IBM was not planning any further developments or enhancements for the 1500 CAI system, the time was ripe for some other firm to take over where IBM had left off. The other development was the TICCIT system (Time-shared,

Interactive, Computer Controlled Information Television) centred at the MITRE Corporation, which was developing the hardware, and the University of Texas, and later Brigham Young University in Utah, which developed the courseware. The TICCIT system was unique in that it contained a built-in instructional strategy, provided the student with some control over movement through a course, and contained a true television display screen. (Other systems, such as the IBM 1500 had "TV screens" but were not capable of displaying a true video picture.)

During this period microcomputers had not been developed, although it has been rumoured that SRA had developed a small desktop computer that used the language called "A Programming Language" (APL) designed by Ken Iverson who obtained his education in Canada.[5] A research and development team, that included a number of Canadians, helped to develop the concepts of APL at IBM's Yorktown Heights laboratory in New York state.

COMPUTERS AND CANADIAN EDUCATION

Although Canadian developments have been very much influenced by the American development of computers, terminals, and software, the Canadian applications cannot be considered a duplicate of those in the United States. In retrospect, factors that likely contributed to the differences were the following:

1. Although more funds were available on a per capita basis in the United States for computer projects, much of the funding was through federal grants. One disadvantage of the U.S. research grant support system was that it was subject to prevailing political interests and frequently directed towards special mission-oriented needs (e.g., disadvantaged children, minority groups, and the like). In Canada, funding was provided, although at a lesser level, through budgets of universities and the research budget of NRC, and funding at the universities was not mission oriented.

2. There was some national scope to the development of computer use for instructional functions in Canada while much less so in the United States. This is understandable given the size of the United States, the many levels of government in the states from which cooperation would have had to have been sought, and the fact that each major computer company had its own research and development program. In Canada, NRC has been, and is today, respected for its impartiality and research interests that are not constrained by provincial boundaries.

3. Although the number of CAI installations in Canada was small, they were almost entirely resident in universities where a considerable degree of freedom existed to explore a variety of research avenues. In addition, almost all the installations were strongly influenced in their operations by researchers interested in educational psychology, measurement, and evaluation. Frequently, these same researchers brought experiences with computers from numerical computation. Although there were installations in the United

States that had similar environments, there were also many installations that had staff who were using computers for the first time, and with little interest in the psychological foundations of learning.

4. Because of the mission-oriented and politically defined areas of financial support in the United States, a large number of computer installations were devoted to instruction with children in the public school systems. This was much less so in Canada, with the result that little experience was gained from actual classroom experimentation in Canada.

Many of the applications of computers for educational and, more specifically, for instructional functions in Canada, can be traced to the work of three groups: the Ontario Institute for Studies in Education (affiliated with the University of Toronto), the University of Calgary, and the University of Alberta. In addition to influencing the applications of computers by directly creating courseware, these three institutions made major contributions through their graduate programs and training of educational researchers who took positions in other Canadian universities.

THE USE OF MICROCOMPUTERS

Because of the relatively low cost, some provinces in Canada, through their departments of education, encouraged the use of microcomputers in the classroom soon after they appeared on the market. British Columbia was one of the first provinces in which the government initiated the use of microcomputers by funding the purchase of 250 for test purposes. Shortly afterwards, Alberta's Department of Education made arrangements for a bulk purchase of one thousand microcomputers, which were resold to schools in the province. Ontario has been particularly active in recent years with financial support to industry and schools for the development and use of a Canadian microcomputer called the Icon. In the latter case, undoubtedly, there appeared to be a desire on the part of the Ontario government to support an indigenous microcomputer industry.

During the last couple of years a number of very sophisticated microcomputers have entered the marketplace. Many micros that have been in schools for the last two or three years have capabilities equal to or greater than the computer capabilities that were available to many universities in the 1960s. For example, the University of Illinois' Illiac I computer, which served a campus of 18 000 students in the early 1960s only had a main memory of approximately 4 000 characters, and a secondary memory (rotating drum) of about 100 000 characters. Micros available in schools today may have as many as 400 000 to 500 000 characters of main memory and as many as 20 million characters on a secondary memory (disk).

More recently, with the availability of microcomputers, a shift away from computer assisted instruction has occurred in the schools, yet most microcomputers have a computing power in excess of those systems that were initially used for computer assisted instruction. A number of reasons exist for this trend. In addition to CAI taking many hours of development time that are not readily available to a teacher, microcomputers do not have the authoring languages and support systems that are needed for the development of instructional material. In addition, even if one has an authoring language for the development of courses, an instructional support system is also required. For example, elements of an instructional support system would include capability for monitoring student progress and examination results, being able to move a student about in a course, review of examination answers, and restructuring the order of course content to suit individual needs—all become important to instructors once a course is operational. Some of these features are being provided on microcomputers, but only through communication with a much larger host computing system. Because of these restrictions, many teachers have moved to the use of computer programs in support of classroom instructional activities, rather than using the computer as the primary source of instruction.

There are two general types of programs that are frequently used by teachers in support of instruction in the regular classroom: a) programs that allow the student to explore ideas and concepts, and b) programs that are tools for the direct support of the subject matter of the classroom. A good example of a program that allows the exploration of mathematics is APL (A Programming Language). It has sufficient versatility that would allow a Grade 1 child to explore simple arithmetic concepts, and yet enough power for use by an applied mathematician. Another example would be the Logo programming language with its robot "turtle" that can be used to draw figures on paper.[6] Examples of programs that are used as tools in the support of instruction are word processors and "spread sheets." Word processors provide the student with an easy method by which essays and reports can be constructed. They are considered easy to use because of their powerful editing capabilities. "Spread sheets" typically refer to accounting-like tabular systems for holding data and which can be manipulated by various arithmetic procedures. In most instances, word processors and spread sheets have been constructed for general use, and they almost never contain special features designed specifically for classroom use.

ISSUES RESULTING FROM THE USE OF COMPUTERS IN EDUCATION

One reason that prompted NRC to support the creation of the NATAL authoring language was to promote the exchange of courseware across Canada. There was concern, supported by prevailing trends, that exchanges were being more easily made north and south across the Canadian-American border than among the provinces. There was evidence to support this concern as the University of Alberta had special education operational courses obtained from Pennsylvania State University, and an electrical theory course from the U.S. Army at Fort Monmoth.

Concerns regarding the development and distribution of the curriculum are not new. However, in the case of computer-based instruction, special concerns are raised in a number of different areas.

IN THE AREA OF INSTRUCTION

1. Since the special education course from Pennsylvania State provided university credit there, if the course is operated at another university, should the latter university also give credit? Should Pennsylvania State give credit?

2. Perhaps some subject matter areas are more acceptable for exchanges. Is an arithmetic drill program so different for children in Alabama, that it could not be used in Manitoba? What might be the long range implications in using instructional programs developed in the U.S.?

3. With the emphasis in teacher training faculties to encourage teachers to create their own curriculum, can this continue with computer-based instruction that may require from 50 to 100 hours of design time for each one hour of student instructional time? If this much effort is required for the design of a computer-taught course, why does it take so much less time for a teacher to prepare lessons for a regular classroom session?

4. Perhaps arithmetic drills and lessons in science can be exchanged across national borders, but can this be accepted in the social science areas? For example, how acceptable would a course on the development of Canada be if it were written by someone in the United States, and vice versa?

5. Should instructional programs in the language arts be exchanged across national borders?

6. What risks are there that computer-based instruction would make it easy to distribute propaganda? Some might argue that this would be easy, but might be more quickly identified especially if the program could be operated on a computer at home where parents might view the content.

7. Since it takes considerable effort to produce computer-based instructional material, is it possible that good and poor material will not be revised and thus contribute to maintaining a rigid curriculum?

8. What contribution might computers have towards multiculturalism in Canada? Consider the fact that CAI courses could be developed in many different languages, for example, in French, Cree, Inuit, German, or Ukrainian, since there is no problem in defining the appropriate character sets that are required.

9. Opponents of CAI frequently claim that it is dehumanizing, while supporters claim that a poor human-based relationship is far more dehumanizing than that which a computer might produce. Consider those factors that you think contribute to dehumanization, and then contrast a typical classroom and CAI using these factors. Which will hurt a student more, a poor teacher or a computer?

10. Some CAI courses represent a complete curriculum for one course and take an average student a hundred or more hours to complete. Is the development of such courses desirable? What are the advantages and disadvantages of such courses?

11. Much has been learned about those factors that promote learning (e.g., instructional design, motivation, perception, memory). How easily are these factors applied and maintained by a CAI course and by a regular classroom teacher?

IN THE AREA OF EVALUATION

1. Should the effectiveness of a computer-taught course be evaluated by comparison of results with those of a regularly taught class? Should the effectiveness of a teacher be judged by contrasting student achievement with that in a computer-taught course?

2. How should a computer-taught course be evaluated for its effectiveness? What criteria should be used: results on standardized tests? attitude towards the subject matter? the degree to which students enjoyed taking the course?

3. If effectiveness of a computer-taught course is judged by contrasting student learning with the learning produced in the regular classroom, should the computer-taught course only use techniques a teacher can use?

4. Kulik et al.[7] report generally positive results in the use of CAI. In particular, there is a saving of instructional time, and students are more likely to have a positive attitude towards the subject matter. What factors in CAI could explain such results?

5. When computers are used to simulate medical patients, how should such tests be scored when frequently each student takes a different route to handling the problem? This becomes a critical problem when a licensing body such as the Royal College of Physicians and Surgeons uses this approach for assessment of medical practioners for their R.C.P.S. degree.

IN THE AREA OF GENERAL COMPUTER USE FOR INSTRUCTION

1. How should the computer be used in the classroom? Should the teacher's approach be eclectic or be concentrated in the area of computer-assisted instruction, computer-managed instruction, or enrichment through use of the computer in an explorative mode? Should the computer be used for testing, diagnosis, and remedial work or as a tool (such as the use of a word processor or a spread sheet)?

2. Should the computer be used where instructional costs are high and numbers of students small, such as in the area of special education involving the handicapped and the gifted?

3. Some view the computer as an amplifier of intelligence. Is this statement a reasonable one and, if so, what experiences should students have

with computers? Should, for example, students learn how to program, or only how to use the computer as a tool?

4. Although the costs of computers continue to decrease, poorer rural school boards may still find it difficult to make them available to their students. Within urban school systems children from the wealthier families are likely to have computers at home. What can be done to ensure equality of access for all students?

5. What can be done to ensure equality of opportunity for both boys and girls to use and learn about computers?

IN THE AREA OF TESTING

Most formal testing today that uses both teacher-made and commercially made tests follow what might be called "classical testing theory." More recently, models for adaptive testing have been developed, and these models lend themselves more easily to computer administration than any other method. In adaptive testing, a large pool of test items is first "calibrated." Calibration involves the administration of the test items to a large pool of students just as is required for norming a standardized test. Once items have been calibrated, they then form the basis of a testing procedure that involves only those items that best estimate the student's ability or achievement. Selecting the particular questions that will best estimate a student's ability can easily be done using a computer system. Best is frequently interpreted to mean an estimate with the least amount of error. Thus, different students are likely to take a different number of questions as well as different questions.

1. Is it fair to have some students take tests with differing number of questions, as well as different questions, and yet make comparisons among results?

2. If adaptive testing were used as a basis of admission to a selective educational program, such as medicine, could the testing procedure be challenged as being discriminatory?

3. How can important examinations be kept secure when they are administered by a computer? Are tests administered by a computer any more or less secure than pencil-paper tests?

4. Since the results of a test can usually be given to the student immediately, is this likely to increase test taking anxiety?

5. When an examination is given in the regular classroom it is always possible for the teacher to "take up the test" and review each question and answer. Is this possible when the test is given by the computer?

Another form of adaptive testing involves a simulation of some complex event. For example, the use of a simulation of a patient in a medical context has been used by the Royal College of Physicians and Surgeons in Canada. If an emergency situation is simulated, initial actions by a student may cause a patient to "die," while other actions are likely to "prolong life." In the case where a student's patient "dies," no further questions are asked, while for another student many more questions would follow on diagnosis and treatment.

1. If a student makes a single, but critical error in a simulation, resulting in the simulation being terminated, should the student be given a second chance? How should such examinations be scored?
2. As a student progresses through a simulation, different problems may arise depending upon the actions taken. For example, one student's actions may result in a patient developing complications that must be treated in addition to the primary problem. Thus, can one really argue that the same test has been administered to all students?

GENERAL ISSUES INVOLVING COMPUTER USE IN EDUCATION

1. Usually a teacher does not develop curriculum material in such a form as to allow its publication. In the case of computer-based instructional material, because of its high cost of development, costs can be recovered to some extent by sales. In order to protect the investment made in the material, attempts have been made to copyright the computer instructional program. If a teacher develops computer-based material, who owns the copyright, the teacher, or the school board?
2. As more and more computers enter homes and schools, some people have questioned the need to develop computer literacy programs for students and teachers. Will students and teachers become computer literate on their own, or will special educational programs be required?
3. If a large amount of curriculum material is available, and a student can proceed quickly, should the student be slowed down to keep in step with peers, or allowed to progress as quickly as possible? Suppose rapid progress takes the student into the curriculum of the next grade level, should this be allowed?
4. Some have argued that introduction of computers into school systems is detracting from the serious consideration of more basic and important issues and needs. For example, in the U.S. context some have argued that many students would do better in school if they did not come underfed and undernourished. Perhaps the funds being spent on computers should be used for social programs, such as supplementary meals for young children at school?

LOOKING AHEAD

Today, it is likely that over 100 000 computers exist in Canadian classrooms even though there has been restricted financing of education by the provinces and a drop in enrolment during the last ten years. The use of computers for instructional functions at the post-secondary level in Canada has taken a different route in the college and technical school system than at the universities. Many colleges and technical schools in Canada operate computer-managed instructional programs (CMI). Computer-managed instruction provides a system for testing student skills and then prescribing traditional educational resources that the student is required to access. Universities in Canada generally have not operated any CMI programs, and have frequently limited the number of CAI programs that they offer. The University of Alberta, however, does operate an extensive CAI program using a Plato system as a campus-wide service, and a small research facility using a mini-computer in its Faculty of Education. The Plato service, for example, provides an extensive set of courses to medical students including a cardiology program that has been operated in CAI mode for over fifteen years. A notable entry by a commercial firm into CAI has been made by B.C. Telephones, which operates a TICCIT CAI system for educational programs required for training its technical staff.

The daily task of educating millions of students and workers is so large that, even today, the contributions of the computer in this regard must still be considered very small. However, a number of developments and trends suggest that the eventual impact of computers upon the educational system will be a major one, and therefore their introduction will affect the role of teachers, students, and educational institutions. As the cost of computers continues to decline and their power continues to increase, many tasks considered today as belonging only to the domain of human endeavour will become amenable to computer application. The short history of computer development suggests that computers are created in the likeness of cognitive humans, particularly so with the development of software. Even concepts of computer architecture can be found in information processing models of human cognition. Research and development in the area of artificial intelligence has already lead to the creation of expert systems that behave as accurately as an expert human in handling the analysis of complex problems requiring experienced judgments. These developments are parallelled by rapid advances in production and recognition of speech. All these developments can be easily related to instructional needs. It would be unwise for teachers and educators in general to be so complacent as to think that their domain of interest will be left untouched by these developments. The primary challenge for the educational system will be to determine how best to take advantage of the computer developments now on the horizon.

NOTES

1. M.L. Westrom, *NATAL-74 National Authoring Language Specifications Manual* (Ottawa: National Research Council, 1974).
2. B.L. Hicks and S. Hunka, *The Teacher and the Computer* (Toronto: W.B. Saunders, 1972).
3. B.A. Sherwood, *The Tutor Language* (Urbana: University of Illinois, Computer-Based Research Laboratory, 1974).
4. P. Suppes, M. Jerman, and D. Brian, *Computer-Assisted Instruction: Stanford's 1965–66 Arithmetic Program* (New York: Academic Press, 1972); E. Macken, P. Suppes, and G. Poulsen, *Evaluation Studies of Computer Curriculum Corporation's Elementary School Curriculum, 1971–1976* (Palo Alto, Calif.: Computer Curriculum Corporation, 1976).
5. H.A. Peele, *APL: An Introduction* (New Jersey: Hayden Book Co., 1974).
6. S. Papert, *Mindstorms: Children, Computers, and Powerful Ideas* (New York: Basic Books, 1968).
7. J.A. Kulik, C.C. Kulik, and P.A. Cohen, "Effectiveness of Computer-Based College Training: A Meta-Analysis of Findings," *Review of Educational Research* 50, 4 (Winter 1980).

COMPUTERS IN CANADA: COMMUNICATIONS AND CURRICULUM

RONALD G. RAGSDALE

The goals in this paper are to discuss three main issues. The first deals with our inability, in most instances, either to predict future events in education or to know what our goals are, to know what future we want. The second deals with the problems that arise in attaining goals, even when they have the support of the majority of the people concerned. The third part is directed at ways of guiding the development of computers in education in such a way that the maximum benefits for students are realized.

THE FUTURE OF COMPUTERS IN EDUCATION

There is an abundant supply of people who are willing to predict the effects computers will have on education, but unfortunately there is little agreement among the pundits. The opinions range from those who believe that computers are just another educational fad like the language lab, to those who believe that education in the not too distant future will be computer-based, with schools abolished.

These divergent predictions are made for a number of reasons. Among the most important bases for forecasts is a deep understanding of both technology and education, but perhaps equally important is a strong desire to see the predicted events actually occur. Because of these sources of bias, it is very difficult to evaluate the prognosticator's art.

Similarly, one might consider the probable effect of predictions about the future of technology and/or education. In some cases, it seems clear that the predictions are made in order to alert the populace to possible pitfalls in the use of technology, as in Orwell's *1984*. Nevertheless, the more general case is to describe the potential of what *could* or *should* happen when computers are used in education, as in Papert's *Mindstorms*.[1]

PREDICTING THE USE OF COMMUNICATIONS MEDIA

Since we interpret events in the context of our own experience and expectations, we might say that the answer to the question about future computer uses is unobtainable. That is, we might say the answer is unobtainable regardless of our background, or more precisely, because of our backgrounds. An illustration of this is seen in the inability of people to forecast the effects of new communications media when they appear. When a new long distance telephone service was initiated in 1878, the President of the United States spoke a few sentences over the phone and then commented that it was an interesting invention, but he wondered why anyone would want to have one. At about the same time, a British newspaper asserted that the telephone would never be needed in Britain, because there was an ample supply of messenger boys. Meanwhile, business made little use of telephones until they had been in operation for several years.

The book *Forecasting the Telephone*, by Ithiel de Sola Pool, is a collection of predictions that have been made over the years about how telephones were going to be used. Many of them are quite accurate, but some involving the phonograph are off the mark for both media. The phonograph was being developed to allow people to make long-distance telephone calls, since telephones in those days did not have enough power. The ideas was that one would phone to a machine, which would make a record to be played into another telephone, with this process repeated until the call had reached its destination. It was a slow version of what microwave repeater stations do today. This cumbersome ritual seemed plausible to people of that day, since it compared favourably with alternatives such as the telegraph and the mail system (which was no better then than it is today). Again, it was the comparison with the current way of doing things which led to this result.

It is amusing to us that people responded to telephones in what seem to be inappropriate ways, but fifty years from now, our response to computers may seem just as amusing. At the present time, it is clear that the ways in which computers are used have changed a great deal over the last two or three decades, but the experience of those decades does not guarantee that our predictions have improved. In 1928, the Benz company (now the makers of Mercedes automobiles) hired a consulting firm to estimate the total number of cars they might sell in the next forty years. The estimated total for forty years was given as up to 40 000 cars, provided that enough chauffeurs could be trained. After several decades of computer use, it is still likely that the applications of computers will continue to change over the coming decades. The most realistic view of computer use may be that the ultimate effect of computers is not yet known, but we can be almost certain that there are major effects that we have not anticipated.

Lias discusses the potential effects of computers as communications media, and, in so doing, presents eight general principles of media, among them, "New media are accepted with little forethought or planning," a problem also addressed by Sullivan.[2] But Lias also presents other, more disturbing principles, in particular, "Each medium biases or distorts the messages it carries in significant ways"; "New media often generate their own market, their own need for existence"; "New media reshape societies, their governments, bureaucracies and institutions"; and "New media cause underlying social values to change through the metaphors which they instill."[3]

THE BIASING EFFECT

One example of the way in which television biases a message is that it develops in the spectator the expectation that any worthwhile event (a good play in a hockey game, for example) will be shown again in "instant replay." A result of this expectation is likely to be a lack of attention to events as they occur. The comparable bias arising from the use of computers in instruction is the expectation that any question from the student will evoke an immediate response.

Even more ominous is Lias's suggestion that the original reasons for using a medium are often lost as new reasons "suggest" themselves. As an example he describes the growth of government records in the United States.

> In a 1977 census, 6,739 files of information were carried by federal agencies, averaging 18 records for each person in the country. Since then many millions of dollars of computer equipment have been added each year to carry more and more files on the computer, for easy access and cross-reference. Such record-keeping could not be managed manually, but with computers, since it *can* be done, it *is* done.[4]

These principles of media certainly support Francis Schaeffer's earlier warning about technology—"that which can be done, will be done"—and its clear applicability to computer uses in government.[5] Moreover, it is also clear that human intentions and media outcomes interact continuously. That is, unanticipated outcomes (modified by media effects) alter human intentions, which again produce different outcomes, and so on. The intentions of humans are probably less important in determining how computers will be used than are the unintended outcomes, the "side effects" of technology as media.

On the basis of this section, we might conclude that favourable benefits of computers (and other technology) are not guaranteed, but must be gained through human direction. In other words, we have to know what we want, if we are, in fact, to get what we want.

COMPUTERS AS COMMUNICATIONS MEDIA

Although the initial predictions about computers, such as predicting that ten computers could serve all the computing needs of the United States, were off the mark there are changes in use that have occurred since that time, and they should allow us to have a better idea of where new applications are developing.

One major change in computer use, and a trend that is continuing, is the decreasing emphasis on mathematical applications of computers. The link between computers and numbers can be described as primarily historical, with punched card equipment being invented in the 1890s so that the data collected in one U.S. census could be tabulated before the next census was upon them. The first computers were constructed to calculate artillery firing tables, with the first large computers used to do extensive calculations for atomic energy research. This emphasis was perpetuated by schools that assigned mathematics teachers to handle the computer courses and made mathematics a prerequisite for these courses.

The drift away from mathematical applications began when the prices of computers sharply decreased and the variety of devices that could be attached to computers increased. When high quality printers became available, word processing became a popular and effective use of computers. The development of high quality graphic display devices has led to the increased use of computers in animation, with a recent sale of one of the largest computers in the world being made to a Hollywood film studio for animation use.

These applications, word processing and graphic animation, are just two consequences of the greater emphasis on non-mathematical applications. They illustrate the general impact that computers are having on communications. Some of the effects are clearly visible and some are hidden. We take the current level of telephone service for granted, but it has been estimated that, in the U.S., half of the population would have to work for the telephone companies in order to maintain today's level of telephone services if computers were removed from the system. On a more visible level, many companies and universities are using electronic message systems to enhance the communications within their communities. One popular form of electronic communications is seen in the hundreds of "bulletin boards" that have sprung up all over this continent. The bulletin board allows any user with a telephone-connected computer or terminal to read notices, add notices for other users or send and receive electronic mail, and share microcomputer programs with other bulletin board users. Many bulletin boards are for groups with special interests, such as users of a particular microcomputer or librarians.

That the connection between computers and communications is not trivial is illustrated by the business battle of the 1980s, currently raging throughout North America between IBM and AT&T. These two giant corporations, one based in computers and the other in communications, are in direct competition for a major market. What products these two companies will be selling twenty years from now is not known by us or by them, but we can be sure that the products will involve computers and be used for communication.

PREPARING FOR COMPUTERS IN EDUCATION

If we know that computers are important to communication, but don't know how they are going to be used, how do we prepare ourselves and our children? How can we do research on the use of computers in education, if we don't know what we are looking for? Our answers to these questions should probably have two main components, the first emphasizing our values and the importance of basing our goals on these values. The second part stems from the first, being a needs assessment, with strong links to underlying values, and a requirement that the needs assessment be a repeating cycle.

NEEDS ASSESSMENT

For those who lack training in philosophy, the relationship between assumptions and their consequences is often ignored. In applied mathematics and other physical science courses, one passes quickly over the assumptions and spends most of the time on the theory—the consequences of the assumptions.

Our educational practices are strongly shaped by our assumptions, usually implicit, including both our group assumptions and individual ones. They include our expectations about what students will have learned before reaching a certain level, what they can learn in a fixed period of time, and what factors external to the student, such as materials, mode of presentation, classroom structure, etc., will influence learning.

The topic of discussion at this point, however, is not the general role of assumptions, but the specific role that assumptions play in the application of computers to education. In particular, this discussion will be concerned with the assumptions made about what students require and the assumptions made about how computers can help to satisfy those requirements.[6]

ASSUMPTIONS OF NEEDS ASSESSMENT

Due to the evolving nature of computer characteristics, the assessment of needs will be a continuous process. However, the focus of the process must be on the curriculum (future, as well as current), not on the attributes of the technology. It may be that experience with computers will be more of a hindrance in determining these needs, since the experience will tend to bias our expectations. The outcome of the process should be in the form of software attributes, based on curriculum goals, independent (as much as possible) of hardware characteristics. (It should be noted that, in practice, this is very difficult to do. Hardware requirements must usually be set well in advance of the creation of software because the software must have hardware on which to be created. This can be a difficult timing problem, since it is important to work with advanced hardware to develop new techniques, but one must not get too far ahead of the potential users.)

CURRICULUM ORIENTATION

This includes what we do now, as well as what we would like to do. It is almost impossible to focus on the curriculum without any knowledge of computer potential, but it is worth trying. This phase might be followed with one that explicitly considers computer characteristics.[7]

CONTINUOUS PROCESS

Any needs that are identified can only be tentative. Alterations will occur because of changing curriculum goals, technological advances, and the results of previous need-assessing cycles. The most important force in changing the needs will be the changing applications of the new technology. For example, word processing would not have been an identified need a few years ago, but its use brings other needs into focus.

PROCESS STEP 1

Initially we would focus on the needs that teachers, students, and others (parents, etc.) can identify in all curriculum areas, without directing their attention to the use of computers. As a follow-up, we would then ask the same groups to identify needs that seemed to be related to computer functions (possibly supplying them with some computer background in the interim). There is a trade-off between unbiased views from non-users and the more informed views of computer users. In either case, there is a danger that the "needs" will be based on intuition, which may not be supported in practice (such as touch screens, which seemed intuitively very desirable, but which, in practice, can be a negative factor due to arm fatigue.)

PROCESS STEP 2

After the lists of general and computer-specific needs have been created, the next task is to identify the "critical competitors" for satisfying those needs, paying particular attention to those that might be satisfied by computer applications. Critical competitor is a term used by Scriven in discussing product evaluation. He stresses that a great deal of imagination may be required to identify critical competitors. He gives an example from an incident in Berkeley in which there were complaints about the time spent in waiting for the elevators on the main floor of a new building. There were no indicators on the main floor to show what floor the elevators were on and this seemed to make the delay longer. The solution of putting floor indicators on the main floor was too expensive, but the problem was solved effectively and inexpensively when someone proposed the critical competitor of installing full-length mirrors next to the elevators. When this was done, the problem vanished. (Scriven also stresses the need to consider printed materials as alternatives to computer-assisted instruction.)

PROCESS STEP 3

From the lists of needs and critical competitors, the next task is to identify the computer functions that seem most appropriate for the various curriculum areas. It is possible that a major need might require more teacher time, which might be obtained through the use of computers for less important, but time consuming tasks. Therefore, appropriateness is not restricted to the highest priority needs.

PROCESS STEP 4

At this point we would look for patterns among the needs, the critical competitors, and the computer functions. It may be that a particular computer function is a marginal solution to one need, but could be an optimal solution to a collection of needs. For example, even mundane applications can be useful in getting teachers started in using computers.

After the completion of step 4, and the implementation of procedures designed to satisfy these needs, the cycle repeats with new needs being detected. Often these new needs may arise as a result of the steps taken to satisfy previously identified needs. The new needs may be a direct and anticipated result of the previous measures, such as the new needs created by new skills acquired through word processing practice, or they may be side effects, or unanticipated effects. An example of side effects might be the increased need for social skills that could arise from use of a peer approval process implemented to relieve the teacher from the pressure of increased written production. The impact of side effects, an impact that is likely to grow as we become more aware of their existence, should lead to a greater appreciation that not all applications of technology that can be done, ought to be done.

WHAT CAN (OUGHT TO) BE DONE

Most readers would agree that what can be done is not necessarily what ought to be done. In the area of computer technology, as in the U.S. space program and mountain climbing, the desire to do something "because it is there" is extremely strong. Therefore, the needs assessment base from the previously described process is a crucial component of technology implementation.

However, the "rational systems" approach is often not adequate for the task of accomplishing the intended goals.[8] Seidman describes the rational systems approach to educational change as beginning with legislation or judicial decisions, then proceeding through the development of program guidelines, implementation by local school authorities (driven by the rewards or sanctions in the guidelines), and including evaluation to determine compliance with the guidelines, as well as the quality of the program. Unfortunately, after the first step in which legislators or jurists agree on vaguely stated general goals, there is a series of compromises in the other steps that may result in outcomes that are the opposite of what was intended. That is, what can be defined in a guideline, implemented by a school board, or evaluated quantitatively is often different, in important ways, from what was originally intended.

Examples of irrational behaviour of organizations might include the automobile industry's use of robots (when full employment is essential to their required level of sales); newspaper staff (both labour and management) insisting on work arrangements that meant the end of many newspapers; railway people apparently working to make the railroads a second choice to trucks and buses; or postal workers and management combining to greatly reduce the amount of mail being sent, particularly during the Christmas season, by their consistent failure to provide adequate service.

CHANGES IN THE EDUCATIONAL SYSTEM

In looking at the components of the educational system, it seems clear that the choices to be made in the selection of appropriate technology should be based on the needs of the students, teachers, and parents. It also seems clear that many of these needs, at least as they intersect with the potential benefits of technology, have not been completely determined. The result is the substantial possibility that technology will be selected in a manner unrelated to the real needs of the people in the educational system.

When the needs of the people, particularly the students, are not clearly identified, or are ignored, there are several other sources of needs that might be filled. The most dangerous of these are probably the needs of technology itself. By this is meant the kind of technology implementation that focusses on the attributes of the technology and attempts to maximize the use of unique characteristics. It is equivalent to asking, "What can computers (or some other technology) do best?" Much of the planning and prediction in education seems to be based on this same faulty assumption.

A second source of potential needs is at the management level, including not only the administrators within school boards, but also those within ministries of education. The needs that they might like to see satisfied by technology include those of replacing teachers, or making teachers conform to procedures set by administrators. Several years ago, in what may have been an example of wishful thinking, a provincial minister of education was quoted as predicting that teachers would be replaced by computers. Other predictions have said that the use of computers would allow (or require) the use of programs that would standardize the curriculum (and teachers' practice). Technology can also be seen by management as a means of monitoring the employees and evaluating their effectiveness. There is a danger that these needs that ease the life of management may be seen as more important than the learning needs of students.

Although teachers might be targets of management needs, they can also be a source of competing needs. Just as in industries such as newspapers and postal services, the staff in schools may have strong desires to see the status quo maintained. Technology that is used to implement the old system in new garments, such as the exclusive use of computers to assist the teacher in lecturing to the class, is a threat, not only to the students, but also to the (successful implementation of the) technology itself. Technology that is misused, or underutilized, be it overhead projectors or programmed instruction, can be thwarted by the very people who use it. If true benefits of technology are possible, the needs of teachers may serve to obscure these benefits.

Finally, the students themselves may be a source of competition to their own needs, if their expressed *wants* are given greater weight than their actual *needs*. One of the assumptions made about the use of computers in education has been that students will be able to learn more when they are given a choice of the way in which they will learn. This feature, called "learner control," has generally been unsuccessful in practice due to the fact that students do not seem to be able to choose the learning style that is most effective for them.[9] A more obvious instance of the clash between user wants and needs can be seen in the offerings on television. Basing choices of technology on student wants might lead to an instructional wasteland to rival the wasteland of television.

On the basis of this section, we may conclude that knowing what we want is not sufficient. There must be some process that reminds us of our goals and the values on which they are based. This calls for some type of monitoring system.

MONITORING THE NEW COMPUTER USES

One reason we do not know what the future of computers will be is that we are too bound up in the non-computer age. Our context affects our expectations and leads us to see computers being used to do present-day tasks, but do them more effectively. The people who are most likely to see new applications for computers are those who are not steeped in the culture of the present, namely young children. Children who grow up with computers are likely to create applications that we have not anticipated.

To get a clearer idea of the innovative ways in which computers might be used, and to see how these applications will affect our lives, we should consider not only providing young children with computing resources, but also observing and monitoring how they make use of these resources when they are not being directed by adults. Already we find that some of the most exciting new hardware and software creations are being produced by very young people, and some of the best educational materials are coming from people who are working closely with very young children. If we monitor the creations of young computer users, we can support those that are consistent with our own values and goals.

But why provide young children with computers, if there is truth in the predictions made by some experts that discarded personal computers will soon fill our closets? The reason for bringing children and computers together is two-fold. One is to help children to learn more effectively, while the other is to prepare them for a world in which computers will play an increasingly important role. We must distinguish between the viability of computers themselves, and the many applications of computers. It will not be surprising if many of our current computer applications are discarded in the next decade, but the use of computers will still increase. If we limit children's exposure to computers because we believe that educational applications of computers will not survive, we may be denying them valuable preparation for adult life. If the exposure to computer use is valuable and, in addition, the predictions about the death of educational applications are also wrong, then we will have doubled our mistake.

Thus, we not only want our children to be ready for the computer age, but we also need them to create the computer age. This is the cornerstone for the arguments in favour of introducing computers into the elementary grades. The younger the children are when they begin using computers (initially in very simple ways), the fewer preconceptions they will have about computers, and the longer they will have to refine their ideas and develop new concepts. The role of the educational system is less to teach young people about computers than it is to provide them with a value base for their uses of computers.

The question about the ultimate effects of computers is still unanswered, but the location of the answer, and the procedures for finding it, are defined. It is through careful observation and encouragement of the children who will use computers as part of their education, through elementary, secondary, and post-secondary levels, that the answer will be found.

AN EXAMPLE FROM COMPUTER PROGRAMMING

These conclusions about the location of the answer and the means for finding it can be supported on the basis of experience in the area of computer programming. Great concern has developed over the most effective methods for creating computer programs, because an increasing portion of programming budgets has had to be allocated to modifying and correcting existing programs, mainly because they were poorly programmed when they were created. One response to this concern was to do a number of scientific studies in an attempt to identify effective programming techniques. The general results of these studies have been disappointing, however, primarily because they usually fail to show any differences between the techniques being compared. On the other hand, there have been some successes in developing more effective programming methods, generally by people who have been or have worked closely with computer programmers over a number of years. It is similar to a comparison between science and folklore, and our experience with health care has shown that some (but not all) of the folklore regarding health care is a useful source of information.

We should not get the idea that folklore is better than science, but rather that they are best used in a complementary manner. The problem in studying programming, and in studying computer effects in general, has been that there has not been a sufficiently long period of careful observation that enables the "folklore" to develop. Without informal but intensive observations, the carefully controlled scientific studies are likely to be directed at studying the wrong events.

DETECTING SIDE EFFECTS

Observations are important. But, when dealing with a new medium such as computers, the observer must be especially alert to unanticipated outcomes or side effects. Searching for the unexpected is not an easy task, since you cannot know what you are looking for. Attention to detail is essential and should be based on neutral expectations: no information should be excluded because of the observer's expectations. One of the techniques of looking for unanticipated outcomes or side effects is called "goal-free" evaluation.[10]

In the goal-free method, the observer avoids (if possible) knowledge of the stated goals of the project and attempts to determine the actual outcomes (which might be the same as the stated goals) through observation. In a second phase; the observations can continue after the stated goals have been learned. The main advantage to goal-free evaluation is the removal of the blinders that knowledge of objectives can put on the observer. If you do not know what someone is trying to accomplish, you may see very different things.

Some examples of side effects from the use of computers in education are already evident. In some of the instructional programs we find that students are "encouraged" to give wrong answers because the programs give more interesting responses to wrong answers than they give to right answers. One observer noticed a student giving an immediate wrong answer to every question, in order to get a hint before making a real attempt.[11] Some programs are described by their authors as developing one skill, while actual practice shows that they develop entirely different skills.

TEACHER AS RESEARCHER

This is a time when it is especially difficult to define the variables that need research, since the variables change rapidly and we may not know the variables initially. The teacher can be the source of hypotheses, if we can find a way to gather these observations. The ability to observe the impact of computers on their users is an important part of the training for the information age.

HOW TEACHERS CAN ACQUIRE THIS ABILITY

1. Give teachers knowledge about computers through their use of application programs *relevant* to them. That is, the teacher should not be asked to use a computer to accomplish (what seems to the teacher to be) an irrelevant task.

2. Make teachers sceptical of the claims being made about the effects of computers and provide them with a few tools to help them in evaluating these claims. The stories that appear in the popular press are strongly biased toward extreme views, both positive and negative, since these create more reader interest, while the more rational compromise views are rarely published.

3. Help teachers to be more sensitive to the changing needs of students, particularly in the areas of computer use, but maintaining a sensitivity to all other areas as well.

As the number of computers in classrooms increases, it becomes more important that teachers observe their students' use of them in a careful manner. What are the side effects of their use? How can positive side effects be increased while negative side effects are minimized? These are the important research questions as we attempt to discover the ultimate effects of computers in education.

NOTES

1. S. Papert, *Mindstorms: Children, Computers, and Powerful Ideas* (New York: Basic Books, 1980).
2. E.J. Lias, *Future Mind* (Boston: Little Brown, 1982); E.V. Sullivan, "Computers, Culture, and Educational Futures: A Critical Appraisal," *Interchange* 14, 3 (1983): 17–26.
3. Lias, *Future Mind*, 31.
4. Ibid., 28.
5. F.A. Schaeffer, *Back to Freedom and Dignity* (Downers Grove, Ill.: InterVarsity Press, 1972).
6. For a more extensive discussion of the role of assumptions in computer applications to education, see R.G. Ragsdale, *Computers in the Schools: A Guide for Planning* (Toronto: OISE Press, 1982).
7. This approach is similar in some ways to the "goal-free" evaluation approach suggested by M. Scriven, "Pros and Cons About Goal-Free Evaluation" in *Evaluation in Education*, edited by W.J. Popham (Berkeley, Calif.: McCutchan, 1974).

8. W.H. Seidman, "Goal Ambiguity and Organizational Decoupling: The Failure of 'Rational Systems' Program Implementation," *Educational Evaluation and Policy Analysis* 5, 4 (1983): 399, 413.

9. R.E. Clark, "Reconsidering Research on Learning from Media," *Review of Educational Research* 53, 4 (1983): 445–459.

10. Scriven, "Pros and Cons About Goal-Free Evaluation."

11. G.M. Della-Piana, "Film Criticism and Micro-computer Courseware Evaluation" in *New Directions for Program Evaluation: Field Assessments of Innovative Evaluation Methods*, edited by N. Smith (San Francisco: Jossey-Bass, 1982).

BEYOND THE MANIA: CRITICAL APPROACHES TO COMPUTERS IN EDUCATION[1]

C. PAUL OLSON AND E.V. SULLIVAN

The past few years in education have witnessed a mania sparked by computers. But the flurry of activity and speculation is everywhere. The January 1983 cover of *Time* magazine gives a glimpse of the cultural ebullience of the topic. The issue is normally devoted to the "man of the year" and features a person on the cover but, in this issue, there is no man on the cover; in his place, there is a plaster model sitting on a chair, looking at a computer. Instead of the 1983 award going to the "man of the year," it is presented to the computer. The title of the cover story is "The Machine of the Year: The Computer Moves In." The view that the computer is the wave of the future is widely shared in the popular culture. Yankelovich's study of American public opinion, reported in the same *Time* issue, showed that eighty percent of Americans expect that in the very near future the computer will be as commonplace in the household as the television. Sixty-eight percent of the same sample believe that the computer will ultimately raise production and improve the quality of their children's education. There are great cultural expectations for the computer.

In Canada there are also great expectations for the computer. By September 1984, there were approximately 27 000 microcomputers across Canada; in schools, on average, there was one computer for every 200 children.[2] While this ratio currently creates a "politics of scarcity" around the computer, a number of ministries of education have two- to five-year plans designed to increase dramatically the hardware and software support available to schools in their provinces. In Ontario, for example, the Ministry of Education has agreed to fund seventy percent of the purchase cost of the Ontario-built Icon system. Similar schemes are in existence everywhere across Canada. School boards seem to share in the belief that computers have an inherent capacity to assit in mathematics instruction, to teach word processing and programming, and in general to enhance the learning environment.

The general interest in educational computing mirrors a wider transformation within the society itself. Canadians seem to share an enthusiasm for computers in many areas of life. In a recent report by the Canadian Department of Labour, the computer is pictured as a "triggering technology."[3] A "triggering technology," according to the report, is industry that will improve economic growth by utilizing or developing computers and "high" technology. The report advocates supporting further development of microelectronics because of the supposed benefits of technological innovation. Questions about computer deployment are proposed in this light as essentially technical ones; that is, as a matter of developing adequate hardware and software to get on with the job of delivering the new order. Questions of implementation, the delivery of the fullest social benefit, and the impact of the new millenium are seen as primarily technical, even if pressing, issues.

There is an underside, or alternative view, of educational computing that relates to a blindness within educational theorizing; this is the tendency to underplay or to ignore the fundamental issue of power distribution. There is every indication in the history of technological innovation in the twentieth century, that innovations become a means of control and have differential results for different classes, racial groups, gender divisions, and so on.[4] There is also sound historical evidence that schooling serves the needs of dominant groups within the work world.[5] Thus, the computer, as well as other information technologies, may possibly accentuate and amplify power inequalities within our society. The whole issue of how "computer literacy" will affect job and status opportunities is an open one at this point, but there is every reason to believe that new status divisions in the labour force, created by changes in production facilitated by computers, will create power differentials in society itself, acting to "skill" some workers (thereby giving them more power) while "deskilling" others (thereby lessening their power).

Michael Apple's work on the effects of computer-assisted instruction in the United States shows that standardized computer-based programs often act to deskill teachers by "modularizing" the curriculum and thereby effectively limiting what an individual teacher may undertake.[6] Even more powerful is the potential impact of such standardized curricula on the presentation of particular points of view. In the Canadian textbook industry, for instance, the selection of texts can be influenced by decisions made in a few U.S. states, particularly California and Texas. The decision to follow the standards set by these states is not a pedagogical or educational one but, instead, an economic one. If a text is approved in Texas or California or, better, in both (together they have a population greater than all of Canada), then it is virtually assured success. If a text fails to make the approval lists in Texas and/or California, it is open to question how successful it will be. This essentially means that a full range of views, including views held by many Canadians, is not presented. The reason is that such views may prove offensive to particular constituencies of Americans. The most notorious example of this kind of information control occurred at Ginn Publishing when that U.S. company summarily fired its entire textbook staff for failing to get Ginn textbooks approved on the Texas state curriculum.[7] This incident may seem irrelevant to our concerns about educational computing in Canada, but we would like to suggest that it provides a lesson.

While computing may seem to be a general, technical skill, the content of computer programs is highly susceptible, in much the same way as textbooks, to social pressures that determine and stratify the educational curriculum. Such seemingly remote social processes have effects ranging from the banal to the profound. Thomas Malone's review of children's preferences and motivations in the use of computer games, for instance, shows that sensationalism and sensory stimulation were chief components in determining children's interest levels.[8] From a content level, the most popular games featured hangings and explosion-games that presented the joys of domination. Listed at the bottom of the preference list were programs that aimed to be educational. The microchips for many of the "invader" games, which were very popular with school-aged, computer-oriented boys, were originally developed, not coincidentally, by the U.S. military. While we are not suggesting that computing promotes militarism or anti-social behaviour, there is little evidence indicating that the content or medium of computing has inherently superior pedagogical, never mind moral, properties for teaching children. Harold Innis and Marshall McLuhan were instrumental in pointing out that particular forms of communication convey biases, and that changing the form, or power structure, of the media changes how information is processed.[9]

The computer is individually operated by the child. In this respect, it is a "personal" medium. The machine requires an initial level of competency to master, which is also engaging for the child. This initial interest quickly becomes routine. The act of having to interface with a machine that also "responds," and is thereby interactive, leads analysts such as Turkel[10] to posit that the "personal" form also provides a projective medium to establish a reflection of oneself. Yet, as a medium for this type of analysis, the computer has a rather limited range of sensory feedback that it can furnish. What the child watches, after all, is a flashing dot screen. Various media analysts have argued that vitacon-based media such as television often function as passive media. Because the initial stimulation of the feedback of the medium is quickly routinized, lessons rapidly become boring unless they are structured to have an interest that involves the child cognitively in ways that go beyond the innate qualities of the medium. Otherwise, if the medium is used in a passive manner (where one effectively watches rather than mentally participates), higher and higher levels of stimulation are needed to maintain full interest. Boys who are games enthusiasts, for example, seek models that are increasingly violent and reflect a worldview that is desensitized to possible consequences for others. Computers as a medium are surely not alone in conveying this idea, but the form of the medium is quite well suited to expressing this type of message. The "innate" utility of the computer as tutor can only be judged as it is used in particular applications.

In evaluating the possible impact of the computer medium, there is the question of how computer instruction will affect established trends of school performance for various groups. For instance, a number of historical reviews of schooling and the curriculum document how social sorting in schools, on the basis of class, gender, and ethnicity, results in differential access to society's opportunity structure.[11] Although computers are nominally classless and sexless, their use-patterns are filtered through institutions, like the school, that have, as part of their *de facto* work, the perpetuation of dominant systems of thought and language, leading to class, gender, and racial inequalities in schooling. It is not hard to imagine how such divisions will occur again with computers. The reciprocal relationship between schooling and technology is well established. It seems most probable that the level of skill training in high technologies will increase. The pattern for market demand seems to be well established; for example, the Economic Council of Canada in "Jobs for the Eighties" reports that high technology is a key area of vocational growth in Canada.[12] Similarly, the national assessment of education in the U.S. suggests that, "The gap between the number of highly-skilled workers needed and the number of students prepared for high-level jobs is widening. Clearly we are not cultivating the raw material, our future workers, who will be vital for both economic progress and ultimately for economic survival."[13] This view has been eagerly taken up by a variety of key Canadian educational leaders. The former Ontario Minister of Education, Bette Stephenson, for example, was quoted as saying, "As this specialized edition of *Education Ontario* will demonstrate, education will have an even more important role in shaping the computer age we are entering. Our technological future can be what philosophers have dreamed of for centuries...or it can be a nightmare of mechanization. Schools will have strong influence in which future awaits us."[14]

With the dawning of the Age of the Chip, the link between the implementation of the micro-technological revolution and the transformation of the economic and educational order are widely postulated.[15] Anticipation is in the air. Virtually all researchers in this area emphasize that computers will have an impact that will pose special problems for the form and content of schooling. But how all this will transpire (and for whose benefit) is still an open question.

Indeed, the assessments of the exact nature of the computers' impact on schooling are filled with contradictions at this early juncture. We are, for instance, assured by one group of notable scholars that the *medium* of technology will revolutionize the forms of learning.[16] With this bit of hopeful wisdom in hand, we proceed toward our next socio-educational insight. Quickly, however, we are greeted with the sobering news from equally eminent researchers that, when controls are made for exogenous factors (e.g., Hawthorne effect, variances and the method of instruction, quality of teachers, etc.), there are no long-term benefits provided by computers or other slick-trick educational innovations.[17] First we go east; then we go west.

Inconsistent conclusions abound with respect to the most interesting issues raised by the social impact of computers on schooling. Some examples are listed below.

1. Do schools "skill" or "deskill"?[18] Canadian data seem to suggest that they do both. Jane Gaskell's work at the University of British Columbia shows how girls' education varies radically depending on whether one is taking computing in the business stream or in the academic stream.[19] The contrasts are revealing. Within the business stream, for instance, there is repeated emphasis upon *mechanical* and *routinized* tasks to *service* the machine. There is very little learning of general skills (e.g., underlying logics, programming skills, symbolic codes, etc.) that might later be translated to another context. The girls interviewed by Gaskell were aware that mechanical skills would not lead to high-level careers. Nonetheless, they felt that, in relation to other studies, the business stream was "the most practical."[20] This pattern contrasts dramatically with programming in the academic stream. Here the emphasis is on *general* and "symbolic" processes that lead to long-term *control*, regardless of the systems that may evolve. The emphasis is on high-level programs and forms of technical knowledge that give this control. What we are witnessing, in effect, is the use of computers to stratify knowledge, hence establishing a new entrance gate for "achievers" and a new barrier for those destined to less desirable fates.

2. Do computers reduce or increase differences in class-based learning? In our own studies we tentatively have found on a limited sample that middle-class children have more frequent access than working-class children to advanced computers in both home and community situations.[21] Since we know that such non-school settings have a powerful impact on how children perform within schools, there is every reason to believe that this will also influence the level, availability, and ultimate uses of knowledge, based along class lines. Since this knowledge, even more than conventional education, is capital intensive (you need an expensive computer, peripherals, software, training books, etc.), it leads to a possible powerful basis for further class division between those who can pay and those who cannot. Pat Campbell, in an overview article of U.S. results, found that in 1983, sixty-seven percent of wealthier U.S. school boards had computers while only forty-one percent of poor schools had microcomputers; that one study of schools in New Jersey found gaps in programming usage between white and black schools by margins of 3 to 1; that richer suburban boards teach programming skills while poorer schools use CAI.[22] Campbell's survey also reviewed learning gaps between poor and rich blacks and whites in computer usage such as those found in curricular areas. A study comparing Newark, New Jersey, city children to their suburban counterparts found differences in availability of both hardware and software. The same study also found that, even the best Newark inner-city children tended to be two years behind their suburban counterparts in computer-use ability.

3. Will computers centralize or decentralize education as a source of knowledge? Again, the speculation in the area is highly divided. In Canada, our colleague, Robert Logan, working from the McLuhan and futurist perspectives, argues the common position that computers offer us unlimited

potential for highly individualized instruction and for making knowledge more available.[23] However, another colleague of ours, Ted Humphries, argues that computers create powerful data bases capable of invading privacy and automating the workplace, thus representing a fundamental erosion of individuality (and privacy).[24]

4. Does the implementation of computers assist the curriculum and the development of individual autonomy, or does it lead to greater dependence on rigid learning packages and rote form? Our own work in the area suggests that the answer is highly dependent on how the program itself is *implemented* and that *teaching* is an influential determinant of computing outcomes.[25] How computer use is integrated with the curriculum also appears to be an influential factor in this area. Nonetheless, there is no single, clear answer provided by the literature.

The list goes on. At any turn, if you name your preference, you can readily garner evidence that you are headed in the right direction. It is plain that a new day is upon us. But where we are going is in question.

THE COMPUTER AS SINNER OR SAINT

If the computer has failed to fire us with unified resolve about its effects, it has certainly not failed to spark our passion and our imagination. There is a plethora of technical material about the computer, but there is little that is without bias. Almost none of this material is without an opinion on where computers can (and should) take us. And, again, sharp division exists about effects.

The views, again, tend to be organized around sharp polarities: one extreme is pro-technological or *millenialist*, while the other is anti-technological, or *cataclysmic*, seeing such technological innovations as hyperextensions of the state's bureaucratic and mechanized control.[26] Within these conflicting archetypes, there is considerable variability in the form of argumentation and the sophistication of proponents. Nonetheless, there are those favouring such technology who argue that computer-based learning will lead to greater individualized freedom and to the breakdown of authoritarianism and standardized classroom forms and mentalities.[27] Again, they see the use of computers as resulting in an expansion of literacy, economic opportunity, and generalized decentralization of social control. Various theorists within the pro-technological camp draw upon McLuhan's work to argue the decentralizing nature of the medium, comparing its impact to that of the alphabet in extending individual knowledge and control.[28] Opponents of the new technologies argue that the use of computers to "deskill" work represents an extension of technical control.[29] They link the technology to an increase in the gap of wealth and power between classes and between nations—between industrialized countries, like Canada, and Third World countries. Others in this camp emphasize the disastrous effects on dislocated workers, particularly the historically disadvantaged such as minorities and women,[30] and/or on fundamental civil liberties such as the protection of privacy.[31] What we are witnessing in the research on the impact of computers on schooling is the emergence of a discourse based less on overt facts about the computer's *technical* effects than on covert treatises about what schools can and should do. In essence, in the guise of a *research* debate is a *moral* debate.[32] This discourse is akin to a theological debate between the believers in the computer and the heretics.[33]

THE POLITICS OF LITERACY

Schooling itself has always been promoted for the sake of a people's future, social, moral, and technical development. That it has in fact been a contested terrain for competing ideologies is plain in schooling's history.[34] The current debates on computing and schooling also mirror the older ideological debates on schooling. The arguments used in these debates conform even more closely, however, to futurist debate on the general social effects of computers. It is within the arena of combative ideologies that we must understand *Time*'s choice of the computer as "Man of the Year," and, conversely, the thesis that the "Third Wave"—the vision put forward by futurologist Alvin Toffler that the industrial era has come to an end and been replaced by a "post-industrial" or communications-based society—should be greeted apprehensively, since such an era will see increasing bureaucratic control of liberty and imagination by technical domination.[35]

We submit that, in order to comprehend both the plurality of effects attributed to the computer and the moral tone of discussion, it is vital to examine how the so-called consequences of computer implementation affect different individuals and serve different social interests. It is also useful to examine how individual or group intentions, which computers should serve, come to represent explicitly or to establish differential relationships of utility for different persons in critical interactions such as those among schools, technology, and homes. The issues here range from career patterns and marketing strategies to micro-social issues (such as teacher/student interactions) to the ways in which computers have radically re-ordered market possibilities. What we are arguing is that a historical and contextual approach is needed. We are not denying that the debate around computing is (and should be) a moral one; but, rather, that assessment of trends needs to be grounded in particular understandings of how different aspects of computer use affect various groups.

The computer has become in our own lives a metaphor for using ideas of social living. Part of this metaphor is placed in the material realm of reorganized productive relations. Another part of the computer metaphor draws substance from our fantasy and projects about this device. Sherry Turkel, in her widely quoted book, *The Second Self*, raises the issue of how "artificial intelligence," as symbolized by the computer, brings into question what is fundamental to our humanness.[36] This type of reflection is in part a basis for our sense of computers.

But part of our relationship lies in material reality. And still another part is given to us in images about the computer. These latter images about computer capabilities are important to our understanding of computers (and their metaphoric use) because they are constructed "for us." Computer companies, for instance, have a vested interest in "portraying" computers as solely positive factors or necessities in schooling. The trade-off in terms of the costs of the machines, the time they divert from other activities, the appropriateness or procedures for integrating their use with curriculum and other studies are seldom discussed. The drawbacks of the vulnerability of hardware, the limits of number of machines available, and their relative non-interactiveness are not discussed in glowing advertisements. These are very real issues. In one school in Ontario, the principal had to choose to increase the number of computers in the school by three (at a cost of several thousand dollars) or to fund a music program to an adequate level to support a group large enough to constitute a band. In tight economic times for education, even a small computer purchase can expend as much as ten to twenty percent of a school's discretionary funds. What we see in both corporate advertising and in ministries of education releases is only the glowing side to computers. Ministries of education, like corporations, "sell" themselves by trying to show their relevance and awareness. Claiming that computers are fully integrated into schools often placates media, even where software, hardware, support instruction, and/or appropriate usage frequently do not exist in anywhere near the form claimed by ministries' optimistic portrayals when one looks closely at the local classroom level. Yet, even more than these distortions, discussion of computers is done a disservice by the relative absence of questioning of how computers come to be controlled by human agency.

The debate suffers from lapses within educational research, which, in the last five decades, has been dominated by a liberal or universalist model portraying schooling as equal and occurring by consensus. Whatever may be its other advantages, steadfastly holding to this position tends to downplay or ignore the existence of very real structural, cultural and other power relationship conflicts within schools and society.[37] But this consensus by these oversights also eclipses the role of "intentional agency" as a part of the educational planning process. Such eclipses, Sullivan says, are tantamount to tunnel vision;[38] but a discourse that assumes that technology such as computers can be introduced "neutrally" or in an "objective" fashion without reference to the larger context of who benefits and also who suffers from such change ignores the social context and thereby reflects an inherent bias that favours *technical* solutions and efficiency models. These positions, while appearing technical, can become implicit value positions and can, for instance, lead to a view that a technology of touchtones is good for society.[39]

This is why *Time* can centrestage the computer to the exclusion of all forms of personal agency, be they male or female. This is one reason why we are presently looking to solve problems by the use of machines as if there were no trade-off. The digital computer, with its incredible capacity for speed and memory, out-performs the computational paces obtainable by humans. Our romance with speed, once vested in the automobile, was enhanced with the advent of the computer.

THE MATERIAL AND THE SPIRITUAL REMADE

In order to understand computers and information technologies, we must understand what they are and what they can do. What they are, very plainly and simply, are efficient *tools* for information processing. This statement is simple enough on the surface; yet, as we are continuously rediscovering in a host of diverse settings, the full range of the impact of the computer as a tool is complex. Knowledge of how and where computers can be efficiently used will doubtless remain an ongoing discovery. But technical understanding of possible usages is not enough. No tool autonomously organizes and employs itself alone from *tabula rasa* to the operational program. Tools are used by people for particular ends (good and bad). Understanding who uses them, how, and for whose benefits—the structure of intentional action—is necessary if we are to assess how computers are likely to be actually employed. Computers announce a remarkable technical advance because they facilitate the rapid execution of a multiplicity of work processes. The introduction of computer technology alters the parameters (and the cost) of executing work and, in some cases, is necessary if work is to be undertaken at all. The level of technology theoretically limits productive capacities—work loads, etc.—but what work is to be done, by whom, and for whose benefits—questions of distribution and processes of production—cannot be given by technology alone. Understanding how computers affect schools, labour markets, and models of social organization, therefore, requires that we look at the various interests that are served and the organizational as well as purely technical decisions. This is a most appropriate project if we are to adequately evaluate the effects of computer implementations since the computer as a tool *does* fundamentally *reorganize material relationships and organizations of production*.

Because the computer directly affects so many of the most important areas of human activity—the organization of information, processes of production, our psychological sense of the possible, and so on—it also potentially changes relationships of social power. Many of these are structural relationships—for example, changes in how work gets done (essays are now word processed, math drills in schools are computer assisted; tickets are booked globally by computers). Who controls such information very much affects one's level of power within society, one's ability to get a job, and even how much of some kinds of knowledge one may obtain. Industrial societies count on computers for the "competitive edge." Yet all these structural changes are ultimately made by people. Not everyone's interest is the same. Understanding this is massively helpful to separating authentic educational benefits of computers from vested claims. When we move beyond the mania of hopes and fears that cloud our perceptions about computers in education to a critical evaluation of how they work in practice, we will best be able to use the potential computers hold for schools.

We must take a hard look at the applied uses of computer technology and ask ourselves if these methods are authentically better ways of doing work. We must calculate the effects of deskilling, the depersonalization of learning, and the areas where computers are pedagogically helpful. We must be practical in our assessment of whether they are more or less expensive (and fashionable) toys. At the same time, we should explore ways to use the computer to assit us in education. If some drill is better done on a computer than at a desk, then we should do the work in this manner. Where computers free us from drudgery or open new avenues of art, science, printing, and the like, we should foster their growth. What is most essential, however, is that we consciously understand what is happening in practice, how it is happening, and who it serves. Ultimately, it is we as conscious actors who must generate the metaphors about computers and control the practical uses of computers. The principle of critically evaluating what our education is about is equally applicable to computerized and non-computerized learning. The computer simply re-opens old questions about technology, equality, and whose school interests should be served.

It can be concluded for now that the effects of computers are mixed. We must be both *empirical* and critical in our claims about their impact. Dreams and fears are part of being human. But if we are to use computers as tools, tutors, and machines to serve our students, we must examine the full range of their actual use and, in conducting our examination, be resolved to keep control and have this new cultural invention serve democratic ends. Democratic ends, not fashion, not technical analysis, not market forces, should control the use of computers. Knowledge ought to bring us greater flexibility and freedom, not new forms of subordination.

NOTES

1. Parts of work described in this piece are based on research funded by the Social Science and Humanities Research Council of Canada. The authors gratefully acknowledge this support.
2. D. Sharon and A. Mehler, *Microcomputers in Teaching and Learning: An Inventory of Canadian Research* (Toronto: TV Ontario, 1985).
3. Canada, Department of Labour, *In the Chips: Opportunities, People, Partnerships*. Report of Labour Canada Task Force on Microelectronics and Employment (Ottawa: Queen's Printer, 1982).
4. Harry Braverman, *Labor and Monopoly Capital: The Degradation of Work in the Twentieth Century* (New York: Monthly Review Press, 1974).
5. R.W. Connell, *Teachers' Work* (Sydney: Allen and Unwin, 1985); Connell et al., *Making the Difference* (Sydney: Allen and Unwin, 1982).
6. M. Apple, *Ideology and Curriculum* (London: Routledge and Kegan Paul, 1979); M. Apple, "The Political Economy of Text Publishing" in *Excellence, Reform and Equality in Education: An International Perspective* (Buffalo and Toronto: SUNY Buffalo and OISE, 1984).
7. Apple, "The Political Economy of Text Publishing."
8. Thomas Malone, "Towards a Theory of Intrinsically Motivating Instruction," *Cognitive Science* 4 (1981): 333–69.
9. H.A. Innis, *The Bias of Communication* (Toronto: University of Toronto Press, 1951), and M. McLuhan, *The Guttenberg Galaxy: The Making of Typographic Man* (New York: New American Library, 1969), *Explorations: Studies in Culture and Communications. Nos. 1–9, 1953–1959* (Toronto: University of Toronto Press, n.d.).
10. S. Turkel, *The Second Self* (New York: Simon and Schuster, 1984).
11. A. Prentice, *The School Promoters: Education and Social Class in Mid-Nineteenth Century Upper Canada* (Toronto: McClelland and Stewart, 1977); E. Sullivan, *Critical Psychology; Psychology as Interpretation of the Personal World* (New York: Plenum, 1984).
12. Economic Council of Canada, "In Short Supply: Jobs and Skills in the 1980s" (Ottawa: Supply and Services Canada, 1982).
13. United States National Commission on Excellence in Education, *A Nation at Risk: The Imperative for Educational Reform. A Report to the Nation and the Secretary of Education* (Washington: U.S. Department of Education).
14. *Education Ontario: The Computer Age and Education* (Toronto: Ontario Ministry of Education and Colleges and Universities, Jan. 1982), 1.
15. L. Berg and W. Bramble, "Computers and the Future of Education" in *Applications of Microcomputers for Instruction and Educational Management* 17, 1–2 (Fall-Winter 1983): 101–88; Canada, Department of Labour, *In the Chips*; S. Papert, *Mindstorms: Children, Computers, and Powerful Ideas* (New York: Basic Books, 1980); H. Schiller, "The World Crisis and the New Information Technologies: A Way Out or Deeper In?" (unpublished paper, University of California at San Diego, March 1983); Science Council of Canada, "Planning Now

for an Information Society. Tomorrow is too Late" (Ottawa: Science Council of Canada, Report 33, 1982).

16. D. Jamison, P. Suppes, and S. Wells, "Effectiveness of Alternative Instructional Media: A Survey," *Review of Educational Research* 44 (1974): 1–67; Papert, *Mindstorms*.

17. J. Kulik, R. Bangert, and G. Williams, "Effects of Computer-Based Teaching on Secondary Students," *Journal of Educational Psychology* 75 (Feb. 1983): 19–26; J. Kulik, "Synthesis of Research on Computer-Based Instruction," *Educational Leadership* 41 (Sept. 1983): 19–21.

18. Apple, *Ideology and Curriculum*.

19. Jane Gaskell, "Sex Inequalities in Education for Work," *Canadian Journal of Education* 6 (April 1981): 54–72, and "Gender and Course Choice: The Orientations of Male and Female Students," *Journal of Education* 166, 1 (March 1984): 89–102.

20. For girls from working-class families, the decision to pursue a secretarial course, when the girl does not expect to attend university, shows a recognition of where jobs for women are currently to be found. In British Columbia, for instance, a full fifty percent of women who work outside the home are employed in clerical occupations. Among women from working-class families, this figure becomes three out of four.

21. E. Sullivan, C.P. Olson, and R. Logan, "The Development of Policy and Research Projections for Computers in Education: A Comparative Ethnography," (Report submitted to the Social Science and Humanities Research Council of Canada, Ottawa, Oct. 1986).

22. Pat Campbell, "Computers in Education: A Question of Access" (paper presented to the Annual Meeting of the American Educational Research Association, Montreal, April 1983).

23. R. Logan, "The Axiomatics of the Innis-McLuhan School of Communications" (unpublished paper presented to the Culture and Technology Seminar, University of Toronto, Dec. 1982).

24. E. Humphries, *Privacy in Jeopardy: Student Records in Canada* (Toronto: OISE Press, 1980).

25. M. Fullan, *The Meaning of Educational Change* (Toronto: OISE Press, 1982).

26. E. Sullivan, "Computers, Culture, and Educational Futures: A Critical Appraisal," *Interchange* 14, 3 (1983).

27. Papert, *Mindstorms*; J. Martin, *Telematic Society: A Challenge for Tomorrow* (Englewood Cliffs, N.J.: Prentice-Hall, 1981).

28. Logan, "Axiomatics of the Innis-McLuhan School of Communications."

29. D. Noble, *America by Design: Science, Technology, and the Rise of Corporate Capitalism* (New York: Knopf, 1977).

30. Canada, Department of Labour, *In the Chips*; Bluestone and Harrison, *The Deindustrialization of America* (New York: Basic Books, 1982).

31. E. Humphries, *Privacy in Jeopardy: Student Records in Canada* (Toronto: OISE Press, 1980).

32. A. Wootton, *Dilemmas in Discourse: Controversies about the Sociological*

Interpretation of Language (London: Allen and Unwin, 1975); Sullivan, *Critical Psychology*.

33. Sullivan, "Computers, Culture, and Educational Futures."

34. Prentice, *The School Promoters*; M. Archer, *Social Origins of Educational Systems* (London: Sage Publications, 1979); B. Bernstein, *Class, Codes and Control*. Vol. 2 *Towards a Theory of Educational Transmission*, 2nd. ed. (London: Routledge and Kegan Paul, 1979); P. Bourdieu and J. Passeron, *Reproduction in Education, Society, and Culture*, translated by Richard Nice (London: Sage Publications, 1977); M. Apple and L. Weis, eds., *Ideology and Practice in Schooling* (Philadelphia: Temple University Press, 1983); G. Whitty and M. Young, eds., *Society, State and Schooling* (Sussex: Falmer Press, 1977); J. Harp and J. Hofley, eds., *Structural Inequality in Canada* (Scarborough, Ont.: Prentice-Hall, 1980); Livingstone, *Ideologies and Educational Futures* (Sussex: Falmer Press, 1983).

35. G. Grant, *Technology and Empire* (Toronto: Anansi Press, 1967); J. Ellul, *The Technological Society* (Toronto: Vintage Books, 1964); H. Schiller, "The World Crisis and the New Information Technologies."

36. Turkel, *The Second Self*.

37. H. Giroux, *Theory and Resistance in Education: A Pedagogy for the Opposition* (South Hadley, Mass: Bergin and Garvey, 1983).

38. Sullivan, "Computers, Culture, and Educational Futures."

39. W. Feinberg and K. Rosemont, *Work, Technology and Education: Dissertation Essays on the Intellectual Foundations of American Education* (Urbana: University of Illinois Press, 1975).

SECTION 3:
STANDARDS AND STANDARDIZED TESTING IN CANADIAN EDUCATION

Standards and standardized testing continue to spark hot and contentious debate. As educators, we are constantly under attack from some quarters for perceived declines in academic standards and for our use of what are seen as unrealistic or inappropriate methods of assessment. Within academic circles, too, there is considerable disagreement about the longitudinal stability of standards and the merits of standardized testing.

In the first paper in this section, Nyberg discusses the issue of standards in Canadian education. He examines data from studies of achievement carried out over the years in nine of the ten provinces and concludes, among other things, that there is little evidence that standards have declined over the years or that achievement is well below standard in any subject area.

In regard to the standardized testing issue, there are those who would move to abolish all forms of standardized assessment in the school setting because they are viewed as perpetuating discrimination and inequality of opportunity. On the other hand, there are those who would argue that promising advancements in test construction and administration techniques may overcome several of the previously perceived inadequacies and shortcomings.

In his article, Ungerleider reiterates the cautionary position regarding the use of standardized testing in reaching educational decisions. He outlines past injustices and warns against employing standardized tests, particularly intelligence tests, to determine the educational futures of students.

Fitzsimmons, on the other hand, describes the historical background of standardized achievement testing in Canada and identifies new trends in the psychometric movement, such as item response theory, which may have the potential to make the results of standardized testing much more useful for academic decision makers. Fitzsimmons also notes that, given new theories of information management, new technology, and new applications of testing, educators are being confronted with new responsibilities in the assessment and evaluation of students, and he raises the spectre of courts deciding issues that were once within the domain of professional associations or the practitioners themselves.

EDUCATIONAL STANDARDS IN CANADA
VERNER RICHARD NYBERG

INTRODUCTION

A frequently asked question in educational issues is, what is happening to achievement standards in Canadian schools? Frequently the query is made in the various news media and by groups not directly connected with education, and sometimes by concerned parents. Despite the fact that the question has cropped up many times over the years, no clear answer based on hard data can be provided. Usually, when someone asks the question about standards, it is in the context of a complaint that there has been a serious decline. Unlike the United States, large organizations devoted to testing students across the nation do not exist in Canada. There are no Canadian counterparts to the College Entrance Examinations Board nor to long-established achievement measures such as the Metropolitan Achievement Tests, the California Achievement Tests, and the Iowa Tests of Basic Skills. While the various provinces conducted some form of school leaving or university entrance examinations for many years, these were discontinued in the 1970s and are only now being reinstated. These tests, however, provided little longitudinal information on standards of achievement.

The scene with respect to information on educational standards in Canada might be changing. The Canadian Tests of Basic Skills, similar in nature to the well known Iowa Tests of Basic Skills, and the Canadian Achievement Tests, produced by the publishers of the California Achievement Tests have been in use in Canada for several years. It might be expected that information on achievement standards over time would be forthcoming. Also, some form of province-wide testing has been reintroduced in several of the provinces, and, in most instances, one of the purposes is to monitor achievement over the long term. While very little information on national standards is available in research journals, most of the provinces have made, or are conducting, studies intended to check on achievement over time.

A hard look at trends in achievement standards is overdue, particularly in the light of the so-called "Test Score Decline" in the United States. In the late

1970s, various publications appeared giving firm evidence that, beginning in the mid-1960s, achievement scores of American students were going down. Perhaps the best known publication was one released by the College Entrance Examinations Board.[1] Comparisons over the years indicated that scores on the verbal Scholastic Aptitude Test (SAT) gradually increased until 1963, then declined steadily. For example, in 1963 the mean was 478, and in 1978 it had dropped to 429. Similarly, the SAT quantitative scores dropped from a mean of 502 in 1963 to 468 in 1978. According to Stedman and Kaestle, the decline in SAT scores ended in or near 1980.[2] These score declines were surprisingly large, in view of the fact that the data were based on test results of several million students, and that the standard deviation of the tests was about 100. The SAT verbal scores, therefore, dropped about half a standard deviation.

Many causes of the decline in test scores of American students were hypothesized. As might be expected, when there was no hard evidence immediately available, many writers listed their own "pet peeves." Among them were activist educators, permissiveness with respect to behaviour, general moral decline, hedonism, intimidation of teachers, Vietnam, Watergate, unstructured curricula, single-parent families, and increased proportions of minority students writing tests. One interesting comment, worthy of some though by Canadian teachers, was expressed by Bruning.[3] Referring to studies of how little knowledge American young people had in comparison to those in other developed countries (a problem different from, but perhaps related to, the test score decline), he stated that this led inevitably to questions about the ability of teachers. He took the view that the teacher competency tests that were made mandatory in several states were probably a result of a general feeling that low student achievement was caused by low-ability teachers.

Whatever the American picture regarding achievement standards in schools might be, we do not have data to make similar studies in Canada. There exists, however, a considerble volume of information, available largely from provincial departments of education, that sheds light on the matter.

The matter of standards is usually approached in one of two ways. The traditional statistical method is to gather data, using a standardized measuring instrument, in two or more instances, separated in time by several years. For example, students in the ninth grade might be given the STEP reading test in 1978, and then in 1985 the same test might be administered to the current crop of Grade 9 students. There are obvious problems. The characteristics of the group being tested might change, as, for instance, where a school system has a substantial influx or exodus of students in the interval between the tests. The tests, also, might become less valid over the years, owing to changes in curriculum. The second approach is less research oriented but more attuned to public opinion. Opinions of various groups such as parents and educators might be sought to determine the degree of satisfaction with standards. This approach sometimes involves administering tests, then asking experts to identify areas of strength and weakness by studying students' responses to test questions.

In this paper, the descriptions of the various studies were grouped by province. Much of the information given was taken from study reports supplied or recommended by officials of the various provinces. There was no doubt that individual school systems have conducted many of their own studies. However, only a few of these were reported here. Inclusion of these studies by individual systems was often a matter of whether the final reports had been made public.

BRITISH COLUMBIA

In 1977 the Ministry of Education, Province of British Columbia, instituted the first Mathematics Assessment project. The objectives of this study were, primarily, to evaluate students' achievement in mathematics; to evaluate students' attitude toward mathematics; and to identify and clarify various curriculum models. The second and third Mathematics Assessment projects, conducted in 1981 and 1985, listed the additional objective of determining changes in achievement from one study year to another.

The assessment projects involved three grade levels in every instance but, because of administrative changes, the same three grades were not tested every year. In 1977 and 1981 students in grades 4, 8, and 12 were selected, while in 1985 grades 4, 7, and 10 were chosen. The reports were extensive but some of the aspects studied were of no direct interest to this report on achievement standards—for example, qualifications of teachers, instructional practices, and sex differences. While achievement of students was listed as one of the objectives of the study, this problem was not addressed in the traditional manner of comparing results on repeated administrations of standardized tests. Instead, the approach was to have panels of teachers evaluate achievement in terms of expectations in each of several content areas. For example, each assessment dealt with student performance in the topic Number and Operation. In 1977, for Grade 8, it was judged to be satisfactory, in 1981, for Grade 8, it was judged to be marginal; and in 1985, for Grade 7, it was judged to be marginal. Only in the case of Grade 4, which was selected for study in all three assessments, was there an opportunity to make direct comparisons so as to check on achievement over time. At this grade level, special provisions were made to make these comparisons. While the tests were different, a core of common items was included in each of the three assessment years.

Results of the three assessment projects are given in tables 1 to 6 below. The code employed for ratings is as follows: S = strong, VS = very satisfactory, S = satisfactory, M = marginal, W = weak. A minus sign (-) or a plus sign (+) following a rating indicates that the achievement was deemed to be slightly lower or slightly higher than the code letter would indicate.

TABLE 1[a]
MEAN ACHIEVEMENT SCORES (PERCENTAGE) AND RATINGS BY YEAR, GRADE 4

	1977		1981		1985	
CONTENT AREA	%	RATING	%	RATING	%	RATING
Number & Operation	—	VS	70	VS	66	S
Geometry	N/A	N/A	62	S	63	S
Measurement	—	M	60	M	62	S–
Algebraic Topics	—	S	58	S	66	S+
Problem Solving	—	–	—	–	47	S–

[a] Tables 1 to 6 are adapted from David Robitaille and James M. Sherrill, *The B.C. Mathematics Assessment Summary Report* (B.C. Ministry of Education, 1977); David Robitaille, *The 1981 B.C. Mathematics Assessment Summary Report* (B.C. Ministry of Education, 1981); and David Robitaille and Thomas J. O'Shea, *The 1985 B.C. Mathematics Assessment Summary Report* (B.C. Ministry of Education, 1985).

TABLE 2
COMPARISON OF ACHIEVEMENT SCORES (%) FOR 1977, 1981, AND 1985, GRADE 4

CONTENT AREA	NO. ITEMS	1977	1981	1985
Number and Operation	12	71	72	74
Measurement	10	57	57	58

TABLE 3
MEAN ACHIEVEMENT SCORES (%) AND RATINGS BY GRADE FOR THREE YEARS, GRADES 7 AND 8

	GRADE 8, 1977		GRADE 8, 1981		GRADE 7, 1985	
CONTENT AREA	MEAN	RATING	MEAN	RATING	MEAN	RATING
Number & Operations	—	S	63	M	63	M
Geometry	—	-	58	M	53	S–
Measurement	—	-	46	M	54	M
Algebraic Topics	—	-	52	S	52	S
Problem Solving	—	-	—	-	—	S

EDUCATIONAL STANDARDS 113

TABLE 4
COMPARISON OF ACHIEVEMENT SCORES FOR 1977 AND 1981, GRADE 8

CONTENT AREA	NO. ITEMS	1977 MEAN %	1981 MEAN %
Number & Operation	15	58	61
Geometry & Measurement	12	54	58

TABLE 5
MEAN ACHIEVEMENT SCORES (%) AND RATINGS BY GRADE FOR THREE YEARS, GRADES 10 AND 12

CONTENT AREA	GRADE 12, 1977 MEAN	GRADE 12, 1977 RATING	GRADE 12, 1981 MEAN	GRADE 12, 1981 RATING	GRADE 10, 1985 MEAN	GRADE 10, 1985 RATING
Number & Operations	—	-	59	M	58	M
Geometry	—	-	61	S+	47	M
Measurement	—	-	57	M	55	S
Algebraic Topics	—	-	54	S	52	M
Problem Solving	—	-	—	-	—	S

NOTE: It was pointed out in the reports that mathematics was not a required subject after Grade 10.

TABLE 6
COMPARISON OF ACHIEVEMENT FOR 1977 AND 1981, GRADE 12

CONTENT AREA	NO. ITEMS	MEAN %	MEAN %
Number & Operation	10	65.4	66.9
Geometry & Measurement	9	57.2	61.6
Algebraic Topics	10	59.0	58.8

Ratings for the 1977 assessment were based on three "domains" entitled Computation and Knowledge, Comprehension, and Applications rather than the five categories shown in the table. As a result, ratings for 1977 had to be inferred from the ratings of the subcategories of the three domains, but in most cases even this was not possible. The percentage scores could not be determined for 1977.

Results of the Mathematics Assessment projects indicated that, for Grade 4, achievement of the students went from marginal, in 1977, to nearly satisfactory in 1985, and that there was a modest increase in achievement as measured by the core of common test items which appeared in all three years. The ratings given depended, of course, on the achievement levels of the student and the expectations of the panel of raters. Both of these variables were subject to changes with time. In grades 7 and 8 and 10 and 12, the ratings awarded were marginal or satisfactory. This indicates that the panels were not generally satisfied with the achievement levels of the students. Comparisons, based on common items, generally indicated that there were modest gains in achievement scores for Grade 8 and for Grade 12 over the four-year period from 1977 to 1981.

The British Columbia Assessment program involved other subjects besides mathematics. Studies involving science[4] and reading[5] were also conducted. The methods used were similar to those employed in the mathematics assessment and the results also were similar. That is, there was general satisfaction, but some areas were judged to be in need of improvement. For example, in 1982, the Grade 4 group was judged very satisfactory in one area, satisfactory in another, and marginal in two. In the same year the Grade 8 sample was rated very satisfactory twice and satisfactory and weak once each. Achievement in Grade 12 was judged marginal in one category and satisfactory in the other.[6]

ALBERTA

In Alberta, reports of declining achievement scores for students in the United States, Great Britain, and other countries, and the resulting fear that a similar situation existed in Alberta, led to the formation of the Minister's Advisory Committee on Student Achievement (MACOSA). Several studies were completed, of which three were directly related to educational standards.

The first study, conducted by Dumont,[7] addressed a general question, what has happened to the quality of education since compulsory Grade 12 examinations were dropped in 1973? The answer was sought by posing three research questions:

1. What are the current Grade 12 student evaluation policies and practices at the school system and school level across the province?

2. What changes have taken place in the distribution of marks awarded by schools in Grade 12 subjects in the five years from 1973 to 1978?

3. What does the public think has happened to quality of education since accreditation, and what does it think ought to happen now?

An answer to the first question was sought by surveying opinions of school superintendents. The responses indicated that there was a real concern with respect to evaluation procedures. The vacuum left when Grade 12 examinations were withdrawn was filled with a multiplicity of procedures for assigning grades. Different schools, supposedly adhering to uniform policies defined by a system, employed different criteria and standards. The superintendents also claimed that the public had little confidence in education, especially regarding the basic skills, and that the expected modification of programs to meet local needs had not materialized.

The answer to the second question was clear-cut. Data provided by Reid[8] were cited as indicating that there had been a sharp increase in grades from 1973 to 1975, after which there had been a small decline that had lasted through 1977. The term "grade inflation" was commonly used to describe the phenomenon that followed the withdrawal of departmental examinations.

The third question was considered by constructing and distributing a questionnaire to a sample of adults from the public in general and to samples of special groups such as students, teachers, administrators, etc. In addition, interviews were conducted to check on the validity of the questionnaire. The responses indicated a pattern dependent upon the stakeholder groups. People within the educational community, on the average, thought that educational standards had remained about the same, while people from other groups felt that changes for the worse had taken place.

The Dumont study did not provide, nor was it intended to provide, hard data on achievement standards. It did, however, indicate that, for the four-year period following the phase-out of the Grade 12 examinations, the general feeling was that achievement in mathematics and science had remained constant or had improved, but that achievement in English was lower.

The Alberta Language Arts (Reading and Writing) Achievement Study[9] investigated language skills of students enrolled in grades 3, 6, 9, and 12 in Alberta. The immediate goal of the project was to describe achievement in several aspects of the language arts, such as word parts, sense of sentence (context), main idea, etc. The descriptions were based on percentage of items correct only, therefore no statement regarding standards could be made. However, a second purpose was to provide benchmarks for future assessments; that is, the foundation for checking on standards subsequent to 1979 was laid. Similar projects were conducted in the fields of mathematics, science, and social studies.

MACOSA also sponsored a study of Grade 3 achievement,[10] for which the main purpose was the establishment of benchmarks for reading, language, and arithmetic. A companion study[11] addressed the matter of standards directly by administering a battery of tests identical to a battery administered twenty-one years previously.

In 1956 virtually all Grade 3 pupils in the Edmonton Public School system were given the Gates-MacGinitie Reading, Vocabulary, and Comprehension Tests, and the California Achievement Tests of Reading, Mathematics, and Language. In 1977 the identical forms were administered to all the Grade 3 pupils in the Edmonton Public School system. Results of the companion study indicated that the performance levels in reading and language had been maintained or improved over the time interval despite the fact that the 1977 group averaged 1.7 months younger than the 1956 group. Achievement in arithmetic was the same or slightly lower; however, the small shift was attributable to curricular changes (for example, roman numerals had been de-emphasized between 1956 and 1977). The provincial study, which involved more up-to-date versions of the tests, included a sample of Edmonton Public School students. From the results it was inferred that achievement standards for Grade 3 had improved in Alberta between 1956 to 1977.

Departmental examinations were re-instituted in Alberta in 1984, but in many aspects they were different from those previously in effect. Tests were conducted in grades 3, 6, 9, and 12. In Grade 12, all academic subjects were tested each year (actually twice a year because of semestering) but, in the lower grades, subject areas were tested on a cyclical basis, so that in any one year all students in these grades would be tested, but only in a few subjects. The primary focus of the examinations, especially for grades 3, 6, and 9, was to monitor achievement. In future years, therefore, hard data should be available on the question of standards over time.

SASKATCHEWAN

In Saskatchewan several projects have been carried out that have indicated a concern for standards by the authorities. A report entitled *Student Evaluation*[12] made strong recommendations intended to ensure that teachers were competent in evaluating student achievement. This was in response to concerns regarding the accreditation policy that had been evolving for several years and that was formulated in 1972. The effect of this policy was to discontinue departmental examinations for all except a few students whose teachers were not accredited. This report made no direct reference, however, to changes in standards.

A study conducted under the auspices of the Saskatchewan School Trustees Association[13] was more directly related to standards. The project had several purposes, all related to achievement or to evaluation of achievement. One of these was to develop norms applicable to the province for the Canadian Tests of Basic Skills and for the Stanford Test of Academic Skills. These norms, when compared to the Canadian norms developed by the publishers, served as a check on achievement standards in Saskatchewan. As a result of the tests administered to students in a representative sample of school systems, it was concluded that achievement was up to the norms established for Canada by the publishers.

A testing project by Randhawa[14] for the Saskatchewan Department of Education had six objectives. One was to provide benchmarks of achievement in the basic skills—reading, language, and mathematics. The second was to compare student achievement in Saskatchewan to national norms. The third was to compare test results with those of a test survey conducted in 1958. The method of the study was to administer standardized tests of mental ability and of achievement in the basic skills to a sample of students in each of grades 4, 7, and 10. Approximately 5 000 students in the three grades were tested. The major conclusion was that the Saskatchewan students scored higher than the Canadian norming sample in most of the tests. With respect to the 1958–78 comparisons, no conclusions were reached because of the dissimilarities in the test forms used in the two instances. If there were differences, they seemed to be in favour of the 1978 group, but this contention could be disputed.

ONTARIO

An extensive study on standards was conducted by Hedges[15] in Ontario. The project dealt with achievement of pupils enrolled in grades 5 to 8 in the St. Catharine's public schools over a forty-year span ending in 1976. Test results for the four grades were available for classes enrolled in (approximately) 1938, 1954, and 1976; that is, at intervals about one generation apart. Four question were posed:

1. How does pupil achievement in language arts and mathematics in 1976 compare with achievement in 1938 and 1954 based on the same tests and schools?

2. How would a *comparable* group perform at present on the same tests? This made adjustments based on socio-economic background, age, etc.

3. How would a comparable group perform at present on a "fair" test? This took into account such things as changes in school objectives and changes in vocabulary usage.

4. What other factors may account for differences in achievement that remain after these factors have been taken into account?

The researcher employed three standardized tests, Dominion Tests, Niagara Mathematics Test Series, and Thorndike-McCall Reading Scale for the Understanding of Sentences (Form 2). Rather than dealing with samples, all students in the specified grades were involved, resulting in approximately 10 000 test papers to be processed.

Results were as follows:

1. Figures indicated that Grade 8 students performed at a lower level in

arithmetic concepts and reasoning in 1976 than did the students in earlier years.

2. Grades 5 to 7 students in 1976 outperformed earlier counterparts in fundamental operations in arithmetic. This conclusion was based on a test of fair comparison.

3. Grade 8 students, in 1976, performed as well as, or marginally better than, the earlier groups in paragraph reading.

4. Over the forty-year interval, Grade 6 paragraph reading had shown a small but steady improvement.

5. Grades 5 to 8 students' ability to initiate vocabulary from descriptions was sharply improved.

It was noted that age-grade figures available for the spring of 1935, 1954, and 1975 indicated that pupils in 1975 were slightly older than pupils in the earlier classes. For grades 5, 6, 7, and 8 the differences were .2 years, .6 years, .1 years, and .6 years respectively. The age increases were primarily due to changes in admission policies.

The researcher cautioned against making broad generalizations regarding achievement changes over the years in Ontario. It was noted that the study involved one school system only. It was stated also that longitudinal studies of this kind in Ontario are almost completely absent.

Another study in Ontario[16] dealt with mathematics achievement of students enrolled in some of the grade 12 and 13 subjects. A comparative analysis of the Ontario Mathematics Achievement Test (OMAT) was conducted for results of test administrations carried out in 1968, 1976, and 1982. The procedure employed was to examine item difficulties and total test scores for the three sets of data. No achievement decline was found. The researchers stated, "the levels of mathematics achievement remained remarkably constant over the time period." This conclusion was reached despite the fact that the 1968 sample consisted of volunteers who were seeking university admission while the later samples were made up of randomly selected students enrolled in several mathematics courses. The researchers suggested further that an improvement in achievement may actually have been recorded if consideration had been given to replacement of outdated items that had formed part of the test.

QUEBEC

In Quebec, the Ministry of Education has issued a number of reports that reflect on standards. One of these,[18] involving students whose first language was French, dealt with reading comprehension and written and oral expression. Student achievement in French with respect to six objectives was studied; three dealt with reading, one with writing, one with oral comprehension, and one with oral production. The report indicated a general satisfaction with student achievement in creating a strong setting. There was less satisfaction with sequencing of dialogue in writing, and a marked weakness was noted with respect to written grammar and written usage.

NEW BRUNSWICK

A study conducted by Nadeau[19] for the New Brunswick Department of Education investigated, for Francophone students, the degree of relationship between grades in high school subjects and subsequent achievement at l'Université de Moncton. A secondary purpose was to check on levels of achievement. Results indicated, first, that correlations between high school marks and university marks, in corresponding subjects, varied a great deal. A second finding was that achievement levels for the three high school grades were going down.

NOVA SCOTIA

In Nova Scotia the matter of standards over time is studied on an annual basis, but the approach is unique. Each year, the Nova Scotia Department of Education prepares examinations for students in Grade 9 and Grade 12 in seven subjects: social studies, science, mathematics computation, mathematics basic concepts, reading, mechanics of writing, and English expression. There are two primary purposes for the tests.
 1. To provide provincial norms and means for each school in each subject.
 2. To "see how students are achieving in the seven test areas from year to year."

Pursuant to the first purpose, each school enrolling Grade 9 and/or Grade 12 students is issued a printout of provincial results and local results. The school, therefore, is informed, on an annual basis, as to how its students fare compared to all of the students in the province.

The second purpose involves the Department of Education only. No report comparing achievement levels from year to year is prepared. Instead, the results are for internal use in identifying weaknesses and strengths and for providing information for groups making adjustments in the various curricula.

NEWFOUNDLAND

The Newfoundland and Labrador Department of Education instituted the Elementary Standards Testing Program in 1975, which was designed to fulfil three purposes:

1. To monitor educational standards in the basic subjects;
2. To establish norms for the province; and
3. To make information avilable for use in formulating educational policy.

Prior to 1975 there had been a system of external examinations at various grade levels, but a gradual reduction in the testing resulted in Grade 11, only, being assessed. In 1974 standardized testing of grade 8 pupils, using the Canadian Tests of Basic Skills, was begun, and in 1975 this was extended to grades 4 and 6.

The new program called for testing in the fall of the year. While three grades were involved, only one was designated for examination in any particular year. The pattern of testing was designed so that all students would, at some time during their elementary school years, be exposed to the battery of examinations. By the spring of 1986, results were available for several cycles of the tests. Grade 4 had been tested in 1975, 1978, 1981, and 1984; Grade 6 in 1976, 1979, 1982, and 1985; and Grade 8 in 1974, 1977, 1980, and 1983.

A summary of the results is shown in table 7. The percentile norms are based on national samples of Canadian students. Data were extracted from Fagan's reports.[21] Test results showed a general improvement in test scores for all three of the grades over the decade or so of testing. It was pointed out by Fagan,[22] however, that evidence indicated a general improvement across the nation, such that Newfoundland and Labrador students remained in approximately the same relative position they held in the mid-1970s. This did not apply to mathematics, where there was a relative gain compared to the nation as a whole. The fact remained, however, that achievement in grades 4, 6, and 8, as measured by the CTBS, showed an improvement over a ten-year period ending in 1985.

A High School Standards Testing Program was instituted in 1982, involving May examinations for a representative sample of Grade 12 students only. One of the primary purposes of the battery was to enable educators to compare achievement of students in the final year of the traditional eleven-year program, discontinued in 1982, with achievement of students in the new twelve-year program. The 1982 results, therefore, were for Grade 11 students, and subsequent results applied to Grade 12. No testing was carried out in 1983 as there were no Grade 12 students. The test employed was the Canadian Tests of Basic Skills, High School Edition. This battery consisted of four subtests: reading comprehension, mathematics, written expression, and using sources of information. A composite score was computed, in addition to scores for each of the subtests. A 1985 report[23] gave an analysis of the results for 1982, 1984, and 1985. Table 8 shows the results of the tests.

In her conclusion, Fagan states, "the 1985 testing of Level 3 students confirmed the 1984 results which showed a significant increase in student performance on basic skills achievement with the introduction of the new high school program."[24] It is evident that the Department of Education of

Newfoundland and Labrador has taken steps to monitor achievement standards over the long term. It is also evident that there has been an improvement in students' scores on the CTBS over the decade ending in spring 1985.

TABLE 7
PERCENTILE RANKS OF GRADES 4, 6, AND 8 STUDENTS ON CTBS COMPOSITE SCORES AT THREE-YEAR INTERVALS

GROUP	YEAR	PERCENTILE RANK
Grade 4	1975	27
	1978	43
	1981	48
	1984	38
Grade 6	1976	36
	1979	45
	1982	41
	1985	46
Grade 8	1974	27
	1977	35
	1980	48
	1983	43

TABLE 8
STANDARD SCORES FOR GRADUATING CLASSES FOR THREE YEARS

SUBTEST	NORMS	1982	1984	1985
Reading Comprehension	194.5	180.5	187.9	188.5
Mathematics	188.5	180.4	182.1	183.8
Written Expression	190.5	177.5	189.3	188.2
Using Sources of Information	190.5	176.5	186.0	186.3
Composite	191.0	178.9	186.7	186.9

Source: Lenora Perry Fagan, *Report of the Elementary Standards Testing Program 1984* (Government of Newfoundland and Labrador Department of Education, 1985), 8–9.

PRINCE EDWARD ISLAND

The Director, Educational Services, Department of Education, Prince Edward Island stated that no research reports were available at present. He noted that the Canadian Tests of Basic Skills are administered at grades 3, 6 and 9, but that the results are used internally, only. He suggested also, that there may be a change in the policy resulting in availability of the data.

COMMENTS AND CONCLUSIONS

The studies described in this report are by no means exhaustive. If, as no doubt is the case, pertinent information on the matter of standards over time in Canada has not been included here, sincere apologies are submitted by this writer. A lame excuse that might be offered is that government reports are typically very difficult to locate in libraries and are all too often not available in university libraries.

In the case of the province of Manitoba, no reports could be found on educational standards. This was despite requests for information and library searches. This does not suggest that there are no reports, but that they are not easy to locate outside of the province.

Another problem that should be mentioned is that many reports are written (perhaps as they should be) for readers in a particular province. An outsider who is not familiar with details of administration or procedures, which are very obvious to people in the target province, might easily misinterpret important data. If such is the case in this summary, the indulgence of those who are more knowledgeable is requested.

The studies cited here tend to deal with individual provinces, or with small subdivisions of the provinces. As a result, it is not possible to state clearcut findings that apply to Canada as a whole. With this caution, then, some tentative conclusions can be drawn.

1. There is as much evidence that achievement standards of students have improved over the last few decades as there is that they have declined.

2. While there are feelings that some aspects of education should improve, there is no widespread feeling that achievement is well below standard in any broad area.

3. Provincial departments of education are generally more concerned with standards of achievement than they were in previous years, and as a result, most of them have provisions for monitoring standards over time in future years.

4. There is no convincing evidence that there was a pronounced decline in achievement in Canada as was the case in the United States. If a decline occurred, it was not great, and it was limited to small sectors of the content domain. It is indeed possible that achievement in some areas has risen over the last number of years.

RECOMMENDATIONS

At the conclusion of their studies, researchers often feel compelled to give a set of recommendations, presumably to enlighten those whom they consider to be less informed (which includes most everybody). In order to uphold the tradition, the following gems of wisdom are offered.

1. Researchers in Canada should be urged (nay! earnestly entreated) to distribute copies of their reports to libraries (especially university libraries) across the nation.

2. Researchers should bear in mind that most studies, especially on the topic of standards, are of interest to many Canadian educators. The reports should therefore include sufficient descriptive details of programs and procedures unique to the province under study so that readers in other parts of the nation can readily comprehend the narrative.

3. Officials in charge of testing programs, whether at the school system or the provincial level, are urged to make provisions for long-range comparisons of achievement. Procedures such as storing samples of test papers and retaining students' work samples are simple but effective ways of providing data for longitudinal research. There are also some sophisticated, but more expensive, methods that might be considered.

NOTES

1. College Entrance Examination Board, *On Further Examination: Report of the Advisory Panel on the Scholastic Aptitude Test Score Decline* (New York: College Entrance Examination Board, 1978).

2. Lawrence C. Stedman and Carl F. Kaestle, "The Test Score Decline is Over: Now What?" *Phi Delta Kappan* (Nov. 1985).

3. Fred Bruning, "An Education System Under Siege," *Maclean's* (21 Apr. 1986), 11.

4. Hugh Taylor, *1982 British Columbia Science Assessment Summary Report* (British Columbia, Ministry of Education, 1982).

5. Peter Evans, S. Allen, R. Chester, T. Johnson, W. Muir, and K. Pye, *British Columbia Reading Assessment 1977 Test Results* (British Columbia, Ministry of Education, 1977).

6. Taylor, *1982 British Columbia Science Assessment Summary Report.*

7. F. Dumont, *Alberta Grade 12 Examination Study* (Alberta Education, 1977).

8. J.E. Reid, *A Comparison of Grade 12 Academic Achievement 1976 to 1982* (Alberta Education, 1982).

9. Canadian Institute for Research in the Behavioural and Social Sciences, *Alberta Language Arts (Reading and Writing) Achievement Study* (Alberta Education, 1978).

10. S.C.T. Clark, V. Nyberg, and W. Worth, *Alberta Grade 3 Achievement Study* (Alberta Education, 1978).

11. S.C.T. Clark, V. Nyberg, and W. Worth, *Edmonton Grade 3 Achievement Study* (Alberta Education, 1977).

12. Minister's Advisory Committee on Student Evaluation, *Student Evaluation* (Saskatchewan, Department of Education, 1975).

13. Leigh Calnek, *SSTA Student Achievement Monitoring Project* (Regina: Research Centre, Saskatchewan School Trustees Assn., 1979).

14. Bikkar S. Randhawa, *Achievement and Ability Status of Grades 4, 7, and 10 Pupils in Saskatchewan* (Saskatchewan, Department of Education, 1978).

15. H.G. Hedges, *Achievement in Basic Skills Project* (Ontario, Ministry of Education, 1977).

16. Merlin Wahlstrom, Dennis Raphael, and Les McLean, "Comparative Analysis of Ontario Senior Division Mathematics Achievement 1968–1982," *Canadian Journal of Education* (Spring 1986): 174–79.

17. Ibid., 178.

18. Lise Ouellet, *Rapport Détaillé Concernant les Résultats à L'Épreuve de Fin de Cycle de Français Langue Maternelle au Premier Cycle du Secondaire* (Gouvernement de Québec, 1985).

19. Gilles Nadeau, *Sommaire Exécutif Projet de Recherche Institutionnelle* (New Brunswick, Department of Education, 1986).

20. Nova Scotia, Department of Education, *Guide to the Nova Scotia Achievement Tests, Level 12* (Nova Scotia Department of Education, 1985), 17.

21. Lenora Perry Fagan, *Report of the Elementary Standards Testing Program (1982 and 1983)* (Newfoundland and Labrador Department of Education, 1984), 27; and *Report of the Elementary Standards Testing Program 1984* (ibid., 1985).

22. Fagan, *Report of the Elementary Standards Testing Program* (1982 and 1983), 5.

23. Fagan, *Report of the Elementary Standards Testing Program 1984*.

24. Ibid., 17.

TESTING: FINE TUNING THE POLITICS OF INEQUALITY[1]

CHARLES S. UNGERLEIDER

Educational rhetoric and policies reflect the political climate in which they develop. In periods of political conservatism, such as the one in which Canada, the United States, and Great Britain currently find themselves, a dominant theme is that education plays an important part in achieving economic superiority over rival nations. Emphasis is placed upon the part education plays in technical as opposed to moral socialization. Demands that educators equip students with the knowledge, skills, and attitudes related to the development of respect for people and social justice are overshadowed by demands for technical, job-oriented skills.

There are many dimensions to the demand for increased attention to marketable skills, but three deserve special consideration. One important dimension is the call for a closer connection between the attributes of the individual, the education to which the individual is entitled, and the outcomes that the individual is considered capable of achieving. A second dimension is the call for increasing differentiation among and within educational institutions. Rising enrolment in private schools and greater demand for the public support of such schools are only two of the manifestations of the call for increasing differentiation.

A third dimension of the demand for increased attention to technical, job-related skills is the emphasis placed upon testing. Testing is seen as a method for increasing both the efficiency of educational institutions and their quality. Testing is regarded as a means for deciding the type of education that individuals will be eligible to receive as well as a means for ensuring that teachers possess the skills and knowledge to provide such education. In addition, testing is considered an appropriate technology for certifying outcomes that the individual has achieved from his or her education. Testing is an important educational technology for fine tuning the politics of inequality to which conservatives ultimately subscribe.

THE ECONOMIC AND SOCIAL ORIGINS OF TESTING

Over the course of the twentieth century, standardized testing has grown from infancy into an enormously profitable and influential industry. The rapid growth of the testing movement and its general acceptance were related to a number of developments, including the expansion and transformation of the economy, the gradual sophistication of testing methods, the belief in innate intelligence, and the expansion of the educational system and its functions.

The change from an agricultural to an industrial economy deeply affected social conceptions of human worth. The shift of economic power from the countryside to the city and the emergence of an achievement-oriented social system permitted the development of a set of social beliefs that could not have existed in an agrarian society where attempts to change one's social position were inconsistent with the idea of the social hierarchy, which was based upon birth. With industrialization, achievement became increasingly important in determining one's place in the social structure.

During the latter part of the nineteenth century, influential people such as Herbert Spencer, William Graham Sumner, and Francis Galton began to apply ideas from the biological and physical sciences to society. Spencer, who coined the term "survival of the fittest," believed that social homogeneity was inherently unstable. He reasoned that the process of increasing social differentiation would eventually result in "the establishment of the greatest perfection and the most complete happiness." According to historian Richard Hofstadter, Spencer held the view that "the pressure of subsistence upon population must have a beneficent effect upon the human race. This pressure had been the immediate cause of progress from earliest times. By placing a premium upon skill, intelligence, self-control and the power to adapt through technological innovation, it had stimulated human advancement and selected the best of each generation for survival."[2] Spencer felt that social theory should recognize the selection principle from biology and refrain from violating it by "the artificial preservation of those least able to take care of themselves."[3]

It was within this *laissez-faire* context that standardized testing developed. Underlying its development were several premises:

1. Inequality is a natural condition affecting all human relations.
2. Equality is incompatible with economic progress.
3. Competition is the mechanism by which progress is achieved.
4. Personal denial and self-control are necessary for economic and social progress.
5. Fitting education to the individual and the individual to the job is the most effective way of ensuring progress.
6. The state should not tamper with the competitive forces that produce progress, nor should it intervene in the lives of its citizens.
7. It is immoral to resist the inevitability of the forces that will produce economic and social progress.

The rapid development of the use of standardized tests of intelligence and ability depended in large part on their claim to be scientific and unbiased. Francis Galton, a cousin of Charles Darwin, believed that intelligence tests could be used to divide humanity on the basis of innate differences and thereby provide the means to control the production of "fine human offspring." Galton's *Hereditary Genius: An Inquiry into its Laws and Consequences* was published in London in 1869. Galton proposed to arrange people "according to their natural abilities, putting them into classes separated by equal degrees of merit, and to show the relative number of individuals included in the several classes."[4] Galton coined the term *eugenics* to refer to "the science which deals with all influences that improve the inborn qualities of a race; also with those that develop them to their utmost advantage.... The aim of Eugenics is to represent each class or sect by its best specimens; that done, to leave them to work out their own common civilizations in their own way."[5] Galton, who founded the Eugenic Society in 1870, was persuaded that nature was much more influential than nurture and that the upper social strata would naturally produce a larger number of talented individuals than would the lower classes.

The development of the concept of "statistical correlation" by Galton's protégé, Karl Pearson, and the enunciation of the idea of "factor analysis" by Charles Spearman furthered the belief that it was possible to design scientific, objective, and unbiased tests of innate intelligence.[6] Pearson, who was Galton Professor of Eugenics at London University and Director of the Francis Galton Laboratory, argued that biological factors "are dominant in the evolution of mankind; these and these alone, can throw light on the rise and fall of nations, on racial progress and national degeneracy." He estimated that ninety percent of a person's capacity was determined by heredity. He was among those of the period who argued that education should vary for individuals and groups in relation to their abilities.[7]

In North America, Lewis Terman, Henry Goddard, and Robert Yerkes were the leaders of the testing movement. As early as 1912, Henry Goddard had begun to administer the Binet-Simon intelligence test (produced in France in 1905 by Alfred Binet and Théodore Simon) to immigrants. Then, in 1916, Lewis Terman of Stanford University translated and adapted the Binet-Simon scale and published the first Stanford-Binet intelligence scale. This scale was revised in 1937 and again in 1960, and is still one of the most widely used tests. In 1917, Robert Yerkes of Harvard University developed the "Alpha" and "Beta" intelligence tests, which were administered to two million American army recruits.[8] Although Binet had been careful to state that the Binet-Simon scale measured competence and not a genetic quality, the scale was soon labelled as a measure of innate intelligence. Without evidence, educational psychologists of the period made a leap of faith to the position that general intelligence as measured by intelligence tests was an innate quality. Terman, Goddard, and Yerkes were among those who subscribed to this belief.

In the first two decades of the twentieth century, industry experienced a period of soaring production, rapid growth, and the concentration of capital. These changes demanded an increase in the number of workers with specific productive, managerial, technical, and clerical skills. Corporate capitalism was faced with the problem of having to select suitable trainees who would provide the largest return on the investment involved in training them. Intelligence, achievement, and vocational tests offered corporations an ideal way of selecting from the mass of available workers those trainees who would most efficiently repay the costs of training through their contributions to production.

The First World War increased the need for more educated and skilled labour organized into a pyramid-shaped structure. New tests helped to provide justification for this hierarchy. Because of the "scientific" stature accorded to the belief that intelligence was innate, workers could be classified on the basis of "intelligence" scores and taught to accept their location in an inequitably structured workplace. Psychological tests provided both the means by which workers could be efficiently selected for training and the rationale for the maintenance of an acquiescent workforce.

Standardized tests of intelligence and ability were also considered scientific tools that could be used to classify people by race and social class in order to determine who should be educated. "Intelligence" and associated achievement tests were thought ideally suited to the rapidly expanding education system, which was geared to serve the industrial structure. These tests offered what seemed to be an unbiased scientific means of measuring students and maintaining the hierarchical education system.

The rise of universal education systems and the expansion of higher education in Britain and North America paralleled the vast economic changes taking place during the first two decades of the twentieth century. In Britain, the educational system was gradually extended largely as a result of pressure from members of the working class who were demanding better education for their children. In North America, working-class pressure and the massive tide of immigrants helped bring about the expansion of the educational system. Intelligence and ability testing made it possible to select and stream the increased numbers of people who wished to have access to the educational system.

North American school systems were based on an ideology of equality. Schools and colleges used the new tests to classify students and to preserve the appearance of equal opportunity. The scientific status of these tests provided an easy and seemingly legitimate way to select students by ability. Educational reformers argued that these tests would allow schools and teachers to "fit education to the individual needs of students." Education had become a hierarchical meritocracy firmly supported by "objective and unbiased" test scores.

CANADIAN TESTING IN HISTORICAL PERSPECTIVE

Testing figures prominently in Canada's education system. As of March 1985, the provinces of British Columbia, Alberta, Saskatchewan, Quebec, and Newfoundland administered compulsory final examinations to students at the secondary level. The number of examinable courses ranged from a low of seven in Alberta to nearly 150 in Quebec. In the five provinces administering compulsory final examinations, examination marks are combined with the marks awarded by teachers to determine the final marks awarded to students.[9]

Seven provinces—British Columbia, Alberta, Manitoba, Quebec, Nova Scotia, Prince Edward Island, and Newfoundland—are engaged in student assessment programs designed to assist in the evaluation of curricula and programs of study. Three of the seven—Nova Scotia, Prince Edward Island, and Newfoundland—use commercially prepared tests.[10] In most provinces, commercially published tests, including the Canadian Test of Basic Skills, Canadian Cognitive Abilities Test, Differential Aptitude Test, Gate-MacGinitie Reading Tests, Metropolitan Achievement Test, Stanford Achievement Test, and the Stanford Test of Academic Skills, are used to make a variety of educational decisions ranging from the placement of individuals to the efficacy of programs.[11]

The use of standardized tests has always figured prominently in Canadian education. The use of such tests has typically reflected nativism—protection of the interests of majority inhabitants against those of immigrants—and a prejudicial view of the educational capacities of children from working-class backgrounds.

In 1925, in Canada's first comprehensive survey of a provincial school system,[12] Peter Sandiford undertook an "objective survey of the intelligence and school achievement of the pupils of the Province [of British Columbia]." Sandiford wrote:

> The object of this study was to determine the influence of immigration from various centres upon the general intellectual level of the B.C. community. If the people coming into the Province are of higher intelligence than those already in it, the general level will be raised. This, of course, is a result greatly to be desired. On the other hand, continued immigration of inferior stock can end only in disaster.[13]

Sandiford then elaborated upon this nativistic theme:

> The low intelligence of pupils born in Continental Europe and the rest of the world is the outstanding feature of this investigation. These high school pupils, normal school and university students have a median intelligence quotient lower than 100; that is, lower than that of the community as a whole. Immigration from these areas lowers the average intelligence of the population.[14]

Later in the report, Sandiford described the mental capacity of the Japanese and Chinese pupils enrolled in Vancouver schools. Recognizing that "tests involving a use of English language would not be fair" to Japanese and Chinese pupils, the testers used a battery of fifteen tests to assess the intelligence of 155 Chinese and 150 Japanese pupils. In subsequent discussion of this testing, Sandiford contradicts his earlier statement on the desirability of raising the general level of intelligence by immigration:

> It will be seen that the Japanese are superior to the Chinese and both are greatly superior to the average white population. The superiority is undoubtedly due to selection. In the main it is the Japanese and Chinese who possess the qualities of cleverness, resourcefulness, and courage who emigrate to British Columbia; the dullards and less enterprising are left behind. This superiority of emigrant stock is no new phenomenon in world history. There are those who maintain that Great Britain owes her eminent position in the world to the fact that only the clever and sturdy could secure a footing on her shores.... But from the political and economic standpoints the presence of an industrious, clever, and frugal alien group, capable so far as mentality is concerned, of competing successfully with the native whites in most occupations they mutually engage in, constitutes a problem which calls for the highest quality of statesmanship if it is to be solved satisfactorily.[15]

Sandiford argued that intelligence testing should be a routine part of Canadian immigration practices.

> In the first place we should avoid the obvious mistake of the United States who "pumped in population" irrespective of the intellectual calibre of the immigrants. No one who dispassionately studies the facts can deny that the average intelligence of Americans has been seriously lowered by the reckless immigration policy she has pursued. But there was some excuse for her. Her high tide of immigration was in the pre-intelligence-test days. Ours is coming at a time when intelligence can be measured with a fair degree of reliability.[16]

Sandiford went on to advocate three principles for immigration. He said that Canada should not accept any immigrant with "defective mentality," advocating selection of only those who were above the Canadian average. Acknowledging that medical examinations were sufficiently reliable to permit the separation of the fit from the unfit, Sandiford said that Canada should not admit any immigrant whose health was seriously impaired. And, lamenting the fact that tests of morality were still in their infancy, he nevertheless advocated that the morality of immigrants should meet Canadian standards.[17]

The discussion of intelligence was not confined to the expression of nativistic sentiments. It also evinced the class distinctions of the time. "There is a distinctive change of intelligence level with parental occupational grouping.... In all cases, children of professional workers head the list by a wide margin. Intelligence sufficiently high to achieve success in a profession is handed down to children. This is a matter of social significance."[18]

There is little doubt that eugenics provided part of the frame of reference for the interpretation of Sandiford's data. In the conclusion to the section concerned with socio-economic differences and intelligence, Sandiford expressed the connection clearly: "the children of professional people are, on the whole, more intelligent than others and, eugenically, this is the group in which large families should be encouraged."[19] And, it was implied, it was also this group for which the most extensive education should be provided.

During most of this century, examinations were used to control access to secondary and postsecondary education for the majority of students in Canada. The demands of working-class and immigrant groups for more and better education were blunted by the use of standardized tests. The "scientific" status of these tests provided justification for the restriction of educational opportunities. Today, the practice of making opportunities available on the basis of what are typically regarded as in-born abilities is as strong as it was a half-century ago. "All students should have access, within the constraints of what a given school can offer, to a program of studies that is challenging, *yet appropriate to their needs, abilities, and aspirations.*"[20]

Standardized tests tend to reinforce the disadvantages imposed by students' economic or cultural background. That members of particular ethnic and economic groups are consistently overrepresented in some educational programs and underrepresented in others is due at least in part to standardized testing and the subsequent streaming of students into "suitable" programs. In Canada, participation rates in postsecondary education differ substantially by social class and region, revealing an inequitable distribution of opportunity for young people from different backgrounds.[21]

In Britain, the "Eleven Plus" examination provides a clear example of the way tests have been used to determine which type of education students would receive. Following the Second World War, a tripartite system of secondary education was established and a battery of tests was administered to all students in publicly financed education. Students who performed well on the examination went on to the grammar schools, which offered an academic curriculum leading to a professional occupation. Students who performed less well were assigned to technical schools, which offered a curriculum leading to skilled technical occupations. Students who performed least well, by far the largest group of students, were assigned to secondary modern schools, which offered a general curriculum that was designed to prepare them for the unskilled jobs they were expected to fill.

When the basis for educational decisions rests upon information provided by standardized tests of intelligence and ability, one can be certain that the inferences being drawn from the test data are influenced by some estimation of the person within an economic, political, or social frame of reference. Because of their bias in favour of white, middle-class students, and their use in determining the opportunities available to students in school and people in the work force, standardized tests have helped to perpetuate discrimination against people from low-income and minority backgrounds and preserve existing social inequalities. In a study of children in Regina in the 1960s, Kennett found evidence of a positive correlation—favouring children of high socio-economic status—between social class and test scores.[22] A similar relationship was found by Holmes in a more recent study in B.C.[23]

THE CONSTRUCTION, USE, AND IMPACT OF STANDARDIZED TESTS

Standardized tests have traditionally served three major functions: evaluation, selection, and restriction. In the construction of standardized ability or intelligence tests, developers seek to have the individual items that make up the test differentiate among the individuals taking the test. Test items are produced so that, on some items, only half of the people in a particular age group will respond accurately. The same population will correctly answer most of the items developed for younger people and will not correctly answer very many of the items developed for older people. In addition, test items are developed to minimize their correlation with each other. As a consequence, the size of any given test score is determined by many independent responses of equal influence. Although we tend to think of intelligence as something tangible, it is, in fact, simply a convenient label for the sum of a person's responses to the individual items that make up the test.

In constructing tests, developers assume that all people of a given age have had the same opportunity to develop the capacities being measured. This assumption is buttressed by the related assumption that the abilities being measured are genetically determined. These assumptions are further bolstered by the development of tests that are *reliable*. Clearly, there are problems with all of these assumptions. In a pluralistic society, there is a wide discrepancy in experiences, values, and opportunities, even among children of the same age group. Moreover, abilities that may, to some extent, be genetically determined, are influenced to an enormous degree by factors such as class and region and expectations associated with ethnicity and gender. If standardized tests take no account of these factors, in what sense can the tests be said to be a reliable measure of the intelligence or potential of a given child?

Another problem is that standardized tests are constructed to be insensitive to change.[24] This runs counter to the purposes of education. The process of education assumes that people change over time and that the rate and nature of the changes can be affected by systematic instruction. Standardized intelligence tests assume that what people are, today, is what they will be in the future. In other words, most standardized tests assume the inequities among people are immutable and will continue to characterize the same individuals in the future.

The technology of standardized testing is of limited utility in improving student performance. It is nevertheless the case that standardized tests of intelligence and ability provide the basis for the comparison of student performances. Such comparisons have inevitably led to selection. Based upon the notion that one should fit education to the needs of individual students, schools have used standardized tests of ability and intelligence as the means for deciding whether and what types of instruction should be made available to students. Standardized tests have been used as the basis for grouping elementary students within classrooms, for deciding whether secondary students should be allowed to pursue vocational, academic, or commercial programs, and for moving students out of the school system into the work force.

The use of standardized tests for grouping elementary students within classrooms and streaming them into particular programs at the secondary level is based upon two related assumptions. The first is that there is a connection between student abilities and instructional method or program. The second assumption is that student achievement can be maximized if students of different abilities receive different types of instruction. Grouping by "intelligence" and ability has a long record of failure in producing increases in student achievement. Results of studies indicate quite clearly that groups of mixed ability do about as well as groups of students with similar abilities.

> The notion of ability grouping is appealing: logic seems to dictate that teachers can teach most effectively when differences in student ability are minimal. However, several authoritative reviews suggest that ability grouping *per se* is unlikely to have a positive effect on student achievement. In fact, the typical results are that such grouping has no effect or only a minor positive effect on the achievement of students in the high-ability classes, but has clearly negative effects on the achievement and attitudes of students assigned to low-ability classes.[25]

The idea of individual achievement determining one's place within the socio-economic hierarchy has its origins in the economic and social transformation that accompanied industrialization and in the rapid development of a technology for testing human abilities. Emphasis upon achievement and the development of a technology for measuring intelligence and other abilities provided a social environment in which three basic ideas could develop:

1. People should be judged by their abilities;
2. Abilities can be represented by a mathematical distribution that depicts a few people standing out from the masses; and
3. Human beings of extraordinary ability are not bound by the same conventions which bind "normal" people.[26]

These ideas continue to shape our ideas about human worth, and they have had a profound effect on our view of education. The pattern of attitudes that grows out of this social imagery creates social, educational, and occupational consequences that are deeply disturbing. Standardized tests are administered and interpreted within a particular social frame of reference. The consequences of how one scores on tests affect one's life chances—for education, for jobs, and for self-esteem.

It is ironic that standardized tests, ostensibly a method of achieving equal educational opportunity, should instead provide a "scientific" rationalization for the denial of such opportunity to minority groups—groups that, whether because of ethnicity, gender, or class, fare less well on these tests than majority-group candidates in whose favour the tests are biased. Minority students achieving lower scores are accordingly streamed into the less rigorous academic programs, in effect guaranteeing, for at least another generation, the educational and, by extension, economic disadvantage of the group.

The decision to provide or withhold certain opportunities on the basis of standardized test scores is an economic and political one. The neo-conservative politics that is currently in the ascendancy in Canada, Great Britain, and the United States grows out of a social philosophy that essentially accepts inequality among people as a natural social condition in which the state should not intervene. In such a context, it is not surprising that education is supported primarily as a means to economic ends and that testing is regarded as an important educational technology.

NOTES

1. An earlier version of this article, entitled "The Social and Educational Consequences of Standardized Testing: A Point of View," was published in the *McGill Journal of Education* 20, 3 (Fall 1985): 281–91.
2. R. Hofstadter, *Social Darwinism in American Thought* (New York: George Bazilier, 1944, 1969), 39.
3. Ibid., 44.
4. F. Galton, *Hereditary Genius: An Inquiry into its Laws and Consequences* (London: Macmillan, 1869), 26.
5. S. Collini, *Liberalism and Sociology* (Cambridge: Cambridge University Press, 1979), 201–2.
6. D. Martindale, *The Nature and Types of Sociological Theory* (Cambridge, Mass.: The Riverside Press, 1960).
7. C. Spearman, "'General Intelligence,' Objectively Determined and Measured," *American Journal of Psychology* XV, 2 (Apr. 1904).
8. L.M. Terman, *Stanford Revision of the Binet-Simon Scale* (Boston: Houghton Mifflin, 1916); L.J. Kamin, *The Science and Politics of I.Q.* (Toronto: John Wiley & Sons, 1974).
9. H. Schulz, "Summary of Provincial Assessment Practices in Canadian Public Education" (Council of Ministers of Education, Canada, Mar. 1985).
10. Ibid.

11. Educational Research Institute of British Columbia, "Testing Service Reference Guide" (Vancouver, 1984).

12. J.H. Putman and G.M. Weir, eds., *Survey of the School System* (Victoria: Charles F. Banfield, Printer to the King's Most Excellent Majesty, 1925).

13. P. Sandiford, "The Mental Capacity of B.C. Students According to the Place of Birth," in ibid., 458.

14. Ibid., 459.

15. Ibid., 508.

16. P. Sandiford, "The Inheritance of Talent Among Canadians," *Queen's Quarterly* XXXV, 1 (Aug. 1927), 18.

17. Ibid.

18. Sandiford, "The Mental Capacity of B.C. Students," 455–56.

19. Ibid., 458.

20. B.C. Ministry of Education, "Graduation '87" (Victoria: B.C. Ministry of Education, 1984), 10.

21. N. Guppy, "Education Under Siege: Financing and Accessibility in B.C. Universities" (Vancouver, 1984).

22. K.F. Kennett, "Intelligence and Socioeconomic Status in a Canadian Sample," *The Alberta Journal of Educational Research* XVIII, 1 (Mar. 1972).

23. B. Holmes, "Individually Administered Intelligence Tests: An Application of Anchor Test Norming and Equating Procedures in British Columbia," (Ph.D. diss., Faculty of Education, University of British Columbia, 1981).

24. R. Feuerstein, *The Dynamic Assessment of Retarded Performers* (Baltimore: University Park Press, 1979).

25. T.L. Good and J.E. Brophy, *Looking in Classrooms*, 3rd. ed. (New York: Harper & Row, 1984), 273–74.

26. R. Sennett and J. Cobb, *The Hidden Injuries of Class* (New York: Vintage Books, 1973).

ADVANCES IN ACHIEVEMENT TESTING: SOME IMPLICATIONS FOR THE CLASSROOM

GEORGE FITZSIMMONS

DEVELOPING CANADIAN TESTS

The historical perspective on the development of Canadian achievement tests provides an essential foundation for understanding new directions in the field. The changes in achievement testing have ranged from those developed by ministries of education, through importing foreign instruments, to developing our first truly Canadian and nationally normed scales.

In the 1950s, the majority of provincial departments of education produced "Departmental" examinations that all students in specified grades or subjects were required to complete. These tests were taken, usually at the end of the school term, and determined the final grade or standing of all such young citizens. System-wide school testing programs of the day often included the administration of an imported standardized achievement test. The most common were the Iowa Test of Basic Skills, the Metropolitan Achievement Test, and the Stanford Achievement Test. These were American scales requiring from three to six hours to administer. They had been carefully constructed according to the standards of the day to represent the typical U.S. curriculum across the grades, and the content of the items often betrayed the country of origin. Maps, city names, currency, and flags were clearly American. So were the norms. Our children were being compared to an American norming sample that was not representative of our population. Usually, average achievement per grade was slightly higher than the norms, which made interpretation of results even more difficult. Given all these limitations, it is surprising how well the imported tests sold in Canada, but there were no available alternatives.

By the mid-1960s, we were all feeling a surge of nationalism. Canada was soon to celebrate one hundred years of self-government. Expo '67 was coming to Montreal and the Bilingualism and Biculturalism Commission was much in the news. Unfortunately, there were not any Canadian achievement tests. Astutely, the publishers of the Iowa Test of Basic Skills decided to Canadianize their product for grades 3 to 8. Dr. Ethel King, of the University of Calgary, became project leader. Art work was revised, spelling edited, and a few minor changes were made to the items. Perhaps most important of all, the name reflected our nationalism: the *Canadian* Test of Basic Skills (CTBS).[1] While the content of the test was essentially that of the Iowa Test, the norming was exclusively done in our country. The Nelson sales force was very convincing. Within a few years, the majority of all school systems with standardized achievement testing programs used the CTBS. The publishers have maintained the test with minor revisions and a recent re-norming, primarily with customer data in the early 1980s.

Back in the United States in the early 1970s, federal legislators were hoping to improve the educational systems with special grants known as the Title series. One of the conditions of receiving the Title funding was to demonstrate that specified educational objectives were being achieved. At the same time, "competencies" and testing for competence were fashionable talk within the psychometric community. The Monterey-based California Test Bureau had been purchased by McGraw-Hill, which in turn was looking for someone to collaborate in bringing a test to market that would help school systems qualify for Title funding. They hired a Canadian, J. Douglas Ayers, who turned the concept of "Objective Competencies" into the California Achievement Test.[2] Over half of the states adopted the California Achievement Test for Title funding purposes. Perhaps the fine variety of computer-printed reports helped to capture such a large market.

Beside the usual subtest and total battery scores per student, a variety of other informative reports help administrators and teachers understand their students and plan for more effective use of their resources. Over sixty objective competencies are identified for each grade or level of the test. For instance, in reading, competencies include "consonants/digraphs, character analysis, figurative language," and so on. By reviewing reports for each student or class the educator can group children for enrichment, re-teaching, or remediation. The achievement testing information provides a basis for enhancing instruction, and later for accountability to demonstrate the effectiveness of teacher interventions or administrative policies. This new concept in testing serves the dual purpose of assessing the broad view of proficiency in "basic" skills while also offering insights into the status of achievement in many of the fundamental elements of the curriculum.

By the late 1970s we in Canada were grappling with the adjustment to System International metrication. Temperature was being reported in degrees Celsius, and children coming home from school wondered what feet and inches were. Unfortunately, there were no standardized tests of achievement that were ready for the new units in mathematics. The Americans, after a flirtation with metric, had decided to stay with the Imperial/U.S. units of measure. Our readily convertible or adaptable source of tests had vanished. Staff in Toronto, at McGraw-Hill Ryerson, began to explore the feasibility of developing a truly Canadian achievement test, reflecting national curricula and the new metric requirements. By 1979 they decided to build a new testing battery for grades 2 through 12. Dr. J. Douglas Ayers, of the University of Victoria, agreed to be project leader. In the ensuing months, curriculum experts from every province identified the objectives to be achieved by grade in their region. These experts later assembled in Toronto for a week to produce a balanced statement of what was being taught across the country grade by grade. The resulting taxonomy provided the scope and sequence information needed for planning and developing the first truly made-in-Canada standardized achievement test battery. Some of the objective competencies were similar to those found in American education, while others were different. The test scales were designed to provide both norm-referenced and criterion-referenced information. Some items from the California Achievement Test series were found to be suitable but many hundreds of new items were written and tried out in Canadian schools. By the spring of 1981 this project was reaching its climax. The use of a random stratified sample of over 76 000 students in grades 1 through 12 from all provinces and territories stands as the largest national norming study of its kind ever done. By the fall of that year, the Canadian Achievement Tests[3] were available for school use.

SCREENING FOR LEARNING-DISABLED AND GIFTED CHILDREN

The identification of exceptional children has traditionally been a labour-intensive and expensive process. Teachers and parents refer to a coordinator who usually asks a consultant or psychologist for an assessment of the candidate. Some time later, the child is "tested" for as long as half a day. About fifty percent of the time the student does not qualify for inclusion in the special program. The teacher is given some suggestions for building on the child's strengths and left with her or his negative feedback. Investigations began for a more efficient and cost effective screening method.

Building on the work of John McLeod at the University of Saskatchewan, Fitzsimmons and Macnab have produced an interesting solution.[4] They asked teachers to rate students on their suitability for referral to a learning disabilities assessment or to a "challenge" program for gifted students. Identified children in learning disabled and challenge programs were included with those in regular classrooms. Beside the teacher ratings, results of the Canadian Achievement Test and the Test of Cognitive Skills[5] were obtained for these children in grades 4 to 6. They calculated a separate multiple regression equation to predict the achievement test scores for every subtest measured by the achievement battery from the cognitive ability subtests. Then a predicted achievement score was calculated for every student. That is, by referring to the intelligence or aptitude test scores and using them in the regression equation, predicted achievement scores are calculated for each of the achievement subtests. The predicted achievement is subtracted from the student's observed achievement to yield discrepancy scores.

Children who achieve "better" than one would expect, on the basis of their Test of Cognitive Skills scores are as easily identified as those who score "lower" than expected. Using the computer to rank the discrepancy scores from highest positive to lowest negative simplifies the screening process. Those students with low negative scores were correctly identified ninety-four percent of the time by discriminant function analysis as members of the "learning disabled" classes. Those with high positive predicted achievement scores were correctly identified as members of the "challenge" classes seventy-six percent of the time. With this new application, consultants or educational psychologists can screen their entire system for potential candidates for enrichment or remediation. Such a service appears to be more cost effective and time efficient than the present barrage of well intended referrals. A number of school systems are beginning to use the multiple regression discrepancy method to facilitate a comprehensive first look at their pupils before commencing individualized assessment of exceptional children.

RESURGENCE OF PROVINCIAL AND SYSTEM-WIDE TESTING

In the 1950s, all the provinces required students to take standard examinations in specified grades and subjects. These tests were usually constructed by teachers of the subject who also supervised the *in camera* marking. Since such large numbers of students were tested, the assumptions made with standardized testing were also applied to the provincial examinations. This occasionally led to some strange "adjustments." If a test were particularly difficult and too high a percentage of students failed, distributions were normalized and a specified percentage received Honours (First Class), A (Second Class), B (Pass), etc. This provided complete control over the number receiving matriculation, which in turn held implications for the size of the next freshman class at universities, colleges, and institutes of technology. Virtually all adults had experienced these provincial examinations, and many wished that they would be abolished. Arguments usually followed two lines of thought:

1. Teachers are making the tests now for the province. Why not let the local classroom teachers make their own exams? After all, they are professional people.

2. Teachers are teaching to the test rather than preparing their students for the real world.

Both statements contain an element of truth but also a fallacy. In the first case, precious few teachers have been, or are being trained in the science of test development. Less than five percent of the graduates from the bachelor of education program at the University of Alberta have received any formal preparation to make tests. It is likely that graduates from other teacher training institutions are similarly limited. They may be employed in a profession but the majority are lay persons when it comes to designing and writing tests. The second statement ignores the direct relationship between the curriculum and the examination. If the teacher is teaching the curriculum, and the test is designed to measure the concepts of the curriculum, then to "teach to the test" is to teach to the curriculum, which is precisely what educators are entrusted to do.

The desire to have provincial examinations abolished held sway. Gradually, in the 1970s, policies were revised province by province, and teacher grades came to replace department of education examinations. Only Newfoundland continued with province-wide testing.

Soon teacher grades began to fail essential tests of validity. Suddenly a particular high school's students would have graduating averages many points higher than they had been with provincial grades. Admissions officers kept track of the students from such schools and found them to have inordinately high failure rates in their freshman year. Other schools with "high standards" would have graduating averages many points lower than they had been with provincial grades. Those who were admitted did much better than might have been expected on the basis of their teacher grades. In either case, there was the potential for misrepresentation of achievement with shattering consequences to individuals' educational/vocational career plans. The standard of excellence and of comparison was lost.

In the hopes of restoring some order to this chaos, a number of boards began to develop system-wide tests, in fact replacing the provincial standard with a local standard. The resulting local norms provided some help. However, various large boards were taking the initiative in curriculum development. This meant that, in some provinces, while grades within a system were *more* meaningful, there were significant discrepancies in grades and content *between* boards. Small and rural boards often continued faithfully with the provincial curriculum and teacher grades.

The 1980s are seeing a return to provincial examinations. Some ministries of education are sampling designated grades and subjects on a rotational basis for their own information about curriculum mastery. Other provinces are setting final examinations for all major or matriculation subjects in specified grades. In these latter provinces, the teacher's final grade and provincial final grade are either both reported on the transcript or are combined in some weighted fashion. Whether we will go full circle and only report provincial achievement scores for final grades, as was done in the 1950s, remains to be seen. Through this decade and a half of disruption in the validity and reliability of high school transcript grades, the standardized achievement test with national norms continued to provide an essential bench mark or point of reference for educators. Some institutions have moved to requiring applicants to submit standardized achievement test results for reading, language, writing, and mathematics. Philosophically, this raises the spectre of moving the standard of admission from the provincial authority to a commercial test publisher, fairly common in the United States, but not in the Canadian tradition.

NEW DIRECTIONS IN EDUCATION AND ACHIEVEMENT TESTING

The remainder of this paper will explore more recent developments in the world of testing to serve education. There are new advances in statistical analysis that hold promise for improved instruction. Technological enhancements with microcomputers and desk-top scoring devices invite increased use of sophisticated equipment at the school and now the classroom level. With all this information at the educator's fingertips, the ethical issues of responsible behaviour are more pressing for the classroom teacher than ever before.

THEORETICAL CONTRIBUTIONS

One of the first cautions given to a teacher using any test is to beware of its shortcomings. Formally, that is referring to the confidence that can be placed in the resulting score or grade. Recognizing that the test is made by a fallible human, it is unlikely that it measures the skill or domain as accurately as the user would like. The amount of error present is something analagous to friction; test developers are always trying to reduce it while accepting that it will continue to be part of the reality of testing. The quest to reduce error has led to the advancement of item response theory (IRT) as a partial solution.[6] If you assume that knowledge of any concept can be described from simple to complex along a continuum, then any test item measuring that concept can be described as existing at some point along that continuum. Take the concept of addition. Test item "one plus one" would be located near the left or simple end of the continuum. "Two plus five" would be to the right of that, "twelve plus nine" would be further to the right, and "twenty-eight plus thirty-six" would be even further along the continuum. Through the use of item response theory, it is possible to establish the location of items on the concept continuum. Any item occupies a spatial region or area of knowledge along the continuum. Thus, an item can be described by its location and the breadth of knowledge it samples. Using this additive and sequential model, it is theoretically possible to determine the extent of knowledge a student has about a concept by asking very few questions. The objective is to query the student near his or her ceiling. Items asked to the right of the ceiling would all be failed and items asked to the left of the ceiling would all be passed. Thus, it theoretically could be possible to design an automated questioning system that would determine the location of a student on a subject matter continuum very efficiently. While no such system is commercially available, one likely will be in the next few years.

The implications for the classroom teacher are very exciting. After determining each child's upper limit of skill or knowledge, it would be possible to print out what could be the next sequence of lessons or learning activities for each student. Such aids to individualizing instruction may not help the children learn, but would certainly help target the next element for mastery. At some predetermined location on the continuum, we could say that the work in that domain for that grade had been completed.

The second use of item response theory is already among us. That is computer test scoring to obtain a better estimate of the individual's true achievement than can be obtained by just summing the number of correct answers. Traditionally, we have established the items to be included in a test, administered the test, and added up the number of correct answers to obtain the raw score. With IRT, remember, each item has its location on the continuum. Usually near the student's ceiling the passing and failing of items is not as clearly demarked as the theory above would have it.

Imagine for a moment items of increasing difficulty along the continuum having numbers 44, 45, 46, 47, etc. If a student passed 44 and all items to the left of it in the continuum, and also the much more difficult item 47, what should be the student's score? If we were using the traditional method, we would say the student had a total of 45 items correct so the raw score is 45. With IRT, the reasoning is different. Item 47 is much more difficult than 44, and represents a significant increment in knowledge. Therefore the student should be placed on the continuum somewhere above 44, and probably higher than 45, but not all the way up at 47 because he or she failed two intervening items.

Already CTB/McGraw-Hill is offering IRT scoring on their Test of Cognitive Skills and California Achievement Test forms E and F. Other publishers are soon to follow suit with their instruments. As often happens, the users, namely teachers, will be expecting their local testing services to follow the industry standard. Probably by the turn of the century, IRT scoring will be reported alongside or instead of raw scores. We will have the added accuracy of estimating a student's knowledge or ability. We may still suffer the present lack of understanding to communicate these scores into action with the child, parent, and other teachers.

Individualizing instruction has been a particularly popular buzz word in the past few years. Ideally, the teacher has unlimited, and always current information about what the children know, their level of functioning and where to move next for them in their learning experience. Standardized testing can only provide this information once or twice a year. At the time of testing, the comprehensive status of the student is nicely pinpointed. Within a few months, however, we expect new learning to have taken place and the achievement status of each individual to have changed in personally unique ways. Of course, it would have been nice if the teacher could have kept track of all these spurts of growth and personal learning victories, but that was really asking too much. Not any longer.

Programmers have developed comprehensive automated record-keeping systems that offer a currency unimagined even two years ago. Now it is possible to maintain individual records that contain standardized test results that are updated by classroom tests within minutes of taking them. The students' academic status is cross-referenced to a multitude of teaching resources, texts, series, and innovative ideas. This means that a teacher can administer a mathematics test, collect the machine readable answer sheets, pass them through a desk top scanner, generate number correct scores and other statistics, copy the students' achievement into their updated personal data files, and then, in the light of their progress, generate personalized learning activity programs for each student, which are cross-referenced to the learning aids within the school. What would have taken the traditional teacher an evening to mark, and a weekend of planning, can now be dispatched by the available personal computer using only five minutes for a class of thirty students. Granted, Microcomputer Instructional Management System[7] has only been on the market recently, but such products portend a revolution in information management for classroom teachers and their students.

NEW RESPONSIBILITIES

In the face of new theories of information management, new technology, and new applications of testing, we are all confronted by new responsibilities. Just how those duties and rules of conduct will unfold is not clear, but the method of their derivation has been changed for all time. Previously, our professional associations specified and supervised the practice of ethical behaviour. As we move into the twenty-first century, the Supreme Court of Canada will be defining our new morality with respect to the Canadian Charter of Rights. Much of what has been enacted in legislation and in the Charter itself will be subject to legal interpretation. If we can learn from our American colleagues, we see that much of their jurisprudence is founded upon interpretations of the Constitution. A continuing and costly process of suits, judgments, and appeals to higher courts.

While our Canadian experience will no doubt be different, special interests groups may want the Court to decide on questions like Who owns testing information? Is it the student, the parent, the teacher, the principal, or the board? What obligations does ownership entail? Depending on the answer to the first question, the obligations that follow could be very different. Just suppose that the student, or the parent on his or her behalf, owns the information. Then who should pay for it? All taxpayers or just the student's family? If students own the information, can they withhold it from the school authorities? On the other hand, suppose the board owns the information. Then, is it fair, unbiased, accurate, error free? Are the policies for governance of the information within the bounds of the Charter of Rights? Whatever the outcome, the new responsibility of test users will likely include a more comprehensive appreciation of the theory, science, and technology of the continuing advances in achievement testing.

NOTES

1. *Canadian Test of Basic Skills* (Toronto: Nelson, 1982).
2. California Achievement Test (Monterey: CTB/McGraw-Hill, 1979).
3. Canadian Achievement Test (Scarborough, Ont.: McGraw-Hill Ryerson, 1981).
4. John McLeod, *Psychometric Identification of Children with Learning Disabilities* (Institute of Child Guidance and Development, University of Saskatchewan, 1981); George Fitzsimmons and Donald Macnab, *Screening for Learning Disabled and Potentially High Performing Students* (Edmonton: PsiCan Consulting, 1984).
5. Test of Cognitive Skills (Monterey: CTB/McGraw-Hill, 1981).
6. Ronald J. Hambleton, *Item Response Theory: Principles and Applications* (Boston: Kluwer-Nijhoff, 1985); Fredric M. Lord, *Applications of Item Response Theory to Practical Testing Problems* (Hillsdale, N.J.: Erlbaum, 1980); Benjamin D. Wright and Geoffrey N. Masters, *Rating Scale Analysis* (Chicago: MESA Press, 1982).
7. *Microcomputer Instructional Management Systems* (Monterey: CTB/McGraw-Hill, 1985).

SECTION 4:
IMPLICATIONS OF ETHNIC DIVERSITY FOR CANADIAN EDUCATION

Canada is a land of ethnic diversity where people are encouraged to retain ties with their past rather than forfeit their traditions to a cultural melting pot. This emphasis on the preservation of heritage results in a number of special and complex problems and issues for Canadian educators and educational institutions. The articles in this section reflect, at least in part, problems posed by our insistence on weaving a multicultural social fabric.

Samuda, Chodzinski, and Marissen examine the problem of assessing and placing students from ethnic minorities in our educational systems. They advocate the abandonment of intellectual aptitude and prediction testing for minorities and the adoption of a team approach that assesses acculturation, adaptive behaviour, primary language, and social, cultural, and ethnocultural background. They contend that this shift coupled with the reorientation and retraining of teachers and counsellors will assist in the understanding and acceptance of cultural pluralism.

Mulcahy and Marfo discuss the assessment and instructional programming issue in regard to Native children and argue that the assessment of cognitive ability in *all* populations should place greater emphasis on the processes underlying learning and performance. They describe the cognitive processing models of Jensen and Das, outline current issues in cognitive functioning, and highlight two specific approaches that they believe hold considerable promise for the assessment and enhancement of cognitive abilities in Native children.

Couture addresses the question of what is fundamental to Native education. He compares Native and Euro-Canadian values and behaviours and notes that major differences are evident in child-rearing practices, in extended family systems, and in the fostering of the autonomy of the individual. He concludes that what is needed is a holistic philosophy and psychology of education founded on Native values but incorporating modern technology. In this manner, according to Couture, affective and cognitive capacities will be developed as well as the intuitive/metaphoric abilities and analytic thinking.

Cummins briefly describes the varieties of immersion programs in Canada and summarizes the research findings in this area. He draws particular attention to the achievement of French immersion students in English and other academic subjects, the predictors of achievement in French, and the issue of the suitability of French immersion for all students. He points out that it is on the basis of these findings and related research on bilingual education that predictions can be made about academic outcomes under differing social and educational conditions. He concludes his chapter by identifying problems that have surfaced in Canadian immersion programs and suggesting possible solutions and future directions for immersion education in general.

Carey explores the purpose, philosophy, and programming of Francophone and immersion schools outside of Quebec in an attempt to clarify the surrounding controversies. He discusses the cultural, economic, and political factors that influence parents to enrol their children in these schooling alternatives, pointing out that parents generally prefer what they perceive as quality schooling so that their children will have the best opportunity to compete in society as a whole.

Bain and Yu evaluate second-language learning practices in Canada with the objective of proposing a more suitable model. They discuss problems and issues preventing the implementation of a new model, emphasizing that many of our current procedures can be faulted because language is a process, not a product, and is therefore not reducible to mere grammar. Using an historical review of immigration patterns in Canada and examples from other countries, they discuss the effect of assimilation policies on language and cultural and economic success. Bain and Yu recommend a model of mutual accommodation and justify their view with several examples and persuasive arguments.

The article by Kach and DeFaveri is rather provocative. They question both the legality and the morality of our multicultural commitment. Kach and DeFaveri suggest that we are at a crossroads in our journey toward a fully multicultural society and, if inappropriately directed, we may be in danger of violating individual rights in order to promote collectivist ideals. On the other hand, continuing to proceed toward expansive multiculturalism may allow for the unity in diversity to which we as Canadians have traditionally aspired. The choice, it seems, is up to us.

ASSESSMENT AND PLACEMENT OF ETHNIC MINORITIES IN CANADIAN EDUCATION

RONALD J. SAMUDA, RAYMOND T. CHODZINSKI, AND HARRY MARISSEN

INTRODUCTION

With the great influx of ethnic minority students into Canadian schools in the past few years, it has become clear that changes in educators' attitudes towards and practices in testing are essential to maintain an equitable and suitable educational system in Canada. The purpose of this paper is to review developments in this area, by outlining the etiology and by summarizing one research study. Then, with reference to the findings, the problems of testing, assessment, and placement of minorities will be discussed.

MULTICULTURALISM IN CANADA

To place the issue in context, it must be understood that a massive influx of ethnic minority immigrants followed the change in Canadian immigration policies that occurred in the early 1960s. An additional factor was the official establishment of a policy of multiculturalism within a bilingual framework, which the Liberal government of Prime Minister Pierre Trudeau established in October 1971. Those two factors—the new immigration policy and the acceptance of cultural pluralism as a principle for social and political relations among the various ethnocultural groups of Canada—were to have far-reaching consequences for the social and economic institutions of the country. More particularly, they affected schools in significant ways, since teachers, especially in Ontario, were faced with an entirely new population of students, different in terms of language, ethnic background, and cultural heritage.

It is important to pinpoint in precise detail what is meant by "different" in order to understand and emphasize the difficulties faced by counsellors and teachers when they attempt to assess and place new Canadian students with fairness and intelligence. For example, from a mere handful of privileged

South Asians and West Indians arriving in Canada in the two decades following World War II, the numbers for the period 1968 to 1977 rose to almost 100 000 from Jamaica and Trinidad alone. Similarly, between 1968 and 1977 non-white immigrants from Asia and Africa continued to swell the mounting "Third World" population in Canada, with 271 598 immigrants from Asia and 54 485 from Africa. In that same period, European immigrants numbered 614 536, of whom Portuguese, including those from the Azores, were particularly plentiful.[1]

ONTARIO RESEARCH STUDY

In May 1977, the Ontario Ministry of Education accepted a proposal by the Ontario Association for Curriculum Development for a research project that would address the problems of assessment and placement of ethnic minorities in the schools of Ontario. Samuda and Crawford, of Queen's University in Kingston, were granted funds to conduct a study in boards and schools that would be representative of the province of Ontario as a whole.

The first difficulty facing the team of researchers was the paucity of available data and the administrative hurdles encountered in trying to identify the areas and institutions that catered to significant numbers of ethnic minorities. Soon after the initial inquiries, it was learned that identifying individuals according to their ethnic origins contravened the Human Rights Code. Another difficulty was in obtaining the co-operation of the boards of education whose officers stood firmly on the ground that the study would not be permitted until its design had been completed and the kinds of questionnaires and sampling procedures could be presented to the boards. It was, in fact, a catch-22: a design could not be created without the statistical data, and board approval could not be obtained without a research design, which required a "fix" on the statistics of concentrations before headway could be made. Moreover, the boards were adamant that interviews and questionnaires should be restricted to teachers and board officers. In other words, direct contact with the students was not permitted.

Much political manoeuvring and compromise was needed before the strictures of the board officers could be overcome. Because of the complexities of the ethnic mix in the schools of Metropolitan Toronto especially, it was decided to limit the study to certain specific minority immigrant groups who, it was felt, would be most representative of the more atypical youngsters in the Ontario school system. Consequently, the study was limited to immigrant students from the West Indies, Southern Asia (India and Pakistan), and Portugal (including the Azores). The choice was based on the fact that these were the most numerous minority immigrants (excluding persons from the United Kingdom and the United States). Furthermore, these three groups satisfied all the conditions of student atypicality in terms of colour, culture, religion, and so forth, and they were, at the same time, representative of newcomers from the Caribbean, Europe, and Asia.

SAMPLING PROCEDURES

The strong objections from board directors and their aides precluded the case studies that had originally been planned to accompany the interview data from administrators, teachers, and counsellors and other program officers employed to cope with the special needs of the student population. The study, therefore, focussed on policies, trends, concepts, projections, and practices as they relate to the testing, assessment, counselling, and placement of ethnic minority students.

It was necessary to depend on available data gleaned from immigration sources and from such documents as the Toronto Board's *Every Student Survey*,[2] and, wherever possible, corroborative board estimates of the ethnic mix throughout their jurisdictions. To assure representativeness, school boards were categorized in terms of small, medium, and large and according to degree of low, medium, or high concentrations of ethnic minority student population. The same procedures were used for identifying public as well as separate school boards. Forty-four school boards were identified that fitted the criteria. They included 300 schools, representing a 16 percent proportion in Metropolitan Toronto (about 140 schools) and an 8 percent sample from outside Metro (about 170 schools). However, since some schools and school boards declined to participate in the study, 245 schools comprising 34 school boards actually participated in the research.

ANALYSIS OF THE DATA

The data on which analysis could be carried out came from three sources: numerous interactions between the research team and groups and individuals from school boards; the completed schedules from the structured interviews carried out at the board and school level; and written documents obtained from the boards participating in the study.

The interview schedule contained 58 numbered questions, a professional data sheet, a student data sheet, and a post-interview assessment sheet to be filled in by the interviewer. There was a total of 279 schedules, 245 from school interviews and 34 from board interviews. Essentially, the schedule examined four main aspects of the intake and review process for new students: placement, testing, counselling, and special programs.

DISCUSSION OF RESULTS

The findings demonstrate some basic problems that have yet to be solved in our attempts to cope with the reception and placement of immigrant minority students. These problems stem from the obvious and significant discrepancies between the social, cultural, and economic backgrounds of immigrant minority students and those of mainstream students. The study pinpointed certain fundamental problems in educational practices, in language, and in assessment and methods employed in the teaching/learning process. But, more particularly, the results emphasized in bold relief the dilemma of adapting the Ontario educational system to a new immigrant clientele, while many teachers still cling to certain underlying assumptions that are essentially redundant and counterproductive, if the ideal of non-discriminatory assessment and fair practice in placement is to be achieved. What the study showed was that, if we aim to provide quality education for *all* students, then reorientation and retraining of teachers and counsellors must become a priority.

THE PROBLEM OF ASSESSMENT

Most teachers are quite proficient in dealing with Canadian students who are either Anglo-Celtic, French-Canadian, or whose cultural and linguistic background is not radically different from that of the Northwestern European. In fact, many of the latter often become quickly assimilated into the Canadian mainstream and "fit" quite nicely into the normal Ontario school. The difficulty arises when students arrive at school from the Azores or Trinidad or India with no recognizable documentation by which the principal and her or his aides can match levels of achievement with available programs in the school. Some teachers tended to fall back on what they interpret as the democratic approach in the schools by claiming that "We treat them all alike." *That* is precisely the point. Treating them all alike does not meet the democratic ideal, nor does such a policy make sense in terms of meeting the needs of the atypical individual. In fact, it represents the very antithesis of good pedagogical practice. What needs to be done instead, is to treat them in terms of their cultural, ethnic, linguistic, and developmental backgrounds.

It was found, especially in Metropolitan Toronto, that the administrators and counsellors had long since abandoned the practice of using tests of intelligence to establish placement upon arrival at school. Instead, they would wait for a period of two years before using such tests to establish the functioning level of students. It is of some interest to note that boards with high ethnic concentrations tended to eschew the use of tests completely in the initial assessment of minority students. In contrast, tests for initial placement were used by 38 and 22 percent of boards having low and medium concentrations respectively. Evidently, the greater the exposure to the inherent difficulties in the testing of minorities, the more administrators realize the absurdity of such pedagogical approaches.

There is no shortage of evidence to document the unfairness of the use of tests that were built, in the main, by white, middle-class American psychologists, and normed on white, middle-class children in Canada, especially when the results of such tests are used to place children in classes that might permanently affect their level of achievement, their understanding of the basics, and their rate of learning in the later grades. Scholars like DeAvila and Bruner have persuasively argued that tests are necessarily embedded within a cultural frame of reference, and can do nothing to distinguish between performance and capacity when such tests are applied to individuals whose experiential background has been different from the norm group.[3] Yet some teachers still cling to the notion of "cultural deprivation" to explain the discrepancy without stopping to think that the values used to measure the ethnic minority individual are monocultural and that the tests are necessarily heavily loaded culturally and linguistically. The end result is that the minority scores are invalid.

In which ways are tests invalid? Why are psycho-educational assessment instruments unfair in establishing the intellectual functioning and placement of minorities?

A dramatic way to answer those questions is to administer what is referred to as the Chitling Test[4] to an "average Canadian" group, such as a university class. This test was constructed to deal with the Black American cultural and linguistic context. Let us suppose that the average Canadian was rated on such a test and that, on the basis of the score on the Chitling, he or she was placed in a class of slow learners or in a special education class for the learning impaired. How would such a procedure be rated in terms of fairness? Would it be justified to treat the average Canadian like everyone else in the Black American milieu?

Or consider the prison environment. A teacher at the Millhaven Penitentiary, near Kingston, Ontario, created a test he called the "Rounder Test."[5] In a fashion similar to the Chitling, it emphasizes knowledge or lack of familiarity with the cultural environment of the correctional institution. When inmate scores on the test were compared to those of a graduate class at Queen's University, inmates from the correctional system scored three times as high as the graduate students who had never had contact with prisons. As these two examples demonstrate, tests are often invalid from the points of view of content and construct, and, what is more pernicious, from the predictive point of view. It is difficult to ascertain how many ethnic minority students have been assessed from the perspective of the monocultural mainstream assumptions and placed in classes for the mentally handicapped.

It was just such an issue that was tackled in California in the case of *Larry P. v. Wilson Riles and the State of California*. The case involved six minority children in a school for the mentally retarded. It was found that, when re-tested, these children were all able to perform above the cutoff score of 75 on the Stanford-Binet test. It was on the basis of the evidence produced at the trial in San Francisco that a moratorium was placed on the use of IQ tests for determining the placement of minority children. Similar attacks have been made on the use of tests to determine tracking (as it is called in the United States), streaming (as it is called in the United Kingdom), or grouping (as we call it in the schools of Ontario). Such practices have been shown to benefit only the teacher, whose job is made easier by having a homogeneous class of students to whom he or she can direct a particular average presentation in the hope that all will benefit. But that sort of pedagogical arrangement does not benefit the students as a whole, especially those who are different and who, in some cases, are labelled as deviant on the basis of performance on a biased test or other assessment device.

What is the most demeaning for ethnic and racial minorities is the claim by certain genetically-oriented social scientists that the native mental endowment of minorities is properly measured by the tests of mental ability and that substandard achievement in school is indicative of genetically determined intellectual deficits. That kind of reasoning is not merely fascist; what is worse is that it can sometimes be made plausible and can lead some teachers to excuse themselves for failing to produce the proper kind of climate to reach and touch those ethnic minority individuals who differ markedly from the regular mainstream student. One may well ask at this point: How can we move toward some kind of non-biased techniques? How can we help to optimize the education of ethnic minority children? How, indeed, can we provide quality education for all students in accordance with their needs and backgrounds?

COMPREHENSIVE INDIVIDUAL ASSESSMENT

So that we may avoid simplistic non-solutions, let us recognize them immediately. It would be useless to:
 1. ban IQ tests without addressing the educational failure of students;
 2. use pluralistic norms with conventional tests, unrelated to programming and remediation; or
 3. use IQ tests as screening or placement devices that lead to disproportionate classification of minorities in special education classes with resultant ineffective programming.

The recent research suggests that we should abandon the notion of intellectual aptitude and prediction when we use regular tests with those students whose backgrounds are radically different from the milieu and context of the test. The presumption of internal pathology or deficits should be abandoned except for those very obvious and demonstrable cases of subnormal physiologically-based pathology. In this context, mental retardation becomes very difficult to demonstrate.

Instead of focussing on the causation of lowered performance, we should rather seek to foster those classes that address the perceived needs of the minority student in such terms as "English as a Second Language." But such reforms should not merely be cosmetic; they should involve a serious effort in terms of in-service education for all teachers in urban, bilingual, and minority education.

Comprehensive individual assessment would stress the need for a broad variety of information prior to making any diagnostic decision. The placement of minority students would require a team approach involving some measure of acculturation, adaptive behaviour, primary language (or language dominance), and social, economic, and ethnocultural background. A comprehensive assessment program would be geared to provide an accurate appraisal of the student's present level and mode of functioning within the context of her or his cultural background and experience. It would identify the specific needs of the individual as well as focussing upon particular assets and strengths he or she brings to the academic situation so as to form the basis on which new skills can be developed. Since it would go hand-in-glove with placement and programming, assessment would necessarily be an ongoing process, helping to monitor and to reinforce academic progress and/or cognitive restructuring. The comprehensive assessment system would involve a team, including the teacher, school administrator, counsellor, or other professionals providing data through observation, consultation, and formal testing procedures. Most importantly, in a humane and democratic society, it is the prior right of the parents to become an integral part of the decision-making process.

Two strictures should be borne in mind in connection with operationalizing the system of assessment: special education should be the very last option; and psychological assessment should come last, after all other data have been collected so that the results can be interpreted in the light of comprehensive and vital background information. In other words, the comprehensive individual assessment portfolio would be obtained from:

1. Observational data
2. Other data available
3. Language dominance
4. Educational assessment data
5. Sensory-motor and/or developmental data
6. Adaptive behaviour data
7. Medical and/or developmental data
8. Personality assessment data, including self-report
9. Intellectual assessment data.

RECOMMENDATIONS AND CONCLUSIONS

The recommendations of the *Provincial Review Report*[6] issued by the Ontario Ministry of Education are germane to the goals of this paper and they coincide very closely with its findings and conclusions.

1. The initial placement of immigrant pupils should be made on an individual basis, monitored regularly, and adjusted as needed.

2. Social adjustment for all immigrant pupils appears to be promoted by a combination of factors, including the English-as-a-second-language/dialect (ESL/D) and guidance teachers, proper placement in ESL/D classrooms, support from classmates, the buddy system, and the positive support of the principal and other staff members.

3. Immigrant pupils acquire facility in English at different rates, depending on their attitude, aptitude, need, age, and ability. The length of time spent

in Canada (the most significant criterion employed by some boards) seems to be questionable as the main criterion for ESL/D placement or formal assessment.

4. Additional appropriate academic programs are needed for adolescent ethnic minority students who have little or no elementary schooling.

5. Programs for immigrant students aged eleven to eighteen need further study and development.

6. Teachers and school administrators need to recognize and emphasize the role of immigrant parents in the education of their children.

7. Secondary schools in particular, should make greater use of parent and community volunteers and aides.

In more general terms, the business of assessment and placement cannot be separated from other considerations in the education of minority students. They are necessarily part and parcel of a new perspective, one that takes into account the minority's culture and background. That is the key issue. School boards need to take special cognizance of the fact that the personnel they place in the schools are equipped by means of inservice programs to cope with the special demands of the atypical new Canadian student.

NOTES

1. R.J. Samuda, "Assessing the Abilities of Minority Students within a Multi-ethnic Milieu," in *Multiculturalism in Canada: Social and Educational Perspectives*, edited by R.J. Samuda, J.W. Berry, and M. Laferriere (Toronto: Allyn and Bacon, 1984).

2. Deosaran, *Every Student Survey* (Toronto: Toronto Board of Education Research Department, 1975).

3. E.A. DeAvila, "Mainstreaming Ethnically and Linguistically Different Children: an Exercise in Paradox of a New Approach?" in *Mainstreaming and the Minority Child*, edited by R.L. Jones (Reston, Va.: Council for Exceptional Children, 1976); J.S. Bruner, "Poverty and Childhood," *Oxford Review of Education* 1 (1975).

4. "Chitling Test" in *Readings in Psychology* (Guildord, Conn.: Duskin Publishing Group, 1972), 237.

5. J. Lewis, *The Rounder Test* (Kingston, Ont.: Queen's University, 1982).

6. *Provincial Review Report*, no. 8 (1983).

ASSESSMENT OF COGNITIVE ABILITY AND INSTRUCTIONAL PROGRAMMING WITH NATIVE CANADIAN CHILDREN: A COGNITIVE PROCESSES PERSPECTIVE[1]

ROBERT F. MULCAHY AND KOFI MARFO

Over the years there has been a continued and often heated debate regarding ability testing of minority students. In Canada, this debate has at times raged with respect to the assessment of cognitive ability in Native children of the North. The argument has often been fought on emotional grounds with little regard for substantial empirical data to support one view or the other. Much of this debate revolves around the concern that the traditional notion of ability testing and the purpose for which such testing was done in the past (i.e., to obtain an IQ score, which was presumed to measure global intelligence) are no longer tenable.

Ability tests have been blamed for the overrepresentation of ethnic minorities in the enrolment figures of classes for the mildly retarded.[2] Critics argue that such tests have served as the critical decision-making instruments for assigning children to special classes. However, this argument has been disputed.[3] Reschly[4] points out that psychologists test only those children who are referred by teachers and that the admittedly meagre evidence available suggests that minority overrepresentation may lie inherently in the referral process preceding the actual assessment. Reschly also argues that, since minority children are overrepresented in school failure and difficulty, factors that lead to their referral in the first place, the question of test bias should not be allowed to overshadow the issue of adapting instruction.

The foregoing arguments have not stopped critics from addressing the issue of test bias itself. The unfairness of specific individual items (item bias) on a test has often been cited as a major factor responsible for low performance by minority groups. This would appear to make sense; however, the research has failed to find that individual biased items are responsible for the differences in performance of minority groups.[5] There has as well been a failure by studies to identify categories of items on ability tests that could be responsible for the minority group differences.[6]

In much of our own work with Inuit youngsters in the eastern Arctic, we have also failed to find specific items or groups of items indicating bias with respect to the Weschler Intelligence Scale for Children-Revised (WISC-R).[7] We have found significant differences in performance on the verbal subtests of this particular measure, a finding that is typical. The differences were greater for children under the age of eleven than for those aged eleven to fifteen. This may be due in large part to differences in language as well as educational experiences. We know, for example, that absenteeism is a significant problem in these far northern schools. Also, the construct validity for the WISC-R appeared to be adequate for those children aged twelve to fifteen but not for those in the age range of seven to eleven.[8]

Several methods have been put forth by various experts with respect to minority group testing to reduce test bias if it is a concern. Among the more extreme is the suggestion that a moratorium be placed on all ability testing of Native children. This, however, is not a positive solution, especially because it fails to recognize the place of assessment in the educational process. It has been suggested also that, if the administration of ability tests to Native children is desirable, then both test content and instructions should be translated into the native language. While this approach may alleviate problems of communication, it is doubtful that it would resolve problems pertaining to Native children's lack of experience with or exposure to test content. In certain circles it has been argued that the test administration process itself is a potential source of bias, especially when minority children are tested by psychologists outside the culture. This has led some to suggest that minority children should be tested by members of the minority culture who should also interpret the rest results, but available empirical research has not found this approach to be necessarily an effective solution.[9]

The importance of administering a wide range of both formal and informal measures assessing a variety of skills has often been stressed. This procedure has been adapted in the instrument developed by Mercer and Lewis,[10] entitled *System of Multicultural Pluralistic Assessment* (SOMPA). This particular device utilizes conventional ability measures as well as extensive sociocultural data to provide a more complete picture of the minority child's performance. The SOMPA obtains three types of information; medical, social system, and pluralistic. Information is obtained on intellectual ability (WISC-R), visual motor ability (Bender Visual Motor Gestalt Test), medical (including physical dexterity, weight by height, visual acuity, and auditory acuity), and from parent interview data with respect to adaptive behaviour, sociocultural aspects, and health history. The sociocultural scales are utilized to adjust the intellectual ability scores to compare with those of students from the same general sociocultural environment. These new scores are then used to derive an "Estimated Learning Potential."

Although the SOMPA has found considerable use in the southern United States, its applicability to the Native Canadian scene has not been demonstrated. In fact, even in the United States, it has not received overwhelming acceptance nationwide,[11] the argument being that it may be a good procedure if the purpose of the test is to know how an individual's performance compares to others of the same group. However, as DeAvila and Havassy[12] point out, the procedure of deriving new ability scores provides little information as to why the minority group in question may tend to score lower on the particular measure in the first place.

Re-norming of tests before using them with minority populations has been suggested as another way of reducing test bias where it is a concern. In our own work,[13] we have adopted this approach with the Inuit population of the Keewatin and Keetemeot region of the Northwest Territories. The Weschler Intelligence Scale for Children-Revised, the Bender Visual Motor Gestalt Test, and the Draw-A-Man and Draw-A-Woman tests were re-normed with 366 children aged 7 to 15 years. As well, norms for the Bender Visual Motor Gestalt, Draw-A-Man, and Draw-A-Woman tests were derived for 400 urban and 400 rural children in Alberta of the same age range as the Inuit youngsters.[14] This approach can be very helpful as it allows comparisons to be made within as well as beyond the cultural group. However, the procedure of re-norming has the same difficulty as is the case with the SOMPA approach in that it does not provide any information on why Native youngsters perform more poorly on the verbal measures of ability in the first place.

Developing tests to better measure the psychological processes by which children learn has often been put forward as a solution as well, although little progress has been made in this direction. This may be one of the more relevant approaches to take with respect to reducing the difficulties in assessment of and educational programming with our Native youngsters. The general goal of most ability and achievement testing is to attempt to provide the most relevant information to the teacher on how best to assist students in the educational mainstream. What one needs to know in terms of making the most appropriate suggestions for programming is not just what level of performance the child reaches but what type of cognitive processes he or she uses to get to that level.

In this chapter we take the position that assessment of cognitive ability in all populations should place greater emphasis upon cognitive processes underlying learning and performance. Consistent with the wide recognition of individual differences in learning and performance styles, an emphasis on cognitive processes should make cognitive assessment more individualized than it has been so far. It is heartening to note that advances in the field of cognitive psychology over the past several decades are paving the way for a major shift away from traditional psychometric approaches to the assessment of cognitive ability. It is to this changing emphasis that we shall now turn.

TRANSITIONAL MODELS OF COGNITIVE PROCESSING

We will begin this discussion by presenting an overview of cognitive processing models we refer to as *transitional models* because they represent the transition between traditional psychometric theories of intelligence and more contemporary models of cognition, which emphasize cognitive and metacognitive strategies underlying intelligent behaviour. Generally, these transitional models represent efforts to develop cognitive processes models of intelligence based on analyses of traditional psychometric tasks. We have chosen to present the work of Arthur Jensen and J.P. Das and his associates as representative examples of cognitive processes models of the transitional type. The rationale for this choice is that in rather different ways each of the two models has instructional implications that are worth examining for minority children.

LEVEL I AND LEVEL II ABILITIES

Jensen may not be considered a cognitive theorist,[15] but his two-level theory[16] represents an attempt to identify broad cognitive processes that underlie psychometric tasks. Mental abilities, according to Jensen, fall on a continuum of cognitive processing. Tasks differ in terms of the amount of cognitive processing or transformation required to perform or learn them. Certain tasks (e.g., serial memory tasks) require very little or no cognitive transformation of the stimulus input; instead, they require the establishment of simple associations. On the other hand, other tasks (e.g., reasoning tasks) call for more complex and active transformation of the stimulus input. Jensen has referred to the processes underlying these two categories of tasks as level I and level II abilities respectively. In a more basic language, level I abilities correspond with associative learning, while level II abilities underlie cognitive learning.

Jensen's two-level theory is relevant for the present discussion for two important reasons. First, he has applied the theory to explain social class and ethnic differences in intellectual ability. Level I abilities are supposedly distributed evenly across social class and ethnic groups but level II abilities are not. Thus social class and ethnic differences in intellectual ability are mainly attributable to differences in level II abilities.

Second, and related to the foregoing differences, Jensen[17] has derived some provocative, if not outrageous, educational implications from his theory. In more general terms Jensen appears to be proposing that, because associative learning (level I ability) is distributed much more evenly across social class and ethnic groups than cognitive learning (level II ability), educators should look for ways to capitalize on associative learning. While this recommendation appears to argue for equity in educational programming, his other more specific recommendations can only lead to inequity in educational services, if they are implemented. Jensen seems to be suggesting that, because children of lower socio-economic status (SES) and minority ethnic groups learn associatively and white middle-class children learn cognitively, the two groups of children should be taught differently.[18] The premise for this differential instruction—that children should be instructed or treated according to their individual needs and capabilities—is a very sound one. However, the theorizing and the data behind the proposition are suspect, and, to say the least, the sociopolitical implications of implementing this recommendation are bound to be catastrophic. The social and political ramifications of Jensen's model are of particular importance to any discussion on minority group education; the model can become a tool for subjecting minority group children to an inferior quality of education and thus deny them the skills and competencies they need to compete equally in society.

It is important also to examine weaknesses of Jensen's theory purely on theoretical grounds. At stake is the proposition that cognitive activities are of two kinds only and that what differentiates one kind from the other is the amount of stimulus transformation required for stimulus input. Current experimental psychological research into cognitive processes demonstrates that Jensen's model is untenable. First, it is simplistic to suggest that there are only two kinds of abilities. Second, it is misleading to suggest that these two abilities are memory and reasoning.[19] The variety of cognitive and metacognitive strategies that individuals employ across a wide variety of tasks cannot be subsumed under the so-called level I and level II abilities. In fact, memory and reasoning are not mutually exclusive processes, as the model presupposes. Some amount of memory is involved in the performance of reasoning tasks. Third, it is misleading to associate memory with associative learning. There is strong evidence from contemporary information-processing research that even very simple memory tasks, such as digit span, require the use of high level cognitive strategies.

SIMULTANEOUS AND SUCCESSIVE COGNITIVE PROCESSING

Das and his associates[20] have proposed a cognitive model of information integration that describes two principal information processes—simultaneous and successive—both of which are considered fundamental and essential to proper cognitive functioning. Simultaneous processing involves the representation or processing of information such that "any portion of the result is at once surveyable without dependence upon its position in the whole."[21] Successive processing, on the other hand, involves the processing of information in a serial or sequential manner. In their research Das and his associates have, through factor analyses of various psychometric measures, isolated specific tasks that require successive or simultaneous processing. Although their data show that some tasks may require both successive and simultaneous processing, in general the Raven Progressive Matrices, figure copying, and memory for designs have been presented as tasks requiring simultaneous processing, while successive processing has been demonstrated largely on digit span, serial recall, and visual short-term memory tasks.

The simultaneous-successive processes model differs from the two-level theory of Jensen in several respects but we will address only those differences that are pertinent to the present discussion. First, unlike Jensen, Das and his associates do not impute a genetic basis for differences in or preferences for the use of one strategy or the other; they have been interested in cultural differences only to the extent that these differences help in understanding what cultural variables interact with the particular demands of a given task to determine which strategy will be employed.[22] Second, while Jensen implies a hierarchical dichotomy between associative and cognitive tasks, the Das model does not view cognitive tasks as strictly requiring either simultaneous or successive processing. "Simultaneous and successive processes are neither modality- nor stimulus-specific. Any type of stimulus information can be processed through simultaneous or successive means; however, certain functions are processed much more efficiently through one process than the other."[22]

Third, the two models differ in terms of the instructional implications they engender. Jensen's genetic deterministic view of cognitive abilities prescribes a differential system of instruction premised on the assumption that learning within SES and ethnic groups is modality-specific. We have already alluded to the serious social and political ramifications of such a view and would not belabour the issue further. The Das model, on the other hand, acknowledges that although cultural and experiential differences may dictate preference for one or the other strategy, children across SES and ethnic groups can be taught to use both information processing strategies efficiently. So far, however, cross-ethnic research using the Das et al. framework has focussed more on remediation in successive information processing. Das and Krywaniuk[24] and Krywaniuk[25] reported that Native Indian children in Alberta showed poor successive processing skills. Training these children in successive information processing resulted in significant improvements in visual and auditory memory.

Some of the critical observations made on the Jensen model apply equally to the Das model. It is doubtful if successive and simultaneous processing adequately capture the entire spectrum of cognitive strategies that individuals bring to the problem solving or learning situation. The later addition of a *planning* strategy to the model speaks to the complex nature of cognitive processes. Planning itself, as an executive function, is a complex process involving many component strategies each of which could constitute a source of individual or group differences. Notwithstanding these criticisms, the Das model is a major contribution to cognitive psychology.

SUMMARY

Notwithstanding the differences discussed earlier, Jensen's level I-level II abilities model and the Das et al. simultaneous-successive processes model share some important common characteristics. Both models rely on traditional psychometric tasks in their identification and classification of underlying cognitive processes. Although such tasks are known to predict success at school very well, their immediate relevance for educational programming and remediation is not readily apparent. More importantly, if individual students, regardless of social class or ethnic identity, are to be helped on the basis of the unique strategies they employ in performance situations, it is imperative that we adopt approaches to strategy assessment that focus on the individual and not the group. The nomothetic approach (focussing on group characteristics), with its emphasis on factor analysis as the method for deriving underlying cognitive processes, has serious limitations in this regard. Knowing how middle-class white Canadian or Native children as a group tend to process certain kinds of information does not tell the teacher very much about how to proceed to instruct individual members of the group. In essence, the danger of prescribing a similar intervention program or procedure to whole groups of students—whether on the basis of social class, ethnic, or diagnostic identity—is a real one.

We must point out in all fairness that with the emergence of individually administered assessment tools like the Kaufman Assessment Battery for Children (K-ABC),[26] which among other things measure "mental processing" strategies, the danger of treating individual children on the basis of their group identity would be reduced. The point needs to be made, however, that the mental processes that the K-ABC measures—simultaneous and successive—were derived through factor-analytic techniques and are subject to the same criticisms as those raised with respect to the Das model.

CURRENT EMPHASES ON COGNITIVE PROCESSES: IMPLICATIONS FOR ASSESSMENT AND INSTRUCTION

The most recent views of what makes up cognitive ability and why it is that some individuals perform better than others on particular measures of cognitive ability have shifted towards a more specific emphasis on the examination of cognitive *processes* as opposed to cognitive *products*. The idea here is to attempt to determine what it is that an individual did (process) that gave rise to a certain score on a particular test or subtest (product). Some experts are therefore now defining cognitive ability in terms of sets of *learning-thinking* skills that an individual brings to the task in an interactive fashion, stressing that students should be taught these sets of learning-thinking skills in a direct way in order to increase their level of cognitive functioning.[27] This approach appears to hold a great deal of promise for the assessment of cognitive ability in our Native Canadians—indeed, with all youngsters.

The typical standardized measures of cognitive ability are basically what have been termed *static* or *product* measures of ability. These measures (e.g., the individual intelligence tests referred to earlier in the chapter) are static in that they set out the same identical testing procedure for each testee. There is little room, if any, for ongoing interaction between tester and testee beyond the set instructions and tester restricted responses set out in the manual. The types of response provided by the tester are essentially neutral and provide little room for determining the testee's ability to learn new information through the tester-testee interaction. This is somewhat incongruous with the goal of ability tests because these tests are presumed to measure the individual's learning potential but instead might better be considered as measures of the individual's acquired knowledge. One way to more directly measure potential to learn would be to utilize a *test-teach-test* procedure. This has been used by Feuerstein[28] to develop an instrument termed the Learning Potential Assessment Device (LPAD). The idea here is to try to take the individual through a series of cognitive tasks in a test-teach-test fashion and thus determine more specifically how the youngster learns in terms of strategies used in order to design appropriate educational programs.

Schubert and Cropley[29] have noted that northern Canadian Native children with presumed low intellectual levels were able to improve their performance on some subtests of the Weschler Intelligence Scale for Children as measured by the test-teach-test procedure. The Native youngsters were able to improve their performance on two subtests (block design and similarities) to a significantly greater extent than Anglo-Saxon youngsters with similar presumed intellectual levels. Matheson[30] pointed out that this may have been due, to some extent, to the language difficulties under original testing conditions, which may have been alleviated through instruction after original testing had been completed. Nevertheless the test-teach-test approach to determine learning potential appears to be an extremely positive one. (We do acknowledge the similarity of this approach to the idea of *testing the limits* as indicated in some of the literature.)

It should be noted that in educational programming as in cognitive ability assessment for Native youngsters more reliance must be placed on examining the information processing activities (cognitive strategies) underlying their performance on tasks, which may then lead to more direct intervention. This focus circumvents the problem of test bias (not tester or teacher bias) in that the emphasis is first on determining what particular type(s) of cognitive strategies the individual has in his or her repertoire and how those strategies are being applied and, then, on providing systematic instruction in the application and evaluation of more appropriate strategies. Thus, the important directions with respect to assessment and programming may be to attempt to determine the types of processing strategies these children use when solving intellectual, academic, and social tasks and how they go about co-ordinating these learning-thinking strategies for task solution. This would be an important first step towards providing the necessary data for more appropriate programming.

Initially, one might examine carefully what cognitive processing strategies the highly successful Native children (academic and social problem solvers) utilize as well as the strategies of those who do not perform well in the academic and social domains. This would include, of course, consideration of motivational and experiential factors. Classroom and home observational data would also be made a part of this strategy assessment development. Through a systematic process beginning with initial exploratory analyses of existing strategies (both in the home and at school) to a more refined and focussed assessment, utilizing a test-teach-test approach, new, more comprehensive and educationally valid assessment devices might be made available for working with these children. Several initial attempts to do this in a systematic manner that may pave the way for more appropriate assessment and intervention with our Native youngsters are identifiable in the literature. Among these are Feuerstein's Learning Potential Assessment Device (LPAD) and his intervention program, Instrumental Enrichment,[31] and the Strategies Program for Effective Learning and Thinking (SPELT) developed by Mulcahy and his associates.[32] The end goal of these programs is to have the youngster *learn how to learn* through the spontaneous use of self-generated effective learning thinking strategies in a variety of academic and social contexts.

In the sections that follow, we will present Feuerstein's Instrumental Enrichment program and our own Strategies Program for Effective Learning and Thinking as two instructional approaches—both with far reaching implications for strategy assessment—that have potential relevance for the education of Native children. Both programs appear to be particularly suitable for our northern Native youngsters because of their focus on the development and nurturing of the cognitive skills and competencies that are crucial for success both in and out of school. Native youngsters often demonstrate a lack of motivation for school work, difficulties in verbal skills and in general problem solving skills in the academic areas. Native youngsters live not only in a rapidly changing local environment but also in a broader society whose technological advances and intricate sociocultural demands call for high-level cognitive and social skills necessary to compete equally with peers in the mainstream of a multicultural society. Both programs place emphasis on these skills. Instrumental Enrichment was originally developed with culturally disadvantaged adolescents in mind and SPELT is being developed within a Canadian context (rural and urban north-central Alberta). It could be said, then, that it is ecologically valid to use both programs with Native Canadian children, although we do acknowledge the need for a direct validation of the program using Native Canadian samples.

FEUERSTEIN'S INSTRUMENTAL ENRICHMENT (IE) PROGRAM

Originally designed for culturally disadvantaged children and youth, Feuerstein's program is now used with a broader population of children in upper elementary schools and junior and senior high schools. The program is based on Feuerstein's theory of structural cognitive modifiability through mediated learning experience, a theory that suggests that cognitive deficiencies that youngsters exhibit as a result of impoverished experiential backgrounds can be corrected if a knowledgeable adult, usually a parent or a teacher, intervenes between the youngster and her or his environment. Such mediation involves the intentional transformation, reordering, organizing, grouping, or framing of environmental stimuli in a way that transcends the immediate stimuli and reveals new meaning and insights hitherto unknown to the youngster.

Poor or inadequate mediated learning experience—or lack of it—leads to cognitive deficiencies related to the three phases of information processing: input, elaboration, and output. Feuerstein has described as many as twenty-one such deficiencies. They include the following: impulsivity; lack of regard for precision and accuracy; unplanned and unsystematic exploratory behaviour; inability to recognize and define problems; failure to make comparisons spontaneously; failure to appreciate the need for logical evidence; etc. It is these and several other cognitive deficiencies that the IE program is designed to correct.

In IE, social interaction is important in that it is not the content, but the means of interacting that is internalized by the child. An adult mediator elicits behaviours from the child that lead to the solving of a problem. The child then comes to understand the goals and strategies of the task. Thus, the sequence is response followed by analysis, with the mediator providing only as much help to the child as is needed for the child to come to a newer understanding of the task. The program, which at present consists of fifteen instruments of paper-and-pencil tasks, is designed to be content-free. The term content-free is intended to convey that the contents of any particular exercise are merely a vehicle, or an instrument, to achieve the overall goals of the program. The major goal of IE is to enhance the cognitive modifiability, that is, learning potential, of the individual, and this is achieved by the implementation of the following six subgoals:

1. the correction of deficient cognitive functions;
2. the teaching of specific concepts, operations, and vocabulary required by the IE exercises;
3. the development of an intrinsic need for adequate cognitive functioning, and the spontaneous use of operational thinking by the production of crystallized schema and habit formation;
4. the production of insight and understanding of one's own thought processes, in particular, those processes that produce success as well as those that result in failure;
5. the production of task-intrinsic motivation that is reinforced by the meaning of the program in a broader social context; and
6. a change in orientation towards oneself from passive recipient and reproducer to active generator of information.

Although the achievement of all the subgoals of the program depend on an active interaction between the three elements of student, teacher, and instruments, subgoals (2) and (4) rely heavily on the teacher's contribution. The remaining subgoals are achieved by the nature of the instruments themselves with the exception of the last subgoal, which is a product of all the others together. The motivation component of this program is particularly noteworthy. One of the reasons offered by Feuerstein for developing a content-free program is that such a program presents students with learning activities and contexts with which they have not experienced failure before. As they succeed on and enjoy doing the IE instruments, students build up or regain their confidence, a process which may transfer to learning in regular academic contexts.

Feuerstein[33] has claimed that IE is effective in increasing school achievement, social skills, intellectual skills, and motivation to learn. In recommending IE as a potentially useful program for Native children, we are cognizant of the need to subject the program to rigorous evaluation to determine its true efficacy with these children. Our own currently on-going four-year longitudinal evaluation of the program in a large number of upper elementary and junior high school classrooms in north-central Alberta should throw a great deal of light on the program's efficacy as well as on the feasibility of implementing it as a permanent curriculum feature. Despite the absence of such evaluative data we feel comfortable recommending the program on the basis of its sound theoretical and instructional principles.

THE STRATEGIES PROGRAM FOR EFFECTIVE LEARNING AND THINKING

In a recent paper,[34] we described several important characteristics of our SPELT approach in some detail. Because the present volume is directed at teachers-in-training, we find it necessary to present as complete a picture of the theory and principles of SPELT as is possible within the space available to us. Consequently, we have deemed it appropriate to present here substantial portions of that paper. The interested reader is referred to the SPELT manual for details pertaining to specific strategies and their teaching sequences.

Theoretical and Philosophical Issues

The impetus for learning/thinking strategies instructional programs originates largely from theoretical perspectives that view human intellectual functioning as deriving from how humans represent and process information mentally. Specifically, a great deal of the theoretical direction is coming from information processing perspectives on intelligence, in general, and from specific theoretical domains, such as metacognitive theory,[35] neo-Piagetian theory,[36] schema theory,[37] and problem solving theory.[38]

There is now a trend toward defining intelligent behaviour as being made up of a number of components, and to emphasize those components that are amenable to change through training. For example Haywood and Switzky[39] identify two requirements of intelligent behaviour—native ability and cognitive functions. Native ability is genetically determined, but cognitive functions, which include such components as "operations, principles, and strategies, as well as a host of 'nonintellective' variables such as attitudes toward learning, work habits, and motives,"[40] are largely acquired. In his componential subtheory of intelligence, Sternberg[41] describes three distinct types of cognitive processes: knowledge-acquisition components, performance components, and metacognitive components, the last of these representing higher-order control processes that the indiviudal uses for executive decision making during problem solving. Because cognitive functions or processes are acquired, they are modifiable through systematic instruction. Learning and thinking strategies instruction is premised on the assumption that we can systematically analyse cognitive performance into specific component processes and strategies, and that we can enhance cognitive performance by training students to employ efficient strategies consciously in their day-to-day learning and performance encounters.

In the context of learning and instruction, cognitive strategies are conceptualized as internally organized skills or control processes by which the learner regulates her or his cognitive behaviour.[42] A learner's repertoire of strategies may thus be seen as a set of tools that enables him or her to activate and regulate more effectively and efficiently such important cognitive activities as attention, comprehension, retention and retrieval of information, thinking, and problem solving. The teacher plays the role of a mediator between the learner and the external world, structuring the learning environment and providing opportunities necessary to establish and improve strategic behaviour in learning, thinking, and problem-solving situations. This mediational role involves, among other equally important actions, raising the student's awareness of her or his own role in the learning-thinking process; encouraging the student to practise the use of cognitive strategies in a variety of novel situations; and structuring the teaching-learning environment (including presentation of information and instructional materials) in a way that constantly challenges the student to make decisions relating to the generation of new strategies or to the modification, extension, and application of existing ones.

The current emphasis on the development and nurturing of cognitive strategies in children as a major instructional goal reinforces the age-old philosophy that instruction should be geared to ensuring that the students we teach become efficient self-learners who are capable of self-motivated self-instruction. Today, preparing students toward *learning how to learn*, and toward organized, active, and purposive thinking and problem solving behaviour is the prime objective of a number of intervention programs aimed at college students[43] and at children with learning problems.[44]

The Program

The Strategies Program for Effective Learning and Thinking represents an effort to translate contemporary cognitive psychological theory and research into a practical and easy-to-implement instructional program that seeks to train children to become active and purposeful learners, thinkers, and problem solvers. One distinguishing characteristic of SPELT is its breadth of coverage; its goal, unlike some of the programs cited earlier, is not just the teaching of strategies for effective acquisition, retention, and recall of information but also the development of effective thinking skills.

The dominant model in learning strategies instruction is the *teacher imposed* model. Under this model, the entire learning strategies program consists of expert-designed and tested strategies that are taught to students as recipes for dealing with a variety of problems. This approach literally leaves no room for students to participate in the determination of which strategies are appropriate for what purposes. Unfortunately, however, the *teacher imposed* approach, if used as the sole technique, runs counter to the cognitive goal of instruction, namely, to facilitate active participation of the student in the learning process. French[15] has elaborated on the active role of the student in the learning process. Stragety imposition, no doubt, is incongruous with the notion of the learner as an active, independent organism. Consequently, SPELT adopts a model of strategy instruction in which the individual student is taught to ultimately assume responsibility for determining when a strategy is needed, what strategy is appropriate, and how to generate and implement it in a way that maximizes performance.

The SPELT instructional model involves a progression from the lowest level of strategy acquisition (acquisition through teacher imposition) to the highest level of acquisition (acquisition through self-generation). There is both theoretical and empirical support for the student-generated model of strategy acquisition which SPELT espouses. Kanfer and Seidner[46] have indicated that, for many everyday cognitive, affective, and behavioural problems, the most effective strategy may be one that is self-chosen on the basis of habitual preferences. Wagner and Sternberg[47] have cautioned recently that, while there is a good case for teaching metacognitive skills to children, "the effects of metacognitive activities may be reduced when they are externally imposed rather than spontaneously generated by students."[48] Empirical evidence from the work of Brown[49], French[50], and others[51] supports this view. For example, Slee has provided interesting anecdotes from her research on visual imagery indicating that externally imposed strategies may, in fact, be detrimental to some students.

Components of the SPELT Instructional Approach

The SPELT instructional approach has three major components: a general teaching style or orientation; the teaching of both recommended and teacher-generated strategies; and teaching toward student control and generation of strategies.

General teaching style refers to that orientation to teaching whereby the teacher's goal in all planning and direct instruction is to involve the student actively in the learning process. Among the principal hallmarks of this orientation are: raising students' awareness about their own cognitive processes and how to control them; leading students to discover rather than revealing or teaching facts to them; and constantly challenging students to be critical, systematic, and strategic in their behaviour and attitude to learning and problem solving. In this orientation, the teacher seeks to use instructional techniques that constantly cue, demonstrate, and reinforce the use of learning and thinking strategies.

The second and third components—the teaching of a set of recommended and teacher-generated strategies, and teaching toward student control and generation of strategies—represent two separate phases of the instructional progression. A three-fold rationale underlies this two-phase continuum. First, teacher-imposed strategies at the initial phase expose students to the fact that there are cognitive strategies that, when employed, will facilitate meaningful learning and problem solving. Second, it is easier and more effective to illustrate the value of strategic behaviour in the context of well-established and tested strategies presented to the teacher during training. Finally, the process of beginning with well-tested strategies that are taught to teachers during training allows teachers enough time to grow and gradually develop their own unique skills and strategies (within the broad framework provided by the SPELT methodology) for teaching toward strategy generation by students.

SPELT and the School Curriculum

Our program targets three curriculum areas: academic learning; thinking and problem solving; and social competence. With regard to academic learning, SPELT is designed to offer the teacher a methodology that integrates the teaching and nurturing of learning and thinking strategies into the teaching of curricular content across all subject areas. Thinking/problem solving and social competence are two important domains of children's development that current educational practices fail to address adequately. In fact, the prominence in recent years of programs for teaching thinking[52] reflects efforts to redress this woeful failure of schools to promote thinking skills. The teaching of social competence even lags behind the teaching of thinking in our schools. With these concerns in mind, SPELT has been designed to teach and nurture not only thinking and problem-solving skills but also social competence.

The major strategies taught or nurtured through SPELT include the following:
— general problem-solving strategies;
— social problem-solving strategies;
— math problem-solving strategies;
— reading strategies;
— knowledge-acquisition strategies;
— memory strategies;
— study skills and time-management strategies;

- test-taking strategies;
- support (mood-setting) strategies;
- general metacognitive strategies.

Under each of the above strategy domains, several strategies pertaining to specific subject matter and/or instructional goals may exist.

Distinguishing Characteristics of SPELT

Unlike many other programs of its kind, SPELT is aimed at a younger population of children—those in the elementary and junior high school grades. The overwhelming focus on high school and college students by existing learning strategies programs (known as developmental education programs in certain circles in the United States) is perhaps an indication that it is easier to work with older students when developing innovative programs. However, in both theoretical and practical terms, it makes sense that potentially valuable interventions be instituted as early in the child's school life as possible. In fact, there is compelling empirical evidence to support learning/thinking strategies instructional programs in the early grades. Research has taught us that one qualitative difference between adults and younger children lies in the fact that, unlike older children and adults, younger children fail to spontaneously utilize techniques, procedures, or strategies that facilitate learning and problem solving. This difference between older and younger children appears to be true also of comparisons involving intellectually high and low functioning children. We have learned from this line of research, too, that it is possible, through a systematic program of instruction, to train young or intellectually low-functioning children to be strategic in their learning and thinking behaviour.

Another area where SPELT differs from other learning/thinking strategies programs is the instructional context. Nowadays it is fashionable to design educational interventions as structured packages to be taught independently of existing curriculum content or subject matter. An important philosophy underlying the SPELT approach is that the teaching of learning and thinking strategies should take place within content and not as an independent or isolated curricular activity. First, one of the dangers of independently taught, non-content programs is that they seem to reinforce the perception by students that there is a time for thinking and a time for other learning activities. To some extent, this is actually another way of saying that the out-of-content approach presents problems with regard to generalization. That is, unless a special effort is made to train for generalization of skills taught in such a program across different content areas, students will generally have difficulty applying such skills beyond program activities. We know, of course, that unless a program leads to generalized effects of training its utility is seriously compromised.

Second, anyone who is familiar with the way schools function, especially with regard to timetabling, will agree that out-of-content program packages present several administrative and philosophical problems for principals, staff, and parents alike. The implementation of such programs almost always requires that some other content areas be curtailed. The decision as to which subject matter to sacrifice is a problem that can potentially pitch administrators, teachers, and parents against one another. The other disadvantage of out-of-content programs is that even when they are accommodated on the timetable, they are the first to be eliminated whenever schools either require more time for other extra-curricular activities or suffer funding cutbacks and have to reduce program offerings as a consequence. Each of these factors can make it extremely difficult to sustain out-of-content programs over the duration of time necessary to make the anticipated impact on student learning and competence.

A corollary to the last issue is the principle that learning and thinking strategies should be taught by the regular classroom teacher and not by a specially trained person who sees the students only periodically for strategy instruction. For the goals of strategy instruction to be maximized, it is imperative that both the program and the instructor be an integral part of the student's day-to-day learning environment in the school. Problems of generalization, as outlined earlier, are reduced when the same teacher sets the goals and learning tasks in all subject areas and reinforces strategies across various content areas. This ideal situation in which the same teacher is responsible for instruction in all subject areas is, however, only achievable in the elementary school context.

The SPELT approach recognizes that, in the junior high school context, the scheduling of instruction around subject specialist teachers (in fact, in some schools this practice begins at the upper elementary grades) makes it impossible to achieve the ideal situation whereby generalization can be maximized in the manner described above. It becomes important, in the context of the junior high school, to design supplementary techniques to ensure that strategies taught or generated in one content area transfer to other content areas and instructional contexts. These techniques may include the involvement of other subject teachers, even if in a limited way, to ensure that key strategies that have potential for broad application are reinforced and cued for generalization during lessons in other subject areas. Assignments that force students to apply learned strategies to more than one content area constitute another potential tool that requires co-operation among teachers from different subject departments. Finally, students may be trained to cue one another when a strategy is perceived to be applicable to content areas that are different from the one in which the strategy was originally taught or generated.

Finally, SPELT differs from other programs in yet another way. SPELT is premised on the view that all categories of children—gifted, normal achieving, mildly learning disabled, and mildly mentally handicapped—can benefit from strategy instruction. In consonance with the movement toward mainstreaming of different categories of children, learning strategies instruction, we believe, should take place in the regular classroom where high-, medium-, and low-achieving students can benefit from the strategic behaviour of one another.

Although SPELT has yet to be formally evaluated within the context of northern Native classrooms, its emphasis on the development of learning/ thinking strategies directly within the curriculum would seem to make it appropriate for all categories of children, in particular for children who by virtue of their different cultural experiences may have difficulty coping with the mainstream curriculum. Also, as the program is designed to teach children how to learn—not necessarily what to learn—it could be applied within the context of any specific curriculum or content area for any given population of youngsters. Because it is designed to capitalize on individual students' existing repertoire of cognitive strategies, it is not the type of program that will impose strategies that may be counter to effective strategies already in use by any particular individual or group of individuals. In other words, the program recognizes that different categories of children, depending upon their unique learning styles, cultural experiences, and prior knowledge may possess a variety of strategies that work for them. It is the intent of the program to build upon those strategies that work, while providing the context for learning new strategies or modifying existing inefficient strategies.

The ultimate goal of all strategy instruction is to put the student in control of the learning process. A basic rationale underlying this goal is that as students gain more and more control over the learning process, they become increasingly motivated to learn and to perform. This effect of strategy instruction is particularly important in light of our knowledge that the high drop-out rates among school-age Native youngsters may be partially linked to motivational problems.

CONCLUSION

In this chapter, we have attempted to address two central issues pertinent to the education of Native Canadian children—assessment of cognitive ability and instructional programming. We have reviewed a number of concerns with the traditional psychometric approach to the assessment of cognitive ability, noting several recommendations for increasing the validity and usefulness of such assessments. We have taken the view that assessment of cognitive ability in all populations should place greater emphasis upon cognitive processes and strategies that underlie learning and performance. On this score, there is overwhelming consensus that traditional psychometric assessments have limited value for instructional programming and remediation. However, until such time as more appropriate cognitive strategy assessment tools of the kind we envisage become available, traditional psychometric assessment procedures will continue to be used.

It was demonstrated that, since the early 1970s, the need to shift towards the assessment of *underlying cognitive processes* rather than *resulting products* of such processes has received the attention of cognitive psychologists. Unfortunately, some of the major efforts towards a process orientation have not departed completely from the psychometric tradition. We examined the level I-level II abilities theory of Jensen and the simultaneous-successive processes model of Das and his associates as representative examples of such efforts, noting their implications for the education of minority populations.

In presenting an alternative to current assessment practices we have adopted a cognitive process approach that emphasizes learning and thinking strategies in a manner that portrays assessment and instructional programming as two inseparable activities in the teaching-learning process. Programs like IE and SPELT have been designed to make individual strategy assessment an integral part of the instructional process, and it is in the light of this attribute that we have presented the two programs for use with Native children. The two programs are highly complementary and provide a continuum from a non-content emphasis upon the development of essential cognitive processes to a curriculum content-based application of learning and thinking strategies.

Preliminary results from our ongoing evaluation of the two programs are very encouraging in the sense that both programs appear, in the short term, to lead to increased positive self-esteem and perceived competence. Data from direct student assessment and from teacher and parent perceptions of student change all point to a positive affective impact.[53] These results are significant because of the known relationship between affective variables and school achievement, and point to the potential efficacy of the programs in the long term.

NOTES

1. We wish to acknowledge the Planning Services Branch of Alberta Education, in particular Dr. Clarence Rhodes, for supporting the project that provided the context for writing substantial portions of this chapter. We would like also to thank the following members of the Cognitive Education Project team for their input: David Peat, Jac Andrews, Laurie Clifford, Seokee Cho, Helen Henderson, and Judy Maynes. This chapter was written while Kofi Marfo was supported by a United States National Academy of Education Spencer Fellowship.

2. D.N. Bershoff, "*P. v. Riles*: Legal Perspective," *The School Psychology Review* 9, 2 (1980): 112–21; P.B. Madden, "Intelligence Tests on Trial," *The School Psychology Review* 9, 2 (1980): 49–53.

3. D.J. Reschly, "WISC-R Factor Structures Among Anglos, Blacks, Chicanos, and Native-American Papagos," *Journal of Consulting and Clinical Psychology* 46 (1978): 417–22; J. Condas, "Personal Reflections on the Larry P. Trial and Its Aftermath," *The School Psychology Review* 9, 2 (1980): 54–58.

4. D.J. Reschly, "Psychological Evidence in the Larry P. Opinion: A Case of Right Problem, Wrong Solution," *The School Psychology Review* 9, 2 (1980).

5. R.L. Flaugher, "The Many Definitions of Test Bias," *American Psychologist* 33 (1978): 671–78.

6. R.L. Flaugher, *Bias in Testing: A Review and Discussion* (TM Rep. 36) (Princeton, N.J.: ERIC Clearinghouse on Tests, Measurements, and Evaluation, 1974).

7. H.H. Mueller, R.F. Mulcahy, L. Wilgosh, B. Watters, and G.J. Mancini, "An Analysis of WISC-R Item Responses with Canadian Inuit Children," *Alberta Journal of Educational Research* 32 (1986): 12–36.

8. D. Matheson, "Confirmatory Factor Analysis of WISC-R for Inuit Children" (M.Ed. thesis, University of Alberta, 1983).

9. J.M. Sattler, *Assessment of Children's Intelligence and Special Abilities*, 2nd ed. (Boston: Allyn and Bacon, 1982); R.M. Kaplan and D.P. Saccuzzo, *Psychological Testing: Principles, Applications, and Issues* (Monterey, Calif.: Brooks/Cole Publishing Co., 1982).

10. J.R. Mercer and J.F. Lewis, *System of Multicultural Pluralistic Assessment* (New York: Psychological Corporation, 1977).

11. Sattler, *Assessment of Children's Intelligence and Special Abilities*.

12. E.A. DeAvila and B. Havassy, *IQ Tests and Minority Children* (Austin, Tex.: Dissemination Center for Bilingual Education, 1974).

13. E.g., R.F. Mulcahy and B. Watters, *Phase 1: NWT Norming Project Final Report* (Yellowknife, N.W.T.: Government of the Northwest Territories, 1982).

14. L. Wilgosh, R.F. Mulcahy, and B. Watters, "Identifying Gifted Canadian Inuit Children Using Conventional IQ Measures and Nonverbal Performance Indicators," *Canadian Journal of Behavioural Science* (forthcoming).

15. J.R. Kirby, "Individual Differences and Cognitive Processes: Instructional Application and Methodological Difficulties" in *Cognition, Development, and Instruction*, edited by J.R. Kirby and J.B. Biggs (New York: Academic Press, 1980).

16. A.R. Jensen, "How Much Can We Boost IQ and Scholastic Achievement? *Harvard Educational Review* 39 (1969): 1–23; and *Educational Differences* (New York: Barnes & Noble, 1974).

17. Jensen, *Educational Differences*.

18. S.R. Yussen and J.W. Santrock, *Child Development: An Introduction* (Dubuque, Iowa: W.C. Brown, 1982).

19. Kirby, "Individual Differences and Cognitive Processes."

20. J.P. Das, J.R. Kirby, and R.F. Jarman, *Simultaneous and Successive Cognitive Processes* (New York: Academic Press, 1979).

21. Ibid., 49.

22. See ibid., passim.

23. C.R. Reynolds, "The Neuropsychological Basis of Intelligence" in *Neuropsychological Assessment and the School-Age Child: Issues and Procedures*, edited by G.W. Hynd and J.E. Obrzut (New York: Grune and Stratton, 1981), 107.

24. J.P. Das and L. Krywaniuk, "Memory and Reasoning in Native Children: An Effort at Improvement Through the Teaching of Cognitive Strategies" in *A Report on Indian Education*, edited by A. Berger and J.P. Das (Edmonton: University of Alberta, 1972).
25. L.W. Krywaniuk, "Patterns of Cognitive Abilities of High and Low Achieving School Children" (Ph.D. dissertation, University of Alberta, 1974).
26. A.S. Kaufman and N.L. Kaufman, *Kaufman Assessment Battery for Children Administration and Scoring Manual* (Circle Pines, Minn.: American Guidance Services, 1983).
27. E.g., R. Feuerstein, *Instrumental Enrichment: An Intervention Program for Cognitive Modifiability* (Baltimore: University Park Press, 1980); R.F. Mulcahy, K. Marfo, and D. Peat, *A Strategies Program for Effective Learning and Thinking: A Teachers' Manual* (Edmonton: University of Alberta Cognitive Education Project, 1985).
28. R. Feuerstein, *The Dynamic Assessment of Retarded Performers: The Learning Potential Assessment Device* (Baltimore: University Park Press, 1979).
29. J. Schubert and A. Cropley, "Verbal Regulation of Behaviour and IQ in Canadian Indian and White Children," *Developmental Psychology* 7 (1972): 295–301.
30. Matheson, "Confirmatory Factor Analysis of the WISC-R for Inuit Children."
31. Feuerstein, *The Dynamic Assessment of Retarded Performers* and *Instrumental Enrichment*.
32. Mulcahy et al., *A Strategies Program for Effective Learning and Thinking*; R.F. Mulcahy, K. Marfo, D. Peat, J. Andrews, and L. Clifford, "Applying Cognitive Psychology in the Classroom: A Learning/Thinking Strategies Instructional Program," *Alberta Psychology* 13, 3 (1986): 9–12.
33. Feuerstein, *Instrumental Enrichment*.
34. Mulcahy et al. "Applying Cognitive Psychology in the Classroom."
35. J.G. Borkowski, "Signs of Intelligence: Strategy Generalization and Metacognition" in *The Growth of Reflection in Children*, edited by S.R. Yussen (Orlando: Academic Press, 1985); A.L. Brown, "Knowing When, Where and How to Remember: A Problem of Metacognition" in *Advances in Instructional Psychology*, vol. 1, edited by R. Glaser (Hillside, N.J.: Erlbaum, 1978); J.H. Flavell, "Metacognitive Aspects of Problem Solving" in *The Nature of Intelligence*, edited by L.B. Resnick (Hillsdale, N.J.: Erlbaum, 1976).
36. R. Case, "Implications of Neo-Piagetian Theory for Improving the Design of Instruction" in *Cognition, Development, and Instruction*.
37. P.W. Thorndyke and B. Hayes-Roth, "The Use of Schemata in the Acquisition and Transfer of Knowledge," *Cognitive Psychology* 11 (1979): 82–106.
38. A. Newell and H.A. Simon, *Human Problem Solving* (Englewood Cliffs, N.J.: Prentice Hall, 1972).
39. H.C. Haywood and H.N. Switzky, "The Malleability of Intelligence: Cognitive Processes as a Function of Polygenic-Experimental Interaction," *School Psychology Review* 15 (1986): 245–55.
40. Ibid., 249.
41. R.J. Sternberg, *Intelligence Applied* (Toronto: Harcourt Brace Jovanovich, 1986).

42. R.M. Gagné, *The Conditions of Learning*, 3rd ed. (New York: Holt, Rinehart and Winston, 1977).

43. E.g., D. Dansereau, "Learning Strategy Research" in *Thinking and Learning Skills*, vol. 1, *Relating Instruction to Research*, edited by J.W. Segal, S.F. Chipman, and R. Glaser (Hillsdale, N.J.: Erlbaum, 1985); C.E. Weinstein and V.L. Underwood, "Learning Strategies: The How of Learning" in *Thinking and Learning Skills*, vol. 1.

44. E.g., D.D. Deshler, M.M. Warner, J.B. Schumaker, and G.R. Alley, "Learning Strategies Intervention Model: Key Components and Current Status" in *Current Topics in Learning Disabilities*, vol. 1, edited by J.D. McKinney and L. Feagans (Norwood, N.J.: Ablex, 1983).

45. F.F. French, "Learner Strategies Enabling Thinking" (unpublished manuscript, University of Alberta, 1983).

46. F.H. Kanfer and M.L. Seidner, "Self-Control: Factors in Enhancing Tolerance of Noxious Stimuli," *Journal of Personality and Social Psychology* 25 (1973): 381–89.

47. R.K. Wagner and R.J. Sternberg, "Alternative Conceptions of Intelligence Testing and Their Implications for Education," *Review of Educational Research* 54 (1984): 179–223.

48. Ibid., 206.

49. E.g., A.L. Brown and S.S. Smiley, "The Development of Strategies for Studying Texts," *Child Development* 49 (1978): 1076–88.

50. F.F. French, "Cognitive Strategy Assessment and Intervention with Educable Mentally Handicapped Adolescents" (Ph.D. dissertation, University of Alberta, 1985).

51. E.g., J.P. Richards and G.J. August, "Generative Underlining Strategies in Prose Recall," *Journal of Educational Psychology* 67 (1975): 860–65; J.A. Slee, "The Use of Visual Imagery in Visual Memory Tasks: A Cautionary Note" in *Mental Imagery and Learning*, edited by M.L. Fleming and D.W. Hutton (Englewood Cliffs, N.J.: Educational Technology Publications, 1983).

52. E.g., de Bono's CORT program; Covington's Productive Thinking Program; Feuerstein's Instrumental Enrichment program; Lipman's Philosophy for Children, etc.

WHAT IS FUNDAMENTAL TO NATIVE EDUCATION? SOME THOUGHTS ON THE RELATIONSHIP BETWEEN THINKING, FEELING, AND LEARNING

JOSEPH E. COUTURE[1]

It was unheard of, prior to the late 1960s, that traditional Native values and behaviours should be and could be the foundation for a relevant philosophy and psychology of Native education. Since that time, an awareness of the potential of traditional sources as inspiration and sound guidelines has slowly and steadily developed.

In Alberta, at the political level, awareness of the value of Native tradition in education dawned during the winter of 1968–69 after months of intense struggle by such burgeoning organizations as the Indian Association of Alberta, the Métis Association of Alberta, and the Native Communications Society. During the preceding summer each of these societies had come under new leadership. All three organizations initially shared a common office, from which they lobbied for hearings and hard-to-find program moneys, with no significant breakthroughs. A joint meeting was called in January 1969 to review the activities of the recent months. After hours of depressing assessment, and during a brooding silence among the leaders, someone blurted out: "We've tried everything Whitey has laid on us, but it doesn't work.... What we haven't tried is our culture. Let's go and talk to some Elders." With that the return to the roots began.

A series of workshops, under the title of "Elders' Think Tanks," was organized across Alberta over a two-year period. The series climaxed in the fall of 1972 at Long Beach, Vancouver Island. Of the many memorable declarations made at that gathering, one was uttered by Elder Louis Crier:

> In order to survive in the twentieth century, we must really come to grips with the White man's culture and with White man's ways. We must stop lamenting the past. The White man has many good things. Borrow. Master and apply his technology. Discover and define the harmonies between the two general Cultures, between the basic values of the Indian Way and those of Western Civilization—and, thereby forge a new and stronger sense of identity. To be fully Indian today, we must become bilingual and bicultural. We

> have never had to do this before. But, in so doing, we will survive as Indian People, true to our past. We have always survived. Our history tells us so.

Elder Louis Crier spoke on behalf of Elders assembled to reflect on and to discuss current Indian problems. There were nine Elders present, representing the eight tribal groupings from Alberta (i.e., Beaver, Blackfoot, Cree, Chipewyan, Sarcee, Saulteaux, Slavey, Stoney), in addition to some forty employees of the Indian Association of Alberta. That IAA-initiated conference, a first of its kind, and now regarded as a milestone, marked the emergence and revitalization of Native culture in Alberta in the early 1970s.

The importance of Louis Crier's declaration is simple and dramatic. Elders, as the historians and the experts on survival, interpret for their own people the current meaning and direction of their own history. The declaration clearly indicates several desirable connections between general Native and western cultures. Notably, Indian identity is redefined in terms of the twentieth-century. Fundamental, traditional elements are re-expressed and presented as fresh inspiration for renewed action. The poignancy of Louis' urging is with us still, a standing and pointed challenge to the children of this generation and to their children's children. "And it is good that it is so," as the Old People say.

The effort to "master and apply his technology" is indisputably one visible feature of Native development during the past fifteen years. Through the media, for example, one can easily trace Native attempts to access Canadian society's institutions and to understand and apply its technologies. One can observe the Native struggle with value reinterpretation and identity redefinition. This is a drama that is evident now in all areas of Native social, cultural, political, economic, and educational activity.

PURPOSE AND METHOD

The purpose of this paper is to explore some of the basic cultural differences that seem to distinguish Native from Euro-Canadian culture and to comment on their implications for Native educational policy. Recognition of diversity is fundamental to our discussion. It is widely agreed that Natives today live on a continuum ranging from highly acculturated urban Natives through to traditional outback Natives. This continuum is manifested in many different languages (including English and French) and in many differing customs and traditions. It includes those groups who have retained their cultures intact as well as other groups who exhibit varying degrees of cultural and social breakdown, personal disorganization, and near-complete identity loss among their members.[2] Many factors contribute to this diversity, which derives largely from legal and regional differences, different histories of inter-tribal relationships, and Native/white relationships mediated through a variety of dominant social institutions.

What follows identifies a number of basic traditional values, some of which can be perceived as "value bridges" between the two general cultures and as functional, defining, or organizing principles that can be applied to solving Native education problems. It is essential that both components be borne in mind if the present alarming conditions and acute learning needs of Native students—especially of Native undergraduate students—are to be responded to in comprehensive, culture-sensitive ways.

It is the intention of this paper to explicate several principles that can help both to delineate the cultural factors that make for significant, contrasting differences between Natives and non-Natives, and to suggest meaningful guidelines for a pragmatic and sensitive response in the many areas of Native educational need. To that end, the question of what are characteristic traditional Native values and behaviours is pertinent, as is the question of how these might best be applied to education. This is a "good theory/good practice" approach, for it assumes that an examination of traditional values as manifested in behaviours is a source of "good" theory, and that this thereby presents sensible guidelines to "good" application as an insightful response to Native educational need.

A two-fold approach is followed to describe the characteristics of traditional Native values. First of all, this analysis sets forth historical-philosophical characteristics that describe the nature of traditional values. Secondly, a brief description of what I regard as traditional behaviours common to most Native groups is presented. These two sections provide a basis for a general discussion of how Native learning conditions could be significantly improved. The final section, on pedagogical requirements, makes it possible to consider other practical and related issues.

HISTORICAL AND PHILOSOPHICAL CHARACTERISTICS OF TRADITIONAL NATIVE VALUES: SOME OBSERVATIONS

Elder Louis Crier's statement reflects an awareness of a historical Native capacity to endure. Oral tradition teaches that when certain values or laws are upheld and observed, the People survive: it devolves to Elders to provide these precepts. However, as Crier's statement indicates, both the interpretation and application of the directives of Elders are the responsibility of the younger generations. Evidence of what these "younger generations" are thinking and seeking can be found in several contemporary sources. One area of interpretation of both Elder oral tradition and aspirations of the People can be found, for example, in the writings of such Native authors as Vine Deloria. In *God is Red*[5] Deloria reveals a deep understanding of the relevance of the Native presence on this continent and of the distinctive qualitative nature of the Native relationship to the land. A second important source is official documents of several national Native organizations. A comparative analysis of their respective statements reveals a consensus on a number of distinctive, inter-related characteristics of traditional Native values and attitudes. The agreement among the several official Native views, condensed below, is striking.

1. Native cultures are dynamic, adaptive, and adapting, not limited to the past.

2. These cultures are authentic and valid, inherently creative, capable of distinctive and sophisticated human development and expression, and therefore they can invent structural forms and institutions as needed to assure and strengthen group/individual survival. They are capable of a social and political rationality of their own, and are as creative in this regard as the dominant culture. It is in this that a basis for legitimate and valid differences between the two general cultures is to be found.

3. Native life-ways are rooted in a perception of the inter-connectedness between all natural things, all forms of life. Within this, the sense of the land is a central determining experience.

4. There is a characteristic sense of community, of "The People," a collective or communal sense that contrasts sharply with western individualism and institutional forms based on private ownership.

5. The current Native situation presents a wide spectrum of variation and diversity of Native behavior and attitude, of history, and of social and political systems, and, as well, a wide continuum of behaviour, encompassing the traditional unacculturated Native together with the highly acculturated.

6. Modern Native behaviour includes responses to highly specialized relationships with the dominant Canadian society, to a greater extent than any other Canadian group, at different levels (e.g., government, churches, special interest groups such as stores, and oil/mining corporations).[4]

A seventh concept is implicit in the preceding. As a thread running through the value statements above is a concept of being that is primarily concerned with the process of the individual's being and becoming a unique person, responsible for his or her own life and actions in the context of significant group situations. This stance contrasts sharply with such western ways as having, manipulating, objectifying—all three carried out in "rugged" individualistic fashion. The traditional Native being-becoming posture requires trust of self and others, a non-manipulative relatedness, and a sense of oneness with all dimensions of the environment—components that, without exception, are experienced and perceived as possessing a life energy of their own. Native philosophies of life manifest a characteristic person-centredness, a holistic personalism that regards the human person as a subject in relationships: both the subjects and the relationships exist in a dynamic process of being-becoming.[5]

General Canadian society has overlooked virtually all of these values. It is a matter of record, as the Reports by the Task Force on Canadian Unity clearly indicate, that the Canadian public and its governments have tended to ignore or downgrade Native cultural distinctiveness. At best, the Canadian habit has been to reify selected aspects of Native cultures and to incorporate them as part of the national heritage—in, for example, the prizing of aesthetic and folkloric elements. This, of course, has been the path of least resistance, and it repeats the historical tendency of most, if not all, majority cultures worldwide.

It is much more difficult not only to acquire an understanding of fundamental Native cultural values, but to create the conditions for maintenance and reproduction of those values. For example, the history of relationships between Francophones and Anglophones in Canada illustrates the fundamental difficulty Anglophones have had in understanding and accepting Francophone uniqueness, despite the European origin and history of both groups, and the sharing of a number of western values. The difficulties are understandably compounded when one considers that the traditions, values, and histories of Native cultures differ radically on many basic points from dominant Euro-Canadian culture.

PSYCHOLOGICAL CHARACTERISTICS OF TRADITIONAL NATIVE VALUES

The basic Native cultural values described above constitute a vital, inner source of strength. These values are the roots to a number of characteristic behaviours, the understanding of which must be regarded as essential to educational planning and development. A working knowledge of these underlying values—as exhibited in such concrete areas as extended family systems, child-rearing practices, the fostering of individual autonomy—is crucial to effective Native educational planning. One is further enriched if one learns several special behaviours and relationships, such as joking and the use of humour as a form of feedback in place of direct criticism, avoidance behaviour, age-graded sensitivities and requirements, the hurt/anger/distrust syndrome, the existence of hereditary leadership patterns, the use of analogy in place of linear logic in teaching and problem-solving, and consensus decision making.

Several features of the above behaviours can be better defined through comparison with some generally recognized dominant-society behaviours.

Historically, each Native nation or group had its own ways, developed over centuries and deriving from internal needs and values in particular environments, with individuals learning defined roles within the community. Across this range of behaviours, there are a number of practices and support systems that clearly contrast with dominant-society patterns (e.g., extended family systems, child-rearing practices, the role of Elders, interpersonal dynamics, and learning styles).

The traditional extended family[6] is a social institution found virtually in all nations. Child-rearing practices must be perceived within the extended family context. Traditionally, child-rearing includes not only the parents but grandparents and aunts and uncles who also share in this process. In addition, siblings and cousins, nearby or under the same roof, help with the rearing of their relatives' children. Economic reasons may require children to move from one nuclear family to another, but it is within the extended family network that help will be obtained in times of crisis. Advice from Elders, who are respected and listened to, is also sought. Finally, traditional child-rearing customs give children emotional and physical room to make mistakes, to succeed as well as to fail, a practice that tends to foster emotionally free, autonomous, responsible individuals.

Within the context of extended family and child-rearing practices, Elders of both sexes play a central role. Traditionally, Elders are the guardians, purveyors, and teachers of the oral traditions and history of the People—they are the doctors and healers, the expert survivors. Traditional Native people often display unusually rich personalities and sophisticated mind development. Their minds are manifestly capable of expounding, for example, on concepts of a metaphysical, epistemological, or moral order. One still finds examples of remarkable intelligence and wisdom animated by a patient sense of humour, excellent memory recall, discursiveness, a sense of caring, and finesse in teaching and counselling. These abilities and qualities are little suspected by non-Natives and now, unfortunately, by growing numbers of Natives, particularly among the urban born and raised.

Ideally, knowledge of the "truth" of the Elder is indispensable to educators. However, this principle presents a practical problem to non-Native and Native alike. The problem stems mostly from the limited number of Elders, their restricted availability, their manner of teaching, and their "rhythm," which is that of the seasons and not that of the watch and calendar. Much time is required to learn their ways and their teachings. For the serious student of Native life, there really is no way but to relate consistently over time with Elders. In the present day, finding time for such teaching relationships is a problem. Pending such an apprentice relationship, the next best thing for the student preparing for Native-related work would be to enter into daily Native interpersonal relationships. Once within these patterns of living, one can learn over time to discern at least some of the underlying traditional values described earlier.

It is a commonplace that non-Natives are often frustrated by much of Native behaviour. This has resulted in frequent and repeated reference to Natives as being uncooperative, stubborn, belligerent, "dumb," impossible, etc. It would be useful to try to discern subtle behaviours: self-reliance, easily perceived as stubbornness; aloofness that is really a reluctance to ask for or receive help other than in an emergency or crisis; the tendency not to interfere, on a basis of live-and-let-live, for to do so is to be discourteous, threatening, even insulting; confrontation avoidance, which is sometimes interpreted as non-cooperation or immaturity, but which is a tendency to avoid direct disagreement with the individual.

It is a matter of record that, with good intentions, Canadian society imposed an educational philosophy and system to which Natives were forced to submit. Natives had no control or say over this, and it led to loss of dignity, decades of miseducation, and a weakening of parental and group responsibility for their children.[7] Since the early 1970s, Natives have been enrolling in growing numbers in a wide range of courses and programs at colleges and universities across Canada. On the face of it, this should be regarded as an encouraging and promising phenomenon. At the same time, however, many Native students who enrol in post-secondary programs often fail to complete their certificates and/or degrees. Recognition of increasing enrolments together with high under-attainment against a continuing history of high drop-out levels from secondary school systems, remains a disquieting backdrop to this whole discussion.

Dominant society's behaviour seems to stem from a Canadian ethnocentrism, a kind of cultural addiction that holds tenaciously to its ideas about knowing and knowledge, about the disadvantaged, education, segregation, ethnicity, and Native "problems." This state of mind steadfastly prizes middle-class individualism, private ownership of property, aggressive "getting ahead," and competitiveness, and exhibits a patronizing, colonizing, custodial mentality towards Natives on the part of those in positions of power (e.g., teachers, missionaries, bureaucrats, guards, business and industrial development people, etc.). The dominant system is hierarchical, perennially and unilaterally imposing decisions, whereas traditional Native systems are based on consensus decision making and respect for the individual.

Given the general characteristics of Native and dominant Canadian cultures, several dilemmas confront us. One of these arises from the fact that Natives generally know what they want and need, and that they have repeatedly voiced their concerns through various representative organizations. With a little help, they can and do develop their own solutions, which are more effective than the disastrous "solutions" imposed by the majority culture. Can a new, functional model, inspired and defined by culture-sensitive philosophies, be developed and implemented, so that getting an education ceases to be a source of failure, if not punishment? Can this new model be implemented to survive in community settings marked by increased suicide and alcoholism rates, growing family breakdown and child neglect, rising violence and general social degradation? At this point, I can only argue from personal and professional experience and from an understanding of traditional values and behaviours in the direction of some operational principles that should and could, in my view, be readily applied.

PEDAGOGICAL REQUIREMENTS OF TRADITIONAL NATIVE VALUES

The Canadian approach to Native education is a dismal failure. The recorded views of Native peoples, regionally and nationally, repeatedly describe the causes of this failure. Alberta has witnessed many indignant Native protest about educational conditions in the provincial school systems. These are typically followed by government attempts to downplay the situation as not as bad as Natives perceive it to be, and by calls for yet another task force on the issue.

The need for appropriate and insightful action in Native education remains urgent, given Native need and the nature of such obstacles as government ignorance and condescension. Another major obstacle to Native educational development is due to an almost total absence of systematic and sustained investigation in all areas of Native educational need. While it is now possible to gather provincial and federal government literature on Native curriculum development, analysis reveals little or no work in terms of the primary values and behaviours described earlier. We also know little about how to develop in Native and non-Native teachers and administrators appropriate understanding of Native behaviours, customs, and ways. There is no general, organized attempt in Canada to draw on compatible western resources relative to Native learning and identity needs.

All this may seem discouraging to teachers, counsellors, and administrators. There are, however, directions to be followed and things to do.

Earlier I suggested that the ideal, traditional way to learn basic Native values and behaviour would be to apprentice to an Elder, and that the next best thing would be simply to live among Natives and learn from social interactions. Both methods work, but they require long periods of time. From a professional training standpoint, there are several other helpful projects that can be more easily undertaken.

One of these can be found in the longstanding western tradition of theory and experience that is holistic, humanistic, person-centred. Since the 1960s, this has been promoted by humanistic educational thinkers and writers, such as Rogers and Samples,[8] and by such Third World proponents as Freire. The common distinction used by many writers between non-formal or informal education and schooling would be useful if applied to Native educational planning, curriculum development, and school administration, for traditional values through the ages are taught through informal means. This contrasts with prevailing educational practice, which tends to objectify and rationalize learning, and treat it as a commodity.

There are now some exciting school-related and cross-cultural learning related endeavours to heed. Examples include the takeover of federal schools by local communities such as the Fort Alexander Band in Manitoba and the Alexander Band in Alberta. The latter community has succeeded in drawing on the Waldorf and Anisa curriculum development and teacher training models in such a way that the community's perception of traditional values and behaviours is readily incorporated. The work of Feuerstein and other researchers and institutions in this regard hold much promise.[9]

There are areas of western philosophy and psychology that provide more comprehensive educational paradigms than do current reductionist varieties.[10] They can provide reference point concepts and models through which undergraduate institutions, for instance, can meaningfully bridge a number of cultural, cognitive, and affective gaps.

Highly important to any discussion of educational planning for Natives is what I regard as traditional Native patterns of learning. It is my view that the traditional Native learning style and conditioning induce development of both the analytical and intuitive capacities of the human mind. Recent research, notably that of Ornstein,[11] and of such followers as Samples[12] and others, strongly suggests that there is left-brain activity distinctive from right-cerebral function, and that our school systems and post-secondary institutions have done little else but develop the left brain. These researchers contend that the left hemisphere of the brain is the area of intellectual analysis, linear thinking, and language, whereas the right side of the cerebrum is the seat of metaphorical symbolic perception, the area of intuition. These investigators of right-brain behaviours also claim that the next major revolution in education will be in right-brain development. In my judgment, it is a question of mind and not of brain function. The new development should ultimately and simply make for pragmatic approaches to total or whole-mind development, regardless of the physiological location of either general mind function. In other words, teachers should learn how to develop affective and cognitive capacities, intuitive/metaphoric abilities, and analytical thinking in their students. Then, traditional Native learning and western educational endeavour could truly meet.[13]

More concretely, "experiential learning" or "learning by doing" models have much to offer (e.g., human relations training, assertiveness training, basic communications skills development, Perlsian and Rogerian encounter learning). Such strategies are in tune with the demands of identity development, human relations, cross-cultural communication, and holistic development.

CONCLUSION

I regard the systematic study and application of holistic approaches not only as both plausible and feasible, but as necessary. To point to what is needed is one thing; it is quite another to determine what is possible, given Canadian cultural and political realities in general, and those of educational institutions in particular.

Since Canadian universities are largely responsible for training professional educators for all levels of teaching, it is at such institutions that new thinking and the development of additional competencies are urgently required. This may be asking too much of universities, however, for they are notoriously slow to change.

So much of what university people do stems from what may be likened to a bourgeois appetite for success, a striving for control and possession. Many Native American and Third World critics, including Freire, consider this kind of academic performance a form of colonialism, a rule-and-conquer syndrome, a compulsion to name what will be, a form of unilateral control. Such behaviour, although understandable, is not excusable. It is behaviour that stems from a predominantly rationalistic, analytical, non-intuitive mind, linear in its modality. Such a mind tends to dissect reality into controllable pieces in the name of "objectivity" and scientific "method," overlooking the loss of gestaltic meaning that such analysis unavoidably entails. Such a mind fails to perceive and esteem another mind that is characteristically intuitive, actively metaphoric, and symbolic in expression, in addition to being analytical. That is one basic reason why the conventional academic mind fails to develop a full perception of the Native. A significant change in attitude and an expansion of the existing epistemological paradigm are obviously needed.

The general North American non-Native educational scene provides a broader context that further underscores the need for a paradigmatic shift in education. In the 1960s in both Canada and the United States, educators and policy makers struggled with concepts of equality and excellence in the name of the "democratization of education." Passow describes the general situation and highlights the basic issue of cultural differences and attendant tensions within an encompassing, and historically unfavourable context:

> In various ways the concepts of uniformity and diversity have raised issues with regard to all aspects of education—goals, curriculum, instructional strategies, staff deployment, resource allocation, organization, evaluation, etc.... Just as the goals of equity and excellence are both deemed desirable, uniformity and diversity are both considered desirable even though they are often in conflict with one another....
>
> In striving to attain the twin goals of equity and excellence, curricular and instructional uniformity and diversity are needed. When uniformity and common curriculum are appropriate and when diversity and differentiated curriculum and instruction are appropriate raises questions which do not respond to either-or solutions. Basic philosophical positions affect decision-making and doctrinaire decisions are not likely to move schools and school systems toward resolution of questions concerning curriculum and instruction. How to blend uniqueness, individuality, and differences with commonalities, group and societal needs without subordinating one to the other is the continuing quest of the curriculum developer in selection of content, instructional strategies, resources, and evaluation procedures.[14]

The education of underprivileged groups in Canada, in the words of the OECD report, is a "major Canadian problem," and the education of Native people is a "special case of perpetuated underprivilege."[15] The standard offering to Native students through provincial systems was assumed to be "adequate" when this is clearly not so. Canada has not defined "an overall concept" for the improvement of the educational opportunity for Native children; this is so because Canadian educators are "characteristically unreflective."[16]

It seems clear to me that a holistic philosophy and psychology of education rooted in traditional Native values can provide an "overall concept." While Passow's comments indicate the nature of the inequality issue relative to the American educational scene, his analysis applies equally to Canada. The discussion of educational inequality must take into account the broader dimensions of economic inequalities and political influence. Canadians need to recognize that, in the graphic words of the OECD Report:

> many of the school related practices that reinforce societal inequalities have occurred and endure precisely because they serve certain economic and political interests. All the good will in the world among educators will not then suffice to eradicate such practices, for that requires a more profound change in the distribution of power in society and the goals which power is made to serve.[17]

Balancing the tension between dominant-society interests and culture-specific hopes is a fundamental and inescapable challenge. There is an ongoing struggle in opposites at play (e.g., recognizing the strengths in persons and communities as opposed to describing weaknesses and pathologies; cultural action as the opposite of cultural destruction; holistic perspective and problem-solving in contrast to the piecemeal and static solutions proferred and imposed over the decades; authenticity as the opposite of lying). There is no mistaking the daily realities of the struggle for enlightened Native educational development: one struggles always with both the results of unsuitable educational resources and inadequate or damaging forms of social services, and with institutional racism and limited attention to social and cultural development.

The purpose of Native education is not to provide an inferior education but to provide a *different* education, the objective of which is to develop knowledge, skills, and values rooted in a centuries-old tradition in order that students can contribute to the betterment of their community and their People.

The solution can be found at the heart of the two general traditions:

> The centred and quartered Circle is the sign of wholeness, of inclusiveness of all reality, of balance and harmony between man and nature. (Amerindian tradition)

> The subject and object of education is the whole of man, in the whole of his environment for the whole of life. (Western tradition)

Each tradition is a testimony to life.

NOTES

1. The author is a Métis of Cree ancestry. His Ph.D. training and experience are in the areas of native development, psychology, and education. This paper is intended primarily for a non-Native audience. The views expressed, unless otherwise specifically indicated, substantially reflect a prolonged professional and personal experience amongst various Native peoples, an experience rooted in and guided by the teachings of Alberta Elders. The frequent references to his own writings are witness to a dearth of relevant academic literature.

2. That something of a "Native" identity remains despite absolute cultural changes is argued by McNickle, a Flathead Indian, and by Miller, a Six Nations Tuscarora. McNickle observes that cultural changes can and do occur without necessarily obliterating personality structure. Natives remain Natives, he writes, "not by refusing to accept change or to adapt to a changing environment, but by selecting out of available choices those alternatives that do not impose a substitute identity" ("The Dead Horse Walks Again" *The Nation* 25 Dec. 1967, p. 11). The precise nature of what does persist is not entirely clear. It is perhaps some kind of psychological pan-Indian core. (G. Miller, "Native Values and Attitudes" (unpublished paper, 1979).) That certain behavioural characteristics seem to survive, in a qualitative sense, and this despite centuries of Indian-white association, is commonly acknowledged amongst Natives.

3. V. Deloria, *God is Red* (New York: Dell, 1973).

4. This quote is based on an analysis by the author of official documents of present-day national Native organizations. Cf. Joseph E. Couture, *Socio-Cultural Development—Policy Recommendations. A Discussion Paper* (Ottawa: Native Directorate, Secretary of State, Sept. 1981), 6–7; National Indian Brotherhood, "Presentation to the Standing Committee on Indian Affairs and Northern Development regarding Indian Government, 27 Nov. 1979," *Parliamentary Liaison 1980* (Ottawa: NIB, 1980). "National Indian Brotherhood Presentation to the Standing Committee on Indian Affairs and Northern Development regarding the Ft. Nelson Bill C-26, 10 July 1980," *Parliamentary Liaison 1980* (Ottawa: NIB, 1980); "National Indian Brotherhood Presentation to the Standing Committee on Indian Affairs and Northern Development regarding the Constitution, 8 July 1980," *Parliamentary Liaison 1980* (Ottawa: NIB, 1980); *National Indian Brotherhood Presentation to the Parliamentary Task Force on Employment Opportunities for the 1980s* (Ottawa: NIB, 13 Feb. 1981); National Native Alcohol Addiction Program, *A Report on the Problems and Needs, Alberta NNAAP Projects with Recommendations* (Ottawa: NNAAP, 1979); National Office for the Development of Indian Cultural Education, *A Discussion Paper on Indian Control of Indian Cultural Education Centres Program* (Ottawa: NODICE, June 1981); Native Council of Canada, *Native People and the Constitution. The Report of the Métis and Non-status Indians Constitutional Review Commission* (Ottawa: Mutual Press, April 1981).

5. Underlying these several qualities, in turn, is a principle of spirituality. For a general discussion of this and related aspects see Joseph E. Couture, "Traditional Aboriginal Spirituality and Religious Practice in Federal Prisons. An Interim

Statement on Policy and Procedures" (Working Paper #1, Draft #2. Prepared under contract for Correctional Services of Canada, Native Inmate Programs, July 1983); Joseph E. Couture, "Indian Spirituality. A Personal Experience," *Kerygma* 16 (1982): 77–92.

6. I.e., a basic kinship unit or system combining relatives on either or both sides, often including non-related friends, in a network of responsibility and interdependency relative to the welfare of each member, and relative especially to child-rearing needs.

7. The OECD Report, although it praises Canadian pragmatism, condemns the general Canadian educational system for its unreflectivity in its treatment of students. Cf. Canadian Association for Adult Education, *OECD Report* (Toronto: CAAE, 1977); V. Hesp, "Native Studies at Athabasca University. Need Project" (June 1984).

8. Carl Rogers, ed., *Studies of the Person*, 12 vols. (Columbus, Ohio: Merrill, 1969); R. Samples, C. Charles, and R. Barnhart, *The Wholeschool Book: Teaching and Learning in the late 20th Century* (Reading, Mass.: Addison-Wesley, 1977); R. Samples, *The Metaphoric Mind. A Celebration of Creative Consciousness* (Reading, Mass.: Addison-Wesley, 1976).

9. Feuerstein's work with the multi-subcultures of Jewish immigrants to Israel, and especially with such a radically different culture as that of black Ethiopian Jews, is most suggestive. His basic distinction between the "culturally different and the culturally deprived," and his assessment approach to determining skill needs relative to dominant society adaptation requirements is attractive and feasible and warrants close consideration. R. Feuerstein, "Cultural Differences and Cultural Deprivation: A Theoretical Framework for Differential Intervention" (paper presented at the First International Jerusalem Convention on Education, Hebrew University, 19–23 Dec. 1984). A second springboard to theoretical model development and pedagogical invention is the common treasure of "competency based education" and "experiential learning." The latter developments arose inductively out of the experience of several American colleges and universities. This promising movement is now sponsored nationally by the Council for Advancement of Experiential Learning. Cf. M. Chickering, *Experience and Learning: An Introduction to Experiential Learning* (New Rochelle, N.Y.: Change Magazine Press, 1977); M. Keeton and P. Tate, eds., *Learning by Experience—What, Why, How* (San Francisco: Jossey-Bass, 1978); D. Kolb, *Experiential Learning: Experience as the Source of Learning and Development* (Englewood Cliffs, N.J.: Prentice-Hall, 1984). Through its member institutions, CAEL has produced and continues to present sound work at the level of adult learner need in the areas of prior assessment of learning and curriculum development. The CAEL sponsored work is noteworthy because it takes into account not only knowledge or content assimilation, but skills and attitude development as well. It is also felt that the Keller-initiated work in personalized student instruction (PSI) would be extremely useful. P.S. Keller, "Goodbye Teacher," *Journal of Applied Behavioral Analysis* 1 (1968): 69–89. The pool of knowledge and techniques, to which CAEL and PSI activity is contributing, especially into the four areas of prior assessment of learning, knowledge mastery, skills, and attitude development, is relevant since Native students in community colleges and universities presently tend to be of the "adult

learner" category. A growing consensus among some Native developers and educators is that Natives wishing to train in any one of the services areas, notably teaching, counselling, and social work, need knowledge and skills that prepare them to work in three interrelated areas regardless of choice of profession (i.e., teaching, adult learning, and community development). It is felt that the CAEL and PSI insights are relevant to that end.

10. Much of mainstream psychology, for example, is based on a reductionistic/mechanistic model of human behaviour, which has had a direct and disproportionate influence on modern educational theory and practice. The reductionist oriented mind, as far as Natives are concerned, is arrogant, patronizing, insensitive, excessively systematized, ignorant of other ways of knowing. Don Juan frequently chastises Castaneda for the shallowness of his rationalist mind.

11. R. Ornstein, *The Psychology of Consciousness* (San Francisco: Freeman, 1972).

12. Samples, "Learning with the Whole Brain," *Human Behavior* (Feb. 1975): 17–23.

13. This is truly an intriguing area that awaits analysis and application to Native learning issues. For principles and examples of application to non-Native children see Samples, "Learning with the Whole Brain"; R. Schmuck and P. Schmuck, *A Humanistic Psychology of Education: Making the School Everybody's House* (Palo Alto, Calif.: National Press Books, 1974); E.L. Simpson and M.A. Gray, *Humanistic Education: An Interpretation. A Report to the Ford Foundation* (Cambridge, Mass.: Ballinger, 1976); R. Valett, *Humanistic Education: Developing the Total Person* (St. Louis, Mo.: C.V. Mosby, 1977). Readers interested in total person development theory and practice are referred to the entire twelve book series *Studies of the Person*, prepared under the general editorship of Carl Rogers.

14. A.H. Passow, "Uniformity and Diversity; Curricular and Instructional Issues" (paper presented at the First International Jerusalem Convention on Education, Hebrew University, 19–23 Dec. 1984), 1, 18.

15. Canadian Association for Adult Education, *OECD Report*, 145–54.

16. Ibid., 20.

17. Ibid., 87.

IMMERSION PROGRAMS: CURRENT ISSUES AND FUTURE DIRECTIONS

JIM CUMMINS

The term "immersion" usually refers to educational programs designed to teach second language skills by "immersing" students in instructional contexts in which all or most of the school day is conducted through the medium of the second language. The term is most frequently associated with the Canadian French immersion programs, which were initiated during the 1960s in the Montreal area but which have spread rapidly across Canada since that time. Currently there are about 178 000 students in various kinds of French immersion programs in Canada. What distinguishes the Canadian programs from previous attempts at second language immersion programs (such as those in Ireland since the 1920s) is the fact that the Canadian programs have been extensively evaluated and their success documented empirically. In the case of previous attempts at language planning that involved immersion programs, the goals were primarily social and political rather than educational. For example, in the attempt to revive Gaelic through early immersion programs, it was assumed by educators and many politicians that there would be educational costs to students' academic development but that these were justified by the social importance of the language revival effort. The importance of the Canadian research is that it has established the *educational* credibility of immersion programs and also some of the conditions under which these programs can succeed.

In this paper I will first briefly describe the varieties of immersion programs as they exist in Canada and then summarize the findings of research on immersion. Then the theoretical principles that emerge from the immersion research together with other research on bilingual education will be outlined. It is crucial for language planning purposes to make these theoretical principles explicit because it is only on the basis of these principles that predictions can be made about academic outcomes under different social and educational conditions. Next, certain problems that have emerged in Canadian immersion programs will be discussed and solutions to these problems and future directions for immersion education generally will be suggested.

VARIETIES OF FRENCH IMMERSION PROGRAMS

The original French immersion program initiated in the St. Lambert area near Montreal[1] was an early immersion program that involved one hundred percent French instruction in kindergarten (age five) and Grade 1, after which one period of English language arts was introduced in Grade 2 and the proportion of English instruction was gradually increased until about half the day was spent working in each language by Grade 5. Reading was introduced in French (L2) in Grade 1. From grades 7 through 12 approximately forty percent of the time was spent working in French. This program has continued to serve as the model for other early immersion programs, the only significant change being that currently in many programs the introduction of English (L1) language arts is delayed until Grade 3 or 4.

A second variety of immersion is termed "intermediate" or "middle" immersion. These programs begin in Grade 4 or 5 with anywhere from fifty to one hundred percent of instructional time in French. After Grade 6, the amount of instructional time is similar to that of early immersion programs and sometimes students from early and middle immersion programs are combined in the same classes. The rationale for this is usually administrative rather than educational.

The third major variety of immersion program is termed "late" immersion and usually instruction through the medium of French starts in Grade 7 or 8 for about eighty to one hundred percent of the school day. After Grade 8, the proportion through French drops to about forty percent.

These are only the major program varieties and, within each, there is considerable variation. For example, some early immersion programs may have up to fifty percent of English-medium instruction from Grade 1 and reading may be introduced in English rather than in French. Similarly, some late immersion programs may involve as little as forty or fifty percent of initial instruction through French.

FINDINGS OF RESEARCH ON IMMERSION

The goals of all the immersion programs are similar, namely, to develop high levels of French proficiency at no cost to students' English proficiency or achievement in other academic subjects such as mathematics or science. In general, the research has shown that all three major types of program meet their goals to a very large extent. Expectations with respect to the different programs vary in accordance with the amount of exposure to French. For example, it was expected that the French achievement of students in early immersion would surpass that of students in the other two program types because considerably more instructional time is spent through French in early immersion. Although, some long-term advantage has been found for early immersion, the differences in French proficiency have generally been much less than expected. For example, several studies have reported minimal differences between students in early and late immersion in French skills measured at the Grade 8 or 9 level. However, no differences are found in English skills despite the fact that the early immersion students have had considerably less instruction through English. In short, with respect to academic achievement there is little to choose between the three major varieties of immersion program, *as they are currently implemented*. It will be suggested in a later section, however, that the French (and English) achievement of students in early immersion programs could be improved significantly if certain pedagogical changes were made in the program.

The specific findings of the research will be described only for the early immersion program since the same pattern is observed in the other program types. There are five major categories of finding, the first three dealing with English achievement, achievement in other academic subjects, and French achievement. The other findings relate to predictors of achievement in French and the issue of whether immersion is suitable for all students. Description of these findings will be brief since detailed accounts can be found in many sources.[2]

ENGLISH PROFICIENCY

Students show no long-term lag in the development of English academic skills. Prior to the introduction of English language arts, immersion students generally perform less well on measures of English skills than comparison groups in regular programs. However, for most aspects of English skills the gap has closed within one year of the introduction of English instruction; with respect to spelling, two years is usually required for immersion students to catch up with their regular program peers.

CONTENT SUBJECTS

Generally there is no lag in the development of content subjects taught through French in early immersion, although in middle and late immersion students often perform at a lower level during the initial year. In subsequent years, however, differences in academic achievement usually disappear.

FRENCH SKILLS

By the end of Grade 6, early immersion students have developed French reading and listening skills that are close to those of native French speakers. However, their expressive skills in speaking and writing remain far from native-like. When components of proficiency are considered in terms of grammatical, discourse, and socio-linguistic skills, it is found that differences between immersion and native French speakers are greatest in grammatical skills and least in discourse skills.[3] The relatively good performance of immersion students on discourse tasks is likely due to the fact that performance on these tasks requires well-developed cognitive as much as linguistic skills.

PREDICTORS OF PERFORMANCE IN IMMERSION

A consistent finding of research is that cognitive ability (IQ) scores predict academic performance (in both French and English) in immersion programs just as they do in regular English programs. However, oral communicative skills (e.g., fluency, accent, etc.) are not significantly related to cognitive ability scores in either early or late immersion. Personality variables have not shown strong or consistent relationships to success in early immersion, although relatively few studies have been carried out in this area, probably because "personality" is a notoriously difficult construct to measure, especially at younger ages.

SUITABILITY OF IMMERSION FOR ALL CHILDREN

The data reviewed above show that research has failed to uncover any pattern of cognitive or personality traits that *differentially* predicts success in immersion as compared to English-only programs. Children with lower cognitive ability (as measured by IQ tests) perform as well in immersion programs as in regular English programs. There is controversy, however, over the issue of whether immersion is appropriate for all children and whether schools should institute screening of children prior to acceptance into an early immersion program. Trites had argued that some children suffer from "a developmental lag in the temporal lobe regions of the brain" and, as a consequence, experience difficulty in early immersion.[4] He also argues that children experiencing difficulty should be transferred to the English program without delay. Both these conclusions are questioned by other researchers who tend to concur with the conclusions of Bruck's research,[5] which suggests that even children with language impairments can succeed in early immersion and that, consequently, there is no need for screening of applicants to immersion programs; children who experience difficulty should be provided with remedial assistance within the context of the immersion program itself. Bruck points to the potentially damaging effect on children's self-esteem as a result of transfer to the regular English program.

In short, there is still controversy among researchers and confusion among practitioners about whether immersion is suitable for all children. Some children certainly experience difficulty in early immersion, but it is not at all certain that this is due to intrinsic characteristics of the children (as Trites suggests) as compared to inappropriate teacher expectations and/or inappropriate pedagogy. The fact that there is an alternative to the immersion program may lead some teachers to assume that problem children would be better off in a regular class. This suggestion is strengthened by Bruck's finding that a high proportion of children with behaviour problems tended to be transferred from immersion to the English program.[6]

Other research that has been carried out on immersion suggests that there may be some subtle cognitive advantages for children who attain high levels of bilingual skills in immersion,[7] that students use minimal amounts of French outside the classroom even in bilingual cities such as Montreal and Ottawa,[8] and that the pedagogy in immersion programs tends to be considerably more teacher-centred than in many regular programs, particularly at the upper elementary grade levels (grade 4, 5, and 6).[9] In a later section it will be suggested that some of the difficulties that students experience in expressive aspects of French are, at least in part, due to this teacher-centred pedagogical orientation in early immersion programs.

The next section outlines three theoretical principles that have emerged from research on bilingual education in a variety of contexts and that are consistent with and help to explain the immersion findings.

PRINCIPLES OF BILINGUAL ACADEMIC DEVELOPMENT

THE ADDITIVE BILINGUALISM ENRICHMENT PRINCIPLE

In the past, many students from minority backgrounds have experienced difficulties in school and have performed worse than monolingual children on verbal IQ tests and on measures of literacy development. These findings led researchers in the period between 1920 and 1960 to speculate that bilingualism caused language handicaps and cognitive confusion among children. Some research studies also reported that bilingual children suffered emotional conflicts more frequently than monolingual children. Thus, in the early part of this century, bilingualism acquired a doubtful reputation among educators, and many schools redoubled their efforts to eradicate minority children's first language on the grounds that this language was the source of children's academic difficulties.

However, virtually all of the early research involved minority students who were in the process of replacing their L1 with the majority language, usually with strong encouragement from the school. Many minority students in North America were physically punished for speaking their L1 in school. Thus, these students usually failed to develop adequate literacy skills in this language and many also experienced academic and emotional difficulty in school. This, however, was not because of bilingualism but rather because of the treatment they received in schools, which essentially amounted to an assault on their personal identities.

More recent studies suggest that far from being a negative force in children's personal and academic development, bilingualism can positively affect both intellectual and linguistic progress. A large number of studies have reported that bilingual children exhibit a greater sensitivity to linguistic meanings and may be more flexible in their thinking than are monolingual children.[10]

Most of these studies have investigated aspects of children's metalinguistic development—in other words, children's explicit knowledge about the structure and functions of language itself. A problem in interpreting these studies is that the notion of "metalinguistic development" is not yet clearly defined in the literature. Bialystok and Ryan have recently attempted to clarify this notion in terms of two underlying dimensions: namely, children's analysed knowledge of language and their control over language.[11] They predicted that bilingualism would enhance children's control over and ability to manipulate language but not their analysed knowledge of language. These predictions regarding the likely consequences of bilingualism for metalinguistic development have generally been borne out in a number of studies.[12]

In general, it is not surprising that bilingual children should be more adept at certain aspects of linguistic processing. In gaining control over two language systems, the bilingual child has had to decipher much more language input than the monolingual child who has been exposed to only one language system. Thus, the bilingual child has had considerably more practice in analysing meanings than the monolingual child.

The evidence is not conclusive as to whether this linguistic advantage transfers to more general cognitive skills. McLaughlin's review of the literature, for example, concludes that:

> It seems clear that the child who has mastered two languages has a linguistic advantage over the monolingual child. Bilingual children become aware that there are two ways of saying the same thing. But does this sensitivity to the lexical and formal aspects of language generalize to cognitive functioning? There is no conclusive answer to this question—mainly because it has proven so difficult to apply the necessary controls in research.[13]

Hakuta and Diaz[14] and Diaz[15] have recently reported evidence that bilingualism may positively affect general cognitive abilities in addition to metalinguistic skills. Rather than examining bilingual-monolingual differences, Hakuta and Diaz employed a longitudinal within-group design in which Hispanic primary school children's developing L2 (English) skills were related to cognitive abilities with the effect of L1 abilities controlled. The sample was relatively homogeneous both with respect to socio-economic status and educational experience (all were in bilingual programs). L2 skills were found to be significantly related to cognitive and metalinguistic abilities. The positive relationship was particularly strong for Raven's Progressive Matrices—a non-verbal intelligence test; further analyses suggested that if bilingualism and intelligence are causally related, bilingualism is most likely the causal factor.

An important characteristic of the bilingual children in the more recent studies (conducted since the early 1960s) is that, for the most part, they were developing what has been termed an *additive* form of bilingualism.[16] In other words, they were adding a second language to their repertory of skills at no cost to the development of their first language. Consequently, these children were in the process of attaining a relatively high level of both fluency and literacy in their two languages. The children in these studies tended to come either from majority language groups whose first language was strongly reinforced in the society (e.g., English-speakers in French immersion programs) or from minority groups whose first languages were reinforced by bilingual programs in the school. Minority children who lack this educational support for literacy development in L1 frequently develop a *subtractive* form of bilingualism in which L1 skills are replaced by L2. Under certain sociopolitical conditions, these children fail to develop adequate levels of literacy in either language.[17]

This pattern of findings suggested that the level of proficiency attained by bilingual students in their two languages may be an important influence on their academic and intellectual development.[18] Specifically, there may be a threshold level of proficiency in both languages that students must attain in order to avoid any negative academic consequences and a second, higher, threshold necessary to reap the linguistic and intellectual benefits of bilingualism and biliteracy.

Diaz[19] has questioned the threshold hypothesis on the grounds that the effects of bilingualism on cognitive abilities in his data were stronger for children of relatively low L2 proficiency (non-balanced bilinguals). This suggests that the positive effects are related to the initial struggles and experiences of the beginning second-language learner. This interpretation does not appear to be incompatible with the threshold hypothesis since the major point of this hypothesis is that, for positive effects to manifest themselves, children must be in the process of developing high levels of bilingual skills. If beginning L2 learners do not continue to develop both their languages, any initial positive effects are likely to be counteracted by the negative consequences of subtractive bilingualism.

In summary, the conclusion that emerges from the research on the academic, linguistic, and intellectual effects of bilingualism can be stated thus: the development of additive bilingual and biliteracy skills entails no negative consequences for children's academic, linguistic, or intellectual development. On the contrary, although not conclusive, the evidence points in the direction of subtle metalinguistic, academic, and intellectual benefits for bilingual children.

THE LINGUISTIC INTERDEPENDENCE PRINCIPLE

The fact that there is little relationship between amount of instructional time through the majority language and academic achievement in that language strongly suggests that first and second language academic skills are interdependent (i.e., manifestations of a common underlying proficiency). The interdependence principle has been stated formally as follows: "To the extent that instruction in Lx is effective in promoting proficiency on Lx, transfer of this proficiency to Ly will occur provided there is adequate exposure to Ly (either in school or environment) and adequate motivation to learn Ly."[20] In concrete terms, what this principle means is that in, for example, a Gaelic-English bilingual program in Ireland, Gaelic instruction that develops Gaelic reading and writing skills (for either Gaelic L1 or L2 speakers) is not just developing *Gaelic* skills, it is also developing a deeper conceptual and linguistic proficiency that is strongly related to the development of literacy in the majority language (English). In other words, although the surface aspects (e.g., pronunciation, fluency, etc.) of different languages are clearly separate, there is an underlying cognitive/academic proficiency that is common across languages. This "common underlying proficiency" makes possible the transfer of cognitive/academic or literacy-related skills across languages. Transfer is much more likely to occur from minority to majority language because of the greater exposure to literacy in the majority language outside of school and the strong social pressure to learn it. The interdependence principle is depicted in figure 1.

FIGURE 1. THE LINGUISTIC INTERDEPENDENCE MODEL

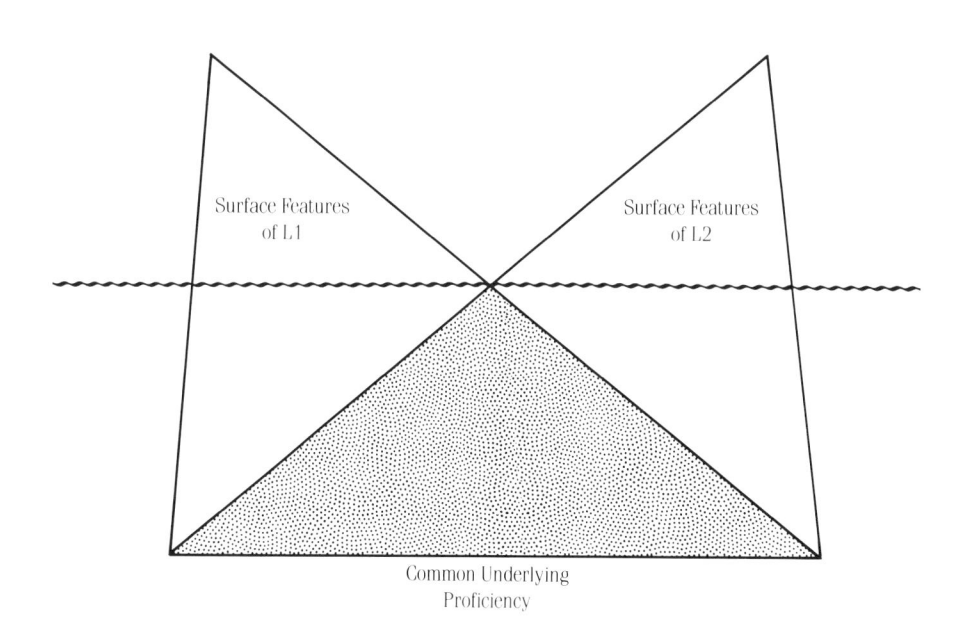

Surface Features of L1

Surface Features of L2

Common Underlying Proficiency

A considerable amount of evidence supporting the interdependence principle has been reviewed by Cummins[21] and Cummins and Swain[22]. The results of virtually all evaluations of bilingual programs for both majority and minority students are consistent with predictions derived from the interdependence principle.[23] The interdependence principle is also capable of accounting for data on immigrant students' L2 acquisition[24] as well as on studies of bilingual language use in the home.[25] Correlational studies also consistently reveal a strong degree of cognitive/academic interdependence across languages.

Recent studies continue to support the interdependence principle. Kemp,[26] for example, reported that Hebrew (L1) cognitive/academic abilities accounted for forty-eight percent of the variance in English (L2) academic skills among 196 Grade 7 Israeli students. Treger and Wong[27] reported significant positive relationships between L1 and English reading abilities (measured by cloze tests) among both Hispanic and Chinese-background elementary school students in Boston. In other words, students above grade level in their first language reading also tended to be above grade level for English reading.

Two longitudinal studies also provide strong support for the notion of linguistic interdependence. Ramirez[28] followed seventy-five Hispanic elementary school students in Newark, New Jersey, enrolled in bilingual programs for three years. It was found that Spanish and English academic language scores loaded on one single factor over the three years of data collection. Hakuta and Diaz,[29] with a similar sample of Hispanic students, found an increasing correlation between English and Spanish academic skills over time. Between kindergarten and Grade 3, the correlation between English and Spanish went from 0 to .68. The low cross-lingual relationship at the kindergarten level is likely due to the varied length of residence of the students and their parents in the United States, which would result in varying levels of English proficiency at the start of school.

An on-going study of five schools attempting to implement the theoretical framework developed by the California State Department of Education in 1981 showed consistently higher correlations between English and Spanish reading skills (range r = .60 to .74) than between English reading and oral language skills (range r = .36 to .59). In these analyses, scores were broken down by months in the program (1 to 12 months through 73 to 84 months). It was also found that the relation between L1 and L2 reading became stronger as English oral communicative skills grew stronger (r = .71, N = 190 for students in the highest category of English oral skills).

Finally, Cummins, Allen, Harley, and Swain[30] have reported highly significant correlations for written grammatical, discourse, and sociolinguistic skills in Portuguese (L1) and English (L2) among Portuguese Grade 7 students in Toronto. Cross-language correlations for oral skills were generally not significant. The same pattern of linguistic interdependence has also been reported in other recent studies.[31]

In conclusion, the research evidence shows consistent support for the principle of linguistic interdependence in studies investigating a variety of issues (e.g., bilingual education, memory functioning of bilinguals, age and second language learning, bilingual reading skills, etc.) and using different methodologies. The research has also been carried out in a wide variety of sociopolitical contexts. The consistency and strength of support indicate that highly reliable policy predictions can be made on the basis of this principle.

THE SUFFICIENT COMMUNICATIVE INTERACTION PRINCIPLE

Most second language theorists[32] currently endorse some form of the "input" hypothesis, which essentially states that acquisition of a second language depends not just on exposure to the language but on access to second language input, which is modified in various ways to make it comprehensible. Underlying the notion of comprehensible input is the obvious fact that a central function of language use is meaningful communication; when this central function of language is ignored in classroom instruction, learning is likely to be by rote and supported only by extrinsic motivation. Wong Fillmore has clearly expressed this point:

> Wherever it is felt that points of language need to be imparted for their own sake, teachers are likely to make use of drills and exercises where these linguistic points are emphasized and repeated. And when this happens the language on which students have to base their learning of English is separated from its potential functions, namely those that allow language learners to make the appropriate connections between form and communicative functions. Without such connections language is simply not learnable.[33]

A limitation to the term "comprehensible input" is that it focusses only on the receptive or "input" aspects of interaction, whereas both receptive and expressive aspects appear to be important.[34] Swain and Wong Fillmore have expressed the importance of meaningful interaction for second language learning by synthesizing the view of leading researchers in the field in the form of an "interactionist" theory whose major proposition is that "interaction between learner and target language users is the major causal variable in second language acquisition."[35] It is important to emphasize that meaningful interaction with text in the target language and production of text for real audiences is also included within this interactionist framework.[36]

The principle of sufficient communicative interaction also characterizes first language acquisition. Young children rarely focus on language itself in the process of acquisition; instead, they focus on the meaning that is being communicated and use language for a variety of functions, such as finding out about things, maintaining contact with others, etc. In Gordon Wells' phrase, children are active "negotiators of meaning,"[37] and they acquire language almost as a by-product of this meaningful interaction with adults.

APPLICATION OF THEORETICAL PRINCIPLES TO IMMERSION PROGRAMS

The first two theoretical principles—additive bilingual enrichment and linguistic interdependence—have important implications for the educational credibility of immersion as well as its public acceptance, while the sufficient communicative interaction principle is important for understanding both the success of immersion programs in the early grades and unresolved problems that have emerged in recent years. The large number of evaluations that have been carried out on immersion programs in Canada is attributable in part to the need to reassure educators and parents that early bilingualism would not confuse children and that children's English skills would not suffer despite being immersed in French. The increasing popularity of immersion is evidence of the extent to which initial concerns about the educational viability of immersion have been resolved. The additive bilingualism enrichment principle and the linguistic interdependence principle account for the pattern of research findings and allow the immersion findings to be incorporated within a broader theoretical framework that is applicable to bilingual education generally.

However, the research does not present a totally positive picture of French immersion programs. Two major problems have emerged; first, the fact that some children apparently do not succeed in early immersion and are transferred to the regular English program; second, the fact that, around the Grade 3 or 4 level, students appear to reach a plateau in the development of their French skills, at least as far as grammatical competence is concerned. Certain errors persist and are extremely difficult to eradicate. This pattern has led many teachers to spend much of the instructional time devoted to French language arts on grammatical drills designed to force correct forms into reluctant heads. Different groups of researchers[38] have reported that there is a considerably higher proportion of teacher-led lessons and much less small group work in immersion programs than in many regular English programs. Furthermore, Allen et al. report that, since teachers do most of the talking (especially in the later elementary grades), students have little opportunity to actually use French in the classroom. There also appears to be considerably less creative or expressive writing in immersion programs than in many English programs. In short, in the later grades of elementary school, the meaningful interaction that students experience in French tends to be confined to the receptive sphere. Given this pattern, it is hardly surprising that students' oral and written French skills remain inadequately developed.

FUTURE DIRECTIONS

Few would quarrel with the assertion that French immersion programs have been among the most successful second language teaching programs ever implemented. The extremely rapid increase in enrolment in these programs across Canada attests to the extent to which they are perceived to be successful. However, I would argue that continued success and perception of success will depend upon the extent to which solutions are found to the problem of students experiencing difficulty in the early grades of immersion and to the inadequate development of students' expressive written and oral French skills. Elsewhere,[39] I have suggested that these problems are symptomatic of a deeper malaise in the way French immersion programs are frequently implemented—specifically, the assumptions about teaching and learning that are embodied in the delivery of many early immersion programs. These assumptions reflect what a number of researchers have termed a "transmission" model of teaching in which teachers view their task as transmitting a body of knowledge and skills to the student. The interaction is dominated by the teacher, with little genuine dialogue (in oral or written modalities) between students and teachers or between students themselves. As noted earlier, research has documented the greater prevalence of this teacher-centred orientation in immersion as compared to regular programs, especially in the later grades of elementary school.

Given the importance of interaction for second language acquisition, one could argue that an "interactionist" orientation to pedagogy[40] is even more significant in immersion programs than in regular English programs. This approach to pedagogy would allow for much more individualized instruction and genuine dialogue (again in both oral and written modalities) between teachers and students. When all children are expected to march to the same tune—played by the teacher—then any child who fails to keep up is likely to be identified as a failure and, in all probability, transferred to the English program. Within an interactionist framework, on the other hand, children are being compared to their point of departure rather than to the "standard" of the class and consequently there is less likelihood of children being "pushed out" of immersion.

Two pedagogical innovations that derive from an interactionist framework appear to have considerable potential to address the problems that have emerged in French immersion. These are the encouragement of creative writing through the "process/conference" approach popularized by Donald Graves[41] and his colleagues and the use of computer writing networks, which permit students to interact directly with peers in different locations: for example, students in French immersion programs could exchange written documents (e.g., collections of stories written by the class) with native French speakers in Quebec or France.[42] The emphasis in process writing is on writing for real audiences (peers, teachers, parents), discussing drafts of the work with teachers and peers, and publishing final drafts of the work within the classroom. Children are motivated to correct grammatical and spelling errors in their final drafts because they do not want their published work to display such errors. In other words, the motivation to acquire formally correct French becomes intrinsic rather than extrinsic. This motivation is likely to be greatly enhanced when the audience is an audience of native-speaking peers in a different province or country.

In short, if the credibility of immersion programs is to remain high, then important realignments in pedagogical assumptions are required. Children must be permitted to become actively involved in literacy—creators of literature rather than consumers of grammar and spelling: they must also be encouraged to *use* French actively for purposes of interaction with peers both in the classroom and in other locations (by means of computer networks). Interaction rather than transmission must become the dominant force both in the development of curricula and in the conduct of the classroom.

NOTES

1. W.E. Lambert and G.R. Tucker, *Bilingual Education of Children: The St. Lambert Experiment* (Rowley, Mass.: Newbury House, 1972).

2. J. Cummins, *Heritage Language Education: A Literature Review* (Toronto, Ont.: Ministry of Education, 1983), and *Bilingualism and Special Education: Issues in Assessment and Pedagogy* (Clevedon, England: Multilingual Matters, 1984). Lambert and Tucker, *The St. Lambert Experiment*; M. Swain and S. Lapkin, *Evaluating Bilingual Education* (Clevedon, England: Multilingual Matters, 1982).

3. P.A. Allen, J. Cummins, B. Harley, and M. Swain, "The Development of Bilingual Proficiency," Final report to the S.S.H.R.C. (Toronto: Ontario Institute for Studies in Education, 1986).

4. R.L. Trites, "Children with Learning Difficulties in Primary French Immersion," *Canadian Modern Language Review* 33 (1976): 143–46.

5. M. Bruck, "The Suitability of Early French Immersion Programs for the Language-Disabled Child," *Canadian Journal of Education* 3 (1978): 51–72.

6. M. Bruck, "The Feasibility of an Additive Bilingual Program for Language-Impaired Children" in *Early Bilingualism and Child Development*, edited by M. Paradis and Y. Lebrun (Lisse: Swets and Zeitlinger B.V., 1984).

7. B. Harley, D. Hart, and S. Lapkin, "The Effects of Early Bilingual Schooling on First Language Skills," *Applied Psycholinguistics* 7 (forthcoming).

8. J. Cummins and M. Swain, *Bilingualism in Education: Aspects of Theory, Research and Practice* (London: Longman, 1986).

9. Allen et al., "The Development of Bilingual Proficiency."

10. Cummins, *Bilingualism and Special Education*.

11. E. Bialystok and E.B. Ryan, "Metacognitive Framework for the Development of First and Second Language Skills" in *Meta-cognition, Cognition, and Human Performance*, edited by D.L. Forrest-Pressley, G.E. MacKinnon, and T.G. Waller (New York: Academic Press, 1985).

12. E. Bialystok, "Influences of Bilingualism on Metalinguistic Development" (paper presented at the symposium "Language Awareness/Reading Development: Cause? Effect? Concomitance?" at the National Reading Conference Meeting, Petersburg, Fla., 1984).

13. B. McLaughlin, "Early Bilingualism: Methodological and Theoretical Issues" in *Early Bilingualism and Child Development*, 44.

14. K. Hakuta and R.M. Diaz, "The Relationship Between Degree of Bilingualism and Cognitive Ability: A Critical Discussion and Some New Longitudinal Data" in *Children's Language*, vol. 5, edited by K.E. Nelson (Hillsdale, N.J.: Erlbaum, 1985).

15. R.M. Diaz, "Bilingual Cognitive Development: Addressing Three Gaps in Current Research," *Child Development* (forthcoming).

16. W.E. Lambert, "Culture and Language as Factors in Learning and Education" in *Education of Immigrant Students*, edited by A. Wolfgang (Toronto: Ontario Institute for Studies in Education, 1975).

17. Cummins and Swain, *Bilingualism in Education*.

18. J. Cummins, "Linguistic Interdependence and the Educational Development of Bilingual Children," *Review of Educational Research* 49 (1979): 222–51.

19. Diaz, "Bilingual Cognitive Development" (forthcoming).

20. Cummins, *Bilingualism and Special Education*, 143.

21. Cummins, *Heritage Language Education*, and *Bilingualism and Special Education*.

22. Cummins and Swain, *Bilingualism in Education*.

23. Cummins, *Heritage Language Education*.

24. E.g., J. Cummins, *Heritage Language Education*, and *Bilingualism and Special Education*.

25. E.g., J. Bhatnagar, "Linguistic Behaviour and Adjustment in Immigrant Children in French and English Schools in Montreal," *International Review of Applied Psychology* 1/2 (1980): 141–58; D. Dolson, "The Effects of Spanish Home Language Use on the Scholastic Performance of Hispanic Pupils," *Journal of Multilingual and Multicultural Development* 6 (1985): 135–56.

26. J. Kemp, "Native Language Knowledge as a Predictor of Success in Learning a Foreign Language with Special Reference to a Disadvantaged Population" (M.A. thesis, Tel-Aviv University, 1984).

27. B. Treger and B.K. Wong, "The Relationship Between Native and Second Language Reading Comprehension and Second Language Oral Ability" in *Placement Procedures in Bilingual Education: Education and Policy Issues*, edited by C. Rivera (Clevedon, England: Multilingual Matters, 1984).

28. C.M. Ramirez, "Bilingual Education and Language Interdependence: Cummins and Beyond" (Ph.D. dissertation, Yeshiva University, 1985).

29. Hakuta and Diaz, "The Relationship Between Degree of Bilingualism and Cognitive Ability."

30. Allen et al., "The Development of Bilingual Proficiency."

31. E.g., S.R. Goldman, *Utilization of Knowledge Acquired Through the First*

Language in Comprehending a Second Language: Narrative Composition by Spanish-English Speakers (report submitted to the U.S. Department of Education 1985); V. Guerra, "Predictors of Second Language Learners' Error Judgements in Written English" (Ph.D. dissertation, University of Houston, 1984); L.T. Katsaiti, "Interlingual Transfer of a Cognitive Skill in Bilinguals" (M.A. thesis, Ontario Institute for Studies in Education, 1983).

32. E.g., S.D. Krashen, "Bilingual Education and Second Language Acquisition Theory" in *Schooling and Language Minority Student: A Theoretical Framework* (Los Angeles: Evaluation, Dissemination and Assessment Center, California State Department of Education, 1981); M.H. Long, "Native Speaker/Non-native Speaker Conversation in the Second Language Classroom" in *On TESOL '82: Pacific Perspectives on Language Learning and Teaching*, edited by M.A. Clarke and J. Handscombe (Washington: TESOL, 1983); J. Schachter, "Nutritional Needs of Language Learners" in *On TESOL '82*; L. Wong Fillmore, "The Language Learner as an Individual: Implications of Research on Individual Differences for the ESL Teacher" in On TESOL '82.

33. Wong Fillmore, ibid., 170.

34. M. Swain, "Communicative Competence: Some Roles of Comprehensible Input and Comprehensible Output in Its Development" in *Bilingualism in Education*.

35. M. Swain and L. Wong Fillmore, "Child Second Language Development: Views From the Field on Theory and Research" (paper presented at the 18th Annual TESOL Conference, Houston, Texas, March 1984), 18.

36. Cummins, *Bilingualism and Special Education*.

37. G. Wells, "Language, Learning and the Curriculum" in *Language, Learning and Education*, edited by G. Wells (Bristol: Centre for the Study of Language and Communication, University of Bristol, 1982).

38. Allen et al., "The Development of Bilingual Proficiency"; R. Wilson and M. Connock, "An Assessment of the 50/50 Programme in the English Sector Schools" (Ottawa Roman Catholic Separate School Board, Feb. 1982).

39. J. Cummins, "Special Needs in French Immersion" (paper presented to the Canadian Parents for French Conference, Whitehorse, Yukon, Oct. 1985).

40. Cummins, *Bilingualism and Special Education*; Cummins and Swain, *Bilingualism in Education*.

41. D. Graves, *Writing: Children and Teachers at Work* (Exeter, N.H.: Heinemann, 1983).

42. J. Cummins, "Cultures in Contact: Using Classroom Microcomputers for Cultural Interchange and Reinforcement," *TESL Canada* (forthcoming).

THE FRANCOPHONE SCHOOL–IMMERSION SCHOOL DEBATE IN WESTERN CANADA

STEPHEN CAREY

The fact that the rights of French-Canadian minorities to education in their native tongue has been enshrined in the Constitution raises an important question as to how Francophones can best preserve their cultural and linguistic heritage in provinces outside Quebec. In Alberta, until recently, Francophones who wanted their children to be schooled in French were required to send them to either immersion programs that were originally designed for Anglophones or to mixed programs where Francophones and Anglophones were schooled in a common facility but streamed in terms of Francophone and Anglophone classes. In other provinces outside Quebec, such as Ontario and Manitoba, Francophone schools have increasingly been promoted, since the Bilingualism and Biculturalism Report of 1965, as avenues to promote the maintenance of the French language and culture. The question is, which of these two schooling options is appropriate if Francophone parents wish their children to develop bilingual skills and an appreciation of French-Canadian culture in western Canada?

The Francophone school differs in at least two major ways from the relatively recent immersion school concept. First, in a Francophone school, it is argued that the curriculum is taught using French as a first language rather than as a second language, as is done in immersion schools. Secondly, the Francophone school can provide a greater degree of French-Canadian cultural awareness due largely to the fact that the student body comes primarily or exclusively from Francophone families. As such, the school may be viewed as analogous to an ethnic minority community school with the proviso that the language of instruction is an official language and often the defining property of the ethnic group. Thus, Francophone schools can serve as a vital focus for the Francophone community, a role that is not played by the immersion school in the Anglophone community. Moreover, the Francophone school can also serve the need of the minority group for cultural and linguistic security, identity, and a sense of historical continuity.

While Francophone schools have existed in several provinces outside Quebec for many years,[1] the implementation of the Canadian Charter of

Rights, in particular sections 23 and 15, has re-emphasized the potential role that these schools can play for Francophone minorities, as recently documented in the 1985 case of *Mahe v. R.* in Alberta. This landmark court case was precipitated as a result of the desire of a group of French, Québécois, and western French Canadians to create an exclusively Francophone school for their children in lieu of the mixed Francophone-Anglophone immersion program that existed. These Francophones argued that, whereas in immersion programs the Anglophone children benefited from acquiring French as a second language, their own children were used as models for the other students and were often schooled in French as a second rather than as a first language. More generally, the Francophone parents believed that their children would advance more rapidly in their French language and schooling if they had schools and perhaps curricula that were developed for their needs. Furthermore, it was believed that Francophone schools would provide the focus for promoting a needed cultural and ethnic identity for a group that was in the process of rapid assimilation.[2] These arguments were accompanied by the realization that the creation of separate French schools would also create further teaching, administrative, and support positions, which would further the creation of a unified Francophone community with a stronger voice in the future governance of their school, community, and political destiny.

However, across Alberta the emergence of the Francophone school movement was perceived very differently by various segments of both the Francophone and Anglophone communities. Some Francophone and Anglophone parents of immersion students, who perceived themselves to be progressive in their promotion of immersion programs and their potential to produce bilingual and bicultural children, were surprised that other Francophone parents would want to segregate their children from the mainstream of the population promoting bilingualism and to limit their children's educational exposure to teachers from the Francophone community. These Anglophone and Francophone parents did not perceive that this was in the best interests of the minority children since the view contravened the enrichment principle of a bilingual and bicultural education, which espouses exposure to schooling in both languages and cultures. The most extreme sceptics of both the Francophone and Anglophone parents saw the creation of Francophone schools as being at the expense of the minority children who were segregated from a more enriched education in the larger community. They found this reminiscent of the American case of *Brown v. the Board of Education of Topeka*, which argued that blacks had been segregated in black schools.

It must be remembered, however, that enrolment in Francophone schools is entirely voluntary, and establishing the rights to such schools does not place a responsibility on parents to enrol their children in them. Indeed, most Francophone parents in Alberta and elsewhere in Canada have not enrolled their children in Francophone schools because, among other things, they believe there is insufficient English usage in these schools. Moreover, some unilingual Francophones from French-speaking countries enrol their children in regular English programs as soon as practical because they are not impressed by the quality of French spoken in western Canada, and they believe that speaking a good quality of French at home and having English immersion at school represents the quickest way to assure a high quality of bilingualism. Just as some Francophone Canadians argued that their children were used as role models and therefore were unchallenged in immersion programs for Anglophones, so these unilingual Francophones from France argue that their children are not challenged by the quality of French that is spoken in some Canadian Francophone schools. In short, they argue, as do the Francophone parents of Francophone children in immersion programs, that their children are used only as models for the other Francophone students in Francophone schools and that their fluent unilingual French children would learn more by improving their English in regular English schools. This logic can, of course, lead to an infinite regress but is given recognition and respectability in the minority legislation of the Charter of Rights under sections 23 and 15.

At the other end of the continuum, some parents and educators held the view that Francophone schools were a necessity not only from the point of view of providing specialized education for students with a unique language background but because such schools provided an ethnic focus for a community that would otherwise be further divided and thus rapidly assimilated.[3] Moreover, proponents of this view also proposed that, because of the overpowering influence of the Anglophone socio-economic and cultural environment, French is the language that needs to be maximally promoted in the school for minority Francophones if the language is to be maintained and the culture developed.[4]

Other Francophone and Anglophone immersion parents felt that the Francophone parents who wished to withdraw their children from the immersion programs represented a partial defeat of the natural goal of immersion programs, namely, the promotion of co-operation and tolerance between Anglophone and Francophone populations. Anglophone parents who had sent their children to immersion programs so that their children might have more understanding of and appreciation of Francophone culture were somewhat dismayed by the insistence of some of the Francophone parents that permitting their children to be schooled with Anglophones would diminish the French cultural ambience present in the school. It is important to realize, however, that both the Francophone and Anglophone communities remain divided on these issues. This is best illustrated by the results of a recent survey commissioned by the Association canadienne française de l'Alberta,[5] which showed that the majority of the Francophone population would prefer to send their children to the immersion programs because they felt, as do most Anglophones, that in a predominantly Anglophone (96%) province it is more important to ensure English language skills than French language skills for economic survival. For many Francophone parents, their lack of English-language skills had been a fundamental obstacle to their attainment of better education and employment, and they were resistant to placing their children in the position of disadvantage that they had fought so hard to escape. Furthermore, although federal initiatives to stimulate provincial governments to promote bilingualism have been successful in job creation for Francophones, these positions have been primarily in the government and education-related fields, which has led to a culture of professional Francophones as is attested to by the fact that the single initiative that has created the most employment for Francophones outside of Quebec remains the immersion school movement. Consequently, these efforts have not been sufficient to reverse the rapid assimilation rates of Francophones outside Quebec or to change many Francophones' attitudes towards the importance of French language maintenance. Nevertheless, for some Francophones, and "nouveaux Francophones" who saw it as a political vehicle to power, the promotion of the Francophone school was the *cause célèbre* and served as a much needed rallying call to unite the Francophones in a common purpose of action against the very real threat of further assimilation.[6]

Thus, within the Francophone community, as in the Anglophone community, there is a variety of perceptions and interpretations of the Francophone school concept and the motivations for enrolling children in French-instructed programs. Some Francophones, because of the direct career and economic advantages they enjoy as a result of their language, have a common perception or career directive to promote the advantages of the Francophone school whereas other Francophones outside Quebec perceive English to be the language of primary importance for their children's education in preparing them ultimately to be able to compete with the larger population. These Francophone parents, like Anglophone parents, willingly promote the acquisition of bilingualism but will not accept a loss in English language skills to attain this goal. Because of the lack of consensus among Francophones, an initial challenge for the Francophone schools is to maintain an adequate number of students that will create a critical mass for the school to function without depriving students of the normal social environment.

This issue of a critical mass of students functionally supercedes that of reducing the legal phrase "where numbers warrant" to one, since the social aspects of schooling are critical to the normal development of the child.

The second challenge is to find an appropriate language maintenance model that will promote a high quality of French usage in the school. Whereas French may be acquired concurrently with English by pre-school Francophone children outside Quebec, there are instances in which neither language is acquired in a complete form but rather a mixture of the two is acquired.[7] The children who may have been exposed to diverse language models present an additional challenge since such students require special education programs in order to develop normal reading and writing proficiency. The finding that a substantial proportion of Francophone elementary students experience reading and writing difficulties[8] is highly predictable if one considers the fact that some of these children may not have mastered French as their first language to the same degree that Anglophone children have mastered English as their first language at the time of school entry due to the inevitable predominance of English in the environment and the consequent highly anglicized usage of French. Moreover, since a proportion of the Francophone population has not perceived French as more than an oral tradition for the last decade or more, there is not a community-wide commitment to de-anglicize the spoken language. Indeed, some Francophones tout their non-standard usage as one of their unique characteristics that should be promoted. Therefore the Francophone school is faced with an added challenge since the usage of French in the home and environment is not always comparable in quality to the standardized usage in their texts or the standardization of English models that Anglophones are exposed to, and this has implications for the teaching of reading of standard French or English.

It is important to emphasize that the relative success of French immersion programs for Anglophones has often been attributed to the fact that Anglophone students have a rather complete mastery of their first language, which acts to develop their social and linguistic identity before being immersed in a majority second language. Furthermore, the mastery of English is a prerequisite to immersion in the second language and the success of immersion programs is attributable in part to the fact that English skills are well developed prior to school entry and continue to be well modelled outside the school by the peer groups in the playground, by teachers in the English language arts programs in the school, and in the home by adult and media models. For minority Francophone children, it is not always obvious that the first or dominant language is French. Furthermore, substantial consideration must be given to the adequacy of the individual's history of the language models in the home, schoolground, and environment due to the limited access that many Francophones have to a socio-linguistically rich usage of the language and the relatively low ethno-linguistic vitality of some Francophone families and communites.

Because of the heterogeneity of the linguistic experiences of Francophones outside Quebec and the fact that section 23 of the Charter of Rights predicates the admissability of children on their parents' childhood language experiences rather than on the child who is entering the program—thus theoretically denying access to fluent French-speaking children while admitting other children who speak little or no standard French—the Francophone schools may not be superior to immersion schools for some section 23 Francophone children[9] in some Anglophone-dominant settings. Minority language children of parents who represent good models of language usage of French as their first or second language and who value the language and are employed in government or education-related positions where it is possible to maintain the language, should show more rapid language gains than these same students would in immersion programs. This may not be the case for some mixed-language children due to their lack of exposure to appropriate language models in the home and their selection of poor language models for their social peers outside of the school. In such cases, although these children would legally qualify as admissable to Francophone schools, French is neither their dominant nor first language, and they may progress in both French and English more rapidly in an immersion setting due to their need to master English (their first and/or dominant language) more completely prior to second-language acquisition. Alternately stated, those students who come from socio-linguistic backgrounds where the English and French language models represent an amalgam may benefit more from a schooling experience that provides a clear distinction between two quality models of language usage. In such cases, either extensive early language acquisition must be considered in the Francophone school, such that there are separate Grade 1 classes for English- or French-dominant Francophones (reminiscent of the mixed Francophone-Anglophone program prior to the creation of Francophone schools), or alternate schooling should be considered.

In placing students in Francophone or immersion programs it must be stressed that immersion programs provide greater socio-linguistic richness of French usage than do core programs or bilingual programs, but French remains a school- or class-based language that is not extensively used outside the classroom and thus these children may be exposed to appropriate language modelling and usage compatible with the standardized materials through which they will learn to read. Therefore, for Anglophone immersion students, French remains primarily a school-based language.

Francophone schools, however, provide the potential for making French the authentic *lingua franca* by integrating the minority school with the minority enclave.[10] Indeed, the minority school has the potential to revitalize the minority enclave and reverse the progress of assimilation. However, this is a delicate balance and is predicated on the assumption that the quality of the minority language usage in the enclave is not eroded[11] to such a degree that it actually operates against the French that is being taught in the school. This situation is common in French enclaves throughout Canada and around the world. In some instances where the minority enclave is particularly small or lacking ethnolinguistic vitality and the language is excessively anglicized, creolized, or pidginized in the community, some role models may have to be imported from outside the community. This is the case in pidginized or creolized situations in the Seychelles, in French Africa or in certain areas of Louisiana or for any other of the 5 000 minority language situations. Moreover, because there is a substantial heterogeneity in the French spoken by Francophones in French schools outside Quebec,[12] the challenge of developing a methodology for providing instruction through French as a first language remains.[13]

A third challenge to the future growth of Francophone schools outside Quebec would include several rather dynamic socio-political and economic variables. The first of these variables is the committment to Francophone schools by the Francophone populations themselves. Many Francophone parents outside Quebec prefer to send their children to regular English-speaking schools while others prefer to send their children to immersion programs due to their priority of ensuring that their children will be proficient in English, which is, in their view, more useful in the career world. Secondly, many Francophone parents feel that Francophone schools promote ethnocentrism and are too narrow culturally and linguistically. Such parents feel that the Francophone schools will ultimately lead to a narrow education and world view, an argument that is frequently associated with other ethnic minority schools. Other parents are concerned with the relatively small number of Francophone schools and the problems in transferring their children should they have to move to other locales, an argument that was also associated with immersion schools in the past. Finally, some Francophone communities see the Francophone school as a means for the English majority to segregate Francophones from the mainstream of society by denying them sufficient education in English. Other Francophones argue the converse, saying that they want Francophone schools so that they will not witness the assimilation of their children to the linguistic majority by sending them to either regular English or immersion programs.[14] At present, the variety of aspirations among Francophones makes it difficult to estimate the future development of Francophone schools. The complexity of the situation is compounded by other Francophone groups who require traditional Catholic or public schools as well as those who prefer academic Francophone programs and schools as opposed to other general programs with special education alternatives.

Clearly, it appears that Francophone parents, like Anglophones, make educational choices that are often dictated by instrumental and practical motivations that seem best explained by their beliefs as to what situation will provide their children with financial, career, and social security rather than a high degree of academic, intellectual, or cultural mastery. Moreover, this concern with employability will increasingly affect student and parent decisions in the next decade due to high unemployment, necessary government deficit financing and the consequent cutbacks correlated with a return to the basics in education as well as an unavoidable emphasis on high technology at the post-secondary level. Thus, once again the social, economic, and political climate will play an important role in the viability of Francophone schools as it has in the past.

NOTES

1. E. Beniak, S.T. Carey, and R. Mougeon, "A Sociolinguistic and Ethnographic Approach to Albertan French and its Implications for French-as-a-First-Language Pedagogy," *Revue canadien des langues vivantes* 41, 2 (1984): 308–14.
2. Peter Li and Wilfrid B. Denis, "Minority Enclave and Majority Language: The Case of a French Town in Western Canada," *Canadian Ethnic Studies* XV, 1 (1983).
3. Ibid.
4. Beniak et al., "A Sociolinguistic and Ethnographic Approach to Albertan French"; S.T. Carey and J. Cummins, "Achievement, Behavioral Correlates and Teachers' Perceptions of Francophone and Anglophone Immersion Students," *Alberta Journal of Educational Research* 29 (1983): 159–67, and "Communication Skills in Immersion Programs," *Alberta Journal of Educational Research* 30 (1984): 270–83.
5. P. Perreault, in Report of the Association Canadienne des Franco-Albertans, 1982.
6. S.T. Carey, "Trends in Enrolment and Needs for French-Instructed Programs at the Post-Secondary Level," *Canadian Modern Language Review* 41, 5 (1985), 877–86.
7. Beniak et al., "A Sociolinguistic and Ethnographic Approach to Albertan French"; Li and Denis, "Minority Enclave and Majority Language."
8. Carey, Turcotte, and Bissonette, in *Proceedings* from the 1985 Conference of the Canadian Association of Immersion Teachers, Edmonton, 8–10 Nov. 1985.
9. Carey and Cummins, "Achievement, Behavioral Correlates and Teachers' Perceptions of Francophone and Anglophone Immersion Students."
10. Li and Denis, "Minority Enclave and Majority Language."
11. Beniak et al., "A Sociolinguistic and Ethnographic Approach to Albertan French."
12. R. Mougeon, M. Heller, E. Beniak, and M. Canale, "Acquisition et enseignement du français en situation minoritaire: le cas des Franco-ontariens," *Canadian Modern Language Review* 41, 2 (1984): 315–35.
13. Beniak et al., "A Sociolinguistic and Ethnographic Approach to Albertan French."
14. O. Silla, *Les écoles unilangues ou bilangues pour les franco-albertains* (University of Alberta, 1976).

ISSUES IN SECOND-LANGUAGE EDUCATION IN CANADA

BRUCE BAIN AND AGNES YU

Language, in one form or another, is at the centre of many of the historic and economic tensions in Canada. In recent years, these tensions have increased as Canadians refuse to accept language-based social, economic, and educational discrimination. Issues of language and language instruction have thus become particularly significant in the Canadian educational field.

If individuals are to be protected against discrimination, and if, under the Charter of Rights and Freedoms, educational and economic opportunity cannot be denied on the basis of language, it matters very much how language is defined. If we conceive of participation in a speech community as consisting of more than a knowledge of grammar, as consisting as well of knowledge of appropriate use, and if we understand how misuse of speech codes can hinder individuals from full participation in social, economic, and educational life, then the social and cultural issues that have been of concern to ethnic minorities would be brought within the scope of the Charter.

The current appreciation in Canada of the tension between the individual, language, and social relations, which is central to analysis of English/French bilingualism, is not as pronounced in the study of ethnic second-language learning.[1] Classes in English/French-as-a-second-language often amount to narrow linguistics-inspired drills in one of the official languages, with little concern for the state of the mother tongue of a student and her or his particular psychosocial circumstances or ethnocultural consciousness. What is necessary is consistency in the research and delivery of language programs for all groups and individuals in Canada.

This paper attempts to formulate a model for such language programs. To that end, we begin by examining changes in immigration patterns and the conflict between ethnocultural pluralism and assimilation. We then discuss language programs in other countries and suggest why traditional models of language education do not fulfil current needs. Finally, we present a model of language education in keeping with Canada's national and international goals.

TRENDS IN IMMIGRATION

Over the past decade or so, the world has seen a new era of immigration. The sheer volume of peoples of differing languages and customs who are coming into direct contact with each other is unlike any seen in history. In the past, stages of hectic immigration to Canada tended to be interspersed by periods of relative calm that allowed for a measured pace of acculturation. Following the cataclysm of the Second World War and the economic realignment of the 1950s and 1960s, immigration has taken on a whole new face. The movement back and forth between and within countries in search of a better life has become standard practice since the mid-1970s. UNESCO demographers[2] estimate that, by the year 2000, six out of every ten people will either have moved from one country to another or from one region to another of the same country and, in many cases, will be using or studying in a language other than their mother tongue.

The new immigrants tend to be far less passive than their predecessors. They are less timid about insisting on their linguistic, cultural, and individual rights in their new homelands. Cries for "multiculturalism" are being heard virtually around the globe. It should be made clear that we are not witnessing a new breed of individual. What we have is a new historical epoch in which individual rights are more a concern than in bygone days. The Canadian Charter did not create the concern; rather, the Charter is a reaction to contemporary world-wide trends.

Inevitably, there have been backlashes against the new "pushy" immigrant. Competition in the marketplace, in education, in housing, and in social services has sometimes resulted in a "foreigners-in-our-midst" reaction. Western European countries, with little experience in taking in immigrants, have been particularly prone to this type of hyper-sensitivity to "the other." The recent riots in England and Holland, and Japan's protracted anguishing over allowing non-Japanese to become citizens, can, at least in part, be seen as a consequence of that type of reaction.

A striking feature of this new era of immigration is that formerly homogeneous societies are becoming pluralistic. Consciousness of the inherent value of ethnocultural pluralism by members of the host communities, and, ironically, in some cases by members of the ethnocultural groups themselves, will likely determine whether the evolution to pluralism will be rough or smooth. Nonetheless the thrust toward social and educational pluralism seems inevitable and, in our judgment, altogether healthy for life in the contemporary world.

PLURALISM AND ASSIMILATION

In established pluralistic societies, different social and ethnic groups often live side by side, but separated, within the same community. In such communities, true pluralism is possible only if no group tries to be dominant in all spheres. If the dominance of one group in all or almost all spheres is complete, the other groups are put into what is referred to as the "forced status" of a minority. History shows us that forced status creates inevitable pressures for assimilation. Social and educational planners trained in the old school have not always understood that, in the modern era, the well-documented negative consequences of assimilation are frequently the result of having one's identity defined by others; that is, of being the victim of the dominant group's cultural hegemony. Today, minorities in virtually all parts of the world are resisting forced assimilation by seeking counter-hegemonic means and insisting on an acceptance of their own definitions of themselves. Researchers are also beginning to find empirically what minority parents have long known intuitively—that forced or no-choice assimilation is the source of many of the educational and social problems of their children.[3]

To be sure, forced assimilation does not necessarily reflect government policy. Although it would be difficult to argue sensibly that domination of certain minorities was not on the agenda of certain governments, the more charitable view is that there simply tends to be a naive assumption by some policy makers that minority groups need to be "like us" in order to get ahead. The idea that minorities could be "like us" in some spheres and "as they wish" in others seems to have been understood only with regard to token issues (such as a Heritage Day) and not substantive issues (such as being equal partners in education and economic development).

In 1970, Americans Daniel Moynihan and Nathan Glazer published a compelling book, *Beyond the Melting Pot*,[4] in which they put forward a cogent argument about how the U.S. melting pot ideology has in fact been an "un-melting pot," with assimilation being more apparent than real. They also put forward a conflict theory with respect to whether majority and minority groups agree or disagree about the goals each group has for the other. Although there is a danger in seeing too many parallels between Canadian and American social history (e.g., attempting to understand multiple inter-group relations in the Canadian French/English ethnic mosaic in terms of the mainstream-majority American model), Moynihan and Glazer offer a distinction that has a certain merit in the Canadian context. They suggest that when social and educational planners deal with the problem of assimilation, it is useful to make a distinction between cultural assimilation and economic-structural assimilation. These heuristic guides are understood in the literal sense of becoming like the majority linguistically and attitudinally, and becoming equal participants in the economic-structural life of the community. Moynihan and Glazer also put forward an interesting, if somewhat static, model of the various types of agreements/disagreements that could occur between majority and minority goals. The utility of their critical distinction is apparent in a number of cases.

THE CALIFORNIA/MEXICO EXAMPLE

According to the traditional U.S. melting-pot ideology, minorities should adopt the American way of life in order to become good Americans. Simultaneously, the American ideal suggests that everyone should be given equal educational and occupational opportunities. The opinion of the majority, so the myth goes, is that there should be both cultural and economic-structural assimilation. Moynihan and Glazer point out that, in reality, the opinion of some minorities is radically different. In their own comprehensive study, they found that the Hispanic population of the Southwestern U.S., for example, wants economic-structural assimilation, but cultural-educational pluralism. The battle for this particular type of pluralism has been given impetus by the rise in the number of legal and illegal immigrants from Mexico, by the advent of an educated class of Hispanic-Americans, and by the recognition of the economic and political power of the Hispanic community. Moynihan and Glazer unfortunately neglected what, in our judgment, is probably the most significant set of influences, namely, initial collaboration with some sensitized members of the majority community, and continued co-operation in good faith by all concerned.

For years, the state governments, which control education in the U.S., have been resisting anything but English language education, but attitudes and educational policies are beginning to change. The bilingual Spanish/English programs, and the English-as-an-alternate language programs that have been introduced to meet the new social situation seem, in our judgment, poor in quality. With but few noteworthy exceptions, where individuals or boards are more informed about modern developments in this area, those programs still tend to be old-fashioned grammar exercises. In the broader scheme of things, it could be argued that their existence is probably a necessary first step. More importantly, however, there are signs that the American majority is coming to accept the idea that someone can speak Spanish and English and still be "one of us."

Events in Southern California are a good indication of this attitudinal change. After many years of false starts, a teacher exchange program has been instituted with school districts in northwest Mexico. The thrust of this program is that Spanish-speaking classroom teachers from Mexico would be exchanged with English-speaking teachers from southern California. The exchanges are for short terms, mostly semesters, with local arrangements made for specific concerns like housing, social, and medical services. This exchange program, however modest, also has the advantage for the American teachers, who are mostly Spanish-language teachers, of upgrading their language skills while in Mexico. A reciprocal advantage accrues to the Mexican teachers.

It would be misleading to suggest that all segments of the American majority are in favour of this type of program, or that the pressure for cultural assimilation of the Hispanics has stopped. It obviously has not. It is also difficult to predict the long-term ramifications of Reaganomics and related neanderthal policies on education and social services. These policies notwithstanding, the historical forces re-defining what is American will be hard to stop. Consciousness of the social value of ethnocultural pluralism is of itself a powerful motive force. The momentum is such that citizens in this part of the world are cautiously but assuredly working toward a genuinely pluralistic society.

THE FINLAND/SWEDEN EXAMPLE

The constitution of Finland guarantees the Swedish-speaking minority (6.6 percent in 1979) the right to satisfy its language and educational needs on the same principles as the Finnish-speaking majority. Moreover, to continue with Moynihan's and Glazer's distinction, the majority and minority in Finland seem to be in agreement about cultural pluralism for Swedes and Finns. In Finland, for example, Swedish and Finnish children can be taught in their respective languages from kindergarten to university.[5]

There is, at the same time, considerable dispute about economic assimilation of the variety well known in Canada. Like many Anglophones in Quebec before the Quiet Revolution, the Swedes in Finland are overwhelmingly middle class. They have also long controlled the industrial sector in Finland. And, like the Québécois quest to be *maîtres chez nous*, the conflict in Finland concerns how to bring about a genuine economic assimilation of the Finns themselves! How the resolution of this conflict will affect the agreement on cultural independence remains to be seen. Contemporary Quebec, without some of the heavy-handedness of Bill 101, could serve as a good role model in this valid desire for economic assimiliation.

In Sweden the situation is quite different. There is no apparent majority/minority consensus on how the Finnish (17 percent in 1979) minority should be treated. The reason for this, we suspect, is that these ethnic Finns are overwhelmingly working class. They have long constituted an alienated, cheap labour pool for Swedish industry. Officially, the Swedish school curriculum states that the Finns should be provided with education in Finnish corresponding to the education of Swedish children. In practice, however, rather drastic forced assimilation measures were pursued for a good part of this century. For example, in a scene reminiscent of Native education in Canada, up to the mid-1950s, Finnish children were, in some cases, punished for speaking Finnish in a Swedish classroom, even when they were the majority in a school; and, despite the official curriculum, classes were taught entirely in Swedish.[6]

In the late 1950s, the curriculum was significantly modified to teach the Finnish children in Finnish, with Swedish-as-a-second-language as part of the daily activities. Unfortunately, these second-language program were too often modeled after the English-as-a-second-language program used in Canada and elsewhere at that time. The essentially negative outcome of the linguistics-based programs then in vogue become apparent to social scientists and school authorities only after a generation or two.[7] Unfortunately, what happened is virtually the opposite of the Finland experience; that is, within a very short period the ethnic Finns in Sweden ended up knowing both Finnish and Swedish in an equally dysfunctional way.[8] The educational experience of the Finns in Sweden gave rise to the phrase *halve sprach*, or semilingualism, which is now common coin. Lambert's phrase "psycholinguistic limbo"[9] perhaps more aptly captures the nature of this often terrible intellectual and emotional predicament. We will return to this predicament shortly.

After considerable research, coupled with vocal activism by local and international social scientists, ethnic Finns and concerned Swedes, ethnic Finnish children are today, officially, and in most cases in practice, being taught in Finnish *before* being introduced to Swedish as a language of instruction. It has come to be appreciated that, in bilingual situations where cultural hegemony has prevailed, and where there is a severe dysfunction in both languages, education programs should facilitate a reasonable mastery of the mother tongue as an affective and intellectual first step toward other school goals.

By "reasonable mastery" is not meant poetic lucidity. The research suggests that the pupil has to become critically aware that the same language being used to speak with is also being used as a tool to aid in the thinking and feeling processes. As opposed to the traditional approach of trying to use a poorly developed tool to try and diagnose the intricate metastructure of yet another language, a difficult task with the best of equipment, the more practical approach is to polish up the basic tool (the mother tongue) by using it in progressively more complex social-communicative *and* academic-intellectual situations so that the pupil can then generalize the acquired critical competencies to include mastery of another language.[10] In the broader scheme of things, reminiscent of the Hispanic situation in southern California, there remains a tangle of educational and political issues that might mitigate against short-term success for the ethnic Finns in Sweden. It is another sign, however, that minorities in other parts of the world, in collaboration with sensitized members of the majority, are struggling toward a more equitable form of economic assimilation with ethnocultural pluralism.

In this new era of pluralistic consciousness, certain ethnocultural groups may wish to follow the path of their predecessors and assimilate into the mainstream society. But, in general, the trend is becoming one of resistance to automatic, one-way assimilation. Mutual accommodation is the new advocacy. Moreover, ethnocultural groups are also insisting on the institutional privileges of the mainstream society, that is, economic-structural assimilation is not being sought at the expense of cultural-linguistic pluralism. The old trade-off of self-worth for a piece of the economic pie is seen as an unnecessary compromise. In pursuit of the new social contract, however, at least two points seem clear. First, if minorities are to attain some acceptable form of cultural and linguistic pluralism, and at the same time attain economic-structural assimilation, research suggests that they must be able to master both their mother tongue *and* the language of the majority community. Second, if these seemingly contradictory goals are to be achieved, it will not be by seeing them exclusively as "ethnic or minority goals."

BILINGUALISM

In the Canadian context, the idea that ethnocultural or minority groups might want a type of language education suited to their needs, one that might even be as good as that provided for the middle-class segment of the majority, leads to the topic of bilingualism.

Defining bilingualism is not a simple task. Most definitions can be divided into those that emphasize linguistic structural concerns (i.e., how well a person knows the linguistic features of language) and those that emphasize communicative competency concerns (i.e., how well a person can use the languages in various psychosocial and educational situations). The former is what is too often taught and tested in schools to the exclusion of the latter. It is not uncommon to find students who have taken a second language throughout their school years, who can perform well on a test of word definitions or other linguistic features of a language, but cannot speak the language in social situations or use that language to perform ordinary educational tasks. Some experts claim that such a student should be considered bilingual. Other experts have their reservations. Still others insist that we are justified in calling a person bilingual if she or he possesses, even to a minimal degree, a capability either in speaking, reading, listening, or writing in a second language. This would mean, in effect, that if a person learns a few words of a second language from radio or television, she or he could be classified as bilingual.

Concerned minority parents (e.g., Francophones in the western provinces), often speak to their toddlers in the heritage language with the hope that their children will grow up speaking the parents' mother tongue. They often find, however, that by preschool age the *lingua communis* (the predominant community language, in this case English) has become so dominant that it is but a sentimental fiction to consider the language first spoken as the "mother tongue." In this case the designation of someone as "French" is more a statement of identity than language facility. These preschoolers characteristically understand something of the parents' tongue. But, over time, they increasingly initiate conversations in the progressively more dominant language. This passive form of usage has legitimate status under the rubric of bilingualism. But definitions are elusive. For example, on the basis of otherwise valid theoretical constructs, some researchers in the field of diglossic studies seriously argue that a person who masters different stylistic or dialectical variations is also bilingual. This would suggest that everyone is bilingual or multilingual because we all alter our speech codes to suit the demands of specific contexts.

Another distinction that should be made is between "natural" and "school" bilingualism. Natural bilingualism is acquired in the home or neighbourhood, without formal tutoring, and is often acquired before school age. School bilingualism is largely a product of formal tutoring. One of the many myths found among educators is that certain ethnic children are, to some extent, natural bilinguals when they start school. It is assumed that they have learned their heritage language at home and something of the majority language either at home or in the community in which they live, and, therefore, are functionally bilingual. Pedagogical practice is often built on this assumption without finding out whether or not it holds true.

In China, for example, which has a most ambitious second language program, the elementary curriculum is predicated upon the assumption that the pupils are natural bilinguals. The Chinese school authorities had originally hoped that, by the time the pupils had completed elementary school, they would have mastery of both their regional dialect (Cantonese, Shanghainese, etc.) and their *lingua communis* (Poutonghua). They are now finding, after some three and a half years of the bilingual program, that the assumption of natural bilingualism is misleading. As with many linguistics-based models, the diagnosis of natural bilingualism mistakes the ability to utter a few words and phrases for the ability to productively use the language to achieve social and psychological ends. A redesigned curriculum, along the "contextual use" reasoning, is expected to redress some of these concerns.

In other parts of the world, the picture is much the same. For some minority children, particularly those who live in tightly knit communities and who are further isolated from the mainstream because of race or religion, the reality of natural bilingualism is even more problematic. These youngsters tend to speak their mother tongue at home and with their playmates. Even if the community in which these children live is, at the adult level, bilingual, it is usually the case that the two languages are used for different purposes. Typically the mother tongue is used in the family, among peers, friends, relatives, and in the immediate neighborhood. Because children under school age are not involved in the broader community in which the *lingua communis* is used, they usually have little opportunity to learn it in any generalizeable way. Even if the children have older siblings who more or less know the *lingua communis*, the older siblings typically revert to the mother tongue when they communicate with their younger brothers and sisters. Even if some of these ethnic children have learned something of the *lingua communis*, their linguistic skill is often misconstrued because it is usually assessed on the architecture of a language and not on language as it is lived and used.

Many minority children are simply not naturally bilingual. They may be able to utter and understand a few words or phrases in the *lingua communis* or, conversely, as the *lingua communis* becomes dominant, they may become able to recognize certain parts of their slowly retreating "mother tongue." But, in either case, they are bilingual only in a linguistic sense, not in a practical (psychological use) or communicative (social use) sense. The facade of bilingual competency quickly drops away when faced with ordinary educational, personal, or social situations. The acritical acceptance of skill in phonetics to the neglect of the real thinking and communicating purposes to which a person puts a language has left many a teacher, parent, and pupil wondering about the effectiveness of second-language programs.

It seems obvious from all this that the chronically uneven research findings on bilingual education for minority and majority children stem, in part, from researchers not taking sufficient care to identify the type of bilingualism they are assessing. Another part has to do with the fragmented nature of research into bilingualism. A definitive history of the policy flips and flops in this area—which in the past has tended to parallel public mood and political convenience—remains to be written. When it is, one theme is likely to stand out, namely, that a good deal of the traditionally conceived research lacks generalizability beyond the axioms of narrowly conceived disciplines. Fortunately, there are indications that the research community is seeking more holistic theories and methods.[11]

TOWARD A CANADIAN MODEL OF LANGUAGE EDUCATION

There is no escaping the fact that minority children need a complete mastery of their mother tongue *and* the *lingua communis* if the goals of cultural pluralism *and* economic-structural integration are to be genuinely achieved. The challenge is to find productive ways of achieving these goals.

When pedagogical practices are being planned, attention should be given to another set of important (we suspect the most important) variables: many minority children come from working-class families (and even if they do not, teachers often believe they do), and their heritage languages are often of low prestige in their respective communities. These social class and language prestige issues are integral to the delivery of appropriate educational services.

There is no single solution to this problem, or, at least none that is acceptable to the entire Canadian nation. Each school district will have to find its own solution in terms of its own context. Be assured, however, that wherever the curriculum has reflected these goals and concerns, the results usually have been reassuring.[12] For example, in addition to honing their reflective skills, official concern for teaching in the heritage language often results in the children developing a healthier self-image, and more positive feelings towards their families and their own language. A positive self-image, as has long been known, is a good predictor of academic success in all fields, including second-language learning.

The difficulties of these minority children are partly the same as those of the children in the lower socio-economic classes in general. The difficulties are compounded in various subtle and obvious ways when these children speak different languages whose specialized codes are geared to a different system of social relations.

The idea of ethnic pride and opportunity to master the heritage language and the *lingua communis* in the early years of school is positive but, before it can be fulfilled, the problems of tradition, of vested interests, of economic assimilation and cultural pluralism, will all have to be wrestled to the ground. At the same time, it will have to be recognized that one reason for the failure to achieve these goals in the past has been that curriculum planners have been using a dysfunctional method of second-language instruction for working-class ethnics and other minorities. They sometimes have been indiscriminatly using the elite or middle-class bilingual model—the much heralded immersion model.

It has long been known that it is possible for middle-class children, who have a positive self-image and adequate mother-tongue mastery, to become bilingual by having their formal instruction through the medium of a second language. There are a few rough spots at the start of these programs but, by and large, after four or five years of this type of immersion experience, middle-class children typically have developed fairly equal linguistic and communicative competencies.[13]

Unfortunately, a pseudo-version of this elite model is sometimes indiscriminately used for some minorities in various school districts. Pupils are placed in what resembles an immersion program. The goal here, however, is not to add another language while facilitating the development of the mother tongue. The goal is to try and add another language while providing sympathy and little else that is productive for the development of the mother tongue.

The problem with these pseudo-immersion programs for certain minority children is that a second language usually can be acquired by most children if they have a positive self-image and adequate mother-tongue development. The correlation between positive self-image and mother-tongue competency, on the one hand, and second-language acquisition skill on the other is well documented.[14] These dual needs have scant chance of being met by many minority children who are simply intellectually and emotionally submerged by the pseudo-elite model. Finding ways of assessing and placing these pupils in programs suitable for their individual needs is a major challenge. Coupled with this is the need for second language teachers in general to be trained in substantive matters. Teacher-training programs that stress a broad exposure to the relationships between individual development, language processes, social context, and education are sorely needed in Canada.

A whole new way of thinking about education in pluralistic communities is necessary. On the one hand, because a heritage language and its related way of life are often of low prestige, ethnic children can develop a poor self-image. Moreover, when ethnic children are from a lower socio-economic background, there may be limited language and literary resources in the home. Such children not infrequently arrive in school with a poorly developed facility in their mother tongue compounded by a negative self-image. Research evidence indicates that a child who has a poorly developed mother tongue and a poor self-image has decided difficulties in learning a second language or most things deemed academically useful.[15]

Although the parameters of this problem are poorly understood, there is a circular negative relationship that can occur: children can become "semilingual." Instead of mastering two languages, these children master neither. They become unable to master the *lingua communis* because the means being used to master it (i.e., the mother tongue) is itself poorly mastered, and these children find themselves in a psycholinguistic limbo.

Without consideration for their particular pedagogical needs, the psychosocial prognosis for a number of minority children is predictably gloomy. Instead of being victimized by pseudo-immersion models, many minority children need a different pedagogical model, one that allows them to develop normal fluency in their mother tongue by initially being taught in it. This practice would also go some way toward improving the perceived value of the minorities' mother tongue in their own eyes, which, in turn, can have a positive effect on their self-image. This practice tends to decrease home and school tensions by ensuring that these children can adequately communicate with their parents and with their teachers. The working language of the community can initially be introduced as subject matter rather than as the language of instruction. Over a number of grades or years, the amount of time allocated to subject matter being taught in the *lingua communis* would gradually be increased. In the early years, the amount of classroom time allocated to schooling in the heritage language would predominate, with the *lingua communis* being used as a medium of instruction for a period or so during the day; then, as the individual child progresses, she or he would be introduced to more and more curriculum topics in the *lingua communis*, with the heritage language eventually becoming the language of instruction for a topic or so.

We are not insensitive to the curriculum, materials, personnel, and assessment problems that such procedures create. But these difficulties seem a small price to pay to resolve the larger problems. We feel confident, on the basis of the studies that have been reported here and pilot projects going on elsewhere,[16] that this model of language education will bring many benefits to the home, the school, the society, and particularly to the individual.

NOTES

1. A word on this idiosyncratic use of the terms *second language* and *bilingual* in Canadian educational circles. We tend to use second language in contexts such as core French/English or English/French-as-a-second-language (ESL/FSL). The term bilingual is usually used to refer to full or partial immersion programs in French/English. If the immersion program is in other than the two official languages, we tend to refer to it as a *heritage* or *ethnic language* program. What is not always recognized is that each of these terms tends to carry certain agendas concerning goals and teaching practices and the social backgrounds of students.

2. Personal communication, Henri Barre, UNESCO, Paris.

3. P. Perrenoud, "Compensatory Education and Perpetuation of Social Classes. Outline of a Political Sociology for the Democratization of Education," Documentation Centre for Education in Europe, *Council of Europe Information Bulletin* 1 (1974): 66–76; L. Ekstrand and M. Finnocchiaro, "Migration Today: Some Social and Educational Problems" in *Viewpoints on English as a Second Language*, edited by M. Burt (New York: Regents, 1977); B. Bain, *Edmonton Public Schools, E.S.L. Needs Assessment* (Edmonton: EPS, 1981).

4. D. Moynihan and N. Glazer, *Beyond the Melting Pot* (Cambridge: MIT Press, 1970).

5. Bilingualism and multilingualism often prevail in these situations. Conducive language policies, public support, family expectations, and a curriculum based on the *use* of the target language in various educational and social contexts are the recognized ingredients of this trend. *Use of*, as opposed to *teaching about*, is stressed because of the effectiveness of this strategy.

6. T. Erasmine, *Language Development and Social Influence* (Kbenhaven: SUB, 1976).

7. T. Skutnabb-Kangas and P. Toukomaa, *Teaching Migrant Children's Mother Tongue and Learning the Language of the Host Country in the Context of the Socio-Cultural Situation of the Migrant Family* (University of Tampere, Finland, 1976); J. Cummins, "Educational Implications of Mother Tongue Maintenance in Minority-Language Groups," *Canadian Modern Language Review* 3 (1978): 395–416; B. Bain and A. Yu, "The Development of the Body Percept Among Working- and Middle-Class Bilinguals" in *Neurolinguistics*, vol. 12, edited by Y. Lebrun and M. Paradis (Amsterdam: Swets, 1984).

8. P. Toukomaa and T. Skutnabb-Kangas, *The Intensive Teaching of the Mother Tongue to Migrant Children at Pre-School Age* (University of Tampere, Finland, 1977).

9. W. Lambert, "Bilingualism and Language Acquisition," *Annals of the New York Academy of Sciences* (1981): 9–22.

10. Note that we are not describing what is necessary in all minority second-language situations. The concern here is with that type of pupil whose family lifestyle has been alienated from its roots, and who, for his or her age, arrives in school with poor mastery of the mother tongue, or is using a pidgin-like amalgam of two or more languages.

11. R. Samuda, J. Berry, and M. Laferrière, eds., *Multiculturalism in Canada* (Toronto: Allyn and Bacon, 1984).

12. Skutnabb-Kangas and Toukomaa, *Teaching Migrant Children's Mother Tongue*; E. Hernandez-Chavez, "Language Maintenance, Bilingual Education, and Philosophies of Bilingualism" in *Language and Linguistics*, edited by H. Giles (Georgestown University, 1978); A. Yu and B. Bain, "Language, Class, and Culture," *New Horizons* 24 (1983): 51–62.

13. We would be remiss if we left the impression that, in the Canadian context, these elite immersion programs are models of quality education and social justice. They are, in fact, hampered by a pair of intertwined and easily predictable problems. On the one hand, by the end of elementary school, the curriculum content and teacher capability is often insufficiently challenging for the children. On the other hand, the elite immersion programs reproduce a more systemic problem: by becoming bilingual in the two official languages, already advantaged classes are ensuring further advantage, fostering new forms of social inequality. Another challenge is to find ways of making suitable second-language programs available to pupils from a broader range of social backgrounds.

14. T. Slama-Cazacu, *Langage et context* (The Hague: Mouton, 1961); R. Titone, "Second-Language Learning: An Integrated Psycholinguistic Model" in *Sociogenesis of Language and Human Conduct*, edited by B. Bain (New York: Plenum, 1983); M. Akoodie, "Identity and Self-Concept in Immigrant Children" in *Multiculturalism in Canada*, edited by Samuda et al,; J. Berryman, "Immigrant Children and the Importance of Self-Esteem in Second Language Learning," *Multiculturalism* 2 (1984): 13–17; Bain and Yu, "Development of the Body Percept."

15. Slama-Cazacu, *Langage et context*; Titone, "Second-Language Learning"; Akoodie, "Identity and Self-Concept"; Berryman, "Immigrant Children and the Importance of Self-Esteem"; Bain and Yu, "Development of the Body Percept."

16. A. Yu, "Unilingualism, Bilingualism, Social Class, and Cognitive Development: A Sociolinguistic Study of Orientals and Westerners" in *Proceedings of the 47th Annual Conference of the Hong Kong Psychology Association*, edited by J. Precker (Hong Kong: UHKP, 1978).

WHAT EVERY TEACHER SHOULD KNOW ABOUT MULTICULTURALISM
NICK KACH AND IVAN DEFAVERI

INTRODUCTION

> I have visited in England one of those models of Gothic architecture which the hand of genius guided by an unerring faith, has moulded into a harmonious whole. This cathedral is made of marble, oak and granite. It is the image of the nation I would see Canada become. For here I want the marble to remain marble, the granite to remain granite, the oak to remain oak and out of all these elements I would build a nation great among the nations of the world.
> Sir Wilfrid Laurier

Though improbable, ethnic revivalists such as the late Senator Paul Yuzyk have seen the genesis of multiculturalism in "Sir Wilfred Laurier's metaphor of Canada-as-a-Gothic-Cathedral."[1] But this radical public policy was really initiated by Lester Pearson in the House of Commons on 17 December 1962. Addressing the House, Pearson announced that, if elected, his government would establish a Royal Commission to examine the issue that appeared central to national unity: Quebec's newly awakened economic, political, and cultural consciousness. The following year, the Royal Commission on Bilingualism and Biculturalism was struck by the Liberal government. Though designed to placate the seething discontent in Quebec, the commission did little to stem Quebec's nationalistic sentiment. "The federal government was prepared to accept bilingualism only at a time when Quebeckers, declaring themselves a majority in their own country, were taking on attitudes and political stances which went far beyond bilingualism. As in every colony, it's a case of too little or too late."[2]

Nor was Quebec's rejection of the commission's report the only negative reaction. While the commission's mandate was to recommend steps to develop confederation on the basis of an equal partnership of two founding races, it was to do so by:

> Taking into account the contribution made by the other ethnic groups to the cultural enrichment of Canada and the measures which should be taken to safeguard that contribution.

> [However] it will be noted immediately that while the terms of reference deal with questions of those of ethnic origin other than British or French, they do so in relation to the basic problem of bilingualism and biculturalism.[3]

From a series of meetings across the nation, the commission learned that "other" Canadians had unanticipated aspirations. Objecting to a policy that would relegate non-English and non-French Canadians to the status of second-class citizens, spokespersons for other ethnics demanded equal treatment. Spearheading these demands were ethnics who could not return to their homelands, for example, Ukrainians, Lithuanians, and Latvians.

> "What the Ukrainians, the Baltic peoples, want desperately in Canada is what the French Canadians and the native people want"...[said] Manoly Lupul, [then] President of the Ukrainian Canadian Professional and Business Federation, "A recognition of their special predicament and an end to dealing with the problem with slogans and clichés."[4]

Such demands resulted in the publication in 1969 of Book IV of the B & B Report, *The Cultural Contribution of Other Ethnic Groups*.[5]

In reaction to such political pressures, in October 1971 "multiculturalism within a bilingual framework" was offered as a concession to Canada's "other" ethnic groups. "Won by force, constructed in haste and under pressure, this historic reversal of the assimilationist ideal is [considered] a political necessity. Its appeal, however, is centered mainly in the 'other' ethnic groups."[6] More important is that the implementation of the policy has proven to be not only problematic but, in addition, has led to undesirable practices.

MAJOR CONCERNS

THE QUESTION OF DEFINITION

Since the 1960s, considerable literature on multiculturalism has been written in Canada, Australia, Great Britain, and the United States. The term, however, is used to mean a variety of things and, in some cases, has become nothing more than a cliché or political slogan. That both Canada and Australia have official government policies of multiculturalism has not lessened the confusion. In fact, it has been compounded now that multiculturalism is indissolubly part of discussions about race, ethnicity, class, power, economic distribution, and social justice.

Examples of the confusion mentioned are numerous. Appelton and Glasson, for instance, tell us that they will try to shed light on the literature they describe as "confused and contradictory."[7] They have, instead, added to the confusion by submitting a new concept of multiculturalism that they refer to as a "two-tier pluralism." However, this presents us with more difficulties than prevailing notions. The major difficulty is that their proposed pluralism would invite us to tolerate practices that ordinary moral consciousness tells us are intolerable or are violations of fundamental human rights.

Nor does C.J. Jaenen, historian and purported expert in the field of multiculturalism, cast any light on this issue. In a public address presented at the University of Alberta in the fall of 1985, Jaenen presented a wealth of historical information putatively supporting the conclusion that multiculturalism is a "sensible cultural ideal, an enlightened policy and an evident social reality." The evidence he presents just as easily supports the conclusion that it is a confused cultural ideal, a muddled political policy and, except for such isolated groups as the Hutterites, a far-from-evident social reality.

That the opposite conclusion follows just as logically from the evidence he presents is due primarily to the fact that the term has no clear meaning in Jaenen's address. To illustrate, Jaenen announced that multicultural programs in British Columbia and Ontario are geared to integration and not to ethnic perpetuation. That programs are given titles that suggest an end result exactly the opposite of what the program brings about is indicative of the terminological confusion that prevails. That programs designed to eliminate pluralism and create a single culture are called muticultural programs, while other programs with an identical title try to enhance pluralism, tells us the sad state of repair the term is in.

Other contrasting perceptions about multiculturalism corroborate this point. On the one hand there are laudatory exegetics about multiculturalism.

> The very definition of what makes an educated person suggests a pluralistic *Weltanschauung*—by virtue of one's acquired *breadth* of knowledge about other cultures, performing arts and comparative and international studies in general. Monoculturalism in today's over-educated society should be an anachronism. Monoculturalism suggests ignorance and fear. It is prevalent among those who are semi-illiterate and biased.
>
> Pluralism [multiculturalism] is the beginning of freedom, of light, of harmony, and happiness.[8]

This view is compatible with the perspective of those who see multiculturalism as a way in which various ethnic groups can flourish in their individual and unique ways. B. Bullivant, on the other hand, in his book *The Pluralist Dilemma in Education*, argues that multiculturalism is a manipulative device used to perpetuate control over ethnic groups. He belongs to the camp to whom multiculturalism represents social injustice. For example, "Vallee argues that any collectivity has limited resources and energy and cannot spend them maintaining ethnic-specific institutions and at the same time prepare its members for achievement in the larger society of which it is a part."[9] And Porter adds a crowning touch to the confusion. Regarding this issue he states that,

> while bilingualism is possible and multilingualism is difficult, I am not able to...understand how biculturalism and multiculturalism

> have any meaning in the post-industrial world into which we are moving. Those who read government pronouncements and royal commission documents on the subject might agree that attempts to deal with these concepts and the related one of ethnicity have generated some of the most complex sophistry ever written.[10]

And then there is Charles Lynch who could only describe multiculturalism as "one huge ethnic howler."[11]

By now it must be evident that multiculturalism means whatever a writer or speaker on the topic wishes it to mean, a case of Humpty Dumpty's logic.

> "There's glory for you!" "I don't know what you mean by 'glory'." Alice said. Humpty Dumpty smiled contemptuously. "Of course you don't—till I tell you. I meant 'there's a nice knockdown argument for you'." "But 'glory' doesn't mean 'a nice knockdown argument'," Alice objected. "When I use a word," Humpty Dumpty said in a rather scornful tone, "it means just what I choose it to mean—neither more nor less."[12]

Given this state of affairs, we can only look at individual conceptions of multiculturalism. In doing so it is found that what some of the apologists advocate leads to or can lead to undesirable consequences. We propose to identify and briefly discuss some of these undesirable and presumably unanticipated consequences.

THE QUESTION OF IMPLEMENTATION

On 8 October 1971 the federal government tabled its response to Book IV prepared by the Royal Commission on Bilingualism and Biculturalism. It said in part:

> We believe that cultural pluralism is the very essence of Canadian identity. Every ethnic group has the right to preserve and develop its own culture and values within the Canadian context. To say we have two official languages is not to say we have two official cultures, and no particular culture is more official than another. A policy of multiculturalism must be a policy for all Canadians.[13]

To ensure that Canada's cultural diversity continues, the government outlined, among others, the following principle: "The Government of Canada will support all of Canada's cultures and will seek to assist, resources permitting, the development of those cultural groups which have demonstrated a desire and effort to continue to develop."[14]

And, in Gwyn's terms, "to butter these fine words" Cabinet approved a $10.1 million appropriation for 1973–74 to facilitate the realization of the principles of multiculturalism.[15] But despite this appropriation and subsequent financial support, successful implementation of multicultural policies has been less than overwhelming. One obvious problem is that of jurisdiction, particularly with respect to multicultural education. Multiculturalism was introduced as a federal policy; education is a provincial matter. Therefore, to implement multiculturalism in the field of education is to rely on the co-operation of the provinces and their agreement to pursue a common policy. This has not been accomplished.

There are other jurisdictional obstacles. To illustrate, the first recommendation of Book IV of the Royal Commission on Bilingualism and Biculturalism reads as follows:

> We recommend that any provinces that have not yet enacted fair employment practices, fair accommodation practices or housing legislation prohibiting discrimination because of race, creed, colour, nationality, ancestry, or place of origin, do so; and that this legislation be binding upon the Crown and its agencies. We further recommend that all provinces make provision for full-time administrators of their human rights legislation.[16]

How can the federal government enforce such recommendations? It is only with the adoption of the Charter of Rights and Freedoms into Canada's Constitution that an avenue for federal appeal has been created. However, this Charter is still in the very early stages of legal testing.

THE QUESTION OF LEGALITY

As was stated in the *First Annual Report of the Consultative Council on Multiculturalism*, the government of Canada will support *all* of Canada's cultures and will assist those groups that have expressed the desire to continue to develop in the Canadian context. This could be interpreted to mean that any culture has the legal right to perpetuate its own traditions and conventions among its own population, as long as it does not interfere with what is being done in any other culture. According to this view, any identifiable culture should be allowed to perpetuate itself with full legal protection. This presents us with serious difficulty.

Some cultures display institutionalized inequality and thus run counter to the laws of the land—the Canadian Charter of Rights: for example—the same laws that on other occasions are seen as means by which cultural integrity is protected.

John Friesen, a staunch advocate of multiculturalism, writes approvingly of Canada's willingness to allow Hutterites their own lifestyle. In his descriptive account of the Hutterites he notes that "Women are believed inferior to men...and they [the women] seem prepared to accept [this]."[17] Nor is this a case of an idiosyncratic interpretation of Hutterian values. John Hostetler who, according to Friesen, has written the best known work on the Hutterites, confirms Friesen's observation.

> Women are believed to be inferior to men intellectually and physically and to need direction, protection, guidance, and consideration. For while it is believed that man was molded in God's likeness, reflecting something of God's glory, woman was taken from man and has weakness, humility, and submission. "Women are just inferior."[18]

Such a belief determines action; for example, Hutterite women are not permitted to participate in colony decisions. Relevant to the thesis of this chapter is that many actions based on the belief that women are inferior to men would probably be found to be illegal if brought before the courts. Any institutionalized sexism, or racism or ageism, will run afoul of the Canadian Constitution, regardless of its status as a cultural value.

Lest it be thought that the Hutterites are being singled out unfairly, let it be noted that the list of cultural groups that may wish to perpetuate practices that will be found illegal whenever the Charter of Rights is taken seriously is quite long. The Koran gives a man the right to take multiple wives if he treats them equally, but a woman cannot have multiple husbands. Not all Hindus have rejected the caste system. In some cultures the sexist practice of female circumcision continues. Infanticide is not universally condemned. Not all subcultures have repudiated slavery. According to modern Japanese law, a failed attempt at *oyako-shinju* (suicide and killing of progeny to avoid dishonour) results in a suspended sentence, probation, and supervised rehabilitation. In most other countries it would be dealt with as a case of attempted murder. Machismo is well established in some cultural groups but who, besides those who display it, would want it perpetuated?

In Canada the 1981 Charter of Rights has come down firmly on the side of individual rights rather than on the so-called rights of groups to dictate to their members how they should live. It is, then, absurd for Canadians who give fundamental importance to their Charter of Rights to give equal respect to all cultural groups when some of these groups do not treat all their internal members equally. The solution to the problem is obvious to all those who take the Charter seriously, but the problem must be seen and faced, and not ignored.

THE QUESTION OF ACCEPTING INTOLERANCE

> [The multicultural policy of 1971] was based upon the assumption that an individual who is to be open in ethnic attitudes and have respect for other groups must have confidence in his or her own cultural foundations. Given this assumption, the policy was also designed to "help break down discriminatory attitudes and cultural jealousies."[19]

The same theme is presented by Valverde in his article "Strategies for the Advancement of Cultural Pluralism":

> Originally, cultural pluralism programs were designed to "counter negative self-concepts and images of racial and ethnic minorities...." Today, the concept of cultural pluralism includes educational experiences so that all students will learn to explore and respect their own culture as well as those of others.[20]

Since the latter proposition is cited without *qualification*, the implication is that every culture or subculture has values that are no better or no worse than those of any other, and that one should be equally accepting of all. While some might find this immediately appealing because it prevents one from making invidious comparisons, it is easy to see that this view is not acceptable.

Note first that, in the judgment that all cultures are equally valid, there is an attempt to escape the relativism that it claims applies everywhere. It attempts to claim that all values are culture bound, but at the same time that affirmation or tolerance should apply across the board. This is clearly inconsistent. The relativism it subscribes to makes such universalistic pronouncements impossible.

Note also that the tolerance that is recommended to all must also be extended to those cultures that are intolerant. It demands tolerance toward groups that act in a systematically intolerant manner toward all but their own members. In at least one important aspect, the Old Believers in northern Alberta are a case in point. Refusing to accept the ritualistic reforms introduced by the Patriarch of the Russian Orthodox Church in 1659, the Old Believers were subjected to extreme persecution. Confronted by an overwhelming adversary, the "faithful" fled to various countries—Romania, Kazakhstan, and northwest China. When communist regimes assumed control in these countries, the Old Believers fled to Hong Kong. From Hong Kong, with the aid of the World Council of Churches, they migrated to Brazil, then to Oregon, and from Oregon to northern Alberta. The most important dimension in the life of the Old Believers is, of course, their religion.[21] And it is in this that the Old Believers exhibit "gross" intolerance. They believe "spiritual adultery" is the consequence of certain forms of contact with nonmembers. For example, confirmed Old Believers at Berezovka (or Nikolaevsk in Alaska) will neither eat with nor drink from a utensil that was used by anyone not of their faith. To impute, if only by implication, spiritual impurity toward all but their own members is "institutionalized intolerance" in this subculture.

The task, then, of the advocates of multiculturalism is not simply to foster tolerance, but to specify with some precision which acts of tolerance we find laudable and which repugnant. We must foster tolerance when tolerance is appropriate, and refuse to tolerate those things that ought not to be tolerated. Multicultural statements and policies, then, should promote not tolerance *simpliciter*, but tolerance *when appropriate*.

THE QUESTION OF MORAL RIGHTS

Some forms of multiculturalism do not take seriously the ideal of an educated person, and for that reason are suspect. To be educated is to have the skills, dispositions, and knowledge needed to assess one's culture rationally, and the internal freedom to act in accordance with that judgment. To be educated means to be able to choose one's cultural orientation on the basis of a free and autonomous rational choice.

If this ideal is accepted, it follows that any child, regardless of the cultural orientation of his or her parents, has the right to an education; that is, the child has the right to those experiences that are most likely to enable her or him to become free, autonomous and rational. The child has, to use Joel Feinberg's apt expression, a "right to an open future".[22] Those cultural groups that restrict this right or do not take it seriously, or give it only verbal expression but otherwise ignore it, must be seen as morally offensive. Some cultural groups, it must be admitted, restrict the lives of their children in just this manner.

It is quite clear that some cultural groups consider the continuation of their culture more important than the child's right to an education and an open future. They try, instead of encouraging their children's freedom and autonomy, to structure their environment so that they will accept the cultural conventions, attitudes, and states of mind typical of their cultural ancestors. Dryden, using the word "education" in a different sense, that is, to mean mere perpetuation of existing states of affairs, captured the flavour of this kind of imposition when he wrote:

> By education most have been misled;
> So they believe, because they were so bred.
> The priest continues what the nurse began
> And thus the child imposes on the man.[23]

For parents to see their children as metaphysical extensions of themselves is a common enough occurrence, but anyone who takes education seriously will not be satisfied with the cultural practices that are associated with this belief. The child's right to an education must be seen as more fundamental than the parents' right to transmit their view of the world. Children must be seen as ends in themselves, and not seen merely as a means to satisfy the parents' cultural ambitions. That human beings should be seen as ends in themselves and not merely as means to other people's ends is a moral principle more fundamental than any other, and we should not lose sight of it on those occasions when it means surrendering some other cherished belief. Those cultural groups that see children merely as a means of perpetuating their culture and not as ends in themselves must be seen as morally flawed. Multiculturalism ought not to be interpreted in such a way that the child's rights are violated.

IMPLICATIONS FOR EDUCATION

Throughout its brief history (the term entered public debate in the 1960s) "multiculturalism" has tended to have positive emotional connotations. Advocates of multiculturalism have profited from this favourable emotional appeal. The term suggests tolerance and a glad affirmation of differences, as opposed to an attempt to force people into a monolithic mold. It suggests that we will let a thousand flowers bloom, and will allow people to pursue their lives in ways that suit them, without interference from central authorities or imposed ideologies. But beneath the rhetoric and the pleasing connotations, there lie some genuine difficulties to be uncovered the moment we insist on a clear statement of just what multiculturalism means.

Pity the poor classroom teachers amidst all of this, who are receiving conflicting messages from the various people to whom they are responsible. They are faced with the fact that there is no unambiguous definition of multiculturalism that can serve to guide classroom activities. There are, instead, competing definitions and competing policies from the various jurisdictions that have some control over education. The federal policy asserts the need to perpetuate cultural characteristics while naively making no mention of the changes that will inevitably result when cultural groups interact with each other. When different cultural groups exist within the same country, the mutual influence and resulting changes will be all the greater, since there will be a single criminal code, a single foreign policy, and the unifying and unique ethos created by sharing the same geographic location. Jean Burnet makes the point well when she describes the situation in Canada:

> the name [multiculturalism] itself implies something that is hardly possible.... Except for such isolated groups as the Hutterites, no ethnic group brings a total culture to Canada, and none can maintain intact what it brings under the impact of the new environment, social as well as geographical. It is ethnic identity that can and does persist, and selected cultural patterns as symbolic expressions of that identity.[24]

The teacher will have to decide, with little guidance from those who make the policy, which cultural patterns to reinforce and which to let die a natural death. Similarly, teachers will be told little about which expressions of ethnic identity it is appropriate for them to reinforce, which to ignore, and which to discourage.

Ambiguities and difficulties in the theory are compounded when an attempt is made to translate it into practice in a particular social setting. Cornelius Jaenen has argued that one must conclude, "if one examines them carefully," that the policies of multiculturalism in B.C. and Ontario "are geared essentially to integration of newcomers, and not to ethnic perpetuation."[25] In other provinces, Alberta, for example, the policy of multiculturalism stresses the perpetuation of ethnic and linguistic diversity. Thus, it is not simply that different aims are pursued at the provincial level under the heading of multiculturalism, but *radically different* aims are pursued. One wonders how many more conflicting interpretations and recommendations are added when the policy is shaped at the local level. It is at the local level that teachers will face a new set of demands. If they encourage the perpetuation of cultural differences, they will immediately encounter the resistance of many recent immigrants whose primary aim is to adjust to the new country, rather than to continue the conventions and customs of the country from which they came. If, on the other hand, they insist on integration, they will meet opposition from many second- and third-generation immigrants who often assert the need to find "roots."

And what is the teacher to do when asked to take the Charter of Rights seriously—the Charter, which insists that no individual is to be discriminated against on the basis of sex (section 15)—but who is at the same time asked to take seriously the federal government's policy of multiculturalism, which states that the government "will seek to assist all Canadian cultural groups,"[26] some of which are, unhappily, sexist?

There are further difficulties for practising teachers when it is realized that they are told both to educate each child and at the same time to socialize the same child into the prevailing cultural practices of his or her forebears. But to educate is, at least, to encourage the child to develop those skills and dispositions needed to critically assess the socialization process she or he is undergoing. It involves insisting that unexamined socialization is not worth being perpetuated. If the notion of education is taken seriously, we have to allow for the possibility that the student will autonomously decide to depart from the cultural patterns of the group into which she or he has been born. This will antagonize those who believe that the group's right to perpetuate itself is greater than the child's right to choose when capable of doing so. But it will be found to be necessary by those who insist that, if multiculturalism is to be interpreted simply by reference to group rights, at the expense of individual rights, it has become a reactionary ideology poorly suited to a world that is no longer regional and one in which a global culture is emerging.

Teachers, then, are at the vortex of several fundamental disputes and are asked to satisfy contradictory demands. Under these difficult conditions, they will have to become as informed as possible, so that they will be able to defend the judgments that they will have to make, knowing full well that some will be disappointed regardless of the decision.

The movement toward a multicultural society is at a crossroads, and individual teachers are thrust into a position where they will help determine future directions. This movement, if used by manipulative and imperialistic people, could be used to violate individual rights in order to promote collectivist ideals. If this were done, the ideals of individuality and autonomy of persons would run the risk of being undermined in the attempt to maintain the cultural integrity of groups over time. On the other hand, if promoted in a context where the autonomy of the person and the respect for individual human rights is taken seriously, a policy of multiculturalism may allow for the kind of unity in diversity to which Canada has always aspired. In this case, multiculturalism would be built upon certain common and fundamental moral and legal principles that would provide the unity necessary for a shared social life, while at the same time allow for the diversity that results from an ethnically pluralistic society.

NOTES

1. S. Gwyn, "Multiculturalism: A Threat and a Promise," *Saturday Night* (Feb. 1974), 17.
2. M. Rioux, "Quebec in Question" in *Two Nations, Many Cultures: Ethnic Groups in Canada*, edited by J. Eliot (Scarborough, Ont.: Prentice Hall, 1979), 56.
3. Canada, Royal Commission on Bilingualism and Biculturalism, *The Cultural Contribution of Other Ethnic Groups* (Ottawa: 1969), 4: 3.
4. Gwyn, "Multiculturalism," 17.
5. E. Kallan, *Ethnicity and Human Rights in Canada* (Toronto: Gage, 1982), 165.
6. K. Mazurek and N. Kach, "Educational Ideologies and Multicultural Canada," *New Education* 5, 2 (1983): 52.
7. N. Appelton and J. Glasson, "In Support of a Two-Tier Pluralism," *Educational Theory* 36, 1 (1986): 43.
8. J. Zajda, "Review of *Multiculturalism in Great Britain,*" *New Education* 7, 1/2 (1985), 124.
9. J. Porter, "Dilemmas and Contradictions of a Multi-Ethnic Society," *Transactions of the Royal Society of Canada*, Series IV, vol. X (1972), 197.
10. Ibid., 198.
11. Gwyn, "Multiculturalism," 18.
12. L. Carroll, *Alice in Wonderland and Through the Looking Glass* (New York: Grosset and Dunlap, 1946), 229.
13. House of Commons, *Debates*, 8 Oct. 1971, 8580–81.
14. Ibid., 8581.
15. Gwyn, "Multiculturalism." For a detailed account of these principles or goals refer to Book VI of the Royal Commission on Bilingualism and Biculturalism.
16. Royal Commission on Bilingualism and Biculturalism, *The Cultural Contributions of Other Ethnic Groups*, 228.
17. J. Friesen, *When Cultures Clash* (Calgary: Detselig, 1985), 131.
18. J. Hostetler and G.E. Huntington, *The Hutterites in North America* (New York: Holt, Rinehart and Winston, 1980), 131.
19. R. Samuda, J.W. Berry and Laferrière, eds., *Multiculturalism in Canada: Social and Educational Perspectives* (Toronto: Allyn and Bacon, 1984), v.
20. Ibid., 150.
21. D. Scheffel, "The Russian Old Believers of Alberta," *Canadian Geographer* (Oct./Nov. 1983).
22. J. Feinberg, "The Child's Right to an Open Future" in *Whose Child?*, edited by W. Aiken and H. LaFollette (New Jersey: Rowman, Totawa, 1980), 124.
23. John Dryden, *The Hind and The Panther*, III: 389.
24. Samuda, Berry, and Laferrière, eds., *Multiculturalism in Canada*, 22.
25. "Multiculturalism: an Historian's Perspective" (Department of Educational Foundations, Occasional Papers, 1986) 17.
26. Statement by the Prime Minister in the House of Commons, 8 October 1971, reprinted in John R. Mallea and Jonathan C. Young, *Cultural Diversity and Canadian Education* (Ottawa: Carleton University Press, Ottawa, 1984), 518.

SECTION 5:
VALUE CONFLICTS IN CANADIAN EDUCATION

The concept of the school system as a purveyor of values inevitably leads to conflict in a complex society. Whose values should the school system reflect? What values should be taught? Which group's values should be paramount? Such questions may force intense pressure onto the educational system and onto the educators within that system. The three chapters in this section illustrate some of the value conflicts occurring in Canadian education.

Hague untangles the confusion of values, morals, and rules, stressing that values are not rules but the guides for choosing rules of behaviour. He discusses three ways in which the teaching of values has traditionally proceeded: first, through indoctrination where values are presented through reward and punishment; second, through school-based values-clarification programs in which the student is encouraged to explore his or her values and choose the ones he or she wishes to keep; and third, the cognitive developmental approach advocated by Lawrence Kohlberg and his followers. A new direction in values education is charted by Hague wherein the student examines her or his values, determines which values she or he wishes to retain, and then establishes a hierarchy for these personal values. Hague points out that this tack involves an affective as well as a cognitive appraisal of one's values, guided by a teacher who is not only cognizant of his or her own values but also directed toward an appreciation of other's values.

Shapiro and Davis highlight a specific instance of a value conflict in their paper on the public funding of religious private schools in Ontario. The authors examine the three most common arguments for the public funding of private schools: the right of parents to choose the education they wish for their children, the discriminatory element of public funding for Roman Catholic but not other religious private schools, and the double taxation dilemma of parents sending their children to private schools. The authors then balance the scales by discussing the three most common arguments against public funding of private schools: the current financial constraints, the homogeneity of private schools increasing the risk of students becoming prejudiced and intolerant, and the jeopardizing of the intent of equality of educational opportunity for all students by the financial and ideological support of private schools. Shapiro and Davis outline their rationale for accepting or rejecting these arguments and provide their own recommendations on the public funding of private schools in Ontario.

Emerson discusses the longstanding debate concerning the teaching of evolution and creation in public schools. He attempts to clarify the controversy in this sensitive area by illuminating both the fundamentalist and the evolutionist positions as well as the stances that each of the provinces has taken. He argues that advances in science and the rapid growth of fundamentalism are polarizing the conflict and that it is becoming increasingly difficult to adhere to the two views as fairly compatible versions of human origins. Emerson also makes thoughtful recommendations for the presentation of the two approaches in our elementary and secondary school systems.

TEACHING VALUES IN CANADIAN SCHOOLS

WILLIAM J. HAGUE

There is pressure on today's teacher from all sides: "Teach our children values; make them good." "Don't teach our children *your* values; teach them *our* values—the right ones." "Don't teach them any values at all; teach them how to think, and they will come to values on their own." If the pressure on teachers comes from all directions, it also comes with a strong, sometimes strident, emotional intensity, for, with values, we are dealing with something important—the practical realm of how people behave. People have great personal and emotional investment in values education. It evokes discussion that, though never lacking in fervour, is sometimes lacking in conceptual depth. It is the purpose of this paper to achieve some degree of conceptual depth without destroying this fervour. To do this, I will come at the issue of teaching values in Canadian schools from four perspectives:

1. What values are and what they are not.
2. The challenges we generally face when teaching values, and the special challenges of values education today.
3. Some of the ways in which values education has been conducted.
4. New directions we might take in Canada to meet today's needs.

WHAT VALUES ARE AND WHAT THEY ARE NOT

Values is a broad term for the concept we have of things or actions when we place a positive or negative weighting on them. Some of these value loadings are moral; some are not. Let me illustrate: fishing is just fishing until I say, "I like fishing." Now I have made a value statement. The same is true if I say, "The fishing is good in this lake; I catch a lot of fish." Now I am saying the lake is good for fishing, and that is why I value this lake. But if the lake is on private property, and the fish belong to someone else, I am now in the realm of morality; my fishing in this lake now touches on someone else's rights, and I must ask the value questions, which are now moral judgments, "Is it right to fish in this lake?" and "Ought I to be fishing here?" I have moved from a statement of general value (the fishing is good here) to a moral value (the owner has a right to his or her private property), and that imposes a certain moral imperative on me—some way in which I *ought* to behave, if I wish to preserve that value.

The distinction between values in general and moral values is an important one to keep in mind when talking about values education—and when *doing* it. But there is another distinction that seems to get lost when people are involved in values education, particularly when it touches on moral values. Values are not rules; values and rules are two quite different things. Values are conceptions of the desirable that lead us to choose from among various modes of behaviour. Values are the guides for choosing rules of behaviour. Our values lead to our behaviour. Particularly when we are making choices about moral behaviour, our values are there, whether we are conscious of them or not, like a foundation underlying specific choices of behaviour, supporting and guiding us to make these choices. But frequently there is a large gap between this theoretical understanding of the relationship of values to action, and the practice of "values education" in our schools. Often what goes under the name of values education does not get at the conscious consideration of values themselves, but stays at the more superficial level of discussing rules, regulations, and ways of behaving. A classroom discussion that starts out with a school's rule prohibiting smoking is not "values education" if it stays with the specifics of rules or even the various ways students "feel" about the rules. It must dig deeper and bring into consciousness the values each student holds that cause those feelings and reactions to the rules—values such as respect for other people, health, freedom to choose for oneself.

These deeper, enduring values are the real meat of values education. If we talk only about the rules of behaviour, we may be moralizing, but not really conducting values education since we are not getting down to the sources of that morality that are to be found in the values underlying behaviour. Values are enduring, relatively stable things. Rules, on the other hand, are norms we derive from our values; they are specific, adaptable to the occasion, constantly changing. As an example, look at the various rules about dress and clothing that people have made to express the value "modesty." An Australian Aborigine's interpretation is very different from that of an Australian lawn bowling club. Today's interpretation of what is "modest" beachwear is very different from that of fifty years ago. We only have to flip through our grandparents' photo albums to see that. So rules that interpret values vary according to time and place. The value itself goes on undisturbed by varying interpretations—even by erroneous interpretations. The key is that rules, if they are to be good rules, must truly reflect lasting values.

The image that best illustrates this relationship of rules to values is that of surface versus bedrock. It is on the surface of the earth that all the activity takes place when people are searching for oil. But, to find oil that is deep below the surface, a seismic crew sends soundings into the depths of the earth and "listens" for the responses that come back from the bedrock. The return message tells them something about the depth and configuration of the bedrock, giving them some rules to guide their decisions about where to drill. The activity on the surface is guided by rules that come from sounding the bedrock. So with values and rules of behaviour. When we want some specific guidelines, some laws or rules, we should sound out the bedrock of our values, making our rules a conscious interpretation of our values.

In summary, values are concepts of the desirable that lead us to choose how we will act. Some values are moral values; some are not. It is important to distinguish values from rules of behaviour, so that education will not limit itself to discussing behaviour alone, but can deal with those deeper forces that influence behaviour—the values we hold.

THE CHALLENGES WE FACE IN VALUES EDUCATION

The first challenge thrown up to a would-be values educator is: what values are you going to teach? If the world were unchanging, the answer would be relatively simple: "I will teach the rules of behaviour that were passed down to me from my elders; they were good enough for them; they are good enough for me; and they will be good enough for all time." If the world were static, that might be a satisfactory answer, and, indeed, those who try to create a static, unchanging society in a protected environment for their children do give this traditional command: teach unchanging, traditional values; guard our children from change of any kind. (By the way; have you noticed that, in presenting this approach, I have deliberately fudged the argument by using "values" and "rules" as though the words were interchangeable?)

But the real world is not static, not protected from the winds of change; it is in flux. Manners, mores, and even morals change. Political, economic, scientific, and military developments create new challenges to old ways of acting. Religious revelations that for some have been the authoritative guide for behaviour are challenged by a world with new insights, and to cling unquestioningly to an authority, even a religious authority, may blind us to possibilities of new insights into how one might be more fully human in a world in flux. Does one then respond to a changing world by saying "Everything is up for grabs; everything is relative; nobody knows what is valuable"? This was the response of some educators a few years ago, and it influenced some theorists to try to introduce a complete relativity into values education. At the present time, a reactionary, conservative swing of the educational pendulum is attempting to counter this relativity of values with a return to indoctrination of "traditional values." I would maintain that neither of these two extremes, neither relativity nor conservative indoctrination, is the answer. The answer hinges on the distinction between values and rules that we considered in the first section of this essay, and will develop in the last section after a brief overview of some of the ways values education has been approached in the last few years.

HOW THE CHALLENGE OF VALUES EDUCATION HAS BEEN APPROACHED

The term *values education* has frequently been used interchangeably with *moral education*. They are not exactly the same thing, *values* being a broader term than *morals*, but, as we will see, moral education theories with any depth ultimately get back to values.

Perhaps the two theories of morals/values education that have had the most influence on Canadian education are *values clarification*, as initiated by Raths, Harmin, and Simon,[1] and spelled out for school practice by Simon, Howe, and Kirschenbaum,[2] and the *cognitive-developmental approach* of Lawrence Kohlberg.[3] We should look at what these theories have to say, noting some of their similarities and differences. One similarity between values clarification and Kohlberg's approach is that each was conceived in an American context and tailored to meet North American philosophy and educational needs. Consequently, their powerful influence on Canadian values education was inevitable. North American society is pluralistic, and diversity of views, educational approaches, and values prevails. There is no established church, for example, imposing dogmatic or moral unanimity on society. In fact, the United States is in the throes of a rather lengthy debate as to whether God should be in or out of the school curriculum. One cannot, in this context, presume, as might have been the case in other times and other places, to present a method of values education built upon a set of moral rules more or less generally accepted by society. That would be the traditional approach we discussed earlier in which the task of the values educator is to accept the rules of his or her society and pass them on unchanged to students who will accept them through the power of indoctrination and the rewards and punishments that follow good or bad behaviour.

VALUES CLARIFICATION

Raths, Harmin, and Simon, following John Dewey, deplored this "keeping dreary watch over ancient values" as not worthy of a citizen in a democracy. They proposed, as good Deweyites, that each individual should "clarify" his or her own values. All people should, through education, be given the opportunity to explore their values, freely select those they want to maintain, and proudly live by them. Raths, Harmin, and Simon, in their book *Values and Teaching*, generated seven criteria for judging a value, and they created exercises in which students were guided in becoming conscious of their actual values. But, underlying the whole values clarification approach, was a philosophical premise of vast proportions that was destined to have profound repercussions on values education in the United States, and, in turn, in Canada, where in some provinces it was accepted as the theoretical framework of a value-based social studies curriculum. The important philosophical premise on which values clarification was built was that of value relativity. In a democracy envisioned as a society in which each person decided for himself or herself, there was no room for outside authority or really even guidance in choosing one's own individual values. A hierarchy of values was one's own subjective choice, judged only by the extent to which one understood the options, freely chose, was proud of the choices, and lived by them. Judging the worth of one's values against some outside criteria was destructive of the individual's inalienable freedom. The scene created by values clarification was a road without guideposts, each individual being left to her or his own subjective resources to discover and choose values.

KOHLBERG AND THE COGNITIVE-DEVELOPMENTAL APPROACH

Kohlberg also built a philosophy, a psychology, and a methodology of moral education suited to a pluralistic society. He deplored what he called the "bag of virtues" approach of traditional character education, claiming that teaching specific virtues had been shown by research to have little real effect on moral development, and, besides, people could not agree on which virtues should be taught, or, even more fundamentally, could not agree on what words like honesty, love, and kindness really meant.

Instead, Kohlberg proposed a model for moral education based on a framework of six stages of moral development. Following Piaget,[4] Kohlberg discovered through his research that moral development took the form of levels of reasoning, the higher levels taking one closer to the core of all morality—justice. The "just person" and the "just society" were the goals of Kohlberg's approach to moral education. In this way he claimed to have objective norms of moral development, and thus avoided the value subjectivity of some approaches, while, at the same time, not getting into the confusion of the "bag of virtues" presented by traditional character education.

For Kohlberg, moral education, far from inculcating a plethora of individual virtues, was to be aimed at improving the reasoning powers of individuals so that they would come to moral decisions that were just, not haphazardly or from egocentric ways of thinking, but from abstract reasoning that was universal and generalizable. The educational technique to be used was to expose children through classroom discussions of moral dilemmas to reasoning that was just one stage above their own stage; they would be capable of understanding thinking just one stage above their own; they would be attracted to it, and ultimately incorporate that next higher stage as their own. A just society in the school would create just citizens for the larger society.

Kohlberg's ideas, like values clarification, had a strong influence on values education in Canadian schools, synopsized all too often in the neat six stages of moral development, and popularized all too often in the many kits and programs that flowed out of the theory. A "Kohlberg bandwagon" developed, and many a harassed classroom teacher, called upon to do values education with little preparation, jumped on it without critiquing Kohlberg's research or considering the narrowing effect of bringing values education down to the confines of reasoning alone.

In Canada, a reaction developed to values clarification and Kohlberg, and was researched and popularized by such books as Kathleen Gow's *Yes Virginia, There is Right and Wrong*.[5] Gow and others reacted on scholarly grounds to the weaknesses of research in the values education area, and, as the book's title implies, reacted, too, against the value subjectivity that they saw as rampant in values education in Canada. There is no point in reviewing here the objections of Gow and others; they have been amply documented. But I think it is important to point out that many of the horror stories these critics recount of how values education was conducted in the classrooms of Canada were abuses of values education perpetrated by individuals who did not understand the philosophy of the methodology they had adopted, or who, in their enthusiasm, got carried away into conducting moral education in a way that was itself immoral because it was hurtful to students. Asking children, even in a game, to rank order their peers as to who deserves most to live, is not the way to teach worthwhile values or moral behaviour.

In summary, the challenges of values education have been approached from several directions. We have concentrated on only three of them here: 1) traditional values education aimed at preserving "tried and true" values by teaching and rewarding the expression of these values in "good" behaviour or punishing "bad" behaviour; 2) values clarification, creating situations in which the students are called upon to examine the values they hold, and to make free, independent, and subjective choices of what values they want to continue to hold and to live by; 3) the cognitive developmental approach, incorporating the idea that individuals go through stages of moral reasoning development, the goal of moral education being to encourage better moral reasoning.

NEW DIRECTIONS IN VALUES EDUCATION

We began this essay by saying that values are important. Perhaps we can best begin this concluding section by returning to that theme and developing from there some new directions that will have practical import for those who are engaged in values education in Canadian schools.

Values are important because they set direction in our lives; some values answer the question, "What is worthwhile?" Simple values may determine nothing more than that we prefer Coke to Pepsi. But if they are major values, they may determine what we give our lives to and, ultimately, what gives our lives meaning.

Each person has an "ultimate environment," the farthest horizons of one's personal world within which and in relation to which one makes meaning out of life. But life, if we reflect on it, is for most of us a vast circumference, and could for many be empty and confusing, like the empty horizon may be for a sailor in mid-ocean, bereft of landmarks. Life landmarks are centres of value, guides in our navigation, things to which we can commit ourselves. In turn, we ourselves feel valued and sustained, because values give direction, security, and ultimate meaning to life.

But when we become values educators ourselves, we realize something new: the task of the values educator is not really to *teach* values in the sense of giving students something they never had before. Everybody has some values already. The task of values education is to dig down to the values we each have deep within us, to provoke the values into consciousness, and to examine them, deciding which are real values by examining whether they actually influence action in our lives, and making decisions on whether we want to keep those values or not, and in what order, what hierarchy we want to place them. That is what values education gives students—an opportunity to raise values into consciousness and to choose the hierarchies that will give form and proportion to the way values influence actions and shape the meaning of their lives.

The concept of hierarchy is important when we are working out new ways of values education. If we already have values, then our first task in values education is to bring them into conscious awareness. This is the essence of the process of values education: getting in touch with the values we already have, and then making some deliberate, conscious choices of which values we want to keep, and which are most important to us. The first revelation we will get from this reflective approach is the realization that most of our values are good, and that we do not want to throw any of them out. But we do have to decide which come first, which values supersede others. One can, for example, value both freedom and security. But if the situation arises in which I have a choice of one or the other, which will I give up? Some people have given their lives for freedom; others (recruits to religious cults, for example) have given their freedom to someone or some institution that promises them security. One must make decisions in specific cases as to which value shall prevail: that is how our value hierarchies become clear to us.

But value hierarchies become clear in another way: when they clash with the values of other people. That is why so much values education takes place in the form of discussion of dilemmas. When our values clash with someone else's values, we are called upon to do two things: 1) re-examine our own values, and 2) put ourselves in the other person's shoes and try to see the problem from his or her point of view.

To pull a few themes together before we go on: values are important because they put meaning and direction in our lives, giving us a sense of personal continuity and worth. The task of values education is to bring into consciousness those values that are already within us, directing our lives. Values education affords us the opportunity of discovering what values we have, and the order of the hierarchy in which we hold them. Most important, it forces us into making *conscious* choices of the values that direct our lives.

Values education sounds below the surface of action for the depths of value hierarchies that ultimately direct those actions.

This little recapitulation allows us to see that we have been coming at the whole task of values education in a way that is so typical of values educators—backwards! It is backwards because we have talked about doing something for our students before we have done it for ourselves. We have discussed the necessity of students becoming conscious of their values, leaving out that essential step of the teacher first becoming conscious of his or her values. What we say in values education is frequently overshadowed by what we are and what we do. It is absolutely essential that would-be values educators work on what their values are and how their personal values direct their lives. Techniques of values education fade into insignificance in the face of this imperative.

As a teacher, clarifying my own values is necessary if I am to be able to respond to questions or demands from students to take a stand. It is imperative that I am able to recognize the direction in which my values are influencing the values and behaviour of others. The teacher's own reflection and the constant passing back and forth from the surface of actions to the depths of values that guide those actions will save many a values education class from being a mere discussion of rules, making it instead a real opportunity for deep value clarification.

At the beginning of this chapter I made the distinction between values in general and moral values in particular: moral values are a subset of values in general. So far, I have let our discussion roam over the range of general values. I would like to conclude with a consideration of values education in the particular sense of morals education.

MORALS EDUCATION

R.S. Peters, the eminent British moral philosopher, has reminded us that the ultimate question of morals education is "How do children come to care?"[6] How do we teach empathy, that kind of justice that means putting oneself in other people's shoes, seeing the situation as they would see it, thinking as they would think, feeling as they would feel, or, more precisely, feeling as I would feel if I were in that situation.

That last phrase, ("feeling as I would feel if I were in that situation") is a loaded statement. It carries two main themes of moral judgment making—the emotional component in moral judgment making and the central role of experiencing authentic feelings in moral development. Too many theories of morals education have emphasized the cognitive, rational approach to moral judgments, giving the impression that the best moral judgments are made with cool logic alone, precluding all feeling and passion. This is a misleading way of looking at moral judgments, as though we could and should cut off our feelings about vital issues.

It is a whole human person that makes moral choices. Rather than avoiding feelings as misleading us or clouding the issue (which has been the view of some cognitivists), the task of the morals educator is to develop feelings, hone their edge, polish them like a mirror until they are authentic reflections of the surrounding world—sensitive perceptions of how one would feel in another person's dilemma. Emotions developed to high levels can be sure guides to judgments about how one ought to behave. Again I have slipped in another phrase that is crucial— "Emotions developed to high levels." Not just any emotion will do, but feelings that are empathic responses to a situation, in which I feel a sense of responsibility for myself and for others, founded on a sense of oneness between myself and others. Empathy, that response one has of feeling with and for another, is at the heart of higher level emotions. Or rather, it could be at the core of our responses if it did not get squashed by a world that does not really encourage authentic feelings.

Children feel deeply. But if we are not careful, they can grow up without being able to experience deep feeling. It seems strange to have to talk about actually experiencing real emotion. We live in a world full of intense emotion; the trouble is it usually comes to us in those neatly packaged containers that fill the spaces between advertisements on TV. In front of the TV set in a single evening, a child can witness a dozen deaths, and yet not participate emotionally in any of them. So much of the "drama" is played out by cardboard-thin characters who can never really draw us in because they are not real; they work through their story line of violence in a pre-programmed system that is meant to raise the viewer's attention just before the commercial to keep you riveted to the screen. Commercialism can be absurd in its lack of sensitivity to other values. Is it not obscene to cut from two men who are clobbering each other to death to remind us not to offend our neighbours with underarm perspiration? Such travesties of real emotional involvement contribute to the development of numb, nonparticipant persons, not necessarily bad persons, but ones who are glassy-eyed, bored, overstimulated, and emotionally undernourished. Someone has said, "Our young people know the price of everything, and the value of nothing." If we have people confused about what is worthwhile, is it because they have never really participated in living, never really been called forth to feel as another may feel. If their motto is "Don't get involved," is their apathy not the result of a feeling of impotence because there are no value guidelines from without, and no sense of real moral choices from within that would make them feel that they belong on planet earth?

The challenge to the values educator, particularly the morals educator, is to let children feel the appropriate emotional responses to their own and others' situations. Let them experience fear, disappointment, loneliness, confusion; they are all part of the human condition. These experiences are schooling in being able to feel for others, to identify with others, to know their hurts as though they were one's own, and to act morally to prevent those hurts to oneself and to others. This is justice, not just an abstraction calling for purely cognitive understanding. It is a passionate sense of justice that we are striving for—a justice that people must "hunger and thirst after."

Morals education asks the teacher to accept the child's spontaneous expression, "It's not fair," and to challenge the child to jump the gap between "It's not fair to me" to "It's not fair to you—or really to me either" because he or she has come to think and to feel, "My good must be your good or it is really no good at all." That is asking a lot; it is asking the child to move from lower levels of selfishness to higher levels of empathy and altruism. It is asking teachers to have made that move themselves before they can pass it on to others. Those ways of thinking and feeling that are lower and not reflected upon must, in the course of moral education, disintegrate, and be replaced by that which is higher, more an integrated part of the personality because it is felt deeply and reflected upon. That really is what morals education is all about.

If we accept the premises that people are at various levels of moral development; that moral judgment making involves the whole person and is neither just a logical exercise of pure reason nor an experience of whimsical emotionality; and that real values education (including moral education) means getting at deeper level values and not staying in the more superficial realm of rules and regulations, how then should we proceed with morals education? Not by the route of utter value subjectivity as in values clarification, leaving moral judgments up to the individual—*any* individual—regardless of his or her personal capacities to make those judgments. This is only pseudo-freedom, leaving each person the victim of his or her own immaturity. Not by the route of total indoctrination, for this takes away the individual's responsibility for her or his own value choices, imposes conformity, and provides at times what is only a pseudo-objectivity, for indoctrination can be a way of imposing one's own set of subjective judgments onto others. Not by the route of over simplification—either seeing moral judgment-making as an exercise in rational thinking alone, or, on the other hand, as a totally emotional, irrational response of the passions. Neither approach is holistic, and that is what we are dealing with in moral judgments—whole, living, breathing, real human persons making judgments with all the data their senses can provide, all the reason their intelligence gives, and all the emotional maturity available at their level of development, deciding how they shall work out the course of their lives in the most caring way possible.

How then, do we teach people to care? We can do so first by recognizing the power and vitality of the "informed heart," the emotions working in collaboration with what we call intellect. The human person is far from being a kind of moral computer that can be carefully programmed to come up with the "right" answer to any moral dilemma. Nor should we encourage feeling that is merely whimsical, subjective, and uninformed. We must recognize that all of us are at various levels of emotional development and need to be drawn from lower level to higher level functioning, the lower, more instinctual, unreflected ways of functioning giving way to higher level reflected ways. The infant's egocentrism must, in the long run, give way to the reflective ability to put oneself in another person's shoes, to see the world as others see it. Childish conformity for the sake of "keeping out of trouble" must yield to a real concern that justice be done. Adolescent rebellion and emotional distancing must give way to real involvement, care, and concern. Adult feelings of inferiority must be transposed into a healthy feeling of dissatisfaction and a quest for the moral ideals of what one ought to be.

Morals education is that part of values education that teaches people to care. Of all the delicate and demanding tasks of the values educator, perhaps morals education is the most demanding and most delicate, but its course can be more surely guided by seeing the need for morals education to go beneath the surface of moral rules and find firm roots for moral behaviour in hierarchies of values that are truly humanizing.

NOTES

1. L. Raths, M. Harmin, and S. Simon, *Values and Teaching* (Columbus: Charles E. Merrill, 1966).
2. S. Simon, L. Howe, and H. Kirschenbaum, *Values Clarification* (New York: Hart, 1972).
3. Lawrence Kohlberg, "Moral Development" in *Encyclopedia of the Social Sciences*, vol. 10 (New York: Macmillan, 1968), 483–94; Kohlberg, *The Philosophy of Moral Development* (San Francisco: Harper & Row, 1981).
4. Jean Piaget, *The Moral Judgment of the Child* (Glencoe, Ill.: Free Press, 1948).
5. Kathleen Gow, *Yes, Virginia, There is Right and Wrong* (Toronto: Wiley and Sons, 1980).
6. R.S. Peters, *Ethics and Education* (London: Allen & Unwin, 1969).

THE PUBLIC FUNDING OF PRIVATE (RELIGIOUS) SCHOOLS IN ONTARIO: A CONFLICT IN VALUES[1]

BERNARD J. SHAPIRO AND BRIAN K. DAVIS

The designers of the Canadian federation believed that, with regard to education, differences in religion, language, and culture required decentralized responses, if public consensus was to be achieved. The end result has been that Canada possesses an array of educational institutions and arrangements that vary along regional, class, racial, ethnic, linguistic, and religious lines.[2]

It is not surprising, therefore, to find that arrangements for the provision of, and/or public funding of, private schools, the great majority of which are religiously based, also show considerable variation between provinces. In Newfoundland, where public school districts are established on a denominational basis, private schools receive no public funds and, in the Maritimes, funding is limited to no more than assistance with the purchase of textbooks.[3] In the Yukon and Northwest Territories, there are neither private schools nor any provision for their public funding should such schools come into existence. On the other hand, there are detailed provisions for the partial public funding of private (mostly religious) schools in Quebec, British Columbia, Alberta, Manitoba, and Saskatchewan, and, in both Alberta and Saskatchewan, the public treasury provides fully for both a non-denominational and a religiously defined separate school system. In Ontario, in 1984–85, there were 535 private elementary and secondary schools serving 87 126 students. Of the 535 schools, approximately forty-eight percent were elementary and twenty-four percent were secondary schools, while the balance offered programs at both levels. Analysed from another perspective, seventy percent of Ontario private schools enrolling eighty percent of Ontario private school students were religiously defined. Further, enrolment data provide evidence of growth in the Ontario private school sector in recent years. Thus, in the period 1973–83, elementary and secondary private school enrolment increased by sixty and ninety percent, respectively. In 1973, private school students represented 2.3 percent of the total number of elementary and secondary students in Ontario. In 1984, the comparable percentage was 4.7.

In Ontario, although the government's policy is for full public funding for both non-denominational public schools and Roman Catholic separate schools, private schools do not have access to either local education taxes or direct provincial grants for operating or for capital expenses. It would not, however, be correct to conclude that these private schools receive no public assistance. Most of the direct aid programs (e.g., access to the Ministry of Education's book purchase plan) are, however, quite minor in scale. Of greater importance is the indirect aid to private schools in the form of exemption from property taxes on non-profit schools; income tax deductions for tuition attributable to religious instruction; and income tax deductions for charitable purposes. The annual cost to the public treasury of these indirect programs—at the local, provincial, and federal levels—is not known. In fact, this cost is very difficult to estimate, for such an estimate would depend on currently untested assumptions such as the market value of private school properties; the marginal tax rates for parents receiving tuition tax receipts and for parents or other contributors receiving tax receipts for charitable donations; and the proportion of tuition that is attributable to religious instruction. Moreover, in each of these areas, there would be wide differences among individual private schools, although the aid programs clearly favour those schools with a religious orientation. In a paper prepared for the Commission on Private Schools in Ontario, Lawton suggests that the actual level of aid "amounts to about one-sixth of the average total in cost per pupil enrolled in a private school."[1] We believe that this is a conservative estimate, and there are certainly some individual private schools where the aid level is at least twice Lawton's average estimate.

There is, of course, no absolute answer to the question of the extent to which public moneys should be used to support the education of persons attending elementary and secondary schools not owned or operated by government bodies. In a democratic and heterogeneous society, any existing policy in this area is the result of the interaction of many factors, and the current arrangements can and should be expected to alter over time. Further, considering what, if any, change(s) would be appropriate, one cannot simply look to available research results and/or the policy and practice of other jurisdictions for easy guidance. With regard to the available research, there are two problems. First, although the pace of inquiry has quickened recently, research in the area of private schooling has not, in fact, been extensive. Thus, the results of the research tend to be fragmentary and suggestive, rather than cumulative and definitive. Second, the "facts" yielded by research studies cannot in themselves respond to the public policy question of whether to provide more public funds to private (religious) schools. The response to such a question is not so much a matter of facts as it is a matter of values. With regard to other jurisdictions, their experience, though often informative, is conditioned by such peculiar contextual factors as their special social and cultural history. It would, therefore, be unwise to assume that the system extant in any one province or geographical region could (even if judged by many to be successful) be easily transferred to another jurisdiction. For example, within Canada, only Saskatchewan, Ontario, and Alberta possess both public and separate (but publicly funded) schools. Thus, the policy and implementation issues for these provinces—to say nothing about the even more complex situation in Quebec—will be quite different with regard to the funding of private (religious) schools than those for British Columbia, Manitoba, New Brunswick, etc.

In Ontario, it was the decision of the provincial government (in June 1984) to fund grades 11-13 of the Roman Catholic separate schools that refocussed public attention in Ontario on the funding of private schools—at least those private schools that were religiously defined. The Commission on Private Schools in Ontario was, therefore, established and, during the course of its work, it received 514 written briefs. In terms of the public policy recommendations proposed, the writers of these briefs put forward a wide range of options—all the way from the full funding of all private schools to the withdrawal of public funds from all schools, public or private. The various arguments provided as rationales for the particular proposals were rooted in the particulars of the Ontario experience. Quite naturally, they reflected commitments to a wide variety of value priorities. Nevertheless, these arguments were often sufficiently general to be worthy of consideration not only in Ontario but elsewhere.

The most common arguments put forward in support of the public funding of private schools were the following:

1. Not only should parents be able to choose school environments that affirm and extend their own values, but they also have a prior right to select the kind of education they believe to be appropriate for their children. The function of the state is—within recognized limits of costs and standards—to enable parents to make this choice free from financial constraints, constraints that now threaten, through the economics of schooling, the right of many parents to choose a private school.

2. It is discriminatory and, therefore, inappropriate for Ontario to continue to offer its Roman Catholic community an educational option not offered all other Ontario communities—at least to all other Ontario communities that are religiously defined.

3. Parents who choose to send their children to private schools should not have to bear the "double taxation" of paying both private school tuition fees and their share of the education taxes in support of publicly funded schools.

These arguments were urged not only on the grounds of justice but also with repeated reference to the view that there is room for many different ways of realizing public goals. It must be recognized, it is argued, that diverse communities have, within them, differing preferences for educational goods and services, thereby creating a need for differing models of school organization. Thus, while education should be public in the financial structure and the opportunities it provides, it need not be public—or at least exclusively public—in its organization. Finally, it was suggested that the current near monopoly of the state in elementary and secondary schooling reduces competition, raises costs, lowers efficiency, and degrades the quality of the product being delivered while, at the same time, it imposes majority ideologies and lifestyles upon the minority, and makes dissent less legitimate. By contrast, the Commission was assured that the provincial funding of private schools would: ensure the diversity appropriate to a pluralistic society (compulsory education was never intended to mean that all children should be schooled in the same way); reconcile individual freedom with majority rule—the very difficulty that has so bedevilled the attempt of boards of education to act as a socially cohesive force; stimulate competition and, therefore, quality; rid parents of double taxation; and allow the free exercise of conscience and religion within all income levels. Moreover, the existing public school system would not be threatened by this policy change, since it was not imagined, by some, that there would be large-scale enrolment shifts from public to private schools as a result of any decision to provide new provincial funding to the latter.

Forceful arguments against public funding were also presented. Of these, the three most common arguments were:

1. Whatever one's view in principle, the current financial constraint on the Ontario treasury and, consequently, on the funding of public schools, makes any extension of public funding to private schools inappropriate, at least at this time.

2. Allowing the use of public funds to support and create private schools, many of which by their own admission would be segregated along lines of, for example, religion or class, would be unwise, since it would sanction the isolation of students in homogeneous groups and thereby not only abandon the advantages of a common acculturation experience but also foster a tendency among the students to think of other people as outsiders—an invitation to prejudice and intolerance.

3. Support of private schools erodes financial and ideological support for public schooling and thereby denies equality of educational opportunity to large groups of students by fostering a two-tier system of schooling inimical to the democratic traditions that public schools are intended to serve.

In support of these arguments, reference was made not only to the various financial restraint programs of the provincial government but, more importantly, to the experience of other jurisdictions—most frequently Australia and Great Britain—where private schools are seen as having played a major role in keeping alive and legitimizing the ideology of class and, therefore, in exacerbating the divisions within society.

Overriding all of these concerns, however, was a commitment to the public school as a source of common (not in the sense of "low" but in the sense of "shared") experiences and common opportunities and, therefore, at least potentially, of a socially integrating sense of purpose. Stress was laid on the great extent to which private schools were seen as catering to individual needs rather than the social ends of public policy. No claim was made that the rights of individual students and their parents were irrelevant. What was emphasized was the likelihood that only in the public schools and through the public schools could social decisions be funded and reinforced. Those arguing against the public funding of private schools also suggested—since the custom-tailored can be expected to fit better than the ready-made—that such public funding would result in substantial shifts in enrolment away from public schools, probably removing from the public constituency the most articulate parents, those who represent the most likely impetus for change, development, and improvement in the public schools themselves.

In terms of the three most common arguments advanced by the proponents of public funding for the private schools (i.e., parents' rights, discrimination vis-à-vis the province's Roman Catholic community, and double taxation), the double taxation argument, although psychologically strong (a private-school parent is, in fact, paying both a tuition bill and education taxes in support of the publicly funded schools), is in our view, without merit. First, the argument arises at least partly as an unintended consequence of a tax system that happens to separate certain educational levies but not other objects of public tax expenditure. Second, the argument confuses an education tax with a tuition bill, which is not the case. What the education tax represents is a general levy in support of what society has identified as a common good (i.e., a public school system). The levying of this or any other tax does not entitle a citizen to an opting-out process. Decisions concerning the raising and allocation of tax revenues are political decisions, and legal redress is available to individual citizens only through the periodic election process and/or the courts. Finally, the double taxation argument would seem to imply that: taxpayers without children (and, perhaps, those without children currently of school age) would not be expected to pay education taxes; taxpayers with more than one residence would be not only double-taxed, but triple-taxed, quadruple-taxed, etc.; taxes for education should be in proportion to the number of children in a family. Each of these options is, of course, a potential public policy, but not a single one of them is supported by any individual or group raising the double taxation argument itself.

The argument arising from parents' rights is, it seems to us, somewhat stronger. Parents are the first educators of their children, and their continued active involvement in the schooling of their children can contribute mightily to the success of that schooling. Further, it is reasonable to suppose that providing parents with a greater range of choice and, therefore, increasing the chances that they will identify closely with the option actually selected, will, in turn, increase the likelihood of their active engagement with their children's schooling. Finally, in a democratic society, choice for individuals is of considerable value for its own sake. Still, although the idea of choice is important, it does not in itself define self-government or democracy, as there are some things (e.g., slavery) that a democratic society cannot reasonably choose. Thus, we would favour the enhancement of parental choice, but we do not regard such a choice as a prior right. Rather, parental choice is seen as a desirable objective, but one whose claims must be measured against the competing claims of other social policies and goals.

In contrast to our rejection of the double taxation argument and our partial support for the argument from prior parental rights, we believe that the argument against the Ontario status quo (or, indeed, the status quo in any jurisdiction that supports one religious community but not another) on the grounds that it is discriminatory (in this case against non-Roman Catholics) is a very strong one. On moral grounds, providing public support to Roman Catholic schools and excluding other religious denominations from that support seems indefensible, for the constitutional provisions usually advanced to justify the special status of Roman Catholic schools serve only to describe their history. They do nothing to inform us about what we *ought* to do. In terms of this moral choice, it does seem inappropriate for Ontario to continue to offer to its Roman Catholic community an educational option not offered to other communities as well. It is true that a strict application of equity in this matter might limit any extension of this option to other religious communities, but it cannot be that the public good will be served by involving government in decisions as to whether or not particular communities are to be considered as religiously defined.

On legal/constitutional as well as on moral grounds, the special status of the Roman Catholic schools is discriminatory. The relatively permissive nature of section 93 of the British North American Act—it specified only which schools must be funded and not which others could or could not be funded—when read together with the anti-discrimination provisions of the Canadian Charter of Rights and Freedoms provides a strong argument for the extension of public funding to private schools. The strength of this argument is increased by the recent extension of public funding in Ontario to Roman Catholic secondary schools, since this appears to be more clearly an act of political will than a fulfilment of a constitutional obligation. The government is, of course, clearly entitled to exercise this political will, but not on a discriminatory basis. On the other hand, the arguments for maintaining the unique status of the Roman Catholic separate schools do not seem convincing. Thus, for example, the argument deriving from the large size of the Roman Catholic community, while of some political and, perhaps, economic interest, is not convincing on either moral or legal grounds. Similarly, the argument based on historical and constitutional status is, as suggested above, morally unconvincing. Further, its legal basis would seem only to find firm grounding if one suggests that the development of a publicly supported denominational school system was an unfortunate historical mistake, one that might have to be supported or tolerated, but that certainly should not be repeated. Given, however, the recent Canadian constitutional exercise during which the historical policy with regard to denominational schools was reaffirmed, the "historical mistake" argument seems unconvincing with regard to the development of public policy. Since Ontario appears much more than nominally determined to maintain and publicly fund Roman Catholic schools, only very strong arguments about other public benefits could justify a continued policy of discrimination against private schools from other than Roman Catholic communities.

In terms of the three most common arguments advanced by those advising against the public funding of private schools, that is, social cohesion and tolerance, equality of educational opportunity, and spending priority, we find that the spending priority argument is of little merit. We do accept the two most common premises of this argument, that the public schools should be the priority public investment in education and that, at present, the public schools are underfunded. Nevertheless, we do not draw the conclusion that there should, therefore, be no extension of public funding to private schools.

The cost of such extension (even at full levels) at no more than $200 million annually, is not sufficiently large—when compared to the $6.5 billion per annum already being expended on the public elementary and secondary schools in the province—to be determinative of public policy. Second, since educators are in the best sense fully engaged in maximizing the funds to be made available to their work and then fully expending these funds in the interest of their students, we find it hard to imagine a funding context in which the public school community—or any other school community—would see itself as having sufficient financial support to enable the funding of other systems to assume a first priority. Therefore, we reject the spending priority argument.

The social cohesion argument is, we believe, on stronger ground. The argument has two facets. First, its posits the need, in a heterogeneous society, for more, rather than fewer, common cultural touchstones, and then argues that the public schools (rather especially the board of education schools) represent the only institutional vehicle that is readily available for providing a common but non-commercial experience for young Ontarians of, at least potentially, widely different personal and family backgrounds. We have some sympathy with this view, although we recognize that in many actual settings (e.g., the neighbourhood school, the separate school) the student body of a particular public school may be quite homogeneous. Nevertheless, a society should strive to realize some common socialization experience for its young people, and the public schools represent the most likely setting for this effort. It is not easy to imagine that largely segmented schools will lead to a sufficiently cohesive social environment, even though one cannot totally dismiss the alternative argument by minority groups that common settings can be very destructive to their distinctive needs.

The second aspect of the social cohesion argument relates to the question of tolerance. It is argued that, in a multicultural society, tolerance is among the supreme civic virtues. It is, however, our unfortunate experience that, with some exceptions, schools—whether public or private—do not actually take this matter seriously in the development of their own programs. The public schools too easily assume that the mere physical presence of various groups within their student bodies somehow breeds tolerance and understanding. On the other hand, private schools, most of which are religiously defined, rather too easily assume the equivalence between piety and good citizenship without taking into account that, for at least a number of religious groups, the claim to universality has often meant the spiritual repression of other religions and cultures. It must be admitted that no one knows just which schooling experiences are most likely to produce tolerant and understanding adult citizens and that, from the point of view of minority groups, large-scale common settings are often repressive settings. One cannot help but recall, for example, Egerton Ryerson's own opposition to cultural diversity when he wrote in 1846 about the arrival of the Irish Catholic victims of famine:

> It is therefore of...importance that every possible effort should be employed to bring the facilities of education within the reach of the families of these unfortunate people that they may grow up in...industry and intelligence...and not in the idleness and pauperism, not to say the mendicity and vices of their forefathers.[5]

Nevertheless, in the absence of sure knowledge, it does seem intuitively plausible that tolerance and understanding are more likely to arise from settings in which various groups interact than in settings that are segmented and segregated, whether voluntarily or otherwise. Indeed, if the opposite is true, that is, if familiarity breeds contempt or, what is worse, contamination, then the very concept of a multicultural and pluralistic society becomes a contradiction in terms. Thus, we would argue that the context of the public school represents, whatever its past failures, the most promising potential for realizing a future characterized by a more fully tolerant society.

It is, however, with regard to the equality of educational opportunity that we find ourselves in strongest agreement with those advising against the funding of private schools. One of the historic missions of the public school has been to act as a kind of ladder of social mobility for young people who do not bring to their schooling special advantages of background, experience, or wealth. It cannot be claimed that this mission has always been achieved, and that the public schools have always risen to Thomas Jefferson's historic call for an "education to enable every man to judge for himself what will secure or endanger his freedom."

Further, on occasion, the public schools are said to actively prevent citizenship and promote the stifling of self-government. Nevertheless, there have also been many successes and, more to the point, the alternative arrangements seem even more unattractive. The great advantage of the private school is that it can focus its priorities and its programs to fit, rather precisely, the particular students (and their families) that such schools may wish to admit. It is hardly surprising therefore, that those for whom the school is designed find that it suits their needs more admirably than the public school, which must, perforce, provide a program of much broader and less focussed dimensions. Thus, readily recognized individual advantage is provided by the private school, at least for those for whom the school is designed and who can afford its cost. The funding of these schools might make such advantages available without regard to parental income, and it is, therefore, not unlikely that this would result in an increased interest in attending such schools, although the actual extent of this new demand is very difficult to forecast. The resulting benefits would be individual benefits, but their cost would be a social cost, one encountered in the growing realization that the seemingly legitimate desire of parents to procure advantages for their children is something that can be fully accomplished only at the expense of others. In any case, if such funding should result in any large transfer of either the higher achieving or the more affluent students from the public to the private schools, then the inability of the public schools (as the schools of "second choice") to offer equal educational opportunity will have been destroyed. It is, of course, by no means certain that this outcome would occur. It would, however, be a rather large risk to take.

The very brief summary given above of both the arguments brought forward to the Commission on Private Schools in Ontario and our response to these arguments reveal the essential difficulty in all substantial matters of social policy, that is, the conflict of values. Thus, the emerging difficulty of the present writers in terms of imagining coherent response to the issues raised on both sides of the "public funding" issue was how to envision a future set of school arrangements for Ontario that would increase parental choice and address the problem of discrimination while not only maintaining but also enhancing—in the name of social cohesion, tolerance and understanding, and equality of educational opportunity—the integrity and the promise of Ontario's public schools.

In considering this matter, the popular language of rights (whether individual rights, group rights, national rights, language rights or, in fact, human rights), although attractive in principle, was difficult in practice. Since the language of rights tends to be so absolutist in its sweep, it is not helpful when the conflicting rights of social policy need to be adjudicated. Further, in the particular matter of schooling, it is children's rights that are of central importance, and, relative to these rights, it was not easy to determine whether it was society's (or the government's) vision of these rights or the parents' vision that should take precedence. Nevertheless, the underlying question of rights, that is, the matter of values, could not appropriately be circumvented.

Social viability is always based on a shared system of values, for it is only on the basis of common values that a truly shared existence (as opposed to mere co-existence) is possible. Thus, in multicultural societies, such as Ontario, among the common or shared values must be a conception of tolerance that demands respect for others and for alternative points of view. This, in turn, is based on a commitment to other values such as the minimal order required for dialogues; a respect for truth; the need, sometimes, to act for the sake of others, etc. Of course, in any society, there are also conflicts of values and, therefore, alternative visions of what constitutes justice and appropriate social policy. It is, in fact, just such conflicts that have historically shaped Ontario's policies in education. Thus, a commitment to common schools and/or private schools starts with values and, therefore, alternative visions of what constitutes justice and appropriate social policy. It is, in fact, just such conflicts that have historically shaped Ontario's policies in education. Thus, a commitment to common schools and/or private schools starts with values that are not themselves subject to empirical demonstration. It starts with beliefs about what sort of society Ontario should become. That is, it starts with a vision of a preferred future expressed as a particular kind of schooling for the young. Policy-making in education is, therefore, primarily a political process. As such, it must be seen—within a democracy—as a question to be settled, in the final analysis, not by social scientists but by elected officials and/or the courts. Thus, the importance of values and the implications that different values and value systems have for public policy with regard to schooling would be difficult to overestimate.

Education is one of society's dominant concerns and, although schooling is only a part of society's much wider arrangements for education, the more complex and dynamic the society, the greater is the need for clarifying the function of its schools and the role they should play in the ongoing attempt to realize a better society. In this context, and without any claim to a complete and comprehensive view, we believe that:

1. Elementary and secondary schools are important institutions whose goal is to develop, nurture, and enhance the intellectual and moral autonomy of the young. This goal and its attendant responsibilities are shared with parents and other societal agencies.

2. In a democratic society, this goal of intellectual and moral autonomy is a social and individual good of sufficient importance to justify the compulsory schooling of children.

3. Such schooling should be made available in such a way as to:
a) maximize the equality of educational opportunity; that is, the likelihood that each person will be prepared to realize her or his potential and to make informed and independent choices as to his or her own future;
b) provide for the shared responsibility of government and family exercising its natural interest in and responsibility for the welfare of the child and the government acting on behalf of the interests of the wider society and as a protector of the rights of individual children; and
c) ensure that, in a pluralistic and multicultural society, schools can contribute to the strengthening of the social fabric by providing a common acculturation experience for children.

It is clearly not logically necessary for governments to both provide and finance educational services, but we believe that the requirements of accessibility and accountability make such a double role entirely appropriate. Further, such a double role provides, in a way that no other policy can, a context in which publicly funded schools are tied not only to the private purposes of self-interest and individual mobility—principles heavily weighted in favour of those already advantaged—but also to the public purposes of providing a public service committed to improving collective and democratic traditions. Further, discussion and action about public and common schools present at least a potential opportunity for citizens to become concerned, not simply about what is good for themselves or their children, but also about what is necessary to bring about a more just and efficient society for others. Finally, to the extent that the public and common schools are the schools of choice for the great majority of families, these schools may be able to respect group differences while at the same time helping their students to perceive the common concerns that transcend such differences. Schools are better able to teach common understanding and shared values if they are less homogeneous and can, at least potentially, bring children of different backgrounds together. Thus, we believe that:

4. It is appropriate for the government to finance and provide an effective system of common public elementary and secondary schools that:
   a) meet society's educational requirements for schooling;
   b) are accessible and open to all;
   c) are tuition-free;
   d) provide substantial opportunity for parental and community participation;
   e) represent the primary, but not necessarily the exclusive, public investment in education; and
   f) are the schools of choice for the great majority of young people and their families.

5. *Relevant constitutional issues aside*, no further obligation for the public funding of elementary and secondary schools exists.

Constitutional issues must, of course, be considered. In addition, none of the above denies the value of private schools. Thus, for example, in a heterogeneous society, the arguments for a common acculturation experience can be overstated, so that all dissent and variation is suppressed in favour of some single, necessarily imperfect, vision, and it is an unfortunate truth that the public school community has not always avoided this pitfall. Past failures should not, however, rule out the present potential of the public schools in which it should, in principle, be possible to both widen and deepen the existing social consensus by capitalizing on our differences without unnecessarily institutionalizing them. Thus, we believe that:

6. There should be no legal public monopoly in education, and that private schools that meet the minimum standards specified by the government in terms of the obligations to both society and individual children should have a clear status in recognition both of the rights of citizens to make alternative choices and of the general value of diversity.

7. Moreover, diversity within the public school system should also be encouraged.

Finally, although—again, constitutional issues aside—no obligation for the public funding of private schools may exist, some public assistance to private schools should, nevertheless, be a feature of a creative public policy. We believe that:

8. As a matter of public policy, and so long as the public policy objectives outlined above are not substantially eroded, new initiatives, both in public support of private schools and in the relationship of these schools to the public schools, should be actively developed and tested.

The appropriate nature of these new initiatives will vary from jurisdiction to jurisdiction, and should be a matter of explicit public debate. For example, there is the question of religious education. Both religiously defined and non-sectarian private schools have identified the lack of religious education in the public schools as a real deficiency. We would agree to some extent, in that it is our belief that the provision of religious education in public schools has the potential to provide a basis, not only for the understanding of one of the most significant aspects of human experience, but also for the development of tolerance and understanding among the members of a multicultural society. This benefit can only be realized, we would argue, if the religious education within the school is non-confessional in nature, that is, is not designed to inculcate a specific system of belief, but focusses, instead, on a theological point of view and general issues in ethnics. We recognize that the ability, in practice, to differentiate confessional from non-confessional approaches is not easy to maintain, but the potential benefits seem well worth the effort. Basic confessional training or understanding is, we would suggest, more properly the task of the home and the church than the school.

In any case, whatever the new initiative—whether in the public schools, in the private (religious) schools, or both—an element of risk will be involved in all cases, since the consequences of new policies cannot be forecast with any assurance. On the other hand, there are also substantial risks associated with the status quo (one need only think of the increasingly tenuous commitment of the Canadian middle class to the public school system). Thus, the only real question in social policy is not whether to take a risk, but which risk to take. In each case, the choice made will depend to no small extent on the values given greatest priority at that point in time.

With particular regard to Ontario, given both the framework of belief outlined above and the importance, in our view, of dealing more equitably with the constitutional issues of discrimination raised by the funding of the Roman Catholic separate schools, we further believe that it is important for Ontario to modify its current arrangements with regard to private schools, especially those religious private schools that are not Roman Catholic in nature.

The particular recommendations of the Commission on Private Schools in Ontario can be found in the Commission's report, but, although these recommendations were regarded by the Commission as appropriate, we cannot argue that they are, in some logical sense, the uniquely correct way to proceed. Different sets of values, or alternative understanding of just what specific values imply, will yield different recommendations. What is important to stress, however, is that whatever policy route either Ontario or any other Canadian jurisdiction is proposing to elect, the proposed policy is likely to succeed only if all of those involved are prepared to summon up their resources for co-operative, perhaps even conscionable, behaviour. Interestingly, Green[6] has described a variety of aspects of conscience among which are the conscience of membership (i.e., the recognition that we must sometimes act for the sake of others) and the conscience of sacrifice (i.e., the willingness to override the pursuit of self-interest and act beyond the limits of mere duty). The success of any proposed program will, in fact, depend to no small degree on the extent to which these aspects of conscience are exhibited by the government, by the board of education schools, by the private schools, by the separate schools, and by the many communities and individuals to which each of these relates and responds.

NOTES

1. This article is based on and drawn from the authors' work for the Commission on Private Schools in Ontario. The Commission's work is more fully reported in *The Report of the Commission on Private Schools in Ontario*, Bernard J. Shapiro, Commissioner Toronto: Government of Ontario, Oct. 1985.

2. J.R. Mallea, "Cultural Diversity in Canadian Education: A Review of Contemporary Developments" in *Multiculturalism in Canada*, edited by R. Samvoa (Allyn and Bacon, Toronto: 1984).

3. The data concerning Canadian policies in this area refer to 1984–85, and were drawn primarily from the following sources: *Public Funding of Private Schools in Canada* (Toronto: Canadian Education Association, Nov. 1984); L. Perras, "Summary of Legislation Regulations, Policies for the Funding of Private Schools in Each of the Provinces of Canada Other than Ontario" (paper prepared for The Commission on Private Schools in Ontario (Toronto, Feb. 1985).

4. Stephen Lawton, "Alternative Methods of Financing Private Schools in Ontario" in *The Report of the Commission on Private Schools in Ontario* (Toronto: Government of Ontario, Oct. 1985), Appendix, pp. 81–108.

5. Egerton Ryerson, *Journal of Education for Upper Canada*, Vol. 1 (Toronto: J.H. Lawrence, 1948), 300.

6. Thomas Green, *The Formulation of Conscience in an Age of Technology* (San Antonio: John Dewey Society, 1984).

THE TEACHING OF EVOLUTION AND CREATION IN PUBLICLY SUPPORTED SCHOOLS

GOLDWIN JAMES EMERSON

Most people are content to view the theory of evolution and the various biblical accounts of creation as compatible versions of human beginnings. According to this view, opposing evolution to creation leads to counterproductive arguments. Where apparent discrepancies exist, adherents of this position are generally content to let religion be religion and science be science. Along with this popular view, there is an indefinable faith that as scientific and religious thinking progresses, whatever discrepancies remain will converge into a unified whole at some point in the not-too-distant future. For the sake of simplicity, this popular view may be characterized as the "let sleeping dogs lie" view. This position accommodates both scientific and religious thinkers, many of whom lay claim to being both at one and the same time. Unfortunately for these adherents, in the past ten to fifteen years, forces are emerging that make the "sleeping dogs" position less comfortable. The rapid growth of fundamentalist religions and the steady advancement of science appear to have polarized the evolution-creation conflict so that it becomes more difficult to embrace both positions simultaneously.

THE FUNDAMENTALIST POSITION

The fundamentalist position is deeply rooted in religious faith in a supreme being who exists eternally and is independent of the natural world. The evidence for this creator-god is thought to be the Bible and, since most fundamentalists are of Protestant origin, the particular Bible that is generally held to be the most authoritative is the King James version. Bible stories are interpreted in a literal manner, and the fundamentalist regards the more liberal interpretations of non-fundamentalist Christian believers to be a sinful departure from God's word. The fundamentalist refers to *the* creation story, overlooking the fact that there are a number of versions of creation within the King James translation of the Bible,[1] to say nothing of other translations of the Bible or the many other sacred writings of non-Christian religions and of secular writings.

In general, Christian fundamentalists form an uneasy alliance with modern science in those areas where science appears to lend support to their religious views. However, when science runs counter to literal interpretations of the Bible, science is regarded as the product of misguided attempts to make sense of a universe that is beyond human understanding.

THE MYTHOLOGY OF CREATION

There are many very serious problems inherent in finding an answer to the question of human origins; so many pieces of information are missing. Yet the question is sufficiently important to have engaged serious thinkers throughout human history. There are literally hundreds of explanations written in the form of creation myths. Creation mythology is an extremely useful tool in understanding the social and logical thinking of various cultures as they have searched for their own answers to human origins. Charles H. Long emphasizes the importance of creation myths as follows:

> There is a rather widespread notion that creation myths are prescientific attempts to give an explanation of the world; in other words, they are primitive science without proper method. We must admit that most myths are products of a prescientific age and that they came into being before the strict functional separation of forms of thought and society were predominant. We must further admit that creation myths do perform an explanatory role in the life of the society which believes in them.[2]

Since there are not sufficient facts to tell how the universe began, it is necessary for the originators of creation myths to be very creative thinkers themselves.[3] In order to endure, a myth must provide a suitable explanation where hard data is missing. It must contain answers that are compatible with the values, the everyday wisdom, and the known truths of a culture. For this reason myths provide important information about the culture that embraces them.

RECURRING THEMES IN CREATION MYTHOLOGY

A study of creation mythology from early Egyptian and Babylonian cultures to those found much later among Navaho and Polynesian cultures reveals that there are many recurring themes regarding creation stories.[4] Many of these parallel the Genesis accounts of creation. For example, the creator, according to the Babylonian epic, created man in his own image and later created a second being out of the body of his first creation. Mythology has many stories of lesser gods who compete for power, and eventually one

Supreme-God emerges over all. This Supreme Being typically resides in highest heaven and is jealous of other gods who compete for the attention of humans.

Women are represented as the cause of releasing evil into the world due to a weakness in their character. In Greek mythology, Pandora is overcome by curiosity and releases evil into the world by opening the forbidden box of good and evil. In Genesis 3:6, Eve is tempted by the serpent and tastes the forbidden fruit, which brings hardship and evil to mankind. An early Japanese myth tells of Izanami who talks too much and does not remain subservient to her husband Izanagi. As a result, their offspring are abnormal and humans are condemned to suffer imperfections because of her lack of judgment. In Ecclesiasticus 25:13 and 25:15–19, women are regarded as a source of great evil.

> 13. No wound is as serious as wounded love. No troubles are as serious as the trouble women cause....
> 15. No poison is deadlier than the poison of a snake, and no anger is deadlier than the anger of a woman.
> 16. I would rather live in the same house with a lion or a dragon than with a bad wife.
> 17. When a wife is in a bad mood, her expression changes until she looks like an angry bear.
> 18. Her husband has to go and eat with the neighbours, where he can't hold back his bitter sighs.
> 19. Compared with the troubles caused by a woman, any other troubles look small. May such women suffer the fate of sinners!

A number of myths, such as those found in the Australian, Mayan, Egyptian, and Hebrew cultures include the concept of creation from nothing.[5] There is some ambiguity in the various translations of the Bible as to whether God created the universe out of nothing or created order out of a pre-existent chaos. The King James version is usually interpreted, especially by fundamentalists, to mean that God created something from nothing. On the other hand, many creation myths suggest that structure and order emerged from a sea of darkness and chaos and in time this order produced imperfect gods who competed with one another.[6] Eventually, a Supreme Being gained control over the lesser gods and brought meaning and structure and human life to the universe.

The fundamentalist version of creation is particularly problematic. It is hard to have either a logical or intuitive sense of how something could be produced out of nothing. Hebrews 11:3 indicates the writer's struggle to answer this same problem. "It is by faith that we understand that the universe was created by God's word, so that what can be seen was made out of what cannot be seen." In addition, the "something from nothing" creation myth raises the question of God's own genesis. If God always existed, as the "first cause" argument claims, presumably it is equally logical to believe that the universe could also have an eternal existence. The Hindu writer in Rig Veda

X.129, mused over the same dilemma in the opening and closing stanzas of this "creation from nothing" myth.

> Was neither Being nor Non-Being then,
> Neither Air nor Space beyond.
> What was It, forcefully stirring?
> Where? In whose Keeping? Was it
> water deep beyond sound?...
> This creation, where it came from,
> Whether a foundation or not, He who
> surveys from highest heaven, Alone knows—
> unless He knows nothing about it?

Many parallels exist in creation mythology, and modern biblical scholars recognize that these myths have been both borrowed by, and borrowed from, the early biblical writers. Graves states as follows:

> Since 1876, when two versions of an ancient Creation Epic were discovered in the ruins of the Assyrian King Assurbanipal's library, all serious Biblical students, except confirmed fundamentalists, have come to realize that the first four chapters of the Book of Genesis are not of unique authority, because [they are] paralleled in these and other Oriental works dating from a far earlier period than that of Moses, the reputed author. It is now also widely accepted that Genesis, as we have it, was reduced to writing as late as the fifth century B.C. and is unlikely to have been current beforehand in oral form.[7]

THE EVOLUTIONIST POSITION

"Essentially, evolution is the belief that all living things descended from a few simple forms of life or from a single form of life that has progressed from a simple to many complex forms."[8] Included in the evolution theory is the idea that, in each generation the most fit, that is, the best adapted, are more likely to survive. This assumes variations within each population gene pool and it assumes that the variations can be passed on to offspring. Since some variations offer a survival advantage, in time a new species will evolve. When further variations in the new species offer yet further survival advantages, these in turn will cause changes within the population moving the organism on to a better adaptation each time.

The epistemological basis for evolution is, generally speaking, the scientific method. Although there are a number of approaches to the scientific method, most traditional approaches follow a procedure that begins either with observations or by identifying a problem. Next, one or more hypotheses are formulated to explain the data or the problem. Each hypothesis is tested by further experiment, if possible, to see which is the most effective explanation. In addition, the evidence is verified by replication, which may be carried out by independent scientists or other objective observers. Finally, a hypothesis becomes a generally accepted theory, by weight of the evidence, or by its ability to predict further observations.

Although the theory of evolution does not depend upon sacred writings nor religious faith, many, indeed most, evolutionists, are religious believers who interpret the Bible in a non-literal sense. A much smaller proportion of evolutionists are atheistic and discount the Bible as an authority on the question of human origins. Both religious and non-religious evolutionists believe that the validity of the theory of evolution is based on scientific evidence.

SOME MISSING LINKS

In science, the term *theory* refers to a belief that is well-founded in evidence at the same time as there is a recognition that all the facts are not yet in. Atomic and genetic theory are two examples of scientific theories that have already been proven very useful models, based on the available evidence. While a scientific theory provides a reasonably workable model, there is the understanding that new evidence may serve either to support the theory or to require its revision or even its abandonment. It is this concept of theory that underlies the scientists' view of evolution. Unfortunately, the same understanding of theory may be overlooked by well-meaning and enthusiastic teachers who confuse the present evidence for evolution as a theory with what they regard as the "fact" of evolution. Or, if the distinction is clear in the mind of the teacher, he or she may fail to communicate the distinction clearly to the students being taught.

HISTORICAL BENCH MARKS CONCERNING THE TEACHING OF EVOLUTION AND CREATION

Early ideas about evolution can be traced back at least to Anaximander in sixth-century Greece.[9] However, in more modern times, the conflict between evolution and creation was brought to a head by Darwin's books, *Origin of Species* (1859) and *The Descent of Man* (1871) as well as by Andrew White's, *A History of the Warfare of Science with Theology and Christendom* (1896). Many people assume that the conflict between evolution and creation was settled by the Scopes "monkey trial" in 1925 although, in fact, the legal result of the Scopes trial was that Tennessee's anti-evolution law was upheld.[10] It was not until 1967 that the law was repealed when another Tennessee high school teacher, Gary Scott, was dismissed for teaching evolution. In 1968, the United States Supreme Court declared that state laws forbidding the teaching of evolution were unconstitutional. This decision, combined with the Supreme Court's 1963 ruling banning state-imposed devotional exercises but upholding the objective study of religion, required the creationists to adopt new tactics.

One approach of the creationists has been to argue that the theory of evolution has many missing links and that it is, in effect, a theory based more on faith than on scientific evidence. Moreover, the creation of organic life from inorganic chemicals cannot as yet be repeated in the laboratory in spite of some interesting work with the production of amino acids. Creationists argue that the theory of evolution is in fact a form of "secular religion" or a "humanistic religion" rather than a true scientific theory. Consequently, they argue that, as a religion, it should be forbidden under the 1963 Supreme Court ruling.

A second, and more effective approach for creationists has been to argue that, in the interest of fairness, all views of human origins should be taught in science classes. Actually creationists do not mean *all* views. What is usually meant is the literal interpretation of one of the biblical stories of Genesis along with the theory of evolution, which is permitted by the Supreme Court ruling of 1968. It is interesting to note that in privately run fundamentalist schools, giving equal time to all views has a very low priority since the theory of evolution is often not taught in science classes at all. The argument for equal time for creation and evolution depends in part on the mistaken notion that there is much disagreement and ambiguity among scientists regarding evolution. Politicians, ranging from school trustees to the president of the United States, are sensitive to the importance of capitalizing on their audience's confusion about evolution. The following account by John Skow tells of Ronald Reagan's pre-election speech to a group of church leaders in Dallas where he stated that:

> Evolution was "theory only," which has "in recent years been challenged in the world of science." He [Reagan] added that "if it is going to be taught in the schools, then I would think that also the biblical theory of creation, which is not a theory but the biblical story of creation should also be taught."[11]

A number of modifications to the theory of evolution have been made by scientists since Darwin. Rather than weakening the case for evolution by these modifications, scientists have been able to fill in many gaps. For example, geologists, astronomers, and nuclear physicists corroborate the fact that the universe is billions of years old.[12] Geophysical and geochemical studies indicate that the earth's surface has been drastically rearranged for a period of history much longer than that claimed by fundamentalist creationists who believe the earth to be between 6 000 and 10 000 years old. Studies in genetics indicate that chimpanzees have a biochemistry in common with humans down to such fine details as the amino acid sequence of particular proteins. Carbon dating of fossils indicates a sequence of animal life on earth that parallels the evolutionary development of species. These and other recent developments in science serve to add new evidence confirming the theory of evolution rather than raising doubts about its validity.

The creationist's argument for equal time in science class for both the creationist and evolutionist points of view has had its impact on education. Some states, including Arkansas and Louisiana, have passed bills requiring equal time in science classes as well as equal space for the provision of textbooks, library materials, and educational programs.[13] Both in Canada and the United States a number of textbooks have recently been modified to cut down on the pages devoted to evolution, and in some Canadian provinces department of education science guidelines now discuss how animals adapt to their surroundings but omit or greatly reduce references to evolution. Many teachers find that it is easier to avoid the teaching of evolution because the topic is too controversial.

A third approach of the creationists is to argue that creation study belongs in science classes because it can be supported by scientific evidence. Proponents call this view "scientific creationism" and refer to themselves as "creation scientists."[14] Generally, they have faith in the infallibility of the Bible, and they interpret it in a literal manner. Nevertheless, proponents claim that support for their beliefs is scientific rather than religious.[15] One such creation scientist, Robert Gentry, contends that the mysterious radioactive polonium halos in granitic rock are "signs of creation left by God for scientists to uncover."[16] Another, Henry Morris, author of a book called *Scientific Creationism*, claims:

> Evolution is inconsistent with God's personality. If man in HIS own image was the goal of the evolutionary process, surely God would not have waited until the very tailend of geologic time before creating personalities. No personal fellowship was possible with the rocks and seas, or even with the dinosaurs and gliptodons [sic]. Evolution is inconsistent with God's omniscience.[17]

The creation scientists appear to start with a particular position of faith drawn not from observation but from the Bible. Their unwillingness to revise their position in the light of observation or to critically examine new evidence that runs counter to their position lacks intellectual honesty. Needless to say, creation scientists are not highly regarded in the scientific community.

THE CANADIAN SCENE

In order to assess present Canadian school systems, it is helpful to look at what policies have been established regarding the teaching of creation and/or evolution in each province in publicly supported schools. The following is an overview of the responses given by representatives from the various provincial ministries of education.

NEWFOUNDLAND

There have been some representations in Newfoundland on behalf of creation science groups. Since the province is organized according to a number of denominational schools, each school system deals with the concept of creation through its religious education programs. This fact tends to alleviate parents' concerns for students' religious needs.

Evolution is taught in the high school biology program. The department of education urges teachers to teach evolution as a plausible *theory* in science rather than "blandly assuming that it is true" or "presenting it as fact and extending it beyond its present range of application." Nevertheless, "the Department of Education intends to continue a major emphasis on the principles and theory of evolution in its science programs."

PRINCE EDWARD ISLAND

There have been relatively few representations from creationist groups in P.E.I., and a formal policy on the teaching of creationism and/or evolution has not been established. However, "creationism is not considered as science and, therefore, need not be taught as part of the science program." Teachers are encouraged to be sensitive to alternative approaches to knowledge in addition to science. Evolution is presented as an option within the senior secondary science curriculum.

The school system operates as a secular system, and no religious courses are included in the curriculum although, within local areas, some religious instruction may be presented on an optional basis.

NOVA SCOTIA

Nova Scotia public schools are secular in nature and there have been no representations from local groups for the teaching of creationism. Science curricula include the teaching of evolution at the secondary school levels both in Grade 10 and in Grade 12. Teachers are encouraged to make their students aware of the role of modifiable theories within science. Although religion and creationism are not included as part of the school curricula, teachers are encouraged to deal with students' questions with sensitivity and with respect for a variety of views.

NEW BRUNSWICK

New Brunswick schools, under the provincial Schools Act, are non-sectarian and religion is not prescribed in the curriculum. There has been little or no pressure from organizations to include concepts of biblical creation within the science curriculum. The minister of education "has indicated that concepts in the teaching of a social-religious nature are not appropriate content to be prescribed within scientific disciplines and that creationism is one of these." However, teachers are encouraged to deal with students' questions on religious topics with sensitivity and with good judgment regardless of the particular course being taught.

ONTARIO

The draft document for the curriculum guidelines *Science, Intermediate and Senior Divisions*, includes the teaching of evolution as a core unit for Grade 13 biology. In Grade 11 biology, "Plant Adaptations and Behaviour" is included as a core unit.

Religious instruction, including the biblical accounts of creation, is given on a regular basis within the elementary Roman Catholic separate schools and on a more sporadic basis within the elementary public schools depending upon the preferences of local school boards and individual teachers.

The ministry of education is presently formulating "a statement on the teaching of sensitive issues, including the creation/evolution issue." The statement on sensitive issues will be included eventually as part of the *Science Program and Policies*. Present indications are that the statement will encourage teachers to be sensitive to the great variety of social attitudes among the students and their parents and that, while science may provide information, it does not dictate moral values *per se*.

MANITOBA

A statement of policy on the teaching of creation and/or evolution is now being developed and it will soon be included in the new biology curriculum guides. Present indications are that the policy will reflect the concept of science as a discipline that proceeds through observation and experimentation. "As data are collected, theories are advanced to explain and account for observations." Theories are modifiable, and "the theory of evolution should be presented as one that is still modified on the basis of newly discovered data."

Creationism is considered to rest "upon spiritual direction and entities that are outside the domain of science," although creationism "could be included within a school initiated course in either Religious Studies or using a Theory of Knowledge approach."

The policy statement will comment on possible local input as well as describe the provincial position.

QUEBEC

The biblical accounts of creation are taught in a systematic manner within Protestant and Catholic schools. "For the elementary level in the first year, God is presented as Father, Creator, and Source of life; in the third level God as Creator is taught even more explicitly." In the first year of Roman Catholic secondary schools, a unit is included on "God Who is Creator." In the fifth year of secondary school, under the rubric of "The great questions of existence," the pupil studies biblical accounts of origins.

In the Protestant secondary system, one unit of the religious curriculum deals with various creation myths, and distinctions are made between myths and fables in terms of their epistemological bases.

Evolution, as such, is not taught as a distinct part of any course although the topic of evolution may come up in an incidental way in some classes.

SASKATCHEWAN

Representation from creationist groups has been more frequent and persistent than in most other provinces. The department of education has developed a policy on the teaching of creation and evolution, and this policy is soon to be circulated as part of the curriculum guidelines for teachers. The policy states that the guidelines that "are developed at the department level will continue to reflect science principles and theories accepted by practising scientists participating in the discipline as valid content for study."

Evolution is taught at the junior high school level under the curriculum areas of anthropology and social studies and also within the Grade 12 biology course. Textbooks and reference books, in accordance with the Education Act, are selected for use from a list of authorized texts. However, with the approval of local principals and superintendents, school boards may choose additional reference materials for the science programs. This latter practice has been one route by which some local creationist groups have attempted to introduce creationist materials into the science programs under the aegis of "creation science."

Creationism is also taught within the religion and Christian ethics courses. In addition, the separate school systems within the province provide for religious instruction.

ALBERTA

The Alberta Department of Education is sensitive to potential difficulties in teaching controversial curricula. In 1972 a policy regarding controversial issues was established, and in 1979 that original policy was expanded to include "the treatment of the theory of evolution in school science programs." Evolution is included in the high school biology curriculum, and the policy statement is an integral part of the instruction to teachers. On one hand, the policy emphasizes the importance of scientific accuracy and observable and reproducible facts as necessary parts of the scientific method. On the other hand, much is said about developing positive attitudes of "tolerance, understanding, and respect" for the opinions and beliefs of others. The policy statement cautions teachers that "care should be taken that neither theories nor beliefs are presented as dogma." The policy statement also encourages involvement "at the local level regarding the treatment of sensitive and controversial topics."

BRITISH COLUMBIA

There has been some representation from creationist groups to teach biblical creationism within science programs. A policy on the teaching of sensitive issues is in the process of being developed, and science teachers tend to take the view that evolution theory belongs within science courses while creationism does not. Nevertheless, science teachers are encouraged to be sensitive to the many views on the origins of the universe in addition to the theory of evolution.

Evolution and adaptation are optional parts of the Grade 8 science course under the heading of paleontology. Evolution is also included as part of the present biology course in senior secondary levels.

Although there are courses in world religions at the secondary school level, there are no religious studies *per se* in other grades. However, opening exercises include reading of the Bible, and occasional references to creationism are included in these exercises.

In summary, most provinces include the teaching of evolution within the biology curriculum at the senior secondary school level. In some cases, evolution is not a core unit within biology courses and in most cases the study of biology itself is not a requirement for secondary school graduation. Consequently, students may or may not receive instruction in evolution.

Creationism is not regarded by departments of education as a legitimate part of science curricula *per se* although, within local areas, some creationist reference materials occasionally have been included.

Courses in religious education are included within half of the provinces and concepts of creationism are included in these courses. All provinces urge their science teachers to deal with issues such as creation and evolution with sensitivity, good judgment, and respect for the views of others.

RECOMMENDATIONS FOR THE TEACHING OF EVOLUTION AND CREATION

The following recommendations pertain to publicly supported school systems at the elementary and secondary levels; that is, schools that are supported by public funds and that are open to students from a variety of religious persuasions.

1. When the theory of evolution is taught, teachers should emphasize that it is a "theory." By doing so, the children of fundamentalist parents are not forced into making an immediate either-or choice between evolution and creation.

2. Science teachers should teach the scientific method. The term *scientific method* may tend to be over-used in our society without students actually understanding its meaning. Students should learn that the scientific method differs from other forms of inquiry such as reliance on authority, religious faith, intuition, tradition, and simple observation.

3. Teachers should cherish and protect the discipline of science. There is a tendency for groups such as religious fundamentalists and commercial advertising agencies to use the term *science* loosely and inappropriately in order to give credence to non-scientific conclusions. Teachers who are vigilant can assist students to be aware of inappropriate scientific claims.

4. Science teachers should not teach the creation view in science classes. Nevertheless, it may be helpful for teachers to comment that creationism is an explanation held by many religious believers. Occasionally, science teachers present the creation view in response to arguments for "fair play." Public pressure to teach creation in science classes is analogous to medical students being required to spend equal time on studying faith healing to that spent on anatomy, pharmacology, or surgery.

5. Where religion is taught in publicly supported schools, it should be presented in an objective, non-devotional manner. When it is properly taught, courses in world religions, religious literature, and religious customs can assist students to be more objective about their own religion and more tolerant of the religions of others.

6. Every teacher of every subject has some responsibility for the moral development of students. It is almost impossible to teach without conveying some value systems to students. Unfortunately, the popular view is that children can learn moral values only through religion. Moreover, science, because of its objectivity, is often thought to be valueless. This idea gives rise to the unfortunate notion that, while religious classes are concerned with moral good, science classes are totally amoral, if not immoral. Yet many moral values can best be taught in science classes. Examples include sharing and conserving of natural resources, appreciation for the beauty of nature, protection of endangered species, and the role of science in increasing and sharing world food supplies. Science teachers have an important contribution to make toward the moral development of their students.

7. Science curricula should include the teaching of the theory of evolution since it is a major theory within the scientific community and presumably it has considerable educational merit if one is to proceed in understanding geology, biology, astronomy, and other related sciences. Moreover, it is difficult to imagine a suitable alternative scientific explanation of the earth's origins that incorporates the present body of scientific facts.

NOTES

1. J. Skow, "The Genesis of Equal Time," *Science 81* (Dec. 1981): 53–60.
2. Charles H. Long, *Alpha: The Myths of Creation* (Toronto: Ambassador Books, 1963).
3. M.L. Von Franz, *Creation Myths: Patterns of Creativity Measured in Creation Myths* (Texas: University of Dallas, Irving, 1978).
4. Long, *Alpha*.
5. Ibid.
6. D. MacLagan, *Creation Myths: Man's Introduction to the World* (Singapore: Thames and Hudson, 1979).
7. R. Graves, *Adam's Rib and Other Anomalous Elements in the Hebrew Creation Myth* (London: Trianon Press, 1955).
8. J. Bergman, "Teaching About the Creation/Evolution Controversy," *Phi Delta Kappa Fastback* 134 (1979).
9. B. Rensberger, "Darwin versus Dogma," *Science 81* (1981): 5.
10. Skow, "Genesis of Equal Time."
11. Ibid.
12. A. Hammond and L. Margulis, "Farewell to Newton, Einstein, Darwin..." *Science 81* (Dec. 1981): 55–57.
13. Rensberger, "Darwin versus Dogma."
14. J. Raloff, "They Call it Creation Science," *Science News* 121, 3 (Jan. 1982): 44–46.
15. H. Siegel, "Creationism, Evolution, and Education: The California Fiasco," *Phi Delta Kappan* 63, 2 (Oct. 1981): 95–99.
16. Raloff, "They Call it Creation Science."
17. Quoted in Skow, "The Genesis of Equal Time."

SECTION 6:
CANADIAN EDUCATION IN RELATION TO SOCIAL PROBLEMS AND ISSUES

Canadian educational systems are reverberating to the largely unpredictable and cumulative impacts of concurrent forces that are reshaping our institutions and our social conscience. These forces include the breakdown of the extended family and the faltering of the nuclear family unit, the rightfully enhanced role of women in our society, revolutionary advances in communication and transportation technology, the corporate benefits of sophisticated automation and the decreased demands for personnel, the accelerating pace of life and the growing alienation of increasing numbers of our citizens, and the manifestation of the global village with its manifold attendant persecutions and ultimate threats to human existence. The issues dealt with in this section result, at least in part, from these forces.

The section begins with an article by Wilson who attempts to clarify the term *social issues* and its development in the Canadian context. He maintains that effective teaching of social issues is not common due to the lack of appropriate resources, concern over the reaction of the community, and the absence of suitable training in this area for teachers. Wilson proposes four strategies for teaching social issues and discusses the requirements and ramifications of each. He also examines two Canadian programs that have been developed to teach social issues.

Given the increased awareness of the role of women in our society, Lips suggests there is a need for redesigning our educational system to empower female students. Steps to initiate the achievement of this goal lie in the examination of role models, curriculum content, interactions in the classroom, and nontraditional career choices. Role models must overcome sex stereotypes and encourage valid male and female self-images, rights, and responsibilities. Curricula that are influenced by societal norms must instead inform the student of the hidden restrictions and direct him or her to all possible choices. Attention and response must be equitable across sexes in the classroom to avoid valuing females more for appearance and good behaviour. Despite the predominant tendency for the career-minded woman to bear the demands of both family and work, there should be encouragement and support for students to confront and attempt to change social conditions that impose this double burden on women. To Lips, the resolution of these contentious issues is the present challenge for teachers.

Friesen contends that, although the family and the school have often been perceived as being in "partnership" regarding the education of children, this has not always been the case and it is at best an "uneasy partnership." He notes that, with the growing resurgence in family-related research, there is mounting evidence that the family exerts the most powerful influence on the developing child's educational expectations, verbal skills, affective relationships, discipline, and beliefs, and consequently, on her or his academic performance. Friesen develops this theme, purporting that parents should assume a greater role in the education of the child by developing a stronger, "co-operative partnership" between the home and the school.

Somewhat in contrast to the position of Friesen on the relationship of the family and the school, Pense examines the "new reality" wherein increasing numbers of preschool children are experiencing peer socialization and institutionalization external to the family at a very young age. Pense outlines the history of family and school life, the nature of our current state of social and institutional transition, and discusses the issues that face us in this area as individuals, as educators, and as a society planning for the future.

Herold reviews the history of sex education in Canada and discusses the objectives of sex education. He identifies a number of issues pertinent to the inclusion of sex education in the curriculum and discusses popular misconceptions, the attitudes of students and of the general population, and the preparation of teachers to conduct sex education classes. He concludes by speculating on the prospects for sex education in Canadian schools.

Eberlein and Mason and Swindlehurst outline the specific roles and responsibilities of teachers and schools in regard to child abuse and discuss the surrounding legal and moral issues. They address questions such as: What is child abuse? Is corporal punishment child abuse? Should society intervene? When should a report of child abuse be made? Who must report child abuse? What happens when a report of child abuse is made? Who keeps track of abused children?

After summarizing recent statistics on drug use and abuse among Canadian youth and outlining the resultant problems and legal consequences, Goodstadt examines the role of drug education in our schools—what it is and what it could become. He discusses the cognitive, behavioural, and affective objectives of drug education, describes the implementation of such programs, and makes specific recommendations for teachers.

Young focusses on the role of schools in dealing with the issues of prejudice and discrimination. He identifies several factors he believes are relevant for developing the attitudes and behaviours necessary for a tolerant multicultural society: the development of a suitable knowledge base for a multicultural curriculum, the opportunity for positive emotional experiences with ethnicity, the opportunity for adequate cognitive and moral development, the purging of prejudice from our language, and the modifying of the pedagogy of instruction. He also attempts to delineate the teacher's role in developing students who are committed to a multicultural reality for Canada.

Nevison concentrates on the specific challenge of counselling in a society in transition. She discusses the economic situation in Canada, the level of our educational preparedness, and our patterns of response to personal stress as indicators of change in our society. Nevison stresses the need for developmental counselling, in particular, to assist individuals coping with changes at various stages of their lives.

Given increased awareness of our global community, Close makes a strong case for the teaching of world affairs in our schools. He notes that the study of foreign affairs and comparative government accounts for a diminutive portion of the existing curriculum. He points out that the school social studies program may currently be the only avenue for systematic analysis of world issues available to most of our citizens. Close reviews relevant research on the learning of social issues and how children develop concepts of international relations and suggests directions for the preparation of courses that will enable citizens to respond to international affairs and crises in a more sophisticated and knowledgeable manner.

Mitchell concludes this section with a sobering chapter. He discusses why we deny the danger of nuclear war, why we do not comprehend the magnitude of the peril, and some of the effects of the threat of nuclear war on the development of our children. He argues that we must bring the issue of nuclear annihilation into our classrooms *now*, even though we may have disagreements about how to proceed in this controversial area.

SOCIAL ISSUES IN CANADIAN SCHOOLS
DONALD C. WILSON

No other social institution receives as much public attention as the school. As an institution of society, it is both supported financially and held accountable by the public at large. What the school does, or does not do, is constantly being examined in reference to a range of societal expectations and interests. In particular, the curriculum, or what is commonly known as the program of studies, is often the focus of public scrutiny.

A curriculum is organized and taught for the purpose of preparing students for a personally meaningful and socially useful place in society. For example, the 1981 Alberta Social Studies Curriculum states that "social studies is the school subject in which students learn to explore and, where possible, to resolve social issues that are of public and personal concern."[1] To achieve a goal of this nature, a school transmits to youth the knowledge, skills, and values that are viewed as necessary for the development of young people. In most cases, the knowledge to be learned is classified according to subject areas and is organized sequentially in grade levels. Knowledge considered appropriate for school programs is derived from what scholars have developed as a body of knowledge, studied either as a discipline (i.e., mathematics) or as a field of study (i.e., social studies). Teaching of skills is included in schools either as something to be learned in conjunction with the transmission of knowledge (i.e., the scientific method) or as a sequence of skills associated with a particular task a student is expected to learn (i.e., typing forty words per minute or being able to write a grammatically correct sentence).

The value component of knowledge and skills within the school mandate receives widespread public attention and debate. Values are taught explicitly and are rooted implicitly in social traditions. Transmission of knowledge and skills involves the transmitting of specific sets of values that sometimes cause concern among various groups in society.

Values are central to our society, because they represent what is worthwhile in daily life. They serve as foci for human expectations. Values guide the choices available in solving social problems, preserving a free and just society, and ensuring a meaningful existence for each member. There are values of many kinds—moral, ethnic, economic, cultural, and social. Each can become a referent for an issue and a focus of aspects of schooling.

While knowledge arises from scholarly pursuits, and skills are related to the application of knowledge in socially relevant ways, an issue evolves from societal concern related to human expectations and group interests. Issues become of public or social concern when the beliefs and actions of one group are challenged by those of others. Each issue, therefore, arises within particular social situations. These situations need to be studied in order to understand not only the conflicting value positions held by various interest groups but also the values implied in the process for resolving the issue. It is the explication of such values and beliefs, however inadequate or biased they may be, that forms the essence of individual points of view and that causes the ensuing public debate among social groups.

Often an individual develops a strong commitment to an issue because certain beliefs and values are being questioned. This may be the case in supporting the plight of the unemployed, addressing the proliferation of nuclear arms, or lending support for the protection from spillage of toxic waste. In instances such as these, the individual may read widely, participate in informal discussion, and attend information sessions. Each individual participates to become personally informed and to formulate a defensible position in terms of moral standards. Each one may also take some form of action.

In other situations, an individual may participate with persons of similar belief to publicize their position to others, be it an individual, a company executive, or a government official. Pross suggests "issue-oriented groups" become prominent when political parties fail in immediately promoting the views of individuals.[2] The existence of these groups is often short-lived. They disband after the group has made its point or has floundered in public debate. Often more organized pressure groups are a successful means by which to promote the views of individuals who may live far apart, by serving as a lobby to influence government policy and to focus public concern on a matter of social controversy. Thus, there is increased action by professional lobbyists in Ottawa and nation-wide demonstrations on such issues as nuclear weapons and legalized abortion.

Educators need to be aware that group actions can provide a public voice to influence other individuals, and therefore can effectively shape how other people, community organizations, and governments view an issue. The process of creating and sustaining public awareness is of paramount importance in the successful formulation and resolution of an issue. For without public awareness, a social issue soon becomes an non-issue.

A second and perhaps more powerful force in creating a social issue is mass media. Tuchman contends that the making of news by television and newspapers is a socially constructed process.[3] A news organization, such as the Canadian Press, provides information about events that are seen as significant for people to know. Issues that receive the greatest media coverage are likely to be those that audiences identify as the most pressing social issues. For this reason Tuchman argues that the media have the power to shape people's thinking on the issues of the day. A case in point is the publication of Canada's weekly magazine, *Macleans*, which features national and regional issues written in an accessible style. The cover of the magazine highlights a national issue and frequently provides a handy listing of issues for the interested reader. A feature article may be an expansion of a current event (i.e., an airplane crash, an earthquake, a government policy) or a discussion of the viewpoints concerning a social or economic issue that has been smoldering for some time (i.e., capital punishment, prostitution, free trade). In covering national issues the magazine strives to report the details of the issue in an accurate and fair manner. Yet, regardless of the detail and accuracy of reporting, what remains important is that the magazine has the power to shape public thinking about social issues. Consequently, when teaching issues, there is a need to identify the values and interests of key actors and to recognize that the information the media convey shapes public perception of national issues. Moreover, teachers presenting issues in classrooms should not pretend to be "neutral," but acknowledge that, like anyone else, their thinking is a product of the forces that shape public thought.

Issue-oriented programs are not new to Canadian education. An examination of a comparison of Canadian social studies curricula prepared by the Council of Ministers of Education reveals that all provincial curricula address societal concerns.[4] However, some curricular statements are explicit, while others are implicit. Perhaps the most explicit statement concerning the teaching of issues is contained in the 1981 Alberta Social Studies Curriculum, which states:

> The social issues that form the basis of the 1981 Alberta Social Studies Curriculum exist in the political, economic, and sociocultural life of the local community, the province, the nation, and the world. They have been selected to acknowledge that the real world is neither "all good" nor "all bad" and that human achievements, enterprise, and ingenuity represent a significant, though not total dimension of social reality.[5]

Such statements, although removed from the practicalities of the classroom, do give a shape and form to what ought to be taught as well as to how teaching should occur. Specific curriculum and instructions questions need to be continually asked if improvements in school programs are to result. What options are available for schools to deal with issues? How should the teaching of issues be organized? What must teachers do to deal successfully with social issues? Who should decide whether or not issues are to be taught in schools?

ORIENTATION OF SCHOOL PROGRAMS

Over time people have developed beliefs on how school programs ought to be organized. Eisner identifies five major orientations that underlie the content and aims of school programs.[6] The basic tenet of one of those five orientations is that schools are institutions established to serve the interests of society. The difficulty in utilizing this orientation is that, in a diverse society, there is often debate and even disagreement as to what interests a school must address. Eisner suggests that programs rooted in societal interests can be classified into two very different orientations: those advocating social adaptation and those favouring social reconstruction.

Programs interested in helping students adapt to existing structures and demands of society are designed according to societal needs. Once a social need is identified, the task of schools is to design a program that is relevant to meeting the specified need. The problem of identification arises, however, when agencies or community groups differ over what needs are worth addressing. For example, some community associations may want schools to offer programs that address social ailments such as child abuse and the use of drugs, while other groups expect schools to focus on English as a second language, women's studies, or a native people's program. To meet community demands, school districts integrate socially oriented programs into provincially prescribed curricula, establish community schools that offer special programs for local needs, and provide night school offerings ranging from language instruction to food preparation. By having students become more knowledgeable and acquire skills associated with the topic, educators assume the gap between "what is" and "what ought to be" will be resolved. By being responsive to social needs, school programs maintain the status quo and make little attempt to change the fundamental structures of society. Thus, the development of school programs having a social adaptation focus accommodates existing conditions and maintains established structures in society.

School programs having a reconstructive orientation are more radical in nature than programs for adaptation. Their aim is to make students aware of societal problems and encourage them to seek solutions and even take action to resolve the problems facing society. The concern to bring about significant societal change is sometimes reflected in provincial social studies or science programs, organized around controversial issues such as racism, technology, the environment, and world peace.

Designing programs around social controversies places profound demands on schools. First, the content of what is taught is derived from persistent social problems that are related to such school subjects as the social studies, general science, and the fine arts. Such a focus requires schools to collect socially related resources and to make use of community resources by means of speaker programs, field trips, and social action projects.

Second, a school may need to alter its social and bureaucratic structures in order to become a societal model for student and teacher examination, and a forum for possible resolution of social controversies. For most schools, major organizational changes may not be possible. As a consequence, there are alternative forms of schooling intended to cultivate attitudes and skills that will encourage youth to build a new society. The decision for alternative schooling is best exemplified in the 1980s by the movement of Christian education schools in western Canada.

Both socially adaptive and reconstructive programs are important components of provincial curricula in Canada. These programs assume that goals for education reside in societal concerns and that the promotion of social understanding is the basic intent underlying school programs.

PEDAGOGY OF SOCIAL ISSUES

By nature, teaching addresses the historical and/or contemporary issues facing society. Issues may arise spontaneously from classroom discussion or may be a planned venture. Teaching of social issues may be supported by a provincial curriculum that encompasses social issues at each grade level and by related instructional materials. A case in point is the Alberta Social Studies Curriculum, which outlines such topics as industrialization, Canadian unity, international cooperation, and social problems as areas of study. In addition, the Alberta Department of Education provides all schools with sixteen multimedia "Kanata Kits," each of which includes a collection of resources, to support the teaching of issues from grades 1 to 12.

Personal commitment, support from curriculum guides, and availability of instructional resources encourage teachers to conduct a variety of issue-related studies with students. Such teaching activities can be classified as follows.

1. Current events sessions. Conducted on an irregular basis, these class activities are based on a personal conviction that students should be aware of world happenings and controversies. Students collect news stories and give oral presentations to the class. Sometimes the class will follow related news events to study how a series of events can lead to the development of a public issue.

2. Local or community studies. Usually conducted as class projects, these types of activities stress research skills associated with an inquiry process. The result is often the collection of large amounts of information that may lead to some form of social action by the class such as a letter to a newspaper or a presentation to a community council.

3. Specific valuing exercises. These activities rely on commercially produced materials that outline procedures for simulation games and small group work that stress a problem-solving approach to issues. The resources are used for a short duration of time and are often selected because of their purported high student-interest level.

4. Analysis of moral issues. This type of activity stresses development of students' reasoning skills that requires knowledge of factual and value claims and ability to justify one's judgments and actions in terms of normative principles. To be successful, valuing activities require a high degree of procedural understanding on the part of both the teacher and student.

In spite of the efforts of a few dedicated teachers, assessments of provincial social studies teaching in Alberta[7] and in British Columbia[8] report that the teaching of issues is not a widespread phenomenon in either province. Some reasons educators advance for the limited teaching of issues include: concern among teachers for the uncertainty that arises from classroom discussion; school concern for community protest over what is taught; lack of appropriate instructional resources; limited teaching skills in leading class discussions that question social values and norms; and the often "conditioned" expectation among students of the need for answers or solutions.

During the "golden age of curriculum development" in the 1970s Canadian developmental efforts were focussed on improving classroom teaching of issues by formulating valuing processes to enhance moral reasoning abilities of students and by designing materials organized around case studies and moral dilemmas. The success of these efforts is exemplified by the work of the Canadian Public Issues Project at the Ontario Institute for Studies in Education, and by the Association for Values Education and Research at the University of British Columbia. The orientation of these efforts to improve instruction and learning were rooted in either American or British curriculum development that stressed logical reasoning and the learning attributes of students. Recent efforts however, have expanded classroom teaching of issues to include the social analysis of Canadian life. To illustrate this renewal of issues-related materials and a pedagogy for classrooms, two development efforts will be examined. The examination, albeit brief, will include the efforts of a non-educational institution, the Jesuit Centre for Social Faith and Justice, and an educational group, the Public Issues in Canada project, centred at the University of British Columbia. Developmental work, exemplified by these two groups, represents the belief that there are certain processes students should learn for examining controversies. Elements inherent in examining social issues are:

1. a reflective stance by both teacher and student;
2. analysis of issues in terms of the position of interest groups;
3. importance of the social and historical context of issues;
4. recognition of societal diversity;
5. resolution of issues in terms of social and political consequences; and
6. instructional use of small groups.

In its publication, *Getting Started on Social Analysis in Canada*,[9] the Jesuit Centre outlines a process of analysis oriented toward social justice and in-depth accounts of contemporary issues such as environmental hazards, health care for Native peoples, and the social impact of microtechnology. The suggestions advanced by the Jesuit Centre challenge the status quo of Canadian society by advocating that individuals become involved against social injustices, instead of remaining detached from the social concern.

Thus, social analysis means raising questions and seeking answers about the inequities and structural problems that characterize Canadian society. Action-oriented in nature, the analysis:

> may entail looking up more information, organizing a local interest group, making a small gesture of protest or contributing to a national campaign that is tackling an important issue. Whatever the action, it will in turn raise new questions and involve people more deeply again in the process of social analysis.[10]

The Jesuit Centre contends that social analysis should help people become critical, not in a negative sense, but in a reflective manner that fosters discerning attitudes for probing behind surface meanings. In some cases, collection of information is necessary to uncover social injustices, to establish connections between issues, or to reveal the political consequences of social issues. Group analysis is preferred as the method for studying social issues:

> where one comment can spark new thoughts, and opinions get refined by coming up against other points of view. As a group gains a picture of an issue, it moves easily from analysis to a discussion of possible action, to making decisions, distributing tasks, contacting other groups, and acting to do something about a problem that has been identified.[11]

As a handbook, *Getting Started* is divided into three parts that are linked by a reflective section. Part one illustrates how individual problems can be explained in terms of the connection to larger social issues. Reflection stresses understanding the language of analysis. Part two shows how the Canadian economy is interconnected in terms of economic patterns. Once individuals understand basic economic structures and roles of media, reflection encourages an awareness of the dominant ideologies that govern what is happening. Part three explores the experiences, troubles, and actions of minority groups such as the elderly, women, and Native peoples. Reflection encourages better understanding of personal meaning and of the processes of social analysis such as examining social priorities and political power. Each section of the book provides a set of readings on background information and points of view for use by community groups or by school classes. The process is enriched by illustrations of cultural expressions and social stereotypes, boxed quotations taken from church reports, questions to help initiate and guide discussion, and a listing of supplementary resources.

Efforts to promote the teaching of issues by a group of educators associated with the Public Issues in Canada Project are portrayed in a teacher resource book entitled *Teaching Public Issues in a Canadian Context*[12] and fourteen instructional booklets. Based on the notion advanced by Hodgetts and Gallagher that Canada is a political community with multiple interest groups,[13] the developers identify the topics of quality of life, Canada and the world, multiculturalism, and Canada's relations with the United States as significant issues of continuing societal concern. Developing a pedagogy for each topic was a collaborative venture of university and school educators.

Based on the notion that a public issue is created when the values and actions of a group are challenged by others, each of the four groups of contributors developed an approach for teaching one of the issue areas. This assumes that "a pedagogy of issues must go beyond the 'information about' an issue and the 'instructional strategies for' the classroom" and suggests that "what is needed is a quality of mind that will help us to use the information to develop in ourselves and our students an understanding of what is happening in society. Hopefully, such understanding will encourage us to some form of social action."[14]

A second assumption is that teaching must be "imaginative" in that an approach to social issues requires teachers and students to become aware of their own experience and to realize the significance of the issue by relating personal experience to the larger societal context. Both large and small groups may need to investigate the historical background, identify the value being questioned by individuals and interest groups, and become familiar with the social, cultural, and political forces that have the power to both create and resolve a public issue.

To illustrate the practicality of the four approaches, an instructional booklet series was developed that focusses on fourteen teachable issues of concern to Canadians.[15] Issues include trade and the Third World, cross-cultural communication, stress in the workplace, life of the unemployed, free trade, cruise missiles, resource-based towns, acid rain, and Native land claims. The booklets are prepared by teachers and university educators, who were initially involved in project work, and by others, who subsequently expressed an interest in developing issue-oriented materials.

Each booklet contains five or six classroom activities that provide suggested teaching procedures and student readings concerning positions of individuals and groups involved in the issue. Many activities that include group work require students to identify group interest and personal meanings, analyse cultural, social, and economic influences, role play in decision-making situations, and consider the personal and national significance of resolving the public issue. For example, the life of the unemployed booklet provides a series of statistical, personal, and policy portraits for students to understand quality of life issues. Class activities enable students to be reflective, not only in terms of their own life, but also with reference to the lives of other Canadians. A second example is the free trade booklet, which requires students to understand how the interaction of interest groups has made free trade an issue in terms of Canada's relations with the United States. Activities encourage students to know about trade relations and to be critically aware of the social consequences of such an agreement to their personal life, the lives of other Canadians, and the national interest. A third example is the cruise missile booklet that illustrates how government decisions are made in terms of Canada's position in the world. Activities facilitate an awareness of the ways in which interest groups can participate in the government decision-making process to resolve world issues. A fourth example, focussing on multiculturalism, involves two cross-cultural communication booklets that outline a series of episodes designed to increase student understanding of other cultures. All booklets are prepared as instructional materials for integration with existing social studies curricula or for use as separate units for short-term study.

Both the Jesuit Centre for Social Faith and Justice and the Public Issues Group have developed issue-oriented pedagogies and related materials that stress social analysis. Their procedures are more suggestive than prescriptive, more reflective than detached, and more open-ended than structured. They differ from previous efforts in advocating how issues ought to be examined in the classroom, yet they share the vision that school should be a place where students systematically examine issues facing individuals and society.

LOOKING FORWARD

Deciding what schools should teach, particularly those committed to some sense of social idealism, is a complex and timely process. The difficulty of developing new programs is evident in the six years of drafts and revisions of the British Columbia Social Studies program, the call for a task force to initiate changes in social studies in Saskatchewan, and the need for special mention of social studies in the 1985 Policy Statement for Alberta Secondary Education. The reasons for such debate and delay are often explained in terms of differing beliefs among educators of what should constitute citizenship education. However, hardships associated with economic restraint and a growing mood of societal conservatism have increased the participation of politicians in curriculum decision making. Thus, within the last decade, government policies and intervention have strongly influenced the nature of curriculum revision. The growth economy of the 1970s encouraged a range of "unchecked" program innovations that reflected the ideals of the developers. In many ways, the power of influencing what should be taught was diffused because it resided with the efforts of developers. However, the 1980s is a time in which power for deciding the nature of school programs is concentrated more with government officials and elected politicians. This has minimized opportunities for educators, both in terms of financial support and conceptual avenues, to participate in program revision.

Changes in the decision-making process are of central interest to the teaching of social issues. Decisions by elected politicians tend to be made in the interests of the public purview, while those made by educators tend to be in terms of ideals. As a result of the increasing involvement of government officials, policies regarding program revision tend to reflect the conservative mood of the day. In times of restraint, this means a belief in social adaptation rather than reconstruction. Current revision of social studies programs features an increased emphasis on "knowing about" Canada's past and present and the effective skills for participating in the Canadian community. The Government of Alberta publication entitled *A Policy Statement for*

Secondary Education, clearly indicates that the means of achieving "effective citizenship" is not "through a firm grasp of process," but rather "depends upon a firm grasp of facts."[16] This policy, sponsored by politicians, established a review and revision of the 1981 social studies curriculum that defined social studies as "the school subject in which students learn to explore and, where possible, to resolve social issues that are of public and personal concern."[17]

In terms of pedagogy, change in social education is portrayed as a debate concerning the merits of process versus product. However, from a political perspective the issue is one of "who decides what is worth teaching." Often educators are persuaded that the process-product controversy is the issue at hand. In fact it is not, for of central importance is the need for educators to recognize the increasing influence of government policies in shaping program development. Focussing on the political process suggests that discussion among curriculists is no longer the means by which improvements in programs are achieved. Instead, it is political action in the decision-making arena that brings changes to school programs. To foster the continued teaching of social issues, there must be opportunities for healthy debate among educators and, at the same time, avenues for participation in the political process to ensure the continuation of those democratic ideals that are at the root of social change. For this reason, educators need to realize that the development of an issues-oriented program itself is a social issue in which some form of political action is necessary. Development of social issue programs can therefore bring a needed renewal and a vitality to Canadian schools.

NOTES

1. Alberta Education, Curriculum Branch, *1981 Alberta Social Studies Curruculum* (Edmonton, 1981).
2. Paul Pross, "Pressure Groups: Talking Chameleons" in *Canadian Politics in the 1980s*, edited by Michael S. Whington and Glen Williams (Toronto: Methuen, 1981).
3. Gaye Tuchman, *Making News* (New York: Free Press, 1978).
4. Council of Ministers of Education, *Social Studies: A Survey of Provincial Curricula at the Elementary and Secondary Levels* (Toronto, 1982).
5. Alberta Education, *1981 Alberta Social Studies Curriculum*, 1.
6. Eliot Eisner, *The Educational Imagination*, 2nd ed. (New York: Macmillan, 1984).

7. Lorne Downey, *The Social Studies in Alberta: A Report of an Assessment*. (Edmonton: Downey Associates, 1975).

8. Ted Aoki, Caroline Langford, David M. Williams, and Donald C. Wilson, *British Columbia Social Studies Assessment: A Summary Report* (Victoria: Ministry of Education, 1977).

9. Michael Czerny and Jamie Swift, *Getting Started on Social Analysis in Canada* (Toronto: Between the Lines, 1984).

10. Ibid., 15.

11. Ibid., 14.

12. Donald C. Wilson, ed., *Teaching Public Issues in a Canadian Context* (Toronto: OISE Press, 1982).

13. Bernie Hodgetts and Paul Gallagher, *Teaching Canada for the '80s* (Toronto: OISE Press, 1978).

14. Wilson, *Teaching Public Issues*, 3.

15. Donald C. Wilson, ed., *Public Issues in Canada: Possibilities for Classroom Teaching* (Agincourt, Ont.: Dominie Press, 1983–86).

16. Alberta, *A Policy Statement for Secondary Education* (1985), 33.

17. Ibid.

EDUCATION AND THE STATUS OF WOMEN: A CHALLENGE FOR TEACHERS

HILARY M. LIPS

One of my university colleagues was recently asked to serve on a graduate thesis committee for research on the topic of pay equity. When she responded that she was too busy, but that another member of her department was well-versed in the area under investigation, the caller said in desperate tones that he especially wanted her on the committee because she was a woman. She replied irritably that there were enough people asking for her help on the basis of her academic expertise, and she failed to see why anyone should want her on a committee simply because she was in possession of a uterus! Her response may have been less than diplomatic, but it epitomizes the frustrations often experienced by women in post-secondary education, whose jobs usually place them in a minority position. Because there are so few of them, they are deluged with requests to serve on committees, make speeches, and lend support to various issues involving women. They tend to be overworked, more visible than they would sometimes prefer, and often unsure that they are valued for their talent and knowledge rather than their gender.

In elementary and secondary education, the role lived out by most female teaching professionals is different from the one I have described above. In these spheres, women are not tokens or minorities: they form the majority. It is a majority, however, that most frequently finds itself under the direction and supervision of the male minority in pre-university education. Recent statistics from my own province, Manitoba, indicate that more than 96 percent of superintendents, 84 percent of assistant superintendents, 83 percent of principals, and 80 percent of vice-principals are men, despite the fact that men make up only 44.5 percent of the total teaching force.[1]

The women who first carved out a place for the female sex in higher education might be hard pressed to suppress a smile at the difficulties catalogued here. To those who, to pursue serious study, had to fly in the face of the conventional wisdom that too much intellectual work would permanently damage a woman's all-important reproductive system, the discovery that women now make up the majority of elementary and secondary school teachers, though not administrators, would no doubt come as a welcome surprise. To those intrepid female scholars who, despite the completion of all requirements and the recommendation of their supervisors, were denied degrees at such respectable universities as Harvard and Johns Hopkins in the 1890s or who, like Emily Stowe, were refused admission to the University of Toronto because, as its president said, "The doors of this university are not open to women and I trust they never will be," the idea of being asked to serve on a thesis committee *because* they were women would probably trigger bouts of uncontrollable, disbelieving laughter.[2] Indeed, women's access to education and to positions of status and authority within educational institutions has improved dramatically in North America during the twentieth century. Yet, at all levels of education, female teaching professionals find themselves faced with enormous challenges. Still facing sex discrimination themselves, they are expected to help their students prepare for a world in which traditional assumptions about the sexes are no longer accepted automatically, where economic necessity frequently dictates that women participate in the labour force, but where that labour force is strongly segregated, vertically and horizontally, by sex. The role that teaching professionals, especially women, are expected to play in this preparation is multifaceted; it includes providing role models, ensuring that the curriculum incorporates the new knowledge about gender, monitoring their own classroom interactions for the presence of inequities, and helping students to give serious consideration to nontraditional career paths.

PROVIDING ROLE MODELS

By their very presence, teachers provide role models for their students. It has become popular in recent years, however, to remind *female* faculty members at every level that they have a special responsibility in this respect. Girls and young women, watching their female teachers, are helped to form an idea of their own future—of what a career might be like, how demanding, how satisfying, it might be.

Certainly there is some validity to the exhortation to women to be conscious of their status as role models. Particularly when holding positions that are infrequently filled by women, they can help others to find images that the media, or their own imaginations, cannot provide. For instance, what would it be like to be a woman who is also a professor of engineering, or what kind of a job could be done by a woman as superintendent of schools?

Perhaps even more importantly, the presence of women in positions of authority within educational institutions should lend legitimacy to the concerns of female students. Women or girls who have been the victims of sexual harassment by male teachers, for example, may well find themselves with more support, in the form of both sympathy and righteous indignation, from female than male teachers. Certainly, it is the case that explicit policies on sexual harassment within educational institutions did not begin to be widely formulated and implemented until women's presence began to be felt in positions of authority and status.

But, is it really fair to place on women alone the whole burden of ensuring justice to female students and attention to their concerns? It is, after all, abundantly clear that we are all in the same boat—that dramatic changes cannot occur in the self-images, dreams, aspirations, and activities of women without concurrent changes in the lives of men.

When students look at their male teachers, what do they see? Do they see people who continue to act as if they believe that they belong to the superior half of the human race, whose words and actions imply that females are incapable of tackling certain academic disciplines or careers, who model a family situation in which their own career always comes first and all domestic duties are relegated to their wives? Or do they see people who are willing to take both their female and male students seriously, who work consciously to overcome gender stereotypes built into curriculum materials, who do their own share of the routine tasks required for day-to-day survival?

It is highly unlikely that many people, male or female, are willing to embrace a career path that precludes family and intimate relationships. Yet research suggests that women (but not men) often feel that they must make a choice or trade-off between career and family, even when they want both very much. Female students who are deciding what to do with their lives need to know that there are men living a lifestyle that is not based on an ideology of female subservience, but on the conviction that women and men have equal rights and responsibilities, both inside and outside the family. And if any of our male students are going to turn out to be that kind of man, they need role models too!

MONITORING CURRICULUM CONTENT

It is crucial that teaching professionals use their degree of control over what goes on in the classroom to make sure that knowledge about women's lives is not lost or trivialized. For example, the history of women's entry into higher education can provide both female and male students with a new perspective on their own experiences, yet most students are not aware of it. Some examples from my own discipline, psychology, illustrate the tendency toward, and the dangers of, ignoring scholarship that deals with women.

Simone de Beauvoir's observation that woman was regarded as the "other" has not really gone out of date in the psychology curriculum, nor, in some ways, has Freud's complaint that women were too mysterious to understand. We continue to design our curriculum as if women were some special small interesting group with strange and unusual ways of thinking, as if women were different from the norm rather than having a quite legitimate numerical claim to being the benchmark for that norm. Students who are interested in women take courses in the psychology of women, or in sex differences, or in the psychology of gender.[3]

Knowledge about women's experience and behaviour is still treated as peripheral in psychology, ghettoized into separate courses or separate chapters in textbooks, categorized as trendy and "soft." An undergraduate student who avoids (or is not given the opportunity to take) a psychology of women course can quite easily graduate from many psychology programs, having majored in the study of human behaviour, without ever having been exposed to anything more than the most cursory information about the process and impact of sex stereotyping, the complications thrown into the career achievement process by the double-duty of home and job that is assigned to women, psychological aspects of menarche, pregnancy, menopause. These are not peripheral issues: they affect the majority of human beings. A course of study of human behaviour that ignores these issues ignores a large portion of reality.

Kenneth Gergen[4] began arguing years ago that social psychology should be characterized as a historical rather than a scientific enterprise, in part because psychology has a tendency to reflect the accepted values of society when labelling behaviour at any given period in time. Moreover, in a kind of vicious circle, the labels psychology applies to behaviour in turn affect society's evaluative biases. Gergen's analysis is enormously useful in pointing out the interaction between psychology and the culture in which it takes place: how our culture influences the biases we bring to our study of behaviour, and how the evaluative biases built into the way we (and the media) report our findings influence the way the public views certain behaviours and tries to tailor its own behaviour. A classic example of this phenomenon is Sigmund Freud's approach to understanding the differences between women and men, as reflected in his psychoanalytic theory.[5] His understanding of women was clearly shaped by the era and culture in which he lived. His theory was widely reported and found its way into twentieth-century western popular literature. There it continues to influence, not only psychologists', but also the popular perception of gender differences and the reasons for them. While Freud's theory is no longer in vogue in psychology, practically everyone in North America has heard the term "penis envy" and knows the type of woman to whom the term can be applied.

One of the ways that Freudian theory gets into and stays in the public's awareness is through introductory psychology courses in universities. Tens of thousands of North American students take this course every year. Most of them emerge with a superficial knowledge of Freudian theory: they have heard of the Oedipal complex and penis envy. But how many of them have seen this theory placed in the context of more recent, thoughtful treatments of the possible role of unconscious processes in the development of family bonds?[6] How many of them have been led to think about the role of psychological theories in reinforcing a culture's stereotypic beliefs? One of the really valuable things that happens when the new scholarship on women is brought into mainstream courses is that it models for the students a questioning of the accepted (but often untested) notions about what is "natural" in human behaviour, and a re-examination of the most basic assumptions on which theories and research in psychology are based. The juxtaposition of the new scholarship on women, based on more feminist assumptions, with the traditional scholarship, based on orthodox assumptions about the appropriateness of certain behaviours for women and men, models clearly for students the basic truth that, in psychology as in other disciplines, the answers we get depend to a large extent on the ways we frame our questions, where our blind spots are, and our acknowledged or unacknowledged beliefs about "human nature." This awareness that scholarship is not value-free, but shaped by culture is exactly what we should want our students to acquire. We want them to approach psychology as a discipline dedicated to learning the truth—the whole truth—about human behaviour, not just wallowing placidly in the conventional beliefs of its time and place. We want them to approach education as a process of being open to new information and ready to re-evaluate theories in the light of new thinking and new findings.

The last few years have been filled with examples of psychological research on women leading to new insights about basic social and psychological processes. Probably the most familiar at this moment is the work of Carol Gilligan,[7] who, in her attempt to look carefully at women's understanding of morality, has suggested a whole new dimension, hitherto ignored, along which the moral development of both women and men might be examined. There are many other examples. Out of attempts to understand the experiences of rape victims and battered wives, a whole psychology of victimization has grown up.[8] Out of attempts to clarify the reasons for the difficulties faced by women in organizations, an understanding of the psychology of tokenism has developed.[9] Monolithic approaches to the understanding of anger, stress, power, responsibility have all been challenged by research on women's experience. Importantly, the challenge is not just to psychology's understanding of women, but to its understanding of human behaviour. The same challenge is experienced in any discipline that is opened to the new perspectives provided by feminist scholarship.

As Bernice Lott pointed out in her excellent article in a recent issue of *American Psychologist*,[10] a focus on the new research on women currently taking place in psychology leads to a renewed appreciation of the impact of social context on human behaviour. The focus on the social conditions that encourage or discourage the appearance of particular behaviours in women and men implies some belief that an understanding of these forces by psychologists, and a communication of this understanding to students, might lead to change. Women and men might rethink and revise their roles and goals. Some people shy away from this notion, arguing that, as educators, communicating information, not making change, is our role. But, as Gergen[11] argues, knowledge can lead to behavioural liberation. If we know about the impact of gender-role stereotyping on our behaviours and how it happens, we are more able to liberate ourselves from its effects. That is a final argument for the inclusion of the new scholarship on women in the curriculum: it will help to promote change in the sense of broader horizons for the students in our educational institutions. It will help them to be more aware of their choices, and more aware of the forces acting on them to restrict their awareness of these choices. Surely, such awareness is one of the main purposes of education.

INTERACTIONS IN THE CLASSROOM

The process that takes place in the classroom is, in many ways, as important as what is taught. Studies show that the classroom process is often disadvantageous to female students. In elementary school classrooms, teachers allow boys to talk and to interrupt them more than they do girls—a practice that ensures not only that more time will be spent on boys' than girls' problems, but that both groups will learn that male concerns take priority and that interrupting others is a more acceptable practice for males than for females. Moreover, teachers punish boys and girls for different kinds of behaviour—boys for being unruly and girls for academic mistakes. On the other hand, when praise is handed out to girls, it is likely to be for good appearance or conduct, while for boys it is usually for good academic performance. The lessons are obvious: girls learn that the route to appreciation is by being "good" while boys learn that they are appreciated for their academic efforts. Most damaging of all, perhaps, is the way that teachers encourage girls and boys to react to their own mistakes. A boy giving the wrong answer is more often encouraged to keep trying until he gets it right; a girl is frequently told not to worry about a mistake, and the teacher spends less time suggesting new approaches and encouraging her to keep working on a problem until it is solved. Thus, boys are more likely to learn to respond to an unsolved problem as a challenge, while girls are given the message that failure is beyond their control.[12]

Even in preschool, teachers behave in ways that perpetuate gender stereotypes. They pay more attention to boys, and respond more to boys who are aggressive and girls who act dependent.[13] Yet teachers are apparently unaware of the differences in their treatment of boys and girls.

Higher education is not exempt from charges of inequities in the classroom. There are suggestions that women experience the classroom atmosphere as less encouraging for themselves than for men because of an aggregation of small, nonconscious discriminatory actions on the part of teachers. Students report that instructors know the names of more male than female students, and that female students are more likely than males to be "squeezed out" of lab projects and demonstrations, and are more hesitant to intrude on instructors' time by asking for help and talking with them outside of class.[14] Even more serious, it is becoming clear that sexual harassment is a common problem faced by female students. In one recent survey of more than eleven hundred university students, two percent of the men and seventeen percent of the women reported being sexually harassed by their teachers. In other studies, the reporting of sexual harassment ranges from ten to thirty percent of female students.[15]

The cumulative effect of all these problems with student-teacher interactions is to decrease the self-confidence of female students. Whereas education should be nothing if not empowering, it cannot be counted on to have that effect on girls and women as long as the subtle messages behind teacher-student interactions remain that females are valued less than males, that females are valued more for their appearance and good behaviour than for their competence and intellectual skill, and that sexuality can be used as a weapon against female students.

ENCOURAGING STUDENTS INTO NONTRADITIONAL COURSES

Despite the encouraging news that the number of women in Canadian medical, law, and business schools is increasing, the majority of women in high school are apparently still aiming for traditionally female (thus low-status and low-paid) employment. Research shows that Canadian female high school students tend to plan to marry and have children, and to assume that their employment will have to take second place to domestic responsibilities. They thus aim for careers that will fit fairly painlessly into this traditional pattern.[16]

The job of educators is not to berate women for continuing to make these traditional choices, despite the new rhetoric proclaiming that women can be anything they want to be. Rather, it is to understand and help to change the conditions to which women are responding in making these traditional choices. As long as women who marry and bear children must take responsibility for most of the housework and childcare *along with* whatever employment they undertake, as long as adequate, affordable childcare is not available to mothers who work outside the home, it is eminently realistic for women to fear and shy away from the double burden of family and high-powered career. Educators must help their female students to analyse and confront the social conditions that make it so much more difficult for women than for men to aspire to demanding careers. They must also help their students to confront one aspect of reality that young women still try hard to ignore: that there is a very high probability that they will have to support themselves, and perhaps their children, without a male partner's assistance.

Among the young women who *are* ready and able to make the sacrifices necessary to pursue demanding careers, only a small minority choose the fields of mathematics, science, and technology. Indeed, the scarcity of women in these areas has aroused deep concern in some circles,[17] and a variety of experimental programs to encourage women into science have been launched.[18] It appears that there are some serious problems with the way science is taught to women (and perhaps to men as well); research with Canadian female university students indicates that the majority of those who avoid mathematics and science courses say they do so out of lack of interest.[19] The problem may start early in the educational process. Researchers have found that teachers' negative feelings about mathematics and science are related to similar negative feelings among their students, and that many teachers feel anxious and less than competent when giving instruction in these area.[20] Clearly, it is important for teachers, particularly women, to confront and conquer their own anxiety about mathematics and science, so that they will not inadvertently pass that anxiety along to their students. It is also crucial that female students be made aware of the extent to which opting out of mathematics and science in high school will limit their career options in a society increasingly dominated by technology.

SUGGESTIONS FOR CHANGE

Education should make a person more powerful, more able to meet a variety of challenges, more competent and confident. For female students, an increased sense of their own power might begin with an educational system on which and within which they feel able to have an impact. Experiencing power within the system might well lead to a sense of power stretching beyond the boundaries of that system.

How might the educational system be designed to empower female students instead of reinforcing the pervasive social message of female inferiority? The four areas discussed in this paper—role models, curriculum content, teacher-student interaction, and presentation of nontraditional career choices—offer a framework for some suggestions.

Both female and male students must be presented with role models of achieving, accomplished women and of men who are comfortable with and supportive of equal status for women and men. The nonverbal message that is communicated by the structure of the educational system must be consistent with the verbal one in favour of equality. That means that it will not do to have a few token women in positions of educational administration or to make sure there is at least one woman teaching in a university mathematics department. Students must see as many women as men holding such positions. That is the only way they will believe that the old adage "a woman has to work twice as hard as a man to be thought half as good" has gone out of style. That is also the only way that most of them will have the opportunity for contact with a woman in educational administration or in postsecondary education who is not too burnt out from trying to live up to her own token status to be of any significant help to them.

Curriculum content should be changed to incorporate the emerging body of scholarship on women and on gender roles. The simple addition of an optional course in women's studies will not suffice. Courses in history, English, geography, social studies, and science should be oriented in ways that avoid masculinist biases and include significant material on women. Textbooks should be chosen with care to this same end. No educated person should graduate with the unchallenged view that women have played an insignificant role in the drama of human accomplishment.

Training workshops should be held to help teachers become aware of the ways in which they tend to treat female and male students differently both inside and outside of the classroom. These workshops should emphasize *behaviour*, since many instructors already say they believe in female-male equality and honestly do not know the extent to which their treatment of male and female students differs.

The issue of sexual harassment should be tackled in an open and structured way. Students should know where to take a complaint, and clear procedures for dealing with these complaints should be set down. In some institutions, such as universities, this procedure might involve the creation of a position of "sexual harassment officer," who has the responsibility and the power to investigate and keep records of complaints and to recommend appropriate action. Whatever the mechanism, it is extremely important that students not be abandoned with the problem of sexual harassment. They must receive a clear message that the institution will not tolerate their victimization through the illegitimate use of a teacher's power.

Educators should do what they can to broaden students' awareness of the vocational choice available to them. In particular, they should take every opportunity (and *create* opportunities) to urge female students not to dismiss mathematics, science, and technology as career options. Even more importantly, though, teachers should explore with their students the problem of the double workload faced by employed women with families. The latter issue is clearly one that receives consideration by young women as they ponder their future work. It should be brought out into the open and discussed with both female and male students. While discussion will not solve the problem, it will help students to understand their own and others' behaviour, putting them in a better position to make intelligent choices and gain a sense of control over their lives.

Over the last decade, a number of people have called for the kinds of changes advocated here. The relative slowness of the response is testimony to the difficulty of changing a large and complex system, despite a growing sense of concern among the educators who staff that system. Nonetheless, the evidence has continued to mount that experiences within the educational system are crucial ones in shaping female-male relations within the larger society. The ongoing challenge of designing and running an educational system that promotes equality between the sexes, working in the context of a larger society that frequently flouts these ideals, is an enormous one. However, if we care about equal status for women, it is a challenge that must be met.

NOTES

1. D. Blackwell, "Affirmative Action.... How Successful Have We Been?" *Women in Education* (Dec. 1985): 6–7.

2. See R. Rosenberg, *Beyond Separate Spheres: The Intellectual Roots of Modern Feminism* (New Haven: Yale University Press, 1982) for an engrossing history of the obstacles placed in the way of women's education.

3. Interestingly, the latter kinds of course titles have become code words for psychology of women among students and faculty alike. There is a tacit and prevalent assumption that, in the main, issues like sex and gender are of interest and relevance mostly to women, in the same way that issues of race and ethnicity are often assumed to be of concern only to minority groups. This situation reminds me strangely of the unsettling way the use of the word "chairperson" has made its way into the language at many universities: the word "chairman" is used in the "normal" cases where the person in question is male, while "chairperson" signifies a female!

4. K. Gergen, "Social Psychology as History," *Journal of Personality and Social Psychology* 26 (1973): 309–20.

5. E.g., S. Freud, "Some Physical Consequences of the Anatomical Distinction Between the Sexes" in *The Standard Edition of the Complete Psychological Works of Sigmund Freud* (London: Hogarth Press, 1925, 1974).

6. See, e.g., P. Caplan, *Between Women: Lowering the Barriers* (Toronto: Personal Library, 1981); N. Chodorow, *The Reproduction of Mothering: Psychoanalysis and the Sociology of Gender* (Berkeley: University of California Press, 1978); D. Dinnerstein, *The Mermaid and the Minotaur: Sexual Arrangements and Human Malaise* (New York: Harper Colophon Books, 1977).

7. C. Gilligan, *In a Different Voice: Psychological Theory and Women's Development* (Cambridge: Harvard University Press, 1982).

8. E.g., D. Miller and C. Porter, "Self-Blame in Victims of Violence," *Journal of Social Issues* 39 (1983): 139–52.

9. R.M. Kanter, *Men and Women of the Corporation* (New York: Basic Books, 1977).

10. B. Lott, "The Potential Enrichment of Social/Personality Psychology Through Feminist Research and Vice Versa," *American Psychologist* 40 (1985): 155–64.

11. Gergen, "Social Psychology as History."

12. C. Dweck, "The Role of Expectations and Attributions in the Alleviation of Learned Helplessness," *Journal of Personality and Social Psychology* 31 (1975): 674–85; Dweck, W. Davidson, S. Nelson, and B. Enna, "Sex Differences in Learned Helplessness: II. The Contingencies of Evaluative Feedback in the Classroom and III. An Experimental Analysis," *Developmental Psychology* 14 (1978): 268–76.

13. L. Serbin and K. O'Leary "How Nursery Schools Teach Girls to Shut Up," *Psychology Today* 9, 7 (1975): 56–58ff.

14. J. Schnellmann and J.L. Gibbons, "The Perception by Women and Minorities of Trivial Discriminatory Actions in the Classroom" (Paper presented at the annual convention of the American Psychological Association, Toronto, Aug. 1984).

15. A. McCormack, "The Sexual Harassment of Students by Teachers: The Case of Students in Science," *Sex Roles* 13, 1/2 (1985): 21–32.

16. M. Baker, *What Will Tomorrow Bring? A Study of the Aspirations of Adolescent Women* (Ottawa: Canadian Advisory Council on the Status of Women, 1985); J. Gaskell, "Young Women Choose Paths to the Future" (paper presented at the annual convention of the Canadian Research Institute for the Advancement of Women, Saskatoon, Nov. 1985).

17. E.g., Science Council of Canada, *Who Turns the Wheel? Proceedings of a Workshop on the Science Education of Women in Canada* (Ottawa: Minister of Supply and Services, 1981).

18. M. Ferguson, "Job Shadowing: An Educational Initiative to Advance Women in Science," *Canadian Woman Studies* 6, 4 (1985): 80–81; P. Rogers, "Overcoming Another Barrier: Real Women Don't do Math—With Good Reason!" *Canadian Woman Studies* 6, 4 (1985): 82–84.

19. H. Lips, "Math/Science Self-schemas and Curriculum Choices Among University Women" (paper presented at the annual convention of the American Psychological Association, Toronto, Aug. 1984).

20. L. Chiarelott and C. Czerniak, "The Development of Science Anxiety in Elementary and Junior High School Students: Implications for the Preparation of Elementary Teachers" (paper presented at the annual convention of the Association of Teacher Educators, Las Vegas, Feb. 1985).

FAMILY AND SCHOOL: AN UNEASY PARTNERSHIP

JOHN D. FRIESEN

Reaction in the 1970s and 80s to intrapsychic and individualistic explanations of human growth and development has brought into sharp focus the impact of environmental influences, particularly those of the family and school, on the developing child. A wide range of studies has been undertaken in the last fifteen years, to determine the influence of the family on the child's intellectual, emotional, and career development, as well as his or her school achievement. It is now generally accepted in the research literature that the family is the most powerful and optimal context for the developing child and that it has a significant influence on the child's academic performance.[1]

This article consists of three parts. The first part traces the historical relationship between the school and the family as partners in the educational process. The second section examines the research regarding the family's influence on the cognitive, academic, and career development of the child, and the third part will consider applications of child development research on educational theory and practice.

THE RELATIONSHIP BETWEEN FAMILY AND SCHOOL

Historically, as Cremin has shown in his work on the history of education,[2] many seventeenth- and eighteenth-century families taught their own children to read, write, and count. Education occurred primarily in the home and church, and the family functioned as the transmitter of moral, psychosocial, cultural, and legal information.[3]

During the first half of the nineteenth century, the public school increasingly took on the major responsibility for educating the child. This shift in educational responsibility from the home to the school has led, in extreme cases, to parents being bluntly told by teachers not to "interfere" in the education of their children. Many things contributed to this shift in responsibility. Among these were the difficulty families had in finding the personal and financial resources to educate their children on their own and the greater efficiency of appointing teachers to perform teaching tasks for the whole community. Teachers were appointed to carry out educational responsibilities as society moved from an agrarian to an industrial society and role differentiation became more formal.

Along with societal changes, the early political and educational philosophers also promoted the movement of education from the home to the school. For example, Horace Mann[1] in his famous report on the teaching of reading, spelling, and composition, did not once make mention of the family as a place where some of this instruction might take place. Similarly, Dewey,[5] although he was aware of the danger of school education becoming abstract and bookish, was also of the opinion that the school served as a special educational institution in "advanced" society, and he associated "participant education" with "low grade society."[6] Dewey did not recognize the importance of families in the intellectual and cognitive development of children and the contributions parents potentially make to the educative process. Similarily, Parsons,[7] although he recognized its expressive qualities, reinforced the view that the family was losing its overall usefulness. He took the position that families in advanced societies would become "factories which produce human personalities," and that education would occur outside the home in schools and factories.

The view that parents are unimportant as educators of their children was not only held by leading educational and political philosophers of the past, but is also held by many teachers today. In a recent study designed to assist learning- and behaviour-disabled Grade 3 children, an intervention strategy designed to involve parents actively in helping a child to read was vigorously opposed by some school staff.[8] It was assumed by some teachers that teaching reading was the role of the school, and that parents could not be trusted to read to their children. This illustration is not uncommon, for often parents tell stories of meetings with teachers who complained that parents should not have tried to teach their children to read and that, by doing so, they had created problems for the child. The overall attitude of many teachers is "leave the educating to us."

It is the thesis of this paper that parents should assume an important role in a child's education, and that a co-operative partnership between the home and school needs to be promoted. In the following section, research data will be presented to illustrate ways in which families influence the academic and cognitive development of their children. Because there is a large body of literature in this area, I have been selective in my coverage of the topic. The reader may refer to several comprehensive reviews of the literature,[9] which provide extensive references and research designs of significant studies dealing with the impact of the family on school performance.

PARENT PARTICIPATION IN SCHOOLING

In the last ten to fifteen years, there has been growing pressure for parent participation in schools. Such participation has taken many forms, such as parental involvement in instruction as aids, volunteers, and tutors; education to improve parental skills and knowledge; community-school movements; and, finally, parent-school consultative committees.

However, many of the programs involving parents in educational endeavours have not been well received by professional educators. For example, in a recent study on parent-school consultative committees in British Columbia, it was revealed that only sixteen percent of school boards in that province have a policy and provide backup support for parent-school committees.[10] Many boards indicated that they had no policies of their own nor any interest in the concept of a district-wide policy to establish parent-school committees.

In contrast to such resistant attitudes toward parent involvement in education, a number of empirical studies concerned with parental participation in the child's education show that parental contacts initiated by the school staff are effective in increasing attendance of chronically absent students, reducing talking in the classroom, increasing the rate of completion of homework, raising the level of performance on daily math assignments, and reducing disruptive/aggressive student behaviour. Similarly, children asked to read to their parents gained in reading skills, compared with children in a control group. Several large-scale community projects, including Home Start and Parent-Child Development Centres, reveal that parental involvement has positive consequences for the child and parent; however, the results of these investigations are not consistent, and thus not conclusive.[11]

FAMILY VARIABLES AND ACHIEVEMENT

A wide range of family variables is associated with school achievement. While it is difficult to summarize the many studies that have investigated these relationships, Hess and Holloway have identified five general categories and obtained considerable research evidence addressing these variables.[12]

1. Parental educational expectations. Boocock maintains that high-achieving children come from families that have high expectations for them.[13] Empirical studies on the relation between parents' expectations and academic performance generally support this contention.[14] Children's school performance is associated with the parents' own achievement orientation, their press for their children's achievement, their aspirations for their child's educational and occupational achievement, and their emphasis on school work generally.

2. Parental verbal interaction with children. Numerous studies have shown the strength of the link between aspects of the verbal environment of the home and achievement in school.[15] The findings show that school achievement is related to how much the parent reads to the child, the amount of verbal interaction in the family, the children's participation in interaction at meals, and parental playing and talking with children.

3. Parental affective relationships with children. A series of research reports show that parental warmth facilitates performance in school. Representative studies reveal that school achievement is related to parental warmth and avoidance of restriction and punishment and is negatively correlated to maternal rejection.

4. Parental discipline. Although research in this area is hampered by definitional problems, the available data show a consistent association between modes of parental discipline and children's achievement. School achievement is positively correlated to authoritative parental control as opposed to permissiveness and autocratic control, the use of physical punishment and discouragement, as well as to the degree of fit between authority structures at home and at school. Hess and Holloway point out that the findings in this area have been impressive, and they encourage more careful theoretical analysis of the data.[16]

5. Parental beliefs and attributions. The effects of parental beliefs on child-rearing behaviour and children's school achievement is becoming increasingly clear as research evidence accumulates. Preliminary studies reveal that parental knowledge of developmental norms is associated with competence in child rearing. Parental beliefs also seem to influence children's self-concepts and expectations for school performance as well as their problem-solving behaviour.

FAMILY EFFECTS ON READING

The family's role in promoting interest and skill in reading has been widely studied. Hess and Halloway identify five general areas of family functioning that have a positive effect on school achievement.[17] These areas include:

1. The value placed on literacy, which involves the amount of reading parents do, the quality of their reading material, and their interest and involvement in reading.

2. The press-for-achievement dimension includes such indicators as parental expectations, involvement in attempting to teach their children to read, interest in having the children watch educational TV programs such as "Sesame Street," and the possession of books and records. All these factors are positively related to reading achievement.

3. The availability of reading and writing materials for pre-school and elementary school children tends to produce more competent readers. Good readers are frequently taken to the library by their parents.

4. The tendency of parents to read to their children is also related to the children's reading interest and performance. This finding was also present when the parents did not speak English but encouraged their children to read aloud to them. In these cases, parental involvement and interest was motivational rather than instructional.

5. Parent-child interactions influenced both language development and competence in literacy skills. Research findings on the impact of the family

on reading performance clearly establish the importance of family involvement in the school.

FAMILY INFLUENCE ON VOCATIONAL DEVELOPMENT

In their comprehensive review of the influence of the family on vocational development, Schulenberg, Vondracek, and Crouter identify four family factors that influence vocational development.[18] The first two of these factors are socio-economic status and family process variables (i.e., socialization patterns, child-rearing practices, interpersonal relationships, and communication patterns). The third factor is family interaction patterns such as acceptance and rejection, dominance and submission, and emotional/rational and assertive/non-assertive behaviour. The final factor is family structure and organization (i.e., family size, birth order, sibling spacing, and single parenthood).

OTHER RELATED STUDIES

While this paper does not purport to provide an exhaustive survey of the literature on the theme of family influence on school achievement, I will nevertheless briefly identify several other areas of enquiry that can be pursued more fully by the reader. They are presented below as areas of potential research activity that show considerable promise.

1. The influence of parents in shaping cognitive skills like perception, memory, cognitive scanning, and selective attention.
2. The effects of maternal communication styles on mental rehearsal in the child.
3. Parental encouragement of children's use of memory strategies.
4. Parental influences on motivational processes such as attempting challenging tasks and working intensively and persistently.
5. Parental influence on the children's moral development.
6. The impact of the parents' cognitive style on the children's performance.
7. The role of parents in facilitating children's language development through knowledge of syntax and vocabulary and communication skills and by monitoring the children's comprehension.
8. The effects of divorce, poverty, employment, illness, number of children, marital harmony, and support networks on the child's cognitive growth and school achievement.

APPLICATIONS TO THEORY AND PRACTICE

As the above review of the child development literature suggests, during the last fifteen years we have entered a new era of family-related research that demonstrates the role of the family as educator and the importance of establishing vital relationships between the home and the school. While some of the data remain somewhat inconsistent and obscure, the fundamental finding that families play an important role in the education of children is supported.

Professional educators must now rethink their practices in the light of current data that points to the family as an important agent of socialization. One of the obvious indications of this research activity is the need of the school and the family to develop a partnership in the educational enterprise. Education is a joint activity of the home and school.

Before outlining the nature of the partnership, I want to make more explicit some of the assumptions and views that have guided my analysis. The first proposition is that children are shaped by their interaction with the contexts in which they find themselves. According to this formulation, as Bronfenbrenner states, "learning and development are facilitated by the participation of the developing person in progressively more complex patterns of reciprocal activity with someone with whom that person has developed a strong and enduring emotional attachment."[19] This viewpoint holds that the individual is embedded in and interacts with ever more expanding and complex contexts. The second proposition, as Hess and Holloway[20] point out, is that in many ways the school and family cannot fully control the cognitive activities of the child that involve remembering, perceiving, forming categories, making associations, and deriving generalizations, for all of these are linked to the biological and anatomical characteristics of the species. The third is that agents of socialization affect the outcomes of basic mental operations by controlling the content or raw materials of experience that children use in developing their mental worlds. School and family may restrict, enlarge, and generally select the material that is to be learned by the child, and thereby give personal and cultural meaning to the knowledge the child acquires, making some of it important and valued and some irrelevant.

Agents of socialization may also influence the child's use of certain cognitive strategies and perceptual mechanisms involved in selecting information, filtering out other information, and using processes to scan the environment for stimulation. It is also generally agreed that these agents have a strong influence on personality development, including the formation of such characteristics as self-esteem, attributions of self, personal monitoring mechanisms, and the internalization of standards and values.

While the home and school are the childs' two most prominent agents of socialization, there are other agents, which may include the mass media (such as television), the peer group, and the community. Where a mismatch exists between the values and information offered a child, her or his learning may be hampered, and inner confusion may result.

One of the characteristics of contemporary society is the existence of great cultural variation in ethnic, religious, political, and economic background. In our multicultural Canadian society, families hold disparate values and beliefs regarding child-rearing practices, the goals of education, and the meaning of human existence. It is very difficult for the school to acknowledge and affirm the wide diversity of opinion and belief that exists among school children. Consequently, schools have a tendency to deny the influence of all home environments, as educators try to equalize educational opportunities for all children. But the school and family are not independent and separate organizations. One cannot disregard the influence of one upon the other. They are part of one system and organization; each influences the other.

In the light of a growing body of literature dealing with the ecology of human development, educators in the future should recognize more fully that schools are built on the educational structures developed in the home. One way of acknowledging the important influence of the home on the child's school performance is for teachers to become well acquainted with families, including their cultures, beliefs, patterns of socialization, and educational purposes and goals. The curriculum needs to be developed with a recognition of the importance of the family. Educational policies need to integrate this information into educational practices through practical administrative and instructional linkages.

In order to utilize more fully the potential resources of the family, schools will need to become more aware of the contribution the family makes to the educational process. In this regard, Hayward suggests: "There are two kinds of knowledge required by the schools to fulfill their role, knowledge about the nature of human mental development and knowledge about the families of the particular children attending each school."[21] By obtaining such information, it will be possible for teachers to develop a keen interest and respect for the family and its traditions, culture, and belief system. Schools and families have a reciprocal relationship that requires the development of a partnership in which co-operation, trust, and mutual understanding exist.

Occasionally, families do not possess the necessary resources to influence their children positively, and families sometimes develop dysfunctional patterns of interaction. When this occurs, the school must go beyond offering programs such as parent education, remedial work, or special education for needy children. While these programs have considerable value, they are all school-based, and fail to involve the families directly.

A program, recently implemented by the author and a colleague, went beyond the school but continued to maintain a close link with it and actively involved families with children who had learning and behaviour disorders.[22] In this program, perceptions of a child's learning problems were shared between the school and the family. The parents' thoughts and suggestions were welcomed, rapport was developed, and school and home interventions were planned. Where dysfunctional family patterns existed, the family was helped to make beneficial changes in such areas as family structure, communication patterns, and child-rearing. The results of the study indicated that, not only did the reading scores of the children in the experiment improve more rapidly than those of the children in the control group, but also the parents indicated that, as a result of the program, their children appeared more cooperative, engaged in less frequent fighting, and were generally less disruptive at home.

SUMMARY

This paper has reviewed the literature and current practices having to do with the relationship between the family and the school as the institutions jointly responsible for educating children. The first section dealt with some historical developments, such as societal changes and philosophical perspectives, that have had a profound influence on educational policies and practice. The second section considered the empirical research studies that have examined the influence of the home on children's school performance. The data from the investigations have provided compelling evidence in support of the view that the family influences school achievement by fostering the child's cognitive development, communication skills, reading competence, and motivation. The third section described some practical ways in which the school could establish a more meaningful relationship with the home. The theoretical underpinning of this paper is an ecological systems perspective that views the child as an active participant interacting with a variety of contexts. The most important of these contexts are the home and the school.

NOTES

1. C.W. Anderson, "Parent-Child Relationships: A Context for Reciprocal Developmental Influence," *The Counselling Psychologist* 9 (1980): 35–44.
2. L.A. Cremin, *Public Education* (New York: Basic Books, 1976).
3. D. Radcliffe, "The Family and Socialization of Children: An Overview of the Discussion" in *The Family and Socialization of Children*, edited by D. Radcliffe (Ottawa: SSHRC, 1979).
4. Horace Mann, *The Republic and the School* (New York: Teachers College Press, 1957).
5. John Dewey, *Democracy and Education* (New York: Free Press, 1966).
6. H. Varenne, *Parental Influences on Child's Education* (paper presented at the meeting of the International Union of Family Organizations, Montreal, 1981).
7. Talcott Parsons, "The American Family: It's Relations to Personality and to Social Structure" in *Family, Socialization and Interaction Process*, edited by T. Parsons and R.F. Bales (Glenco, Ill.: Free Falls, 1955).

8. J.D. Friesen and DuFay Der, "The Outcomes of Three Models of Counselling and Consulting," *International Journal for the Advancement of Counselling* 7 (1984): 67–75.

9. Anderson, "Parent-Child Relationships"; R.D. Hess and S.D. Holloway, "Family and School as Educational Institutions" in *Review of Child Development Research*, edited by R.D. Parke (Chicago: University of Chicago Press, 1984); R. Seginer, "Parents' Educational Expectations and Children's Academic Achievements: A Literature Review," *Merrill-Palmer Quarterly* 29 (1983): 1–23.

10. British Columbia Council for the Family, *Parent-School Committees in B.C.: An Overview* (Victoria: Queen's Printer, 1980).

11. Hess and Holloway, "Family and School as Educational Institutions."

12. Ibid.

13. S.P. Boocock, *An Introduction to the Sociology of Learning* (Boston: Houghton Mifflin, 1972).

14. Seginer, "Parents' Educational Expectations and Children's Academic Achievements."

15. Hess and Holloway, "Family and School as Educational Institutions."

16. Ibid.

17. Ibid.

18. J.E. Schulenberg, F.W. Vondracek, and A.C. Crouter, "The Influence of the Family on Vocational Development," *Journal of Marriage and the Family* 46 (1984): 129–43.

19. U. Bronfenbrenner, *The Ecology of Human Development: Experiments by Nature and Design* (Cambridge: Harvard University Press, 1979).

20. Hess and Holloway, "Family and School as Educational Institutions."

21. B. Hayward, "The Family and Education" in *The Family and the Socialization of Children*, edited by D. Radcliffe (Ottawa: SSHRC, 1979), 185.

22. Friesen and Der, "The Outcomes of Three Models of Counselling and Consulting."

DAY CARE: CHANGES IN THE ROLE OF THE FAMILY AND EARLY CHILDHOOD EDUCATION

ALAN R. PENCE

Few rites of passage are as significant and universal in Canadian life as a child's entry into school. Traditionally, this transition has represented the child's passage from the protective environment of home and family to a broadened social involvement in peer-oriented institutions. Such has been our tradition, but it is no longer our contemporary experience. This chapter will examine the nature of our traditions and of our new reality wherein an increasing number of preschool-aged children experience peer socialization and institutionalization outside the family at increasingly younger ages. The history of family and school life, the nature of our current state of social and institutional transition, and an examination of issues that face us as individuals, as teachers, and as a society in planning for the future will be explored in the following pages.

THE TRADITION

The "traditional" relationship between family and school life referred to above is not one that extends back over a number of centuries in European or North American societies. Indeed, in English-speaking Canada its development can be seen as an essential component of the "framing of the twentieth-century consensus,"[1] the roots of which are imbedded in the nineteenth century.

The traditional relationship between families and schools in Canadian society is based on a particular model of the family and a particular model of education. The familial model with which we are most familiar today, and with which we have strong ties of sentiment and moral sensibility, has been termed the Victorian model.[2] The rise of the Victorian model, with its characteristic strong differentiation of "spheres of influence," or specific roles, for men, women, and children, is closely associated with the rise of industrialization and urbanization in England and in English-speaking North America. The Victorian model supplanted an earlier agrarian-based, domestically centred economic unit that had a less strictly defined conception of "separate spheres" of activity and purpose.

The Victorian model was based on a "father-breadwinner, mother-homemaker, child-dependent" ideal of family responsibilities. The home itself became the nest of family life, a "haven in a heartless world," to borrow Christopher Lasch's image.[3] It was seen as a fortress against the evils of the world.

One of the early challenges against the sanctity of the home, and the inviolability of the family gathered within, was the proposed system of compulsory, public schooling. The resistance of many communities and families to this "violation" of parental rights and responsibilities was strong. Yet, in the space of the nineteenth century, Canada passed from a system of private education for a few, to public education for the majority. "School had begun to rival the family as a determining influence of the formative years."[4]

The line of demarcation between what one was "to give unto" schools and what was "of the family" came, over time, to settle around children six years of age. In a somewhat surprising fashion, both the family and the school ultimately came to honour and support the territorial integrity of the other. The North American "tradition" evolved into the paramountcy of *family* life for the preschool-aged child and the supremacy of *school* life for the child aged six, seven, or older. The line of demarcation became transformed over time, and most of society forgot that the boundary had ever been in dispute.

Public school teachers became some of the strongest defenders of the rightful province of parents (young children) versus that of schools (children six and older). One of the very earliest North American experiments to test the firmness of this evolving division was the infant school movement introduced from England to the United States and Canada in the 1820s. These preschool programs (and first day-care programs in North America) extended from Halifax throughout "all principal cities and towns of the Atlantic States".[5] The reaction of one school board to their introduction was unequivocal:

> It is the decided opinion of every [primary school] instructress in the district who has had any experience on the subject, that it is better to receive into the Primary Schools children that have had no instruction whatever, than those who have graduated with the highest honors of the Infant Seminaries.[6]

The infant schools had died out in North America, leaving hardly a trace, by 1840, but their meteoric rise and fall demonstrate the rapid spread and popular acceptance of the notion that young children belonged exclusively with the family but that they were to be claimed by the school system as they grew older.

At various periods in Canadian (and American) history, a bridge between the domain of home and that of school was introduced. One such bridge was the Froebelian kindergarten. James L. Hughes, a Toronto school inspector, was largely responsible for developing the first public school kindergarten in Canada in 1883. The Toronto school board employed Ada Marean as the first instructor. She later married Hughes, and the couple became the principal promoters of the kindergarten movement in Canada, linking up with similar proponents in the United States. The Canadian advocates of kindergartens were, as historian Neil Sutherland notes, divided into two camps. There were those who saw the kindergartens "primarily as an agency which used young children as agents to improve the family life of the poor," while "others directed their efforts to use Froebelian ideas to reform the whole school system."[7] Both perspectives can be seen in preschool movements from the infant schools of the 1820s to the "head start" movements of the 1960s and 1970s (which impacted on Canadian preschool practice and theory as well as on U.S. developments).

Despite the considerable impact of various preschool movements on pedagogical practice and on community services, the overriding reality of preschool experience for the vast majority of North American children has been family life and family nurturance. More specifically, in the scheme of the Victorian family model, *mothers* have been the central caregivers of preschool children. In surveying the history of early childhood and preschools over the last 150 years, preschool and day-care movements have come and gone with varying degrees of impact and import, but the activity has taken place in the ever-present shadow of motherhood and the Victorian family model. This is beginning to change.

OLD AND NEW TRADITIONS: A SYSTEM IN FLUX

The movement of mothers out of the home and into the paid labour force is the most significant phenomenon in preschool care in Canadian history in over a century and a half. Insofar as mothers and their activities are a part of a number of interrelated social systems, a change in mothers' traditional roles and functions impacts on a great number of other social systems. There are few aspects of Canadian society that have not been affected by women's and, in particular, mothers' changing roles.

In 1951, the percentage of mothers who were part of the outside labour force was approximately ten percent. By 1961 this figure had climbed to twenty percent, in 1971 it was thirty percent, and by 1984 the Abella commission reported that just under sixty percent of mothers with children under the age of sixteen were in the labour force.[8] It is interesting to note that, from 1975 to 1985, the group of mothers who moved most rapidly, on a proportional basis, into the labour force were the mothers of children under three years of age (see table 1).

TABLE 1
LABOUR FORCE PARTICIPATION RATES OF WOMEN WITH CHILDREN, 1976, 1980, 1984,
ANNUAL AVERAGES

Age of Youngest Child	1976	1980	1984
Less than 3 years	31.7	41.7	51.5
3–5 Years	40.9	50.1	56.9
6–15 years	50.0	58.2	64.4

Source: Statistics Canada, *The Labour Force* (Ottawa, Dec. 1984), table 65a, p. 100; *The Labour Force* (Ottawa, May 1982), table 4, p. 106.

These revolutionary changes in mothers' and families' lives have totally redefined the nature of child-care needs in Canada. In 1973, the newly formed Federal Office of Day Care Information in Ottawa noted that there were approximately 26 516 licensed day-care spaces available in Canada to serve the needs of an estimated 543 000 children age birth to five years (a service-to-need ratio of 1:20). By 1982, the child-care need estimate for children age birth to six years was 950 000, and the available licensed spaces had risen to only 108 677 (a service-to-need ratio of one licensed space for every eleven children, aged birth to six years, in need of care).[9]

It is apparent from the above that the licensed services model utilized in Canada has proved insufficient when faced with a greatly altered social model of need. The welfare service model was predicated on the Victorian family model of service need, not on our present, greatly altered need base. The Victorian family service model is a limited-need model, insofar as the principal early childhood caregiving unit is defined as the family and, more specifically, as the mother. Services under such a model are needed only for the limited number of families who do not fit the "norm."

Funding for day care in Canada is on a matched basis of fifty percent federal and fifty percent provincial funds through the Canada Assistance Plan (CAP). Parents eligible for subsidy assistance are described in the plan as: "Canadians who require social services to prevent, overcome, or alleviate the causes or effects of poverty or child neglect."[10] Clearly CAP legislation is reflective of day care as viewed from the Victorian family model, not present-day need. Given this discrepancy, many question whether CAP should continue to be the mechanism whereby day-care funding is generated, or whether more normative-based model that would more accurately reflect the current *majority* of families' need for child-care services should be created. This call for child care to be seen and funded as a social need of the many rather than the few has led some to a review of the history of public education in Canada[11] and has produced calls by some for ministries of education to assume a more central role in the future of preschool child care in Canada.

If children are not in licensed care (as evidenced by the Federal Day Care Information Office), then where are they? This very straightforward question, which is certainly central to current day-care discussions, has yet to be answered. Canada lacks a data base addressing this question, although a proposal with that research intent has been submitted to Health and Welfare Canada.[12] Although we lack a strong and comprehensive data base, preliminary national studies and various regional studies suggest that caregiving in Canada is a complex mosaic of parental and child needs juxtaposed against a wide variety of formal and informal services. The overlay of the needs and services mosaic varies considerably from province to province, across different ethnic groups, and between urban and rural settings, to name but a few critical variables influencing the pattern. Some studies[13] suggest that, for a great number of families, more than one form of care is regularly used in a given week with, for example, a grandparent alternating with a neighbour for part of the week and perhaps a nursery used two or three afternoons a week. Some parents work non-overlapping shifts so they can care for their children themselves, while other parents employ a live-in nanny. The varieties of care used to fill in what used to be primarily a mother's role are endless, and, as the Day Care Information Office points out, most of these arrangements are of an unlicensed, informal nature.

We know very little about the quality of care provided in informal, unlicensed settings and not that much more about care in Canadian licensed facilities. Some Canadian studies suggest that, in utilizing informal, unlicensed arrangements, Canadians face "an epidemic of child neglect,"[14] while other researchers find some parents deliberately seeking out informal arrangements for a variety of reasons and experiencing strong levels of satisfaction with them.[15] To some degree, the question of quality is in the eye of the beholder, with a range of parental and child considerations entering into selection of and satisfaction with care.

The great diversity of needs inherent in a multi-cultural society as geographically dispersed and politically fragmented as Canada leads some to question if the fullest powers of decision making regarding child care should not be left in the hands of individual parents. Following from that position, it would seem that the primary role of government should be to extend and enhance options for parents, rather than to promote a tightly regulated and more restricted range of options such as exists in the public school system.

NEW MODELS FOR A NEW SOCIETY

There are innumerable policy briefs, position papers, and individual statements concerning day-care in Canada. Virtually every Canadian has a position on day-care: how good it is, how bad it is, what families should be doing, what they should not be doing, and so on. The remarkable thing about this range of opinion is the extremely limited nature of the empirical data on which it is based: the mass of opinion threatens to outweigh the available research evidence.

We are at a critical decision point in the history of Canadian day care and the development of Canadian society. The critical nature of this juncture has been recognized by the federal government, as evidenced by the establishment of a federal task force on child care in June 1984 and a parliamentary task force on child care in November 1985.

From the work of the task forces, and from various studies and papers over the last few years, several critical social questions emerge:

1. Whose responsibility is the care and well-being of Canadian preschool children? Is it primarily individual, familial, or societal, and to what degree is it a shared responsibility?

2. Does caregiving responsibility, shared or singular, imply financial responsibility as well?

3. Developmentally, what are "optimal" caregiving experiences and environments for preschool children of various ages?

4. To what degree is a definition of "optimal" dependent on child factors, family variables, and societal dimensions, and is "well-being" defined at an individual or some broader social level such as that of the family, ethnic community, or country?

5. To what degree do actual or potential conflicts exist among the various social levels noted above, and at what level is the decision-making power placed?

6. Insofar as our changing socio-familial dynamics are in large part the result of changes in workforce requirements, to what degree should employers be held accountable for and included in a redefined interactive system of responsibilities that would include families, communities, employers, and governments?

As was noted in the preceding section, one model of preschool-child caregiving that has been proposed is a downward extension of the schooling system, with certain modifications. Such a model is evidenced in the Ontario pre-kindergarten approach. When utilizing a school-based model, it should not be forgotten that this apparently benign model experienced a somewhat turbulent early history as zealous supporters of the "one-best-system" approach imposed its common structure across a diversified human-scape of ethnic, religious, urban, and rural lifestyles. The relative tranquility of schoolyards today belies their history of social discord and confrontation.

The public school model has, over time, addressed in its own unique way the six questions posed earlier. The relationships between children, institutions, parents, community, and the broader society have been spelled out, as have been financing and the pedagogical environment. Definitions of "optimal" are largely institutional decisions that have evolved over time, the "norm" is revered, and the role of employers has never been considered. Conflicts are de-emphasized by the ponderous logic of a professional bureaucracy, which cherishes the certainty of "tradition" in the same way that Tevye could set his life-clock by the traditions upheld in "Fiddler on the Roof."

In Canada's public school system there is a level of "certainty," bred by early victories and reinforced over time, that is both comforting and frightening. It is a uniform system designed to train children for the uniformity of adult work life. Its enforced uniformity exists in sharp contrast to the diversity of post-Victorian Canadian family life with its complexity of single-parent, blended, and one- and two-income families, as well as a host of ethnic traditions and values spread across a landscape of metropolitan centres and rural dispersion.

Children are born into diversity and uniqueness in Canada and, at age six, they enter normative uniformity. What should take place in the years in between?

A very different model from the downward extension of the institution of schools is a model of *planned* diversity. It is true that the existing state of preschool care in Canada is one of diversity: the great majority of children are not in licensed facilities. But the existing state is not one of *planned* diversity; rather, it is the result of an overflow of a limited welfare model. There exist problems of availability, affordability, and quality, which effectively limit parental choice.

One child-care option that has not been developed adequately in Canada is parent-care. Existing benefit structures deny parents viable options to care for their own children (beyond a period of a few months) without endangering the family's financial well-being or parents' career advancement. Given the choice of the family's economic hardship, for possibly extended periods of time, or remaining home to care for a baby over the first years of his or her life, many parents opt for non-parental care. (Supporting this economic hardship theory is a recent study by the Canadian Welfare Council showing that fully fifty-one percent of all two-income families would slip below the poverty line without the second income.) This first and most basic option of child care, through extended parental-care, is built into the social systems of European countries such as Austria, Hungary, and France, but does not provide an available, affordable option for Canadian parents.

Extended benefits for parental care are but one component in an options-oriented model, which is totally underdeveloped in Canada at present. There are similar problems of affordability and availability in the non-parental care sector of child care in Canada as well but, added to the restricting elements of affordability and availability, are questions of quality. As noted earlier, over eighty-five percent of all day-care provided in Canada is unlicensed, and one must be dubious about the quality of care offered even in licensed spaces when Canadian experts such as Dr. Howard Clifford of the National Day Care Information Office could note in 1979 that "Half of the 85 000 licensed day care centres in Canada are not fit to be open."[16]

At present, the basic orientation that must guide Canadian parents seeking child-care arrangements is *caveat emptor*," let the buyer beware. Yet if we as a society have done little to prepare individuals to become "good" parents, we have done even less to provide them with the information and skills necessary to become effective consumers of child care.[17]

It is apparent that, if we are to pursue a parental-option model of child care addressing the six questions posed earlier in new and creative ways, we must resolve very pressing questions of affordability, availability, and quality.

The issue of quality is one that must involve our training institutions, whichever basic model is developed, schooling-extension or a broader parental-option plan. In all likelihood, certain regions of the country will place a greater emphasis on one approach over the other, but the end result will be a mixed model for the country as a whole. Early childhood education and child-care training programs at both college and university levels must present a broad introduction to the child and her or his developmental needs within a social-ecological structure. A definition of quality in early childhood programs cannot be limited to the intra-program elements of curriculum, play materials, and interactions. Isolated learning, independent of family, peers, and cultural and neighbourhood groupings, is an inappropriate training orientation for working with a child of any age, but it is particularly inappropriate for the preschool-aged child given our historic respect for and demarcation of family responsibility for preschool-aged children.

Training for early childhood education and care must see the child as a learner in the broadest possible sense. Students must learn instructional and communication skills that *bridge* the ecological domains of school, family, neighbourhood, and culture rather than *block* that flow of systemic interaction through an over-emphasis on a particular domain or system in isolation.

Such a training imperative represents a serious challenge to many traditional education programs. The us/them orientation between schools and families that characterizes far too many school systems in Canada today, cannot be allowed to dominate the preschool care system without doing great damage to our socio-historical traditions and to the development of our children.

In summary, the rite of passage that school entry represents in our society is shifting, the portico of that passage is in motion. The traditional roles and responsibilities that families and schools have assumed on either side of school entry are in a state of flux, with a variety of future scenarios possible. Decisions that we, as a society, make over the next five years will be critical to the future role of families, educational institutions, and society as a whole, and to our children's development as we approach the twenty-first century.

NOTES

1. N. Sutherland, *Children in English-Canadian Society: Framing the Twentieth-Century Consensus* (Toronto: University of Toronto Press, 1976).
2. C. Strickland, "Day Care and Public Policy: An Historical Perspective" (unpublished paper, Emory University, 1981).
3. C. Lasch, *Haven in a Heartless World: The Family Beseiged* (New York: Basic Books, 1977).
4. C. Gaffield, "Schooling, the Economy, and Rural Society in Nineteenth-Century Ontario" in *Childhood and Family in Canadian History*, edited by Joy Parr (Toronto: McClelland and Stewart, 1982), 69.
5. William Russell, "Intelligence," *American Journal of Education* 4 (1829), 462.
6. John Bigelow, from *Minutes of the Boston Primary School Committee* (1820).
7. Sutherland, *Children in English-Canadian Society*, 174.
8. Statistics Canada, *Labour Force Participation Rates* (Ottawa: Statistics Canada, n.d.).
9. National Day Care Information Centre, *Status of Day Care in Canada* (Ottawa: Health and Welfare Canada, 1973–84).
10. Canada, Department of National Health and Welfare, *Canada Assistance Plan* (1974), 2.
11. *Report of the Task Force on Child Care*, K. Cooke, chairperson (Ottawa: National Council on the Status of Women, 1986).
12. D. Lero, A. Pence, L. Brockman, and H. Goelman, "Where are the Children? An Ecological Survey of Families and their Child Care Arrangements" (research proposal to Health and Welfare Canada, 1985).
13. D. Lero, A. Pence, L. Brockman, M. Charlesworth, et al., *Parents' Needs, Preferences, and Concerns About Child Care: Case Studies of 336 Families*, Report to the Task Force on Child Care (Ottawa: National Council on the Status of Women, 1985).
14. L. Johnson and J. Dinesen, *The Kin Trade: The Day Care Crisis in Canada* (Toronto: McGraw-Hill Ryerson, 1981).
15. A. Pence and H. Goelman, *Silent Partners: Parents of Children in Three Types of Day Care* (forthcoming).
16. H. Clifford, "Fifty Percent of Centres Unfit, Care Seminars Told," *Globe and Mail*, 23 Oct. 1979.
17. A. Pence and H. Goelman, *The Puzzle of Day Care: Guide for Parents and Counsellors* (Toronto: University of Toronto Guidance Centre Press, 1986).

SEX EDUCATION IN CANADIAN SCHOOLS[1]

EDWARD HEROLD

While some people may still believe that young people are better off not knowing the "facts of life," there are many tragic consequences of not properly informing young people. Consider the following:

> At midnight on January 26, 1983 a 15-year-old Hamilton high school student who was alone in her bedroom gave birth. She lay in bed with the baby through the night and in the morning hid the child in a garbage bag. The mother of the teenager had no idea her daughter was pregnant. In court, the defence lawyer stated the girl had no knowledge of childbirth and did not know how her parents would react to the situation.[2]

Another example is that of a twenty-one-year-old university student who felt that, because she received no sex education at home or at school, she suffered unnecessary worry and anxiety about the physical changes she experienced during and after puberty. "My ignorance in the area of sexuality, until I reached the university level, fills me with regret, shame, and a determination that my children will not be left in such an educational vacuum in this area."

Many different agencies and professional groups are involved in sex education, including religious institutions, the medical profession, social service agencies, and birth control groups. Nevertheless, most formal sex education takes place in the school setting. During the 1970s, many Canadian school systems began offering sex education courses. However, very few have developed comprehensive programs and, as a result, most young people in Canada are not receiving adequate sex education.

HISTORY OF SEX EDUCATION IN CANADA

Until the 1960s, there were virtually no organized sex education programs in Canada. In those few cases where sex was discussed, little or no information was given other than vague references to the avoidance of temptation. However, beginning in the late 1960s, in response to the increased sexual activity among young people, and the accompanying increase in unplanned pregnancies, health professionals, educators, social workers, and parents cooperated to develop sex education programs.

In 1967, Ortho Pharmaceutical organized the first national conference on Family Life Education, which was attended by 3 000 participants. In 1972, a conference on family planning was organized under the sponsorship of John Munro, then minister of national health and welfare. In that same year, the Family Planning Division of the Department of National Health and Welfare was created. This division was instrumental in helping to establish new clinical and educational programs in family planning and sex education.

During the 1970s, some of the provinces developed policies and guidelines for the teaching of sex education. Although the implementation of sex education programs was left to individual school boards, the fact of having provincial approval facilitated school board involvement in these programs. Two of the earliest programs were developed by school boards in Calgary and London. Until recently, the Calgary family life program was one of the most comprehensive in Canada with considerable resources, including consultants, allocated to the program.

In 1977 a survey by the Canadian Education Association found that twenty-one percent of school districts in Canada had a family life education program. With the exception of puberty, few topics in sex education were introduced before high school. One of the main problems reported was that few of the teachers had received specific training to teach family life education.

A 1984 survey of school superintendents by the Planned Parenthood Federation of Canada found that fifty percent offered a family life education program.[3] Whereas eighty-seven percent of urban districts had a program, only twenty-five percent of rural districts provided family life education. Of 125 family life co-ordinators surveyed, only twenty-six percent indicated their school board had a policy statement on family life education. Co-ordinators stressed the necessity of obtaining school board commitment to the program in order to push reluctant administrators to act and provide the needed resources and training for the teachers to do a good job. Only one-half of teachers surveyed indicated that they had taken courses to prepare them for teaching family life education. Many teachers said that more in-service training programs were needed to keep them up-to-date on specific topics and resources. Few teachers reported having experienced any opposition to their programs, and most indicated that parents provided overwhelming support.

A major weakness of surveys on family life education is that the concept is so broad it includes many topics that may not really be sex education. Surveys are needed that focus on specific sex education topics such as premarital sex and birth control.

As of 1985, most provinces were leaving the responsibility for sex education to local school boards. Generally, the provinces have provided minimal support for these programs. Quebec is an exception in that it is the only province in which sex education is included under moral and religious education, whereas in other provinces it is usually included under health education. Ontario and New Brunswick provide extensive family planning programs funded provincially through local health units. Many of these programs also include sex education components.

A 1983 national health education study of 29 000 Canadian school children ages nine, twelve, and fifteen showed a considerable lack of sex education.[4] Only thirty-five percent of Grade 7 students knew that it was possible for a girl to get pregnant between the ages of twelve and fifteen. Most thought pregnancy could not happen until after age sixteen. Only twenty-two percent of Grade 10 students knew that usually there are no early symptoms of gonorrhea in females. Only forty-six percent knew that mothers who smoke are more likely to have premature babies than those who do not smoke.

OBJECTIVES OF SEX EDUCATION

What are the objectives of sex education? When sex education courses were first introduced, the emphasis was on the negative pathological aspect of sexuality. Sex was never talked about in positive terms, but rather was viewed almost as a disease that had to be cured by repression. Masturbation, for example, was seen as a filthy habit resulting in various physical and psychological illnesses. The main objective of sex education was to stamp out as much of sexual thoughts and behaviour as possible by instilling in people a tremendous amount of sexual guilt. In more recent years, although the negative aspects of sexuality are still being taught, there is a trend toward examining its positive, life-enriching aspects.

Of course, we need to be concerned with unwanted pregnancy and venereal disease, and an important objective of sex education programs should be the development of sexual responsibility so these problems will be reduced. But there is more to sex education than pregnancy and venereal disease prevention. Today most mental health professionals recognize that healthy sexual functioning is important to the well-being of individuals and of marital relationships. Most people consider a satisfying sex life to be important for their happiness.

What should be the goals of sex education? The first objective is the acquiring of accurate information. A good sex education program should provide students with basic facts about sexuality and clear up misconceptions.

A second objective is the development of greater self-awareness and understanding. When students acquire more information regarding sexuality, it enables them to develop greater insight into their own sexuality. This can lead to a reduction in anxieties about their own sexual development and help young people better manage their sexual problems. A female university student commented:

> I feel I have learned to appreciate sex as natural and healthy behaviour and not as something dirty and not to be talked about. The course has given me a better understanding of myself in this area and has helped me to answer many of the questions I have had about sex.

A third objective is to help students clarify their own values regarding sex so that they are less dependent on the standards of peers and are less likely to engage in sexual relations if they do not feel ready. This should result in more satisfactory decision-making.

A fourth objective is the improvement of communication skills. It is a myth that people are open in their discussions of sex. Most of the openness is carried out in a superficial way, and sex education can provide the opportunity to discuss sex in a serious manner. However, it must be emphasized that many aspects of sex are personal and private. In promoting classroom discussion on sexual issues, it is essential that educators be aware of this and refrain from attempting to impose complete self-disclosure. Students should never feel forced to divulge matters that they believe are personal and that they do not want others to know about.

The development of open communication can only occur in a classroom setting where the teacher is a warm, accepting person who respects the opinions of students. This point cannot be overemphasized. Communication cannot take place if students are reluctant to express their opinions because they fear being ridiculed by the teacher or other students. However, given a supportive atmosphere, students are highly enthusiastic about being able to discuss sexual topics in a serious manner. One student commented:

> I do feel more comfortable talking about sex. I think this is because now I realize I'm not the only dumb one and other people really don't know as much about it as they would like people to think they do. Also what I have learned in this course gives me more background to draw upon when discussing the topic.

Marriage counsellors report that many couples have difficulty communicating. By developing the communication skills of our students, they should be better prepared to discuss problems with their partner.

Being more knowledgeable about sexual issues, having greater self-understanding, and being able to communicate more effectively can increase one's self-esteem. A very important objective of sex education is the fostering of positive feelings of self-worth. A common problem among teenagers today is that of low self-esteem, which in extreme cases leads to suicide. By assisting students to deal with an area of their lives that many find problematic, sex education programs can help to make students feel better about themselves, which in turn will enable them to function more successfully in society.

Another objective of sex education is the development of tolerance for those whose opinions differ from our own. Surely one of the goals of any educational program is that of respecting the opinions of others. Too often our society is divided into conflicting groups that try to impose their views on one another rather than to accept the differing views that exist. Sex education in schools is unlikely to change fundamental values regarding sexual behaviour. Students in sex education courses indicate that their basic values and behaviour are not changed as a result of the course. This is important to stress because of the fear some people have that talking about sex encourages students to engage in it. In actual fact, given a peer group environment that is usually supportive of premarital sex, the teacher can play an important role in providing support to the students who do not want to engage in premarital sex.

Finally, another goal of sex education should be the increasing communication and closeness between parents and their children. Many students who take sex education courses indicate that it provides them with the opportunity to openly discuss sexual matters with their parents for the first time, and that this enables them to feel close to their parents.

TOPICS IN SEX EDUCATION

There are many important topics in sex education. Because my own research has focussed on the topics of premarital sex and birth control, I am concentrating on these areas. Of course, these two topics are integral to any comprehensive sex education program.

CHOOSING A SEXUAL STANDARD

Given the conflicting values about sex in our society, choosing a sexual standard is a serious and difficult matter. Yet it is a decision that every young person has to face.

Ira Reiss[5] has outlined four basic standards of sexual morality: abstinence, the double standard, permissiveness with affection, and permissiveness without affection.

1. The abstinence standard prohibits sexual intercourse before marriage for everyone.
2. The double standard prohibits sexual intercourse before marriage for women, but accepts it for men.
3. The permissiveness with affection standard permits sexual intercourse within a love relationship.
4. The permissiveness without affection standard allows for sexual intercourse outside of a love relationship.

Each of these sexual standards has its costs and benefits.

Since the abstinence code follows traditional religious and parental values, young people adhering to this code do not have to face the turmoil of going against religious and parental beliefs. Sexual decision making is simplified in that one does not have to decide continually whether to engage or not to engage in sexual intercourse. Certainly one does not have to worry about pregnancy or sexually transmitted disease. The major cost of this code is that it might result in considerable sexual frustration as well as conflict if one's partner does not accept this code. If the code is transgressed, then considerable sexual guilt would result. Because of sexual repression, some people following this code may have difficulty adjusting to a sexual life later when they get married.

The double standard is theoretically rewarding to males and exploitative of women. Obviously if the code were strictly applied, males would have a difficult time finding accessible sexual partners. Prostitutes would be about the only women available. Males accepting this code tend to categorize women into two types: sexual or bad and non-sexual or pure. This type of belief system could cause problems in a relationship when the male might have a difficult time adjusting to a sexually experienced woman whom he might perceive as being pure or non-sexual. Similarly, women might have a difficult time adjusting from being non-sexual to sexual.

The permissiveness with affection standard, while allowing for sexual expression when in love, may cause problems in terms of defining when one is in love. Decision making is difficult because the person may be uncertain about whether he or she is ready to experience intercourse. Guilt feelings can arise when the relationship with the sexual partner ends and a new relationship is started. One nineteen-year-old woman stated, "Previously I had rationalized my sexual activity through the expectation that my first sexual partner would be my only one. With a change of partners I had feelings of guilt in that this seemed like promiscuity."

The permissiveness without affection code potentially offers great sexual excitement and the least sexual frustration. However, one has to face the possibility of being labelled promiscuous, which might cause guilt feelings and lowered self-esteem. In addition to the possibility of unwanted pregnancy, there is also the greatly increased probability of contracting venereal disease through casual sexual contacts.

In summary, every sexual standard has its costs as well as its rewards. One of the responsibilities of sex educators should be to discuss the different sexual standards with young people and to point out the costs and benefits of each so that young people can be in a better position to make responsible decisions about their own sexual behaviour. Ultimately, the sexual standard young people choose will be affected by their own values regarding religious teachings, parental views, personal freedom, affection, and sexual pleasure.

Sex educators should be aware that many parents want them to emphasize traditional values, with the abstinence code being presented as the best one for young people. On the other hand, there is not a consensus among parents with respect to how the issue of sexual standards should be presented. In a 1982 national survey, seventy-four percent of Canadians indicated that premarital sex is "not wrong at all" or wrong only "sometimes."[6] When asked if an important objective of sex education should be to discourage premarital sex, only one-third of mothers in Wellington County, Ontario, agreed.[7] Furthermore, seventy-six percent of the mothers agreed that sex education teachers should avoid preaching at youngsters.

Nevertheless, most people would agree that the majority, if not all, younger teenagers are not mature enough to handle the responsibilities involved in having sexual intercourse. Indeed, until about age eighteen, most young people do not have sexual intercourse, either because they do not feel ready or for moral reasons. For this group, it is especially important that sex educators provide support for these values. Also, educators need to stress the building of communication skills, which can help these young people deal with peer and partner pressures that might lead to early sexual involvement. This would include specific examples of how to say no to such pressure. Of course, there are other alternatives to sexual intercourse, such as petting or masturbation, and sex educators should be prepared to present these topics in a sensitive manner.

In providing guidance about sexual decision-making, sex educators should encourage students to consider the following questions:

1. What are the views of your religion regarding premarital sex? Are you conforming with your religious ideals?

2. Are you taking your parents values into consideration? If your decision goes against parental values, how would you feel about acting contrary to them? How would you feel if your parents found out?

3. Will you feel guilty about your decision?

4. Are you being pressured by peers or your dating partner into sexual activity for which you are not ready?

5. Are you exploiting your partner or is your partner exploiting you?

6. Are you expecting too much from sex?

7. How important to you is having a sexual relationship and what does a sexual relationship mean to you?

8. Do you have trust in your dating partner and can you communicate honestly about your needs and concerns?

9. Are you prepared to use effective contraception?

10. If contraception should fail, how would you handle pregnancy?

11. Have you considered the possibility and consequences of contracting a sexually transmitted disease?

BIRTH CONTROL EDUCATION

Too often educators believe that birth control education consists only of a description of the different methods of birth control. This approach ignores the many other factors influencing birth control use, especially attitudes and values. What, then, should be included in the ideal birth control education program?

First, young people should know about the male and female reproductive systems, especially the menstrual cycle. Unfortunately, many adolescents have incorrect assumptions about the cycle of female fertility and attempt to use the old-fashioned rhythm method on a chance basis.

Students need to know about the different methods of birth control and have a clear understanding of precisely how to use them. They should also be aware of the effectiveness rate and advantages and disadvantages of each method. However, educators must avoid presenting too much information and thereby overwhelming adolescents with factual detail. Given that there is no ideal contraceptive, young people need to be familiar with more than one method because they are likely to use several different methods throughout their lives. Attitudes about different methods should also be discussed because adolescents are unlikely to use methods about which they feel uncomfortable.

Teachers and clinicians must be aware of their own biases in presenting the different methods of birth control. For example, consider how you would answer the following: Can the condom and/or foam be used effectively by adolescents? Are IUDs safe for young women to use? Do the benefits of the pill outweigh possible side effects? Educators and clinicians have differing opinions regarding these and other issues in birth control. It is essential that we be aware of these biases and how they can affect our teaching or counselling. Every method of birth control has its positive aspects and these should be stressed. The best method of birth control is one that will be used consistently by the individual.

Adolescents, especially the younger ones, often are not aware of how to obtain birth control services and of the procedures involved in obtaining them. Precise information should be provided about birth control services such as clinics, including their hours, location, and policies regarding confidentiality. This should also include detailed information about the procedures for internal examinations. When clinics provide birth control to young people they should make certain that written instructions are provided for the use of that method and include a description of side effects plus a telephone number to call in an emergency.

Birth control education should be presented at different grade levels throughout the junior high school and high school years. This would overcome the problem of forgotten information and, even more importantly, provide continual reinforcement of responsible sexuality.

Educators are often asked: "Why is it that so many sexually active young people know about birth control but don't use it?" The answer, of course, is that many factors influence birth control use. In order to have adequate sex education, these factors need to be addressed.

We need to make young people aware that, if they have sexual intercourse, there is a good possibility of pregnancy unless they take preventive action. Here statistics can be used to illustrate the large number of pregnancies occurring among adolescents. Also, we need to deal with such myths as "I won't get pregnant if I do it only once or if I only have sex once in a while." In discussing perceived susceptibility we need to make young people aware of the necessity to plan ahead to use birth control. Adolescents seldom anticipate becoming sexually active and find it difficult to think rationally about birth control after they have become sexually aroused.

To increase their perceived seriousness of a pregnancy, we need to make adolescents aware of the costs of childbirth. Teenage mothers face many economic, psychological, and social problems. Also, their infants face greater health and social risks than infants born to older mothers. For those few teenagers who intentionally want to become pregnant, we need to pay attention to the emotional needs they are trying to satisfy through pregnancy. They must be shown that having a baby would more likely increase rather than decrease their emotional problems.

In any discussion of birth control the psychological costs of using birth control need to be presented. Adolescents may be so overwhelmed by the emotional costs of contraception at the time of intercourse that they put aside consideration of the long-term costs of a possible unwanted pregnancy.

One of the major emotional costs is embarrassment in getting and using contraceptives. Teachers and clinicians, by discussing the different methods of birth control in a comfortable manner, can help to decrease student embarrassment. Young women are particularly embarrassed about the internal examination, and it is important that teachers and clinicians carefully explain the procedures involved so that young people will be less fearful of it. Also, when physicians are conducting an internal exam, they should try to reduce feelings of embarrassment.

Underlying many of the costs involved in using contraception is sexual guilt. Many young people cannot use contraception because it would make them feel guilty about having sexual relations. We should encourage young people to accept, as a rule, that they should never have intercourse without using contraception and, if they feel guilty, they should not be having sex.

Educators can play an important role in providing a cue to action for responsible sexuality. One technique is to use a motivating film. In 1972 I produced the film "It Couldn't Happen to Me,"[8] which deals with the psychological costs of using contraception and makes young people more aware of the risk of pregnancy. In producing "It Couldn't Happen to Me," I wanted to encourage birth control use among the sexually active, while at the same time supporting the views of those who did not want to have premarital sex. Indeed, adolescents who are opposed to premarital sex state that their views have been strengthened as a result of seeing the film.

Other factors influencing contraceptive use are age and self-esteem. Sexually active younger teenagers are less likely to use birth control than are older teenagers. Thus, it is important to begin formal birth control education programs during the early adolescent years.

Young people with high self-esteem are less likely to be pressured into having sex when they do not want to and are more likely to use contraception if they do engage in sexual intercourse. Teens with high self-esteem also feel less need to become pregnant in order to satisfy unmet emotional needs. Thus, wherever possible educators and counsellors should use strategies to raise the self-esteem of adolescents.

Sex education should not only be limited to teenagers. There should be education for parents so that they will feel more comfortable discussing topics such as birth control with their sons and daughters. It is easier for teenagers to be responsible for their sexuality when their parents are able to provide positive sex education.

Peer group influence could also be used to encourage responsible sexuality. For example, Family Planning Services of the City of Toronto has sponsored the development of a teenage drama group entitled "STARR" (Students Talking About Responsible Relationships). Through the use of dramatic role-playing, this theatre group presents important decision-making aspects of sexuality and birth control. By providing a role model, the actors help adolescents to feel comfortable about discussing contraception and related issues. To make the best use of techniques such as the drama group, it is essential that students have the opportunity to discuss their own feelings and reactions in a small group setting. In this way, their own peer group in the classroom can be used to reinforce the concept of responsible sexuality.

Most young people find it difficult to communicate about sexuality and birth control. Sexually active couples who discuss contraception are more likely to use it. Therefore teachers should attempt to increase the communication skills of their students. Communication exercises designed to improve the sending, receiving, and interpretation of verbal and non-verbal messages should be incorporated into all sex education programs. We also need to develop contraceptive assertiveness so that a young person can tell the partner that intercourse definitely would not occur unless he or she were using effective contraception.

Often educators assume that sexuality is the female's responsibility and typically female students receive more sex education than males. In Saskatchewan, eighty-three percent of females indicated that they had had some sex education compared with sixty-six percent of males. In particular females were twice as likely as males to be taught about menstruation.[9]

Adolescent males need to be educated about their sexual responsibilities. Here educators could work toward instilling feelings of respect toward the other person and, through values clarification exercises, support the value that it is wrong to use physical or emotional coercion to try to get one's partner to become involved sexually. Males have an equal responsibility in birth control and should be knowledgeable about the different methods. It is sometimes more difficult to teach males than females because males are socialized to present the image of knowing it all. Fortunately, there are audio-visual and other resource materials directed specifically at males that can help the teacher to overcome some of the difficulties involved in teaching and counselling males.

PORNOGRAPHY AND SEXUAL ABUSE

In the 1980s, there has been increasing societal concern over the issues of pornography and sexual abuse. Accordingly, efforts were made by feminists and other groups to have these topics discussed in the classroom. In every province special programs were developed, in at least a few school districts, beginning at the primary grades, warning children of the possibilities and dangers of sexual abuse. In a national survey of the Canadian population, the Badgley Commission on Sexual Offences Against Children reported in 1984 that about one in two females and one in three males are the victims of unwanted sexual acts, with most of these occuring during childhood and adolescence. The Commission recommended that a national educational program be established focussing on the needs of sexually abused children and youths. Similarly, the Special Committee on Pornography and Prostitution, chaired by Paul Fraser, recommended in 1985 that the federal government, in conjunction with the provincial governments, should initiate and support public education programs designed to increase the general understanding of human sexual relations.

DOES SEX EDUCATION CAUSE PROMISCUITY?

One belief of some opponents of sex education is that sex education promotes promiscuity. The research evidence clearly does not support this belief. Instead, research has shown that sex education does not increase premarital sex but may increase the more responsible use of contraception among young people who are sexually active. For example, Zelnik and Kim,[10] in studying a large random sample of American teenagers, found that those with sex education were no more likely than those who had no sex education to engage in premarital intercourse. However, those whose sex education included birth control education were less likely to become pregnant because they were using contraception. Within Ontario, Orton and Rosenblatt,[11] in a study of health districts, found that adolescent pregnancy rates declined the most between 1975 and 1979 in districts with the most developed family planning and sex education programs. Meikle et al.[12] found that, among fifteen to eighteen-year-old Calgary high school students, there was no significant difference in coital experience between those who had or did not have sex education, while among thirteen- and fourteen-year-old girls, fewer of those with sex education had experienced coitus. In the province of Quebec, Dr. Jean Yves Frappier,[13] in a controlled experiment with 1100 students in grades 9 and 11 found that those students who were given sex education were not more likely to engage in sexual intercourse. However, the sex education students did acquire more knowledge, and they showed a more responsible and less exploitative attitude towards sexuality.

There is definitely a need for more research into the effects of sex education. In Hamilton, Dr. Corinne Devlon of McMaster University is directing a major study of the effects of sex education programs on rates of adolescent pregnancy.

CANADIAN ATTITUDES TO SEX EDUCATION

Do Canadians approve of the teaching of sex education? In 1974 the Gallup Poll asked Canadians, "It has been suggested that a course in sex education be given to students in high school. Do you approve or disapprove?" Seventy-three percent approved. Those who approved were asked, "Would you approve or disapprove if these courses discussed birth control?" Eighty-nine percent approved. The strongest supporters were people from large communities and those who were younger and well-educated. Nevertheless, a majority of people over the age of fifty approved of sex education.

In a 1979 survey by the Ontario Institute for Studies in Education, ninety-one percent of adults in Ontario said that the school should be involved in sex education.[14] Over fifty percent said that sex education means more than the provision of medical or factual information on topics such as birth control and includes a fuller treatment of the social and emotional as well as the physical aspects of sex. In a survey of Calgary parents, Meikle et al.[15] found that eighty-one percent of parents agreed that schools should teach contraception. Ninety percent of parents surveyed in Prince Edward Island agreed that birth control information should be included in family living courses.[16] Sixty-nine percent of mothers in Wellington County, Ontario, agreed that schools should inform teenagers about the different methods of birth control; eighteen percent were undecided and only 1.3 percent disagreed.[17] Only two percent believed that providing teenagers with knowledge about contraception would lead to sexual experimentation. A 1984 Gallup survey for the Planned Parenthood Federation of Canada found that eighty-three percent of Canadians believed sex education should be taught in schools.

Every survey of parents that has been done has found the great majority supporting sex education in the schools. This needs to be emphasized because opponents of sex education programs time and again will say parents are opposed to sex education, when what they are really saying is that a small vociferous minority of parents are opposed to sex education. As long as parents are informed about what is being taught and are involved in curriculum design and revision, most will support the school system. A good example of this occurred in Halton County, Ontario, in March 1975 when the Renaissance Committee organized a parents' night featuring the film "Sexuality and Communication." The opponents of sex education had spread so many rumours about the film that the curiosity of parents was raised and several hundred attended the showing. When parents had the opportunity to view the film, their reaction was opposite to that predicted by the Renaissance Committee. Most parents liked the film and wished they could have seen such a film when they were in high school. Rather than remaining to listen to a tirade against sex education, most parents streamed out of the meeting.[18] The opponents of sex education thrive in an atmosphere where lack of knowledge about a program exists and consequently many false rumours arise. The correct action is to provide adequate information to the community.

Further indication of parental support can be seen in the fact that when parents are given the opportunity to refuse permission for their child to take a sex education course, hardly any do so. In many communities, parents have been so involved in the process of program planning and curriculum review that they have requested sex education for themselves.

ATTITUDES OF STUDENTS TO SEX EDUCATION

One concern of adults is the possibility of teaching sex education before the young people are ready. However, young people have the opposite concern—that of being taught too little material presented at a time when it is too late to be of much use to them. In 1972 we surveyed attitudes of grades 10 and 12 students in Wellington County, Ontario, toward family life education.[19] We found the students were overwhelmingly in favour of more family life and sex education being offered in the schools. They also preferred to have the sex education topics introduced earlier than they had been. Over eighty percent said that, at least before the end of Grade 10, they wanted to know about such topics as birth control methods, masturbation, and sexual response. When we presented the statement "Teenagers are better off not knowing about contraception," ninety percent disagreed. When we asked if information on methods of contraception leads to experimentation, almost all disagreed. The students believed that they should be provided with information about birth control and they did not believe this information would encourage sexual activity.

PRINCIPLES OF SEX EDUCATION

For sex education programs to be accepted and supported by parents it is essential that some basic principles regarding the school's role in sex education be established. The following are some fundamental principles that should be considered by all school boards before sex education programs are developed.

1. The primary responsibility for sex education rests with parents and the school's role is to support the parents' role.

2. School sex education programs should reflect both parental values and student needs.
3. Parents and educators should be partners in designing and implementing school sex education programs.
4. Parents who do not wish their children to be involved in sex education should have the opportunity to withdraw their children from these classes.
5. Wherever possible, sex educators should assist both parents and their children to communicate with one another.
6. Many young people do not want to become sexually involved and their views should be supported.
7. The sexual difficulties faced by young people are increased when they are not given adequate information.

SEX RESEARCH

A related development that is having a significant impact on sex education is the rapid increase in sex research. Following from the works of Kinsey and Masters and Johnson, research is being carried out into every conceivable aspect of sexuality. This research has exploded many popular myths surrounding sexuality and has helped to replace ignorance with knowledge. This new information is beneficial both in counselling people with sexual difficulties and in educating people about sexual reality. So much research is being done, and so many articles and books are being published, that it is almost impossible to keep up to date. What this research is demonstrating is that sexuality is not the simple matter it was once thought to be, but rather is a highly complex area of life that is influenced by numerous factors. A responsibility of sex educators and counsellors should be to keep aware of the major research developments.

TEACHER PREPARATION

Sex education is one of the most difficult subjects to teach because there are so many conflicting attitudes and emotions about the topic. Unfortunately, some administrators assume that any teacher, simply because of being a man or woman, is automatically qualified to teach sex education. The importance of adequate preparation for teachers of sex education cannot be over-emphasized. A particular concern of mine is that inadequately prepared teachers are less able to distinguish between value statements and statements of fact and will often state value assertions that may not have factual validity. For example, there are still many people who believe that sexual behaviour rates among young people have not significantly changed over the past twenty years. There are others who believe that women do not enjoy sex and only do it to please males. The following student comments also illustrate the consequences of inadequate teacher preparation:

> While I was in Grade 6, the boys were sent to shovel snow off the outdoor rink and the girls were kept indoors to observe a film on menstruation. It was terribly confusing even when all the facts were laid down in front of me. I felt as though there was something wrong because the boys were not allowed to observe the movie. This increased my negative feelings about the topic of sexuality.

> Every year the school did its duty and showed 'from girl to woman' and 'boy to man' films. No teacher ever asked us what we thought of these films or if we had any questions. At the time, I remember that viewing these films was rather a stressful experience, particularly while we all waited for the film to roll. As I look back on this now I realize that our teachers were uncomfortable too, and that this may have been transmitted to us.

There can be no doubt that a major problem in sex education is the lack of adequately prepared teachers. Fortunately, many teachers recognize this deficiency and are attending courses and workshops in sex education such as the University of Guelph's conference on human sexuality, which brings together more than five hundred teachers and clinicians from across Canada each year.

A related problem is the lack of adequate resource facilities. Very few school boards have a full-time specialist in sex education. Because of this, the responsibility for developing curriculum on sex education or of providing guidance to teachers is given to a consultant who is often busy with other responsibilities and does not have the time to deal adequately with the sex education program. One of the strongest recommendations we can make for improving sex education programs is that funds and personnel be made available at the provincial level as well as at local school board levels for the development, implementation, and evaluation of such programs.

PROSPECTS

What are the prospects for sex education? I personally believe that, despite some controversies, sex education programs in Canada will continue to develop and grow. I am optimistic because our children need and want the information and because most parents approve of sex education. Granted, there will be some difficulties. Nevertheless, parents in the 1980s are more willing to educate their children about sexual matters than parents of previous generations. As parents become more comfortable about providing sex education for their children, they will further increase their support of sex education progams in the schools.

NOTES

1. Portions of this article were originally published in E.S. Herold, *Sexual Behaviour of Canadian Young People* (Toronto: Fitzhenry and Whiteside, 1984). Permission to reprint these portions has been granted by Fitzhenry and Whiteside. The quotes by students are taken from various research studies conducted by the author with Ontario university students.
2. *The Globe and Mail*, 9 Aug. 1983.
3. Judith Nolte, "Sex Education in Canadian Classrooms," *Tellus* 5, 3 (1984): 13–16.
4. A. King and A. Robertson, "Canadian Health Knowledge Survey for Ages 9, 12, and 15" (Queen's University, 1983).
5. Ira Reiss, *The Social Context of Sexual Permissiveness* (New York: Holt, Reinhart and Winston, 1967).
6. R.S. Bibby, *The Moral Mosaic: Sexuality in the Canadian 80s*. PROJECT CAN80, Release 1: Sexuality (Lethbridge, Alta: University of Lethbridge, 1982).
7. J. Marsman, "Mother-Child Communication About Sex" (M.A. thesis, University of Guelph, 1982).
8. Magic Lantern Films.
9. M. Weston, *Youth Health and Lifestyle* (report of work in progress submitted to Saskatchewan Health, Aug. 1980).
10. M. Zelnik and Y. Kim, "Sex Education and its Association with Teenage Sexual Activity, Pregnancy, and Contraceptive Use," *Family Planning Perspectives* 14, 3 (1982): 117–26.
11. M.J. Orton and E. Roseblatt, *Adolescent Birth Planning Needs: Ontario in the Eighties* (Toronto: Planned Parenthood, 1980).
12. S. Meikle, K.I. Pearce, J. Peitchinis, and F. Pysh, "Parental Reaction to Contraceptive Programs for Teenagers" (unpublished manuscript, Department of Psychology, University of Calgary, 1980).
13. J. Frappier, "Evaluation of a Sex Education Program in High School" (unpublished manuscript, University of Montreal, 1983).
14. T. Livingstone and L. Hart, *Survey of Attitudes to Ontario Schools* (Toronto: Ontario Institute for Studies in Education, 1979).
15. Meikle et al., "Parental Reaction to Contraceptive Programs."
16. M.A. Macleod, *Opinion Survey of the Family Planning and Sex Education Needs in Prince Edward Island* (P.E.I. Department of Health, 1980).
17. Marsman, *Mother-Child Communication About Sex*.
18. *The Oakville Beaver*, 19 March 1975.
19. E.S. Herold, K.E. Kopf, and M. de Carlo, "Family Life Education: Student Perspectives," *Canadian Journal of Public Health* 65 (1974): 365–68.

CHILD ABUSE AND THE TEACHER

LARRY EBERLEIN AND BETTY MASON SWINDLEHURST

"Mr. Walters, I was just shocked," Mrs. Lehman explained. "When I finally got Mary Ellen to tell me why she didn't want to go home right after school, she showed me the welts and bruises and started to cry. I know she's been absent a lot lately and Mary Ellen says her mother won't let her come to school unless her clothes cover the bruises from her step-dad's beatings. Mary Ellen says she often has to run outside or hide when her dad slaps her mother around, and then he threatens them with another beating if they tell anybody about it. What can we do?"

Not a daily event for a teacher—but one that is repeated all too often in schools across Canada. What should a teacher and principal like Mrs. Lehman and Mr. Walters do when they suspect physical abuse or neglect? Teachers are often the first to notice the physical and emotional behaviour that can indicate a child is in need of protection.

Mrs. Lehman and Mr. Walters have both a moral and legal duty to act in such cases and their actions should be carefully considered. Our society has a special concern about children who are often unable to protect themselves from more powerful adults. This is why the law treats them as a special population. While the legal issues in this case of child abuse will depend upon the province, the moral issue is the same: "What course of action will be best for Mary Ellen?" This question is not as easy to answer as one might think. It implies both defining the goal of a physically and psychologically healthy child and also evaluating the means by which that goal is reached.

Over the past few years, there has been a dramatic increase in the focus on child abuse and neglect—especially sexual abuse. Briefly, physical abuse can be defined as force resulting in a non-accidental injury to a child. Neglect occurs when the action or inaction of a child's caretaker endangers the safety and development of the child. Sexual abuse includes any sexual behaviour or sexual exploitation of a child. (See appendix for fuller definitions.)

The material that follows is divided into three parts. We deal in the first part of the paper with the roles and responsibilities of parents and children, recent changes in provincial legislation, and the related duty to report child abuse. In the second section we look at the philosophy of treatment and follow the case of Mary Ellen Blair. We explore some of the practical problems and issues that arise, and consider the implications these have for both the legal and moral issues involved. Finally, we focus in the last section on the teachers' and schools' specific roles and responsibilities.

PARENTS, CHILDREN, AND SOCIETY

In almost every country, the parents of Mary Ellen Blair would be responsible for the training and education of their child. This duty includes the authority which, unless there is a specific public policy to the contrary, extends to all areas of Mary Ellen's life. This power includes the right to custody, control, services, earnings, choice of religion, education, and so on. The duty to support Mary Ellen implies the power to make decisions about where she will live, what she will eat, and how she will dress. Because parents have a duty to provide a favourable moral environment, they have the power to censor books, magazines, movies, and TV. Child abuse has always occurred in society but it has generally been ignored or hidden, children having historically been viewed as the "property" of the parents (especially the father), who could use or abuse them at will. Until recently, children were not even permitted to question or challenge their parents' decisions. Courts have been reluctant to intrude upon the sanctity of the family and have tended to consider a child's welfare as being identical to that of the parent.[1]

SHOULD SOCIETY INTERVENE?

Children like Mary Ellen today have more rights than previously. With the introduction of the new Canadian Charter of Rights and Freedoms, this trend will continue into the foreseeable future. Defining a child's constitutional rights vis-à-vis the government is not too difficult; it is a matter of taking adult rights and providing as many of them as possible to children. The difficulty comes when a child's rights conflict with those of a parent, frequently a problem in child abuse cases.

Regardless of the sanctity of parent-child relationships, society has always intervened in the family through governmental agencies, sometimes to protect children from undesirable parental conduct and sometimes to compel obedience to parents. In the current movement towards a paternalistic, welfare state, governments have taken an increasingly active part in child-rearing under the doctrine of *parens patriae*. The origin of this concept was an expression of the monarch's prerogative, since the monarch was seen as the guardian of the people. In return for allegiance, the monarch had a duty to take care of subjects who were legally unable to take proper care of themselves and their property. In the nineteenth century, the purpose shifted away from protection of mere property to protection of the child. During the nineteenth century, societies were organized to prevent cruelty to animals (1824 in Canada), and this led in time to similar societies for the prevention of cruelty to children (1893 in Ontario and Manitoba). Only in the twentieth century did the other provinces follow and did legislation distinguish between delinquent children and neglected children, a transition that involved more state intervention directly into the family.

This doctrine of state intervention has led to the most recent innovation—legally requiring persons who observe child abuse or neglect to report suspected cases to appropriate authorities. The introduction of these laws marks a departure from the usual view of law that citizens are not duty bound to report criminal activity or to intervene in another's personal affairs.

Not all agree with this trend. Hafen[2] concludes that the intrusion of judicial and social service agencies may give children independence to assert their rights, but this will lead to a corresponding decline of parental control and responsibility that will ultimately damage the child and scuttle the traditional benefits of the family structure. He suggests that children must be viewed as developing persons with a basic interest in maximizing their own potential. However, this is almost always inhibited in families in which physical, sexual, or psychological abuse occurs.

IS CORPORAL PUNISHMENT CHILD ABUSE?

Parents like Mary Ellen Blair's stepfather will often claim that the spanking given Mary Ellen was necessary for disciplinary purposes. Since the family is responsible for a child's upbringing, parents have always had a special privilege in the area of child discipline. What would otherwise be seen as child abuse (corporal punishment) has been consistently recognized in the Criminal Code of Canada as a caretaking right.

The Law Reform Commission of Canada[3] found three situations in the home where force is most often used with children. The first is the emergency situation. Force is used for a child's own safety, to safeguard others, or for protection of property. In these situations the use of force is felt to be justified and authorized by the law without need to resort to a specific exception in the Criminal Code. This defence of necessity, however, may not justify physically compelling the child to go to bed at night.

A second kind of situation occurs when a parent resorts to violence in the heat of the moment. A harassed mother, for example, alone in her house with three small children loses her temper and strikes her children. The Law Reform Commission felt that the use of force in this situation was not legitimate even when provoked by the children.

The third situation involves the use of reasonable corporal punishment. A majority of the Commission felt that permission to use force for punishment should continue to be included as part of the Criminal Code. Some felt that to remove the provision would give too much discretion to criminal prosecutors to determine when excessive force had been used. They argued that, since parents have primary authority over their children, the obligation should clearly carry the right in law to use reasonable force as a last resort. A substantial minority argued, however, that the use of force demonstrates that adults view physical abuse as acceptable behaviour and a suitable way of handling life's frustrations. They favoured the elimination of the provision. For the present, however, reasonable corporal punishment is not considered to be child abuse.

WHAT IS CHILD ABUSE AND WHO MUST REPORT IT?

In general, abuse involves a physical or emotional injury to a child. It is usually caused by some overt act by a parent or other caretaker, but can also be caused by carelessness, negligence, or failure to perform a responsibility that the caretaker has toward the child. For example, when Mary Ellen was a baby, if her mother yanked her arm too hard, resulting in a shoulder separation, this could be seen as child abuse. On the other hand, if her mother carelessly left a top rail off her crib and Mary Ellen "accidentally" fell on the floor, this could be seen as child neglect. Since parents have so much responsibility for their children, failure to provide adequate food, clothing, shelter, medical care, and so forth can all be classified as child neglect. Neglect is more widespread but harder to detect than obvious physical abuse. Psychological abuse, which leaves only internal scars, is also very difficult to detect, and more indicators need to be observed before reporting. Wife battering has been considered by some to be an insidious form of child abuse as well.

In 1984 the Badgley Committee surveyed in detail all Canadian provinces and territories in an attempt to determine who is responsible for supplying information when a child has been sexually abused. Although the committee's focus was upon sexual abuse, their findings have wider implications for any type of child abuse or neglect. They found that the responsibility to report child abuse or neglect in every province rests on *all* people. Some provinces, however, add an additional obligation for reporting by professionals, including teachers. As legislation is modified, as in Ontario and Alberta, this special responsibility is being included where it had not been before. Some provinces such as Alberta and New Brunswick have also added a provision that, should a professional not report, the minister responsible may require the appropriate professional society (teachers' association or psychologists' association) to investigate the case. A professional in New Brunswick, for example, includes the school principal, school teacher, or other teaching professional or guidance counsellor.

WHO KEEPS TRACK OF ABUSED CHILDREN?

Most provinces provide for a central child abuse register. What is entered in these registers, however, depends upon the province.[4] In some jurisdictions, information is added to the register only after a complaint has been investigated and verified by a case worker. On the other hand, every received report is recorded in Quebec, Manitoba, Alberta, and British Columbia.[5] Because registers are not uniformly used across Canada, there is frequently no complete listing of verified cases of child abuse. In addition, there is no transfer of information between provinces, and social workers often do not even check their own provincial register.

Two problems with these registers were identified. At least three provinces (Newfoundland, Manitoba, and Saskatchewan) do not notify a person when his or her name has been put on a central registry. In Manitoba, since all reports are recorded in the register, the name of a person who has never committed any form of abuse may be registered without that person even knowing it. In addition, in several provinces there are no procedures available to get a name off a register even though the party may be innocent of any wrongdoing.

PHILOSOPHY OF TREATMENT

Since child protection services are the legal responsibility of the provinces, there is no single model of either administrative organization or philosophy of service followed in Canada. Administration ranges from loosely affiliated local regional children's aid societies to centrally administered services. In addition, the Badgley Committee concluded that the "provincial statutes are of little value in terms of providing any real guidance, or practical assistance to officials responsible for child care and protection."[6]

Almost any child thought by a welfare worker to be living in unsatisfactory domestic conditions or subject to any form of abuse or neglect would come within the purview of the provisions of provincial child care statutes. For practical purposes, a provincial authority can intervene by law in any family situation.[7]

Because of the diversity of policy, it is important for educators to clearly understand the philosophy of the social services department in their own province in order to understand the eventual implications of their reports of child abuse. All provinces have developed some type of policy manuals or guidelines for the use of professional caretakers dealing with abused children. Some are more comprehensive than others. For example, the B.C. Handbook,[8] which combines policy from four government departments, emphasizes that the investigation of a complaint is the responsibility of the Ministry of Human Resources and the police and should not be assumed by school district personnel.

There is also a lack of uniformity in the philosophy of intervention strategies. Two basic models are extant in the North American literature. The family-centred approach focusses on the child in relation to the family. A child abuse report is made to the child protection services, and a family court or civil law approach decides what is in the best interests of the child in the family setting. The child has both a right not to be harmed and a right to life in his or her natural home. The focus is on voluntary co-operation with the family rather than on arresting the offender, although the offender may be expelled from the home.

The second model, sometimes called the child-centred model, emphasizes the criminal law system, the involvement of the police, and the removal of the offender from the home. The adult offender is seen as totally responsible for any abuse. Kempe,[9] a supporter of this approach, argues strongly against the goal of reuniting the family and insists that only the best interest of the child should be served.

WHAT IS YOUR PROVINCE'S PHILOSOPHY?

Recent changes in legislation in some provinces have taken the position that what happens to a child in need of protection should be in the child's best interest. The legislation lists matters to be considered by the courts. Now, for example, Prince Edward Island, Manitoba, Newfoundland, and Ontario offer some direction in this regard. Typical are the following considerations in the Newfoundland Child Welfare Act, amended in 1981:

— The right of a child to love, affection, and understanding;
— The right of a child to an environment to stimulate and encourage her or his development;
— The necessity for appropriate care or treatment for mental, emotional, and physical health of the child;
— The love, affection, and ties that exist between the child and each person to whom the child's custody is entrusted or who has access to the child;
— The views and preferences of the child;
— The effect upon the child of any disruption of the child's sense of continuity;
— The child's cultural and religious heritage;
— The merits of a plan proposed by the government agency in comparison with the merits of the child returning to or remaining with his or her parents.

By contrast, Alberta's new Child Welfare Act, proclaimed in force on 1 July 1985, adopts the family-centred model and provides, among other factors, the following matters to be considered, indicating the importance of provincial support for the family:

— The family is the basic unit of society and its well-being should be supported and preserved.
— The family has the right to the least invasion of its privacy and interference with its freedom that is compatible with its own interest, the interest of the individual family members and society.
— The family is responsible for the care and supervision of its children, and every child should have an opportunity to be a wanted and valued member of a family.

The Badgley Committee survey found that two provinces use primarily the child-centred approach and two others provinces the family-centred approach. Six provinces reflect a mixed philosophy. The result is a wide variation across Canada in terms of whether a child abuser is removed from the home, criminal charges laid, the type of services provided, and so forth. For example, abused children permanently placed in foster care varied from ten percent to forty percent across Canada, depending upon the province. Children remaining in the family without the offender varied from three percent to twenty-eight percent; and in the family with the offender present from sixteen to twenty-three percent. The laying of criminal charges against the offender varied from eight percent in one province to fifty-nine percent in another. Because of the magnitude of these variations, it is important that professionals understand the obligations imposed by their own provincial statutes.

WHEN SHOULD A REPORT BE MADE?

In spite of the vagaries of child welfare statutes from one province to another, one requirement remains constant in all jurisdictions: all persons, including teachers, must report child abuse when they have a reasonable basis for their belief that it has occurred. Such reporters are usually protected by law from any retaliatory action by the parent.

There is a difference, however, between suspicions and a reasonable basis in fact. This is why we encourage consultation before making a report. Were a teacher to report based upon a mere suspicion, and it was found that there was no reasonable basis for such a report, the teacher would not be protected.

The situation is made more difficult when provincial policy prevents a teacher from seeking sufficient additional information to change a mere suspicion into a reasonable belief that abuse has occurred. For example, one of the common indicators of child abuse and neglect is a child's reluctance to go home after school. If Mrs. Lehman had simply reported that she suspected Mary Ellen to be abused because she seemed to be reluctant to go home after school, she may not have been justified in reporting under the law, even though a literal interpretation of the B.C. policy would seem to indicate that she should. When Mrs. Lehman was able to give information about the bruises and the home situation, she was justified in consulting with her principal and then reporting. Indeed, she was obligated to report to the proper authorities.

WHAT HAPPENS WHEN A REPORT IS MADE?

What occurs when a report of an abuse situation is made? Although terminology and guidelines may vary somewhat from one province to another, the basic reporting and follow-up procedures are similar. In each province, child welfare services are provided by a provincial department that operates under statutory responsibilities. The child welfare process involves situations from the time a district office first becomes involved in a case to its ultimate resolution. The basic components of the child welfare process include: receipt and verification of reports; assessment of family difficulties; case management and planning; and follow-up of services provided. This process has two major purposes. First the protection of referred children from child abuse and neglect is ensured. Second, services to referred families are provided to aid, restore, and rehabilitate the family unit, if possible.

Mary Ellen is Reported

When the report on Mary Ellen is received by an intake worker, her case is referred immediately to a social worker for investigation. The social worker assesses the report and the Blair family's situation under the terms of the provincial child welfare act. During the investigation, the worker talks to Mary Ellen, visits her mother and stepfather, and contacts other involved persons and resources, such as Mrs. Lehman, Mr. Walters, the public health nurse, and any other services involved with the family such as mental health services. Further information and verification of details are sought, and support is offered to Mary Ellen and (possibly) her family. The worker may have several contacts with Mary Ellen, her parents, and other resource personnel before making one of the following decisions.

Leave Mary Ellen in the Home

If there is no evidence of abuse or neglect, the case may be *closed*.

If there is evidence of physical or sexual abuse, the offender may be removed but Mary Ellen left at home. This may also be true in some cases of spousal abuse.

There may be concerns about the family's functioning, and the worker may keep the case open on what is called an *open protection* basis. The worker maintains regular contact with Mary Ellen and her parents, and possibly involves other agencies such as the school, public health and mental health services, psychologists, psychiatrists, family aides, homemakers, and so on. There usually is a case conference with involved agencies to exchange information and plan how to best help the family.

Remove Mary Ellen from the Home

Mary Ellen and/or any of her brothers or sisters may be removed from the parents' custody (apprehended) by a child welfare worker at any point in the contact between the worker and the family. This decision is made when the safety of any child in the home is in question. In some provinces, child welfare workers attempt to keep the family intact and provide services to aid the family as a unit (family-centred approach) while other provinces adopt a child-centred approach. The services offered to the family and the punishment/rehabilitation of the abuser depend to an extent on the approach chosen and/or mandated under the particular act.

If Mary Ellen is apprehended, she may be placed in one of several temporary situations including a children's shelter, a receiving home, or a foster home. Legal guidelines ensure that the child's case must be heard in court within a specified time. During the time between apprehension and court, the social worker gathers more information about the family's functioning by talking further with the parents and with involved resources such as the school.

Mary Ellen in Court

After hearing testimony from the social worker, other professionals, and the parents, the judge may choose one of several alternative courses of action. First, the judge may find that there was no neglect or abuse and that Mary Ellen should be returned home. At this point, the social worker may close the case. The worker, however, may decide to remain involved with the family on an open protection basis if there are still concerns regarding care in the home.

Second, Mary Ellen may be returned home under a supervision order, which means that the worker will be involved with the family on a regular basis. This gives the worker more responsibility for maintaining contact with the family than does keeping the case on an open protection basis. In either situation, professional assistance may be provided to the family so that ongoing monitoring is provided.

Third, the judge may make Mary Ellen a ward of the government for a specified period of time, usually three, six, or twelve months. When the child is made a ward, she can be placed in a foster home, group home, or residential treatment centre. Treatment centres usually provide intensive help for children with severe emotional, behavioural, psychological, or social problems. In this latter eventuality, workers maintain regular contact with the child, the placement resources, and the natural parents to prepare for eventual return to the home. Other agencies may be involved at any point to provide assistance to the child, her natural family, and to the placement resources.

Mary Ellen and a Guardianship Agreement

Several provinces have a voluntary, co-operative agreement status that may be used. Under this agreement, the parents would give child welfare the right to provide temporary care and assistance to Mary Ellen. This type of agreement may be ended by the parent at any time.

CHILD WELFARE DILEMMAS

Several dilemmas confront the child welfare worker who is dealing with abusing or neglecting families. First, the worker must skillfully operate within the guidelines of the provincial statute while keeping in mind the safety of the child. At the same time, the worker attempts to engage the parents in a trusting and helping relationship. Often only one parent constitutes the problem but that parent exercises the power in the family unit.

It is important to realize that most of the identified parents were themselves abused or neglected as children. They received little nurturance, guidance, support, or teaching from their own parents. As a result, they have little knowledge of how to nurture, guide, support or teach their own children and tend to treat family members as they themselves were treated. They have a low sense of self-worth, usually do not understand children well nor do they feel empathic toward them. These offending parents are usually socially isolated and distrust anyone who comes to the home. As a result, they are resistant toward intervention and unmotivated to change. It is particularly difficult for child welfare workers and other professionals to engage them in a helping relationship. When a non-abusive parent is freed from the power and control of the offending parent, the non-abusive parent may adjust quite well.

A further dilemma involves the shortage of treatment resources. Foster homes, group homes, and treatment centres are often in short supply. Psychiatric or other assessment services that aid workers and the family in diagnosis and treatment might not be available on a long-term basis.

ROLE AND RESPONSIBILITY OF SCHOOL PERSONNEL[10]

The Child Abuse Handbook compiled by the Province of British Columbia[11] indicates some of the problems facing teachers in the child abuse area. The handbook quite properly indicates the unique role of the educator in identifying and reporting abused and neglected children. "Since educators are in daily contact with children and are trained observers of children's behaviour, they are frequently the first adults to become aware of situations which may be indicative of abuse or neglect. In fact, the school may be the only place where an abused child feels safe and in contact with caring adults."[12] The handbook then indicates that educators who have "reasonable ground" are required by law to report their *suspicions* (emphasis added) of a case of child abuse or neglect. The suggested outline of procedures (a policy, incidentally, with which we disagree) is that the teacher report this suspicion first to a social worker and then notify the school principal. In addition, B.C. policy also requires that police be informed of any suspicions of physical or sexual abuse. Statements made to teachers should be recorded but "teachers should refrain from interviewing the child after receiving the child's first disclosure."[13]

Many school districts have established internal procedures including consultation with the community health nurse, school principal, and the superintendent of schools. The handbook indicates that, while these are desirable, it is the responsibility of the individual teacher to make the report. In addition, parents should not be contacted by school personnel unless specifically asked to do so by the social worker or police.

In each particular school situation, it is important that teachers are cognizant of child abuse and neglect policies and reporting procedures. If policies are not explicit, guidelines must be established by involving the principal, counsellor, child welfare officials, and the teachers.

Our view is that teaching staff who have reasonable and valid suspicions of abuse or neglect should report these instances to the principal of the school. Where a teacher notices a severe case, such as physical injury, the public health nurse should be contacted immediately, as often the nurse is helpful in identifying the type and seriousness of the injury. In more chronic cases of neglect, malnourishment, or unusual behavioural patterns, the nurse or school social worker may provide knowledgeable back-up and support. In a clear case of abuse, the teacher should report, even if the principal does not believe it necessary. Ethics also require that a teacher notify the principal of this course of action.

In most provinces, when physical abuse is apparent (e.g., welts, burns, fractures, bruises, etc.), a report to child welfare must be made immediately. Usually, reports of a crisis nature are funnelled through a child abuse "hotline." In this case, a crisis worker qualified as a social worker will interview the relevant school personnel, the child, and the parents. Medical attention will be provided to ascertain the nature and cause of the injury.

When abuse or neglect of a chronic nature is suspected, a case conference may be held. Necessary in this approach is teacher identification of children "at risk" and pertinent behavioural data that are noted on a daily basis. This latter is essential because often it is only through daily, dated recording of behavioural observations for particular children that parents or social agencies may realize the seriousness of a situation. Records should note positive as well as negative items, as this type of data can focus attention on the seriousness of a situation or, alternatively, may indicate that suspicions are unfounded.

The public health nurse, child welfare social worker, and other school personnel involved with the identified child are helpful in this type of approach. In conference, concerns may be clarified and assistance provided for the child and the dysfunctional family. This type of operation reassures participants that assistance is ongoing and the child's needs and progress are being monitored. The supervision ensures that the assistance is indeed beneficial or, alternatively, that more stringent measures may be required.

THE TEAM APPROACH

It is important to realize that each school has resources within it that can be used to assist children from abusive or neglecting homes. Teachers must first be trained to recognize the signs of abuse and neglect. Lists of indicators are available from a variety of sources including the literature,[14] provincial welfare departments,[15] and the school systems. As an example, a list used by the Edmonton Public School Board is included in the appendix to this article. Note the important differences between physical and sexual abuse indicators. Workshops are also a helpful means of learning identification and reporting strategies. Each teacher should become aware of the types of information that are necessary to assist this special group of children.

Teachers should also become aware of the characteristics of physical abusing and neglecting parents. These parents rarely keep school appointments or, if they do, may be late or unresponsive. They are often difficult to locate and may move frequently, seemingly just one step ahead of help for their children. Parents such as these are distrustful of schools and have a personal history of failure. Because of their social isolation, they are unable to ask for help, and schools and other agencies must reach out to them through volunteer and out-reach programs. Parents who evidence little concern for their children may be expressing personal helplessness and hopelessness and may be indirectly asking for assistance. Often, physically abusive or neglecting parents demonstrate very poor knowledge of child development. They seem to lack understanding of children's physical, emotional, and psychological needs. They seem to either overprotect their child or they may have unreal expectations, expecting or demanding behaviour well beyond the child's years or abilities. If teaching staffs can see beyond these characteristics and reach a very difficult and troubled group of parents, it is likely that there would be fewer occurrences of abuse.

Children too must be sensitized to the signs, causes, and effects of abuse and neglect. Since parenting is learned in the home, an alert younger generation will certainly become more adequate parents in the future. Multimedia presentations of abuse signals and procedures to obtain help are important for children. The optimal presenters are teachers if they have the training and skills necessary for offering these classes and discussions. Child development, family life, interpersonal relations, communication programs, and other similar courses would help prepare young people for parenting. The good touch/bad touch concepts are very important to help younger children identify sexual abuse situations.

Finally, diagnostic testing is often helpful for this special group of children. Such students usually have learning problems that cannot be defined by ordinary classroom methods, but assistance can be provided through the services of the school psychologist, guidance counsellor, reading specialist, speech therapist, etc. Children from these atypical homes *can* learn, but they require specialized methods because of years of physical and/or emotional abuse.

APPENDIX

DEFINITIONS OF ABUSE

Physical abuse is any physical force or action that results in or may result in a non-accidental injury to a child and that exceeds what could be considered reasonable discipline.

Neglect is the failure on the part of those responsible for the care of a child to provide for the physical, emotional, or medical needs of that child to an extent that endangers that child's health, development, or safety.

Sexual abuse is any sexual touching, sexual intercourse, or sexual exploitation of a child and may include any sexual behaviour directed toward that child.

GUIDELINES FROM THE EDMONTON PUBLIC SCHOOL BOARD[16]

RECOGNITION OF POSSIBLE ABUSE

What School Personnel May See

Some of the physical indicators of child abuse and neglect and some child behaviours to be considered include the following. It is important to be mindful of the fact that observation of one or two of the behaviours in any age group does not necessarily mean abuse. Some of the factors included may be indicative of other problems. Documentation of unusual behaviours may help school personnel become aware of an abusive or neglectful pattern.

PHYSICAL ABUSE

Physical indicators include:
— unexplained bruises and welts:
  on face, lips, mouth
  on torso, back, thighs
  numerous bruises of different colours
  reflecting shape of article used (cord, rope, belt buckle, clothes hanger)
  bald spots
  human bite marks
— unexplained burns:
  cigarette diameter (on soles of feet, palms of hands)
  immersion burns (glove-shaped, sock-shaped)
  electric burner or iron-shaped burns
— unexplained fractures
— unexplained lacerations or abrasions
— injuries regularly appearing after absence or weekends

Behavioural symptoms may include:
- wariness of physical contact with adults
- apprehensive when other children cry
- reports injury by parents
- resists changing clothing for school activities
- arrives early, stays late at school, and appears reluctant to go home
- wears clothing that covers body and may be inappropriate for warm months
- cannot tolerate physical contact or touch
- shows extremes in behaviour: aggression, withdrawal
- is a chronic runaway
- is unable to form good peer relationship (many abused children are forbidden by their parents from making friends or bringing them home)
- is fearful (the child may assume that all adults hurt children and is constantly on guard)

PHYSICAL NEGLECT

Physical indicators include the following:
- unattended medical or dental problems such as infected sores, decayed teeth, glasses not provided when needed
- child always seems hungry, begging, stealing, or hoarding food, and comes to school with little food of her or his own
- very poor hygiene and inappropriate, soiled clothing
- may be emaciated or may have distended stomach indicative of malnutrition

In addition the neglected child may:
- be frequently late or absent from school
- inform the teacher that there is no caretaker at home
- exhibit stealing, vandalism, or other delinquent behaviours
- have poor peer relationships, perhaps because of hygienic problems, or a depressed, negative attitude because of low self-esteem
- be fatigued, listless, or falling asleep
- crave affection
- be destructive or pugnacious

SEXUAL ABUSE

Physical indicators include:
- difficulty in walking or sitting
- pain or itching in the genital area
- frequent urinary or yeast infections
- sudden onset of enuresis or encopresis
- frequent, unexplained sore throats

Behaviour symptoms associated with sexual abuse:
- shows unusual interest in sexual matters and seems to have more sexual knowledge than is appropriate for child's age
- does drawings that are sexually explicit, beyond developmental level
- shows an inordinate fear of males or seductiveness toward males
- has large number of gifts, or money from a questionable source
- is exceptionally secretive
- has bouts of crying with no provocation
- is unwilling to participate in physical activities
- talks about or attempts suicide (especially adolescents)
- is a chronic runaway
- masturbates publicly and excessively
- reports sexual approach by an adult

EMOTIONAL ABUSE

Physical indicators may include:
- speech disorders
- severe allergies or ulcers
- lags in physical development

Behavioural indicators of emotional abuse or neglect include:
- constant apologizing even when not at fault
- inappropriate affect to situations
- behavioural extremes (compliant and passive, or aggressive and demanding; sleep disorders; inhibition of play)
- cruelty, vandalism, stealing, cheating
- rocking, thumbsucking, biting
- enuresis
- fears failure, gives up, and will not try again
- is self-deprecating, or makes claims of competence or achievement that are not part of play or fantasy; often daydreams
- sets high standards for own performance in order to gain approval, then cannot cope

Many of the behaviours of emotionally abused children are similar to those of children who have been physically abused: poor self-concept, acting out behaviour. Emotional abuse is often difficult to pin-point: it is not as visibly specific as is physical and sexual abuse or neglect, nor is it as easy to substantiate; nonetheless its effects on children are traumatic.

NOTES

1. R.L. Geiser, "The Rights of Children," *Hastings Law Journal* 28 (1977): 1027–51.
2. B. Hafen, "Children's Liberation and the New Egalitarianism: Some Reservations About Abandoning Youth to the 'Rights'," *Brigham Young University Law Review* (1976): 605–58.
3. Law Reform Commission of Canada, *Assault*. Working paper 38. (Ottawa: Law Reform Commission, 1984).
4. Consider the following report from the Toronto *Globe and Mail* for 9 April 1986. A three-year-old child came home from a day-care centre and told her mother than another child touched her "there," pointing to her crotch. She also rambled on about a carrot and used the work "prickly." The mother hastily took the child to her doctor who assured her there had been no penetration, but that he was required to report the suspected abuse to the children's aid society. The police were informed and they promptly investigated. The officer questioned the mother of the child, talked to the three-year-old, went to the home of the day-care provider (who happened to be the mother of the other three-year-old child). The officer determined that neither child was at risk and reported this to the children's aid society, which independently investigated the incident, and found no problem. However, the case is now on permanent file with the Ontario Ministry of Community and Social Services, the Metropolitan Toronto Children's Aid Society, the Metropolitan Toronto Police, and the Day Care Connection (a Serious Occurence Report was legally required to be filed).
5. R.F. Badgley, *Sexual Offences Against Children*, 2 vols., Report of the Committee on Sexual Offences Against Children and Youth (Ottawa: Government Publishing, 1984).
6. Ibid., 548.
7. As this chapter was being prepared, the Toronto *Globe and Mail* for 29 March 1986 reported a couple suing three social workers and the provincial superintendent of family and child services in British Columbia. In the first such case to come to trial in Canada, the parents challenged the right of the province to take their seven children in 1982, even though they were returned five days later. They were claiming damages for "negligence, false imprisonment, distress, and suffering," and for defamation, because their names were placed on a child-abuse registry. The mother testified that her three younger children were taken from her home by social workers while she was supervising the four older children at a swimming pool. When she returned home, social workers threatened her with jail if she did not give up the other four. The four older children were taken despite advice from the RCMP that there was no basis for allegations of abuse.
8. G.M. McCarthy, *Interministry Child Abuse Handbook*, rev. ed. (Victoria: Queen's Printer, 1981).
9. C.H. Kempe, "Sexual Abuse: Another Hidden Pediatric Problem" in *Child Abuse: Commission and Omission*, edited by J.V. Cook and R.T. Bowles (Toronto: Butterworths, 1980).
10. Case Study: Consider how you would handle the following actual (and not

atypical) case: Trudy Sandich is a sixteen-year-old girl who has run away from home repeatedly since she was twelve years old. She lives with her mother, father, and twelve-year-old sister, Samantha. Her eighteen-year-old-brother, Rick, is in training with the Armed Forces. Her father has difficulty making ends meet and is a strict disciplinarian. You notice that Trudy has many deep scratch marks on her arms. She has been crying. After you ask what is wrong, she responds by asking you what you would do if someone is raped. She mentions she is very concerned about her sister. You spend several hours establishing rapport and trust, asking questions, trying to piece the story together.

She has told you that her brother, her sister, and herself had been repeatedly locked in their rooms, sometimes for days. During these times, her father had beaten them repeatedly with a belt on their backs, buttocks, and stomachs, and had also punched them in the stomach. Trudy has mentioned her concern for her sister several times. You realize that she fears that her sister has been sexually abused by her father, as she has been.

After you talk with Trudy and suggest that this is a serious matter that must be reported to the police or welfare officials, she begs you not to tell anyone about it. She says that her father is a large and strong man. He has had special training in the martial arts. The father has threatened them with death if they break up the home. Trudy says that the worst possible thing that could happen would be any official action to investigate, arrest the father, or take the children out of the home. Trudy sincerely believes her father would carry out the threats.

Trudy tells you that if her dad ever found out someone outside the family knew about the beatings, he would kill Trudy's cat and beat Trudy, Samantha, and their mom until they were black and blue all over. He also has let Trudy know that if they ever tell anyone about anything at home, no matter how long it takes, he will find them and get even with them. Although Trudy wants to move out of the home, she fears that Samantha will be raped and beaten.

Trudy tells you she will be going back home tonight and asks you to promise her you will not tell the authorities.

What would you do? Note that, because Trudy is sixteen years old, some child abuse reporting statutes will not cover her situation. Others cover all children until the age of majority.

11. McCarthy, *Interministry Child Abuse Handbook*. rev. ed.
12. Ibid., 78.
13. Ibid., 80.
14. G. Will and B. Swindlehurst, "Role of the School in Child Neglect and Abuse," *The Alberta Counsellor* 8, 1 (1979): 19–23.
15. McCarthy, *Interministry Child Abuse Handbook*.
16. This material is part of the *Child Abuse and Neglect and Personal Safety Program* and consists of pages 31 to 33 of the information package that is distributed to all schools in the Edmonton Public School District. The information was collected from numerous current research articles and edited by Ruth Mickelson, Edmonton Public School social worker, and is reproduced here with her permission.

SUBSTANCE ABUSE: THE ROLE OF THE EDUCATOR

MICHAEL S. GOODSTADT

DRUG USE AMONG CANADIAN YOUTH

There are two reasons for considering young Canadians as a major subpopulation worthy of special attention in the discussion of drug use and abuse. First, many people consider any drug use, including the use of alcohol and tobacco, by young people as being "risky." Secondly, and most practically, we know more about drug use by young people, especially those of school age, than we do about any other subgroup; this is because young people are a readily available population for research, as well as being a major focus for society's socialization concerns.

Surveys have been conducted in many of the provinces, including Ontario in 1985,[1] Prince Edward Island in 1982,[2] Vancouver, British Columbia in 1982,[3] Nova Scotia in 1979,[4] Manitoba in 1978 and 1979,[5] Alberta in 1976,[6] New Brunswick in 1976[7] and Quebec in 1975.[8] There have, in addition, been a series of national surveys conducted for Health and Welfare Canada, the most recent being in 1985, as well as a recently completed national survey of alcohol, tobacco, and cannabis use by Grade 7 and 9 students.[9]

A number of the surveys have been able to examine trends in drug use as shown by comparisons between survey years.[10] We will concentrate on data obtained since 1980, since, without follow-up data, the results of earlier surveys are of questionable relevance to the task of assessing present-day patterns. The following discussion of drug use will, therefore, be based upon the more recent studies.[11]

DRUGS THAT HAVE THE HIGHEST PROBABILITY OF USE AMONG CANADIAN YOUTH

Prevalence of Drug Use

Studies concerning the prevalence of drug use (i.e., the proportion of the population of young people reporting any use of the drug, for example, within the previous twelve months), indicate that alcohol and tobacco are the drugs of choice among young Canadians (as they are in the adult population). Cannabis use is in a distant third place among those under sixteen years of age, and occupies second place after alcohol among the oldest cohort of high-school students (i.e., Grade 13). Of fourteen other drugs, only the non-medical use (i.e., not from a doctor) of stimulants is currently used by more than a small minority of students. Drug use is related to gender, age, and geographic location. The use of all drugs, other than glue, solvents, and inhalants, is less common in the youngest groups (i.e., those in Grade 7 or 9); peak prevalence rates occur in Grade 11 for all other drugs except alcohol and cocaine, which peak in Grade 13. The use of alcohol among young people is more prevalent in the Western provinces, while tobacco use tends to be more prevalent in the Eastern provinces. Particularly large regional differences are found with respect to marijuana use: British Columbia has twice as many users (thirty percent) as Quebec and the Atlantic Provinces.

As significant as the data concerning drug use in any single year are the trends across survey years. Such trends are difficult to measure accurately since they involve complex assumptions regarding comparability between surveys. Considerable fluctuations have occurred between sample years. Examination of the data suggests that a peak occurred (in Ontario) in 1979 with respect to the prevalence of use of many drugs, with subsequent declines in the use of several drugs, including tobacco, alcohol and cannabis. This stabilization in drug use has also been reflected in other surveys, in both Canada[12] and the United States.[13]

Fluctuations do occur in the use of drugs as fads and fashions change. For example, by 1983, non-medical use of stimulants became the fourth most prevalently used substance in Ontario; by 1985, however, it appeared to have dropped to its pre-1981 level. These same trends have been reported in the United States by Johnston et al.[14] Although LSD showed an increase in popularity in 1981, more recent trends have been downwards.

Frequency of Drug Use

With the exception of alcohol, tobacco, and cannabis use, the use of drugs is infrequent, that is, the majority of users use the drugs only once or twice within a twelve month period. There is, however, a group of "high risk" drug users who use alcohol or other drugs on a regular basis (e.g., daily), in quantities that are abusive (e.g., more than one drink per hour, more than five drinks at one sitting), in situations that are dangerous (e.g., in conjunction with the use of automobiles or other machinery), or for inappropriate reasons (e.g., to cope with or to modify their feelings).

Age of First Use of Drugs

Another important aspect of drug use is the age at which a drug is first used. Age of first use varies with the drug. For example, the use of inhalants and solvents is typically tried for the first time by the young, followed by alcohol and tobacco and, later, by the use of cannabis and other illicit drugs (this time sequence does not, however, imply a causal chain in the progression of drug use). Recent evidence suggests that cannabis use first occurs among few of those younger than twelve years of age; the majority of users, however, report having tried the drug by the age of fourteen, although this is one year younger in British Columbia, and one year older in the Atlantic Provinces. There is no evidence that initial drug use has been occurring at an earlier age.

PROBLEMS ASSOCIATED WITH THE USE OF DRUGS BY YOUNG CANADIANS

Problems arising from drug use are of two kinds: the health-related consequences (e.g., morbidity and mortality), and the legal (and related social) consequences of use (e.g., fines, probation, imprisonment, loss of social esteem, loss of voting rights, employment opportunities, etc.). These measures are notoriously unreliable for reasons related to identification/detection and reporting practices. Other untoward consequences of drug use and abuse are even more difficult to document, although experience and current wisdom strongly suggest that drug use plays a significant role in poor performance at school, problems at home, and other symptoms of retarded development and adjustment.

Prevalence of Health Problems Associated with Drug Use

Perhaps the most significant drug-related health concern relates to the prevalence and consequences of drinking and driving among young people. In 1982, in Canada, 106 alcohol-impaired drivers under the age of eighteen were killed in car acidents.[15] In 1984, in Ontario, 1619 such drivers were involved in motor vehicle accidents.[16] Automobile accidents are the largest single cause of death among young people in Canada. Young people are over-represented in alcohol-related traffic accidents due, in part, to the combination of learning to drive and learning to drink.

Evidence concerning the health consequences of drug use among the young also comes from surveys; in this case, however, data are limited to the effects of cannabis use. According to the 1985 Ontario survey, the majority of cannabis users reported that, while using the drug, they had *never* experienced any of a large number of possible emotional and physical consequences; there was, nevertheless, a sizeable minority (twenty-five to fifty percent) who had experienced mild anxiety, feeling "in another world," confusion, extreme anxiety, suspicion towards others, poor health, and nausea. After-effects of using cannabis included changes in mood, feeling anxious and emotional, tingling fingers, trouble with vision, and seeing things that did not exist. Less than one percent of cannabis users, however, reported having sought medical help. As would be expected, such consequences are more common among frequent cannabis users. The national

Gallup survey found that thirteen percent of the users' sub-sample reported having experienced problems connected with its use, mainly in the form of changes in mood or social problems.

There are relatively few hospitalizations of young people (0–19 years) in Canada due to drug (other than alcohol) complications (671 in 1980–81, the last years for which data are available). The overwhelming majority of these cases are non-fatal consequences of ingesting analgesics, antipyretics and antirheumatics, and psychotropic agents such as tranquillizers. The risks associated with poisonings are related to the drug in question, the user's sex, and the user's age. There is a much larger number of young people who receive treatment for alcohol problems. In Ontario in 1983, for example, 3533 persons under the age of nineteen received hospital or community treatment for alcohol-related problems.

Prevalence of Legal Consequences Associated with Drug Use

One of the most serious inadequacies in crime-related statistics arises from the practice of reporting statistics only with respect to the most serious criminal charge. Many drug offences are, therefore, not identified as such in official statistics, masking the involvement of drugs in crime, or drug use as a crime in its own right. In 1984, 2344 Canadian juveniles (i.e., 12–18 years) were charged under the Narcotic Control Act, principally (i.e., 94 percent) for cannabis offences; a further 91 were charged under the Food and Drug Act for other drug offences. Approximately three-quarters of those charged were found guilty. The disposition of these cases appears to be evenly divided (at least in Ontario) between probation and a fine, reprimand, and suspended sentence. The recent change from the Juvenile Delinquents Act to the Young Offenders Act makes it difficult to predict future enforcement and legal patterns.

Most significant with respect to the legal consequences of drug use are the social and practical implications of a finding of guilt; this always involves the acquisition of a criminal record (even in the case of a conditional discharge), and carries with it both social stigma and practical limitations on future employment, travel, and civil liberties (e.g., running for elections).

DRUG EDUCATION IN CANADIAN SCHOOLS

NATURE AND EXTENT OF DRUG EDUCATION

The data do not exist that would allow us to make general statements about the extent and the nature of drug education in schools across Canada. There is evidence, however, from two provinces (Ontario and British Columbia) that most students recall having received *no* drug (including alcohol) education in the previous school year.[17] Furthermore, the majority of those who report having had some drug education, also report that it consisted of only one or two classes involving teacher-led lectures, films, or discussions, and dealing with the harmful effects of drug use.[18] A 1981 survey found, in addition, that more than half of Ontario school boards did not deal with drugs in any curriculum domain; under these circumstances, it is not surprising to find that the majority of students report receiving no drug education.

IMPACT OF DRUG EDUCATION

No comprehensive evaluation has been undertaken of the effectiveness of drug education in Canadian schools. Very little drug education research has been undertaken in Canada, with the possible exception of smoking education. Relatively small, highly focussed, experimental studies of alcohol and cannabis education have been reported by Schlegel and his co-workers,[19] by Goodstadt and his co-workers,[20] and by Smythe.[21] These experimental studies, as well as those based upon school surveys,[22] indicate that drug education programs do not have uniformly positive effects. This evidence is supported by the more extensive literature available from the United States.[21]

From this collective experience we can draw several conclusions. Little evidence exists regarding the effectiveness of drug education—"little" relative to the thousands of programs that have been developed in North America. Most drug education evaluations have been methodologically inadequate. Research findings have been too inconsistent and/or negative to be directly helpful in the development of further programming. It has also been found that programs sometimes produce "undesirable" effects, such as greater reported drug use or more pro-drug attitudes after the program.

THE CHALLENGE TO CANADIAN DRUG EDUCATORS

Canadian school administrators and teachers currently face a significant challenge, namely, to promote drug education programs, and supportive materials that have been demonstrated to be efficacious, are implemented widely in the most effective manner possible, and have demonstrated effectiveness in producing the expected impact when implemented in the classrooms of the nation. The failure of previous Canadian drug education to address this challenge has been due to combined weaknesses in program development, program implementation, professional training of teachers and administrators, and accountability for both teachers' and students' performance in the field of drug education (and health education in general).

THE POTENTIAL FOR EFFECTIVE DRUG EDUCATION: PROGRAMME PLANNING AND DEVELOPMENT

OBJECTIVES

Drug education has different meanings for different people. For some, it means preventing drug use, for others it means reducing drug use, while for others it means educating the public (or subgroups, such as adolescents) about the hazards of drug use in order to reduce the personal, social, and economic costs of drug abuse. Although the ultimate goal may be the reduction or elimination of problems, most educational efforts are directed at more immediate outcomes. These short-range objectives are usually neither well specified nor well conceptualized. They also comprise a mixture of behavioural, affective, and informational objectives, depending on one's understanding of the origins and nature of the drug-related concerns/problems, and the theoretical model underlying the proposed intervention.[24] These broad categories of variables can themselves include a host of widely divergent aims.

Behavioural Objectives

These may include total abstinence, retarding the onset of drug use, reducing levels of drug use (frequency and/or quantity), retarding the rate of increase in drug use, modification of situations in which alcohol is used (e.g., separating drug use from the use of machinery), changing the drug being consumed (e.g., to "low-alcohol" beer), modification of the manner in which drugs are consumed (e.g., spacing of drinks), or early identification of problem drug use. Some behavioural objectives may not be exclusively related to drug use, for example: improving decision-making skills, modifying "lifestyles," or promoting "alternatives" to the use/abuse of drugs.

Affective Objectives

These may be equally varied, focussing on drugs, drug use, drug abuse, or drug users. More specifically, objectives may include increasing or decreasing positive/negative feelings towards any of these targets, modifying values related to drug use (e.g., regarding health, personal responsibility), making explicit the dissonance between values and drug use, or modifying individual characteristics such as self-esteem.

Cognitive Objectives

These may include raising levels of awareness and understanding of the nature and effects of drug use, the role of drugs in our society, appropriate ways of using drugs, alternatives to drug use/abuse, and sources of help for drug-related problems.

Many drug educators have failed to take adequate account of the research evidence concerning the building blocks of all programs, namely changes in knowledge, attitudes, and behaviours. Research indicates that "knowledge about..." can be easily influenced by a variety of programmatic approaches, not all of which, however, are equally effective. Programs that are exclusively informational have the greatest impact in raising knowledge levels.[25]

Improvement in knowledge, however, is a *necessary* but *not sufficient* condition for behaviour change.[26] There is voluminous evidence that attitudes are difficult to influence in a predictable fashion and that attitude-change does not lead, automatically, to a corresponding change in behaviour.[27] Behaviours are notoriously difficult to change and are associated with the most problematic outcomes for drug educators. For a variety of reasons, some methodological and some programmatic, several studies have demonstrated that drug education may lead to effects opposite to those intended by the educator.[28] It is not yet possible to specify the conditions under which these "negative" effects are likely to occur. The effect may be due to students feeling more at ease about "owning up" to drug use after participating in non-judgmental programs; they might, on the other hand have "unlearned" prior misconceptions about the hazards of drug use and, consequently, experimented with drugs; or, educational programs may produce polarization of attitudes, as documented in other settings. It might be expected that the recent, more psychologically sophisticated and intensive programs would produce more impact than earlier generations of programs.[29] "Undesirable" findings, however, warn against over-optimism in this regard.[30]

Objectives may differ in their time-frames for achievement: long-range, mid-range, or short-range. Most programs emphasize, by implication, the more immediately attainable objectives, which are, at best, instrumental in achieving long-range goals (e.g., raising self-esteem, improving decision-making). The instrumentality of these objectives is often not made explicit and only rarely evaluated. This link between changes in these variables and the achievement of ultimate goals is not examined. Furthermore, since significant ultimate goals are frequently projected into the long-range future, program implementation and evaluation rarely survive long enough to permit adequate assessment of long-range attainment.

TARGET GROUPS

One of the weaknesses of drug education is its apparent inability to recognize the existence of a variety of target subgroups, representing a range of motivations and experiences with respect to drug use. Groups include: the committed non-user for whom the objective may be to reinforce the decision not to use drugs; the potential drug user, for whom it is appropriate to delay onset of drug use; the former drug user, whose decision not to use drugs can be reinforced; the "non-problem" drug user, whom we might encourage to re-examine drug use and, at least, not let the use increase; and the "problem" drug user, whose pattern of drug use we might attempt to alter. Drug educators and programs tend to operate as if there exists only a homogeneous group of students (i.e., non-users) and only one possible objective (i.e., non-use). If we fail to specify target groups and objectives, we will, at best, only have *some* impact on *some* of our students.

PROGRAM FORMAT AND CONTENT

Program content and format can vary in a multiplicity of ways, but they are inextricably related to each other and to program objectives. There is no single entity constituting drug education. The way in which material is developed and presented, or the way in which influence is exercised, depends upon the target audience, the desired outcomes, the available media and resources, and the selected mechanisms of influence.

Recent developments have attempted to influence drug use through factors operating at two levels, namely, personal competence and social competence. Personal competence variables and processes have included: information regarding drugs (all programs do this, to some extent); decision-making/problem-solving;[31] cognitive-coping;[32] coping with anxiety/stress;[33] and values clarification.[34]

Social competence has focussed especially on social assertiveness. This latter, in turn, has been addressed at both the general behavioural level,[35] as well as at the specific level of drug use, emphasizing the enhancement of what have become known as "refusal skills."[36]

COMPETING FORCES

Drug education programs have, typically, failed to take account of the history, diversity, and strength of the rewards and reinforcements competing for influence over students' behaviours. The *incentives* for *not using* drugs compete with the incentives for *using* drugs and, similarly, the *disincentives* for *not using* drugs compete with the disincentives for *using* drugs. Too often, programs have operated as though drug use is associated only with "costs," while the non-use of drugs is associated exclusively with "benefits." This perspective flies in the face of both logic and students' own experiences: they know that alcohol can be a social facilitator, cannabis can produce a pleasant state of euphoria, and giving up smoking can incur a loss of social support and esteem.

Drug educators frequently operate as though they are presented with a *tabula rasa* upon which they can inscribe their own message. The reality, however, is that even the youngest students come to school with a long history of intensive exposure to drug use, through parental and sibling example, advertising, and the portrayal of drug use in mass media programming.[37] As important as taking account of past reinforcement is the need to be aware of the pervasiveness and strength of present and future non-program influences—that is, the reality that begins at the classroom door. Recent programs, as indicated earlier, have begun to give more emphasis to teaching and reinforcing the personal and social skills necessary for students to cope with these forces in a satisfactory manner. In this framework, students are not viewed as passive victims of peer and other influences but, rather, as active players in the process of living their own lives.

PROGRAM INTEGRATION

Although no systematic data have been gathered on the subject, informal evidence indicates that the majority of programs are either stand-alone curricula or form an independent unit of a larger health curriculum. Dealing with drugs in an integrated curriculum would allow for the reinforcement of concepts and principles (e.g., decision-making) common to several areas of health. Even less common is the integration of drug education within the broader (nondrug) curriculum. Recognition is, however, frequently given to the potential value of such integrations: an "umbrella" approach to health education would permit the more efficient use of time, since general principles would need to be introduced only once; these principles could then be reinforced in dealing with discrete areas of health; drug use would be less likely to be seen as an isolated behaviour, or as an isolated target of adult control; and the broader relevance of drug use could be conveyed through its integration into curriculum areas such as history, geography, chemistry, and English literature.

In spite of the arguments in favour of the integration of drug education into the larger curriculum, the cognitive development of most students and the generally unintegrated nature of school curricula limit students' ability to appreciate the relevance of the content on drugs unless it is made explicit. Furthermore, some drug-related content (for example, the pharmacology of alcohol use, and the effects of drug abuse on the family) requires more detailed and focussed discussion. In sum, while there is value in integrating drug education into other curriculum areas (including health), there are also potential weaknesses in such an approach. The solution is the judicious use of both integrated and stand-alone elements.

PROGRAM IMPLEMENTATION

Implementation of programs is probably the weakest link in the educational chain for all curricular domains. The potentially most efficacious program will be ineffective if it is not disseminated to and utilized by teachers. In spite of the extensive resources invested in developing drug education programs, we have not invested sufficient resources in ensuring that these programs are used. There is little empirical evidence concerning the implementation of drug education programs.[38] There is, however, an extensive body of literature concerned with the diffusion of innovations, including educational innovations.[39]

Although there are differences in focus and perspective, there is agreement that implementation involves a sequence of stages.[40] Kolbe and Iverson[41] have provided a synthesis of alternative frameworks involving five generic stages: mobilization of the perceived need for program improvement and the ways in which improvements might be achieved; adoption, or the commitment to the change or improvement; implementation, by which the course of action is put into practice; maintenance of the changes; and further evolution of the changes. Little effort is usually invested in ensuring progression beyond the adoption phase; awareness of the importance of the later phases would render most programs significantly more effective.

RECOMMENDATIONS FOR THE EDUCATOR

The educator has many roles to play in developing, disseminating, and utilizing drug education programs. These roles parallel the positions occupied by those involved in the educational process. In the front line are the teachers and principals, backed up by resource (materials) support staff and consultants specializing in drug education, health education, curriculum development, psychological services, research and evaluation, and community development. There is, in addition, the contribution made to education by elected officials in the form of school-board trustees. What recommendations can be made for this diversity of "players"?

TEACHERS

Teachers are involved in drug education in a variety of ways: as identifiers of the need for change or improvement, as participants in the development of curricula and lesson-plans, as implementers of new curricula, as disseminators of new materials and ideas. Teachers' major role and strength is as classroom teachers; it is this primary function that should be stressed, by encouraging them to do what they are trained to do and what they do best, namely, teaching. We have seen that education about drugs presents many challenges and many opportunities. It involves more than mere teaching *about* drugs; it is concerned with the three classical domains of education—cognition, affect, and behaviour. As we have suggested, this calls for special appreciation of the interrelated functions of these elements, as well as special skill in handling the content and processes needed for the sensitive promotion of cognitive, affective, and behavioural change. It has also been pointed out that it is necessary for teachers to be aware of the limited power of in-classroom reinforcers, in comparison to the world outside. In this regard, teachers are, however, in a position to lay the groundwork for identifying and reinforcing the non-drug-using norms that research has identified as characteristic of the majority of youth. Teachers are also able to introduce and reinforce the social and personal skills required for coping with the influences that students will encounter outside the classroom. Finally, teachers are in the best position to find opportunities within the various curriculum domains through which they can interject elements of drug education content and process, thereby overcoming some of the limitations of time and context imposed by the crowded health curriculum.

PROGRAM PLANNERS AND DEVELOPERS.

Teachers can fulfil additional functions related to drug education. As suggested above, they are originators of change, identifying the need for, and nature of, improvements in drug education curricula. At some point, teachers may collaborate with other educational specialists in developing or revising drug education curricula and materials. In collaboration with the specialists in health, drugs, and curriculum development, teachers are faced with the challenge of developing curriculum content and strategies that are likely to be pedagogically effective, both within the classroom and in the "real world" outside the school. We have suggested some of the elements of planning necessary for this task, including the clear and adequate identification of target groups and objectives. Failure in either respect will doom any program to less than optimal effectiveness. We have also seen that an appreciation for the relevant psychological and social factors suggests that a rich array of educational procedures be incorporated into any program, including strategies that enhance students' personal and social competence. One of the greatest challenges that we have identified concerns the influence of forces that compete with the efforts of the educator; an especially effective educational ingredient, in this regard, is the support derived from involvement by parents and the wider community. Lip-service is often paid to the significance of programs that extend beyond the four walls of the classroom, but little concerted effort is usually made in realizing this objective. Similarly, integration of curriculum content domains is more often spoken about than acted upon.

ELECTED OFFICIALS

The impetus for or against drug education frequently originates from political and community pressure channelled through elected school-board officials. This influence can be positive or negative, depending on the degree to which it is focussed on a genuine and well-defined need in contrast to political self-interest. In the latter case, the resulting drug education program is more likely to be educationally unsound, unaccepted by those responsible for program implementation, short-lived, and, therefore, ineffective. On the other hand, to the extent that politicians respond sensitively to carefully identified local needs, resist hysteria, and support a professional educational response, significant advances are likely to be made in the development and implementation of drug education. Two current weaknesses that elected officials are in the best position to address are support for the non-threatening identification of community drug issues (which school and board staff are frequently reluctant to admit), and support for the allocation of resources needed for adequate professional development and program evaluation. Without these, program development efforts, and the resources spent on them, are merely expressions of hope rather than activities of known effectiveness.

NOTES

1. R.G. Smart, E.M. Adlaf, and M.S. Goodstadt, "Alcohol and Other Drug Use Among Ontario Students: An Update," *Canadian Journal of Public Health* 7 (1986): 57–58.
2. J. Killorn, *Chemical Use Among P.E.I. Students* (Charlottetown: Alcohol and Drug Problems Institute, 1982).
3. M.J. Hollander and B.L. Davis, *Trends in Adolescent Alcohol and Drug Use in Vancouver* (Vancouver: Province of British Columbia Ministry of Health, Alcohol and Drug Programs, 1983).
4. B. Neumann and W.J. Shannon, *Drug Use Among Halifax Adolescents 1976–1979*, Bulletin 80031 (Halifax: Nova Scotia Commission on Drug Dependency, 1980).
5. Alcoholism Foundation of Manitoba, *Beauséjour School Survey, Brandon School Survey, Dauphin School Survey, Portage La Prairie School Survey, Ste. Anne School Survey and Thompson School Survey* (Winnipeg: Directorate of Evaluation and Research Co-ordination, 1970, 1979).
6. W.D. Ratcliffe and D.S. Hewitt, *Alcohol Consumption Patterns Among Alberta Adolescents* (Edmonton: Alberta Alcoholism and Drug Abuse Commission, 1978).
7. L. Stevens, M. Richardson, S. Linton, and W.J. Shannon, "A Survey of the Non-Medical Use of Drugs in Saint John, New Brunswick, 1976," cited by Health and Welfare Canada, *Canadian Drug Indicators: A Compilation of Current Statistics on Alcohol, Tobacco and Other Drugs* (Ottawa: Health and Welfare Canada, 1978).
8. I. Poissant and M. Crespo, *La consommation des drogues chez les jeunes du secondaire* (Montreal: La Commission des Écoles Catholiques de Montréal, 1976).
9. A.J.C. King, A. Robertson, and W.K. Warren, *Summary Report: Canada Health Attitudes and Behaviours Survey* (Kingston, Ont.: Queen's University, Social Program Evaluation Group, 1985).
10. I.e., Ontario, Nova Scotia, Vancouver, and the national surveys.
11. Smart et al., "Alcohol and Other Drug Use Among Ontario Students," covering the years 1977 to 1985; Hollander and Davis, *Trends in Adolescent Alcohol and Drug Use in Vancouver* for the years 1970 to 1982; Health and Welfare Canada, *A Summary Report on Tobacco, Alcohol and Marijuana Use and Norms Among Young People in Canada: Year 3*, Gallop Poll (Ottawa: Health and Welfare Canada, Health Promotion Directorate, 1985), for the years 1980 to 1985; and King et al., *Canada Health Attitudes and Behaviours Survey.*
12. Hollander and Davis, *Trends in Adolescent Alcohol and Drug Use in Vancouver*; I. Rootman and D. Dakers, "Trends in Self-Reported Marijuana Use Among Canadian Teenagers: An Update to 1985," *Chronic Diseases in Canada* 6 (1985): 63–64; N.E. Collishaw, "Percentage of Young Canadians Who Smoke Daily," *Chronic Diseases in Canada* 6 (1985): 61.
13. L.D. Johnston, J.G. Bachman, and P.M. O'Malley, "Press Release" (Ann Arbor, Mich.: University of Michigan, 1985).
14. Ibid.

15. D.J. Beirness, G.C. Haas, P.J. Walsh, and A.C. Donelson, *Alcohol and Fatal Road Accidents in Canada: A Statistical Look at its Magnitude and Persistence*, Impaired Driving, Report No. 3 (Ottawa: Traffic Injury Research Foundation of Canada, 1985).

16. Ontario, Ministry of Transportation and Communication, *Motor Vehicle Accident Facts–1984* (Toronto: Ministry of Transportation and Communications, 1985).

17. M.A. Sheppard, M.S. Goodstadt, and B. Williamson, "Drug Education: Why We Have So Little Impact," *Journal of Drug Education* 15 (1985): 1–6; Hollander and Davis, *Trends in Adolescent Alcohol and Drug Use in Vancouver.*

18. M.A. Sheppard, M.S. Goodstadt, and G.C. Chan, "Drug Education in Ontario Schools: Content and Processes," *Journal of Drug Education* 11 (1981): 317–26.

19. R.P. Schlegel and J.E. Norris, "Effects of Attitude Change on Behavior for Highly Involving Issues: The Case of Marijuana Smoking," *Addictive Behaviors* 5 (1980): 113–24; R.P. Schlegel, S.R. Manske, and A. Page, "A Guided Decision-Making Program for Elementary School Students: A Field Experiment in Alcohol Education" in *Prevention of Alcohol Abuse*, edited by P.M. Miller and T.D. Nirenberg (New York: Plenum, 1984).

20. M.S. Goodstadt, M.A. Sheppard, and G.C. Chan, "An Evaluation of Two School-Based Alcohol Education Programs," *Journal of Studies on Alcohol* 43 (1982): 362–80; M.S. Goodstadt and M.A. Sheppard, "Three Approaches to Alcohol Education," *Journal of Studies on Alcohol* 44 (1983): 362–80.

21. L. Gliksman, R.R. Douglas, and C. Smythe, "The Impact of a High School Alcohol Education Program Utilizing a Live Theatrical Performance: A Comparative Study," *Journal of Drug Education* 13 (1983): 229–48.

22. Goodstadt et al., "An Evaluation of Two School-Based Alcohol Education Programs."

23. See, for example, E. Schaps, R. DiBartolo, J. Moskowitz, C.S. Palley, and S. Churgin, "A Review of 127 Drug Abuse Prevention Program Evaluations," *Journal of Drug Issues* 11 (1981): 17–43, for a review of the general drug education literature; G.N. Braucht and B. Braucht, "Prevention of Problems Among Youth: Evaluation of Educational Strategies" in *Prevention of Alcohol Abuse*, for a review of the alcohol education literature; and B.R. Flay, "What Do We Know About the Social Influence Approach to Smoking Prevention: Review and Recommendations" in *Prevention Research: Deterring Drug Abuse Among Children and Adolescents*, edited by C.S. Bell and R. Battjes, Research Monograph No. 63, DHHS Publication No. ADM 85-1334 (Rockville, Md: National Institute on Drug Abuse, 1985), for a review of the smoking literature.

24. M.R. Wong, "Different Strokes: Models of Drug Abuse Prevention Education," *Contemporary Educational Psychology* 1 (1976): 285–303.

25. Goodstadt and Sheppard, "Three Approaches to Alcohol Education"; Schlegel et al., "A Guided Decision-Making Program for Elementary School Students."

26. M.S. Goodstadt, "Alcohol and Drug Education: Models and Outcomes," *Health Education Monographs* 6 (1978): 263–79.

27. I. Ajzen and M. Fishbein, *Understanding Attitudes and Predicting Social Behavior* (Englewood Cliffs, N.J.: Prentice-Hall, 1980); Gliksman et al., "The Impact

of a High School Alcohol Education Program Utilizing a Live Theatrical Performance"; Goodstadt, "Alcohol and Drug Education: Models and Outcomes"; Goodstadt et al., "An Evaluation of Two School-Based Alcohol Education Programs"; Goodstadt and Sheppard, "Three Approaches to Alcohol Education"; R.T. LaPiere, "Attitudes versus Actions," *Social Forces* 13 (1934): 230–37.

28. M.S. Goodstadt, "Drug Education—A Turn On or a Turn Off?" *Journal of Drug Education* 10 (1980): 89–98; Goodstadt and Sheppard, "Three Approaches to Alcohol Education"; Schlegel et al., "A Guided Decision-Making Program for Elementary School Students"; Gliksman et al., "The Impact of a High School Alcohol Education Program Utilizing a Live Theatrical Performance"; L. DiCicco, R. Biron, J. Carifo, C. Deutsch, D.J. Mills, A. Orenstein, A. Re., H. Unterberger, and R.E. White, "Evaluation of the CASPAR Alcohol Education Curriculum," *Journal of Studies on Alcohol* 45 (1984): 160–69; J.A. Stein, J.D. Swisher, T-W. Hu, and N. McDonnell, "Cost-Effectiveness Evaluation of a Channel One Program," *Journal of Drug Education* 14 (1984): 251–70; A.F. Williams, L.M. DiCicco, and H. Unterberger, "Philosophy and Evaluation of an Alcohol Education Program," *Quarterly Journal of Studies on Alcohol* 29 (1968): 685–702; T.A. Wills, "Stress, Coping, and Tobacco and Alcohol Use in Early Adolescence" in *Coping and Substance Abuse*, edited by S. Shiffman and T.A. Wills (New York: Academic Press, 1985).

29. G.J. Botvin, E. Baker, N.L. Renick, A.D. Filazzola, and E.M. Botvin, "A Cognitive-Behavioral Approach to Substance Abuse Prevention," *Addictive Behaviors* 9 (1984): 137–47; A. McAlister, C. Perry, J. Killen, L.A. Slinkard, and N. Maccoby, "Pilot Study of Smoking, Alcohol and Drug Abuse Prevention," *American Journal of Public Health* 70 (1980): 719–21; M.A. Pentz, "Social Competence Skills and Self-Efficacy as Determinants of Substance Abuse in Adolescence" in *Coping and Substance Use*.

30. Wills, "Stress, Coping, and Tobacco and Alcohol Use in Early Adolescence."

31. Botvin et al., "A Cognitive-Behavioral Approach to Substance Abuse Prevention"; DiCicco et al., "Evaluation of the CASPAR Alcohol Education Curriculum"; Goodstadt and Sheppard, "Three Approaches to Alcohol Education"; J. Moskowitz, E. Schaps, J.H. Malvin, and G. Schaeffer, "The Effects of Drug Education at Follow-up," *Journal of Alcohol and Drug Education* 30 (1984): 45–49; Schlegel et al., "A Guided Decision-Making Program for Elementary School Students"; Wills, "Stress, Coping, and Tobacco and Alcohol Use in Early Adolescence."

32. Wills, ibid.

33. Botvin et al., "A Cognitive-Behavioral Approach to Substance Abuse Prevention"; Wills, ibid.

34. Goodstadt and Sheppard, "Three Approaches to Alcohol Education"; Schlegel et al., "A Guided Decision-Making Program for Elementary School Students"; Wills, ibid.

35. Botvin et al., "A Cognitive-Behavioral Approach to Substance Abuse Prevention"; J.J. Horan and J.M. Williams, "Longitudinal Study of Assertion Training as a Drug Abuse Prevention Strategy," *American Education Research Journal* 19 (1982): 341–51; Pentz, "Social Competence Skills and Self-Efficacy as Determinants of Substance Abuse in Adolescence"; Wills, ibid.

36. Botvin et al., ibid.; E. Duryea, P. Mohr, I.M. Newman, G.L. Martin, and E. Egwaoje, "Six-Month Follow-up Results of a Preventive Alcohol Education Intervention," *Journal of Drug Education* 14 (1984): 97–104; Flay, "What Do We Know About the Social Influence Approach to Smoking Prevention"; Horan and Williams, ibid.; Pentz, ibid.; Wills, ibid.

37. W. Breed, J. De Foe, and L. Wallack, "Drinking in the Mass Media: A Nine-Year Project," *Journal of Drug Issues* 14 (1984): 655–64.

38. I.M. Newman, ed., *Dissemination and Utilization of Alcohol Information* (Lincoln, Neb.: Nebraska Alcohol Information Clearinghouse, 1979); M.A. Sheppard, "Barriers to the Implementation of a New School-Based Alcohol Education Program," *Journal of Alcohol and Drug Education* 27 (1982): 14–17.

39. M. Fullan and A. Promfret, "Research on Curriculum and Instruction Implementation," *Review of Educational Research* 47 (1977): 335–97; M. Fullan and P. Park, *Curriculum Implementation: A Resource Booklet* (Toronto: Ontario Institute for Studies in Education, 1981); R.G. Havelock, *The Change Agent's Guide to Innovation in Education* (Englewood Cliffs, N.J.: John Wiley, 1973); G.E. Hall and S.F. Loucks, "A Developmental Model for Determining Whether the Treatment is Actually Implemented," *American Education Research Journal* 14 (1977): 263–76; C.J. Marsh, "Implementation of a Curriculum Innovation in Australian Schools," *Knowledge: Creation, Diffusion, Utilization* 6 (1984): 37–58; C.J. Marsh and M. Huberman, "Disseminating Curricula: A Look from the Top Down," *Journal of Curriculum Studies* 16 (1984): 53–66; S.J. Virgilio and I.R. Virgilio, "The Role of the Principal in Curriculum Implementation," *Education* 104 (1984): 346–50; M.C. Wang, N. Mehran, C.D. Strom, and H.J. Walberg, "The Utility of Degree of Implementation Measures in Program Implementation and Evaluation Research," *Curriculum Inquiry* 14 (1984): 249–86.

40. M.A. Pentz, "Social Competence Skills and Self-Efficacy as Determinants of Substance Abuse in Adolescence" in *Coping and Substance Abuse*, edited by S. Shiffman and T.A. Wills (New York: Academic Press, 1985).

41. L.J. Kolbe and D.C. Iverson, "Implementing Comprehensive Health Education: Educational Innovations and Social Change," *Health Education Quarterly* 8 (1981): 57–80.

PREJUDICE AND DISCRIMINATION: CAN SCHOOLS MAKE A DIFFERENCE?

JOHN ROWLAND YOUNG

That Canada is a multicultural society is as banal as it is true. Although it was not until 1971 that the federal government announced a policy of "multiculturalism within a bilingual framework," we have been culturally heterogeneous for centuries. According to Burnet, "Even before contacts with Europeans the 250,000 to 300,000 inhabitants of what is now Canada constituted about 50 societies, belonging to a dozen linguistic groups. Some of the societies were nomadic bands of hunters and gatherers; others were highly structured chiefdoms of fishers and cultivators of the soil."[1]

Whether multiculturalism is possible is dependent upon at least two major factors: the desire of minority ethnic groups to retain their linguistic and cultural identities, and the commitment of the majority groups to provide cultural and structural support in all its forms for this retention of diversity. Although the federal government, in its desire to implement the policy of multiculturalism, instituted six programs designed to promote the language and cultural development of "the other ethnic groups," the policy's actual realization is in the hands of average Canadians. Canadians, individually and collectively, must be committed to multiculturalism as a goal and be aware of what is required to encourage it.

In the light of recent developments in Canada, such as the Keegstra affair, one has to ask how successful we have been in breaking down discriminatory attitudes and behaviours and in providing structural support for all ethnic groups in our society. Seldom a week goes by that we are not exposed by the media to examples of violence against some member of a visible ethnic group. Before the goals of multiculturalism—tolerance of all ethnic groups and the full participation of all groups in society—can be achieved, changes must occur not just in people's attitudes towards themselves and others, but also in the reward structure so that all individuals and groups can expect to participate in society and be rewarded accordingly. This paper will not focus on institutions generally, but will deal with the role of schools in attitude development and change and as structural and cultural reproducers. Let us look first at the role of schools in attitude development and change.

For our purposes, we will define attitude, as does Berry, to include "the affective, cognitive, and behavioural characteristics of individuals."[2] We can further assume that attitudes are learned and, consequently, have the possibility of being changed. The specific attitude with which we are concerned is prejudice: a negative and inflexible attitude based in part on incomplete or inaccurate information. Translated into behaviour, this prejudicial attitude is manifested as discrimination, which can be sexist and ageist as well as racist.

Does racial prejudice exist in Canada? In order to answer such a question, it is important to determine what one can use as a reliable measure of prejudice. If one uses media headlines, one could reach the conclusion that there is extensive prejudice and discrimination: "Study shows racism growing in Calgary"; "Racism in article denied"; "Admitting racism first step in cure"; "Keegstras everywhere says race council brief." Do we reach the conclusion that deep-rooted prejudicial attitudes are rampant in society? Or is this simply the media's way of attracting reader attention?

A danger confronting sociologists is to assume that prejudice varies in magnitude directly to the number of reported acts of violent racist attacks. There may be no relationship between the cases reported and those actually committed. An approach more favoured by sociologists is the sampling of a population for attitudes of prejudice. Using this procedure, we find the various conclusions somewhat confusing. So much depends on how prejudice is defined and from what part of Canada the sample is drawn. A generally accepted conclusion comes from Berry, Kalin, and Taylor's classic study of multiculturalism, which argued that, although there is not a great deal of explicit racism or overt bigotry, "there is some evidence that race is an issue and is being employed by Canadians in their acceptance or rejection of groups of people."[3]

From the various approaches discussed, it seems obvious that a degree of prejudice does exist in Canada and that its actual measurement is not that important if it is sufficient to influence behaviour to the extent that the goals of a multicultural society are adversely affected. Also, if teachers are going to do anything about prejudice and discrimination within schools, they are going to have to step back from the frenzy of headlines and look for solutions in rational solitude. Solutions will not come from hysteria or self-condemnation by the majority group. Prejudicial attitudes and discrimination are not the sole prerogative of the majority group. As Jean Burnet says, "if we are to understand one another, we must forego the pleasure of regarding some ethnic groups as more virtuous than others and look instead in a detached way at the kinds of things people—all people—do in various situations—nothing is so devastatingly egalitarian as detachment."[4]

When looking at the nature of prejudice and discrimination from an educational perspective, one must examine not only attitudes at the individual level, but also the role the educational system plays in fostering and perpetuating inequality in its very rewards structure. According to Patel, prejudice and discrimination must be seen "as a form of stratification built into the structure of society; the roots of this division are located in the structure of the division of labour and in the organization of political power."[5] Specifically, prejudice and discrimination are not understood simply as the ideas that one group has about others, but are also the outcome of inequalities within institutions, like schools.

If the school can both harbour and perpetuate prejudice and discrimination, how can a teacher work most effectively towards the goals of multiculturalism? First, we can not assume that teachers should accept full responsibility for changing societal values about multiculturalism and eradicating prejudice and discrimination. Attitudes are the outcome of the influences of all social institutions, including school, family, mass media, government and, increasingly important, the peer group. Secondly, teachers and schools cannot accept total responsibility for the lack of mobility of some students into certain areas of the economy. Inequality of educational opportunity is the outcome of many processes at work in society. However, teachers do have a responsibility to see that all students are rewarded for their talent and motivation regardless of social factors such as class, race, and ethnicity.

What is it, then, that teachers can reasonably be expected to do about prejudice and discrimination? The findings of sociopsychological research indicate that no single practice in education will be sufficient to combat prejudice because of the multidimensional nature of attitude change. According to Ijaz,

> Cognitive and perceptual principles of categorisation may combine with effects of socialisation, personality variables, and emotional and affective factors to produce prejudicial ethnic attitudes.... A truly successful educational program for attitudinal change in youngsters has to combine a variety of approaches, intellectual and factual, emotional and affective.[6]

What will such a multifaceted approach look like? If teachers are committed to developing the attitudes and behaviours necessary for functional multiculturalism, they must be concerned with five specific areas: the knowledge base of the curriculum; positive experiences of ethnicity; cognitive and moral development; purging the language of prejudice; and modifying the pedagogy of instruction.

KNOWLEDGE BASE OF THE CURRICULUM

There has been an increasing trend in the provinces to establish a curriculum reflecting an appreciation and an understanding of all ethnic groups, not just the two so-called founding nations. All attempts have not been successful. Werner and associates[7] analysed various ways in which ethnic groups have been treated within different curricula during the 1970s and have identified six approaches, none of which seems desirable. The study maintains that minority ethnic groups are frequently treated as marginal Canadians, as contributors to the dominant society, as beneficiaries of the dominant society, as minority groups seen as problems, as ethnic groups seen within a hierarchy of cultures, and, finally, as a "museum" of minorities' differences. These approaches are problematic in that they do not promote the goal of multicultural education, that being tolerance and understanding where all groups are seen as beneficiaries of and contributors to all societal outcomes. These approaches do not show the minority groups as active participants in the life of the country. The knowledge base is often not factually accurate, and ethnic groups are often singled out by focussing on their uniqueness as opposed to the many similarities between all ethnic groups.

What would be the basis of a suitable knowledge base for a multicultural curriculum? The information presented must be balanced and factual. Stereotyping must be avoided. It is important that a factual information base be not just accurate in terms of what is presented but that it include a balanced presentation, without the exclusion of cases that might be embarrassing (such as the treatment of Japanese-Canadians during World War II or the wholesale slaughter of the Boethuk Indians in Newfoundland).

Two other factors must be considered in a multicultural curriculum. When cultural diversity is discussed, it can be interpreted by students as simple quaintness if its sources are not discussed and understood. Perhaps most importantly, information must be presented on the commonality of the human situation or the similarities of basic human values. At the level of basic needs and values, Canadians, regardless of their ethnic background, have more in common than is often presented in multicultural curricula.

These curriculum requirements appear to be minimal but necessary for developing the attitudes and values associated with multicultural outcomes.

POSITIVE EXPERIENCES WITH ETHNIC DIVERSITY

Prejudice is not modified by the presentation of information alone, however accurate it may be. Students must have positive experiences with ethnic diversity. Students must be given opportunities for personal association or vicarious identification with members of other ethnic groups. Numerous Canadian studies have confirmed the importance of affective relations with members of other ethnic groups in changing attitudes towards these groups. Kalin concludes that:

> Experience with ethnic diversity is likely to reduce the excesses of bigotry (emotional intensity and inflexibility) and instead promote tolerance (respect, acceptance, and fair treatment of others) and flexibility (ability to suspend stereotypes and ethnic preferences) when dealing with individual persons. This goal is most likely to be achieved through individualised contact with other members of other ethnic groups.[8]

Teachers must take every opportunity to encourage all students to interact as freely as possible without the restrictions that streaming and grouping place on students. For example, in some situations, students who do not speak English as a first language are placed in a stream with students of poor academic achievement. Consequently, they do not interact with all students in the system. Ethnic ghettos are often created within school systems that limit the possibility of the formation of multi-ethnic friendship groups. Where schools attract students who are from a similar ethnic background, it is imperative that students be exposed to other cultures.

COGNITIVE AND MORAL DEVELOPMENT

This approach is based on the assumption that to solve moral problems, such as prejudice and discrimination, a student must be given experiences in developing capacities of reasoning and cognition. An example of this approach is the model supplied by the Association for Values Education and Research (AVER).[9]

The AVER model is based on the assumption that a morally autonomous or morally responsible individual must bring to bear upon any moral problem a number of abilities and dispositions. The AVER Prejudice Unit[10] attempts to make the student conscious of prejudice and discrimination so that she or he can recognize their "irrationality, inconsistency, injustice and lack of humanheartedness." The AVER unit encourages the student to make judgments about ethnic minorities. Basically, the student has his or her consciousness raised and is encouraged to see the importance of justifying the values he or she holds. This is done by increasing the student's ability to distinguish between mere descriptive claims and value claims, to evaluate moral arguments, to determine the role of authority, and to understand the consequences of one's actions as they affect others. In a study of the effects of the use of this procedure, the results suggest that "the *Prejudice Unit* is an effective condition for improving senior secondary students' ethnic tolerance and normative reasoning ability, [and] changes in tolerance and reasoning produced...are reasonably stable over time."[11]

This requirement of a multicultural program is based on the assumption that teachers must accept the responsibility for developing cognitive abilities of students and providing them with opportunities to make mature moral judgments in the areas of prejudice and discrimination. This must become one of the objectives of all teachers.

PURGING OUR LANGUAGE OF PREJUDICE

The negative consequences of ethnic stereotyping and its relation to prejudice has been previously discussed. Related to this is the relationship of language to the development of prejudice. It seems reasonable to accept that the very socialization of an individual's consciousness and her or his personality are to a degree determined by language. Values and attitudes are, to a degree, the outcomes of the language that an individual experiences in gaining access to culture and society. Thus, the language we use in understanding our world shapes how we relate to that world. According to

Luckman, "Language evidently plays a central part in the processes of social objectivation and social transmission of such thought, value, and attitude configurations as have a relevance and validity that go beyond individual experience."[12]

Language itself can be responsible for conditioning the attitudes that students accept about members of other ethnic or racial groups or those singled out on the basis of age or gender. Words like "Wop," "Paki," and "Dago" are obviously demeaning when applied to specific ethnic groups. But there are less obvious words that serve the same function of influencing the attitudes of students about members of minority groups. Words that are common to our vocabulary can change our attitudes when they are used in certain contexts. Moore shows how words like defend, conquest, victory, and massacre, which are common in our history books, shape our understanding of groups of people. Specifically,

> Eurocentrism is also apparent in the usage of "victory" and "massacre" to describe the battles between Native Americans and whites. *Victory* is defined in the dictionary as "a success or triumph over an enemy in battle or war; the decisive defeat of an opponent." *Conquest* denotes the "taking over of control by the victor, and the obedience of the conquered." *Massacre* is defined as "the unnecessary, indiscriminate killing of a number of human beings, as in barbarous warfare or persecution, or for revenge or plunder." *Defend* is described as "to ward off attack from; guard against assault or injury; to strive to keep safe by resisting attack."[13]

These seemingly innocuous words become value-laden when we talk about Western European immigrants being "victorious" in defending themselves against an Indian "massacre." Another common term used to describe certain ethnic groups is "culturally deprived." This is problematic, since no group can be said to be deprived of culture if by culture we mean language, dress, norms, and values. The term itself is probably meant to refer to a cultural difference between two groups, but the word deprived connotes the inferior status of one culture. It consequently serves the function of condemning, demeaning, and detracting from the acceptance of differences between groups.

What teachers must realize is the power of words to negatively condition attitudes. Prejudice can be the unanticipated outcome of the indiscriminate use of certain words that are ideologically and politically loaded. We cannot change the language, but we can change our usage of it. This will not entail avoiding certain terminology, but encouraging students to look at the effect of the language we use on attitudes and perceptions.

MODIFYING THE PEDAGOGY OF INSTRUCTION

Up to this point, emphasis has been placed on changes that can be made to the content of the classroom curriculum. Changes will also have to be made in the pedagogy or the process of transmission of the curriculum. Morgan[14] develops two models of pedagogy, which she labels the *psychometric model* and the *epistemological model*. These two models differ significantly in their assumptions about and treatment of students in educational settings. The psychometric model is the one most frequently found in schools today. It is based on the following assumptions.

> 1. The child is regarded as an *object*, more particularly, as a *deficit system* whose passivity is a necessary condition for being initiated into public thought forms.
> 2. The child is regarded as "having" *intelligence* in the sense of a specific property which can be measured by objective tests.
> 3. The world of knowledge is regarded by those who adopt the psychometric model as composed of pre-existing theoretical forms into which the child must be initiated.
> 4. The pre-existence of such forms and the possession of such by the educator legitimizes a highly *didactic* form of pedagogy.
> 5. As a possessor of such theoretical forms, the educator assumes the role of societal surrogate one of whose main roles is to assess the growing congruence of the child's thought forms with the pre-existing standards.
> 6. *Educational development* consists of growing rationality as the child moves away from the concreteness of his immediate world towards the increasingly abstract theoretical forms.
> 7. *Educational achievement* consists in progressing towards increasingly specialized and highly discipline-bound subject matter and is measured in terms of objective evaluative criteria such as behavioural objectives.[15]

In this model, the student is someone who "has education done to them." Morgan contrasts these features with those of the epistemological model, which has the following characteristics.

> 1. The child is regarded primarily as a *subject*, that is, as a being who is actively involved in constructing and arranging his knowledge of the world in terms of personally relevant interpretational schemata.
> 2. The main property which the child is thought to possess and which is most relevant to the educational setting is the non-quantifiable property of *curiosity*.
> 3. Following the leads of Piaget and Bruner, the world of knowledge is regarded as composed of thought forms which are in a constant process of construction and which are dialectically related to the development of individual subjects interacting with socially approved and socially distributed knowledge.
> 4. Emphasizing the constructive aspect of human knowledge and placing value on intellectual initiative legitimize a pedagogy which is highly *interaction oriented*.
> 5. As a similarly constructive, growing subject, the educator assumes the role of social model in the process of knowledge construction, one of the main responsibilities of which is the

heuristic channelling of the pre-existing curiosity of each individual student.

6. *Successful pedagogy* consists not in the measuring of the achievement level of the students but in the ability of the teacher to apprehend and recreate the intentionality and subjective reality of the students so as to provide greater individual stimulation.

7. Although *educational achievement* is measured in distance from the starting point to present level of development, this is a highly individualized measure. The child is essentially treated as a self-regulative being insofar as he controls the sequence and pace of the experience. In many cases, he controls the content of the experience as well, insofar as his interests and desires are often the crucial curriculum determinants in the setting.[16]

In this model the students would be active in their education and responsible for its outcomes. The epistemological model would be the better model to foster the development of positive attitudes and values associated with a multicultural program. Students would be held responsible for their intellectual and moral growth. It seems to follow that this pedagogy would be less authoritarian and would encourage the acceptance of differences between individuals, the enhancement of self-esteem, the development of critical thinking, the understanding of the consequences of holding certain beliefs and attitudes, and the desire to engage in activities leading to social justice. This model of pedagogy, combined with the four previously discussed conditions of the multicultural classroom could provide a sound basis for the desired educational outcomes of tolerance and understanding.

What role does education play in either creating structural inequalities or bringing about their demise? One is made constantly aware of a recurrent theme in Canadian education, namely that of equality of educational opportunity. The principle of equality of opportunity has been an important part of the general liberal ideology that has influenced the development of public education in the past one hundred years. The guiding principle has been the assumption that education would provide equal opportunities for all individuals to achieve, through the use of their abilities and motivation, whatever position in society they desire. The assumption is that every child should have the opportunity to make fullest use of his or her potential and that the means to achieve this would be the educational system. Although education would not completely eliminate inequality, the argument goes, talent found among children of minority ethnic groups would be encouraged, and the unfair advantages open to the majority group would be reduced. Education would be a means of assuring that children would end up in a position in society commensurate with their abilities and motivation and not merely with their socio-economic status or place of birth.

However, when one looks past this ideology to see what really happens, one finds a very close and persistent relationship between the adult occupational hierarchy and the type or level of education gained by the children of those adults. This is often quite independent of the child's ability and motivation. Those adults who have had their experiences and characteristics recognized and rewarded by the educational system have been allocated higher positions in the occupational hierarchy; in turn, these adults can pass these experiences on to their children, assuring that the latter will be allocated like positions through the educational qualifications they gain. If we relate this to ethnicity, we find that, in a country such as Canada, the hierarchic occupational structure corresponds to the ethnic background of its citizens. Certain ethnic groups are more successful in using the educational system than are others. What results is a hierarchy of ethnic groups. Consequently, ethnic and racial inequalities are by and large reproduced in the next generation by the educational system. This is the structural basis of discrimination discussed earlier.

We have seen that schools have successfully forged clear linkages between educational attainment and the occupational structure. It is clear that faith in the ideal that the educational system can be the means to bring about equality in society is misplaced. Schools have not been successful as vehicles of mobility for children of certain ethnic groups or as agents for social change. Schools reproduce the inequalities that already exist in society, and later the credentials awarded by schools are used to justify an individual's success, or lack thereof, in the social hierarchy. Schools, indirectly if not directly, legitimize inequalities. Contrary to the goal professed by those who control schools of using education as a means of restructuring society by rewarding individuals according to talent and motivation rather than according to characteristics ascribed at birth, schools are themselves directly shaped by the realities of the broader society. Consequently, the goal of social change, which schools often profess, becomes the reality of social control.

It is not just the structural factors outside of schools that have a profound effect on what schools actually do. The hidden curriculum and educators' assumptions about educability and future achievement exert a significant influence on the different values taught to students. Moreover, inequalities and their stratifying outcomes are built into the very structures of schools themselves. Streaming and tracking are two such structures. Raymond Breton[17] showed that academic stratification (streaming) is considerably more important in influencing students' aspirations to higher education than is their measured ability and that this streaming is often directly related to the child's ethnic background.

Children from minority groups differ from children of the majority group not only in their levels of educational attainment and in their rates of educational participation but also in the kinds of education they receive. In that subjects are stratified into a hierarchical structure, children of certain ethnic groups may be exposed to different kinds of pressures and expectations, which create different aspirations and lead to allocation to occupations that are differentially rewarded.

The educational system is not just an innocent bystander when it comes to the creation of inequalities in society. According to Jaenen:

> If we accept the view that Canada is a multi-ethnic and polycultural society, then it would seem to follow that the public school systems of the nation ought to reflect this cultural pluralism. Such a conclusion would seem to impose itself if for no other reason than publicly supported school systems should serve all and reflect the educational objectives of the entire community. The tendency in all public or state school systems, however, is towards uniformity and centralization. Uniformity and centralization, whether defended on grounds of administrative efficiency, in the name of equality, or on grounds of scholarly attainment of stated common objectives, discourage educational recognition of cultural pluralism. Thus, one may declare that it is possible for public schooling, equated in the popular mind with education, to retard the development of a unique and significant culture in Canada, to downgrade what is genuinely and authentically Canadian in our lifestyle, and to depreciate the moral, relevant, and innovative aspects of public schooling.[18]

We have attempted to look "through" what educationalists in Canada say they are doing and better see the reality of educational outcomes. This may have led to a fairly pessimistic conclusion. But it does not mean that teachers are totally helpless. Changes in teacher training, curriculum, and pedagogic practices may be required and useful if for no other reason than providing a more humane and stimulating environment for students who spend the better part of each day for twelve years—or more—within these institutions.

If teachers accept the difficult task of making the suggested changes in the curriculum, pedagogy, language of education, and in their understanding of the cognitive, affective, and moral possibilities of education, then prejudical attitudes and discrimination, which threaten the existence of our multicultural society, can be reduced. Teachers must not just teach about multiculturalism. They must realize the instrumental role they play in creating structures of inequality through the practices common in many schools.

This goal is no less controversial than it would be difficult to obtain. However, if we accept that the inequalities that exist in Canada are costly in both an economic and social sense, inimical to our sense of social justice, and destructive of the realization of multiculturalism, then we may wish to do something about them. And here is where teachers can play their part. It seems reasonable to assume that schools could teach the norms of distributive justice and the principles of equality. Rather than teaching loyalty and commitment to the status quo, schools could teach sincere questioning and critical analysis. Rather than accepting the role of allocator of credentials that reduce students to products, schools could foster knowledge and skills that would lead students to see themselves as producers of reality. If we can create a truly multicultural school system, as has been outlined, our students will leave schools strong, capable, and committed to a multicultural reality for Canada. The challenge is great, but can we ask for anything less of our schools?

NOTES

1. Jean Burnet, "Myths and Multiculturalism" in *Multiculturalism in Canada: Social and Educational Perspectives*, edited by R.J. Samuda, J.W. Berry, and M. Laferrière (Toronto: Allyn and Bacon, 1984), 18.
2. J.W. Berry, "Multicultural Attitudes and Education," ibid, 104.
3. J. Berry, R. Kalin, and D.M. Taylor, *Multiculturalism and Ethnic Attitudes in Canada* (Ottawa, 1976), 127.
4. Burnet, "Myths and Multiculturalism," 27.
5. D. Patel, *Dealing with Interracial Conflict Policy Alternatives* (Montreal: Institute for Research on Public Policy, 1980), 14.
6. M.A. Ijaz, "Ethnic Attitude Change: A Multidimensional Approach" in *Multiculturalism in Canada*, 135.
7. W. Werner, B. Connors, T. Aoki, and J. Dahli, *Whose Culture? Whose Heritage?* (Edmonton: University of Alberta, 1977).
8. R.K. Kalin, "The Development of Ethnic Attitudes" in *Multiculturalism in Canada*, 124.
9. Association for Values Education and Research, *Evaluation of the AVER Prejudice Unit in a Senior Secondary School*, Report no. 7 (Vancouver: University of British Columbia, 1978).
10. Association for Values Education and Research, *Final Report of a Study of Moral Education in Surrey, B.C.*, Report no. 6 (University of British Columbia, Faculty of Education, 1974).
11. Ibid., 18.
12. Thomas Luckman, *The Sociology of Language* (Indianapolis: Bobs-Merrill, 1975), 20.
13. R.B. Moore, *Racism in the English Language* (New York: Racism and Sexism Resource Center, 1976), 11.
14. K. Morgan, "Socialization, Social Models, and the Open Education Movement: Some Philosophical Considerations" in *The Philosophy of Open Education*, edited by D. Nyberg (London: Routledge and Kegan Paul, 1975).
15. Ibid., 126.
16. Ibid.
17. Raymond Breton, "Academic Stratification in Secondary Schools and the Educational Plans of Students," *Canadian Review of Sociology and Anthropology* 7, 1 (1970).
18. C.J. Jaenen, "Cultural Diversity and Education" in *Must School Fail?* edited by N. Byrne and J. Quarter (Toronto: McClelland and Stewart, 1972), 199.

COUNSELLING IN A SOCIETY IN TRANSITION

MYRNE B. NEVISON

Counselling is normally a challenging task. One can never know the best answer for another person; from knowledge of society and people in general, counsellors try to help others understand and evaluate relevant choices. But, when a society is in transition from one age to another, when the job structure is fluid, when the rate of change is geometric and already staggering, and when our economic well-being—indeed, perhaps even our survival on world markets—is in question, then counselling can be an intimidating responsibility.

We are caught up in the middle of such transition now. It is imperative that we seek to understand our predicament: the dimensions of the economic change, the level of our educational preparedness, and our patterns of response to the inevitable personal stress. Then, we may gain some perspective on the counselling issues of our day.

THE ECONOMIC DIMENSIONS

Canada is now being catapulted from a reasonably successful industrial nation to one facing survival issues in new world markets and, as we are a trading nation, we cannot avoid these new realities. We started as a rural society and gradually built strength through selling our natural resources. The decades since World War II have seen significant changes in the economy, which accelerated in the 1950s and soared in the 1960s. The 1970s brought shocks (such as oil prices rising with astonishing speed) and a new awareness of our vulnerability. The 1980s are causing frustration as changes in world markets have begun to affect our economy. Prime Minister Mulroney recently commented that we have been slipping in our share in these markets and that three million Canadian jobs are at stake.

Countries that are succeeding today either combine cheap labour with industrial know-how (as illustrated by the sudden emergence in our automobile markets of South Korea's Hyundai) or invest heavily in education for workers for the knowledge-based industries (as does Japan). Japan is moving ahead so quickly that many expect it to surpass the United States as the major industrial power within fifteen years.

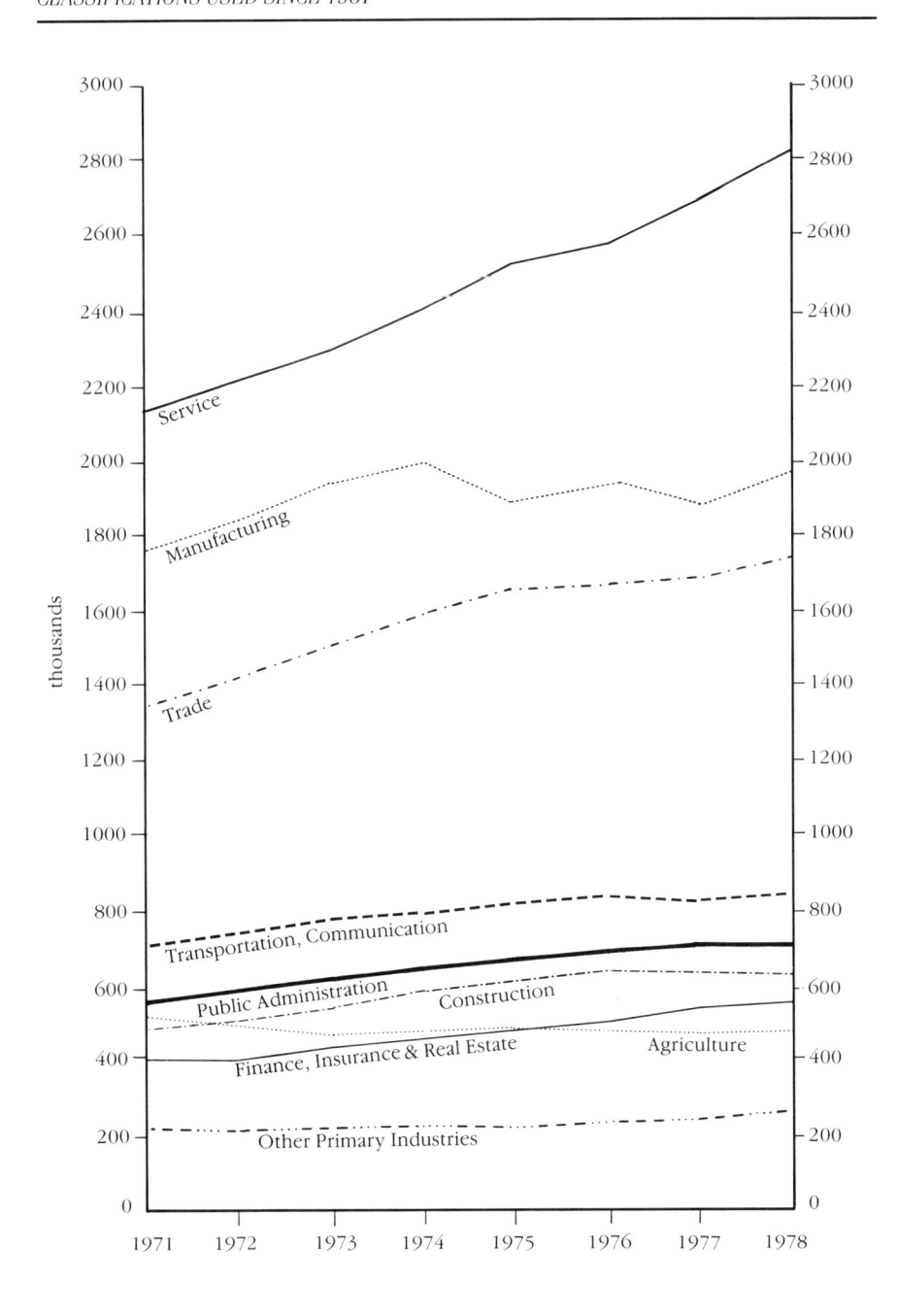

FIGURE 1
EMPLOYEES BY INDUSTRIAL GROUPS
CLASSIFICATIONS USED SINCE 1987

382 SOCIAL PROBLEMS AND ISSUES

Canadians do not want to accept the cheap-labour route and are fighting to prevent our standard of living from falling but have not yet come to terms with the requirements to succeed in knowledge-based areas. For instance, Japanese workers spend, on average, sixty-five hours a year on increasing their knowledge and upgrading their skills; Americans spend twenty-five hours; Canadians, fifteen hours. In Canada, unions are still fighting for job security when they should be trying to get income security through job retraining.

Historically, we began as a nation of farmers. Later labourer and eventually clerk became the largest occupational category. The turning point in this last transition came in the 1950s when, for the first time, white-collar workers outnumbered blue-collar ones. Very soon technicians will probably be the largest single occupational category.

The accelerated sweep of change in occupations is illustrated in figure 1, which shows the change in the relatively stable 1970s. The largest and fastest growing job category is services, where the pay is not as good as in the larger industries. Since there will be fewer jobs in industries (as robots are used increasingly), many people who anticipated working there—even those now so employed—will face a poorer income. And, according to news reports, we have fallen behind in the high-tech industries where knowledge is so important.

OUR EDUCATIONAL READINESS

We have always looked upon ourselves as a people valuing education and, according to traditional guidelines, we have a right to feel proud. But this is a new era and we must ensure that people are prepared for work in the Information Age and that we can staff knowledge-based jobs.

It is generally held that one Canadian in six is functionally illiterate—unable to read work directions or even fill in an application form for a job. Table 1 gives the levels of education of all members of the work force. With fewer unskilled jobs available, it is sobering to note that 1.682 million workers have 0–8 years of education; of these, 1.444 million have jobs, 238 000 do not. Of the population group 25 years or older, a quarter of them, 3.64 million, are in that 0–8 year category.[1]

It is troubling, too, to realize that the attitude of so many Canadians toward schools—and probably toward further education—is quite negative. Historically our schools were designed to give basic learning to all and advanced education to the so-called academically able instead of taking each child, at an individual rate, to his or her potential. Two out of five of the men now in their middle adult years were "overage" by Grade 9 and the major cause of this was failure in school. For women, the figure is three out of ten. A child who has tried to meet standards and is publicly failed is reluctant to seek out more educational experiences.

TABLE 1
EDUCATIONAL LEVEL OF ADULT POPULATION AND WORK FORCE ESTIMATES, MAY 1983

Education	Population (15 years and over) (Thousands)	Labour Force Total (Thousands)	Employed (Thousands)	Unemployed	Participation Rate* (Percent)	Unemployment (Percent)
0–8 Years	3 892	1 682	1 444	238	42.2	14.2
High School	9 390	6 185	5 335	851	65.9	13.8
Some Postsecondary	1 661	1 252	1 079	174	75.4	13.9
Postsecondary Certificate/Diploma	2 001	1 564	1 417	147	78.2	9.4
University Degree	1 755	1 501	1 418	84	85.6	5.6
Total	18 789	12 185	10 692	1 493	64.9	12.3

Source: *Learning a Living in Canada* (Ottawa: Employment and Immigration Canada, 1983), I: 41.
* Percentage of group either employed or seeking employment.

TABLE 2
FULL-TIME ENROLMENT

Province	In College[a]	In Postsecondary Education[b]	In Universities[a]
B.C.	10.2	15.5	14.7
Alberta	10.5	15.8	16.5
Quebec	29.3	27.6	16.1
Ontario	13.5	23.3	23.5
Canada	15.4	21.7	19.7

[a] As a percentage of the 18–21 age group.
[b] As a percentage of the 18–24 age group.
Source: John Dennison, "The Financial Future of Universities and Colleges in Canada: An Approach to Federal-Provincial Relations with Respect to the Financing of Post-Secondary Education" (unpublished paper, March 1985).

Participation in postsecondary education, particularly in universities and colleges, has now become very important. Nationally, we lag behind the United States and far behind Japan in our participation rates. Even within Canada opportunities are not equal. Table 2 shows that young people in Ontario and Quebec have a much better chance of following a program in higher education than do those in the other larger provinces.

Our attitude toward education must change. The Information Age will require that all Canadians be prepared to increase their level of skill and knowledge, and perhaps even to change to new areas of work. Instead of the old pattern of school, work, and retirement, there will be a lifelong combination of work and study. Opportunities for upgrading and retraining occupational skills must be readily available and encouraged.

Instead of schools judging growth in competence by comparing all those in a chronological age group where the mental age of a class of six-year-olds could range from four to eight years and in a group of twelve-year-olds from eight to sixteen years, they must encourage each individual to continue to develop at an optimum rate. Schools will be judged excellent only if all young people leaving them want to continue to learn. Only then will we produce adults with the confidence to be the entrepreneurs now needed. The Information Age cannot tolerate many educational drop-outs, regardless of age.

PATTERNS OF RESPONSE TO PERSONAL STRESS

The new and different demands that are being made on Canadians, particularly in the job area, could easily lead to more people having trouble coping, and it is important to try to identify patterns of reactions. While it is difficult to measure how individuals are responding to the new levels of stress, it is possible to get data on the direction and rate of change in areas of social problems.

Data can be made visible and understandable by converting rates of social problems to the scale of the Consumer Price Index. This is done by converting rates, usually number per 100 000 of the population; the rate in 1971 is scored as 100 and those for other years adjusted accordingly. Patterns of change in levels of problems then become obvious.

In figure 2[2] the rates for alcoholism (using the Bellinek Estimation Formula with the number of deaths from cirrhosis), suicides, and admissions to psychiatric hospitals (prior to the recent change in policy on the use of large institutions) all show a steady rise. The Consumer Price Index, based on the same scale, is included as a familiar reference base.

When we compare the change in the incidence of suicides in young people (figure 3) with a scale for all ages, we find much sharper increases. Recent informal data seem to indicate a continuing rise as joblessness exacts its toll.

FIGURE 2
ABILITY TO COPE: INDEXES FOR ALCOHOLISM, SUICIDE, AND ADMISSIONS TO PSYCHIATRIC HOSPITALS AND THE CONSUMER PRICE INDEX
RATE OF CHANGE (1971 = 100)

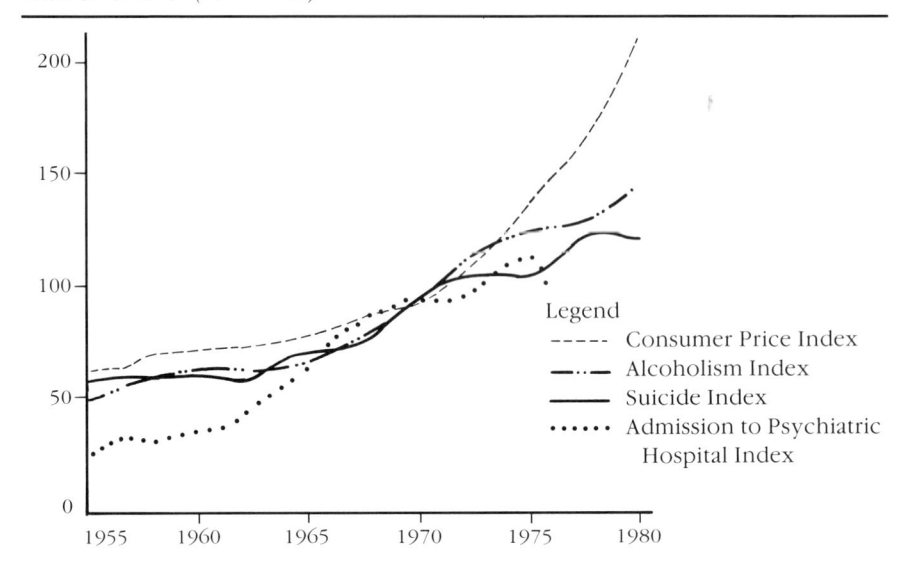

FIGURE 3
SUICIDES IN YOUNG ADULTS
RATES PER 100 000 FOR SELECTED AGE GROUPS

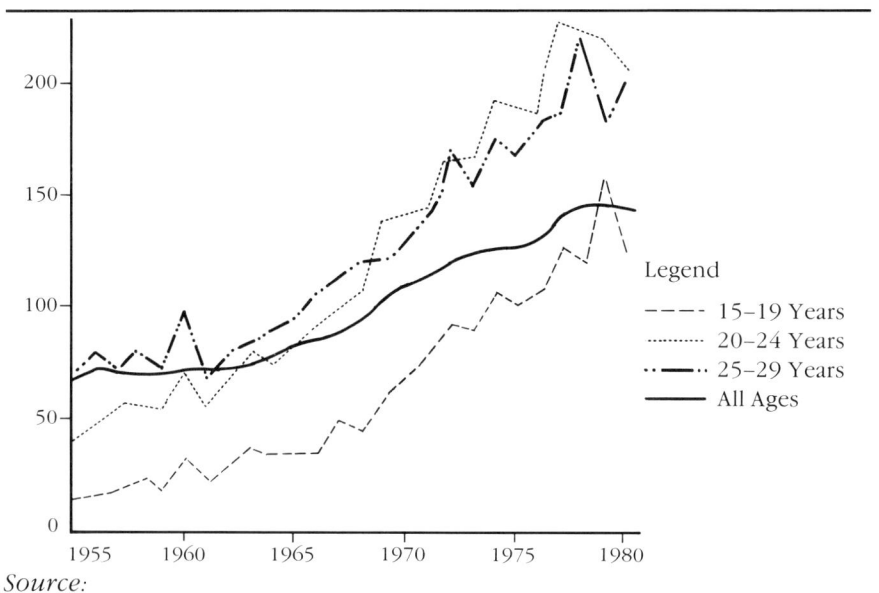

Source:
Rates from Statistics Canada, *General Mortality*, Catalogue 84-531.

FIGURE 4
CRIME INDEX: CRIMINAL CHARGES AND COST OF CORRECTIONAL SERVICES
RATE OF CHANGE (1971 = 100)

Legend
— Criminal Charges Index
—·— Correctional Services Cost Index

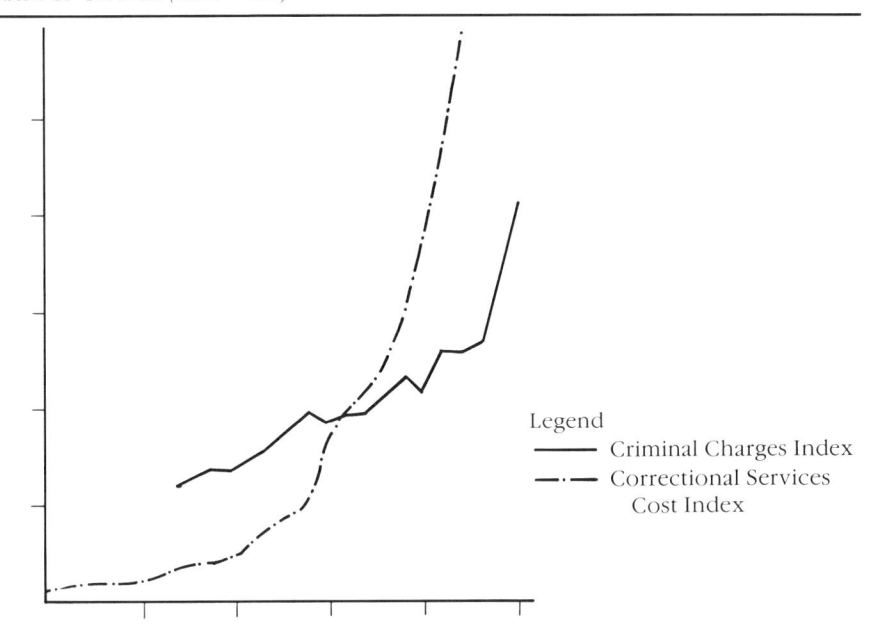

FIGURE 5
FAMILY INDEXES: MARRIAGE DISSOLUTIONS, ILLEGITIMATE BIRTHS, ABORTIONS, CANADA ASSISTANCE PAYMENTS

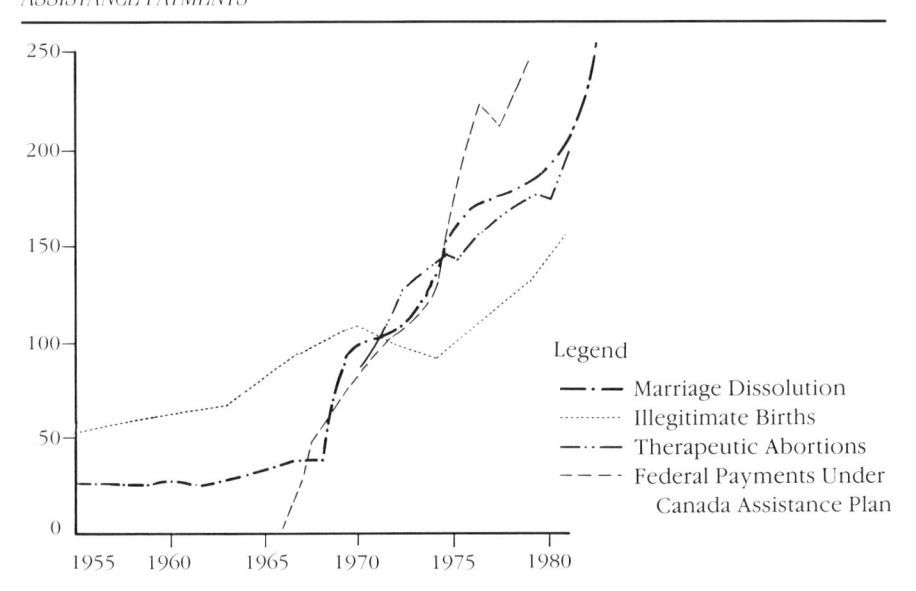

Legend
—·— Marriage Dissolution
······ Illegitimate Births
—··— Therapeutic Abortions
– – – Federal Payments Under Canada Assistance Plan

Aggression against others as indicated by the rate of criminal changes is also increasing (figure 4), but even more dramatic is the soaring cost of correctional services (from a total of $15.2 million in 1960 to $525.8 million in 1982).

The changes in family patterns (figure 5) are profound and worry many people. The change in divorce rates (marriage dissolution) started in 1968 when the laws were liberalized. When the bases for abortions were modified in the late 1960s, the rate of abortion increased but so too, after a preliminary lag, did the number of births to unmarried women. Accompanying these patterns, related financial cost began to soar. Payments under the Canada Assistance Plan (the federal share of welfare bills), started about the same time, began to run out of control.

FIGURE 6
EXPENDITURE INDEXES: RATE OF CHANGE (1971 = 100)

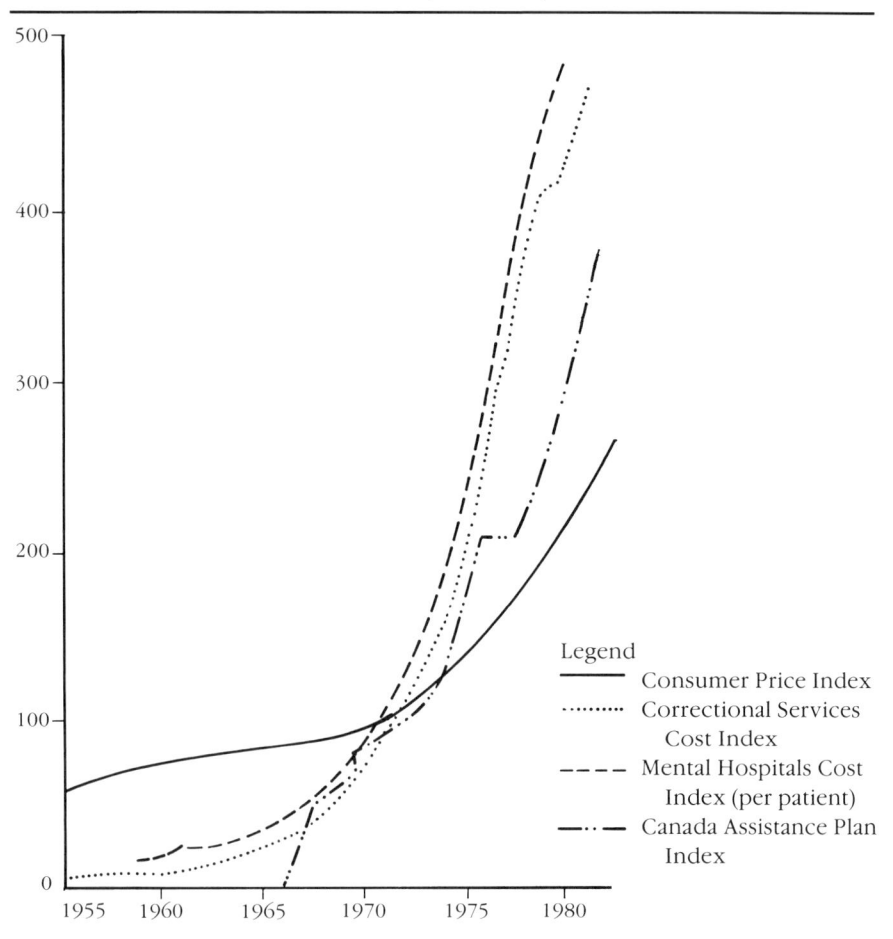

Legend
—— Consumer Price Index
·········· Correctional Services Cost Index
– – – Mental Hospitals Cost Index (per patient)
—··— Canada Assistance Plan Index

The personal anguish of the people reflected in these statistics exacts a heavy toll, and the financial costs have the potential to be a severe drain on our resources as a nation. Expenditures in the key and representative areas included in figure 6 are heading out of control. The total cost of correctional services, the per diem cost of mental hospitals (from $4.67 in 1960 to $114.11 in 1980) and the federal payments to the provinces under the Canada Assistance Plan (from $342.7 million in 1967 to $2887 million in 1982) are all heading up off the chart.

It is essential that, as a society, we somehow intervene to prevent the development of, and increase in, the number of problems that people find crippling. It does not make sense to continue to pay such high costs for stress; some money must be directed into prevention. It may be possible for counsellors to give more strategic help.

COUNSELLING ISSUES

Counsellors have become very aware of the difficulties many people have in coping, whether it be with planning a career or finding personal satisfaction in life. Evidence of drug abuse and violence are all too common. In spite of this general awareness of the increasing social costs, both personal and financial, our counselling services do not seem to be making the necessary impact.

People are generally able to cope when their society is relatively stable and when the older people have prepared the younger for the tasks that they will face. But when a society is not stable and when adults do not know either the probable tasks or the answers to questions facing young people, the stress level can become overwhelming.

With increasing numbers of people having difficulties, our limited resources have gone primarily to provide some relief for those whose situations were critical. Meanwhile, others drift into patterns of inadequate responses and, in turn, need expensive help. The question arises, do we continue to put our resources into helping those with major difficulties or do we fund assistance at an earlier stage? Where do we establish these counselling services so that people who are starting to experience difficulties will seek help before the problem becomes serious?

In reality, we have no option. We cannot afford the crippling costs of early neglect and we must put some money into prevention. We must ensure that information and assistance for each new major stage of life are available to anyone wanting it. If we fail to provide this assistance, we leave the individual to depend on the often grossly inadequate knowledge and attitudes of peers.

This help at important life stages is called *developmental counselling*. It involves assistance in thinking through personal options whether they be adjusting to learning in a group setting in school, understanding adolescence as the transition from childhood to adulthood, mastering the skills for earning a living and parenting, or preparing for a life after retirement. Such developmental counselling is analogous to the medical model now being advocated where preventive care is provided so that people can build a healthy body instead of relying on the emergency and acute care services.

There is also a need for a secondary level of counselling and intervention—*preventive counselling*—that provides more specific information and help for people who are starting to have difficulties with their developmental tasks. Here the counsellor's role is to help the person gain a perspective on his or her problems and to develop the understanding and skills needed to meet life's demands more successfully. People may be facing such difficulties as meeting educational goals, making friends, adjusting to family breakdown, or coping with stress. In developmental counselling the information needed is general and often provided in group settings; preventive counselling is geared towards a special difficulty that an individual is having, and the service is provided, usually, on an individual basis.

Finally, there is the traditional *remedial* or *therapeutic service*—the one that has taken most of our resources and where the returns have been minimal. This service is made available to those who are unable to cope. They are in trouble and need special, and often extensive, assistance. Although the difficulty may be manifested in any area of life, it tends to be caused by a serious lack of self-confidence, a crippling emotional reaction and an inability to see more effective ways of coping. The counsellor's role varies depending on the setting in which she or he works and the level of her or his skills in therapeutic interventions.

If counselling services are to be utilized, and therefore have a chance to be effective, they must be based on local needs and be readily available where people congregate. Certainly schools and other educational institutions would probably provide developmental and preventive services, but resources must also be available for adults. Large businesses are now starting to provide such services and churches have traditionally been helpful but, to reach others, there should be centres in places like shopping malls. These could attract the person interested in knowing more about options, either vocational or social.

The extent of current social disruption requires a significant measure of co-operation, an interdependence rather than merely a belief in rugged individualism. In our global village, the pattern of life is not childhood dependence to independence, but dependence through independence to interdependence. For the effective functioning of a system of counselling services, the community must be involved. All segments of the community representing a diversity of experience and opinions should participate in developing a consensus on what is needed and who should provide it. This is similar to the emerging pattern in business where small, quality groups, directly involved in the task, work together to solve problems.

Issues in counselling reflect the needs of the society. When a society changes, it is necessary to speculate on the type of community that will emerge and the socialization procedures required to prepare individuals for responsible, satisfying lives. When the new requirements, especially in the area of work, differ so markedly from traditional experience, then the larger society must try to supplement the now inadequate help given people at each new stage of life if crippling problems are to be avoided.

The challenges facing us in world markets, the lack of educational and motivational readiness, the number of crippling personal reactions now obvious can become a crisis of enormous proportions. The challenge is to ensure that Canadians are strong enough to find challenges rewarding and to participate successfully in the demands of our new world.

NOTES

1. Ministry of Employment and Immigration, *Learning a Living in Canada*, Report of the Skill Development Leave Task Force (Ottawa: Employment and Immigration Canada, 1983).

2. M.B. Nevison, "Psycho-social Problems and Causes: Indexes of Changes," *Canadian Counsellor* 18, 2 (1984): 51–71.

A CASE FOR TEACHING WORLD AFFAIRS IN CANADIAN SCHOOLS

DAVID CLOSE

Watch the TV news any night and you will see stories about the arms race, the Third-World debt crisis, and current political issues in the United States or some other foreign country. The news reports events from abroad that may influence either what the government of Canada will do or how we in this country will lead our daily lives. A war in the Middle East could bring another oil crisis and higher fuel prices here. A decision by the Federal Reserve Board in Washington to raise interest rates will make it harder to buy a house in Winnipeg. If NATO adopts a new missile or a different strategy on the use of tanks, Ottawa may have to alter Canada's defence policies.

Everyone can see that the world is now so interrelated that Canadians are likely to feel the effects of major political and economic events that happen anywhere in the world. But what people may not see is why these events, over which they have no control, happened in the first place. Are the guerrillas we see the product of hundreds of years of oligarchic mis-rule or the result of a great power's decision to destabilize an unfriendly regime? Are Mexico and Brazil not paying their debts because they cannot or only because they are trying to pry more concessions from us? The ability to make these sorts of distinctions comes only from having both more information than we get in a brief newscast and some experience analysing the complex world of international affairs.

International affairs is the most difficult realm of politics for the average citizen to penetrate. As a result, it is also the area where citizens will be least able to affect public policy because government's claim to "know better" will be harder to dispute. If we lived in a world where foreign events did not greatly influence our national life or in a country that allowed its citizens no role in shaping any policy, this would not matter. But such a state of affairs is surely unacceptable in a democracy that assumes an active role in world affairs.

Since world affairs make up a significant part of a Canadian's political milieu, it follows that citizenship education in this country ought to emphasize the analysis of international issues. While this emphasis should be strongest in the secondary school civic education program, social studies courses at all levels should help students develop the skills and knowledge needed to understand both international politics and how other political systems work. It is thus disheartening to find that the study of foreign affairs and comparative government accounts for only a small part of the formal political education offered in our schools.

At this juncture it would be easy to lament the absence of an important foreign affairs element in Canadian school social studies programs and to condemn the educational establishment for failing to prepare a generation of well trained global citizens. But it would not be a very useful exercise because it would not suggest how this lamentable state of affairs might be altered. One might even argue that it could not be changed. We have already stated that foreign affairs are the least well understood part of politics, so how can we expect school children, who have trouble mastering Canadian history and government, to come to grips with even more complex and unfamiliar material?

The point is well taken. At the very least it makes good sense to ask if international studies could be presented in the same way as Canadian civics. But the point is premised on two assumptions that may be wrong. The first of these is that children learn about foreign affairs later than they do about domestic issues. The second is that even secondary school students will be woefully ignorant of current world issues. Neither assumption is substantiated by research into children's socialization to world politics. In fact, this material suggests that political information and values needed to understand the international system are learned alongside those used to make sense of domestic politics.

Beginning in the late 1950s and continuing through the 1960s, political scientists in Western Europe and North America undertook the systematic study of political socialization to discover how people learn the facts of political life. Most of their attention was focussed on school children, so we have very good information concerning what children know about politics, how their attitudes toward politics are formed, and how their attitudes change and knowledge becomes deeper and broader as they grow up.[1]

Most of these socialization studies concentrated on issues related to domestic politics; for example, how children regard some key political figure or when they are able to give an accurate description of the workings of an important political institution. These are clearly matters of substantial importance to anyone concerned with civic education, as it is usually conceived, because citizenship training has always aimed at building loyalty to and an understanding of the student's homeland. Perhaps it was because these early socialization studies mirrored the concerns of educators involved in preparing the coming generation of Canadians, Americans, or Britons that questions of politics beyond the nation's frontiers were not stressed.

Nevertheless, the child's awareness of international phenomena was not completely neglected, though it was more often psychologists or sociologists than political scientists who carried out the studies. The best known of all these analyses is a 1951 study done by Piaget and Weil examining the development of a conception of "the homeland" among children.[2] They concluded that children are not normally able to understand the idea of "nationality" until they are ten or eleven years old. Replicating this study a few years later, Jahoda[3] found that even children of eight or nine were able to distinguish between their homeland and foreign countries, thus suggesting that some form of international studies could be taught as early as Grade 3 or 4.

Some studies of international political socialization have concentrated on the evolution of children's views of war and peace.[4] The general thrust of these works reveals that children's notions of what peace is about develop slowly and that, when they do, peace is often pictured as a period free of hostilities and not as a positive drive toward co-operation.

More explicitly addressed to inter-state relations are works by Morrison, Targ, and Button.[5] The first of these found that Scottish adolescents evaluated western regimes more positively than they did socialist states, but opposed a pre-emptive American nuclear strike against the Soviet Union because they feared this would bring mutual annihilation. The Targ study on nine- to twelve-year-old Americans discovered "an increasingly positive orientation to the United States...and an increasingly negative valuation of the Soviet Union and China with grade level."[6] He also argues that his "data tended to indicate that children increasingly were socialized to a political world not too dissimilar from Morganthau's theory of political realism [which holds that a state's behaviour in the international arena is governed solely by self-interest]."[7] Button, too, found that children acquired adult perspectives on international conflict early on in life. He paid particular attention to the role of the school, concluding that, after Grade 6, the school became children's most significant source of information about foreign affairs.

Most of the research reviewed above focusses on attitudinal development, but there are a few studies that concentrate on the child's knowledge of international issues.[8] Tolley's attempt to assess how much American children knew about the Viet Nam war at the height of that conflict is particularly interesting. He found that children's perceptions of the war were essentially identical to those held by adults; that is, they were able to give substantial factual reasons why they did not approve of the way President Richard Nixon prosecuted the war, but they still wanted the United States to win. Of special interest was Tolley's observation that, though parents may influence children in such matters as choosing to support a particular political party, it is the school, supplemented by the mass media, that takes the leading role in fostering patriotic commitment.

All these studies indicate a very important role for schools in teaching world affairs. Children are certainly aware of world issues by the time they are ten years old, and it is quite clear that the instruction provided in school is an important shaper of attitudes. It may even be that the school social studies program will be the only systematic analysis of world issues that many children will ever receive.

Surprisingly, none of the literature cited above asked if children learn about national and international affairs at the same age. If they do, it becomes possible to think about developing curricula that link Canada with the rest of the world in a direct and obvious manner. Should the rates of learning about the two spheres of politics differ, this, too, must be known if the material is to be presented effectively.

That such an obvious and practical consideration should have been ignored becomes even more perplexing when we note that analyses of both domestic and international political learning emphasize the same variables—class, age, and sex—in their research. But we still do not know if the relationships between these variables and political attitudes and information that hold in the realm of domestic politics apply to the field of international affairs. Is it, for example, still the rule that upper-class children are better informed than lower-class children at each age level, and that boys are more politically aware than girls their own age? Or do these advantages not transfer to international affairs? We would hypothesize that they do but, in the absence of specifically applicable evidence, we cannot really be sure.

The question of how children's attitudes toward foreign affairs evolve also needs attention. We know that children become both less parochial and more liberal—that is, more accepting of the desirability of extending equal political rights to all—as they mature. If the same process is at work in their thinking about international politics, it should mean children become less likely to choose simplistic, aggressive solutions to international problems as they grow up. If we knew this were true, we could then devise courses for the last years of high school that presented students with complex and innovative approaches to international conflict resolution secure in the knowledge that these would not be dismissed as unrealistic.

My own research[9] has tried to answer some of these questions so as to provide guidelines for in-service teachers and curriculum planners. In particular, I have been concerned to see how a foreign-affairs-oriented course could be grafted on to existing civics courses. Getting this information has meant preparing a survey to be carried out in Canada, as nearly all the existing studies were done in other countries. Although it is improbable that socialization would differ greatly among industrialized western democracies, the fact that Canadians do attach less importance to foreign affairs than domestic issues could produce lower levels of interest in these matters than is the case in the United States or Western Europe. To eliminate this possible source of ambiguity, a Canadian study was needed.

The survey reported here was done in May 1979 and involved 1121 Newfoundland school children. The sample population was drawn from the grades 5, 8, and 11 classes in eleven schools in a rural part of the province. All in the sample responded to a seventy-one item questionnaire; a separate ten-item schedule was added for the Grade 11 students. The schools were selected to reflect a wide range of socio-economic characteristics. These particular grades were chosen because: Grade 5 is the threshold of an awareness of a sense of nationhood in most children;[10] Grade 8 is the upper end of the most important years of childhood political learning;[11] and Grade 11 was the last year of secondary school.

A cross-sectional study of the kind reported here cannot show the development of a child's ideas about world affairs or the precise rate at which her or his knowledge grows; to do that would require a longitudinal panel study lasting five to seven years. Looking at age cohorts does, however, show how a ten-year-old's thinking about international issues differs from a sixteen-year-old's. This provides important benchmark data both for future researchers and for teachers and curriculum designers who need results that can be used immediately.

The results arising from the above study are divided into two categories. The first is built around the question of what children know about international affairs. This has two components, viz., how much they know at each age and how their levels of information about Canadian and foreign affairs compare. The second category contains data relating to the development of attitudes, and again has two component parts—the differences in attitudes held by different age cohorts or class or gender groups and the relationship between information possessed and attitudes held.

A battery of twenty-three questions touching war-peace issues, foreign governments, and international relations was used to measure knowledge of world affairs. Knowledge of Canada was gauged by an eight-question index. Some of these thirty-one questions were grouped into smaller sets for more detailed examination. There were six questions concerned with peace issues (e.g., knowing how many countries had nuclear weapons), eight asked students to identify Canadian or international political leaders, and seven presented national symbols (e.g., a Union Jack) to be matched with their countries.

Table 1 shows that students become better informed about both domestic and international politics at similar rates as they grow older. Although students in each grade know more about Canadian than non-Canadian issues, the difference is not great and could have been affected by the inclusion of especially easy questions in the Canadian index. For example, being able to identify the prime minister from a photo during a federal election campaign should not really be too difficult. Consequently, it may be that the real difference between the Canadian and international politics indexes is even less than it appears. This is an interesting finding because surveys done in the United States[13] have consistently found American students much less well informed about international affairs than domestic events. Whether this means that Canadians are more cosmopolitan than Americans or suggests that children here are growing up with a poor sense of national identity is something future researchers may want to consider.

TABLE 1
INFORMATIONAL INDEX SCORES IN PERCENT CORRECT BY GRADE

Index	Grade 5	Grade 8	Grade 11	Gamma
Canada	41.0	55.6	70.4	.68
International	38.3	52.4	65.6	.66
War-Peace*	47.8	54.3	67.3	.44
Leaders*	30.8	48.1	65.5	.67
Symbols*	46.2	69.0	76.7	.57

* Sub-index; n = 1121.

When we look at the three sub-indexes we see that students in the lower two recorded particularly low scores on the leaders index. Asked to identify the Ayatollah Khomeni, Leonid Brezhnev, Deng Xiaoping, Helmut Schmidt, Jimmy Carter, Pierre Elliott Trudeau, Edward Schreyer, and Brian Peckford, the students most often named the prime minister, the Newfoundland premier, the Iranian leader, and the U.S. president correctly (see table 2). They were much less successful in identifying the major political figures of China, West Germany, and the U.S.S.R. as well as the man who had recently been named Canada's governor-general. This indicates that knowing about public officials with relatively low media profiles is a mark of political adulthood; younger children may only be able to recognize those whom they see frequently.

By way of contrast, political symbols such as flags are well known even in grades 5 and 8. To give one striking example, 34.6 percent of the fifth graders could identify the Soviet flag, but only 9.1 percent of them knew Brezhnev was the Soviet leader. Equally familiar to even the youngest respondents were some of the issues related to international conflict. The vast majority of the Grade 5 sample (72 and 62 percent respectively) knew that countries were talking about stopping the spread of nuclear weapons and that the U.S. and U.S.S.R. had been discussing how to avoid war. Part of the success of the Grade 5 students may be attributable to the phrasing of some questions, which allowed children with only a general image of world issues to deduce the correct response, but it is still surprising to see a large proportion of young children possessed of even a general image of international events.

We now want to know how this sense of foreign affairs is developed. Obviously the school (e.g., children learn to recognize the flags of other countries in geography class), the media, and parents all contribute. One item in the questionnaire gives a glimpse into how children think they should find out about world events. They were asked to indicate which of four sources—parents, teacher, social studies text, or other book—they would consult to get information about a foreign country or foreign affairs. Table 3 shows students relying increasingly on teachers, texts, and other books as they grow older. Children obviously think their school is a key place to learn about the world.

TABLE 2
PERCENT ABLE TO RECOGNIZE NATIONAL LEADERS BY GRADE

		Grade			
Leader of	Method	5	8	11	Total
Iran	a	38.1	39.9	67.8	47.9
U.S.S.R.	c	9.1	24.6	52.6	28.3
West Germany	a	29.3	44.0	47.4	40.9
Peoples' Republic of China	a	11.4	18.0	31.0	20.3
U.S.A.	b	31.1	78.6	88.9	65.0
Canada-Prime Minister	b	66.6	90.7	94.2	84.8
Canada-Governor-General	a	19.1	34.2	52.6	35.7
Newfoundland	d	35.5	60.6	83.3	60.6

a. Multiple choice
b. Photo
c. Photo + multiple choice
d. Fill in blank

TABLE 3
PREFERRED SOURCE OF INFORMATION ABOUT FOREIGN AFFAIRS BY GRADE

	Grade		
Source	5	8	11
Parent	32.7	18.0	15.9
Teacher	12.1	17.5	26.3
Social Studies Text	35.5	34.8	26.3
Other Book	19.4	29.7	32.4

$n = 1067$.

Finally, the relationship between knowledge of public affairs and both sex and class followed the expected pattern. Upper-class children scored significantly higher than their lower-class cohorts on all indexes, suggesting that the greater verbal skills often found in upper-class children play an important role. While boys scored higher than girls on all measures, the difference was not statistically significant on the Canadian affairs index.

Three indexes were used to discover attitudes about international affairs. One was composed of five questions about East-West relations; its purpose was to assess children's acceptance of polarized views of international relations. The second contained four questions focussing on the students' internationalism, and especially the question of whether Canada should aid poor countries. The last index had five questions aimed at determining how students viewed the Canadian politico-economic system. The goal of this index was to see if students held idealized views of their own society that could result in overly harsh judgments of other systems. The resulting indexes are additive, not scalar, and the variables of age, sex, and class are again examined.

Table 4 gives the mean scores on the indexes broken down by age. In each case a higher value means a less parochial or authoritarian view of the world. There is an evident trend toward more critical, perhaps less ideological, perspectives on both the domestic regime and world affairs among older children. This is congruent with the findings of other socialization studies and indicates the acquisition of adult values. The absence of change on the internationalism index may also be explicable in terms of moving toward adult outlooks, for the younger children's optimistic views on aid were replaced by a more sceptical perspective among the Grade 11 students who showed the characteristic North American doubts about the wisdom of spending money abroad.

Class and sex affected attitudes very slightly. The only significant difference between boys and girls was on the internationalism index and derives from strongly negative views on aid held by Grade 11 boys. We should note,

TABLE 4
MEANS SCORES ON ATTITUDINAL INDEXES BY GRADE

	Grade			
Index	5	8	11	Gamma
East-West	6.6	7.2	7.5	.35
Internationalism	10.8	11.0	10.9	.03
Regime	9.1	10.0	10.6	.36

$n = 1116$

TABLE 5
MEAN SCORES ON ATTITUDINAL INDEXES BY SEX AND CLASS

	VARIABLE			
	Sex		Class	
Index	M	F	Lower	Upper
East-West	7.1	6.8	7.0	7.6
Internationalism	10.8	11.1	11.0	11.0
Regime	9.9	10.0	9.9	10.0

though, that girls were more likely than boys to answer "maybe" to attitudinal questions; the evidence does not tell us if this represents ambivalence or disinterest. Turning to the question of class, the only significant difference finds lower-status students holding more conservative views on the East-West conflict (see table 5). As there is no appreciable difference between the groups on their support for Canadian-style democracy, the difference may be related to the upper stratum's greater knowledge of world politics. Because they know more about world affairs, students from the upper classes may conclude that international relations take place in an amoral atmosphere where only might makes right, and thus would be suspicious of both the Americans and the Soviets.

Finally, a correlational analysis of the knowledge and attitude indexes for the entire sample and for sub-samples grouped by age, sex, and class showed weak levels of association. Apparently, what children know about world affairs is a minor factor in shaping their attitudes toward world issues. This could mean that the development of more liberal attitudes toward international issues shown in table 4 was more closely linked to a general growth of tolerance and sophistication than to having received any special knowledge about the international system. Of course, as the schools surveyed offered no systematic instruction in international affairs, we can still only speculate about a possible information-attitude nexus in this realm.

The most important finding of this study is that what we know about how children learn domestic politics applies to international politics as well. Not only is information about both gained at similar rates, the students surveyed showed only slight differences in their knowledge of the two spheres of public affairs. If marks had been awarded, all the fifth graders would have gotten an "F," the eleventh graders a "B," and the eighth graders a "C-" in Canadian affairs and a "D + " in world issues.

It must be stressed that no systematic instruction in comparative government, foreign affairs, or even civics was offered in any of the schools studied. Only the Grade 8 classes who were taking world geography and world history, and those in Grade 11 who were studying world history were seeing any non-Canadian materials. The results obtained can therefore be seen as reflecting the general knowledge of world affairs of children at each grade level and not the effect of a world-affairs-oriented curriculum.

A reasonable conclusion to draw from the foregoing is that social studies courses presenting materials about Canada and foreign countries could be taught as early as Grade 5, while courses on international relations would certainly be appropriate in the high school. Courses comparing Canadian and other political systems, or that analyse the North-South dialogue, East-West relations, or the prospects of nuclear war, will clearly not be beyond the competence of most children from the later elementary years onwards.

Preparing such courses will not be without problems. To begin with, material concerning other countries—especially ones with social and political systems different from ours—will have to be carefully prepared and presented to preclude the unintentional reinforcement of existing biases. This, of course, is a problem all text writers confront, and it is probably easily solved.

A less tractable side of the problem of providing information for use in world issues courses arises in conjunction with their current affairs component. Because we have no idea where the world's next trouble spot will be, we cannot prepare material in advance. So teachers may find themselves in a position where they have to quickly gather enough information on, say, the Sudan to help their students understand a recent coup. If a teacher lives in a big city with a good public library or near a university with a research library, she or he will have no trouble. But what about colleagues who live in a small town far from major urban centres? We can hardly expect them to buy the books and magazine subscriptions needed to examine any and all areas of world affairs, nor should we count on the school being able to provide them with more than a few basic sources. Does this mean that such teachers and their students have to settle for second best?

Not necessarily. An obvious solution lies in the provincial department of education, which could keep some foreign affairs specialists on staff to prepare background information on crisis spots. These same specialists could also do longer analyses of long-standing world issues that would give teachers access to more up-to-date information about these questions than could possibly be found in a curriculum guide.

A program of this kind might be expensive. But when we realize that it will pay dividends in the form of citizens able to deal with international affairs in a more sophisticated and knowledgeable manner, we can see its true costs are minimal.

NOTES

1. H. Hyman, *Political Socialization* (Glencoe, Ill.: Free Press, 1959); F. Greenstein, *Children and Politics* (New Haven: Yale University Press, 1965); D. Easton and J. Dennis, *Children in the Political System* (New York: McGraw Hill, 1969); R. Dawson, K. Prewitt, and K. Dawson, *Political Socialization* (Boston: Little, Brown, 1977); W. Mishler, *Political Participation in Canada* (Toronto: Macmillan, 1979).

2. J. Piaget and A. Weil, "The Development in Children of the Idea of Homeland and of Relations with Other Countries," *International Social Science Bulletin* 3 (1951): 561–78.

3. G. Jahoda, "The Development of Children's Ideas About Country and Nationality (Part I)," *British Journal of Educational Psychology* 33 (1963): 47–60; (Part II), ibid., 143–53.

4. P. Cooper, "The Development of the Concept of War," *Journal of Peace Research* 2 (1965): 1–17; T. Alvik, "The Development of Views on Conflict, War, and Peace Among School Children," *Journal of Peace Research* 5 (1968): 171–95: L. Rosell, "Children's Views on War and Peace," *Journal of Peace Research* 5 (1968): 268–76; M. Haavelsrud, "Views on War and Peace Among Students in West Berlin Public Schools," *Journal of Peace Research* 7 (1970): 99–120; J. Ehly, "Images of Peace: A Comparative Study of Canadian, English, and American Children," in *Socialization and Values in Canadian Society*, edited by Zureik and Pike, vol. I (Toronto: McClelland and Stewart, 1975); D. Close, "Children's Views of World Conflict," *Peace Research* 15 (1983): 9–14.

5. A. Morrison, "Attitudes of Children to International Affairs," *Educational Research* 9 (1967): 197–208; H. Targ, "Children's Developing Orientations to International Politics," *Journal of Peace Research* 7 (1970): 79–98; J. Button, "Youth and Foreign Affairs," *Theory into Practice* 101 (1971): 346–55.

6. Targ, "Children's Developing Orientations to International Politics," 93.

7. Ibid., 95.

8. H. Tolley, *Children and War* (New York: Columbia Teachers College Press, 1973); B. Stacey, *Political Socialization in Western Society* (London: Edward Arnold, 1978).

9. D. Close, "Canadian Youth and the Cold War: Political Education and Perspectives on Global Conflict," in *Perspectives on Political Education in the 1980s*, edited by Bodnan and Gohring (Warsaw: International Political Science Association, Research Committee on Political Education, 1982); Close, "Children's Views of World Conflict"; D. Close, "Canadian Students and World Affairs," *Canadian Journal of Education* 9 (1984): 331–42.

10. Piaget and Weil, "The Development in Children of the Idea of Homeland and of Relations with Other Countries."

11. D. Easton and R. Hess, "The Child's Political World," *Midwest Journal of Political Science* 6 (1962): 229–46.

12. J. Torney, "The International Attitudes of Knowledge of Adolescents in Nine Countries: The IEA Civic Education Survey," *International Journal of Political Education* 1 (1977): 3–20; R. Jones, "National vs. International Learning: Political Knowledge and Interest in the USA," *International Journal of Political Education* 3 (1980): 33–48.

COMPREHENDING THE DANGER OF NUCLEAR WAR: THE ROLE OF EDUCATION

JOHN J. MITCHELL

> It is a fact of the greatest absurdity that we human beings threaten to exterminate ourselves with our own genocidal technology. One must never loose that sense of the absurdity, the madness, the insanity of it all........
> Robert Jay Lifton

At the very moment you read this sentence, the Soviet Union and the United States have thousands of nuclear missiles aimed at one another, awaiting only the command to be fired. If the command is issued, most of the people in Europe and North America will be dead within six hours. The danger of this situation is undeniably real—no one denies the existence of the weapons, no one denies their lethality, and no one denies that these missiles can be fired on command from halfway around the globe (or from satellites in space) in less time than it takes to warm the car on a cold winter day.

However, despite the ghastly danger posed by thousands of missiles being aimed at our cities, many people remain impervious to it. That is, it simply does not appear to them that they should worry about the danger, or, even more significantly, it does occur to them that they should try to reduce the danger. This paper attempts to explain some of the reasons why we *deny the reality of the nuclear world we have created.*

In this chapter, I will describe six reasons why we do not think about nuclear war, and why, when we do attempt to think about it, our thinking is often cloudy or faulty. These reasons include:

1. our inability to comprehend the physical destruction of nuclear war;
2. our inability to comprehend the *psychological* destruction that will be inflicted upon the survivors of a nuclear war;
3. our use of psychological mechanisms that deny the kill-power of nuclear weapons and that encourage us to accept them as a necessary fact of life;
4. our use of deceptions and falsehoods, that delude us into thinking that nuclear war will not be as bad as the experts say it will be;
5. our inability to comprehend mass-death; and
6. our inability to comprehend human extinction.

Each of these reasons contributes to our ignorance about the prospects of nuclear death.

INABILITY TO COMPREHEND THE PHYSICAL DESTRUCTION OF A NUCLEAR ATTACK

A twenty-megaton nuclear bomb detonated over Toronto would crush, incinerate, or vaporize every living creature within a five-mile radius of the blast. Most of the people living within a twenty-mile radius of the blast would die within seconds (if unprotected) or within hours (if protected by their home). "If the bomb exploded on the ground, countless others who live miles away, far beyond the reach of the initial blast and searing heat wave, would be sentenced to a lingering death as radioactive fallout drifted quietly down onto people, buildings, water and food supplies, and the earth itself."[1]

Brutal as this reads, in all probability the actual reality would be far worse because Toronto could be hit by two, three, four, or even five nuclear missiles. The Russians (like the Americans) have far more nuclear missiles than military *or* civilian targets at which to fire them. In 1987, the United States is building, or planning to build, 5 000 cruise missiles, each *one* of which has fifteen times the explosive power of the bomb that destroyed Hiroshima.[2]

A thermonuclear weapon is a holocaust of destruction. Upon detonation, a fireball is unleashed in which the temperature and pressure are about the same as those at the centre of the sun. The blast front moves out in a widening circle at supersonic speed, followed by high winds. "Within a two-mile radius of ground zero nothing can withstand this blast or the 500 mph winds that follow. Even at four miles, only the skeletons of buildings with steel-beam construction would remain, the following winds still having twice the velocity of a hurricane. Out to eight miles from the centre, large commercial buildings would be heavily damaged and all homes destroyed."[3] The most physically complex and structurally durable of all human creations—the modern city—crumbles in the wake of a thermonuclear explosion. Human beings, themselves, are simply vaporized.

A specialist in the study of the consequences of a nuclear attack describes *some* of the consequences which would accrue if a single one-megaton weapon exploded over Vancouver, B.C.

> After a nuclear explosion, Vancouver would be an inferno. Unfortunately, no firemen are going to be around because there is not going to be any water supply.... Essentially, about 400,000 people would be killed outright, and another 300,000 would be severely injured. Most of the latter would be dead within four weeks.... After a nuclear attack on Vancouver, there would be ten times as many severely burned patients as the total burn treatment capacity for North America.... About 70 percent of the doctors and nurses

would be dead or severely injured.... About five days after the attack, heavily exposed people would develop spontaneous bleeding throughout the skin, the internal organs and the brain...followed by death. Diseases like hepatitis, meningitis, pneumonia, and tuberculosis, which are reasonably uncommon now, would become epidemic.[4]

What damage would be inflicted on the people of Canada as the result of a nuclear attack? Based upon the best current data, the following seems reasonable:

In the Windsor, Ontario, to Quebec City axis, almost 55 percent of all Canadians live on 2 percent of the nation's land. A combination of urban centres, many nuclear reactors in both the United States and Ontario, and several other targets, make it clear *that in the event of a nuclear war this area would be devastated far beyond anything that has ever happened in any war, or any natural disaster, anywhere in the world in the history of mankind.*[5]

INABILITY TO COMPREHEND THE PSYCHOLOGICAL DESTRUCTION OF A NUCLEAR ATTACK

Disaster alters psychological functioning in a manner that is unbelievable to those who have not experienced it or observed it. Normal everyday skills (such as calculating the consequences of your actions, or solving simple problems) virtually disappear. The efficiency that characterizes ordinary behaviour is gone. Emotions disappear and are replaced with a zombie-like numbness. In severe disasters, the victims have no genuine sense of overcoming their tragedy because they cannot see beyond the despair and suffering of the moment. They envision only empty outlines of a vacant future. After the nuclear attack on Hiroshima, for example, "survivors not only expected that they too would soon die, they had a sense that *everyone* was dying, that the world was ending. Rather than panic, the scene was one of slow motion—of people moving gradually away from the center of destruction, but dully and almost without purpose."[6]

When horror is overpowering, the mind shuts down. Again, referring to the Hiroshima survivors, Lifton notes that there was "a closing off of the mind so that no more horror could enter it. People witnessed the most grotesque forms of death and dying all around them but felt nothing. A profound blandness and insensitivity...*seemed to take hold in everyone.*"[7]

As important as our knowledge is about how the survivors of Hiroshima and Nagasaki coped with their disaster, we must bear in mind that a future nuclear war will be far more devastating. Nuclear weapons today are a thousand times more powerful, and we have tens of thousands of them. Another important distinction exists. Hiroshima and Nagasaki were isolated disasters. The rest of the world was intact. The rest of Japan was intact.

Human resources, medical equipment, assistance at *every* level was available to these victims. In a future nuclear war *there will be no outside help*. There will be no one to help the survivors. There probably will not be anyone to bury the dead. The psychic disintegration will leave people in a condition for which no parallel exists in ordinary day-to-day life.

> The suddenness and the sheer ferocity of such a scene would not give survivors any chance to mobilize the usual forms of psychological defence. The normal human response to mass death and profound horror is not rage or depression or panic or mourning or even fear; it is a kind of mental anesthetization that interferes with both judgment and compassion for other people.[8]

It is important to remember that even in *minor* disasters, the mind becomes partly immobilized. But in a nuclear attack, the immobilization might be so severe that people might no longer even be connected to their own past, their own community, or to their previous patterns of behaviour. "The resulting scene might very well resemble what we usually can only imagine as science fiction. The landscape is almost moonlike, spare and quiet, and the survivors who root among the ruins seem to have lost contact with one another, not to mention the ability to form cooperating groups and to offer warmth and solace to the people around them."[9]

Interestingly, the leading authorities on nuclear warfare within the Soviet Union make similar predictions about the psychological impact of nuclear war. M. Vartanyan, Deputy Director of the Research Centre on Mental Health, U.S.S.R. Academy of Medical Sciences claims: "The direct [psychological] disorders caused by a nuclear attack include acute brain syndromes, protracted anxiety states, and reactive psychosis...." Furthermore, "It seems clear that the psychological reactions of survivors of a nuclear war will continue for months or years after the disaster." Vartanyan then goes on to comment:

> Let us assume...that approximately 20–25 percent of the urban population of European countries would survive a nuclear attack. *About one-third of the survivors would be in a state of acute anxiety. About 20 percent of the survivors would be so incapacitated by psychological and pathopsychological conditions that they would be unable to care for themselves or others.*

Vartanyan agrees with the majority of medical doctors who have ever examined this issue when he concludes: "...as doctors of medicine and scientists in health-related fields, we conclude that nuclear weapons are so destructive to human health and life that they must never be used. Prevention of nuclear war offers the *only possibility* for protecting people from its medical consequences. There is no alternative."[10]

A nuclear war will, in all probability, decimate "normal human behaviour." The cataclysmic physical destruction, coupled with the death of one's family and loved ones, will shatter those who remain. "Survivors will remain in a deadened state, either alone or among others like themselves, largely without hope and vaguely aware that everyone and everything that once mattered to them has been destroyed.... Virtually no survivors will be able to enact the most fundamental of all human rituals, burying their own dead."[11]

PSYCHOLOGICAL MECHANISMS THAT HELP US TOLERATE THE POSSIBILITY OF A NUCLEAR ATTACK

The reasons presented thus far for denying nuclear war pertain to what we *do or do not comprehend* about the consequences of nuclear war. These, however, are not the only reasons we deny the possibility of nuclear annihilation. In this section, we will examine several psychological mechanisms that yield three significant consequences. These mechanism cause us: to accommodate ourselves passively to the existence of nuclear weapons; to believe that nuclear weapons are necessary to protect us from the Russians; to become emotionally numbed to the human consequences of nuclear war.

ADAPTATION-HABITUATION

Many of us have simply grown accustomed to nuclear weapons. They have existed for so long, without accidental or intentional use, that they no longer seem a threat. Like the residents of Cougar, Washington, a sleepy hamlet at the base of Mt. St. Helens, we have adjusted ourselves to living with a volcano that may or may not explode. And, because it has not done so, we believe it will not.

An interesting corollary of our adaptation to the presence of nuclear weapons is that we also "get used" to our worry about them and our fear of them. That is, we become sufficiently accustomed to our own fearfulness that we can "put it on the back burner." Adaptation of this kind is not unusual. During the latter stages of the Vietnam War, for example, it was reported by U.S. fighter pilots that peasant rice farmers frequently continued working their plots while adjacent plots were being strafed or even bombed. We can become habituated to even the most hazardous situations, if exposed long enough.

SELECTIVE PERCEPTIONS ABOUT OUR ENEMIES (PARTICULARLY THE RUSSIANS)

Groups who oppose one another tend to view the other group as hostile, untrustworthy, and aggressive. In its most elemental form, Americans think that the Russians cannot be trusted and that, if they do not protect themselves, the Russians will destroy them. Conversely, the Russians do not trust the Americans, and believe that, if they do not "protect" themselves, the Americans will destroy them.

One of the most clear-cut demonstrations of this "mirror-image" fear can be obtained by reading two very important books. The first is titled *Soviet Military Power*.[12] It is released annually just before each U.S. budget, and it tells the reader how the Soviets are building and buying weapons at a furious pace. The second book is titled *Whence the Threat to Peace*[13] and it outlines how the U.S. is preparing for war. A former Assistant Chief of Naval Operations in the Pentagon says:

> It is very frightening to read these two books, to discover the degree of mutual fear that exists on both sides, and the resulting arms race that comes of it. The consequence of this is that in 1990 or 1992 we will simply have added to the nuclear arsenals on both sides, made them less stable and more destructive. We will be able to annihilate each other a few more times, but no one will prevail.[14]

Differences of opinion exist as to which side is right (or wrong) in these perceptions. Perhaps both sides are correct; perhaps either power would destroy the other if it were not militarily strong. Not everyone, however, thinks we should risk the major cities of the world on an idea that *may* prove to be true, or *may* prove to be false.

Ralph K. White, a leading authority on East-West relations, believes that many of the perceptions that Americans and Russians have of one another are false, and that they are grounded in fear:

> The "madness" that is carrying the world closer and closer to nuclear war has at its core a psychological explanation: Each side, though fundamentally afraid, misperceives the nature of the danger it faces. Each side imagines that it faces an inherently, implacably aggressive enemy when actually it faces an enemy as fearful as itself—an enemy driven mainly by fear to do the things that lead to war.[15]

Thus, we have the two great superpowers of this century hissing back and forth while, at the same time, perfectly aware that either could destroy the other on any given day. It calls to mind two scorpions in a bottle. If neither attacks, both will survive. If one attacks, the other retaliates, and both die. A stressful situation for the scorpions develops when one has to plot its strategy on the assumption that the other may attack at any time.

Research on conflict (whether between individuals or superpowers) yields some interesting findings. When participants define a conflict in terms of "win" or "lose," several consequences usually occur:

1. Communication is impaired, usually in the direction of increasing the amount of misinformation; also the probability of misperceiving what the "opponent" is saying increases. In *serious* conflict, the opposing parties rarely communicate effectively or honestly.

2. In serious conflict the opponents become increasingly suspicious of each other and are more inclined to believe the "unbelievable" about their opponent.

3. In serious conflict each party becomes increasingly attracted to the idea that the conflict can only be solved by the use of superior power. Whether the conflict occurs before a divorce court or before the United Nations, similar thinking about the "opponent" is likely to take place.

Misperceptions about the enemy sometimes lead to major errors. This is one reason military commanders frequently underestimate the enemy's capacity to endure unbearable conditions, two examples being Germany's failure to believe the Russians could hold on to Leningrad while surrounded for almost three years, and America's failure to believe that the North Vietnamese could endure unprecedented air bombardment.

Misperceptions of the enemy, however, have more disastrous consequences than mere intellectual error. They also encourage a fanatical hatred that may take self-destructive turns. Thus, at the beginning of World War I, the German Kaiser said, "Even if we are bled to death, England will at least lose India." In a similar vein, the Japanese war minister, upon ordering the attack on Pearl Harbor said, "Once in a while it is necessary to close one's eyes and jump from the stage of the Kiyomizo Temple [a Japanese means of suicide]."[16] Thus, one group is willing to take upon itself tremendous suffering and punishment if it will result in severe suffering and punishment for the enemy. A situation of even worse proportions occurs when the leaders of one country develop such an intense hatred for their enemy *that the desire to destroy them is greater even than their desire to stay alive.*

Would the commanders in the field, or under the sea, respond to the orders of leaders obsessed with vengeance or self-destruction? Most likely yes. For example, the commander of a Polaris submarine, when asked how it felt to shoulder the responsibility of firing missiles of such destructive power, replied: "I've never given it any thought, but if we ever have to hit, we'll hit and there won't be a second's hesitation."[17]

EMOTIONAL NUMBING

Because the *possibility* exists that nuclear war will kill us, we have learned to "numb" ourselves emotionally to this possibility. In all likelihood, a similar phenomenon occurred during the devastating plagues of the middle ages. An important difference exists, however. During the great plagues, people saw death daily. Today we do not see nuclear death. Rather, *we anticipate it.* The need for numbing, therefore, is most powerful among those who can envision the human destruction that would be caused by a nuclear war, and among those who believe that such a war could happen. Individuals preoccupied by their day-to-day worries, or who have given little thought to nuclear war, or who are, for whatever reasons, existentially impervious to it, are less emotionally in need of insulation than those who openly acknowledge and fear its lethality.

To insulate oneself against the fear of annihilation is not the only reason for emotional numbing. In addition to the egocentric fear of losing one's life, there exists *a moral revulsion* to the kind of mass murder and global extermination upon which nuclear attack is founded. Religious doctrine distinguishes between those wars that are justified and those that are not. Most individuals, whether schooled in religious doctrine or not, tend to believe the elemental principles of justice by which we assess the rightness or wrongness of war. But most concepts of a "just" (justifiable) war are distinctly *pre*nuclear. Traditional thoughts such as "the blood of a nation ought never to be shed except for its own preservation" seem not to apply to nuclear war because blood spilled in a nuclear war would result in the extermination, not the preservation, of a nation. Or the idea that "war can be justified only on that ground that is necessary for keeping peace" seems difficult to justify when the social fabric of a nation, over which peace is to prevail, has been destroyed. Finally, "the one thing a state can never lawfully do is this: it may not directly intend to kill the innocent." Nuclear attack of cities, however, is nothing less than the planned murder of innocents.

The confusion that bewilders the moral philosopher about nuclear war also burdens the average citizen. There seems to be no moral clarity, only ambiguity, and the human personality does not cope well with ambiguity of any kind. We prefer simply to avoid it. And, on the whole, that is exactly what we do. Emotional numbing is one way we do it.

DECEPTIONS AND FALSEHOODS THAT DENY THE CONSEQUENCES OF A NUCLEAR ATTACK

Few people think about nuclear annihilation in an objective manner. It is too fearful. In this section we will examine some of the deceptions and falsehoods we employ in order to avoid the fear and the anxiety created by "facing the facts" of nuclear war. Most of the ideas in this section are based upon the pioneer work of Robert Jay Lifton.[18]

THE DECEPTION OF LIMIT AND CONTROL

That is, if a nuclear war began, it would *somehow be controlled* before missiles were sent to incinerate the city in which I, or my loved ones, live. Somehow, the deception goes, the persons who ordered the missiles to their targets (each nuclear-tipped missile is computer programmed to strike a specific target) will change their minds after only five, or ten, or twenty cities have been destroyed. This *may* prove to be correct. No one knows. To *assume* that it will occur, however, defies everything we know about how military strategists behave in the face of either winning *or* losing a nuclear war.

Believing that a nuclear war will be limited is akin to the rationalizing of those Ukrainians in 1938 who believed that, when Hitler invaded Poland, they would not be affected because the war would "somehow be limited" to the invasion path. As we know, it was not limited. Over one million Ukrainians died.

THE DECEPTION OF PROTECTION

As Lifton writes,

> This is the idea that something we call "shelters" will live up to their name, again in willful disregard of such truths that, in a large-scale nuclear war, very few people would have the time or capacity to arrive at such shelters; once there, most would be incinerated in them; and those few who were still alive would emerge into a "dead world" of lethal radiation fallout.[19]

Shelters are pointless for *the vast percentage* of urban dwellers because everyone within three miles of the point on the ground directly beneath an atmospheric explosion

> will be killed regardless of whether [they] are in a shelter or not, by crushing injuries, burns, suffocation due to lack of oxygen, and by carbon monoxide poisoning.... To offer any chance for survival, shelters have got to be 200 feet underground, and of reinforced steel and concrete construction. They must have independent oxygen, water, and food supply sufficient to last for 6 to 15 months.[20]

The only such shelter in Canada is the "Diefenbunker," west of Ottawa, and it is reserved for federal officials.

Ironically, many individuals feel that the ultra-technology required to build and deliver nuclear weapons will, in fact, protect them from it. They have faith that technology is foolproof; and that the people in charge of the technology will always remain rational and level headed. They reason that technology and technicians will save us from a nuclear catastrophe. Not everyone buys this. David Suzuki points out that, "The difficulty is that the greatest risk for error is not technological but human. Humans get sick, stressed, and hungover, all of which affect their attention and their response. We are the 'fools' that technology attempts to anticipate. But history teaches that we can never anticipate how foolish humans can be."

THE DECEPTION OF STOIC BEHAVIOUR UNDER ATTACK

This deception suggests that, after a nuclear war, the survivors who are strong of character, disciplined, and "rugged" will make it. Self-discipline and organized behaviour, as we now think of them, will probably be non-existent among the survivors of a nuclear attack. "We anticipate in survivors psychic numbing so extreme that the mind would be shut down altogether."[21]

This deception is most deeply rooted among the young, the healthy, and the strong. Their life experience has taught them that they can overcome most obstacles, and that, in the long run, willpower prevails over any adversity. This practice of projecting the past onto the future will, in all probability, prove completely false after a nuclear attack. Most of those individuals who believe they could "pull themselves together" after a nuclear attack will be either psychotic or something closely resembling it.[22]

THE DECEPTION OF RECOVERY

Most of us believe that "somehow" after a nuclear war, we will be treated, helped, looked after. In all probability, this will not be the case. All thoughtful research indicates that the vast percentage of medical facilities will be destroyed and the doctors, nurses and technicians who staff them will be dead.

> In our systematic presentations of the overwhelming medical consequences of nuclear war, we have rejected outright the concept of medical contribution to recovery. The concept itself is more a product of prenuclear times and wars: the injured would be treated by doctors, who would do their duty and stay at their posts, healing all those who could be healed. Our message in the doctors' movement is, in effect: In a nuclear war, don't expect us to patch you up. You'll be dead and we'll be dead too. And whatever tiny bands of survivors might exist will, at least for a while, be at a stone-age level of struggle for the means of maintaining life, with little capacity either to heal or to be healed.[23]

The net effect of the foregoing is that we deceive ourselves about nuclear war. Our deceptions will probably not cause nuclear war, but they increase its chances because they prevent our thought patterns from responding to new dangers, new consequences of warfare, and new powers of destruction and annihilation. In essence, we are living in a "gap" between what is and what used to be, and we employ a wide variety of deceptions to ensure that climbing out of the gap will be difficult. Even more importantly, we employ deceptions to keep ourselves ignorant about the probable effects of nuclear war. We prefer ignorance because the price of knowledge is a brand of "nuclear anxiety" that is painful to bear. In a nutshell, we would rather deceive ourselves than confront a reality that is overpoweringly fearful.

REFUSAL TO BELIEVE IN MASS EXTERMINATION

Most North Americans refuse to believe that mass extermination could ever apply to themselves. They have virtually no first-hand experience with mass death. (The number of North Americans killed during World War I, World War II, the Korean War, and the war in Vietnam, if added together, would not equal the number of citizens massacred in the small country of Armenia in the single year of 1914.)

Mass exterminations, however, are a fact of the twentieth century, and they will be a fact of far greater magnitude if, or when, anyone ever fires nuclear missiles. Even though we have already witnessed mass extermination on an enormous and diverse scale in this century (the most reliable sources estimate there have been about 110 million "man-made" deaths in the first three-quarters of this century), the numbers are considerably less than those projected for even "limited" nuclear war.

For those readers whose knowledge of history is weak, or whose awareness of it has made their mind grow weary, it is worthwhile to reflect for a moment on some of the episodes of this century that resulted in mass deaths. The Turkish massacre of the Armenians in 1914, for example, resulted in the deaths of at least one million people; the Greco-Turkish War (1919–22) ended with half a million deaths; the Paraguay-Bolivia conflict (1928–35) resulted in half a million killed; the Indian Partition disorders, one million dead; the Nigerian Civil War (1967–69), one million dead; the Cambodian uprising (1975–78) two million dead. These disasters, devastating as they were to the countries involved, are classified among the smaller mass exterminations of this century.

Major episodes of mass death have also taken place throughout the twentieth century, the most dramatic of which include: the slaughter of the European Jews in the early 1940s during which approximately five million people, most of whom were women and children, were killed; and the First World War, for which conservative estimates place the number of dead at ten million. During World War II the Russians incurred ten million civilian deaths, and, in addition, the death of ten million soldiers; other deaths associated with World War II, fifteen million. The Revolution in China resulted in the death (conservative estimates) of twenty million people. Although precise records from previous centuries are not available, it is reasonable to assume that more people have been killed by their fellow human beings (or, more precisely, by hostile governments) during the twentieth century than in *any* previous century.

If the magnitude of these mass deaths could be embraced by the human mind—and it is doubtful they can be—their inexhaustible vastness would be equalled *in the first hour of a nuclear war*.

Elliot, who has compiled the most systematic analysis of mass deaths in the twentieth century, offers a comment that applies directly to our present theme: "It seems...that there is a limit to the extent to which the reality of large-scale violent death can be comprehended.... There is no doubt that this is difficult for the imagination to compute. After a certain stage in assimilating casualties, the rest seems an indigestible piling-on of horror and numbers."[24]

Multiplying one personal death by two million, or five million, or, if you use the numbers of nuclear war strategists, 200 to 300 million is beyond the capacity of the normal person and is another reason why we do not think about nuclear war.

INABILITY TO COMPREHEND OUR OWN EXTINCTION

If comprehending death on a mass scale is difficult for you and me, comprehending human extinction is even more difficult. It is precisely the issue of human extinction, however, that cannot be avoided when we think about nuclear war. It is a *fact* of military technology that, if the Soviets launch only half of their nuclear weapons and the United States does the same, the majority of human beings on this planet will die either from the nuclear explosions, from radiation, from disease, or be frozen to death in "nuclear winter." The concrete facts of nuclear technology force us to contemplate the most esoteric abstraction: this planet without human life, or (and for some this is even more difficult) this planet with sporadic pockets of human life clawing and scratching for survival much as in prehistoric times.

Joanna Macy summed it up rather well: "I especially find it hard to believe that after millions of years of the evolution of life on earth, after millenia of civilization, of spiritual and artistic geniuses, Shakespeares, Mozarts, Einsteins, we should come to this—that we should be developing and deploying instruments to blow up our world."[25]

Psychologists are novices at decoding the precise reasons why we cannot, or will not, picture our own extinction. Schell's statement seems as accurate as any: "It seems not to be given to human beings to hold great horrors unremittingly before their mind's eye, and particularly not when the beholder is...the potential perpetrator of the horror. We falter. We need respite. We forget. Then perhaps we look again. Alertness and stupor alternate. And we seem to lack any way of picturing extinction."[26] Our fear of extinction is one further reason why we do not think about nuclear war.

Thus, even though we find it difficult to envision our own extinction, the facts of technology, plus the facts of twentieth-century history, make the prospect of it uncomfortably real. The once remote *theoretical possibility* of human extinction is, for many individuals, growing into a gut-level fear. The vague disquietude, which formerly rumbled in the marrow of only an apprehensive few, has grown into an easily recognizable anxiety state. More and more people, and certainly not only those living within the Soviet Union or the United States, find themselves re-thinking Carl Sagan's lament: "What a waste it would be, if after four billion years of tortuous biological evolution, the dominant organism on the planet contrived its own annihilation."

IMPLICATIONS FOR EDUCATION

Educating young people *and* their parents about the possibility (*probability* is a better word) of nuclear annihilation is one of the pressing issues facing education in the late 1980s and early 1990s. It is pressing not only for the citizens of the Soviet Union and the United States, it is equally vital to the citizens of Canada, England, East and West Germany, for these countries will also be decimated in a war in which the superpowers fire only ten percent of their nuclear missiles.

How young people and their parents are to be educated is a matter for educators from different backgrounds, different moral and political viewpoints, and different degrees of fear about the nuclear situation to work out on their own. To expect a systematic, unified approach to this question is beyond any reasonable expectation. (After all, educators do not universally agree on such basic topics as the "3 R's," although virtually all educators agree that the "3 R's" are vital to any school program.) However, to think that the issue of nuclear annihilation can be *avoided* in the classroom is naive beyond justification.

Do young people become frightened when they learn that nuclear weapons have the power to destroy entire cities, even entire countries? Yes, they frequently do. Do children have nightmares about nuclear war? Some do. Most do not. Is there any reason why students in school should be burdened with the knowledge of the nuclear predicament we presently face?

One group of psychologists who investigated the impact upon children of learning about the possibility of nuclear disaster stumbled upon an interesting insight:

> Children know that we live in a scary and dangerous world; they want us to acknowledge that fact and their feelings about it, rather than to try to shield them. *When we give them the opportunity to share their deepest concerns, we find it is we adults who gain.* Clear-eyed and truthful, they can cut through our habitual defenses, our lethargy, and our political debates.[27]

Another group of investigators, who interviewed children in the Soviet Union, drew conclusions of special interest to educators:

> We learned that Soviet children, like American young children, are frightened about the nuclear threat. We learned that, far from teaching their young people that nuclear war can be fought and won, these children have been taught that there can be no meaningful survival after a nuclear war. We learned that it is possible to build upon trustful personal relationships between American and Soviet colleagues outside the political sphere to overcome stereotyping and to counter the effects of misinformation.[28]

It is fair to emphasize that, whether our hesitance to teach young people that their lives may end unexpectedly in a fire flash is based upon our love for them, our political beliefs, our fear of the enemy, or our general apathy, one thing is certain: if a nuclear war does occur—even a "small one"—most of the children in Canada will be killed, and they will not be here to ask what the particular reasons were that we did not prevent their extermination.

CONCLUSION

The unreal has not yet happened. Perhaps it never will. Then again, perhaps it will.

We frequently read that nuclear weapons have not been used in anger in over forty years. This, we are told, is encouraging. Forty years, or fifty years is commendable. But what is our time frame to be? Forty or fifty years is significant when measuring the life of a single person; when viewed within the time frame of history, or even that of our own civilization, it is much smaller. Perhaps the important point to remember is that, as far as human history is concerned, the unreal need only happen once.

We citizens generally hold great faith in our political and military leaders. We trust that they will not make the mistakes that will cause a nuclear holocaust. Ironically, we generally hold an equal faith in the political and military leaders of our "enemies." For whether they, or we, make the fateful error, the results for you and me will be the same. Therefore, it is the calm thinking of the Soviets as well as the Americans that each day determines the fate of the earth. When *either* side decides that the time has come for the missiles to be fired, that is the day that civilization dies.

Perhaps when enough individuals garner enough courage to face the nuclear situation honestly rather than with a series of cowardly deceptions, we will be able to create a world where the human future cannot be obliterated merely because a half dozen men in Washington or the Kremlin decide that, for some ideological reason, civilization has seen its last moment.

NOTES

1. T.L. Perry, ed., *The Prevention of Nuclear War* (Vancouver: Physicians for Social Responsibility, 1983).
2. E.J. Carroll, "Current Arsenals: The Balance of Terror," in *Nuclear War: The Search for Solutions* (Vancouver: Physicians for Social Responsibility, 1984), 47.
3. Perry, *The Prevention of Nuclear War.*
4. Ibid., 8–10.
5. D. Bates, D.P. Briskin, L. Cotton, M. McDonald, L. Panaro, and A. Polson, "What Would Happen to Canada in a Nuclear War?" in *Canada and the Nuclear Arms Race*, edited by E. Regehr and S. Rosenblum (Toronto: J. Lorimer and Co., 1983).
6. R.J. Lifton and R. Falk, *Indefensible Weapons: The Political and Psychological Case Against Nuclearism* (New York: Basic Books, 1982), 275.

7. Ibid.
8. Ibid., 276.
9. Ibid., 277.
10. M. Vartanyan, "The Psychiatric Consequences of Nuclear War Demand its Prevention" in *Nuclear War: The Search for Solutions* (Vancouver: Physicians for Social Responsibility, 1984). For a comprehensive statement of the medical and biological consequences of nuclear war, as understood by physicians within the Soviet Union, see Y.I. Chazov, *Nuclear War: The Medical and Biological Consequences: Soviet Physicians' Viewpoint* (Moscow: Novosti Publishing, 1984), 90.
11. Lifton and Falk, *Indefensible Weapons*, 278.
12. Published by the Secretary of Defense in the United States.
13. Published annually by the Soviet Minister of Defence.
14. Carroll, "Current Arsenals," 48.
15. R.K. White, *Fearful Warriors: A Psychological Profile of U.S.—Soviet Relations* (New York: Free Press, 1984), preface.
16. Jerome Frank, "Sociopsychological Aspects of the Nuclear Arms Race" in *Psychosocial Aspects of Nuclear Developments, Report of the Task Force on Psychosocial Aspects of Nuclear Development of the American Psychiatric Association* (American Psychiatric Association, 1982), 7.
17. Ibid., 4.
18. Lifton and Falk, *Indefensible Weapons*.
19. Ibid.
20. Perry, *The Prevention of Nuclear War*, 11.
21. Lifton and Falk, *Indefensible Weapons*, 19.
22. As pointed out earlier, the psychological condition of survivors of a nuclear war is a topic upon which Soviet, European, and North American psychiatrists and psychologists hold considerable agreement.
23. Lifton and Falk, *Indefensible Weapons*, 20.
24. G. Elliott, *Twentieth-Century Book of the Dead* (New York: Charles Scribner's Sons, 1972), 5.
25. J.R. Macy, *Despair and Personal Power in the Nuclear Age* (Philadelphia: New Society Publishers, 1983), 6.
26. J. Schell, *The Abolition* (New York: Alfred A. Knopf, 1984), 10.
27. B.F. Berger, "Children and the Threat of Nuclear War," *Therapy Now Journal* (Summer 1984).
28. J.E. Mack, "What Russian Children are Thinking About Nuclear Weapons," *The New Haven Register*, 19 Oct. 1983.

SECTION 7:
EDUCATION FOR THE EXCEPTIONAL CHILD IN CANADA

The education of the exceptional child in Canada has received widespread and heightened attention during the past fifteen years. We have become much more conscious of the need to provide equality of educational opportunity to all children regardless of their academic capacities. We have become more attuned to considering the needs of children who differ in their manner of coping with educational experiences and we have become more willing to modify school routines or programs in order to maximize each student's potential. The authors in this section address a number of educational and legal issues pertaining to pupils who are at both ends of the scholastic ability spectrum, from those who have mental and physical disabilities to those who may be defined as gifted.

Kysela, French, and Johnston provide an analysis of each province's legislative mandate for the provision of educational services for the handicapped, noting the permissive conditions that apply in some provinces and the mandatory conditions that exist in others. The implications of these provisions for the development and implementation of special education programs are noted and potential issues and concerns in the field are identified.

Gall, in a similar vein, discusses major issues arising from the current provision of special education services for the mentally retarded in Canada. Given the unique sociopolitical fabric of this nation, Gall argues that legislative reform is desirable and necessary so that greater federal co-ordination and financial support can be utilized to provide appropriate educational strategies for special needs children.

The chapter by O'Neill reflects the growing recognition of the responsibility of educators to provide special programs to fulfill the psychological, educational, occupational, and social needs of gifted and talented students. After explaining definitions and identification procedures used in this area of special education, he discusses the goals, implementation, and operationalization of educational programs that he feels are so vital for the optimal development of the gifted student. To O'Neill, the challenge to schools and teachers is to become involved in initiating and continuing to support special programs for the gifted until such programs are a part of every school system in Canada, regardless of size.

LEGISLATION AND POLICY INVOLVING SPECIAL EDUCATION

G.M. KYSELA, F. FRENCH, AND J. JOHNSTON

INTRODUCTION

Educational matters have been traditionally left to provincial jurisdictions in Canada, particularly with respect to the issues of educational principles, policy, regulations, and specific service provisions. Even though the Bill of Rights passed in 1958 by the Diefenbaker government guaranteed specific rights to individuals within Canadian federal jurisdiction, specific provincial statutes or regulations were seldom challenged on the basis of equal opportunities or experiences. However, since that time, a number of legislative, litigative, and social factors have brought this disparity to the attention of lawmakers and the public.

These factors have been particularly focussed, in part, upon the educational experiences of those persons in our society with exceptional or handicapping conditions such as mental handicaps, behavioural adjustment problems, and physical handicaps. Most notably, during the past fifteen years, the Commission on Children with Emotional and Learning Disorders in Canada, Public Law 94–142 in the United States, the Warnock Commission in the United Kingdom, and more generally, the human rights movement in North America, have each provided either legislative or policy changes affecting the educational experiences of exceptional persons. In this chapter, we will focus on the impact of these developments upon the schooling of exceptional children.

It was increasingly recognized in the 1960s that exceptional children were experiencing de facto segregation and exclusion from normal schooling experiences because of the "special environment" institutions provided for their education. Although these provisions were made with the best intentions, under the assumption that similar handicapping conditions in some way resulted in similar educational needs, it was realized that neither the exceptional person nor the other members of our communities were benefitting from this exclusionary process. That is, the exceptional child was completing school without the requisite competencies to function in our communities, and was often unable to read, write, compute, or perform the other academic skills presumably being taught in their segregated schools and institutions.

Respecting the conditions mentioned above, the definition of exceptionalities adopted in this paper includes the following description: the educationally exceptional child is thought of as any child who differs in her or his manner of coping with educational experiences to such an extent as to require modification of typical school routine, program, or practices in order for the child to have maximum opportunity for successful development.

This notion of exceptionality encompasses a wide variety of children with varying degrees and kinds of disabilities. The idea of the school routine requiring adjustment to suit the dynamic needs of each exceptional child[1] provides an initial basis for the special education requirements the school must meet. These children have many needs and strengths common to the majority of children as well as unique needs and strengths relative to their exceptionality. It is now generally accepted that both types of educational needs must be addressed by the educational system. Such an undertaking requires alterations in the typical functioning of the school related to the policy, legislation, and regulations affecting the provision of these educational experiences.

In attempting to meet the children's special needs, schools have extended services to handicapped children through local special programs, integrated learning experiences, and more functional, community-oriented programs of study. In addition, the provinces and the country as a whole have gradually altered statutes of educational relevance in order to provide legislative and regulatory provisions to ensure that the handicapped child will be able to gain access to these special programs on a continuing basis. A major change, in this regard, occurred with the passage into law of the Canadian Constitution and its attendant Charter of Rights in 1982.

THE CONSTITUTION AND PROVINCIAL LEGISLATION

As mentioned earlier, the federal government does not have direct authority regarding the provision of educational experiences to children as is the case in other nations. In the past, however, federal agencies and national organizations such as the Department of Health and Welfare, the Canadian Council for Exceptional Children, and the National Institute on Mental Retardation have provided task force reports, information, and recommendations to the provinces regarding provisions for exceptional children. These groups have also been influential within *some* provinces with respect to the development of innovative legislation.

In 1982, following repeated federal-provincial conferences, the Charter of Rights and Freedoms was passed by the Parliament of Canada. Although not pertaining exclusively to education for exceptional persons, the Charter does specifically outline some basic rights to equality of opportunity for persons with mental or physical handicaps in all provinces and territories of the country. That is, if handicapped individuals or their advocate feel that these rights and freedoms have been infringed upon or neglected, they have the right to appeal to the courts for a ruling to uphold these new provisions of equality.

Although most of the Constitution Act was implemented in 1982, some clauses regarding the Charter of Rights and Freedoms did not come into effect until April 1985. The supposition was that, by that date, each province would bring legislation to a level consistent with the specified rights for all persons, including the handicapped.

In one respect, the Charter of Rights speaks directly to the issue of being handicapped by suggesting that the handicapped require special provisions to ensure that discrimination does not take place. The Charter further states that the law will "allow for the establishment of special programs designed to promote opportunities for the disabled, and will make certain these kinds of programs will be upheld by Canadian law."[2] The use of the phrase "allow for" makes this statement permissive, as opposed to mandatory. The development of special programs is endorsed, but is not insisted upon. Thus, it is unclear exactly what circumstances would arise in which a legal ruling could be made on the basis of this statement alone.

In section 15, the section of the Charter that has the most relevance to special education, the final clause to come into effect, dealing with equality rights, states the following:

> Every individual is equal before and under the law without discrimination based on race, national or ethnic origin, colour, religion, sex, age, or mental or physical disability.

The educational implication of this statement is that all individuals have a right to equivalent educational provisions. Therefore, school acts may no longer make exceptions with respect to the services provided. Furthermore, these services are required to meet each child's unique needs. Thus, to exclude a child from attaining an education that is afforded to every other (non-handicapped) child would discriminate against that child on the basis of mental and/or physical disability. It implies that "equal protection" exists that precludes public funds being spent on some children while refusing the same expenditures for others. This federal statute then holds major implications for provincial legislation regarding special education.

PRECEDENTS FROM OTHER NATIONS

Within the past decade, influences from two major nations have had a significant impact upon Canadian legislation and practice in the field of education of exceptional children. First, in 1975, the U.S. Congress passed Public Law 94-142, the precedent-setting legislation described as the Education for All Handicapped Children Act. From the United Kingdom, the

Warnock Report had a similar, although not a legislative, effect upon services in that country.[3] With respect to the United States, PL 94-142 required the provision of educational services to all children within the least restrictive environment. Thus, although mainstreaming or integration of exceptional children with their non-handicapped peers was not mandatory, this process became more typical of educational provisions for these children. As well, the law prescribed services to such a specific extent, including the use of Individual Educational Programs for each child, that litigation in the courts was an available and clear option when parents or advocates of the handicapped perceived that a child's needs were not being met in terms of the provisions of the act.

The specific impact of the law upon state and local school jurisdictions included not only special educational services to the handicapped children in their charge but also such activities as due process safeguards for appeals, parental consultation and involvement procedures, and evaluative mechanisms.[4] Indeed, the act includes specific provisions for even the most severely and profoundly handicapped children, a population that previously had been all but ignored educationally and placed within institutions far removed from the mainstream of the community. This national commitment to exceptional children has had a major effect upon Canadian law and practice. These changes are due to international co-operative lobbying activities, to Canadian national and regional projects, and to the initiatives discussed below.

Almost simultaneously, the Warnock Report in Great Britain brought attention in that country to the educational inequities experienced by disenfranchised persons with handicaps. The impact of this report has apparently been lessened by the revised education act of the early 1980s, but it did highlight three fundamental areas of need in the country: the provision of education to handicapped children under five years of age; an emphasis upon vocational and community living skills for persons in their teens; and a revision of teacher preparation programs for special education personnel.[5] Thus, the emphasis upon provision of adequate educational experiences at the local level was heightened, as was the need for adequately prepared professionals to deal with the exceptional conditions handicapped children presented when attending community schools.

THE LOGIC OF MANDATORY LEGISLATION

Each of these influences had a significant impact upon thinking and practice across Canada, although the effects were quite dissimilar in the various jurisdictions. Well in advance of these developments, Canadian provinces had been attempting, to a certain degree, to take up the challenge of community-based educational programs. The basic premise of these changes is that all children, regardless of their exceptional needs or handicaps, have the right to remain within their local school jurisdiction and to learn the skills and competencies necessary to live a satisfying life, in so far as is possible. This concept includes such philosophical positions as "normalization" proposed by Wolfensberger,[6] the concept of integration within the least restrictive school environment, and the right to an adequate, appropriate education. Although this notion may seem to be self-evident to some, the handicapped persons in our communities have consistently been denied these opportunities in the past. Only the influence of very powerful lobby groups in some parts of Canada has prevailed over the traditional practice of segregation of school and living for handicapped, particularly more severely handicapped persons.

In the remainder of the article, we will provide an analysis of each province's legislative mandates for education of the handicapped, examining first the permissive conditions which exist in some provinces and the mandatory provisions of others. In the last section of the article, the implications of these legislative provisions will be examined in terms of policy and regulations arising from these statutes as well as a number of specific service issues affecting program development and implementation in special education. Finally, some new directions will be previewed in terms of potential issues to be aware of during the next several years.

PROVINCIAL LEGISLATION

With respect to the provision of appropriate public education to exceptional children, the Canadian provinces differ quite dramatically from each other. Some provinces mandate, through legislation, special education services to all exceptional children, while others are permissive in their legal statutes, in the sense of permitting provision of special programs without requiring local school authorities to supply such services. Each of the ten provinces and two territories do make some legislative statement entitling children between specific ages to attend school. However, this provision is frequently phrased in such a manner as to focus on compulsory school attendance rather than on the right of each child to obtain an education. Thus, the onus is upon the child's parents or guardians to ensure that the child attends school in the face of legal consequences. However, many provinces that make school attendance mandatory include an "escape clause," which specifies that the minister of education may excuse some individuals from attendance for unspecified reasons. Thus, provisions for special education could be avoided legally in these jurisdictions, although this practice is infrequently invoked at this time.

PROVINCES WITH PERMISSIVE LEGISLATION

Several provinces in Canada have still to revise their School Acts to insure, through the law, that all children, especially the handicapped, have access to equal educational opportunities. Prince Edward Island, New Brunswick, Alberta, British Columbia, the Northwest Territories, and the Yukon were included in this group as of April 1985. These provinces thus have in common the absence of mandatory provisions for the education of the handicapped in the "least restrictive environments" within their school jurisdictions.

Prince Edward Island's legislation, for example, makes no mention of specific groups that might require special education. Although special educational programs are in existence within P.E.I. for various groups of handicapped children, these programs have not grown from the legal mandates of the School Act.

The School Act in New Brunswick only "enables" school boards to organize special education services if these boards so desire. The Auxiliary Classes Act contains regulations of a much more specific nature, pertaining exclusively to the mentally handicapped or cerebral palsied child and the education of aurally and visually handicapped children. Consequently, more extensive services are available for these groups of children who tend to be more severely handicapped, although these services may be in "segregated settings," as opposed to integrated classrooms or schools. Children with milder handicapping conditions of mental, learning, and/or behavioural origins are not served as adequately. The directors of special education for the province have stated that individuals in these latter groups often remain on waiting lists for services.[7]

The School Act of Alberta similarly allows school boards to provide services to handicapped students; it does not, however, guarantee these provisions. There is no mention of the appropriateness of education to meet students' special needs. Also, no specialized teacher preparation is required for personnel providing special education programs to handicapped students. Currently, the province does provide a variety of special education programs both through local boards and government funding. The special service provisions are possible through a per pupil grant to each system amounting to $135.00 per child in the school division. However, if these funds become less abundant than is the case at present, financial support for these programs could be withdrawn, and parents would have little recourse via existing legislation. As well the value each jurisdiction places upon services will determine the extent and quality of services offered to pupils with special needs. At this time, Alberta is revising its School Act with specific attention to these aspects of the legislation. Hopefully, the result will be mandatory provision of services to these exceptional children.

The province of British Columbia amended its Public Schools Act in 1958 to include school accommodation and free tuition for *all* children between the ages of six and nineteen. However, "all children" in this context referred to all those students who could function adequately with the curriculum offered. To date, the province's legislation does not guarantee appropriate educational rights to *all* children. Present legislation does address the provision of educational programs for children with learning handicaps, but it is permissive in this regard. As with the provinces previously discussed, British

Columbia school boards offer numerous effective special programs, but these developments reflect local conditions and concerns rather than current legislative support and mandate. As a result, there is an absence of any effective accountability system to ensure special education programs.[8]

Within the Northwest Territories, all education was the responsibility of the federal government until 1969. In that year, a Territorial Department of Education was formed to provide educational services to the children resident there. In 1977, a revision to the Education Ordinance provided legislative support for school authorities, by giving approval to special education programs assisting students who could not be served by regular educational programs. However, essential specifics were neglected, including eligibility criteria for such programs, the types of programs to be provided, and a mechanism for the allocation of funds for support. In the absence of these policy guidelines, the existing legislation is rather ineffective.

The territory has recognized its need for greater special education provisions and has emphasized the importance of children receiving educational assistance as close to their home communities as possible. Unlike other provinces in Canada, the territory must battle problems associated with a sparsely populated jurisdiction having many transient residents and frequent cultural conflicts. Attempts are being made to meet the students' needs as qualified personnel and resources become available.

The Yukon shares many of the basic characteristics of the Northwest Territories; its legislation makes only vague reference to special education services. As such, the law constitutes only enabling legislation. Currently, the Yukon is attempting to provide mainstream programs for children requiring special assistance. Given the lack of adequately qualified regular classroom teachers, however, it seems unlikely that an appropriate educational program will be developed for the exceptional child at this time. The territory is attempting to overcome this difficulty through the provision of relevant in-service training for the classroom teacher. Nonetheless, present legislation does not yet address these issues, leaving current new directions in special education provisions to the discretion of local authorities.

The preceding section has dealt with provinces and territories of Canada that provide special education to a greater or lesser degree without the impetus of mandatory legislation ensuring the future provision of these services. The most certain means to ensure the provision of services to meet the special needs of exceptional students is to entrench the policy and beliefs that are the foundation of special education within legislation. This provision would effectively guarantee that *all* children are provided with a free, appropriate education relative to their individual needs. Without this guarantee, special services remain dependent upon government officials attending to these needs on the basis of good conscience, benevolence, and perceived concerns of their constituents.

If funding becomes increasingly scarce, or belief systems change drastically, the provision of these services could easily be threatened. The provisions of the Charter of Rights and Freedoms raise some substantial concerns in this regard. Are children with special needs in these jurisdictions receiving educational provisions consistent with the equality section in the Charter of Rights? Before attempting to address this question, it should prove instructive to examine legislation regarding special education in the rest of the country.

PROVINCES WITH MANDATORY LEGISLATION

As early as 1971, four years before the passage of Public Law 94-142 in the United States, section 122 of Saskatchewan's School Act delineated the right of all handicapped children to an appropriate and public education, and included specific definitions for the term "handicapped." These definitions of the term were essential for determining both eligibility and appropriateness for judicious funding allocations. The Education Act of 1978 further asserted that a board of education should ensure provision of such services by staff with special training. Teachers within programs receiving special funding were required to have specific qualifications (acceptable to the Department of Education) by September of 1981.

In this way, the province was attempting to make sure that the mandated "appropriate" education was indeed possible. The act also made clear that school boards could not exclude pupils from school without making some alternative service available. Parents or guardians are now able to appeal designations of their child's condition or placement decisions regarding programs for their child through written appeal to regional superintendents of education. Following the first recourse, an appeal committee can make a binding decision. In these ways, Saskatchewan has attempted to anticipate difficulties in these areas and has implemented legislation to avoid unnecessary confusion and misinterpretation of existing legislation.

In 1967, the province of Manitoba passed specific legislation regarding the education of mentally handicapped ("retarded") pupils. Prior to that time, school boards were only required to offer instruction to pupils for grades 1 through 12. Advancing beyond this legislation in 1976, Bill 58, which paralleled Saskatchewan's legislation, was introduced. This statute amended the Public School Act, making appropriate educational alternatives for all handicapped students resident in the province mandatory. In addition, this legislation recognized that "special class" teachers should have a special education certificate in order to teach children requring special programs. Like Saskatchewan, Manitoba was taking steps to ensure optimal appropriate education for each child.

Largely influenced by Saskatchewan's legislation and the American Public Law 94-142, Ontario introduced Bill 82, otherwise titled "The Amended

Education Act, 1980." This bill guarantees an appropriate education to all children between the ages of six and twenty-one, with the mandatory provision of special education services by September 1985.

In the past, these special services were provided on a voluntary basis through local school boards. The formation of Identification, Placement, and Review Committees was mandated through the act to make appropriate eligibility evaluations, placement decisions, and program assessments on behalf of the student. Parental involvement was ensured through these I.P.R. committees, and through the availability of a Special Education Appeals Board. Parents were given a seat at the placement and review case conferences, and the right to appeal to the S.E.A.B. if they disagreed with decisions of the committee or the school personnel. Unlike Saskatchewan or Manitoba, however, Ontario's act does not make any specific statements regarding teacher preparation or qualifications for special education.

In 1978 the Charter of Personal Rights and Liberties (Bill 9) was passed by the Quebec National Assembly. This charter ensured the right of handicapped persons to obtain equitable services and community living experiences. The eleven member "Office des personnes handicappes du Quebec" was established to ensure that these rights were not violated. The Office was to co-ordinate the services provided for the handicapped, inform and advise handicapped persons, promote their interests, and facilitate their educational, vocational, and social integration.

In 1979, the government of Quebec, employing this legislation as a policy foundation, established the principle requiring school boards to provide appropriate education for all school-age children residing in the school district. The policy also emphasized the importance of early preventive measures in special education. Schooling was extended to the age of twenty-one for those pupils requiring extra education, and instruction was to be given in as normal a setting as possible. The Quebec government's Charter was very extensive, sharing the same basic premise as the more recent federal Charter. That is, it explicitly described the necessary modifications required to prevent discrimination against the handicapped. As with Ontario, however, there are no specific recommendations regarding teacher preparation or qualifications for employment within the special education field.

Interestingly, Nova Scotia was the first province in Canada to introduce mandatory legislation within the field of special education. The Education Act of 1973 directed school boards to be responsible for the instruction of physically and mentally handicapped students between the ages of five and twenty-one. Transportation was assured free of charge to the family/school district. Similar to Quebec's legislation, a Public Building Access Act guaranteed that school buildings would be accessible to handicapped students. Thus, discrimination based upon an individual student's handicapping condition would be reduced. The provision for parental involvement was also a component of Nova Scotia's legislation, similar to that in force in Ontario and Saskatchewan.

In 1979, the province of Newfoundland altered previously permissive legislation to mandatory status with the revision of its School Act. Through this revision, all school boards were required to provide appropriate educational programs or alternative arrangements for all categories of exceptional students. As in the Saskatchewan act, no child was to be denied access to an education by being excused from compulsory attendance. In addition, all school buildings were required to be adapted for free and easy access. This aspect was similar to Quebec's and Nova Scotia's regulations. The new provincial regulations also identified the need for early intervention programs to prevent more serious handicaps that can emerge in the absence of early diagnosis and remediation.

From this abbreviated review of the legislation of those provinces mandating special education services for exceptional children, it appears that the requirements of the federal Charter of Rights and Freedoms are adequately met. That is, it seems that all of these provinces are in agreement with the equality section of the Charter supporting the statement that *all* children *must* be provided with educational services suited to their needs and handicaps.

Several points of contention between the provincial statutes and the federal Charter arise regarding the definition of such terms as "appropriate" and "normal setting," and underlying assumptions regarding the nature of equality of services. As well, there are inconsistencies as to the specifications of teacher qualifications, the extent of parental involvement in assessment and placement, and the provision of appeal structures or due process arrangements. These issues will have to be addressed in the future as each province comes to grips with the specific needs of its students in terms of the Charter's mandate for equal opportunities within the mainstream of our society.

FEATURES COMMON TO ALL PROVINCES

Despite the various legislative and policy differences among the Canadian provinces, certain similarities—both positive and less beneficial—do exist. From the positive standpoint, all the provinces have developed extensive services for exceptional children as well as the fiscal and regulatory structures to support these services. There are large discrepancies between the various provinces regarding the nature and scope of services, but each province and territory has striven to meet as many children's needs as possible. Particular areas of emphasis have included schools and programs for students with physical and mental handicaps; in many provinces these services have been provided within segregated schools or separate classrooms but, nonetheless, have been funded through the public purse.

Children with impairment in hearing, vision, or both have also received extensive recognition and service. For example, many provinces have schools for the deaf that are designed to provide residential educational experiences for children with hearing impairment. Although these schools are being replaced, to a certain extent, by programs within local school jurisdictions, many educators still feel they provide an appropriate social and educational milieu for the severely or profoundly hearing-impaired child.[9]

Finally, many provinces have developed a variety of detection, assessment, and educational services for children with "learning disabilities" within school systems and within some children's hospital programs. In the last fifteen years, these services have become more extensive and more sophisticated, identifying more children with learning disorders and providing more effective remedial programs. Thus, in each of these fields, similarities exist between various provincially-funded programs and the fiscal arrangements necessary to support them.

A second area of similarity among many of the provinces is the identification of specific sets of characteristics that make various sub-groups of children appropriate candidates for special educational programs. Often, these "operational definitions" of special needs and conditions are entrenched within provincial regulations or guidelines. This lends an appearance of stability to the provision of the services; however the absence of overarching legislation supporting the need for service to these children may result in the deletion of programs in times of financial restraint. Funding may be based on whim or prejudice rather than on supporting programs where definite needs exist, even when the group with those needs does not have strong advocacy support.

Few provinces require personnel working with children with special needs to have or obtain appropriate preparation. Most believe that the generalist can handle the special needs of these children. It may seem logically sufficient, but there is substantial literature that supports the notion of giving teachers and school personnel working with exceptional children special training in areas such as assessment of educational needs, program planning, remedial instruction, and modest skills in evaluating the impact of their educational programs on the development and well-being of their pupils. This need was recognized in the early 1970s by the CELDIC commission, but has largely gone unheeded since that time.

In another area, few provinces have developed adequate opportunities for post-secondary educational and vocational preparation. Where these opportunities do exist, they vary from locale to locale. Many private organizations provide sheltered workshop experience, but few community colleges, vocational/technological training centres, or universities provide programs that integrate the exceptional student into the advanced educational network. This lack of a continuum of educational opportunities has kept the student with special needs out of the mainstream of education following secondary school, and often out of the vocational mainstream when the student reaches adulthood.

Finally, only minimal provision seems to exist for support for the transition from secondary schools into the community, both vocationally and residentially. Few provinces have actively addressed this problem, either in terms of social skills and adjustment, community living skills, or vocational/occupational competencies necessary to earn a living in the marketplace. At this time, new developments in this are being pursued, but these efforts are specific to one or two institutions, and do not represent a groundswell of development across the country.

In summary then, despite differences between provinces with respect to legislative and policy developments, some similarities do exist in provision of services and supporting financial arrangements as well as in various inadequacies in the field. Often, however, these problems have been the result of unclear legislation and the lack of a policy with an adequate philosophical basis. This philosophical foundation is required to eliminate these inadequacies so far as possible without mandatory legislation.

The last section of this article will attempt to identify policy and policy issues that could stem from effective mandatory legislation. Components necessary for the provision of appropriate special education services will also be discussed in reference to the student remaining within the mainstream of community living and learning.

POLICY DEVELOPMENT AND SERVICE DELIVERY ISSUES

In the introduction to this paper, several major issues were identified that form the basic premise of the provision of special education services to students in Canadian schools. Such premises as the right to life experiences commensurate both with their peers' and with social standards usually form the basis for mandatory legislation. The presence of such legislation makes possible associated policies and regulations that specifically endorse *and* ensure educational programs for students with special needs or handicapping conditions. In this section, the philosophical issues associated with these policies will be briefly examined. Following this is a description of these major policy areas and a service delivery model outlining the steps necessary to provide integration of exceptional students within our schools and communities. The final area to be discussed is new directions identified through these policy areas and the service provision model.

PHILOSOPHICAL BASIS FOR POLICY DEVELOPMENT

The Charter of Rights and Freedoms and mandatory provincial legislation helped educators focus upon the provision of services to *all* children. However, the problem issues discussed under provincial legislation have existed for some time. In attempts to solve these problems, advocacy groups, provincial government departments, school jurisdictions, and teacher preparation personnel have worked towards the indentification of a variety of models to facilitate the delivery of effective and efficient services to all students. It is towards this goal of service delivery that the model below is directed.

A number of previous authors have attempted to describe the contributing factors that facilitate effective and efficient program and service delivery systems. For example, Karnes and Lee[10] and Bryan and Bryan[11] both focussed on teaching techniques of modelling (observational learning) to encourage more appropriate learning behaviours with students having mental handicaps. Yoshida and Gottlieb[12] have also studied the individualized program planning process often touted as an effective means of ensuring adequate school experiences for exceptional students. Maher[13] examined models for evaluating organizational effectiveness, and found no generally accepted conceptualization that would assist in evaluating special educational services.

Perhaps part of the difficulty in identifying an acceptable model stems from examining the specifics before first considering the fundamental principles. Consideration of these principles may facilitate an understanding of the necessary components supporting the effective design, delivery, and evaluation of special programs and services. As well, consideration of fundamental principles should make it easier to understand the reasons for assigning specific roles and responsibilities to the various partners in the educational process.

Conceptually and pragmatically, the most fundamental belief involves the child as the *raison d'être* for all educational programs and services, including those for exceptional students. Given this child-centred focus, the principle of natural justice becomes the major overarching principle in the provision of education to children with special needs. Section 7 of the Charter of Rights and Freedoms uses the phrase "fundamental principles of justice" with its intent appearing to equate these principles with natural justice and "procedural requirements of fairness."

While some doubt exists regarding the exact definition and meaning of natural justice, section 7 supports an existing *right* to schooling and introduces the issue of procedural fairness. It may be that the most direct application of this section is in the areas of suspension and expulsion. However, the areas of program planning and placement, particularly the placement of exceptional students, may well hold equal or greater application.

Program planning and placement decisions appear to require a set of safeguards, so that decisions are not only followed but are perceived to have been derived from a clear, reasoned, objective, and well-explained process that evolved from the informed participation of the persons affected by the educational decision (e.g., parents, student, teachers, etc.). Indeed, students, particularly past the age of twelve, should be partners in the educational decision-making process themselves. Thus the notion of the right to education as embodied in the Charter would appear to require the involvement of students in decisions that affect them.

Another fundamental principle at the centre of the service delivery model includes identifying the ethical considerations in the decision-making process, relevant to the practice of teaching and the practice of school psychology. For example, many provincial psychology statutes describe, in the code of ethics attendant to the act, the ethical stance required to assit the psychologist in the designation of the client. While this process may be clear in the case of a private practitioner dealing with an adult client, the situation is more complicated for a school psychologist employed by a local school jurisdiction involved with clients legally considered "minors." Conflicting views of appropriate professional behaviour are possible, both in the determination of who the actual client is (e.g., the school, the parent, or the child) as well as in the determination of what information should be considered confidential. Kimmins, Hunter, and Mackay[14] have referred to this dilemma in their review of provincial legislation and litigation regarding the practice of school psychology in Canada.

Other principles forming the philosophical bases of any service provision model include the following areas: teacher preparation and qualifications; the provision of due process for review of placement decisions (i.e., an appeal procedure for parents or advocates); administrative, fiscal, and governance support to school systems in the provision of special educational programs.[15] With regard to teacher preparation and standards of qualification, personnel involved with exceptional students should possess the requisite skills and knowledge in order to meet the students' special needs, whether in the areas of assessment, program planning, or program provision. This requirement extends from infancy and early childhood through the developmental stages to early adulthood and the transition into community living. This principle and its attendant policy require attention by almost all jurisdictions in Canada, as the foregoing review of legislation indicated.

The provision of due process or appeal procedures by independent persons for the parent, child, or advocate, ensures their access to the decision-making process. In this way, an attempt is made to maintain the notion of natural justice (vis-à-vis the child's peers and accepted social standards) regarding placement and program decisions. Some may argue that this is unnecessary in Canada, but the very fact that persons with handicaps have continued to experience inequitable treatment, and that provinces vary regarding statutory provisions, *requires* the provision of these safeguards for the student. Finally, the provision of administrative, fiscal, and governance support for special programs provides the vehicles for actually ensuring the provision of services to all students within a jurisdiction. At both the legislative and the policy levels, these provisions will assist school jurisdictions in identifying the means by which to provide special education for exceptional students.

By way of summary, then, the fundamental principles of natural justice, ethical considerations, teacher preparation, provision of appeal process, and administrative and fiscal support are interconnected with federal and provincial legislation, regulation, and policy. Each of these provisions in turn has an impact upon the design, delivery, and evaluation of special education programs and services. Further, these principles and policies influence the roles and responsibilities held by and/or assigned to the partners in the educational decision-making process.

PROGRAM DEVELOPMENT AND IMPLEMENTATION ISSUES

The design, delivery, and evaluation of special education programs can be examined from a molecular viewpoint pertaining to program planning for the child, or as a molar issue pertaining to the provision of programs throughout a school system. Within either analysis, however, a set of hierarchical activities exist in a sequence. These activities move from information gathering and assessment regarding the student and the services available, through information synthesis and program planning to the identification and assignment of resources, followed by program placement and implementation, monitoring, and evaluation.[16] The process provides for feedback, in that the monitoring and evaluation functions lead back to more information gathering and subsequent possible program modifications and changes in placement. For each of these four stages, overarching principles or policies exist that guide actions and determine specific roles and responsibilities of the various partners.

Within this framework, it is necessary to consider a "process approach" to the analysis rather than to identify a single outcome in order to ensure that the principles of natural justice have been followed. This approach is recommended, since the special needs of exceptional students require specific recognition and planning rather than a single solution. Further, it is proposed that a program-planning and decision-making process for both the child and the system will be more effective in meeting student needs than choosing placement options based upon a categorical label of exceptionality. The program-planning approach removes the necessity of using labels to describe student needs. Rather, each student is viewed as an individual with particular strengths and needs requiring attention in program selection and implementation. A brief consideration of each of these four planning phases will now be pursued, including a description of policy issues associated with each step of the process.

Assessment and Information Gathering

At the system or school jurisdiction level, the decision-making process involves setting policies, guidelines, and procedures to ensure early referral for concerns regarding student progress. Such procedures have been perceived by local school jurisdictions as their responsibility, backed up by provincial support.[17] Further, it is proposed that such procedures are more effective when supported by specific referral instruments that document, clarify, and operationalize the reason for referral.

A second systems-level priority involves the provision of specific screening procedures facilitating early detection of hidden disabilities, an important component of an effective and efficient system of special education services. Such procedures should be viewed as general indicators to be supported by individualized follow-up diagnosis. In a review of recent court decisions in the United States, relative to assessment practices, Baker identified a number of specific assessment practices that school jurisdictions should consider as standard policy:

1. The language of assessment should reflect the dominant language of the child.

2. Assessment of students from diverse ethnic backgrounds should reflect the cultural standards of the children's specific group.

3. Placement and program decisions should use a variety of sources of data rather than a single measure of potential and/or actual achievement.

4. The competence of those individuals responsible for assessment should reflect professional practice competencies set out by appropriate professional groups.

5. Parental permission and active involvement relative to assessment including screening, and subsequent placement and program decisions should be guaranteed.[18]

Since the major reason for screening and referral is to ensure the accurate identification of student needs, reports should convey accurate and educationally relevant information that can lead to any one of an array of programs and services. Several models have been advocated to provide a continuum of services to all students, from regular classroom placements through to highly specialized, yet somewhat segregated, placements.[19] The central consideration for placement decisions regarding appropriate programs should be that a student is moved from the regular setting only to the extent that the alternative program is necessary to meet the student's unique needs.

The specific components of the assessment/information-gathering phase of the decision-making model include the use of a functional skills assessment across a variety of learning environments, developmental assessment including several developmental domains, and multidisciplinary assessments addressing areas such as medical, academic, speech, and vocational competencies and family priorities. Information gathered in this phase provides data to collate and interpret into an educational plan.

Information Synthesis

Several responsibilities exist within the phase of information synthesis and planning allocation of resources. As well, a number of critical decision points exist in this phase. For example, it is the responsibility of the school administrator to ensure that the synthesis and planning process is undertaken. The teacher has the responsibility to focus upon instructional strategies that have been effectively used with the student or to modify those that have been ineffective.

Parents have the privilege and responsibility of participating in the discussions. Such involvement allows them to seek clarification of information that is not clearly understood, to outline their perceptions of the goals they have for their child, and to provide specific input relative to the program placement and characteristics available to their child, both within and outside the system. The school psychologist has the responsibility for ensuring the breadth and depth of educationally relevant data presented regarding the educational, personal/social, and career development needs of the student.

Individual educational plans or programs resulting from this process serve both a process and a product function in identifying, documenting, and synthesizing information about student needs, ensuring the implementation of the selected program, and evaluating its effectiveness. While mandatory in only one province (Ontario), the IEP has been the focus of special education during the past fifteen years.

Despite the fact that the IEP, in the spirit of Public Law 94-142 in the United States, was intended to serve both a product and process function, the emphasis in both the United States and Canada has been on the product of this device. This is evidenced by the reliance on a written format more as an end product than as a dynamic tool in service provision.

In considering the role of the IEP, Morgan has identified six key functions: a written commitment of resources; a program-compliance monitoring document; a communication device between home and school; a written focal point in attempts to resolve differences between partners; a management tool to ensure that each student receives the special programs and services necessary; and an evaluation device for determining the extent of student benefit and progress.[20]

Through its development and use, the IEP, as a product or written record, leads to a process. If devised by the partners in an environment of mutual respect and co-operation, and if utilized to document mutually agreed-upon objectives, strategies, materials, and programs, and finally, if utilized to monitor outcomes of intervention, the IEP becomes an actualized process on behalf of the student.

In surveying teachers' attitudes towards the IEP, Hayes and Higgens found that many feared the document and its process as an accountability measure.[21] This concern existed despite the stated intent of Public Law (94-142) regarding IEP's, which indicates that the use of IEPs does not guarantee student progress. In fact, special educators may wish to use the IEP in advocating specified programs and services. The alternative viewpoint is that the IEP states what the partners have agreed upon, a reasonable approach for dealing with the student's learning problems, subject to further modifications through on-going monitoring, data collection, synthesis, and further program alterations.

Program Implementation

School administrators are responsible for securing and allocating sufficient funds to operate the variety of programs necessary for the students in their district. As well, a range of facilities and materials, professional development programs for all staff, and the provision of student transportation require support and maintenance by the administrative personnel. Whether these services, facilities, and programs are provided within the system, or on a contracted basis with other jurisdictions, private schools, or individuals, will be a matter of local philosophy and resources. The important issue is that these principles and policies should be implemented with regard to the notion of natural justice and fairness to the student as the client.

In providing for these services, school jurisdictions must respond to the needs of a variety of students from a range of backgrounds and having diverse goals, abilities, and supports. With respect to rural systems, Harris and Maher identified several additional stressors, including greater problems in transporting pupils, a lower tax base, difficulties in attracting specialized personnel, and sparse support services.[22] The existence of these problems will require rural boards to use innovative and perhaps co-operative mechanisms in order to provide the service options required by their students.

During this program-implementation phase, the above policies support a number of specific activities carried out by the significant partners in the special educational service. Long- and short-term goals are specified, teaching strategies are defined, materials are located and obtained, and the setting for the special education service is confirmed. Peer and family involvement in the student's program is also specified and planned. Finally, some mechanism of on-going monitoring of the student's progress is put in place to aid in the feedback process for program revisions.

Program Evaluation

The program evaluation process may result in immediate, specific program modifications or in reconsideration of both short-term and long-range goals. As well, some evaluative data may indicate that re-assessment and information gathering are necessary, prior to revisions in IEPs. Thus, both formative evaluations that impact upon specific program characteristics, and summative evaluations, often employed to make larger, system-wide decisions regarding program or staff adequacy, require some policy support.

At the systems level, Mollenkopf suggested that evaluation may include the determination of program effectiveness, provide a basis for a public relations program regarding special educational provisions, and assist in the development of more systematic approaches in future program development and service provisions.[23] In this same context, Mollenkopf described a discrepancy model for evaluation that examined program, not individual staff or students, in a constructive manner. Comparisons between what is found and what should be are made in this approach; if a difference or discrepancy is found, further evaluation is carried out to determine whether the discrepancy involves positive or negative features and what further actions may be required.

TABLE 1
REFERRAL/ASSESSMENT/PROGRAM DEVELOPMENT ISSUES

Information Gathering	Information Synthesis	Program Implementation	Program Evaluations
Definition	Development of IEP	Refining Individual Programs	Formative Evaluations
Referral	Parental Reporting	Placement Options/ Decisions	Summative Evaluations
Screening	Responsibilities of Professionals	Physical Faculties	Graduation Requirements
Reporting		Transportation	

Finally, policy regarding graduation requirements should be developed so that students with special needs have end points or long-term goals to aim towards in their educational planning. As well, plans for transitional experiences to the potential sources for advanced education and community living should be developed, so that this process begins long before the student's last year in secondary school. Table 1 summarizes the various policy areas discussed under each of the four phases of information gathering, synthesis, program implementation, and program evaluation. These policy areas will require school jurisdictions and provincial government personnel to examine their legislation and regulations to ensure an equitable experience for those students within their realm of responsibility who have special needs and handicapping conditions.

NEW DIRECTIONS

The interrelated nature of legislative reform and new, appropriate policy development illustrated in this chapter sets the stage for specific implications of these legislative and policy mandates. The "new directions" postulated in this discussion are centred around the need for teachers to become competent in specific instructional domains as required by legislative and policy developments intended to promote effective special education. It would be irresponsible, for example, to insist that teachers assess students and construct appropriate individual programs if they themselves do not have the skills and knowledge required to do so adequately. Several specific areas of teacher competency, emphasized by legislation and policies aimed at providing a better education for the handicapped, will now be described.

One such domain characterizing the beginning point in the educational enterprise is that of assessment. In order for adequate and appropriate program planning to take place, special education teachers are required to have competencies in the assessment of the children they teach. Unlike teachers of the typical child for whom curriculum guides provide a framework for instruction, the teacher of the student with special needs must address each student's unique capabilities and needs in order to design appropriate instruction. Such a task requires that the teacher be able to accurately identify the various strengths and needs of each special student.

In the past, an assessment of any depth has generally been the responsibility of school psychologists and other similar professionals. However, because of the close relationship between assessment, program planning, evaluation, and modification as outlined in the decision-making model, teachers sufficiently competent in assessment would not only aid in initial placement decisions, but could make appropriate program modifications based upon on-going assessment processes.

Closely associated with this set of skills, teacher preparation programs focussing on special education will have to prepare prospective educators in the area of program planning. Skills in this domain address not only identification of appropriate objectives for each student, but also prepare the teacher with a sufficient repertoire of methods to achieve those objectives. Such competencies are prerequisite to the writing of comprehensive I.E.P. statements, a procedure that is increasingly required in many parts of Canada.

Given that a wide variety of professionals from diverse disciplines, and a variety of paraprofessionals, are typically involved in the provision of an appropriate education for each handicapped student, teachers in the field will have to develop skills to work with persons in these diverse roles. Because such a range of professionals is in contact with the exceptional child, it is essential that the professionals communicate well with each other. Therefore, the responsibility not only rests with the teacher, to understand the meaning of such information as specific test results and special terminology, but also with professionals from other disciplines (i.e., physiotherapists, psychologists, speech pathologists, etc.) to relate their perspectives on the child to the educational context in which the educator must work. As well, working effectively with paraprofessionals within the classroom will also require teachers to manage and plan for others besides themselves within an instructional framework.

Legislation and policy addressing the I.E.P. development process includes parents or guardians and/or the students themselves as active members of the decision-making team regarding placement. As such, teachers will have to be sufficiently trained to deal with parents as participants on behalf of their own child. Previously, parents were only perceived as recipients of educational services provided for their child. The absence of mandatory legislation to provide appropriate educational services to children with special needs tended to cast the parents in the role of "grateful recipients" for provision of *any* services within the normal school system. Progressive policy developments, however, that ensure that all children, regardless of the extent of their disability, are entitled to appropriate school services, alter the parents' status to that of active members, making sure that the child's best interests are considered. Particularly where "functional skills" programs are to be continued in the child's home, educators will have to develop skills enabling them to work effectively with parents or guardians.

A final area of teacher preparation concerns equipping special education teachers with specific teaching strategies and techniques so that they are able to employ those best suited to their students. Such approaches include teaching the general case as incorporated into a variety of "mastery learning curricula" and instructing students how and when to apply a variety of "cognitive strategies" to learning material and situations. In both instances, the emphasis is on teaching general rules or skills that the learner can apply in a variety of situations, not just those situations within the classroom.

Similarly, transition into the community will be aided if students are taught to generalize the skills and knowledge learned in the classroom and apply them to other environments. Therefore, in view of education's ultimate goal, that of successful integration of students with special needs into the community where they can maximize their involvement with society, teachers must develop special teaching strategies that can be applied in more than one setting.

These new directions, stemming from the legislation and policies discussed earlier, place major demands upon the institutions responsible for the preparation of the special education teacher. Nonetheless, given that the teacher is the primary agent working with the student and parents for whom the legislation and policies were planned, it is critical that these concerns be seriously addressed. Failure to do so at the teacher preparation level would jeopardize the appropriate education for students with special needs, and, legally, violate Canada's Charter of Rights and Freedoms.

NOTES

1. S.A. Kirk, *Educating Exceptional Children* (Boston: Houghton Mifflin, 1972); M.S. Lilly, ed., *Children with Exceptional Needs* (New York: Holt, Rinehart and Winston, 1979).

2. Constitution Act, 1982, section 15.

3. H.M. Warnock, *Special Education Needs: Report of the Commission of Inquiry into the Education of Handicapped Children and Youth* (London: Her Majesty's Printing Office, 1978).

4. R.S. Gall, "Special Education" in *Dialogue on Disability: A Canadian Perspective*, edited by N.J. Marlett, R.S. Gall, and A. Wright-Felske (Calgary: University of Calgary Press, 1984), I: 27–45.

5. Ibid.

6. W.W. Wolfensberger, *The Principle of Normalization in Human Services* (Toronto: National Institute on Mental Retardation, 1972).

7. M. Csapo and L. Goguen, eds., *Special Education Across Canada: Issues and Concerns of the 80s* (Vancouver: Centre for Human Development and Research, 1980).

8. Ibid.

9. See R.J. Carver, "Integrated Education: A Paradox for the Deaf," *Just Cause* 2 (1984): 9–11.

10. M.B. Karnes and R.C. Lee, *Mainstreaming in the Preschool* (Washington: Institute of Education, 1977).

11. J.H. Bryan and T.H. Bryan, *Exceptional Children* (Sherman Oaks, Calif.: Alfred Publishing Co., 1979).

12. R.K. Yoshida and J. Gottleib, "A Model of Parental Participation in the Pupil Planning Process," *Mental Retardation* 27 (1977): 206–11.

13. C.A. Maher, "Evaluating Organizational Effectiveness of Special Services Departments: Comparison of Two Models," *School Psychology Review* 9 (1980): 259–66.

14. R. Kimmins, W.J. Hunter, A.W. Mackay, "Educational Legislation and Litigation Pertaining to the Practice of School Psychology in Canada," *Canadian Journal of School Psychology* 1 (1985): 1–16.

15. See F. French and G.M. Kysela, "Special Educational Administrative Policies in Alberta and Newfoundland During 1982: Implications for Policy Development and Service Delivery" (unpublished manuscript, Department of Educational Psychology, University of Alberta, 1983) for a completed review of these issues.

16. G.M. Kysela, S. Barnos, N.C. Grigg, and M. Kanee, "The Integration of Exceptional Children Within Preschool Environments: A Decision-Making Model" in *Childhood Disorders: Behavioral Developmental Approaches*, edited by R.J. McMahon and R.D. Peters (New York: Brunner, Mazel, 1985), 116–39.

17. French and Kysela, "Special Educational Administrative Policies."

18. L.E. Baker, *Assessment Issues in Special Education: Dissemination Packet* (Monroe Courts, Ind.: Joint Special Education Co-operative, 1982).

19. M.C. Reynolds, C. Maynard, and J.W. Birch, *Teaching Exceptional Children in All America's Schools* (Reston, Va.: Council for Exceptional Children, 1977).

20. D.P. Morgan, *A Primer on Individualized Education Programs for Exceptional Children* (Reston, Va.: Council for Exceptional Children, 1977).

21. J. Hayes and L.F. Higgins, "Issues Regarding the I.E.P.: Teacher on the Front Line," *Exceptional Children* 46 (1978): 44.

22. W.J. Harris and C. Maher, "Problems in Implementing Resource Programs in Rural Schools," *Exceptional Children* 43 (1975): 95–99.

23. D.A. Mollenkopf, *Program Evaluation: Information Dissemination Packet* (Hamilton, Ind.: Special Education Co-operative, 1982).

DEVELOPMENTALLY-DELAYED CHILDREN AND THEIR RIGHTS TO EDUCATION IN CANADA: AN ANALYSIS OF MAJOR CONTEMPORARY DEVELOPMENTS

R.S. GALL

INTRODUCTION AND LIMITATIONS

This article will attempt to explain several of the major issues arising out of the provision of Canadian special education services generally, and will focus on how such services impact on developmentally-delayed children in Canada's unique sociopolitical context. Several critical historical and contemporary phenomena will be examined in an attempt to explain some of the utopian and dystopian practices that reflect Canada's dichotomous interpretation of the value of education for special needs individuals.

The following principles form the foundation upon which the organization and content of this article unfold.

1. The individual is the most important entity in the Canadian interpretation of the democratic society and, therefore, those individuals who are mentally retarded/developmentally-delayed[1] have unique value and deserve equity within this society.

2. Education is a basic inalienable right of all citizens of Canada; that right must be extended equitably to those labelled mentally retarded.

3. The neighbourhood school is the most logical setting for the formal education of all citizens.

4. Senior Canadian governments can and must mandate the universal right to education in the law and supportive regulations at both national and provincial levels.

5. Constitutional modifications must be enacted without delay and as an urgent priority in order to redress the historical and contemporary abuse of mentally retarded individuals by the official representatives of Canadian society.

6. Educational practice must reflect a commitment to such individuals, and educators must implement and monitor individualized instructional processes that reflect the individual's ability to learn and the education systems' ability to teach.

7. Parents have a right to full involvement in planning for the education of their children towards the end of individualizing and maximizing their educational outcomes.

This article will attempt a general overview of the present status of the Canadian special education enterprise, with particular attention paid to the unique status ascribed to those labelled mentally retarded. The pressures exerted by physical proximity and cultural ties to other countries such as the United States and Great Britain will also be briefly examined.

REFLECTIONS UPON THE CANADIAN ENVIRONMENT

The public school should be the institution with primary responsibility for providing or obtaining educational and related services for all children in need of special assistance.[2]

Over a decade ago, Perkins suggested that, as a "have" country, Canada required a more comprehensive special education delivery system, one that removed geopolitical inequities.[3] Subsequently, an educational task force commissioned by the International Organization for Economic Co-operation and Development investigated Canadian education structures at all levels and concluded that special education services in this country were comparatively impoverished.[4] These simple examples indicate that internal and external criticism has been directed in the past at the special education service system in Canada. Was such criticism warranted then, and has it abated recently? Why does major unrest and debate continue to characterize special education in Canada, and why is it likely that this turmoil among parents, advocacy groups, professionals, bureaucrats, and politicians will extend through the immediate future.

A general explanation of the unique Canadian special education environment will be attempted. Csapo described this environment as an "intricate patchwork quilt of political accident, professional ambition, and pedagogical oversight loosely bound together with provincial permissive or mandatory red tape and federal neglect."[5]

Progress toward the provision of full and appropriate educational rights for special needs children, especially those labelled mentally retarded, can be observed in some Canadian educational jurisdictions, but it can be shown to be both sporadic and piecemeal. A trend toward the placement of children in integrated settings can be noted, if physical proximity and not social integrtion is used as the standard. Indeed, movement toward the application of service concepts such as the "cascade model" and the "least restrictive alternative" does seem to be occurring in Canada, but at a pace and with inconsistency that is not acceptable to this observer.

Acceptance of special needs children as full and legitimate heirs to all service rights involves a sociopsychological commitment to genuine interpersonal integration. Such commitment can be seen in limited individual and group advocacy action, but does not reflect the national mood. Practical problems, attitudinal barriers, and administrative resistance characterize an often hostile environment faced by special needs children and their parents. Developmental and preventive measures (such as the provision of early intervention programs, early childhood education, respite care parent support, and improved professional and paraprofessional training), are not encouraged on a national level. Thus unitary planning and equitable delivery formats for special education, where they do occur, do so on a local or at best regional level.

Does Canada conform to an almost universal code of negligence or is the situation different elsewhere? For over two decades now, Americans have successfully achieved universal educational opportunity for special needs individuals, and often in maximally integrative ("mainstreamed") environments. In the U.S., legal guarantees to service for even the most severely handicapped child have been advanced through the provisions of PL 94-142 (Education for All Handicapped Act). This law:

> has accelerated the development of educational programs for students with severe handicaps. In the past decade, preparation of teachers of students with severe handicaps has received considerable attention.... In addition, increasing research has been addressed to the process of educational integration of students with severe handicaps. Empirically based guidelines have been developed to support
> a) development
> b) instructional procedures
> c) program structure, and
> d) updating the general state of the art.[6]

Now that legal guarantees to educational service have been assured, Americans are focussing on pragmatic problems of service delivery. With reference to the issue of "integration," "In light of the professional consensus and the various legal and programmatic arguments supporting it, the appropriate question is not, 'Should we do it?' or, 'Does it work?' but rather, 'How can we make it work?'"[7]

American interpretations of individual rights are guaranteed by the constitution; there exists in the U.S. a strong historical commitment to the right of the aggrieved individual to employ litigation and court intervention to verify individual rights. Thus, court-imposed standards for special education service delivery are the norm there, and equitable service standards are monitored regularly by government officials and advocacy groups with a spirit and vigour quite discomforting to the Canadian psyche.

Americans are testing the limits of service provision, while Canadians, by contrast, seem unable to achieve consensus regarding a viable political process that would achieve high educational standards in a context where such education is guaranteed as a right. Thus, major inconsistencies in special education policies are the norm in Canadian special education statutes and regulations.

In Canada, the right to appropriate education for all (a primary demonstration of any nation's moral and ethical commitment to its citizens) appears as an elusive challenge to legislators at the provincial level, and an impossible dream at the federal level. "In many districts the goals of special education are still shrouded in mystery, stated in purposefully vague, diffuse and politically non-offensive terms to satisfy the imagination of every potential adversary group."[8] Canada must, in the near future, remove special needs children from the political buffer zone between federal and provincial levels of government.

One indication of the extent of the apparent Canadian malaise is reflected in the recent statement issued by the Canadian Association for the Mentally Retarded, now aptly renamed the Canadian Society for Community Living:

> We know that children with handicaps and children without handicaps learn best and prepare for adult life best when they learn and prepare together in the same schools and classrooms. We know that education is most effective when it starts early, involves the family, and is directed toward acquiring skills, information and experiences that are essential to social and economic participation. *Yet the vast majority of children and handicaps are isolated in segregated schools and classrooms, and are not being given the opportunity to learn those things that will foster the levels of independence and participation of which they are capable.*[9]

DEFINING "MENTALLY RETARDED/DEVELOPMENTALLY DELAYED": A MORAL CHALLENGE

In North America, the most widely accepted definition of mental retardation is that outlined by the American Association for Mental Deficiency (AAMD). The revised 1973 definition states: "Mental retardation refers to significantly sub-average general intellectual functioning existing concurrently with deficits in adaptive behavior, and manifested during the developmental period."

Understanding this definition requires a critical analysis of three elements:
1. low intellectual functioning;
2. deficiency in adaptive behaviour; and,
3. acquisition during the developmental period.

Regarding the first element, the concept of cognitive competence and the valid and reliable measurement of that concept, have come to be seen multi-dimensionally. To illustrate, the 1961 AAMD definition required that the I.Q. score obtained through an individualized test had to fall only one standard deviation below the mean to permit the identification of mental retardation. In 1973 new criteria established a benchmark I.Q. of 70 (two standard deviations below the mean), arbitrarily redefining in one stroke of the pen the entry point for the application of a powerful negative label. Thus, we can see that "low-intellectual functioning" is an arbitrary, subjective, even political concept used more to set apart a disenfranchised segment of the population than to categorize an individual's capacity to learn. This can be verified by examining the widely varying criteria for program eligibility among regions or provinces. Interpretations of "capacity to learn" vary greatly if one examines the impact of being labelled "trainably" or "educably" retarded. This slavish adherence to a norm-referenced simplistic view of individual complexity is a pernicious and unsubstantiated perspective.

The 1973 AAMD definition required the concurrent existence of low intellectual functioning with "deficient adaptive behavior." Younger children thus classified are seen as deficient when communication, socialization, sensory-motor, and self-help skills are addressed; these are relatively objective benchmarks. However, the adolescent's adaptive behaviour incorporates someone's subjective interpretation of the individual's social and academic competence—both environment-specific factors. It can be argued that, while the concept of adaptive behaviour has somewhat humanized the definition of mental-retardation by reducing the primary focus on I.Q. scores, it has also allowed the entry of even more subjective variables.

Perhaps the least controversial component of the AAMD definition is that such retardation must be manifest during the "developmental period," essentially saying that the learning process was impaired to some extent during the "growing years" from birth to full physical maturity in late adolescence. But, during this span of about eighteen years, "retardation-causing" conditions range from powerful trauma such as anoxia and brain damage, to societally induced factors such as deprivation, neglect, and abuse.

It is difficult to accept mentally retarded or developmentally-delayed individuals as an homogeneous group. Indeed, there are individuals with both academic and social delays that cause serious disruption in life-coping abilities. In the light of contemporary social-psychological concepts, however, what is to be served by focussing on this elusive and damaging homogeneous concept? How much further have we advanced over the practice of labelling such individuals "idiots," "imbeciles," and "morons"? How much more reflective is the contemporary practice of identifying them as "trainable" or "educable"? Pervasive negative connotations persist, and our system of identifying such individuals for service can be shown to be largely at fault:

> Because of the important political, social, and economic implications of identification as exceptional, classification systems should have "clear definitions and a coherent, logical structure".... Any definition or any classification system that results in a considerable number of nonhandicapped individuals being identified as handicapped and receiving services designated for handicapped individuals will not, and should not, be acceptable to professionals or to

the general public. Similarly, a system that results in a significant number of handicapped students not being identified, and thus not receiving special services, is unacceptable. The efficiency and effectiveness of a classification are important.[10]

With reference to that population identified colloquially as mentally retarded, there are at least two subcategories:

1. the quantifiably handicapped, including those moderately and severely/profoundly retarded who are relatively easy to identify due to persistent learning difficulties and associated physical anomalies; and

2. the nonquantifiably handicapped, including those "mildly retarded" who are better described as "educationally disordered" in terms of the interaction between the child and his or her school. "Children with differences in learning style, temperament, social and affective patterns and motivation experience major educational problems when they interact with set curricula, methods of instruction, and administrative organizations."[11]

It is important to keep this distinction clearly in mind. Services for the quantifiably handicapped have increased both quantitatively and qualitatively throughout North America during this past decade. Those services for the nonquantifiably handicapped will remain difficult to monitor, and qualitative program standards for them more difficult to obtain and sustain. This is primarily because they are based on a convenient social contract between the schools and the public for dealing with a disenfranchised segment of the school population, and not upon the objective assessment of the needs of such individuals.

One must recognize the pressures brought upon the public school system by external political forces, including the prevailing outlook of the population, the translation of that outlook into legislation, and the modification of that legislative process by litigation undertaken individually or collectively by those whose rights are aggrieved. In any country, and Canada is no exception, the unique interplay of these forces must be carefully examined in order to understand the *raison d'être* for the services given to special needs individuals.

NEW PERSPECTIVES IN SPECIAL EDUCATION: THE POST-1960 ERA

> I lay it down as a prime condition of sane society, obvious as such to anyone but an idiot, that in any decent community, children should find in every part of their native country, food, clothing, lodging, instruction, and parental kindness for the asking.... The children must have them as if by magic, with nothing to do but rub the lamp, like Aladdin, and have their needs satisfied.[12]

In general, the decades of the 1960s and 1970s were periods of widespread if not universal reaction to the medical perspective that had so long dominated special education philosophy and practice. Innovative educators appeared determined to challenge established practices that appeared to create social and intellectual cripples of children in spite of idealistic rhetoric associated with special education. Smith and Greenburg[13] coined the phrase "six-hour retardate" to describe the environmentally competent child forced to appear defective in the school setting by inappropriate exposure to ineffective curriculum and pedagogy. Many special education practices from the past came to be criticized as restrictive to human potential.

During the 1960s, a near-universal renaissance of attitude and cognition occurred that exposed many traditional practices in special education to critical review and challenge. For example, as early as 1962, Johnson suggested that adequate objective evidence to support the effectiveness of special classes was difficult to obtain. He noted, "It is indeed paradoxical that mentally handicapped children, having teachers specially trained, having more money per capita spent on their education and being enrolled in classes with fewer children and a program designed to provide for their needs are not accomplishing more."[14]

Prominent and respected special educators, who had earlier advocated partial segregation and traditional service models began to review their postures. One of the most noteworthy was Dunn who published a revealing article calling for a moratorium on the placement of mildly handicapped students in segregated settings.[15] The general educational community was asked to accept responsibility for serving a more broadly constituted student population, while special educators were challenged to abandon nonobjective and unvalidated teaching practices in favour of data-based empirical procedures.

Special education was emerging as a science based upon single subject (individualized) research-to-practice procedures that challenged the assumptions based on norm-referenced homogeneity. Specialized curricula for target groups of students, such as the Trainable Mentally Retarded curriculum text in Alberta, were increasingly viewed as inappropriate. Special educators were challenged to be "continually surprised at what we can do if we are imaginative enough to find better methods and procedures."[16] Thus, a period of intense research-to-practice endeavours came to dominate special education pedagogy.

Attitudes toward special needs populations appeared to alter as new methods and procedures were developed and disseminated. Even the most severely handicapped were shown to benefit from the application of teaching technologies.[17] Attention was directed to refining methods to teach coping skills to children being integrated into regular educational settings.[18] An ecological perspective emerged in which the focus of special educational intervention altered to incorporate the child's needs into the unique service potential of the educational system and large community environment. Service models were developed that emphasized accountability and the monitoring of service provision. The concept of "zero reject" became the philosophical principle and driving force behind both legislative and academic thrusts to serve special needs children.[19] Other educators looked to the improvement of teacher skill levels as the focal point for a revised educational process that would assist all children regardless of their degree of biologically-acquired deficiencies.[20]

In commenting on the major philosophical and technical adjustments made to the concept of mental retardation during the last two decades, Cegelka and Prehm[21] recounted both the victories and the defeats. On the positive side, they noted the tendency

> to recognize the rights of mentally retarded people to appropriate education and habilitation and to participate in society. These striking changes in social responsiveness to mentally retarded people have been parallelled by a steady increase in knowledge concerning prevention, detection, learning, adjustment, and treatment of retarded development. Despite these important improvements, the agenda of needed research, undelivered services, ineffective practices, and unfulfilled promises is still extensive![21]

SPECIAL EDUCATION DEVELOPMENTS ON THE NATIONAL LEVEL

Having seen the assault upon traditional special education services during the years from 1960 to 1970, let us examine some of the Canadian reactions to this international movement. It will be shown that Canada pursued a unique pattern of policy development somewhat at odds with the processes in other countries.

Canada made global commitments to action regarding special needs in the international arena that were impossible to actualize nationally. For example, Canada formally acceded to the United Nations International Covenant on Economic, Social and Cultural Rights in May 1976, with unanimous provincial consent. Article 13 formally recognized the universal right to a free, compulsory education, at least at the primary level. Principle 5 of the 1959 United Nations Declaration of the Rights of the Child, with which Canada concurred, upheld special treatment, education, and care for the handicapped. Further, the 1971 United Nations Declaration of the Rights of Mentally Retarded Persons called for seven major protections guaranteeing the dignity of life of such individuals, and included the concept of education as an enhancing feature.

The most obvious Canadian expression of commitment was the Commission on Emotional and Learning Disorders in Children (CELDIC), which was established in 1966. A comprehensive study of Canadian special education, which then showed promise of accomplishing in Canadian fashion what other nations would accomplish in their own way and time, was undertaken.

The CELDIC body was sponsored by two leading advocacy groups, the Canadian Mental Health Association and the Canadian Association for the

Mentally Retarded. A document entitled *One Million Children* was published to reflect the consensus of the contributors, and over one hundred recommendations were incorporated in it.[22] Optional models for the organization of Canadian special education services, the personnel required, and the related research priorities were clearly identified. National, not regional, solutions were contemplated in a proposed reorganization of the structure of special education. Consistent with the emerging American posture of the time, CELDIC sought to present special education as an integral part of regular education. The American concept of "mainstreaming" had its first major Canadian interpretation as CELDIC urged a general national reorganization of all aspects of special education service delivery.

CELDIC urged the federal government and the ten provincial governments to establish joint standards for service delivery and training in special education to remove geopolitical inequities. The needs of individual children were to be the focal point for the action required at all levels. Nothing less than a dramatic change in the attitude and policies of Canadians was called for. Given the sociopolitical realities of Canada, the CELDIC report was, in retrospect, a revolutionary document.

Individual agencies then attempted to actualize the spirit of CELDIC. The best example may have been the Canadian Association for the Mentally Retarded (CAMR) and its visionary executive secretary, Dr. Allan Roehrer. CAMR sponsored Dr. Wolf Wolfensberger as visiting scholar to the National Institute on Mental Retardation in the early 1970s, and his milestone publication entitled *The Principle of Normalization in Human Services* emerged at the same time.[23] Thereafter, a powerful series of national level workshops, offered under the direction of CAMR's "ComServ Plan for the '70s," and the corresponding Program Analysis of Service Systems (PASS) training sessions, appear to have awakened Canadian conscience to all facets of service to the handicapped. It is significant to note that these national thrusts represented agency, and not direct government, intervention, and that even these lost their formal impact over time.

In spite of the awareness encouraged by the CELDIC report, legal and social changes regarding special needs education progressed almost exclusively on a provincial basis. Even the publication of *Standards for Educators of Exceptional Children in Canada*[24] was unable to mobilize significant collective will and national political commitment to special education teacher training. Provincial teacher certification boards continued to react individualistically to the implementation of criteria and standards for the training of special education personnel.

Thus, when the Organization for Economic Cooperation and Development (OECD) external examiners released the findings of their 1975 review of Canadian education, a shocking analysis of our neglect of educational rights was portrayed.[25] At best, our heady international expressions of commitment seemed to disappear in the reality of Canadian educational policy forged with section 93 of the British North America Act. The OECD report illustrated many deficiencies and concluded that appropriate and quality special education provision was tragically deficient. It found evidence of the complicity of school officials in extending this negative environment by the enforcement of policies of benign neglect. OECD examiners found Canadian bureaucrats at the front line of resistance to change, and they decried our national status with these words: "Hardly an area [exists] in which lack of co-operation among the various levels of government, and between professionals and parents, produces such harmful results as in the case of the special needs student."[26]

In summarizing the relative Canadian timidity in taking concerted action in the area of special needs education, Csapo noted that only half of the provinces had taken action to see to the physical presence of special needs children in school, and none had fully addressed the issue of quality education.[27] For Canadians, the "Royal Commission" approach has become the norm: study the issue but evade direct action. As Lewthwaite described the situation, "Perhaps the most noteworthy disparities between US and Canadian cultures are the two governments' basic commitments: to life, liberty and the pursuit of happiness in the United States; and peace, order and good government in Canada."[28]

EXAMPLES OF REGIONAL/PROVINCIAL DISPARITIES IN THE PROVISION OF SPECIAL-EDUCATION SERVICES

Federal power to legislate in matters regarding education is limited to constitutionally granted lines of service: to natives, the armed forces, the inmates of federal prisons, and residents of the two northern territories. In contrast, in the U.S., federal legislation (specifically PL94-142, and section 504 of the 1973 Rehabilitation Act) mandates free and appropriate education for all children throughout the country.

Mandatory provision (or mandatory legislation) exists in those provinces where free and appropriate education is provided to all without exclusionary provisions of any kind. In contrast, the term permissive provision (or permissive legislation) can be used to indicate the prevalence of the concept of education as a favour or privilege in those provinces where exclusion of special needs children is permitted.

It is important to note that *mandatory* and *universal* are not synonymous concepts in Canada, as each province interprets the right to school uniquely. Consider the following statement:

> The extent and specifics of the mandate vary significantly from province to province; however, exclusionary clauses may still be used to eliminate services to some students with severe or multiple handicaps. Even in provinces without specific mandatory special education legislation, compulsory schooling acts may be interpreted to include all children regardless of handicap.... Still, children with severe handicaps may be excluded by suspension or

expulsion. While a school board normally would not be allowed to expel a child because of a severe handicap, a board may be able to expel the same child for disruptive behaviour. By labelling the child's behaviour as "disruptive," a school board may escape the responsibility of providing services.[29]

Five provinces have to date enacted mandatory provision for education: Newfoundland (1974), Nova Scotia (1969), Quebec (1979), Ontario (1980), and Saskatchewan (1971). Manitoba has quasi-mandatory status because it has not to date fully implemented statutory modifications suggested in 1976 through Bill 58. Four provinces, at the time of writing, continue to allow permissive provisions to prevail: Alberta, British Columbia, New Brunswick, and Prince Edward Island.

MANDATORY PROVISION: THE EXAMPLE OF SASKATCHEWAN

In 1971, section 122 of the School Act in Saskatchewan made it mandatory that school boards provide special education to all handicapped children. Prior to 1971, special education programs had been funded by the Department of Education through a system of designated teacher grants administered by the Guidance and Special Education Branch. While administratively convenient, these required the identification and grouping of children into classroom units and thus fostered both labelling and segregation. Such grants favoured the larger urban school divisions that had students exhibiting a wide variety of disabilities because such divisions could develop a full set of options. In the smaller (and frequently rural) divisions, inappropriate congregation of children, separation from the mainstream, and concomitant problems of transportation and service inequity were the norm. Such was usually the experience in other parts of Canada that had a large population segment living in rural settings.

Prior to 1971, groups in Saskatchewan challenged segregated special education classrooms as inappropriate; as early as 1968 two urban jurisdictions disbanded segregated classes for the moderately handicapped. With the passage of mandatory legislation, Saskatchewan became the second province (after Nova Scotia in 1969) to move toward such statutory provision. The Department of Education was thereafter challenged to develop more appropriate services at the local level. Innovative methods of funding and service provision were implemented based on the needs of each individual child. The policy of the "least restrictive environment" was implemented as a guiding philosophy.

While the 1971 legislation ensured that handicapped children became part of Saskatchewan education in the broader sense, pressure from various advocacy groups continued to ensure the evolution of improved levels of specialized service to handicapped children. As a result, in 1978 the department assumed direct responsibility, in every respect, for multiply handicapped children.

A new inclusive special education manual was published, and a per-pupil funding structure was established to reflect the new expanded services to special needs children. Even more notably, the government announced that by 1981 teachers had to achieve acceptable and formally identified standards of training in order to be able to teach special needs children.

A visible and identifiable program thrust that gave priority to individual needs was clearly discernible in Saskatchewan during the 1970s. Funding required local program accountability through periodic review of each child's progress. It can be seen that Saskatchewan had, in slightly more than a decade, established an effective special needs service delivery package.

MANDATORY PROVISION IN OTHER PROVINCES

The four other provinces favouring mandatory legislation regarding the universal right to education—Nova Scotia, Newfoundland, Quebec, and Ontario—will be presented briefly in the order of their chronological acceptance of mandatory legislation.[30]

Nova Scotia

A major review in 1969 of the status of Canadian special education provisions reported that only one province, Nova Scotia, had developed mandatory legislation. Over a decade earlier, in 1956, the Department of Education in that province had assumed funding responsibility for special programs. This was formally confirmed and strengthened with the passage of the Education Act of 1973 and the specific Mandate of Regulation that required school jurisdictions to provide for all students, including the handicapped.

Newfoundland

The province of Newfoundland and Labrador created the Division of Special Services in 1969 as an integral part of the department of education, and thereby indirectly encouraged the local boards to develop special programs. This first stage was replaced by mandatory legislation a decade later, when the 1970 School Act was amended in 1979.

Quebec

Quebec took seriously the external and internal criticisms of its special education provisions and underwent a major revolution in services during the decades of the 1960s and 1970s, moving from separate provision of services to mandatory legislation (1978) and a major review and revamping of procedures and regulations. The Quebec Loi Assurant l'exercice des droits des personnes handicapées incorporated regulatory processes to ensure quality education in the most normal environment possible.

Ontario

Ontario's system, one of the most entrenched and segregated prior to 1980, has undergone major revisions. As recently as 1974, the Ontario School Act provided no legal right to education; typically local boards were encouraged but not forced to adopt special provisions. In less than a decade Ontario moved to mandatory legislation. In 1978, a judicial award was granted in Peel Municipality to cover costs for a special needs student's education. This echoed the changing mood reflected in a private member's bill presented in the Ontario Legislature in 1977. The 1978 regulations were introduced to force boards to establish placement and review committees regarding individual enrolments in programs. The Ontario change leading to the 1980 Education Amendment Act brought mandatory legislation and was primarily the result of unrelenting pressure by several parent advocacy groups "who have been successful in setting the priorities of the Ministry of Education, ... acting in part because the school system has failed to act. The number of children on waiting lists, the lack of consistent and high quality educational services are proof of this."[31]

Bill 82 initially included a rejection clause for some categories of children, a moral oversight that was corrected by modifying the exclusionary clause in section 34. Wilson suggested that Ontario had achieved with Bill 82 the principles of universal access, public financial support, appeal procedures, appropriate program monitoring, and a child review process quite similar in impact with that achieved by American legislation. However, Wilson goes on to describe the limitations imposed on the appeal process in Ontario, which is quite consistent with the "play-safe" Canadian attitude described here.[32]

Summary: Mandatory Provisions in Canada

Thus, of the five provinces with mandatory legislation, three continued to resist genuine and full incorporation of all children into their schools. Only Saskatchewan and Quebec appeared to buttress statutes with regulatory safeguards. One could argue that the Canadian social environment is more accepting of a medical/deficiency model, in which the child is viewed as having "the problem" for which special educators magnanimously provide protective service. Categorical treatment and labelling are appropriate and morally defensible given this view: affected children and their parents do not know what is best for them, professionals do! Many professionals feel that the danger of this perspective is that it is "not in the best interests of children and their families, and is potentially open to legal scrutiny, for it leads to the fragmentation of the tasks ... and a lack of accountability."[33]

Canadians also prefer to have less confidence than Americans in the power vested in the courts. Legal confrontation appears to be contrary to British parliamentary tradition and may create a litigative posture that brings harm in the long term. Goguen contends that "litigation per se does not seem to assure comprehensive educational services in Canada."[34]

DEVELOPMENTS IN PROVINCES PRESENTING A PERMISSIVE MODEL

In at least four provinces—British Columbia, Alberta, New Brunswick, and Prince Edward Island—exclusion of children is permitted if not directly encouraged. Permission to attend school is a most fragile and tenuous concept: "attending school is not in itself education. But the right given by provincial law does not include...the right to receive in school anything worthwhile: what the child receives depends on the uncontrolled discretion of the school authorities."[35]

It is this very point of appropriate education that marks the key distinction between the American and Canadian systems: the specific requirements of Public Law 94-142 permit, and in fact encourage, the judicial interpretation of educational effectiveness. In Canada, however, while only five provinces provide universal access to school, the Canadian process universally denies an external assessment of educational adequacy.

Canadian bureaucrats at all levels are overprotected and overpowered; teachers are unorganized and ill prepared to press for change; parents are just beginning to recognize that they can speak up. Unless provincial and federal legislation begins to incorporate measures providing for accountability, the rights of special needs children will remain subject to the arbitrary advocacy of those in power. A more detailed analysis of the situations in Alberta and British Columbia follows.

Alberta

An examination of developments in the province of Alberta can be used to illustrate the major differences that exist in Canada regarding philosophies held by those responsible for special needs education.

The Alberta School Act (1980), under provisions established in section 133, calls for "pupils" between six and sixteen years to attend school, but refutes that requirement in section 134 by allowing school jurisdictions to exclude special education youngsters from attendance. Section 134 is quoted here because it provides a classic example of the vagueness decried by Brennan[36] regarding the British School Act of 1981:

> A board may temporarily excuse from attendance in a regular classroom any pupil whose special educational needs in the opinion of an inspector or superintendent are of such a nature that regular classroom experience is not productive or is detrimental to the pupil or to the school.

In 1978, a challenge was mounted to section 134 by the parents of a ten-year-old cerebral palsied child who had been suspended from her Lamont school under the provisions of the section. The court, administered by Mr. Justice O'Byrne, ruled on behalf of the child in 1978, relying on the "residency" provision in another section of the School Act as the primary argument. The court decision required county officials to enrol the child and to subsequently pay all costs involved in her education, yet concurrently withdrew from the requirement of effective monitoring and implementation procedure on the grounds that such authority was not appropriately described.[37]

The decision clearly reflects the complex problems that ensue when mandatory legislation is not present and powerfully implemented. It is a paradox that Alberta can be faulted for negating its statutory obligation to special needs children by allowing permissive legislation, and yet proceed to develop strong special supports through a variety of modifications in policy and regulatory structures. Two examples will be drawn to prove this point. The Program Unit Grant, established in 1979, enabled severely and profoundly handicapped children (dependent handicapped) to be placed in school, should the local authorities concur. Through such grants, aides and other supportive services are provided to enable school attendance for many such children. Earlier, the Learning Disability Fund, established in 1973, allowed school jurisdictions to tap provincial funds for the assessment of and special provisions for the school-aged learning disabled population. Even earlier, Alberta provided support for pre-school program attendance of handicapped children as young as two-and-one-half years.

It is obvious that the government remains committed to regulatory, if not legislative, support of handicapped children. However, Alberta Education has recently announced the Management Finance Plan, which should dramatically affect the education of special needs children. Block granting supplanted categorical funding for all areas of exceptionality since September 1984. The new special education finance plan incorporates features that could well serve in the future to create a climate similar to the American situation. It has the potential to revolutionize social policy in Alberta. This newly created system will not require labelling as a means for funding special needs students. Each school district will receive a blanket grant based on overall school enrolment to apply to their special needs students, and expenditures will be monitored. Responsibility for the care and education of special needs students will be shifted from the minister directly to the administration within the child's school jurisdiction.

Parents will now have a focal point for their concerns regarding educational planning for their children, as direct planning, budgeting, program development, and implementation of special education services become the direct responsibility of local school divisions. Parents and advocates will be able to use the courts to argue for a child's appropriate school placement as well as school attendance. It remains to be seen if that litigative posture will emerge. What is significant is that no longer can the local school districts reject outright the special needs student, but rather they must attempt to provide the necessary services. This modified position was created solely through a restructured funding regulation and not through legislation.

It is obvious that Alberta has set forth on a unique path for the balance of the 1980s. On the surface, it appears that special needs children will be served through the application of local pressure and without the security of mandatory legislation. The Alberta situation clearly presents the potency of provincial authority and the longevity of entrenched attitudes.

It remains to be seen if the revision of the School Act in Alberta will incorporate universal principles of the right to education or will continue to deny that expression of commitment to all of its citizens.

British Columbia

During the 1968–69 school year, the British Columbia Department of Education created the Special Education Division, thus marking a watershed in the transition of special services in the province. With that move, a specific focus was given to a previously unstructured system of special needs education. Central co-ordination, dispersal of grants, and liaison with other departments and private agencies involved in special education were established.[38]

As in Alberta, the decade of the 1970s was one marked by program expansion at both the elementary and secondary school levels. The name change of the "Special Education Division" to "Integrated and Supportive Services" reflected the willingness of local and provincial authorities to partially integrate almost all special needs children into regular schools and programs. Public policy in British Columbia stipulates that from age five to nineteen years all children are entitled to educational services, and further tht section 158 of the British Columbia Public Schools Act mandates basic educational programming. However, it is still the case that "legislation pertaining to special education services is non-prescriptive and program developments within the province tend to reflect local conditions and circumstances."[39]

Thus, in British Columbia as in Alberta, the standards required for universal and appropriate education for special needs populations are inconsistently administered. In tracing the recent development of special education administrative policies developed by the British Columbia Ministry of Education, Leslie and Goguen commended the province for improved funding and monitoring the incorporation of parental involvement, the development of individual educational plan guidelines, and the formation of a Special Programs branch to oversee all special needs developments. However they condemned the legislative inaction that has characterized the recent past.

"If we could start with nothing we could probably develop a rational, comprehensive and coordinated system.... We cannot, without great difficulty however, divest ourselves of our past. We therefore live with a system that is somewhat short of being ideal."[40] Thus, while advocacy groups pressure for public acceptance of adequate and full legal regulatory provisions for exceptional children, such acceptance remains a favour permitted by the provincial authority.

CONCLUSION

The Canadian special education enterprise is inconsistent, creating a situation that imposes real hardship upon many Canadian children and their families. The needs of Canadian special needs children are too important to allow another decade to pass without change on a national level. While certain elements of Canadian society have pressed for change to the bureaucratic intransigence that has characterized our educational system, the status quo has largely prevailed.

What steps might be taken in the near future to address and correct the negligence of the past? One could postulate at least three scenarios should legislators agree to enact the appropriate modifications necessary to place Canada in a leadership role vis-à-vis humane and appropriate special needs education. Each scenario is dramatic and therefore quite out of character with the Canadian preference for moderation.

Perhaps the most dramatic gesture would be initiated by the federal government if it were to seize direct control of education by first reducing unconditional grants to the provinces and replacing them with direct grants that mandate the right to education for all as a precondition. Such a move could be justified by Parliament on the grounds that Canada's historical tradition has abused special children, that a crisis exists with regard to their educational welfare, and that the complexity of special education service provision can only be overcome by central co-ordination. As is the case with U.S. Public Law 94-142, provinces would be forced to conform or lose significant grants provided for the support of other components of education. Such a move in the present political environment is seen as highly unlikely as it would generate intense debate and litigation and perhaps even further widen regional alienation. The tension regarding energy profit sharing, which marked the past decade, would provide some indication of the acrimony which would accompany such a bold and constitutionally novel act.

A second scenario would see the provinces retain exclusive control of education, but enact mandatory legislation (with potent regulatory supports) on a voluntary but universal basis. This would require leadership by the Council of Ministers of Education acting in a manner totally inconsistent with its past record of developing a broad national perspective on any issue. Such leadership would be required to achieve consensus on a model for service implementation on all levels, perhaps reexamining the CELDIC and SEECC Reports in the light of the Canadian realities of the 1980s. Again, this scenario is improbable in spite of its logic and appeal to common sense.

The third scenario is no less difficult but would essentially respect the present constitutional and historical tradition. It would require commitment by legislators at both levels to raise special needs education to priority status and thus achieve mutual benefit through co-operation. While provinces would retain control of education, federal involvement would be expanded into this one area by the creation of an Office of Special Education under the Secretary of State or an equivalent federal office. Such an office would probably replace the present council of ministers. Federal-provincial cost sharing arrangements beneficial to all parties could be implemented through this office to provide equity of service across geopolitical boundaries. The office would further provide a forum for the resolution of inequities and the establishment of new funding formulas that could strengthen provincial power while still recognizing federal involvement through central co-ordination and financial support.

Legislative reform is desperately needed and long overdue and will probably not occur unless parents and advocacy groups in this country intensify their pressure on legislators at all levels. In recommending the formation of a national office to evaluate and fund appropriate educational strategies for special needs children, Csapo suggested:

> Provincially vested interests in special education and territorial imperatives do not have costs of the same length of those of general education.... Uprooting might prove to be easier and might serve as an experimental demonstration that federal intervention...can produce results before the question of regular education is tackled.[41]

Canadians of moral conscience must now assume a strong posture of personal and collective advocacy on behalf of special needs children.

NOTES

1. The term *mentally retarded* is used interchangeably with *developmentally delayed* throughout this article. Such labels reflect only a historical assumption about the homogeneous character of individuals so labelled, and do not accurately reflect their inherent individuality. In this paper, the terms developmentally delayed and mentally retarded simply indicate a child in need of special services.

2. N. Hobbs, *The Futures of Children* (San Francisco: Jossey-Bass, 1975).

3. S. Perkins, "Shortcomings in the Delivery of Special Education Services in Canada" (paper presented at the meeting of the Council for Exceptional Children, New York, April 1974).

4. Organization for Economic Cooperation and Development, *Review of National Policies for Education: Canada* (Paris: OECD, 1976).

5. M. Csapo and L. Goguen, eds., *Special Education Across Canada: Issues and Concerns for the '80s* (Vancouver: Centre for Human Development and Research, 1980), 215.

6. M. Csapo and D. Baine, "Teachers of Students with Severe Handicaps," *Canadian Journal for Special Education* 1, 4 (1985), 130.

7. B. Wilcox and W. Sailor, "Service Delivery Issues: Integrated Educational Systems" in *Quality Education for the Severely Handicapped: the Federal Investment*, edited by B. Wilcox and R. York (Washington: U.S. Department of Education, 1980), 282.

8. Csapo and Goguen, eds., *Special Education Across Canada*, 216.

9. Canadian Association for the Mentally Retarded "A Statement of Principles, presented to the Canadian Government" (Downsview, Ont., 1985).

10. J. Ysseldyke, B. Algozzine, and S. Epps, "A Logical and Empirical Study of Students as Handicapped." *Exceptional Children* (1983): 160–66.

11. E. Edgar and A. Hayden, "Who Are the Children Special Education Should Serve and How Many Children are There?" *Journal of Special Education* 18, 5 (1985): 531.

12. George Bernard Shaw, *Parents and Children* (1914).

13. I.L. Smith and S. Greenburg, "Teacher Attitudes and Labelling Processes," *Exceptional Children* 41 (1975): 315–24.

14. G.O. Johnson, "Special Education for the Mentally Retarded—a Paradox," *Exceptional Children* 29 (1962): 62–69.

15. L.M. Dunn, "Special Education for the Mildly Retarded—Is Much of it Justifiable?" *Exceptional Children* 35, 1 (1968): 5–22.

16. S.A. Kirk and J.J. Gallagher, *Educating Exceptional Children* (Boston: Houghton Mifflin, 1979), 7.

17. R. Perske and J. Smith, eds., *Beyond the Ordinary* (Parson, Kan.: Words and Pictures, 1977), 9.

18. M.R. Redden and A.W. Blackhurst, "Mainstreaming Competencies for Elementary Teachers," *Exceptional Children* 44 (1978): 615–17.

19. S. Lilly, *Classroom Sociometry* (Eugene, Ore.: Northwestern Regional Special Education Instructional Materials Center, 1970).

20. H.J. Prehm and J.E. McDonald, "The Yet to be Served—A Perspective," *Exceptional Children* 45 (1979): 502–07.

21. P. Cegelka and H. Prehm, *Mental Retardation: From Categories to People* (Columbus, Ohio: Charles E. Merrill, 1982).

22. Commission on Emotional and Learning Disorders in Children, *One Million Children* (Toronto: Crainford, 1970).

23. Wolf Wolfensberger, *The Principle of Normalization in Human Services* (Toronto: National Institute on Mental Retardation, 1972).

24. *Standards for Educators of Exceptional Children in Canada* (published jointly by the Canadian Committee of the Council for Exceptional Children and the National Institute on Mental Retardation).

25. Organization for Economic Cooperation and Development, *Review of National Policies for Education: Canada*.

26. Ibid.

27. Csapo and Goguen, eds., *Special Education Across Canada*.

28. G. Lewthwaite, "So Many Differences. So Much in Common," *Vancouver Sun*, 5 March 1980, 6.

29. D. Sobsey, "Educational Services: Canada, the United States, and Oz," *Canadian Journal for Exceptional Children* 1, 4 (1984): 127.
30. Csapo and Goguen, eds., *Special Education Across Canada*.
31. Ibid., 89.
32. A.K. Wilson, *A Consumer's Guide to Bill 82: Special Education in Ontario* (Toronto: Ontario Institute for Studies in Education, 1983).
33. Csapo and Goguen, eds., *Special Education Across Canada*, 80.
34. Ibid., 182.
35. J.A. Smith "The Right to Education—A Comparative Study" (unpublished paper, University of Ottawa Faculty of Law, n.d.).
36. W. Brennan, *Changing Special Education* (Milton Keynes: Open University Press, 1981).
37. Csapo and Goguen, eds., *Special Education Across Canada*, 182.
38. Ibid., 7–8.
39. P.T. Leslie and L. Goguen, "British Columbia's Educational Policies: A Retrospective Examination," *Special Education in Canada* 58, 2 (1984), 47–49.
40. Csapo and Goguen, eds., *Special Education Across Canada*.
41. Ibid., 228.

THE EDUCATION OF THE INTELLECTUALLY GIFTED STUDENT IN CANADA

G. PATRICK O'NEILL

INTRODUCTION

The education of intellectually (academically) gifted children in Canada, until the last decade, was largely the responsibility of the regular classroom teacher. The results, however, have been disastrous in light of the fact that nearly twenty percent of the high school dropouts in North America have been gifted/talented students.[1] Obviously, this is a sad reflection on the school systems of both Canada and the United States.

The first program for the gifted in Canada dates back to 1928.[2] There were sporadic programs in the 1950s and 1960s, but it was not until the mid-1970s that they became common. Ontario has lead the way,[3] although no province can afford to rest on its laurels, according to a recent survey.[4] In essence, this survey found that: departments or ministries of education did not make special financial provisions for the gifted; school boards generally reported difficulty in finding extra funds for the gifted; gifted education was not a priority among faculties of education; and, with the exception of Ontario, none of the provinces required special certification for teachers of the gifted.

No doubt these embarrassing conditions have improved considerably since the survey was conducted. Lobbying by parents for special funding, schools, and programs[5] has prompted the formation of task forces[6] and, in some cases, concrete legislation.[7] Regardless, many school systems are still struggling with the establishment, or maintenance, of special facilities for the gifted.[8] It is in this context that the following article is written. It provides direction and guidance for those interested in planning, organizing, implementing, and/or refining programs for the academically gifted student. The corpus is divided into four major areas, namely, defining giftedness, identification, implementation, and programming.

DEFINING GIFTEDNESS

The term giftedness has a wide range of applications. Indeed, one could readily get lost in all the jumble and jargon. For example, Levin found that,

> There is considerable controversy in the literature regarding a cut-off IQ score for giftedness. Some researchers maintain that only those in the upper 1% of measured IQ (around 137+) should be called gifted, while others feel that all those within the top 10% of measured IQ (around 120+) should be included. Some view giftedness in terms of a "superior" IQ range (around 116–124+), a "gifted" range (about 132–140+), and an "extremely gifted" range (172–180+).[9]

Others have attempted to make distinctions between the moderately gifted and the highly gifted.[10] Once again, though, divisions are not clear-cut. "Some researchers cite IQs above 145 as indicating highly gifted abilities, while others reserve the label for children whose IQs exceed 165 or even 180."[11] Clearly, then, there are great variations in terminology. What is deemed gifted in one jurisdiction may be high ability, average gifted, or superior in another jurisdiction.

For the purposes of this article, the term intellectually gifted will be defined as that two to three percent of the school-age population that have IQ scores in the 130-plus range.[12] This definition is considered to be functional, pragmatic, and utilitarian as it represents a compromise between practical and philosophical considerations. That is, most boards could not cope with the larger numbers of an expanded definition that included, for example, the superior child (IQ 116–124 plus). If, on the other hand, the definition was restricted to only students with IQs above 140, the numbers would be so low (about two in an average school of four hundred) that it would likewise be difficult to operate a successful program.[13] Hence, the *modus operandi* of most school boards is in the 130-plus IQ range.[14]

IDENTIFICATION

Of course, no operational definition of academic giftedness should be based solely on measures of cognitive ability, rather giftedness should be viewed as a composite of many factors. Hard-line cognitive test scores are extremely important, yet other auxiliary factors such as overall school achievement (grade-point average), biographical data, and performance in specially designed problem-solving situations[15] should also be considered. Thus, indentification strategies should hinge on multiple sources of information.[16] The options are many, but most school systems rely on a combination of behavioural procedures such as student interviews, rating scales, and checklists of various sorts.[17] However, rating scales and checklists are regularly discounted as dependable sources because most lack validity and reliability.[18] Still, there are some supposedly promising instruments on the market, mainly, among others, the GIFT rating scales,[19] the Multi-Dimensional Screening Device,[20] and the Scales for Rating the Behavioural Characteristics of Superior Students.[21] Interviews are usually employed to help confirm or negate a child's score on a test or series of tests.[22] As with checklists, though, interviews are prone to subjectivity and biased reporting. Perhaps this is one of the reasons why interviews are rarely used.[23]

A more attractive alternative, and one that is commonly utilized, is that of parent or teacher nominations, or both. Nominations are based, for the most part, on informal observations. Interestingly, parent nominations, as a rule, correlate more closely with success in gifted programs than do teacher nominations.[24] Teachers often confuse compliance and diligence with giftedness.[25] Plainly, "Gifted children are frequently not 'good' students. Good students sit in the seat, get out the book and work on an assignment, or stand in line until it's time to play the game, just like they are told. Gifted children often don't."[26] For the gifted, "Getting ahead, pleasing and meeting the expectations of society are of secondary importance. When required to learn things they consider meaningless, they resist, ignore or give token acquiescence."[27] Hence, many high-ability youngsters perform poorly in terms of conventional classroom norms.

Teachers unaware of the characteristics of giftedness might label such children hyperactive, socially immature, or emotionally disturbed. Indeed, evidence suggests that untrained teachers tend to be largely inaccurate "spotters."[28] Whitemore,[29] for instance, tells of Bobby (IQ 153) who spent a second year in the first grade because of his disruptive behaviour and his failure to complete daily classroom assignments. It is therefore imperative that teachers, as principal nominators, be cognizant of the traits customarily associated with giftedness.

What attributes then separate the gifted child from the average learner? First, and perhaps foremost, the gifted are seen as being extremely independent[30] because they have an internally structured locus of control.[31] Often, they cannot identify with the society-at-large and, as a result, retreat into "a personal, secret world in which imagination becomes the only reality."[32] Withdrawal is due in part to both peer pressures to conform and to insensitive, ambivalent parents. If the gifted are consistently labelled "different and strange" by their playmates, they may internalize this designation and become eccentric and socially isolated.[33] Parents have also been known to confuse a child who is not a replica of either the mother or the father. On the one hand, the parents may take pride in the child's outstanding achievements but, on the other, fear that special treatment

> will adversely modify relationships within the family or shorten the period of parental influence. Others believe that labelling will cause their child to develop an inflated self-image that can interfere with personal relationships throughout life. Some mothers and fathers want their children to be well thought of and believe that gifted classes may take away from time with age mates, the proper group with whom children should first learn to relate.[34]

This inconsistent feedback confuses the child to the point of not knowing whether it is "good" or "bad" to be highly intelligent.[35] As a result, the child may conclude that it is not smart to be smart and decides therefore to either "hide" his or her ability in an effort to be accepted,[36] or the child may simply withdraw into a make-believe world.

The independence of gifted children is also reflected in their thinking styles. Rather than reasoning in a sequential manner, that is, step by step, they frequently "skip-think."[37] Translated, they solve complex problems without going through the so-called normal channels. Consequently, their work is very imaginative,[38] and distinctly original.[39] As well, they are able to concentrate for extended periods of time,[40] they exhibit unusual levels of task persistence,[41] and they generally prefer solitary activities[42] in which lecture and discussion are kept to a minimum.

In addition, the gifted are self-motivated,[43] very creative,[44] although not always in a conventional fashion,[45] and they are extremely perceptive,[46] in the sense that they are, "alert, keen, observant and respond quickly" to the demands of the situation.[47] In other words, they are the first to notice patterns, trends, and special relationships in seemingly dissimilar subjects and, as a consequence, new material may seem more recognized than learnt.

Other traits commonly associated with giftedness include abounding curiosity, physical and psychological stamina, better memory, although not necessarily more accurate memory, and heightened sensitivity.[48] The gifted, "have often been described as having 'one skin less' than other children; with their above average sensitivities and concerns for problems of society."[49] The tendency, though, to be offended easily or to respond quickly to criticism can lead to feelings of rejection and despair. The gifted, for example, may be ridiculed for overreacting, thereby increasing their feelings of being "odd."[50] Meanwhile, their acute awareness of society's injustices and mammoth hypocrisies can compound their feelings of scepticism[51] and cynicism.[52] Hence, the gifted need a "warm and safe psychological base from which to explore"[53] and they need understanding and support in their pursuit of excellence. Without this extra support, their curiosity is often suppressed and this, in turn, can lead to serious behavioural problems.

In summary, identification procedures should depend on more than one source of information. Although individual and group intelligence tests are the most widely employed screening devices,[54] they are not without problems. Truly, many tests ignore cultural idiosyncrasies and environmental factors,[55] and individual tests, in particular, are expensive to administer.[56] Still, a high IQ score "is a sufficient indicator that a type of giftedness exists. Moreover, an unusually high test score ought to alert us to the possibility that we are in the presence of one of those rare individuals who can make a momentous impact on human thought and civilization."[57]

At the same time, a multidimensional approach can help clarify the type of giftedness and confirm the need for a specific type of facility. Thus, identification strategies,

> should be started early in the school life of children and be continued. Progress should be continually monitored and procedures should be established for withdrawing those who do not

show promise. Withdrawal should not be seen as punishment, but rather as lack of congruence between the program's objectives and the child's specific needs. When many students are not performing well, however, the program should be reassessed and modified accordingly.[58]

IMPLEMENTATION

The development and successful implementation of programs for the gifted depend on a number of factors, most notably, funding, space allocation, and staff, administrative, and community support. The proces will also depend on whether the impetus is grassroots or board mandated. Summy[59] offers a list of ten practical suggestions to help teachers, and other interested parties, launch a grassroots movement. The proposals are aimed at overcoming institutional obstacles, financial barriers, suspicious colleagues, and reluctant administrators. Briefly, the list includes the following:

1. Make a commitment.
2. Be enthusiastic. A positive thinker is a goal achiever.
3. Research G/T theory and programs, thoroughly. Begin by reading books and articles.
4. Formulate a G/T program that fits the needs of your students, school, and community.
5. Set short- and long-term goals. Be realistic about the goals and the time sequence in which the goals are to be achieved.
6. Write your proposal and document it with the research sources you used. Make sure the proposal is consistent with the goals and curriculum of your school.
7. Present the proposal to your immediate supervisor. Be prepared to answer tough questions and do not become defensive; it will only work against you.
8. Do not take it personally if you are not successful in the beginning with your supervisor.
9. Do not ask for money. Design the program so that initial funding is not needed.
10. Be flexible. Change the program if there is need.

Summy concludes his article with some sound advice. Specifically, "What you are about to embark upon is a commitment to do more than you are doing now. It will take more time, planning, risk taking, energy and work. Regular duties will have to be performed, and you will still receive the same pay. Don't start any project unless you are willing to sacrifice!"[60]

Regardless of the impetus, there are two cardinal rules to the successful implementation of a gifted program. The first involves public awareness and the second concerns tailoring activities to the individual needs of a particular school and community. All those involved in the program should have a thorough understanding of what the organizers are trying to accomplish.

Newsletters, introductions at PTA meetings, and mailed requests for volunteers can help increase community awareness and support.[61] Orientation sessions might even include movies or slide/tape presentations that have been developed by both staff and students.[62] Whatever route is taken, it is imperative that all participants, students included, have a clear understanding of the selection strategies, the models of instruction, the goals, the teaching methods, the resource materials, and the evaluation techniques. Further, the participants must be provided continually with up-to-date feedback. Correspondence in the form of progress-reports, bulletins, and periodic invitations to visit the school can help maintain high interest levels.

Faculty can best be briefed through a formal series of inservice workshops, seminars, or colloquia. According to Reis and Renzulli, a minimum of three inservice sessions should be scheduled and each should address a separate topic.

> Sequential subjects to be covered include a detailed structural overview of the entire system; a definition of giftedness and resulting identification procedures; the specific roles and responsibilities of classroom and resource teachers; and, finally, an indepth session on compacting or streaming the regular curriculum to ensure that students have an adequate challenge in the regular classroom as well as the time to participate in the gifted program.[63]

The second cardinal rule, stated simply, is: build in flexibility and maintain program uniqueness. Every gifted facility should be carefully planned with a specific school and community in mind.[64] In other words, the planners should never fall into the trap of copying a model designed for another school. Each district's local administrative priorities, scheduling practices, and budgetary constraints must be fully weighed before a program is launched. Organizers should feel free to borrow ideas, but not exact blueprints.

PROGRAMMING

Programming can be divided into four complementary areas, namely, goals or objectives, structural design, models of instruction, and program evaluation. Naturally, the goals should correspond closely to the design and models of instruction. As well, the goals should be listed in sequential, hierarchical, and developmental terms. In the case of the Purdue Three-Stage Model, for instance, the goals are differentiated explicitly by levels of performance. In short, the goals include "the development of basic creative thinking and problem solving abilities; the development of higher level thinking skills, independent study, and research skills; and the development and maintenance of positive self-concepts through interaction with other gifted students."[65]

There are several structural designs, but most fall within the domain of either acceleration or enrichment. Acceleration involves administratively moving youngsters through regular programs at a faster rate. Such an approach could include early admission to kindergarten or Grade 1, collapsing grades (three grades in two years), enrolment in extra classes to earn advanced credit(s), and advanced placement in some subject(s).[66]

Acceleration has several financial and administrative advantages. Once implemented, for example, there is no need for additional space, materials, or teachers as students can be readily accommodated within the boundaries of existing structures. Acceleration, then, merely requires ingenuity and flexibility on the part of the administration, the staff, and the students.

However, a potential problem with acceleration is that of excessive repetition.[67] Elaborated, schools must guard against merely doing more of the "same" old things. As Renzulli warns, "the word 'course' automatically implies a certain amount of structure and uniformity,"[68] which, in turn, often means fixed time allocations, prescribed textbooks, and limited choices. In such circumstances, there is a danger that quantity, rather than quality, could become the guiding principle.

At present, most programs fall within the domain of enrichment practices.[69] Strictly speaking, there are two levels of enrichment, horizontal and vertical.[70] Horizontal enrichment refers to the provision of a wider range of experiences at the same level of difficulty, whereas vertical enrichment pertains to higher level activities of increasing complexity.[71]

Enrichment programs can be orchestrated on an individual basis within the confines of the regular classroom or outside on a daily or weekly basis depending on space allocations and availability of support staff. Full-time classes can also be arranged when resources and numbers permit

At the elementary level, the pull-out program is the most frequently employed alternative.[72] The term

> describes an administrative arrangement that places gifted students in a heterogeneous classroom for most of their instruction and "pulls them out" to study with other bright youngsters in special classes and a special setting for a portion of the school week. The special classes may meet in the student's home, school or the students may be bused to another school or designated center. Time spent in pull-out classes varies from less than an hour a week to a full day per week or more.[73]

Pull-out programs should either supplement what the children are learning in their regular classes or they should be directly related to the standard curriculum. Teachers must be careful not to fall into the "brain exercises" trap.[74] Problem-solving games, puzzles, and brainstorming sessions are fun but, unless they have continuity and enduring value, they are of little worth.

Pull-out programs allow children the opportunity to socialize and interact with peers like themselves. This opportunity can be a refreshing experience especially if they feel alienated by their classmates. Indeed, evidence suggests that grouping can enhance both their social and emotional development.[75] At the same time, though, pull-out practices can be a disruptive force. Many teachers oppose such programs because they further fragment the school day.[76] There is also the danger of "affective dislocation," where participants may physically feel their difference when they "get up" and go to a gifted class.[77] Their agemates can be cruel, and resentment, expressed or otherwise, can compound their feelings of being different. One solution to both problems, of course, is to schedule pull-out classes for a full day rather than for part of a day.

Another more attractive option is to establish full-time gifted classes. Self-contained facilities have several advantages over pull-out programs. First, there is no disruption and no fragmentation of other classrooms. Second, the teacher can incorporate a wider range of activities that cater specifically to each student's individual skills, talents, and abilities. Third, a permanent family grouping can create a safe environment in which the child can explore freely without the fear of having to constantly defend his or her eccentricity. This freedom can have a profound positive influence on student morale. Truly, there can be "an openness and excitement about culture and the humanities that would quickly be forced underground in a heterogeneous class. Having taught the entire educational spectrum, I can safely say I have seen intellectual curiosity buried for fear of scorn."[78]

Cries of elitism are regularly levelled at full-time gifted programs. Such criticism can be softened somewhat by building in a "pull-in" component.[79] That is, students from regular classes can be invited to participate in some field trips, projects, and in special presentations. Students can also be invited "in" for a game of checkers, chess, or Scrabble, and there can be a sharing of some weekly activities with other classes.

> By opening up certain enrichment sessions and inviting as many students as possible to listen to a lecture or to participate in a workshop on creative dramatics, all children benefit at certain times from the special program. Program ownership is thus extended to students outside the talent pool, and everyone has a better appreciation of and a more positive attitude toward its very existence.[80]

The Enrichment Triad Model[81] is the most widely used instructional paradigm in America.[82] There are other models of instruction but, due to space limitations, this discussion will be confined to the Enrichment Triad Model. The model is divided into three types of activities. The first type deals with general exploration, the second with group training, and the third with individual and small-group investigation.

Type I activities should be deliberately designed to generate personal interest. The teacher should expose students to a wide variety of topics from which they can select problems for independent study. Throughout this stage, the teacher should be actively involved, providing information, provoking curiosity, and encouraging further study. Interest centres, resource personnel, and field trips can help facilitate the process.

Type II activities are concerned with the development of high level thinking and feeling abilities, critical, divergent, reflective, and creative thinking, problem solving skills, inquiry methods, awareness development, and sensitivity training. Certain taxonomies, such as those proposed by Bloom, Krathwohl, Bloom and Masia, and Guilford,[83] can be used to help classify these cognitive and affective behaviours in a progressive pattern. It should be remembered that this stage is devoted primarily to the development and expansion of thinking skills, not the teaching of specific content. Students may acquire factual knowledge as a by-product of the process, but the focus should be procedural, not informational.

Type III activities should be directed to solving "real" problems. According to Renzulli,[84] a real problem has four characteristics.

> 1. A real problem must have a personal frame of reference, since it involves an emotional or affective commitment as well as an intellectual cognitive one.
> 2. A real problem does not have an existing or unique solution.
> 3. Calling something a problem does not necessarily make it a real problem for a given person or group.
> 4. The purpose of pursuing a real problem is to bring about some form of change and/or to contribute something new to the sciences, the arts, or the humanities.

A real problem, then, is genuine when it has meaning for the young investigator. Problems prescribed, presented, and predetermined by the teacher are not real problems. Teachers can focus, suggest, direct, and guide, but they should not structure the learning experience. Although there is nothing wrong with looking up information and summarizing existing facts and figures from encyclopedias and other reference books, such activities are classified as reporting, not researching. Researching involves real problems, problems that go beyond existing knowledge to create new constructs, concepts, or theories based on a synthesis of past research. In a real problem situation students assume the role of a first-hand inquirer.

> They may pursue these roles at less complex levels than adult researchers, artists and other creative producers, but the main point is that they go about their work thinking, feeling and doing like the practising professional. The end product of their efforts is not merely learning about existing knowledge. Rather, the major purpose is to use existing knowledge and methodology to create something that is new.[85]

Once a problem has been researched, the results should be presented to an appropriate audience or published in a newspaper or magazine. Dissemination will depend largely on the format of the final product and on the grade level of the student. With the younger students, it is sometimes best to limit the audience to classmates, parents, and teachers. Type III activities should consume approximately one-half of the time students spend in enrichment classes. In addition, they can, and should, be employed with all gifted students, from preschool[86] to senior high school.[87]

Program evaluation should provide feedback as to the success or failure of the instructional model. The process, however developed, should be closely linked to the goals of the program. In other words, the evaluator(s) should continually monitor the original goals to see if they are being achieved, and, if so, to what extent.

Reis and Renzulli[88] developed a software package that contains structured forms to monitor program activities, questionnaires for those with vested interests in the program, and instruments designed to assess cognitive and affective growth. The items are intended as a set of "friendly enforcers" that help pinpoint areas of deficiency. Another equally attractive alternative was developed by Morris and Fitz-Gibbon.[89] Their book, *Evaluator's Handbook*, describes how to conduct a systematic formative evaluation of a gifted program. The book is divided into a series of four consecutive steps commencing with setting the boundaries for the evaluation and terminating with reporting procedures.

Whatever approach is selected, it is important not to rely entirely on standardized achievement tests. Administering pre- and post-tests can present a distorted picture because most gifted students would be performing initially at the ninety-fifth percentile. In fact, post-test scores may show decreased performance due largely to the phenomenon known as regression toward the mean.

CONCLUSION

This article has looked at the education of the intellectually gifted student. The text defines the term gifted, offers guidelines for identification of members, and provides information on the implementation and operationalization of programs for the group.

In the United States, public support of gifted education has been rapidly increasing to the point where, in 1980, their school systems were "in the midst of enjoying the strongest amount of acceptance and public support that has ever been accorded to the gifted child movement in America."[90] Moreover, there is every indication that the movement has and will continue to "thrive" and "flourish."[91]

In Canada, gifted education has progressed more slowly than in the United States. As late as 1980, for instance, there was little public support of facilities for the gifted.[92] Since that time, the movement has been gaining force. Canadian educators are getting involved and they are starting to provide special services for the gifted.

Ultimately, special programs for the gifted should be part of every school system in Canada, no matter how big or small. At the moment, this challenge may be somewhat idealistic but, in the end, it is the gifted who will brave the unknown and bridge the universe. Let us not forget, therefore, that the more we deny them, the more we deny ourselves!

NOTES

1. Marquis Academic Media, "Gifted and Talented" in *Yearbook of Special Education 1977–78* (Chicago: Marquis Who's Who, 1977), 521–33; B. Rice, "Going for the Gifted Gold," *Psychology Today* 13 (Feb. 1980): 55–67; R.L. Zorn, "A Comprehensive Program for the Gifted/Talented Pupils in Grades 1 Through 12," *Education* 103 (Summer 1983): 310–15.
2. A. Kahanoff, "Educating Canada's Gifted," *ATA Magazine* 60 (Nov. 1979): 27–29.
3. W. Dennis, "Charting a Brighter Course for Genius," *Maclean's*, 19 October 1981, 53–54; Kahanoff, "Educating Canada's Gifted."
4. B. Borthwick, I. Dow, D. Lévesque, and R. Banks, eds., *The Gifted and Talented Students in Canada: Results of a CEA Survey* (Toronto: The Canadian Education Association, 1980).
5. Dennis, "Charting a Brighter Course for Genius."
6. Alberta Education, Planning Services Branch, *Educating Gifted and Talented Pupils in Alberta*, Report of the Minister's Task Force on Gifted and Talented Pupils (Edmonton: Alberta Education, 1983).
7. Ontario Ministry of Education, *Bill 82—An Act to Amend the Education Act, 1974* (Toronto: Ontario Ministry of Education, 1980).
8. G. Adamson, "Giftedness/Creativity: The Coin With More Than Two Sides," *ATA Magazine* 63 (Jan. 1983): 28–29.
9. B. Levin, "Identification of Intellectually Gifted Students. 1: Overview of Issues," *Research Peel Board of Education Bulletin* 3 (Nov. 1981): 1.
10. P.M. Powell and T. Haden, "The Intellectual and Psychosocial Nature of Extreme Giftedness," *Roeper Review* 6 (Feb. 1984): 131–33; W.C. Roedell, "Vulnerabilities of Highly Gifted Children," *Roeper Review* 6 (Feb. 1984): 127–30.
11. Roedell, ibid., 127.
12. F.M. Hewett and S.R. Forness, *Education of Exceptional Learners* (Boston: Allyn and Bacon, Inc., 1977).
13. P.E. Veron, G. Adamson, and D.F. Vernon, *The Psychology and Education of Gifted Children* (London: Methuen, 1977).
14. Adamson, "Giftedness/Creativity."
15. R.J. Kirschenbaum, "Flexible Methods for Identifying the Gifted," *Education Digest* 49 (Dec. 1983): 58–60.
16. J.F. Feldhusen, J.W. Asher, and S.M. Hoover, "Problems in the Identification of Giftedness, Talent, or Ability," *Gifted Child Quarterly* 28 (Fall 1984): 149–51; Kirschenbaum, "Flexible Methods"; R. Swassing, "The Multiple Component Alternative for Gifted Education," *A/C/T* 33 (May-June 1984): 10–11.
17. B.H. Yarborough and R.A. Johnson, "Identifying the Gifted: A Theory-Practice Gap," *Gifted Child Quarterly* 27 (Summer 1983): 135–38.
18. Feldhusen et al., "Problems in the Identification of Giftedness, Talent, or Ability."
19. R.A. Male and P. Perrone, "Identifying Talent and Giftedness: Part I," *Roeper Review* 2 (Sept. 1979): 5–7, Part II (Dec. 1979): 9–11, Part III (Feb.-March 1980): 9–11.

20. B. Krantz, *Multi-dimensional Screening Device for the Identification of Gifted Talented Children* (Grand Fork, N.D.: Bureau of Educational Research, University of North Dakota, 1978).

21. J.S. Renzulli, L.H. Smith, A.J. White, C.M. Callahan, and C.M. Hartman, *Scales for Rating the Behavioral Characteristics of Superior Students* (Wethersfield, Conn.: Creative Learning Press, 1976).

22. G. Lewis, "Alternatives to Acceleration for the Highly Gifted Child," *Roeper Review* 6 (Feb. 1984): 133–36.

23. B.H. Yarborough and R.A. Johnson, "Identifying the Gifted: A Theory-Practice Gap," *Gifted Child Quarterly* 27 (Summer 1983): 135–38.

24. B. Clark, *Growing Up Gifted: Developing the Potential of Children at Home and at School* (Columbus, Ohio: Charles E. Merrill, 1979); Kahanoff, "Educating Canada's Gifted"; W.C. Roedell, N.E. Jackson, and H.B. Robinson, *Gifted Young Children* (New York: Teachers College Press, 1980); R.D. Strom, "Expectations for Educating the Gifted and Talented," *Educational Forum* 47 (Spring 1983), 279–303.

25. W.D. Kirk, "A Tentative Screening Procedure for Selecting Bright and Slow Children in Kindergarten," *Exceptional Children* 33 (Dec. 1966): 235–41; C.W. Pegnato and J.W. Birch, "Locating Gifted Children in Junior High Schools: A Comparison of Methods," *Exceptional Children* 25 (March 1959): 300–4.

26. C. Tingey-Michaelis, "Gifted Kids Are Not All Gift Wrapped," *Early Years* 14 (Apr. 1984): 64–65.

27. J. Yatvin, "Gifted or Bright?" *Principal* (Jan. 1984): 14–16.

28. G.H. Gear, "Accuracy of Teacher Judgment in Identifying Intellectually Gifted Children: A Review of the Literature," *Gifted Child Quarterly* 20 (Winter 1976): 478–89.

29. J.R. Whitmore, *Giftedness, Conflict, and Underachievement* (Boston: Allyn and Bacon, 1980).

30. P.M. Powell and T. Hayden, "The Intellectual and Psychosocial Nature of Extreme Giftedness"; J. Ricca, "Learning Styles and Preferred Instructional Strategies of Gifted Students," *Gifted Child Quarterly* 28 (Summer 1984): 121–26; E.E. Stewart, "Learning Styles Among Gifted/Talented Students: Instructional Technique Preferences," *Exceptional Children* 42, 2 (1981): 134–38; P.L. Vail, *The World of the Gifted Child* (New York: Walker and Co., 1979).

31. R. Dunn and G. Price, "The Learning Style Characteristics of Gifted Children," *Gifted Child Quarterly* 24 (Winter 1980): 33–36; Powell and Hayden, ibid.; Stewart, "Learning Styles Among Gifted/Talented Students."

32. Tingey-Michaelis, "Gifted Kids Are Not All Gift Wrapped," 65.

33. Rodell, "Vulnerabilities of Highly Gifted Children."

34. Strom, "Expectations for Educating the Gifted and Talented," 296.

35. Powell and Hayden, "The Intellectual and Psychosocial Nature of Extreme Giftedness."

36. R.D. Feldman, "Helping the Gifted Grow Up," *Instructor* 94 (Sept. 1984): 92–94.

37. Powell and Hayden, "The Intellectual and Psychosocial Nature of Extreme Giftedness."

38. Strom, "Expectations for Educating the Gifted and Talented."

39. Tingey-Michaelis, "Gifted Kids Are Not All Gift Wrapped."
40. Strom, "Expectations for Educating the Gifted and Talented"; Vail, *The World of the Gifted Child*.
41. Dunn and Price, "The Learning Style Characteristics of Gifted Children"; S. Griggs and G. Price, "A Comparison Between the Learning Styles of Gifted Versus Average Suburban Junior High School Students," *Roeper Review* 3 (Sept. 1980): 7–9; Strom, "Expectations for Educating the Gifted and Talented."
42. Griggs and Price, ibid.; G. Price, K. Dunn, R. Dunn, and S. Griggs, "Studies in Students' Learning Styles," *Roeper Review* 4 (Nov. 1981): 38–40; Strom, "Expectations for Educating the Gifted and Talented."
43. Dunn and Price, "The Learning Style Characteristics of Gifted Children"; Griggs and Price, ibid.; Vail, *The World of the Gifted Child*.
44. Levin, "Identification of Intellectually Gifted Students. 1. Overview of Issues."
45. Vail, *The World of the Gifted Child*.
46. Dunn and Price, "The Learning Style Characteristics of Gifted Children"; Griggs and Price, "A Comparison Between the Learning Styles of Gifted Versus Average Surburban Junior High School Students"; Vail, *The World of the Gifted Child*.
47. Tingey-Michaelis, "Gifted Kids Are Not All Gift Wrapped," 64.
48. Vail, *The World of the Gifted Child*.
49. S.M. Shiner, "Challenge and Commitment for the Gifted: A Task for the 80's," *Orbit* 11 (Feb. 1980): 8.
50. Roedell, "Vulnerabilities of Highly Gifted Children."
51. V. Jones, "Current Trends in Classroom Management: Implications for Gifted Students," *Roeper Review* 6 (Sept. 1983): 26–30.
52. Roedell, "Vulnerabilities of Highly Gifted Children."
53. J. Khatena, *The Creatively Gifted Child: Suggestions for Parents and Teachers* (New York: Vantage Press, 1978), 93.
54. B.M. Mitchell, "An Update on the State of Gifted/Talented Education in the U.S.," *Phi Delta Kappan* 63 (Jan. 1982): 357–58; Yarborough and Johnson, "Identifying the Gifted."
55. Hewitt and Forness, *Education of Exceptional Learners*.
56. Kahanoff, "Educating Canada's Gifted"; J. Payne, "The Gifted" in *Behavior of Exceptional Children—An Introduction to Special Education*, edited by N.G. Haring (Columbus, Ohio: Charles E. Merrill Publishing, 1974), 189–214.
57. M.M. Brown, "The Needs and Potential of the Highly Gifted: Toward a Model of Responsiveness," *Roeper Review* 6 (Feb. 1984): 126.
58. G.P. O'Neill and B.M. Scollay, "The Education of Intellectually Gifted Children: A Challenge for the 1980s and Beyond," *Comment on Education* 13 (Feb. 1983): 12.
59. J. Summy, "Gifted and Talented Program Development: The Teacher As A Change-Agent," *Education* 104 (Fall 1983): 45–46.
60. Ibid., 46.
61. Zorn, "A Comprehensive Program for the Gifted/Talented Pupils in Grades 1 Through 12."

62. S.M. Reis and J.S. Renzulli, "Key Features of Successful Programs for the Gifted and Talented," *Educational Leadership* 41 (April 1984): 28–34.
63. Ibid., 31.
64. Ibid.; Summy, "Gifted and Talented Program Development."
65. P.B. Kolloff and J.F. Feldhusen, "The Effects of Enrichment on Self-Concept and Creative Thinking," *Gifted Child Quarterly* 28 (Summer 1984): 53.
66. Vernon, Adamson, and Vernon, *The Psychology and Education of Gifted Children*.
67. Feldman, "Helping the Gifted Grow Up."
68. J.S. Renzulli, "The Enrichment Triad Model: A Guide for Developing Defensible Programs for the Gifted and Talented," *Gifted Child Quarterly* 20 (Fall 1976): 316.
69. Jones, "Current Trends in Classroom Management."
70. R. Banks, B. Bélanger, I. Bettiol, B. Borthwick, B. Donnelly, and A. Smith, *Gifted/Talented Children* (Toronto: Ontario Ministry of Education, 1978); Payne "The Gifted"; Vernon et al., *The Psychology and Education of Gifted Children*.
71. Payne, ibid.
72. J. Cox and N. Daniel, "The Pull-Out Model," *G/C/T* 34 (Sept.-Oct. 1984): 55–60.
73. Ibid., 55.
74. N. Mirsky, "Starting an Interage Full-time Gifted Class," *G/C/T* 33 (May-June 1984): 24–26.
75. T.E. Newland, *The Gifted in Socio-Educational Perspective* (Englewood Cliffs, N.J.: Prentice-Hall, 1976); F. Speed, "Teaching the Bright Child," *Orbit* 9 (Feb. 1978): 6–11; H.M. Woodliffe, *Teaching Gifted Learners: A Handbook for Teachers* (Toronto: Ontario Institute for Studies in Education, 1977).
76. Cox and Daniel, "The Pull-Out Model"; Mirsky, "Starting an Interage Full-time Gifted Class," *G/C/T* 33 (May/June 1984): 24–6.
77. Cox and Daniel, ibid.
78. Mirsky, "Starting an Interage Full-time Gifted Class," 26.
79. Ibid.
80. Reis and Renzulli, "Key Features of Successful Programs for the Gifted and Talented," 33.
81. J.S. Renzulli, *The Enrichment Triad Model: A Guide for Developing Defensible Programs for the Gifted and Talented* (Mansfield Center, Conn.: Creative Learning Press, 1977).
82. Mitchell, "An Update on the State of Gifted/Talented Education in the U.S."
83. B. Bloom, ed., *Taxonomy on Educational Objectives. The Classification of Educational Goals Handbook I: Cognitive Domain* (New York: Longman, 1977); D.R. Krathwohl, B.S. Bloom, and B.B. Masia, *Taxonomy of Educational Objectives. The Classification of Educational Goals Handbook II: Affective Domain* (New York: David McKay Co., 1974); and J.P. Guilford, *The Nature of Human Intelligence* (New York: McGraw-Hill, 1967).
84. J.S. Renzulli, "Guiding the Gifted in the Pursuit of Real Problems. The Transformed Role of the Teacher," *Journal of Creative Behavior* 17, 1 (1983): 49–50.

85. Ibid., 50.
86. C. Sloan and U. Stedtnitz, "The Enrichment Triad Model for the Very Young Gifted," *Roeper Review* 6 (Apr. 1984): 204-6.
87. Zorn, "A Comprehensive Program for the Gifted/Talented Pupils in Grades 1 Through 12."
88. Reis and Renzulli, "Key Features of Successful Programs for the Gifted and Talented."
89. L.L. Morris and C.T. Fitz-Gibbon, *Evaluator's Handbook* (Beverly Hills: Sage Publications, 1978).
90. J.S. Renzulli, "Will the Gifted Movement be Alive and Well in 1990?" *Gifted Child Quarterly* 24 (Winter 1980): 3.
91. B.M. Mitchell, "An Update on the State of Gifted/Talented Education in the U.S.," *Phi Delta Kappan* 63 (Jan. 1982): 357-58.
92. Borthwick, Dow, Lévesque, and Banks, eds., *The Gifted and Talented Students in Canada*.

SECTION 8:
TEACHER TRAINING IN CANADA

Educators have been under attack from critics who charge that teachers being trained today are inadequately prepared to assist our youth in coping with the complexities of a society in transition, or perhaps more properly, a society in a continuous process of transformation. Some lament the erosion of traditional educational values; others stress the need for change in educational goals and assumptions. The authors in this section identify several of the issues facing those involved in teacher training in Canada and offer possible directions for the future.

To Birch and Elliot, "the paramount issue in teacher education is the formulation of a conception of teacher education of sufficient scope to accommodate the full reality of the task." In discussing this theme, they concentrate on issues surrounding the selection of candidates for teacher training, the appropriate subject-matter preparation for elementary and secondary school teachers, the necessity of adequately linking theory and practice in teacher preparation programs, and the conceptualization of teacher education as being an integral endeavour carried on throughout teachers' careers.

Smith examines four issues that he feels are of national concern: Who should enter the teaching profession? Should faculties of education continue their traditional practice and train teachers for elementary and secondary school roles or should they train teachers who have more generic capabilities so they can work in a number of different settings where some form of instruction may be involved? Should teachers be trained to have a provincial, a national, or a global perspective and orientation? Should we encourage and ensure greater mobility of teachers within Canada? These issues are discussed in relation to the social forces that are creating underlying tensions.

Sackney contends that a growing demand for accountability in education and a burgeoning research base for understanding the dynamics of teaching and learning are resulting in higher expectations for teacher performance and for teacher training. He points out that the responsibility to develop more rigorous entry standards and to develop improved teacher education programs based on research findings rests squarely on the faculties of education and, to this end, he concludes his chapter with a tentative model for teacher training in Canada.

Patterson and Miklos contend that the basic structure, curriculum, and methodology of teacher training has remained relatively static for the past fifty years, and now is the time to identify fundamental issues in order to promote real change in teacher preparation practices. According to Patterson and Miklos, there is still a general failure to effectively instill the process of lifelong learning, to develop decision-making skills, or to promote the fruitful exploration of relevant data bases. They note that these problems are not unique to teacher education but are inherent in the existing university system and occur in other professions such as medicine. Patterson and Miklos discuss the fundamental issues in the areas of curriculum, requirements for admission, instructional strategies, and linkages between teaching professionals and faculties of education. They conclude that teacher education needs a broader definition and the stronger encouragement of alternatives if it is to appreciably accelerate its own evolution.

TOWARDS A NEW CONCEPTION OF TEACHER EDUCATION

DANIEL R. BIRCH AND MURRAY ELLIOTT

How is teacher education to be conceived? While it has not always been recognized as a crucial issue, how teacher education has been conceived—by those preparing to become teachers, by those providing preparation programs, and by the profession generally—has had major implications for the quality of teacher preparation and ultimately for the quality of teaching in society's schools.

Our contention is that teacher education has often been conceived much too narrowly. University students and faculty members alike often refer to the teacher preparation program as the "fifth year"—the one year that graduates spend in a faculty of education between a degree program and a teaching position. Those in concurrent teacher education programs frequently separate in their minds the pedagogical courses and student teaching experiences from the liberal arts and science components of their programs; they regard the pedagogical courses and student teaching as the *professional* part of their degree program—as their *teacher* preparation proper—and the non-pedagogical components as something of an irrelevant intrusion into their teacher education.

Whether concurrent or consecutive, a teacher education program culminates in the award of a teaching certificate or licence—culminates and, in many minds, terminates. The teaching certificate marks the attainment of the status of a fully qualified teacher and the end of an individual's teacher education.

In our view these positions represent serious distortions of how teacher education should be conceived and of how it must be conceived if teachers are to be adequately prepared for the complex challenges facing them, both as individuals and as a profession, in the 1990s and beyond. In this paper we will address selected aspects of this theme. In particular, we will focus attention on:

1. the selection of teacher candidates;
2. the subject-matter preparation of teachers;
3. bridging theory and practice in teacher preparation; and
4. teacher education as a career-long endeavour.

THE SELECTION OF TEACHER CANDIDATES

We regard teaching as fundamentally an intellectual and moral activity. A free and democratic society depends on its citizens' ability to exercise the right and responsibility of making informed choices. Schools and teachers have a substantial role in enabling children and young people to develop the understanding, the critical thinking skills, and the attitudes and values essential to exercising that responsibility. We regard teacher education as the process of enabling teachers to gain the necessary knowledge, understanding, skills, and inclinations to carry out this intellectually and morally demanding role.

We are conscious that the challenge of teaching effectively is great and we will consider below several aspects of what a teacher must know and be able to do. It would seem self-evident that the teaching profession should be populated by the brightest and the best. We have to ask, then, what could make the selection of teacher candidates an issue. First, it is widely perceived that those who enter teaching are not the brightest and the best, and we will explore that perception. Second, in addition to their manifest educational tasks, schools play a part in social role selection. If recruiting members of certain minority groups can mitigate the systematic de-selection of group members for higher status roles in society, that has implications for practice. Third, it may be desirable to increase diversity among teachers merely to increase the richness of the learning resources represented by teachers collectively.

Meet the average Canadian teacher. In 1979–80 she was thirty-seven years old, a woman, held a bachelor's degree, and had ten years' experience working under the supervision of a male principal[1] in a school with a pupil/teacher ratio of 19:1. In the intervening years, decreased mobility in teaching and fewer openings for new teachers mean that today's average teacher is over forty years old, and still female in all Canadian provinces but one.[2] Increased awareness of the folly of overlooking talented women is slowly reducing the percentage of male principals.

And is this "average teacher" perceived by the Canadian public as the brightest and the best? Polls show the public perception of Canadian teachers to be quite positive and markedly more so for respondents with current or recent school contact. Of all public institutions, schools head the list in degree of public confidence followed in order by local government, the church, and the courts.

Teachers are generally seen as performing well in a salient role. Nevertheless, one frequently encounters in the press or among members of the public indications of a belief that those who choose teaching are somehow less able than others. Indeed, Shaw's dictum that, "he who can, does; he who cannot, teaches," is widely quoted, not infrequently with the tag, "and he who cannot teach, teaches teachers."

What causes people simultaneously to hold the views that schools and teachers are doing a good job, that teachers are less intelligent than other university graduates, and that teacher education is less effective than other programs? People rate local schools better than schools in general and rate them even more highly if they have their own children in them. Thus, it appears that many share a vague, general impression that is less positive than local impressions, especially those based on direct experience. But there is more than a grain of truth underlying common views of selection for teacher education.

SELECTION

When compared with other professions, teaching is characterized by a relative lack of selectivity. A major factor is the sheer size of the teaching profession. The number of teachers in Canada's elementary and secondary schools is well over one-quarter of a million (compared to 6500 doctors and 46 233 lawyers). At the peak of teacher demand in the mid-1970s, almost 14 percent of the university undergraduate enrolment in Canada was in education (compared to 2.7 percent each in medicine and law). Thus, whatever the aspirations of the profession, it would be impossible for faculties of education to insist that all students be drawn from the top fifteen or twenty percent of all university students. Relative size alone, apart from status—and the two are not completely independent—makes it impossible for teacher education programs to be as selective as those in medicine or law. Nevertheless, all or virtually all teacher education programs have minimum standards for admission and retention well above those in arts or science (including particularly standards for achievement in arts and science courses). In addition, most programs experience demand exceeding capacity and many have several qualified candidates for every opening.

Probably the majority of candidates for teaching in Canadian teacher education programs are A or B students, with quite a number of C+ students in some institutions. Assuming that society also wants bright and committed engineers, lawyers, physicians, and scientists, we might ask what is a reasonable proportion of the most outstanding students that can be attracted into teacher education. Our view is that the demands of teaching, properly understood, are almost overwhelming. The potential for teacher education, properly defined, to challenge students intellectually and to stretch them also in terms of performance skills is enormous. Consequently, there should be room for the most intelligent and no room for the unintelligent.

It may be true that programs attract the students they deserve. If so, as teacher education becomes more rigorous and more effective itself in providing students with the conceptual tools and the skills needed for effective teaching, it will generate greater demand for admission. As it becomes known for practitioners capable of analysing their experience, of taking a reflective stance, it will prove more attractive to those able and willing to move beyond a superficial, merely technical training. This entails not only intellectual, but above all moral development: the ability to identify with the moral purposes of education and to act autonomously on the basis of considered principles.

Whatever the particular teaching strategy adopted for specific purposes, the effective teacher is fundamentally a communicator, and communication skills are, therefore, an appropriate basis for selection. We propose that, at several points in the formal preparation program, admission or continuation be contingent on achieving a specified level of competence in speech and writing in the language of instruction.

Past behaviour is frequently one indicator of future interest and activity. It is, therefore, sensible to seek in prospective candidates for teaching some evidence of previous interest in teacher-like roles and activities. We, therefore, would ask candidates to provide statements of prior experience and would look for indications that opportunities for relevant experience had been sought out and that some success had been experienced, whether in clubs, youth work, playground supervising, tutoring, or camp leadership.

Perhaps the most important aspect of selection is that it is a continuous or repeated process over an extended period of time. There are many appropriate points for review, selection, testing, and affirmation of achievement. More serious attention to selection is an important element in promoting identification with the profession.

AFFIRMATIVE ACTION FOR NATIVE TEACHERS

Schools function implicitly to sort young people for various roles in life, most often in such a way that their status approximates that of their parents. To recognize this is not to make it a goal of schooling or even to condone it. But deploring this latent function of schools will not change its effects one iota. Any change is likely to require significant social interventions. Such interventions have taken place in the development of teacher education programs with, by, and for Native people. The inclusion of Native people as home/school co-ordinators and as resource people for Native language and culture was an effort to enhance the relevance of the school to Native children. Their inclusion represented important steps toward enhancing the participation and success of Indian children in public schools. Nevertheless, they were typically restricted to marginal and precarious roles. Recruiting and training Indian teachers would not only reduce the distance between Indian cultural groups and the schools but would also provide Indian children and young people with influential role models.

In the past fifteen years many programs have been established to prepare Native Indian teachers. The best have entailed co-determination in the selection of students and staff, substantial cultural content, and extensive tutoring and counselling support. Native Indian people are well represented on staff and serve as administrators. Perhaps the most important single factor is that, although affirmative action is necessary at the time of initial selection and admission, no adjustment of standards or expectations takes place at the time of completion and graduation.

Programs for Native teachers have multiplied many times over the representation of Native people in the profession. In addition some have moved through teacher education and into other fields, particularly law, and graduate programs are now emerging for administrators and leaders. Native young people faced with role models and psychological support are staying in secondary school to graduation.

DIVERSITY IN THE TEACHING PROFESSION

In today's urban schools in Toronto, Montreal, or Vancouver—the major recipients of recent immigrants—the student population is very diverse in cultural and ethnic origin. The students and their families are thus a rich source of multicultural knowledge and experience. The teaching staff, on the other hand, is substantially less diverse. If the school is at once to reinforce the values of unity and diversity in Canada, diversity in the ethno-cultural background of teachers is desirable. Representation of ethnic minorities in the ranks of the teaching profession makes a teaching staff a potentially richer resource and serves to reinforce the identity of students with various ethnic backgrounds. Recruiting a culturally diverse student body in teacher education may be a reasonable end to pursue quite independent of any need for affirmative action.

THE SUBJECT-MATTER PREPARATION OF TEACHERS

Contrary to what is sometimes maintained, we do not accept that studies in the liberal arts and sciences are irrelevant intrusions into a teacher education program. On the contrary, such studies are as essential to the professional preparation of teachers as are studies in the various aspects of pedagogy.

The liberal arts and sciences cover a wide range of human knowledge and a university generally includes in its curriculum both courses of a general survey character and courses narrowly focussed on relatively obscure or highly technical areas of the disciplines. Some of these courses may be designed primarily with the interests of prospective researchers in mind and it is understandable that prospective teachers might find them ill-suited to their objectives. Nor are all subjects offered in a large "multi-versity" equally important areas of study from the perspective of prospective teachers. There are, however, certain disciplines, and within these certain courses and types of courses, that are essential components of the preparation of professional teachers.

THE LIBERALLY EDUCATED TEACHER

We want first to argue for the importance of every teacher achieving a sound liberal education incorporating studies from the major areas of human intellectual and cultural achievement.[3] This is as important for the kindergarten and first grade teacher as for the junior- or senior-secondary teacher. It is equally important for those who will serve as generalist teachers as for those who will specialize in teaching but a single subject.

Education is, fundamentally, an intellectual and moral enterprise.[4] It is concerned at root with introducing people to their intellectual heritage; with helping them to learn how to make valid discriminations within different dimensions of their experience of the natural and interpersonal worlds; and with helping them to master the concepts, the procedures, and the sensitivities necessary for creating and refining meaningful and valid expressions of the longings and achievements of the human spirit. Education is concerned with enabling people to understand their world; to accept, respect, and rejoice in their world; and to interact with and control that world both effectively and responsibly.

If teachers are to be equipped to structure and facilitate young people's education, conceived in these broad terms, they must themselves have the breadth of understanding and perspective represented by the liberally educated person. If they are to assist young people in differentiating and enhancing their various abilities and sensitivities, teachers must themselves have sympathies and achievements in these same areas. Teachers must have developed aesthetic sensitivities as well as the ability to make and build upon reliable empirical discriminations; they must appreciate the significance of the present human potential and predicament in the context of the past achievements of the human will; they must have some substantial awareness and respect for alternative ways and styles of life and of living; and they must acknowledge the importance of moral demands in human interactions.

How are these important understandings, sensitivities, appreciations, abilities, and achievements acquired? In one sense these are the achievements of living and maturing as a person. But these specific human achievements are also the focus of systematic and sustained attention in the academic disciplines that constitute the curriculum of the liberal arts and science faculties of a university: such studies as history; the visual, performing, and literary arts; philosophy, ethics, and theology; the physical, life, and social sciences; and language, logic, and mathematics.

The achievement of a liberal or general education incorporating some or all of these studies has frequently been advanced as an important value, but one different from the demands of professional or vocational education. In the case of the preparation of a teacher, we maintain, this distinction between liberal and professional education breaks down. Given the distinctive task of the teacher, liberal education has not only the importance it has generally for all persons; it has in addition a distinctive professional urgency. Given that educating young people is what teaching is about, acquiring the achievement of a liberal education is, for the prospective teacher, a part of professional education.

The general argument in favour of liberal education as essential for the professional preparation of teachers may be particularized differently depending on the level and specialization aspirations of the prospective teacher. The generalist primary teacher will assume responsibility for teaching the full curriculum. This teacher assumes responsibility for assisting children to differentiate and develop the full range of human sensitivities, capacities, dispositions, and understandings. In order to discharge this broad responsibility, a teacher must have a broad range of developed achievements. Granted, children's target capacities, sensitivities, and understandings will not be developed to a highly sophisticated level in a kindergarten or first grade setting; it is, however, essential that sound foundations be laid there as a basis for more advanced work at a later stage. If children's scientific understanding, aesthetic appreciation, or moral attitudes are distorted or thwarted in the first grade, later recovery and rebuilding is rendered more complicated and less probable. In order to guide and facilitate this learning, the first grade teacher must have a sound, even if limited, grasp of the structure and procedures of the forms of human inquiry being taught.

Senior secondary teachers typically teach only a single subject or perhaps two related subjects. This notwithstanding, we submit, it is still essential for them to have a comprehensive understanding and appreciation of the different forms of human inquiry and of their potential for enriching human understanding and illuminating the fullness of human experience. With the rapid increase in human knowledge and with the greater complexity of many fields of professional practice, university and other post-secondary programs have become more highly specialized and more narrowly focussed. One result of this has been that the breadth of understanding across the full range of human achievements has become increasingly difficult to embrace as an objective of such programs.

Moreover, as such programs have become more sharply focussed, the admissions requirements have become more narrowly defined. The justification for this streaming is to enable students in such programs to attain a higher level of knowledge and skill in their chosen field by the completion of their post-secondary program. An unfortunate consequence of such streaming, however, is that the number and range of elective courses that can be accommodated within either the post-secondary or the preparatory secondary program is limited. Accordingly, students risk having only narrow bands of their total human capacities developed.

In the extreme, when an individual aspires to a program that requires secondary preparatory studies narrowly and exclusively composed of work in, say, mathematics and the sciences, the development of the student's broader capacities and sensitivities depends crucially on the mathematics and science teachers' sensitivities, sympathies, and accomplishments in the arts, humanities, and other areas. The breadth of such students' liberal education is dependent on the abilities of these teachers to present their subjects within a clear context of the total domain of human inquiry and achievement. Similarly, when a student is for one reason or another restricting formal studies to the humanities or the arts, that student's possibilities for achieving broadly based understanding of the full range of human possibilities depends on teachers of these subjects communicating their subjects within the broader context of forms of human inquiry, including the mathematical and scientific.

Breadth of educational achievements of the sort usually referred to as liberal education must thus be a part of the professional requirements of all teachers.

SUBJECT-MATTER STUDIES

Studies in subject fields in arts or science faculties as well as certain other areas are also essential to teachers' professional preparation in that it is precisely these studies that provide the substance of what the teacher will teach.

Clearly not everything that the teacher attempts to teach and that the student is to learn, is knowledge. But much of it typically is and much of the remainder, though not knowledge itself, is knowledge-related—such things as concepts, investigative procedures, the criteria and procedures for assessing factual discoveries and explanatory theories, and such inquiry-related dispositions as inquisitiveness, intellectual honesty, and the propensity to actually test conclusions against the relevant evidential experience or canons of reasoning.

To acquire a base of information and understanding of the content and procedures of the subjects to be taught is one essential objective of including subject-matter studies in the curriculum of prospective elementary and secondary teachers.

It has long been accepted that secondary teachers require substantial studies in the subjects they propose to teach. However, there has not always been full agreement about the proper amount or the ideal nature of such studies. Common consensus frequently favours the equivalent of at least one full year of post-secondary studies per teaching field, spread over several academic years; some maintain that considerably more subject-matter study (i.e., study to the master's level) is essential for those who would teach at the senior-secondary level, particularly for students planning to specialize in that subject later.

The question of the nature and amount of subject-matter study necessary for elementary teachers has not, in our view, been well addressed. This is understandable, for the elementary teacher typically serves as a generalist teacher with responsibility for the full range of subjects in the prescribed curriculum—language, the arts, mathematics, social studies, science, music, physical education, and drama, with subjects like a second language, religion, and/or computer studies added as well. The scope of the elementary teacher's subject-matter responsibility is really quite overwhelming!

Until recently, conventional wisdom tolerated elementary teachers having no post-secondary studies in some or even all of their teaching subjects. Recent research has documented this unfortunate lack of subject-matter preparation in both mathematics[5] and science.[6] The situation is probably similar in other fields. After all, it was argued, the content of the elementary school curriculum is not all that difficult, and any person with secondary school graduation and some pedagogical training is sufficiently beyond the achievement levels of the children to be able to teach. The challenges of elementary teaching are not content challenges, but pedagogical ones.

Precisely such an argument has had the effect of condoning the teaching of distorted and erroneous subject-matter in elementary schools: bad mathematics, bad science, bad art, bad history, bad physical education, etc. In some subjects such as mathematics or science, bad subject-matter has led to confusion, error, or incoherence; in others such as the arts, bad content has resulted in a hardening of human sensitivities and a withering of the creative imagination; in still others such as physical education, bad and ill-selected activities have proven physically damaging to individual students.

In our view, the subject-matter preparation of elementary teachers is at least as demanding as that of secondary teachers, indeed more so because of the greater number of subjects in which detailed preparation is required. With the mushrooming of knowledge in all fields, it is questionable whether the ideal of the elementary generalist teacher is till defensible.[7]

We must not be misled by the apparent lesser sophistication of the treatment of content in elementary than in secondary classrooms. There is a fundamental continuity of the intellectual content of education at all levels. The primary teacher is as much concerned with teaching, within the level of students' capabilities, fundamental concepts, procedures, and skills of inquiry in science, art, or literature as is the university graduate instructor.

Clearly, the primary teacher does not require the same detailed mastery of the advanced content of subjects that is essential to the professor or even to the secondary teacher. The primary teacher can function effectively with a lesser *quantity* of subject-matter mastery than is needed by teachers of older and more accomplished students. But the *quality* of that understanding is no less important. If the primary teacher is to teach faithfully what differentiates concepts and investigative procedures in, say, science from those in ethics or the arts, that teacher must have achieved a sound understanding of the nature of the different approaches to exploring human experience and consciousness; such a teacher must appreciate the scientific, the aesthetic, and the ethical approaches to conceptualizing the relevant dimensions of human experience and to expressing and testing those conceptualizations.

It is trite but true that sound understandings of the content, structures, and procedures of types of inquiry are acquired through the systematic study of these disciplines. Such study must be from both within and without. That is, the subject-matter preparation of teachers must include studies of both these disciplines themselves (science, art, history, etc.) and also systematic accounts of the nature and structure of the disciplines (history and philosophy of science, aesthetic criticism, historiography, etc.).

Admittedly this is a tall order for the adequate preparation of teachers, especially elementary generalists. The foundations of systematic human inquiry are laid in the elementary school, however, and it is important that they be laid well by people who appreciate fully what they are teaching.

PEDAGOGICAL FOUNDATIONS

The systematic study of certain disciplines in the liberal arts and sciences makes a further important contribution to the professional preparation of teachers. It undergirds the study of pedagogical theory and practice.

Teaching, as we have already said, is fundamentally an intellectual and moral enterprise.[8] It is an enterprise in which teachers engage deliberately and in which they make choices both about procedures to bring about specified ends and also about appropriate ends themselves. These choices are not, for the professional teacher, arbitrary choices. They are made on the basis of the results of accumulated professional experience and of systematic pedagogical research.

Pedagogical research is not *sui generis*; it is grounded in certain basic disciplines. Research on the effectiveness of particular instructional strategies generally builds on and applies the investigative procedures and strategies of various of the social sciences: developmental and social psychology, sociology, cultural anthropology, etc. Similarly, debate on fundamental policy questions and question of objectives in and for education is grounded in the same sorts of basic disciplines on which systematic discussion on other questions of social policy is grounded: political, social, economic, and ethical concerns as well as factual material from other pertinent fields.

Accordingly, studies in several disciplines within the liberal arts and sciences, notably, anthropology, economics, philosophy, political science, psychology, and sociology, provide the academic foundation for an understanding of pedagogical research and theory. Such studies are thus, in an important sense, likewise components of the professional preparation of teachers.

SUMMARY

In this section we have not attempted to rank particular studies or to make an "absolute" case for the inclusion of specific studies in preference to others within limited programs of teacher education. We have rather been intent on making the case for a broader conception of professional teacher education than has sometimes prevailed, a conception that incorporates, rather than contrasts with, studies in the liberal arts and sciences.

Nothing that has been said is intended to diminish the importance of pedagogical studies or school experience in the total preparation of elementary or secondary teachers, but to complement those aspects. We now turn to address a major issue about this important dimension of teacher education.

BRIDGING THE GAP BETWEEN THEORY AND PRACTICE

From the time we are born into a society we experience the process of socialization. Through interaction with those around us we transact meanings, attitudes, values, and role relationships. We experience sanctions and internalize norms. The entire complex of shared meanings and values constitutes our culture, and socialization is the label we give to the processes by which the social and cultural molding takes place. Much of the curriculum of socialization is hidden, in the sense that it is invisible to the participants. They are not aware that they are making choices or frequently that there are even choices to be made. This is not to suggest that all socialization is unconscious but that we are frequently unaware and uncritical in taking on the modes of behaviour and belief common to our culture.

Socialization always involves a particular group of people to whose world view and life ways the individual is adjusting. Professional socialization entails internalizing the shared meanings and values, the common role expectations and patterns of belief and behaviour of teachers, or at least of teachers in those institutions the neophyte has experienced. Without rigorously limiting our definition of teacher socialization, we take it to be the product of the whole complex of interpersonal processes and institutional influences that shape the ideas, attitudes, and behaviour of the teacher. Unconscious modelling and conscious emulation, reinforcement of behaviour elicited by pupil actions, communication of parental expectations, approval and disapproval of supervisors are among the elements that combine to ensure that the shared culture of teachers is reflected in those inducted into the profession.

The formal schooling required of prospective teachers is extensive, but the period of general education is much longer than the period of specialized professional preparation. The period of general education, usually fifteen or sixteen years, is longer than that associated with most occupations. Indeed, it is equivalent to the general education requirements of divinity, law, and medicine. It is unique to teaching, however, that the entire period of general education constitutes a potent element in occupational socialization. In the course of fifteen years the prospective teacher has transacted numerous student-teacher role relationships. Although socialization has been in the student role, transacting role relationships requires development of at least a modicum of empathic understanding of the complementary role (i.e., teacher). Every school day, year in and year out, teachers have played out their roles under very close scrutiny of their students and those students have internalized operational norms and expectations for teacher behaviour, however partial and imperfect. From the time the individual begins to entertain the possibility of entering the teaching profession, all of the outcomes of this prior experience become part of that individual's anticipatory socialization. In its contribution to preparation for the teacher role this necessarily extensive prior experience can be more of a bane than a blessing.

Our view of teacher education as a process designed to increase the teacher's ability to make rational choices about the ends and means of education requires the teacher educator to ensure that the process of socialization is understood by the prospective teacher. We would go further and say that teacher education should enable candidates to become active agents in their own development rather than passive recipients of the forces and effects of socialization. Central to this requirement are the analytical skills and reflective inclinations essential to achieving understanding of the teaching and learning process as it is experienced, and insight into the potential effect of alternative choices and courses of action.

One factor affecting the completeness of socialization is the sense of "shared ordeal" of candidates who are selected and who complete extensive and rigorous formal preparation. A second is the sense of induction into the otherwise mysterious complexity of skills and knowledge essential to members of the guild. We have noted that the teaching profession is necessarily less selective than law or medicine, for example. That portion of the formal preparation usually labelled professional is shorter and less arduous. The skills and knowledge seem less mysterious by virtue of being exhibited to the constant scrutiny of the society's entire youth population. To all these characteristics is added an exposure to professional skills that fails to reveal the systematic patterns in their complexity. And the knowledge presented is inappropriate or insufficient to promote an understanding of professional practice or insight into the prospective teacher's own interaction with subject matter and pupils.

The power of socio-cultural molding and the stability of established patterns of behaviour have led Cogan to put forward what he terms a heretical proposal. His heresy is to propose that pre-service education include no less than three full years of rigorous professional study, supervised practice, and "closely and systematically supervised internship."[9] His contention is that in teacher education we grossly underestimate both the quantity and the quality of instructional and psychological inputs required.

Joyce has pointed out that existing teacher education programs have worked to maintain the status quo. Student teaching serves essentially as an apprentice system socializing the neophyte to the norms and practices of the established teacher. Methods courses are designed to deal with current trends in traditional curriculum fields. Separation of methods courses from student teaching minimizes the influence of the methods instructor, particularly if there is a gap between school practice and methods instruction. The foundations courses and subject matter courses in teaching fields are not even expected to meet the criteria of pragmatism implicit in the methods courses. The very structure of the program and organization of the curriculum, with the apparent separation of theory and practice, encourage the student teacher to dismiss radical ideas as mere theory.[10] Joyce's characterization presents teacher education as ideally structured to allow education professors to present whatever they want to present without any great risk that it will affect practice in any way at all. Many professors who consider themselves agents of change may well be merely agents of the rhetoric of change.

In considering the theory/practice gap we must avoid the trap of seeing professional education as consisting ideally of theories to be learned and applied. Theory and practice are not connected in a one-way relationship with the flow always from concepts to skills. The relationship is much more dynamic than that, and the effective teacher's concepts are fashioned from the stuff of actual classroom practice. The challenge of teacher education is to bring within the student teacher's field of perception the relevant samples of practice from which to form concepts and theories in action. In so doing, we will be helping the teacher acquire the tools for interpreting practice and, in turn, guiding further action.

A core issue in teacher education is the need to ground skill development conceptually and to develop practices for doing so, not merely potentially but effectively. Thus teacher training must be integrated with teacher education. Otherwise the actual practice of teaching will be picked up happenstance without conceptual referents other than the folk wisdom of the teaching craft. Equally pointlessly, educational theories will be picked up without behavioural referents and will be no more than excess baggage.

The centrality of a body of theory on which to base practice and the process of developing theory out of practice are among the elements that distinguish a profession from a craft. Members of a profession develop theories in action[11] that guide professional practice and theories of action that guide professional education. An important criterion of professionalism is the ability to select and use skills on a rational basis to achieve desired ends. This entails both a rich resource of ideas and concepts and an appropriate repertoire of skills. Indeed, if rational decision making is an integral characteristic of the professional teacher, then the use of particular skills to achieve particular ends must be grounded in a set of concepts. In the capacity for reflection lies the potential for a communicative relationship between concepts and skills.

PROMISING STRATEGIES

Fragmented teacher education programs that rely on lectures, seminars, and student teaching organized in courses and practica have been unable to guarantee bridge-building between clear concepts and productive skills. Can we, then, identify promising alternative strategies with a greater probability of achieving our goal of the reflective teacher able to marshall appropriate skills in effective strategies to appropriate goals? If so, what are the characteristics of tactics and strategies for effective teacher education? We present several strategies and approaches followed by some general observations about them.

Microteaching

A product of Stanford in the 1960s, microteaching is a strategy designed to focus attention on a limited number of skills at any given time and to provide the opportunity to concentrate on developing them under conditions designed to limit distraction.[12] With advance agreement on the one skill or cluster of skills to be practised, a student teacher teaches a mini-lesson to a small group of real pupils in a campus clinic. The lesson is video-taped and subsequently analysed by student teacher and supervisor together, with particular attention to the agreed-upon skill(s). Goals are then formulated for the next lesson and the cycle is repeated, with the same lesson being taught (sometimes immediately) to a different group of pupils.

Examples of skills emphasized in microteaching are presenting, questioning, and responding to pupils. Microteaching is designed to enhance skill learning by allowing for focussed practice in a non-threatening environment with immediate feedback. Its critics point to weaknesses in the research base establishing links between particular teacher skills and student outcomes. Advocates and critics respectively emphasize the similarity and contrast to the regular classroom when predicting the effectiveness of transfer of training. Microteaching has repeatedly been shown to enhance the initial acquisition of particular technical skills, but evidence of transfer to the classroom in the form of increased use of those skills is less clear.

Minicourses

The minicourse approach was developed in California's Far West Laboratory for Educational Research and Development. Microteaching is incorporated into a complete package that includes description and analysis of the skill(s) to be learned and videotapes of actual classrooms with teachers modelling the skills. Although the minicourses are used in pre-service teacher education, their application is not limited to neophytes. Experienced teachers using minicourses use their own pupils and classrooms as the clinical context for skill development. In these applications, unlike most pre-service applications studied, the minicourse has proven effective not only for the initial learning of specific technical skills but also in extending the range of technical skills used in the actual classroom after the program is completed.

The most obvious explanation of the enhanced transfer of training is the similarity of the training context and the transfer setting (the teacher's own classroom in each case). However, considering the classroom as an ecological system suggests a further explanation. The experienced teacher using a minicourse and practising the skills in the classroom will have induced the pupils to exhibit the expected reciprocal behaviours. As the teacher has practised certain behaviours so have the pupils, and these behaviours are mutually reinforcing. In this context the specific skills learned in the minicourse are more likely to persevere.

Protocol Materials

Demonstration and observation have been traditional means of giving student teachers a sense of the reality of teaching and the nature of particular practices, whether classroom management or teaching strategies. The quality of the demonstration and the effectiveness of the observation vary greatly. A very large number of variables interact in a classroom at any given time, and perception is structured by the concepts available to the observer as well as attitudes and expectations. Moreover, the action is ephemeral and, once past, cannot be recaptured. Protocol materials are written records and audio- or videotape recordings of actual classroom episodes illustrative of specific concepts. The advantage of protocol materials over unstructured observation is that they are selected from a larger corpus of recordings, edited, analysed, and highlighted to focus observation on particular, significant behaviours and interactions. The record can be re-examined as often as the observer wishes. As with microteaching and minicourses, the use of protocol materials has been shown to contribute to skill development, but as yet little evidence has been obtained about the frequency with which teachers use the skills thus developed or the extent to which the skills are maintained over time.

These three practices are examples of efforts to bridge theory and practice by bringing laboratory or clinical experiences to bear, primarily though not exclusively, in those phases of teacher education that take place on the campus. We could equally well have added descriptions of peer teaching used with varying degrees of structure to enable prospective teachers to gain an operational understanding of particular teaching strategies or to develop habits of reflection or the skills of analysis. In fact, many teacher education programs incorporate aspects or adaptations of all of these approaches.

These strategies incorporate some or all of the following. They focus perception on specific teacher behaviours and their effects on student behaviours. In addition to modelling particular skills for student teachers (or experienced teachers), they provide concepts for understanding those skills in action and relating them to one another and to pupil learning. They provide the opportunity to emulate the particular skills and to practise them in an interactive context, to obtain analytical feedback about that practice, and to plan for its improvement. Graphic, focussed modelling of teaching skills and strategies described by clear concepts, detailed planning, guided practice, explicit feedback, and re-teaching are practices that hold promise for bridging theory and practice.

Models of Teaching

In their book *Models of Teaching* Joyce and Weil present sixteen models in four families. A set of concepts is used to analyse and describe each model in terms of its characteristic learning environment. These concepts include the orientation or focus of the model, its syntax or phasing, principles guiding the teacher's reaction to student activity, the social system characteristic of the model, support systems required, the actual classroom implementation (including transcripts or anecdotal descriptions and analysis), and finally the concept of the general applicability of the model.[13]

Including an interaction analysis schema developed for use with the models, this represented a thorough-going attempt by Joyce and his colleagues at Columbia University Teachers College to overcome the kind of fragmentation they had observed to be so characteristic of teacher education. Exploration of a particular model of teaching appeared at first to give student teachers a recipe for action but its effect is to provide a conceptually structured way into discovering layers of meaning in the rich fabric of classroom interaction.

Although it is one of the most ambitious and one of the most coherent, the models of teaching approach is but one of hundreds of alternatives to emerge in the late 1960s and early 1970s. Many new programs developed in response to a continent-wide call for reform in teacher education. Virtually every faculty and college of education in Canada provided prospective teachers with a choice among programs. These programs had several characteristics in common. They were almost always small, and had a distinctive focus reflecting a shared commitment of the staff members working in them. The staff constituted a team and the major teaching assignment of each team member was in the program. In many cases the team included both university faculty and co-operating teachers and not infrequently the program was field-based. Staff and students shared a common location in space dedicated to the program.

In general, it can be said of alternative programs that a distinctive focus contributes to faculty and student identification with the program. This may be enhanced by a shared ideology and shared educational and social commitments, particularly where the students have chosen the program and have the sense of having been selected. A common language of discourse contributes greatly to the level and quality of professional dialogue. When the major teaching commitment of the staff is in the program, their accessibility to students and students' perceptions of their helpfulness are enhanced. The reduced fragmentation in such programs and closer contact makes it more difficult for instructors to ignore problems of practice or to avoid responsibility for responding to the student teacher's concerns. Of course, these characteristics in themselves cannot guarantee effective bridging of the theory/practice gap.

Student Teaching

Most efforts to integrate theory and practice have focussed on student teaching as the means to that end. As Gaskell noted,[14] Dewey addressed the issue directly.

> On the one hand we may carry on the practical work with the objective of giving teachers in training working command of the necessary tools of their profession: control of the technique of class instruction and management, skill and proficiency in the work of teaching. With this aim in view, practice work is, as far as it goes, of the nature of apprenticeship. On the other hand we may propose to use practice work as an instrument in making real and vital theoretical instruction, the knowledge of subject matter and of principles of education. This is the laboratory point of view.[15]

In Dewey's terms the key lies in transforming practical experience from an apprenticeship into a laboratory for testing hypotheses based on existing theory and generating new knowledge and insight to contribute to the elaboration of theory.

Evidence is overwhelming that the student teaching experience serves primarily as an apprenticeship. A "group management" orientation rather than an "intellectual leadership" orientation appears to be fostered by extensive field experience. In contrast to other professions that are practised on individual adults, teaching entails working with large groups of children, frequently with different needs, interests, aptitudes, and cultural backgrounds. The sheer press of events works directly against the ideal of responding to children as individuals. Under such circumstances it is not strange that the neophyte's survival need is to develop skill in maintaining order and managing the flow of events. However, essential though management may be, it can only be considered unfortunate when the concern for management supersedes concern for learning.

The laboratory point of view advocated by Dewey would make school experience an opportunity to examine ethical issues, to reflect on the theories implicit in teacher actions observed and experienced, to consider the decisions made or avoided in curriculum development and materials selection, to study how children think and feel. But in the competition with the practical and the technical, intellectual and ethical concerns are almost always relegated to second place. The immediate and the urgent drive out the important thereby minimizing the potential for developing the concepts and habits of thought essential to the reflective practitioner capable of independent development and renewal thoughout a professional career.

It has been suggested that student teaching experience negates the more liberal effects of university teacher education, but closer examination reveals the fact that university and school influences combine in exerting a common pressure on student teachers to conform uncritically to the expectations of the co-operating teacher and the routine of the school.

On the basis of his study of student teachers in a special summer enrichment program, Gaskell describes several conditions that facilitate the development of an analytic perspective: "responsibility for teaching accompanied by frequent, focussed, visible interaction with co-operating teachers who assumed responsibility for a rational analysis of teaching." These conditions are difficult to achieve in student teaching during the regular school term. He concludes that the quality of supervision is of central importance and that the training of co-operating teachers as clinical supervisors could not only enhance the quality of the student teaching experience but also, in the words of Lortie, encourage "a tilt towards pedagogical inquiry" within a school staff. Time for reflection, opportunities for peer observations, and encouragement of experimentation do not normally characterize the school.[16]

Clinical Supervision

Enhancing student learning by improving the teacher's classroom behaviour is the goal of clinical supervision. Continued growth is inherent in the overriding purpose of achieving "the development of a professionally responsible teacher who is analytical of his own performance, open to help from others, and withal self-directing."[17] These goals are to be achieved through first-hand observation of actual teaching events, data analysis in a face-to-face context, consideration of the meaning of the data and of their implications for student learning, and agreement on goals for both long-term development and also further teaching and supervision. Ideally, the teacher is an active agent and the supervisor is a "colleague" providing skilled feedback and psychological support for behavioural change in directions desired by the teacher. Clinical supervision is explicitly formative in its goals and will be of only transitory value unless provision is made for successive cycles of supervised teaching and systematic, preferably non-directive, feedback.

One of the more helpful metaphors to appear in the dialogue about teacher education is the notion of coaching. The performance of complex skills by an athlete of national calibre is not the product of a few lectures and seminars. Nor is it the product of occasional demonstration and observation. It is unlikely that it has developed solely while serving as equipment manager for the team although an "apprenticeship of observation" is not irrelevant either. An outstanding performance normally follows years of focussed observation and endless practice of bits of the complex sequence of skills involved. It follows analysis and feedback, enhanced today by videotape and even computer graphics, tools to stop the action, to extend perception, to heighten awareness. The effective coach becomes virtually an alter ego, challenging and supporting, ultimately enabling the athlete to achieve performance far beyond previous levels. In the process, the athlete has achieved skills and understandings and the ability to relate each to the other in action—a process of empowerment.

TEACHER EDUCATION AS A CAREER-LONG ENDEAVOUR

One further persistent misconceptualization of teacher education has been the tendency to conceive of it as those studies leading to and *concluding with* the award of a teaching certificate. In our view this is the fallacy of mistaking the part for the whole.

In all professional areas, there is a level of knowledge and skill that is essential before an individual is judged competent to practise that profession independently. But it is a mistake to regard this initial preparation for professional practice as sufficient to inform and sustain a full career in that profession. Initial professional preparation prepares people only to begin practising the profession; it is important that professionals progress beyond this level of competence and that, throughout their careers, they incorporate into their repertoire of professional knowledge and skill new advances in their field. Initial professional education must be supplemented with continuing professional education.

We will address this issue in two parts: first, the experienced teacher's ongoing needs for continuing professional education and, second, the special needs of new teachers for further professional education during their induction year—that first year of teaching following completion of a program of initial teacher education.

CONTINUING TEACHER EDUCATION

The tragedy of continuing teacher education has been its haphazardness. Left at times entirely to the whim of those interested in taking courses, and the happy correspondence of their desires with the offerings of those interested in providing such courses, there has been only fortuitous matching of the work being done with the projected staffing needs of schools.

We must recognize that in our schools our most valuable resource is the competence of experienced teachers and that this resource needs to be managed with foresight and imagination. Management, in this context, involves not only deploying particular personnel where their special strengths can be used most effectively; it involves planning carefully to ensure both that all teachers receive periodic enrichment and renewal in both pedagogical and subject-matter areas and also that appropriate persons acquire new or special competence for which a need can be projected. Continuing or in-service teacher education needs to be planned both in relation to the priorities and requirements of the school or school system and also in relation to reasonable career priorities of and for individual teachers.

Teachers, school administrators, and society generally all must recognize that continuing teacher education can not be only an option for the professional teacher. It is not something that some may take and others may leave: it is essential for all. Moreover, this work must be recognized as part of the proper work of teachers, just as is daily lesson preparation and delivery.

Continuing education must not be viewed as something teachers are expected to do in evenings in addition to their daily marking and preparation. Nor must it be done solely by a few dedicated teachers as a sort of seasonal sandwich compressed between two school years and the annual family vacation. Continuing teacher education must be provided for deliberately in our overall educational planning, as a matter of both right and obligation.

An expectation of regular periods of sustained in-service study for all teachers is required. One- or two-day professional development events, evening study groups, and short courses are all important in in-service education. For extensive enrichment or renewal of subject-matter or pedagogical knowledge and skills, especially before major changes of teaching assignments, teachers should expect to be sent for extended periods of personal study, perhaps as long as a year or more depending on the nature of the task. Such study must not be regarded as "time off" from a teacher's regular duties, but as an essential part of those duties. Nor should such study be undertaken solely on the teacher's own time or at the teacher's own expense. It is in society's interest that children be given the best possible education, and society must ensure that teachers are enabled to provide this.

Consistent with points made earlier, a teacher's personal program of continuing professional education must include a judicious balance of pedagogical and subject-matter components. We would not wish to specify in advance what this proper balance should be; clearly it will vary from teacher to teacher and from situation to situation depending on the specific achievements of the individual teacher and on the current strengths and projected needs of the school or school district. We must note, however, that significant increases in the rate of knowledge-production in all disciplines and substantial changes in school curricula to reflect achievements in human inquiry conspire to make a strong *prima facie* case for subject-matter studies figuring more prominently in the continuing education of teachers than has been so in the past.[18]

Planning for the continuing professional education of teachers must not stop with the design of the content of such work. Thought must also be given to appropriate scheduling, to effective means of program delivery, and to the most suitable "packaging" of the needed studies.

THE INDUCTION YEAR

It is widely recognized that the new teacher's first year in the classroom is crucial in shaping professional style and behaviour patterns and in determining whether the person remains in the profession. A teacher's first year is a "make or break" year. Many teachers retain fond memories of supportive colleagues who helped them through their first year when the sharp shock of classroom reality often seemed more than they could bear. Others, without such collegial support, marvel at how they ever made it. Still others did not make it.

In times of a teacher surplus, the system can perhaps allow some people who complete programs of initial teacher education to drop out of the profession during or after their first year of teaching: "they were not really cut out for teaching," we say to ourselves. Now that a serious teacher shortage once again looms on the horizon, we can ill afford such wastage. We must do a better job of inducting teachers into the profession, of supporting them during that crucial first year so that they emerge from it with increased professional competence and commitment.

This problem needs to be addressed on three interrelated fronts. First, and most important, is the matter of human support for the first-year teacher. Teaching is a lonely occupation. For five hours per day the teacher works behind a closed door with little adult contact. Such contact that does occur is too frequently of a non-professional "coffee break" character; it too rarely includes a sufficiently close association that presents the new teacher with either a vivid and forceful role model or a clear message that the work being done is noticed and valued by colleagues who care about the new teacher, the pupils, and their individual and collective accomplishments.

It is ideal when human and professional support systems develop spontaneously. In organizations and institutions they do not, however, always develop by themselves: they need to be managed. Those responsible for managing schools—principals, department heads, and district personnel—must design into schools both personal and professional support for new teachers. The designation of an appropriately experienced and specially prepared teacher to serve as a mentor for each beginning teacher, with sufficient protected time for both mentor and protege to ensure that the relationship has existence in fact as well as on paper, is one possible structure for facilitating the effective induction of new teachers.

For a mentor-protege arrangement to be effective, the relationship must be carefully conceived and clearly articulated. Of paramount importance is the recognition that whether or not the two individuals might be personal friends, the relationship of mentor to protege is a professional one. As such, the responsibilities and duties of both roles should be recognized within the professional assignments of both teachers. This assignment should include provision for assessing the success of both mentor and protege.

A second and more powerful possibility for the effective induction of new teachers into the profession is through an internship program. We must make clear that, as we understand internship, it is not a component within an initial teacher education program, such as an extended practicum, nor is it an alternative to a carefully designed and delivered program of initial teacher education, such as an apprenticeship. Teacher interns are neither student teachers nor apprentices: they are qualified professional teachers, albeit qualified teachers who are just beginning to practise their profession. As qualified professionals, they have all the rights and responsibilities of other members of the profession: they have teaching credentials, they exercise professional judgment, and they are recompensed on the same basis as others in relation to the magnitude of their assignment.

An internship, as we conceive it, incorporates but is not limited to the features of the mentor-protege relationship sketched above. In addition, it includes a carefully planned experiential orientation to the full range of activities and services of the school and the community, scheduled opportunities to observe and analyse the work of the teaching mentor and others, and a gradually increasing amount and complexity of instructional responsibilities over the year.

There have in recent years been a number of attempts to develop so-called internship programs. Many of these are, in our view, useful and effective for what they are but misdirected and only partially effective in relation to the conception of internship presented here. Some have been designed fundamentally to solve the social problem of unemployment, not the problem of teacher induction. Some have been designed not to induct qualified teachers into the profession, but to give a greater sense of reality to student teaching programs within initial teacher education. And some have been designed to solve the problem of teacher shortage in certain high-demand secondary subject fields by minimizing or bypassing the period of teacher education prior to the assignment of full classroom responsibility.

Not all of these are totally incompatible with the ideal of internship we have presented. What is crucial is the degree to which in the design of the program the paramount consideration is support for and continuing professional development of a newly-qualified teacher.

A third area that deserves special reflection and planning in relation to the induction of new teachers is their continuing professional education. Ideally, an internship program should encompass for all new teachers carefully selected opportunities and requirements for continuing professional education. As for all teachers, this must go beyond the few designated but disconnected days set aside for professional development. And, as for all teachers, continuing education for new teachers must address subject-matter as well as pedagogical concerns. New teachers need to relate their general pedagogical knowledge to their particular instructional situation and they need to attend to gaps in their subject-matter background.[19]

For new teachers, there is a special concern to be addressed, namely the *establishment* of the basic expectations for a career-long approach to continuing professional education. Appropriate professional attitudes, behaviours, and habits need to be nurtured early in the new teacher's career. Responsibility for inducting a new teacher into the profession includes responsibility for helping that teacher develop appropriate patterns and activities for professional enrichment and renewal.

CONCLUSION

In this article we have been concerned with developing a conception of teacher education that transcends some of the traditionally assumed or ascribed limitations.

If, as we maintain, teaching is fundamentally an intellectual and moral enterprise, then an adequate conception of teacher education must transcend narrow behavioural limitations and prepare professionals who are sensitive, compassionate, deliberative, and reflective. If, as we maintain, studies in the liberal and fine arts, in mathematics and the sciences, and in other areas of human inquiry are essential components in the preparation of teachers, then an adequate conception of teacher education must encompass more than what is narrowly pedagogical. If, as we maintain, there are important personal qualities that contribute to teacher effectiveness, then an adequate conception of teacher education must not be indifferent to the means whereby these qualities are developed in prospective teachers. If, as we maintain, teacher education cannot be confined to a single "professional" year, or even to a full undergraduate degree program, but is a career-long endeavour, then an adequate conception of teacher education must encompass programs of both initial and continuing teacher education.

The paramount issue in teacher education is the formulation of a conception of teacher education of sufficient scope to accommodate the full reality of the task. This article has been directed to that objective. In the course of our reflections, we have indicated implications of such an expanded conception for the practice of teacher education. On this, of course, much more needs to be said as the general conception is translated into detailed policies, programs, and syllabi for particular teachers in particular situations.

NOTES

1. In 1980, 85 percent of elementary and 96 percent of secondary school principals were men.
2. Men constitute a bare majority of public school teachers in British Columbia.
3. P.H. Phenix, *Realms of Meaning* (New York: McGraw-Hill, 1964); P.H. Hirst, *Knowledge and the Curriculum: A Collection of Philosophical Papers* (London: Routledge and Kegan Paul, 1974); C. Bailey, *Beyond the Present and the Particular: A Theory of Liberal Education* (London: Routledge and Kegan Paul, 1984).
4. R.S. Peters, *Realms of Meaning* (New York: McGraw-Hill, 1964) and *Ethics and Education* (London: Allen and Unwin, 1966).

5. D.F. Robitaille, *The 1981 B.C. Mathematics Assessment: General Report* (Victoria, B.C.: Ministry of Education, 1981), 216–18.

6. G.W.F. Orpwood and I. Alam, *Science Education in Canadian Schools*, vol. 2, *Statistical Database for Canadian Science Education*, Background study 52 (Ottawa: Science Council of Canada, 1984), 40–43; H. Taylor, ed., *British Columbia Science Assessment: Summary Report* (Victoria, B.C.: Ministry of Education, 1982), 36.

7. M. Elliott, "Can Primary Teachers Still be Subject Generalists?" *Teaching and Teacher Education* 1 (1985): 279–85.

8. H.D. Gideonse, "The Necessary Revolution in Teacher Education," *Phi Delta Kappan* 64 (1982), 15.

9. M.L. Cogan, "Current Issues in the Education of Teachers" in *Teacher Education*, 74th Yearbook of the National Society for the Study of Education, Part II, edited by K. Ryan (Chicago: University of Chicago Press, 1975), 212.

10. B. Joyce, "Conceptions of Man and their Implications for Teacher Education," ibid., 116–17.

11. C. Argyris and D.A. Schon, *Theory in Practice: Increasing Professional Effectiveness* (San Francisco: Jossey-Bass, 1974).

12. D.W. Allen and K.A. Ryan, *Microteaching* (Reading, Mass.: Addison-Wesley, 1969).

13. B.R. Joyce, M. Weil, and R. Wald, *Basic Teaching Skills* (Chicago: Science Research Associates, 1972).

14. P.J. Gaskell, "Developing an Analytic Perspective During Student Teaching: A Case Study" in *Research on Teaching and the Supervision of Teaching: Four Canadian Studies*, edited by M. Arlin (Vancouver: Centre for the Study of Teacher Education, 1984), 51.

15. J. Dewey, "The Relation of Theory to Practice in Education" in *Teacher Education in America: A Documentary History*, edited by M.L. Borrowman (New York: Teachers' College Press, 1965).

16. Gaskell, "Developing an Analytic Perspective."

17. M.L. Cogan, *Clinical Supervision* (Boston: Houghton Mifflin, 1973), 12.

18. J. Lynch and B. Burns, "Non-attenders at INSET Functions: Some Comparisons with Attenders," *Journal of Education for Teaching* 10 (1984): 164–77.

19. Department of Education and Science, *The New Teacher in Schools: A Report by Her Majesty's Inspectors*, HMI Series: Matters for Discussion 15 (London: Department of Education and Science, 1982).

TEACHER SELECTION, PREPARATION, PERSPECTIVES, AND MOBILITY: SOME CRITICAL ISSUES IN TEACHER EDUCATION IN CANADA

DAVID C. SMITH

Teacher education in Canada can never properly be understood in itself, since it is always inextricably connected to the larger educational system and to our society. Issues in teacher education inevitably arise when tensions develop between certain key points in our social system, especially between the universities, the schools, and other social institutions. These tensions remain until a new accommodation is reached between the elements concerned.

There appear to be at least three fundamental areas of tension. The first, and perhaps the most common, occurs when school commissions, ministries of education, and other public and private bodies identify new social needs, which require some response by schools and universities. We have seen such new sensibilities as those for vocational education, the elimination of sexism, the introduction of bilingualism, and the need for human rights education spring primarily from social movements and economic developments actively addressed by schools and teacher education institutions.[1]

In the second place, demands have frequently arisen among the schools and from teacher organizations for smaller classes, higher salaries, better support for professional development, and improved preparation and qualifications for those entering the profession. Such demands have occasionally led to clashes with public bodies, as in cases where teachers work-to-rule or strike. More often than not, the tensions lead to dialogue and to appropriate adjustments in the system.

The third source of tension is that which arises in faculties of education. It usually develops as a result of research, experience, and reflection, and may take the form of educational policy research, the creative development of new curricula or instructional techniques, speculative thinking in the philosophy of education, or the discernment of new needs and trends in education. Disparities between university findings and the system may dissolve quickly through in-service training, teacher workshops, conventions, conferences, and the like, or more slowly through the writing of textbooks, the production of teaching materials, and the entry of a new generation of teachers into educational institutions.

Given this larger context, one can identify many "issues" for teacher education; that is to say, questions confronting faculties of education as a result of pressures from within or without the resolution of which is possible through alternative and competing solutions. Some of the issues are of a local or temporary nature and will not be described here. This paper will examine four major issues that the author regards as the most compelling in the sense that they are matters of national concern in Canada and their resolution will have a major impact in the long term upon the quality of life in this country. They are the issues of teacher selection, teacher preparation, teacher perspectives, and teacher mobility.

TEACHER SELECTION

The question of who should enter the teaching profession has been a continuing issue in Canada largely because we have a rapidly changing society and we are constantly questioning the appropriateness of the criteria for admission to the profession. Essentially, the issue is whether admissions to teacher education should take into consideration such dimensions as ethnic or racial origin, religious affiliation, sex, and other social factors, or whether selection should be based upon desirable personal qualities associated with excellence in teaching as long as there is a basic standard of academic attainment.

Canada has deliberately chosen policies that make for a multicultural, pluralistic society. As immigrants from many parts of the globe have entered Canada, they have changed the composition and distribution of ethnic groups, particularly within our urban centres. In a time of rapid change, the ethnic and racial composition of the teaching force may become quite unrepresentative of the population in primary and secondary schools, since new groups arrive and older groups depart as a result of increased horizontal mobility. As a consequence, we frequently hear of the need for occupational groups such as civil servants, the police force, and the teaching profession to be more ethnically or linguistically representative of the populations they serve.

Because of social change, there may be either implicit or explicit pressures upon universities to actively recruit teachers from specific constituencies, and for the criterion of ethnic, linguistic, or racial background to be considered in teacher recruitment. Behind such a policy is the belief that young people—particularly those who belong to visible minority groups—need to have teachers with whom they can easily identify and who can serve as examples of role models.

The more laissez-faire position holds that the candidates who are recruited should be those who have the qualities and the potentiality to be outstanding teachers, no matter what their background. If the racial or ethnic affiliation of a teacher is different from that of the majority of students, that may be viewed as an advantage because, in a pluralistic society, we should have an opportunity to appreciate the contributions of all the members including those who belong to groups different from our own. That is true not only in education but for occupations in an array of fields such as politics, business, sports, entertainment, and broadcasting. In the opinion of those who hold this position, the proper locus of rights is the individual rather than any group, constituency, or local collectivity.

Much concern has been expressed, and for similar reasons, regarding the ratio of men to women teachers. This concern has manifested itself in a movement to eliminate sexism in education through the promotion of equality of opportunity for men and women and for equality of the sexes.[2] It is a fact that, in most school systems in Canada, the majority of primary school teachers are female and the majority of secondary teachers are male. To continue the imbalance in any sector is to perpetuate the practice of sexism in education.

Those who favour decisive measures to help eliminate sexism would urge that those responsible for the selection of teacher candidates should strive to achieve a balance between males and females, and should go as far as to favour the admission of the gender that is underrepresented. They believe that equal representation at various levels of education is important to allow young people to acquire acceptable ideas of sex role models; otherwise, the schools will continue to be agents for perpetuating sex role stereotypes.

Others, by contrast, affirm that those admitted to teacher education should simply be the most promising candidates, regardless of whether they are men or women. Social processes by which the achievements and aspirations of men and women change and expectations for them alter will, they argue, in due course, bring about a new equilibrium at all levels. In the meantime, we would only be penalizing our young people, if we were to give higher priority to the sex of the candidate than to considerations of scholarship, personality, and potential teaching ability.

Whereas ethnicity, race, and sex in teacher selection have impinged upon teacher education mainly as a result of significant social developments or movements, the perennial question of the academic attainment and intellectual aptitude of teacher candidates seems to have been affected as much by economic considerations as by social ones. Teaching in Canada has traditionally been viewed as an occupation of the middle class, or of those aspiring to middle-class status. There is strong evidence that it has not attracted the same proportion of candidates having high academic aptitude and achievement as have the professions in science, engineering, law, and medicine. From time to time there emerge campaigns for raising the standards of admission into teacher education so that teaching will receive its "fair share" of human resources and, in consequence, there will develop more comparable standards across the professions. The problem is that considerations of prestige and status among the professions seem to result in a disproportionate distribution of scholastic aptitude in spite of measures taken to counteract it.

Others have felt that high grade-point averages and other measures of intellectual attainment used as the most important single criterion of admission to teacher education is misleading, and that the best prospective teachers are not necessarily those who are academically highest in the pool of available students. They cite qualities such as humaneness, energy, perseverance, self-confidence, open-mindedness, ability to work with people, and a sense of humour as co-requisities with an intellectual understanding of bodies of knowledge for admission to teacher education.[3]

TEACHER PREPARATION

A second kind of disequilibrium that has been developing between programs of initial teacher education in our faculties of education and the emerging needs of the educational system lies in both the concept and the scope of education. The discordance arises from two principal sources. One is the change in the age distribution of our population: there are now fewer younger people and a greater concentration of people in higher age brackets. The second is that education has become a lifelong process, involving both formal and informal learning, in order to respond effectively to rapid technological and organizational change. Our society is becoming preoccupied with learning in all its contexts and at all age levels.[4] The issue confronting faculties of education is that they must decide whether they will cling to their traditional role of focussing upon formal education in school systems or embrace larger responsibilities in the broader context of education.

It is becoming increasingly rare for a teacher who graduates from university to spend an entire career teaching either the same subject or at the same level. Today, many teachers are encouraged to acquire new competencies and to have more flexible teacher qualifications. Further, some who are trained for teaching at the school level find themselves teaching languages, mechanics, typing, and a host of other subjects to adults in evening classes sponsored by their school commissions. Graduates in physical education frequently teach in recreational or fitness programs in their community. Some teachers are finding positions involving the training and retraining of adults in business and industry. It is clear that teachers are being drawn into working in a variety of educational contexts and with a range of different age groups.

Given these considerations, should faculties of education then broaden their mandate from preparing primary and secondary school teachers to training teachers who have more generic skills and who, like engineers and lawyers, will work in a variety of settings and with a variety of clientele? Those who favour the retention of the status quo argue that faculties of education are equipped in terms of their current resources to prepare teachers in the traditional specializations and that it would require major expansion and new resources to expand their role effectively to other areas of education. Besides, it has not been demonstrated, they would argue, that the skills of teaching are that easily transferred from one subject or from one kind of clientele to another. They point to the continuing claim of student teachers that training of a more theoretical and general nature is less helpful to the novice than is training that is more specific and more focussed.

The point of view adopted by those who advocate a more general kind of teacher education derives from the belief that change in our system of education is so pervasive and persistent that we should not prepare teachers to have a narrow set of competencies that will have diminishing application upon graduation. Hence teachers should have a more generic type of preparation. That preparation should consist of two parts: first, a good knowledge of their field of study, and, second, very general teaching skills that might include the effective tutoring of individuals, the skilful leading of discussions and seminars, and the effective presentation of subjects to large groups. As future teachers will, in all probability, be required to teach different populations at different levels and in different contexts, they should have the basic knowledge and skills to do so with some degree of comfort but, like all other members of a changing society, they may need to retrain in order to up-date their knowledge of their field, to explore related disciplines, and to utilize techniques of instruction appropriate to the needs and capabilities of the clientele with whom they may successively be dealing. Further, they would argue that faculties of education are rich repositories of knowledge about the process of education and that this knowledge should be harnessed not just for the benefit of schools and colleges but for all those institutions that have an educational role, whether hospitals and rehabilitation centres, businesses,[5] industries, prisons,[6] the armed forces, or voluntary organizations. If knowledge is not shared by the universities, the changes occurring in these organizations will require that they be serviced by private, entrepreneurial consulting firms, which may emerge as parallel formations, or that they develop their own discrete, self-serving operations.

Whether faculties of education will preserve their traditional role, or expand to deal with education in the more general sense, will be determined to some extent by their internal resolve, their ability to assemble resources and to deploy them more widely, and by whether those institutions external to the university will be convinced that teacher education resources can be harnessed for their benefit.

TEACHER PERSPECTIVES

The issue of perspectives in teacher education is a more difficult one to address partly because the forces that have given rise to the need for changing perspectives in our society are less tangible than those related to teacher selection and preparation. Nevertheless, the issue is closely linked both to teacher preparation, which has already been discussed, and to teacher mobility, which is considered as a concluding issue. Essentially, we may ask whether teacher education should have a provincial orientation, a national perspective, or an even broader, global perspective.

In Canada, teacher education and certification is controlled by each province or territory, which sets down not only the pattern of teacher preparation, but also the related programs of study for primary, secondary, and collegial education. Teacher education, then, is aimed primarily at serving provincial needs. For that reason, the education of teachers in most provinces has a strong provincial perspective that includes an appreciation of the history of education in the province, the legal aspects of education in the province, the provincial organization of education, and the content of primary and secondary education as approved for the province.

Recognizing the provincial orientation of education, a number of groups have made conscious attempts to help Canadians to develop wider, national perspectives through education. The Canada Studies Foundation, now officially disbanded, helped, over a period of nearly twenty years, to promote Canadian studies largely in the primary and secondary schools of the nation. The Canadian College of Teachers has, through its national and regional meetings, aimed to focus attention on matters of national importance in education. The Canadian Teachers Federation and the Council of Ministers of Education have striven to facilitate the interprovincial movement of teachers. These latter actions have been based on the belief that some movement of teachers within Canada brings benefits to young people by exposing them to a geographical mix of teachers who have stimulatingly different experiences and perspectives. Of course, where education takes place in non-school institutions, such as national and international corporations, the use of teachers having strong provincial perspectives, it is argued, can be a seriously limiting factor for them.

Many critics of our system of education have begun to assert that there is a serious lack of synchronization between our schools and teacher education systems, on the one hand, and the international realities of the emerging global society on the other. The relationship between school and society has been almost exclusively associated with the school and local or national society. However, the forces at work in our world society, including the increasing development of world systems within which modern nations live, trade, and communicate with each other, is not sufficiently acknowledged. Hence, a tension has grown that requires a re-evaluation of perspectives.

The forces that have produced the disequilibrium in educational perspectives include changes in world population, the competition for scarce resources not only between the developed nations but also between the "have" and "have not" nations, the build-up of armaments to protect territories and resources. At the same time, the growth of global communications networks, the proliferation of international and world organizations, and the increasing economic interdependence of the world's peoples accentuate the need for mutual understanding and co-operation.

Those responsible for teacher education programs, it is argued, have a responsibility to take these new realities into consideration when re-examining the general and professional studies components of their programs. They can do this by considering global as well as local and national perspectives in the teaching of the arts, literature, history, science, technology, and other subjects, and also by including the study of values inherent in educational systems that have ideological and philosophical orientations different from their own, by fostering an appreciation of intercultural education, and by developing relationships with educational institutions in other parts of the world.

The tensions that exist between the schools, the universities, government, and society in the largest sense will only be resolved through continuing efforts to recognize the changing realities in which we live. On the one hand, those who advocate provincial perspectives do so in the belief that the optimal benefits for those who live in the province can be attained if the boundaries of consciousness are circumscribed by relatively narrow geographical limits. At the other extreme, the International Council on Education for Teaching believes that optimal benefit can be achieved through the development of a global consciousness requiring international education. It asserts:

> International education should be a high priority of modern institutions of higher education and specifically for teacher education. The achievement of a global perspective demands a vision that transcends national and cultural differences. All humanity is a single species, on a single planet, sharing a common future. To mold this common future is today's educational imperative."

TEACHER MOBILITY

The issue of teacher mobility is a tug-of-war between the forces that cause teachers to remain fixed in the location in which they develop their careers and the forces that cause them to move from one province to another and, beyond that, to enter or leave Canada for the practice of their profession. Over the past two or three decades we have seen that either one or the other of these forces have tended to dominate.

It is understandable that some teachers may be reluctant to move from one position to another when, for example, they have many years of service, built a good pension with a provincial pension plan, and wish to have some stability before retirement. There are, however, more important factors inhibiting mobility that are exploited by ministries of education in order to protect provincial interests. These include the development of profiles for certification designed to meet local or regional needs but which, at the same time, discourage teachers outside the province from qualifying for that province's certification, and attempts to control teacher supply and demand to ensure that there is an adequate supply of staff and a low rate of unemployment among teachers.

Most of the provinces have given at least lip-service to the need for mobility among the Canadian teaching force. It is recognized that, within Canada, there have been, at certain points, major internal migrations of the population as well as differential population growth rates. The free flow of teachers from province to province has enabled areas where there is a surplus to supply those areas where there is a shortage. That has occurred at differing times between the Maritimes and central Canada, between east and west, and between southern Canada and the Arctic regions. Occasionally, one area of the country has been able to supply teachers having special qualifications to another area where those competencies are in demand as, for instance, in the movement of bilingual teachers from Quebec to Alberta. The flow of teachers in these ways has exemplified the relatively free movement of teachers who form a national pool of professional workers within a common market.

The mobility of teachers, however, has not only an economic advantage, but also an important educational one. Since Canadian teachers work in at least twelve separate jurisdictions, the free movement of ideas is impeded, and there is always the danger the provincial systems of education can become ingrown and parochial in outlook. But the movement of at least some teachers exposes young people to a healthy mix of influences, provided that the teachers have varied backgrounds, different emphases in training, and different perspectives. When that is the case, the students themselves may have a greater possibility for creative personal and intellectual development.

In an effort to promote the mobility of teachers, the Council of Ministers of Education came to a general agreement on the portability of teacher certificates in 1982. The agreement allowed for the recognition of teacher qualifications across Canada where candidates for certificates in any province had a three- or four-year degree awarded by a university accredited by a provincial government, had successfully completed one year of teacher training, and had a valid certificate to teach issued by a provincial or territorial government.[8] In addition, the Canadian Teachers Federation has encouraged the provinces to enter into portability agreements among themselves.

In spite of these efforts, the portability plan was adopted by only half of the provinces, and gradually the teacher certification branches of most governments have introduced provisions that generally make it more difficult for extra-provincial teachers to be certified in their jurisdictions. In Saskatchewan, secondary school teachers must have two teaching fields, a major and a minor; hence, students with honours degrees in a single field are likely not to qualify. In Ontario, professional training must include qualification to teach in two consecutive divisions: either K-6 and 4-10, or 4-10 and 7-13. Such a requirement automatically excludes many qualified teachers from other provinces. In New Brunswick, candidates must have a minimum of eighteen weeks of student teaching in order to be considered for provincial certification. These kinds of regulations have the effect of impeding the free flow of teachers; however, most provinces do have provisions for allowing those who are deficient in the qualifications to overcome the deficiency and obtain provincial certification.

It is not exactly clear what the motives are for the provinces to develop their own unique teacher education patterns that, in effect, create obtacles to mobility. In some cases, a parochial system of education, such as that in Quebec, or a combination of a public and parochial system, such as that in Ontario and Newfoundland, places restrictions on certification. In other cases, it may be an act of implicit protectionism to try to ensure that provincially trained teachers, or those who can demonstrate provincial residence, are fully employed before positions are offered to out-of-province applicants.

The mobility of teachers appears to be a positive feature in Canadian education when teachers are in short supply, due to population growth or population shifts. However, when there is a decline in the school-age population and a surplus of teachers, steps may be taken to restrict the mobility of the profession, although the measures may be rationalized in other ways. Considerations of immediate provincial interest appear to take precedence over the longer-term educational benefits of mobility.

CONCLUSION

The four contemporary issues in teacher education that have been selected and discussed here have all arisen largely because of widespread social movements and economic changes. Indeed, it is as a result of these changes that tensions have arisen between different points of our social system, and educational institutions themselves must make some major adjustments. In some cases, the early discernment of impending change by planning bodies in the universities and other agencies has clarified the need for change and accelerated the review of personnel policies, programs, and perspectives, in order to bring about a new equilibrium. The issues have been labelled "critical" ones, since the ways in which ministries of education, schools and universities respond to them will have an important impact upon education.

It becomes apparent, as we consider these issues, that they are not discrete, but very much related to one another. In fact, one can look very systematically at a set of six interrelationships between the four issues.

1. The way in which we select students for teacher education in terms of such factors as intellectual aptitude and ethnic and racial background may well enhance, or restrict, the mobility of the teaching force.

2. A more generic type of teacher preparation and training for teaching a range of age groups conceivably expands enormously the opportunities for mobility of teachers.

3. Similarly, teachers who have national or international perspectives will usually find it easier to move to positions within or outside Canada.

4. The way in which teachers are selected for professional training affects the kind of preparation they can receive since, for example, the challenge of being inventive and adaptive in teaching at many kinds of institutions and with a variety of clientele requires intellectual aptitude of a high order.

5. The initial preparation of teachers, whether of a general or specialized nature, and whether restricted to one age group or expanded to many, can be related to narrow or to wide perspectives.

6. And, further, if perspectives are extended from the relatively familiar environment of the province to the wider, and in many ways more abstract, global environment, the selection process could conceivably be related to such factors as intellectual breadth and world mindedness.

One final point, and that is that each of the four issues presented here may appear to have alternative solutions of an either-or nature. However, our search for the resolution of the tensions does not necessarily mean that we have to be caught in a sterile dualism. Issues may be resolved by drawing upon some element of each of the posited alternatives. The preparation of teachers, for instance, can be partly generic and partly specific, or it can begin as general and have specific competencies as add-ons. In the same way, the perspectives of teacher education do not have to be parochial or expansive, but can be a judicious blending of the provincial, national, and global. Whatever ways we opt to resolve the issues, we need to realize that the options chosen will have a significant impact upon the quality and character of teacher education in Canada in the years ahead.

NOTES

1. An analysis of social demands on teacher education is given in Geraldine Gillis, "Teacher Education—Today and Tomorrow," *Teacher Education* (Oct. 1981): 6–23, and the effect of population changes in Canada is analysed by Jeffrey W. Bulcock in "Changes in Society Affecting Schooling: With Some Implications for Teacher Training," *McGill Journal of Education* (Spring 1979): 133–47.

2. See, for instance, Kay Sigurjonsson, "Equal Opportunity through Affirmative Action," *The ATA Magazine* (May/June 1985). In fact, this entire issue of the magazine was devoted to the theme "Women in Education."

3. Deborah Roose, Susan Mitchell, and Masha K. Rudman, "Selecting the Brightest and the Best," *Phi Delta Kappan* (Nov. 1985), 219.

4. An interesting discussion of the way school commissions can better serve the whole community is found in Mel Shipman, "The Public School and Our Aging Society," *Education Canada* (Fall 1985): 30–35, and Lorne Rochlis, "Adult Students in Our Schools," *Education Canada* (Summer 1983): 16–21.

5. Tim Kelley, "Education and Business: The Business of Education," *The B.C. Teacher* (Jan./Feb. 1986): 17–18.

6. See, for instance, Mary Nixon and Chester Bumbarger, "Extending Educational Opportunities to Provincial Prison Inmates," *Education Canada* (Spring 1983): 4–8.

7. International Council on Education for Teaching, *A Global Perspective for Teacher Education* (Washington: American Association of Colleges for Teacher Education, 1983).

8. Council of Ministers of Education, Canada, *Communique* (Regina, 19 Jan. 1982).

TEACHER TRAINING: AN EXPLORATION OF SOME ISSUES AND A DIRECTION FOR MODEL DEVELOPMENT

LARRY SACKNEY

I am convinced that the structure of teacher education must change. I am convinced that the structure of schooling must change. I am also convinced that these changes must be forthcoming soon.

My convictions about the need for change are founded on three premises. The first is that we know a great deal about teaching and learning. The second is that the image we have of teachers and the role that we expect them to perform must shape their training. The third premise is that we must examine the image of our teacher training institutions.

In this paper I propose to deal with some of the issues surrounding these premises and to suggest a direction for model development for teacher training in Canada.

THE NEED FOR A RESEARCH BASE

In its simplest terms, teaching is the application of treatments, consisting mainly of teacher performances, verbal and nonverbal. In this regard, it is like such other professions as engineering, medicine, and law, each of which entails interaction with something, be it animate or inanimate.

Every profession has its beginnings as a craft, based on knowledge derived from trial and error and passed on from generation to generation by imitation and informal instruction. As the profession matures, its activities are subject to theoretical analysis and scientific study and improvement by knowledge derived therefrom.[1] This knowledge and the process of discovering it is what distinguishes a profession from a craft.

It is my contention that teaching is well on the path to becoming a profession. We now know a considerable amount about teacher effects, school effects, classroom management, and student achievement, that can be used to make a real difference in the classroom. Berliner in a recent article reviewing the research on teaching, suggests that the "glass is now half-full."[2] He argues that we have sufficient evidence on factors that can be controlled or influenced by teachers and that are known to affect student behaviour, attitudes, and achievement.

Similarly, Brophy argues that research on teaching needs to be modelled and integrated into teacher education programs. He states, "I think it logically compelling that research on teaching should feed into, and provide part of the basis for teacher education."[3] In particular, he argues for the inclusion of classroom management research and teacher effects research in teacher education programs (focussing on linkages between teacher behaviour and student achievement).

A few examples should suffice to illustrate the point. In the area of teacher effects research, we now know that academic learning time is an important contributor to increased student learning. Furthermore, teacher presenting skills are crucial to successful student learning. Lessons tend to go better if there is some kind of advance organizer or introductory statement about objectives and goals. Once the lesson is under way, there is usually some presentation of information. The important variables in presenting information appear to be clarity, structuring, and modelling. The importance of teacher planning to effective instruction has also been noted.

Recently, a good deal of research has been carried out on student perception and mediation of instruction. A very important concept to emerge, and one that we need to convey to teachers, is that instruction is a matter of changing existing beliefs in students, not one of putting information into a vacuum.[4] Brophy claims that teacher expectations research has established beyond a doubt the influence of expectancy on students' achievement.[5]

There has been criticism about the apparent lack of a research base to teacher preparation programs.[6] It seems to me that this kind of information needs to be brought in somewhere in teacher education programs. In other words, we need to focus on the scientific basis of teaching. Based on this knowledge, skill development can take place through the internship, simulations, and classroom modelling by university professors.

At the same time, one of the most serious defects in the preparation of teachers is the failure on the part of teacher educators to recognize that theoretical studies cannot function prescriptively in the work of the teacher. It is too much to expect teachers to derive classroom practices from the principles of psychology, sociology, or any other theoretical subject. Smith argues that these subjects need to be taught as explanatory subjects. According to him, "This means, among other things, that the theoretical principles should be taught in such a way as to enable practitioners to place a given practice in context and to understand why it is effective."[7]

LACK OF COMMITMENT AND STANDARDS

A number of prospective teachers show an inherent lack of respect for and commitment to their chosen profession. Too many teachers view teaching as a "trump card;" if all else fails, they can always teach.[8] Teacher training institutions need to recruit prospective teachers from those who choose teaching as their first choice, not their last.

Moreover, far too many teacher training institutions recruit prospective teachers from the lower quartiles of high school graduates compared to other professions.[9]

Darling Hammond concluded that teaching can never act like a profession without developing more rigorous entry and training standards.[10] A scrutiny of Canadian university calendars leads me to conclude that, in general, colleges of education have lower entrance requirements than other professions. There are a few exceptions, but they are rare. One such exception is the University of Saskatchewan where there is a quota and a 70 percent minimum average is required. Additionally, transferees from other colleges must have a C+ average, and a quota applies to the number of transferees allowed. Thus a student cannot fail in one college and then request to be transferred into education. Such a stance should help remove the stigma attached to many teacher training institutions.

As has been suggested previously, teacher training institutions need to recruit a higher proportion of the top high school graduates. Tyler[11] contends that universities need to spend more time counselling potential teachers. He argues for university personnel visiting schools and encouraging top candidates to apply.

Yet another problem plaguing teacher training institutions is the type of teacher being trained. Too many physical education teachers and too few science and mathematics teachers are being trained for secondary teaching. Various writers have noted the possible long-term consequences of such a development.[12]

What is being argued for, is the need for greater attention to screening potential teachers. The use of entrance examinations, interviews, and references should be considered in addition to marks. A few institutions are utilizing the Teacher Perceiver and interviews for screening the lower quartile candidates with some degree of success. Much more effort is required if we are to select the best candidates for teaching.

LACK OF QUALITY TEACHER EDUCATION PROGRAMS

Schools of education have been criticized for the poor courses offered as well as the inadequacy of the training provided. Lack of rigour in courses and poor role models on the part of professors are frequently mentioned criticisms. The comments made by Susan Ohanian are typical: "I have sat through more stupid education courses than I wish to recall...."[13] She suggests that schools of education need to shape-up their own institutions first, getting rid of Papercutting 306 and having the professor get out in the field to work with student teachers, principals, and children.

Similarly Weaver[14] maintains that lax teacher education programs have had an even more devastating effect; they have destroyed the integrity of the teaching profession. When standards are abandoned, professionalism and the commitment expected from professionals go out the window.

For the sake of all that is professionally sound, teacher education programs must work to put some genuine academic fibre into the programs they offer. Easy certification is what got us where we are today, and reform must begin with the requirement of high-quality preparation.

I hope that education courses can be made truly relevant. We need to get rid of "Mickey Mouse" courses. I am not convinced, for example, that we need all the methods courses. Too many teacher training institutions have methods courses for every subject area. For many secondary students the methods courses become working through the high school course outlines.

Furthermore, there are too many redundancies in course work.[15] In many cases students are exposed to the same theoretical constructs in more than one course. As well, the calendar descriptions of courses, and what actually happens in the university classroom, may be two different events. Too many university professors ride their own "hobby horse."

The assignments structured around course work tend far too often to be mundane. The connection between teaching and the work assigned is difficult to make in many instances, according to Darling-Hammond.[16] Moreover, the marking of assignments and examinations has been found to be lax. Generally teacher educators tend to fail fewer students and to give fewer low marks.

What I am arguing for is for more rigorous coursework. We need to pay more attention to teacher communication skills, both written and oral. Far too many teachers are incapable of expressing themselves correctly. The lessons from teacher expectations research need to be applied by university professors.

THE THEORY-PRACTICE GAP

A frequent complaint by teachers is that theory and practice are not the same. Tyler[17] has noted the importance of preservice experiences with children and practising teachers in helping to integrate theory and practice. Similarly, the Boyer Report[18] has argued for a closer link between theory and practice, and between the colleges and the schools. These studies have also noted the need for university personnel to work closely with the field. Far too many professors are out of touch with the field. Boyer has found that many university professors have not been in an elementary or secondary school in over two decades. Their view of reality is too far removed. This, in turn, is evident in their classroom teaching—the theory-practice gap is increased. Both Boyer[19] and Goodlad[20] found that student teachers preferred university professors who were in active contact with the field. They were generally perceived to be better teachers.

In order to bridge the theory-practice gap, extensive internship programs, similar to those found in other professions, have been found to be useful. The University of Saskatchewan teacher training program, for example, requires the potential teacher to spend time in the school in each year of his or her preparation. Contact with the school and students in the first year of training is designed to orient the potential teacher into the profession. It helps the student to determine whether she or he really want to teach. Contact with the school in the second year is designed to assess skill areas requiring remediation prior to the internship. In the third year, the student teacher interns for a period of approximately sixteen weeks. In the last month of the internship, the student teacher is expected to teach full-time to gain an appreciation of what it is like to be a teacher. To assist the intern in the development of his or her skills, simulations, case analyses, and microteaching are used in the university laboratory setting prior to the internship.

Numerous modifications of the above program are now found across Canada. It is deemed that such programs will better prepare potential teachers. Essentially, I support well-designed internship programs, ones where follow-up, inservice, and close contact with the field is maintained.

TOWARDS A MODEL

It seems to me that a teacher should be a decision maker, not just a technician who links the students, textbooks, and text developers. Teachers who assume roles as technicians are bound to be less inspired and less committed to their work.

Furthermore, the teacher needs to be acquainted with the elements of teaching. The Boyer Report[21] concludes that a beginning teacher needs to know:
— the curriculum priorities of the school;
— how to assess student progress;
— how to organize instruction;
— how to develop and use evaluation instruments;
— how students learn, both individually and in groups;
— how to motivate students;
— how the classroom functions as a social unit; and
— how the school functions as an organization.

Moreover, as has been argued by the Paideia Group, teacher training institutions need to ensure that teachers are on the way to becoming educated persons. A sign that they are moving in this direction is their manifest competence as learners. Another is that they show a sufficiently strong interest in their own education and a sufficiently strong motivation to carry on learning while engaged in teaching. Adler adds, "The teacher who has stopped learning is a deadening influence rather than a help to students being initiated into the ways of learning."[22]

How does a prospective teacher become an educated person? Adler[23] argues that the mind can be improved by the acquisition of organized knowledge; by the development of intellectual skills; and by the enlargement of understanding, insight, and aesthetic appreciation. These are basic requisites for all teachers. Teacher courses should therefore be general and liberal to reflect those dimensions. This does not negate the fact that a mathematics teacher should have a solid background in the subject she or he teaches. It does mean, however, that a potential teacher should have a well-rounded education.

Furthermore I contend that teacher training needs to emphasize the creative aspects of teaching. Too much emphasis is placed on comprehension and recall of information. Far more attention needs to be placed on the synthesis and evaluation of information. Redfield and Rosseau[24] found that teachers who ask more higher-order questions have students who achieve considerably more.

Beyond the classes, the art of teaching can only be learned in the classroom, in which one first spends a sustained period in observation, followed by a sustained period in direct experience. The importance of an extensive internship cannot be underestimated in any teacher training program.

CONCLUSION

This paper has attempted to raise some issues that need attention if we are to train high-quality teachers. I have argued for:
1. the need for a research base for teacher education programs;
2. the need for rigour and standards in preparation programs;
3. the need to recruit high quality candidates; and
4. the need for a field-based approach to teacher education.

Much has been written about the apparent lack of good teaching in our schools.[25] Naisbett, for example, argues that this is the first generation of graduates who know less than their parents.[26] He cautions that, unless this trend is reversed, we will have to accept a lower standard of living.

Perhaps the current emphasis on implementing the research on effective schools is an attempt to refute these charges. Focussed on high expectations for student learning, in a climate that is conducive to learning, and structured within a framework that is readily accepted and understood by everyone, schools are striving for excellence. The attempt is to foster a school culture that is conducive to achievement. It is within such a cultural context that teacher training institutions need to foster the new teacher graduate.

In closing, Peters and Austin best summarize the need for passion for excellence in organizations:

> When you have a true passion for excellence, and when you act on it, you will stand straighter. You will look people in the eye. You will see things happen. You will see heroes created, watch ideas unfold and take shape. You'll walk a springier step. You'll have something to fight for, to care about, scary as it is, with other people.... It takes real courage to step out and stake your claim. But we think the renewed sense of purpose, of making a difference, of recovered self-respect, is well worth the price of admission.[27]

It is time for a passion for excellence in teacher training. Our schools will only be as good as the teachers we train.

NOTES

1. A.N. Whitehead, *Adventures of Ideas* (New York: Macmillan, 1933).
2. D.C. Berliner, "The Half-Full Glass: A Review of Research on Teaching" in *Using What We Know About Teaching*, edited by D. Berliner (Virginia: ASCD, 1984).
3. J. Brophy, "Research in Teacher Education" in *Research in Teacher Education: Current Problems and Future Prospects in Canada*, edited by I. Housego (Vancouver: Centre for the Study of Teacher Education, 1984), 21.
4. J. Eaton, C. Anderson, and E. Smith, "Students' Misconceptions Interfere with Science Learning," *Elementary School Journal* 8, 5 (1984): 27-35.
5. J. Brophy, "Classroom Organization and Management," *The Elementary School Journal* 83 (1983): 265-86.
6. Ibid., and Brophy, "Research in Teacher Education."
7. B.O. Smith, "Research Bases for Teacher Education," *Phi Delta Kappan* 66, 10 (1985), 689.
8. B. Marczely, "Teacher Education: A View from the Front Lines," *Phi Delta Kappan* 66, 10 (1985): 702-03.
9. A.M. Gallegos and H. Gibson, "Are We Sure the Quality of Teacher Candidates is Declining?" *Phi Delta Kappan* 64, 1 (1985): 33; J.I. Goodlad, *A Place Called School: Prospects for the Future* (New York: McGraw-Hill, 1984); L. Darling-Hammond, *Beyond the Commission Reports: The Coming Crisis in Teaching* (Santa Monica, Calif.: Rand Corp., 1984); E.L. Boyer, *High School: A Report on Secondary Education in America* (New York: Harper and Row, 1983).
10. Darling-Hammond, *Beyond the Commission Reports*.
11. R.W. Tyler, "What We've Learned from Past Studies of Teacher Education," *Phi Delta Kappan* 66, 10 (1985): 682-84.
12. J.W. Guthrie and A. Susman, "Teacher Supply and Demand in Mathematics and Science," *Phi Delta Kappan* 64, 1 (1982): 28-31; Goodlad, *A Place Called School*.
13. S. Ohanian, "On Stir-and-Serve Recipes for Teaching," *Phi Delta Kappan* 66, 10 (1985), 699.
14. T. Weaver, "In Search of Quality: The Need for Talent in Teaching," *Phi Delta Kappan* 46, 9 (1979): 29-32.
15. Darling-Hammond, *Beyond the Commission Reports*.
16. Ibid.
17. Tyler, "What We've Learned from Past Studies of Teacher Education."

18. E.L. Boyer, *Report of a Panel on the Preparation of Beginning Teachers* (Princeton: New Jersey State Department of Education, 1984).
19. Ibid.
20. Goodlad, *A Place Called School*.
21. Boyer, *Report of a Panel on the Preparation of Beginning Teachers*.
22. M.J. Adler, *The Paideia Proposal: An Educational Manifesto* (London: Macmillan, 1982), 59.
23. Ibid.
24. D.L. Redfield and E.W. Rosseau, "A Meta-Analysis of Experimental Research on Teacher Questioning Behavior," *Review of Educational Research*, 51 (1981): 237–45.
25. Goodlad, *A Place Called School*.
26. J. Naisbett, *Megatrends* (New York: Warner Books, 1984).
27. T. Peters and N. Austin, *A Passion for Excellence* (New York: Random House, 1985), 419.

IT'S TIME FOR CHANGE IN TEACHER EDUCATION: REAL CHANGE THIS TIME!

R.S. PATTERSON AND E. MIKLOS

What undergraduate student in a teacher education program has not whiled away at least some class time indulging in escapes into fantasy, contemplating actions that would radically alter the content and structure of teacher education? "If only I were in charge of this program," is probably the thought that precedes reflection on a lengthy litany of recommendations for change and improvement. The items are only too apparent to the student as participant-observer. Usually, they are also obvious to the practicing professional, but inexplicably hidden from or overlooked or ignored by those responsible for designing and delivering teacher preparation programs. These would-be reformers do not have reason to take heart over the prospect that their ideas, even if known, would significantly alter the map that charts the course for the preparation of teachers. Others have attempted to redraw the map with limited success.

CRITICISM AND CONSEQUENCES

An examination of the contemporary wave of criticism in Canada and the United States that is directed at public schooling, teachers, and teacher education exhibits remarkable similarity, in scope and content, to the critical outbursts on this same subject that appeared in popular and professional forums several decades ago. Just as in 1963, in *The Miseducation of American Teachers*, Koerner spoke out against "the inferior quality of the Education faculty"[1] and observed that "course work in Education deserves its ill-repute,"[2] recent American critics have claimed that "teacher education is perhaps the biggest running joke in higher education."[3] The earlier critics condemend the course work in education as "puerile, repetitious, dull and ambiguous"; their counterparts of the 1980s are making similar assertions. Reports such as *A Nation at Risk* have not only attacked schooling practices and outcomes, but also have struck out at teacher educators for failing to prepare teachers capable of providing quality public school education.[4]

These instances of criticism, both in the 1950s and the 1980s, first gained recognition and acceptance in the United States. The harbingers of bad news in American education stimulated Canadian observers to voice similar messages of dismay and gloom about the operation of schools, provisions for teacher education, and the well-being of public education in general. One contemporary Canadian source, albeit one of questionable qualification, notes that most teachers "will state that their training had nothing to do with effective teaching and was an out-and-out fraud."[5] Unquestionably, efforts to reform American education have served to encourage similar activity in Canada. Educators and governments in several Canadian provinces have been actively involved in altering school curricula as well as provisions for teacher education. Canadians, in effect, have chosen to accept and respond to criticism, even though, not uncommonly, they may acknowledge with an air of superiority and justification that their system is not plagued with either the range or the seriousness of problems that beset the schools and teacher education in the United States.

The purpose of this article is not to debate the specific allegations of deficiency and weakness directed at schooling and teacher preparation. Instead, it serves as an opportunity to explore what might be done to significantly alter and improve teacher preparation regardless of any judgment as to its current level of adequacy. One thing that should be obvious to the student of educational history is that the nature of teacher education has not changed markedly over the past half century. Some content has been modified, expanded and modernized, some programs have been lengthened, but, essentially, the basic elements of structure, curriculum, and methodology have remained relatively constant. One should not be led to conclude from the introduction of computer technology or the reliance on video recording in microteaching that much has changed. The criticisms of our day suggest that we are still contending with problems similar to those of earlier periods.

PROBLEMS IN PROFESSIONAL PREPARATION

One way of recognizing the need for an examination of improved ways of preparing teachers is to look at arguments for similar reform in other professional fields. Educators who, like many other groups, are wont to emulate the model of professional medicine should be stirred by the fact that the highly respected, revered establishment of medical education is also experiencing criticism. Medical schools are hearing disapproving claims about the appropriateness and adequcy of preparation programs for doctors. The parallels between the conditions warranting change in medical education and those in teacher education are striking. They are adequate testimony in their own right to support the need for reform in most professional preparation programs, including those for teachers.

The president of Harvard University, Derek Bok, is one respected critic who has issued a challenge to the medical establishment for its intransigence in failing to accept and respond to changing societal conditions. As the amount and nature of knowledge continues to increase dramatically in fields related to medicine, the typical response by those preparing doctors has been to increase the content to be taught and learned. An already saturated program is overloaded even further with more information. Efforts to make compensating allowances have resulted in the reduction of time for laboratory work and independent study. Little attention appears to be given to the fact that the "lecture system encourages a static, passive attitude toward education that emphasizes memorization instead of the active, inquiring cast of mind required to keep up in a rapidly changing field."[6] Experienced critics, according to Bok, claim that students are forced to play a passive role without sufficient opportunity to practise the skills of seeking out information, making tentative diagnoses, testing their hypotheses with further information, and eventually reaching a conclusion.[7] In response to student complaints, medical faculties "have tended to increase the number of electives or to provide a bit more contact with 'live' patients."[8] In other words, they administer palliatives rather than confront the serious, underlying malaise.

Doctors and teachers face a similar challenge with respect to rapidly increasing knowledge. Teachers are impacted in several ways by these changing circumstances. Questions arise as to what students need to know. Teachers struggle with changing and expanding knowledge both in school and university curricula. They are confronted by new information within disciplines related to school subject areas and pertaining to child development, learning styles, teaching strategies, and technological aids. Individual student needs and characteristics are changing. The combined effect of these developments should lead to a questioning of the value of continuing to pack more into the curriculum at the expense of not teaching professionals how to foster lifelong learning, how to approach decision-making, and how to access relevant data bases and diagnostic tools as needed.

CHALLENGE OF CHANGE

Several factors operate to inhibit reform. The nature of the university is one serious contributor to an absence of change. If needed reforms are to occur, attention must be given to the alteration of teaching and learning strategies. Yet, consideration of teaching is a low priority activity in medical faculties, as it is throughout universities generally. Bok observes that "basic reforms require a lot of work—to change pedagogic styles, to develop new instructional materials, to endure the frustrating trials and errors of developing novel ways of teaching. Since none of the typical incentives and rewards of academic medicine reinforce such activities, few professors will devote the time required."[9] Unfortunately, even for those in universities concerned with teacher education, this depreciation of the study of teaching as a priority activity is strikingly real. Teacher educators may pride themselves on being more attentive than their university colleagues to teacher-learner concerns. However, as a group they do not distinguish themselves for their researching, modelling, and evaluating of instruction through which alternative teaching strategies might be injected into professional preparation programs.

Another force operating to subvert change in medical and other professional preparation programs resides in the controlling power of the established practice of the profession. As in most occupations, "formal education is shaped to fit the prevailing sense of how practitioners go about resolving the characteristic problems of their callings.... So long as the prevailing conception stays unchanged, faculties are unlikely to alter the curriculum very much."[10] To challenge the established procedures of the medical or educational culture is to put at risk a doctor's or teacher's professional security. The established system has its own way of dealing with "risk takers," of thwarting innovations, or of discouraging changes that would disrupt and drastically alter the recognized way of doing things. Deviance is difficult to tolerate because it alters the map, threatens the system, and fosters the acceptance of new rules and behaviours. Those accustomed to the established order generally find such conduct disruptive, dysfunctional, even painful.[11] Although we tend to emphasize concepts such as leadership, innovation, and reform, in fact these are generally understood to be operative within relatively fixed boundaries of convention and practice. As long as our commitment to a limited view of professional practice prevails, we can, at best, expect to do little more than make minor adjustments in the preparation of those who will fit into this system.

In spite of his rather critical view of the professional preparation of doctors, Bok argues that new practices must emerge, and they must do so quickly. The anachronistic form of medical education cannot be expected to stand against the pressures of our time. The demands of exponential knowledge growth on human memory and on intellectual processing capacity are reaching the breaking point for doctors, teachers, and many other professionals. Help is needed to assist these professionals in analysing situations, framing concerns, accessing relevant information, intelligently and expeditiously applying knowledge, and evaluating outcomes. Ethical dilemmas are gaining in prominence and centrality, compounding the complexity of decision-making. Just as doctors must deal with questions about sustaining life, and at what personal, social, and economic cost, so, too, educators must pay heed to individual rights and social responsibility as vital ingredients in the educational process. In both spheres, an increasingly pluralistic, uncertain value realm complicates already difficult professional decisions. The spiraling costs of medical services and of public education add one further element to the contemporary scene, which accentuates the necessity of drastic change. Governments and the public they represent expect doctors and teachers to look for new, better, more economical ways of providing their services. Traditional practices and structures are subject to question, if for no other reason than the fact that they constitute a serious, mounting drain on public resources.

PROBLEMS IN TEACHER EDUCATION

Of course, it is not necessary to examine the state of medical education to initiate a discussion of reform in teacher education. The professional literature of educators is replete with statements supporting the need for reform and outlining proposed changes for the improvement of teacher preparation programs. Many authors have attempted to describe both the perceived deficiencies and the current state of research in teacher education, using these as the bases for introducing their own recommended solutions. Joyce and Clift capture the essence of the criticisms about teacher education in the following statement:

> Complaints about teacher education are wondrous in their variety and devastating in their implications. Its students are inferior. Its academic components are too brief and too weak. It is too theoretical and irrelevant to the real world of the schools. It is excessively devoted to pedagogy. It gives too little attention to teaching and practical mattters. It squelches the creativity of its students. It resists innovation. Its graduates resist innovation. It is susceptible to faddism.[12]

As one might expect, associated with this recent wave of criticism about teachers and teacher preparation, has been the emergence, particularly in the United States, of a number of alternative ways of supplying schools with teachers. Some changes are based on the assumption that there is not much to be learned about teaching that cannot be learned on the job, perhaps through apprenticing with a master teacher. Several states have introduced changes in certification requirements through state legislatures, others have discontinued traditional preparation routes and institutions. Still others have lengthened programs, and some have instituted forms of competence testing. These and numerous other responses to the problems associated with teacher education, especially as they exist in the United States, are in part, according to Robert Egbert, to be blamed on teacher educators. He argues that:

> teacher educators are at fault for offering programs that have little substance and less rigor, for graduating students without being sure that they can teach, for failing to incorporate the developing information bases in preparation programs, for failing to demand the resources that must be available to produce educated teachers, and for failing to speak out against even the worst teacher education programs.[13]

A similar but more damning point was made by Evertson, Hawley, and Zlotnik after an extensive review of the research on teacher education, when they observed that "the research raises questions about a number of popular proposals for reforming teacher education, but it does not add up to a defence of teacher preparation as it now exists in most institutions."[14] There are many who would be quick to agree with this conclusion, perhaps to legitimate their attempt to offer the ultimate formula for effective teacher education.

Many who enter into the temptation of providing a remedy for ailing teacher education are prone to think the answer resides exclusively in the nature of the curriculum. As a result, they debate the relative merits of general education, in-depth specialization, professional education courses, nature and length of practica, and overall length of program. Others who recognize the importance of the nature of the student tend to focus on requirements for admission. There exists, as well, among some teacher education reformers, recognition of the importance of instructional strategies and linkages between professionals in the schools and faculties of education. To fail to attend to all of these elements is to ensure the existence of a glaring deficiency in a proposal for reform of teacher education. Not only must all four areas be addressed, they must be properly meshed and balanced.

PROPOSALS FOR REFORM

The preceding comments serve as the context for the proposals for reform outlined in the remainder of this discussion. To some extent, the cautions about attempting to identify a limited number of specific actions to solve complex problems are violated. Although significant reform will require substantial changes in a number of areas, we do have to begin somewhere. The gap between the desirable and the possible may be too wide. In the short term, the feasible and the practicable may have to prevail. But this does not mean that our vision must be blurred. Accordingly, the proposals for change fall into two clusters. The first contains those on which progress could be made in relatively short order—if we could find the will to work on the problems. The second set offers more exciting possibilities for fundamental change in teacher education.

MODEST CHANGES

The most important factor in the quality of teacher preparation programs may well be the calibre of students who enrol in those programs. Eventually, the quality of schools is affected directly by the same factor. Teacher education programs can contribute to school improvement by improving the quality of the graduates; the task begins with the selection of candidates. Although there are numerous students of high academic and intellectual capabilities in education, the overall situation is characterized by what Lanier and Little describe as "too many lows."[15] Specifically, teacher education programs attract and admit more than their fair share of students whose readiness for either university education in general or teacher education in particular is marginal. The explanation for this situation is relatively straightforward.

As is only too well known, the operation of educational systems has been plagued by long periods during which there was an undersupply of teachers. Those periods in which teacher education programs were not under pressure to graduate large numbers in order to staff every classroom have been relatively infrequent and of short duration. For most of its history, teacher education has been influenced to a much greater extent by considerations of quantity than of quality. Progress toward establishing teacher education firmly within universities, requiring a degree before initial certification, and having admission standards comparable to those of other faculties has been slow, and there have been many setbacks. Even though these desirable conditions have been established, teacher education appears to attract a higher proportion of students from the lower end of the spectrum than do other areas of study. The time has come for faculties of education to look critically at their faith in being able to develop marginal candidates into effective teachers.

For the historical reasons outlined above, teacher education does not have a tradition of careful selection of candidates at entry. During periods of undersupply of teachers, governmental policies do not permit such selection. When the supply situation does permit greater selectivity, faculties have neither the tradition nor the procedures for screening those who are admitted on other than academic criteria. Even when there is an adequate supply of teachers, the suspicion that this will be of short duration discourages more intensive selection activities. The time has come to take the selection responsibility seriously. Given that relatively little selection takes place during teacher preparation programs, adequate screening at the time of admission assumes even greater importance.

Although increased selectivity could focus specifically on academic criteria, those responsible for teacher education must have the courage to go beyond such basic indicators. Consideration should also be given to interests, attitudes, and aptitudes that are likely to be related to success in teaching. Even though the research evidence may be weak or contradictory, opinions of teacher educators may vary, and the predictive validity of various factors may be low, the assumption that not all who meet the minimum admission standards are suitable for careers in teaching must guide selection. The task of selection is not to find those who will be the best teachers but, more realistically, to try to screen out those who are least likely to be successful. Selection that screens out even a small proportion of potentially unsuccessful teacher candidates will be worth the effort.

The allocation of time and effort at the selection stage has potential for high returns. If some problem cases are prevented from developing, there is obviously time for more productive kinds of activities. Increasing the average intellectual and academic capabilities of students will be reflected in the quality of classroom interaction during teacher education. More capable students from education faculties who are taking courses elsewhere on campus will enhance the status of teacher education candidates in general. There is potential that teacher education programs will become more attractive to other capable students. Clearly, these benefits are speculative at this stage. But the prospect of achieving such outcomes should spur our effort.

In brief, the proposal is that teacher educators must become more modest in their beliefs about their abilities. Although some teachers are born, some are made, and most are a combination of the two, we must recognize that there are probably those who were not born to be teachers and who cannot be made into teachers. Some of our efforts should be directed at identifying these people before they enter a teacher preparation program so that both they and the teacher educators can engage in more productive pursuits.

An enduring debate about teacher education revolves around the extent to which what teachers need to know can be learned through initial teacher preparation, to what extent this is gained through experience, and to what extent continuing education is required. Advocates at the extremes would seek either to accomplish everything in the preservice program or to abandon such programs entirely. Within this range there are those who question the length and content of teacher preparation programs. More generally, there is some consensus that, regardless of the combination of formal education, apprenticeship, and experience, learning to be a teacher is a lifelong process. Although espoused, the belief seems to have had little impact on the nature and design of teacher preparation programs.

If teacher education is and should be a lifelong process, then preservice preparation must be carefully designed to provide the base for initial practice and further learning. Such an orientation does not seem to be reflected in, or to be consistent with, the pressures for longer and more specialized periods of initial preparation. Designers of teacher education programs should realize that not everything can be squeezed into an initial preparation program. Even the proponents of longer periods of initial preparation must give thought to the content so that longer does not mean just more of the same.

Consistent with a model of lifelong teacher education, the initial preparation should be oriented more to the development of general rather than specialized pedagogical content. Although the teacher will develop some specialization in particular areas of subject matter and curriculum, there should be sufficient breadth to open possibilities for teachers to move into a range of grade and subject areas. Narrower and more focussed specialization can come later. In part, the lifelong aspect will involve not only the updating of knowledge and skills but the development of more specialized areas of professional practice. The injection of variety into a teacher's practice may help to reduce some of the routine and boredom that seem to be a part of teaching for too many educators.

A serious commitment to a lifelong teacher education model would, in effect, reduce the pressures for either extending programs or forcing more content into existing programs. Recognition that learning also occurs during service would place pressures on developing effective means for facilitating the transition to teaching. Teacher education programs have a role to play in this process. Furthermore, the fragmented approach to continuing professional development might give way to more deliberate attempts to provide teachers with the kinds of learning opportunities that teacher preparation programs have to offer.

The adoption of a lifelong teacher education model has significant implications for the content and structure of both initial and continuing teacher education. Real change in teacher education would begin by taking these implications seriously.

Teacher education programs are vulnerable to criticism of compartmentalization and fragmentation. Indeed, a harsh commentary might question even the designation of the collection of courses and experiences as forming a program. The major divisions in the curriculum of teacher education are almost universal: general education, subject matter specialties, and pedagogy. The first two of these are mainly, but not exclusively, taken outside faculties of education; consequently, there are major divisions between different parts of the program. In the pedagogical area, there is fragmentation even within education among specific fields such as foundations, educational psychology, and curriculum or methods areas. Practicum components may stand even further apart when these are substantially under the control of teachers in the schools or of school districts.

Within their programs, teacher candidates will encounter a diversity of orientations toward the teacher preparation program, possibly ranging from hostility outside of the teacher education faculty, variable commitment within, and a tendency to question the relevance of university studies generally among teachers. The widespread involvement of different groups in teacher preparation tends to ensure that the integration of various components, if its occurs anywhere, must occur in the minds of individual teacher education candidates.

Real change in teacher education will require acceptance of responsibility for programs by all those who are involved: academics outside of education faculties, administrators of these other faculties, and members of the profession as well as members of faculties of education. Acceptance of that responsibility would mean moving beyond reciprocal criticism to mutual planning of how teachers might best be educated. The distinctive contributions that each part or component can make must be made explicit, and those who offer each part must accept responsibility for the adequacy of the contribution. In addition, we must move to a more adequate level of integration of the different parts through a collaborative approach to program planning and design.

Such a reorientation must begin with the professors in a faculty of education. Without a more coherent approach in the pedagogical area, there is not the base from which to extend the co-operation. For any program, agreement must be achieved on what should be included in the pedagogical curriculum so that there is less variation in content across instructors teaching the same courses. Similarly, more co-operative forms of planning will be required to ensure that the hoped for integration across various components actually does occur.

To move toward more coherent and integrated teacher education programs will require overcoming a range of political problems that serve as deterrents to reform in teacher education.

REAL CHANGE

Apart from selecting some familiar proposals for comment, we have attempted to identify several fundamental changes that, if accepted and introduced, would represent a considerable shift in the way in which teacher education is viewed and practised. They would also serve to alter appreciably the nature and quality of teaching and schooling. The time has come to address change of this magnitude.

Let us begin by arguing for the need to broaden the focus of our schools and faculties of education. This is by no means a novel idea. George S. Counts advocated such a development in the 1930s.[16] Charles E. Silberman voiced a similar message in the 1960s when he observed, "if our concern is with education, we cannot restrict our attention to the schools."[17] These proposals were not denigrating the importance of schools, instead they were giving recognition to their place among a myriad of other educating agencies in our society. Even more recently, Lawrence Cremin, during his presidency at Columbia University, reiterated this message, arguing for teacher preparation institutions to foster a study that examines education both comprehensively and relationally.[18] Such an exploration would help teachers appreciate the impact of other educating agencies on learning and schooling and, also, would provide a basis for determining the possibility that established practices and structures may be in need of change. Each educational agency teaches its particular messages and, in the course of doing so, mediates the messages of other agencies. Schools teach, but they also interpret, evaluate, challenge, and reinforce the teachings of church, television, peer groups, families, and employers.

As long as members of teacher preparation institutions make schooling and education synonymous, they will tend to redefine our problems in essentially the same way and will arrive at similar solutions with little reason to modify the basic approach to teacher education. Teachers in public schools have far more in common with museum curators, television producers, newspaper publishers, and parents than they generally recognize. By looking at education as it occurs in these various settings, we may acquire the ability to shape our views of preparation programs in ways to make them far more effective in stimulating, facilitating, and enriching learning.

We are in need of an educational vision for our day, a vision that will address fundamental questions about the nature of education in a truly humane society and raise corresponding questions about the impact of the process on learners of varying ages, circumstances, needs, and interests. The tensions inherent between the style, substance, values, and aspirations of various educating agencies are the very basis of fundamental change. By awakening ourselves to these considerations, we give hope to the prospect that we will begin to reshape our traditional educational institutions. A remapping of the terrain in creative, imaginative ways will replace the tinkering and adjusting to produce exciting alternatives for the future.

By recognizing, studying, and being involved in education in a variety of institutional and social settings, future teachers will be less likely to allow established schooling practices to control and restrict change. This outcome would be even more likely if practising teachers were encouraged or required to leave their classrooms to spend time in different educational settings outside of public education. By working in adult educational activities, for example, new perspectives could be gained on the necessity of prerequisites, the importance of motivation to achievement, and the value of self-directed learning. The reconceptualizing of schooling and education, which is essential to future well-being, is likely only if we find a way to seriously challenge established principles and procedures.

The second proposal for fundamental change in teacher education is closely linked to a broader definition of education. But attention shifts to a broadened understanding of the process through which learning about professional practice occurs. For a teacher, significant learning can be based in the day-to-day experience of teaching. Even though experience and practice have long been recognized as important for professional development, there has been minimal emphasis on adopting a deliberate and analytic approach to this form of learning.

No one would deny the importance of the learning gained through firsthand teaching experience or even through watching others perform in these situations. Unfortunately, the key to successful performance is usually seen to be little more than observing, imitating, and adopting what seems to be effective. The tendency in this process is toward a limited set of acceptable practices because teachers are not stimulated to consider new ways of defining problems or of creating new methods for dealing with them. Improvements in professional practice are contingent upon teachers who will consider different ways of structuring their tasks. The current socializing effects of teacher preparation programs and of the profession discourage this development. Success is determined largely by fitting into established patterns.

Significant professional development will occur only as teachers begin to place less emphasis on imitating teaching behaviours and to give more attention to the analysis of what occurs in practice. In order for teachers in schools to become reflective in their work, as Donald Schön advocates,[19] they must see this exemplified in the actions of teacher educators. Furthermore, they must be taught in practice sessions how competent performers study their situations, identify needs, determine courses of action, and evaluate outcomes. In effect, such teachers engage in research while teaching. Their questioning and answering is a vital source of professional knowledge; they learn from what they do. Each teaching situation affords the practitioner with multiple ways of setting the task and of finding ways of dealing with it. Even though the teacher enters the class to teach a lesson in a particular way, there should be an openness and a readiness to consider other possibilities. Both during and after the lesson, the teacher analyses and reflects on the process in order to identify ways in which improvement might be made. In the midst of action, the professional teacher should keep alive a wide variety of views of the situation in order to learn from the experience.

If teachers are to become reflective, and if teaching is to be a valuable source of professional knowledge, several supporting changes are necessary. All teaching situations in schools and universities, from those of the novice to those of the experienced practitioner, need to be examined critically and reflected upon openly. Adequate support, both financial and moral, is needed for this activity. Teachers at all levels of competence, qualification, and instruction will need to be taught to be more open and ready to examine what they do. The professional development of teachers must truly become a life-time venture. Experienced teachers, working with practicum students or interns, would learn from their less experienced colleagues. Through the relationship they would find reason to seek new, additional learning and would gain new ways of setting or framing their tasks. The questioning of an established practice opens the door to new ways of viewing the assignment.

One way to establish the commitment to this development would be for teacher educators in universities to pay greater heed to their own instructional practices and to involve their students, who are not only students but also prospective teachers, in the examination of these practices. Efforts could also be made to utilize practicum or internship settings as locations for such discussions about teaching. The key to any of these developments or changes is for teachers to become convinced that the critical examination of practice will lead to professional growth and improvement.

CONCLUSION

In effect, these proposals for fundamental change are part of a view of teaching as an exciting, creative, skillful art. The art requires knowledge of content fields to be mastered by students, of various knowledge areas that provide essential understanding of learners and learning contexts, and of mastery of skills and methods related to effective pedagogy. Teachers who are helped to develop this vision of what they are commissioned to do will find ways of opening doors to enable more people to experience the excitement of learning. Teacher educators, in universities and in school classrooms, should lead the way in providing the model situations where their students can gain the appreciation of the broader meaning of education and of the power of knowledge generated through reflection in action.

But is there any basis for optimism that real changes such as these will occur in teacher education? We believe so. Increasingly, teacher educators themselves are becoming more cognizant of the strengths and weaknesses of teacher education programs. Instead of responding defensively to criticism of present practices, they appear ready to look at ways in which the education of teachers might be improved. Summaries of research such as that developed by Lanier and Little are helpful in defining the nature of the problem.[20] New directions for research such as those proposed by Shulman have potential for increasing our understanding of how students develop into competent educators.[21] Not just the case but also the base for change in teacher education is being strengthened. Perhaps teacher educators will soon act to accomplish the real changes that at present are only vague thoughts in the minds of would-be teacher-education reformers.

NOTES

1. J.D. Koerner, *The Miseducation of American Teachers* (Boston: Houghton-Mifflin, 1963), 17.
2. Ibid., 18.
3. Dennis A. Williams, Lucy Howard, Dianne H. McDonald, and Renee Michael, "Why Teachers Fail," *Newsweek* (24 Sept. 1984), 64.
4. The National Commission on Excellence in Education, *A Nation at Risk* (April 1982), 22.
5. Andrew Nikiforuk, "Why Our Teachers Can't Teach," *Quest* (Sept. 1984), 35.
6. Derek Bok, "Needed: A New Way to Train Doctors," *Harvard Magazine* (May-June 1984), 35.
7. Ibid.
8. Ibid., 34.
9. Ibid., 35.
10. Ibid.
11. R.S. Patterson, "Go, Grit and Gumption: A Normal School Perspective on Teacher Education" (McCalla Lecture, Faculty of Education, University of Alberta, 1983).
12. Bruce Joyce and Renee Clift, "The Phoenix Agenda: Essential Reform in Teacher Education," *Educational Researcher* 13, 4 (April 1984), 5.

13. Robert L. Egbert, "The Practice of Preservice Teacher Education," *Journal of Teacher Education* 36, 1 (Jan.-Feb. 1985), 21.
14. Carolyn M. Evertson, Willis D. Hawley, and Marilyn Zlotnik, "Making a Difference in Educational Quality Through Teacher Education," *Journal of Teacher Education* 36, 3 (May-June 1985), 8.
15. Judith E. Lanier and Judith W. Little, "Research on Teacher Education" in *Handbook of Research on Teaching*, 3rd ed., edited by Merlin C. Wittrock (New York: Macmillan, 1986), 540–542.
16. George S. Counts, "What Is a School of Education?" *Teachers College Record* 30 (1928–29): 647–55.
17. Charles E. Silberman, "The Carnegie Study of the Education of Educators: Preliminary Statement of Intent," (26 Sept. 1966), unpublished memorandum, p. 2), quoted in Lawrence A. Cremin, *Public Education*, (New York: Basic Books, 1976), 12.
18. Lawrence A. Cremin, *Public Education* (New York: Basic Books, 1976), 57.
19. Donald A. Schön, *The Reflective Practitioner* (New York: Basic Books, 1983).
20. Lanier and Little, "Research on Teacher Education."
21. Lee S. Shulman, "Those Who Understand: Knowledge Growth in Teaching," *Educational Researcher* 15, 2 (Feb. 1986): 4–14.

SECTION 9:
CANADIAN EDUCATION IN THE FUTURE

Canadian education at all levels is undergoing change. The process of evaluation and redirection appears to be fostered by many factors including governmental priorities and conflicts, financial restraint, the development of alternative educational settings and delivery systems, technological changes, unemployment and underemployment, and pressing demands for new curricular approaches to prepare citizens more readily for a society in flux. The authors in this section examine current developments that have impact for the future of education in Canada and also speculate on possible scenarios so that we may be somewhat more able to better direct our educational endeavours in the next century.

Awender and Nease discuss Canada's continuing search for an appropriate distribution of federal and provincial powers and responsibilites in educational matters. Governmental relations are treated from both a theoretical and an operational perspective with a particular emphasis on the intrusions of the federal government into the educational jurisdictions of the provinces. Awender and Nease highlight the complexities of Canadian education in terms of constitutional realities and political processes.

Bezeau identifies two issues in the financing of education that will have significant impact on Canadian education in the future. The first is the growing controversy over the public funding of private schools and the second concerns the fluctuations in "dependency" in the Canadian population. Dependency refers to the fact that certain age groups within our population (particularly the young and the old) do not contribute to production and therefore depend on the productive segments of our population to provide for their needs. Ramifications of these two issues are highlighted and discussed.

The plight of community colleges in Canada is described by Dennison. Initially supported by economic prosperity and the political and social goals of provincial governments, the multipurpose public community colleges experienced rapid growth in the 1960s and early 1970s but this development has more recently been curtailed by economic decline and demands for accountability. Dennison discusses four major issues affecting the future of the community college: (1) Their level of autonomy is being questioned and the tendency toward greater provincial centralization is creating a degree of instability in planning. (2) There is a controversy between the demand for specialized training and a more liberalized education that prepares a person for a lifetime of learning. (3) There is a need for a formalized evaluation procedure for operations and staff development. (4) There is a need for enhanced understanding between professionals and unionists to prevent labour confrontations and maintain the flexibility required of community colleges. Dennison offers possible directions to stimulate solutions to these problems that, if unresolved, may lead to the demise of this important postsecondary alternative.

A more optimistic picture is painted by Hayduk who states that the educational prospects of individuals who are employed full-time, or who are physically unable to attend a formal institution may be greatly enhanced through the growth of distance education in Canada. Based on a myriad of media, hardware, and software that permit two-way interaction to bridge the physical separation between the teacher and the learner, distance education still emanates from a formal institution but it requires different interpersonal and organizational skills than conventional teaching. With the philosophy of lifelong learning and the proliferation of advances in communication technology, this promising approach is emerging with an ever clearer profile from the educational mosaic.

Livingstone focusses on a major crisis in Canadian education: the excessive production of qualified people to fill declining job markets. In discussing future routes for solutions to this problem, he considers the reforms suggested by opinion leaders and policy makers, presents a distillation of public sentiments on postsecondary education, and critically analyses the social class forces that will likely come into play in solving this crisis.

Zingle and Dick examine counselling and counsellor education in the future. They identify six existing factors—the baby boom, the new woman, computer technology, social disenchantment, lack of confidence in the monetary system, and the increasing tempo of modern life—that they believe will have tremendous impact on counselling programs. These forces are examined with the view that this type of discussion will help counsellors and counsellor educators to be better prepared for the future and therefore more able to influence it.

In the final article in this section, and indeed in this volume, Pratt discusses how the curriculum planner can help teachers and students with the recognition, construction, and integration of public, interpersonal, and personal meaning. Public meaning refers to the areas of knowledge and technical competence that can be readily communicated in verbal and numerical forms. Interpersonal meanings refer to meanings that can only be understood and shared by those in some sort of relationship. Personal meanings are essentially intuitive and can only be fully comprehended by the person who experiences them. Through this context, Pratt raises many extremely relevant and thought-provoking questions that merit serious consideration by educators at all levels if we are to effectively prepare young Canadians for life in the twenty-first century.

GOVERNMENT CONTROL OF EDUCATION

MICHAEL A. AWENDER AND A.S. NEASE

One of the major dilemmas confronting Canadians throughout most of their history has been that of intergovernmental relations. There has been a constant search for a satisfactory distribution of responsibility and power between the federal government in Ottawa and the governments of the individual provinces and territories. The histories of the provinces have exhibited the same conundrum for they have been equally concerned about their roles vis-à-vis local levels of government. Similar problems of relationship confront the latter when overlapping responsibilities occur between, for example, a municipal council and a school board or between a municipality and a regional agency having a mandate in a particular area of concern. Simplistically diagrammed, federal, provincial, and local intergovernmental relationships may be viewed vertically, whereas relationships between local governments, school board jurisdictions, and regional agencies may be regarded as horizontal in nature (see figure 1).

In this essay, an attempt will be made to deal with the dilemma of Canadian intergovernmental relations through an examination of the process in one program area—that of education. Moreover, this process will be viewed not only from a theoretical but also an operational perspective because, as has often been argued in the past, "federalism takes on meaning only in actual situations, when solutions are sought to substantive problems."[1]

CONSTITUTIONAL ARRANGEMENTS

Any discussion of overlapping government authority in the Canadian context necessitates, in the first instance, reference to the British North America Act, 1867, re-enacted and retitled, the Constitution Act, 1867, by the Constitution Act, 1982. The B.N.A. Act was one of several acts and amendments that comprise the Canadian Constitution. A statute of the British Parliament, its primary purpose was to amalgamate the two provinces of Upper and Lower Canada, which became Ontario and Quebec, and the provinces of Nova Scotia and New Brunswick into one political entity which would be called Canada. As such, the Act had to deal with the question of intergovernmental relations, for it is extremely difficult to create any type of political

FIGURE 1
INTERGOVERNMENTAL RELATIONSHIPS

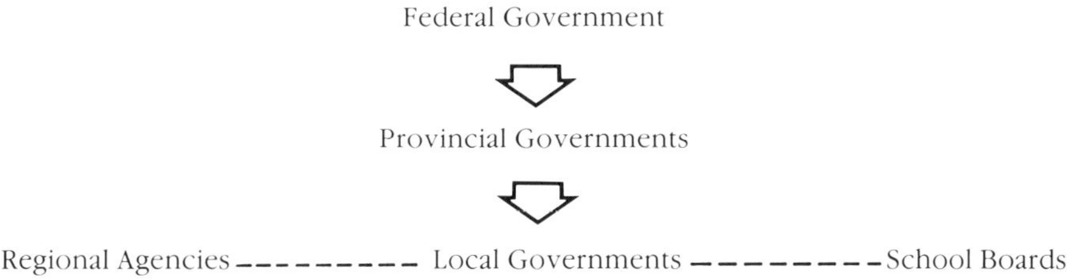

Federal Government
⇩
Provincial Governments
⇩
Regional Agencies _____ Local Governments _____ School Boards

union without dealing with the question of the respective roles of all the entities involved in the process. This was particularly the case in British North America where each of the new provinces that united into "One Dominion" had its own history, cultural traditions, and aspirations under the Crown.

Those who framed the B.N.A. Act had to pay attention to these matters in creating a federal state and finally had to agree on the distribution of powers between the national government and the governments of the provinces. They delineated the responsibilities of exclusive Dominion jurisdiction in section 91 of the Act. The twenty-nine areas outlined in this section, which J.A. Correy and J.E. Hodgetts claim are "illustrative only and not a definite statement of the scope of Dominion power" outline basic functional responsibilities such as, defence, criminal law and penitentiaries, trade and commerce, census and statistics, navigation, currency and legal tender, Indians and lands reserved for the latter, and what is often referred to as a residual clause, appearing in the preamble to the section, "to make Laws for the Peace, Order, and good government of Canada."[2]

Provincial responsibilities were outlined in section 92. They dealt primarily with those areas that were considered to be of relatively minor importance in 1867. A list of a few of these sixteen classes of subjects is as follows: health, welfare, natural resources, municipal institutions, local licences, and local works that did not affect "the general advantage of Canada," property and civil rights, taxation for provincial purposes, and "generally all Matters of a merely local or private Nature in the Province." Although it was determined that education would be primarily a provincial responsibility, perhaps to stress a point, it was not included in the general enunciation of the provincial powers. Rather, its place was spelled out within a separate area of the document.

Section 93 of the Act provides that, in each province, "the legislature may exclusively make laws in relation to education." However, a number of restrictions accompany this right. Cheffins outlines these as follows:

> A province cannot prejudicially affect rights and privileges that had been accorded to denominational schools at the time of union. Furthermore, wherever a province has a separate school system, or one is subsequently established by provincial legislation, the members of the separate school system have the right to appeal to the Governor-General-In-Council [the prime minister and cabinet] any action or decision of a provincial authority, which affects the Protestant and Roman Catholic educational rights that either existed at the time of union or were thereafter established by legislation. If an appeal established a violation of these rights, the Governor-General-In-Council is authorized to make recommendations.... In the event the province does not take appropriate actions, the Parliament of Canada is given legislative authority in subsection 193(4) to "Make remedial Laws for the due Execution of the Provisions of this section and of any Decision of the Governor-General-In-Council under this section."[3]

In summary, then, it must be concluded that the provincial legislatures, though granted authority over education, cannot pass any law that denies "any Right or Privilege with respect to Denominational Schools which any class of Persons have by Law in the Province at the Union."[4] In addition, though section 93(4) permits the federal parliament to pass remedial laws necessary to restore educational rights denied by the provinces, it does not allow the national government to change the rights enunciated in section 93(1). Thus, although education seems to fall exclusively within the provincial domain, the federal government does have a role to play in the protection of rights and privileges and, indeed, has taken upon itself other educational responsibilities as will be noted later in this paper.

Neither should local government units, in this case school boards, be overlooked in a discussion of this nature. Certainly, the fact that the latter are actually creations of the provinces must be taken into account. However, the fact remains that certain functions in the educational field have long been delegated to local jurisdiction and the twin spectres of tradition and public opinion encourage the provincial authorities to tread rather lightly in certain aspects of the educational environment. Thus, the local level is yet another factor to be considered when one attempts to examine the intergovernmental nature of the educative process.

Such, then, are the formal constitutional elements governing intergovernmental relations in education. One may now turn to an examination of the actual division of powers as they have developed since 1867.

LOCAL INVOLVEMENT

Looking first of all at the local situation, it is apparent that school boards have their greatest freedom in the area of administrative matters. Hiring certified teachers and qualified administrators, purchasing supplies and equipment, providing and operating schools, and establishing tax rates, based chiefly on ownership of property within a permissive range, are all examples of such administrative matters. However, even in these areas, the school board does not possess complete freedom of action. Although boards can hire teachers and administrators, they must choose from those certified by the provincial department or ministry of education; while they can purchase supplies, they can do so in some areas, such as textbooks, only after receiving prior provincial approval; while they provide schools, the latter often can only be built with provincial approval and funds; and while a local tax for educational purposes can be levied, its limits, at times, are subject to provincial guidelines. Thus, in these as well as many other administrative matters, the local board's powers are prescribed and limited by the regulations and actions of the provincial legislatures.

Local school boards are also intimately intertwined with other governmental units. In several provinces, the boards use county and city governments as tax collecting agencies. In these instances, the board itself determines the amount necessary for school purposes, and then sends the bill to the local municipal units, which are compelled by provincial statute to collect the moneys and transfer them to the boards prior to specified dates.[5] In addition, county and city governments are usually responsible for certifying standards of health and safety on school property, as well as providing, through the regional office of the department or ministry of health, medical and dental services to local boards on the latter's request. Even when a board undertakes the construction of a new school, its architectural plans must not only be submitted to one of the provincial regional offices for its approval, but it must also satisfy the local fire and sanitary authorities that their regulations can be fulfilled. Moreover, some provinces issue procedural guidelines to follow when a board decides to close a school because of insufficient enrolment. Transportation is another area in which school boards and municipalities often work out co-operative agreements. Quite often, rather than inaugurate their own service to transport their students, the local board will make arrangements with the city or county government to provide the service.

There are many other areas where this type of co-operation occurs at the local level. J.F. Cramer and G.S. Browne point out several of these in their comparative study of different countries.

> There are many areas, such as recreation, parks, and play-grounds, health services, community planning, and others, where the local school district and the local [government] authority must work closely together. The problems of control and of budgetary relations have not been solved.... The trend seems to favor a greater degree of voluntary and legal co-operation between school administration and city [and county] management.[6]

Because it is a creation of the provinces, the local school board is affected greatly by provincial policies and procedures. As was indicated above, while the local government unit, in this case the school board, is responsible for the daily administration of almost all school matters, it can act only within the broad guidelines established by the province. Thus, the province acts as the "guarantor of educational standards and the local school boards the source of diversity."[7] In addition to the areas of personnel, supplies, accommodations, and taxes already mentioned, curriculum also serves as an example of local-provincial interrelationships. For example, within the province of Ontario, the Ministry of Education issues guidelines that outline the general philosophy of program that may be offered by the schools. Local boards are then given the option either of developing actual courses that meet their unique needs from the criteria outlined in these documents, or of developing entirely different courses, which they must then submit to the provincial body for approval. In addition, regional educational offices housing specialized curriculum and administrative consultants have been established throughout the province. These individuals, although formally representatives of the provincial curriculum department, are available to the local boards for program and curriculum development and evaluations. At the same time, however, they are used by provincial authorities to ensure that provincial standards are being met in the region. Thus, it is not difficult to see that, in the area of curriculum, as well as those areas outlined earlier, the local school boards must always be cognizant of a provincial presence.

There is also a local-federal relationship in school matters that deserves mention. First of all, the local school government benefits from grants originating from federal authorities for vocational programs that are offered by the school board. Although these funds are channelled through the provinces, nevertheless, the money and impetus for the program do filter from the federal to the local level, and thus, at least, an indirect relationship does exist. The development of comprehensive secondary schools throughout Canada in the early 1960s, incorporating vocational programs of study, is the result of the federal government's concern about an overall shortage of trained technical personnel in the country. A similar fiscal flow is evident in the areas of bilingualism, including minority-language teacher training, travel bursaries, and the like.

Furthermore, the federal government is also involved in two other local educational matters: the education of Native peoples and children of armed forces personnel. In the first instance, the Minister of Indian and Northern Affairs is responsible for either actually providing schools for Native children or giving them access to public or private schools. In 1985, about half of the Native children in Canada attended public schools, and the federal government reimbursed the provinces in the form of tuition fees or contributions to the school's capital costs. The Department of National Defence also reimburses the provinces on behalf of the children of the armed forces personnel who attend the local schools.

Finally, locally sponsored educational conferences and research efforts are very often given direct federal assistance in the form of financing and personnel. Hence, once again, it is evident that, just as the provinces affect the operations of the educational system within the localities, the federal government also plays a definite role at that level.

PROVINCIAL INVOLVEMENT

As was pointed out earlier, the provinces are formally at the centre of the Canadian educational system. Obviously, how each province fulfills this particular role with respect to the local systems and the federal government cannot help but be coloured by that province's own history, customs, and culture. Thus, a discussion on intergovernmental relations in this field necessitates identification of the province under consideration in the analysis. This is not to imply that the conclusions reached here are unique only to this one province's relations with other government levels. Rather, it is simply a caution offered that a closer appraisal of the other provinces may be necessary before all the generalities of this study could be applied to the total Canadian experience.

Ministers of education and departments in ministries of education exist in every Canadian province as do their counterparts in the territories. However, for the purposes of this paper the Ontario educational apparatus will be the model used.

The individual most responsible for the educational system of Ontario is the elected member of the Legislative Assembly who is assigned the portfolio of education by the premier. As Minister of Education, she or he is directly responsible to the Legislature for all the activities of the ministry. These include all elementary and secondary education matters, all teacher certification, all curriculum development, a great deal of provincial planning and research, vocational training that is not the specific responsibility of another government ministry, all special education schools, all educational exchange between Ontario and other Canadian provinces, correspondence courses, and a substantial share of adult education. In addition, direct responsibilities include the organization and operation of, and teacher training for, provincial schools, such as day and residential demonstration schools for children with severe learning disabilities, and schools for the blind and the deaf. Obviously, there are very few matters of an educational nature that do not fall into one of these categories. Consequently, it is not too difficult to see the pivotal role that the province plays in the educational field.

Scrutinizing the situation more closely, it appears as though the ministry's influence over events at the local level is determined by two different factors: the control of legislative grants, and the related power of supervision. In his book, *Quiet Evolution*, R.S. Harris comments on the power behind the first of these.

> Grants can be withheld unless the department's regulations are fulfilled. Moreover, the department is able to encourage local school boards to adopt measures which can be expected to improve the eductional programs by offering additional grants which pay for all or a sizable portion of the increased expenditures.[8]

To demonstrate, however, that the province must still consider the local government's feelings if it really desires to encourage such programs, Harris adds this: "The [local] school board is normally free not to accept the grant and thus not to introduce the proposed measure."[9]

The second factor extending provincial influence at the school board level is the local director or superintendent of education. Although usually appointed and paid by the school board itself, the superintendent is still "directly responsible to the Minister for the performance of...duties" specified by the provincial authorities.[10] These duties include making certain that the departmental acts and regulations, which touch upon almost every aspect of the local educational system, are carried out.

At the provincial level itself, the activities of the Ministry of Education are intertwined with other provincial government ministries. The closest relationship is with the two ministries that arrange for the Ministry of Education to provide instruction for their educational programs—Health (hospital programs) and Community and Social Services.

The Ministry of Health has the basic responsibility for providing educational programs to individuals within health institutions known as special care facilities. However, the educational programs in these particular facilities, while tailored to local needs, generally follow the guidelines established by the Ministry of Education. Moreover, the latter also hires the teachers employed in the program. The diploma that one receives after the successful completion of the prescribed program of studies is also issued and awarded through the Ministry of Education. Thus, it is not too difficult to see the relationship that exists between these two ministries.

The Ministries of Education and of Community and Social Services combine resources in operating seven developmental centre schools for the mentally retarded, developmentally handicapped, and emotionally disturbed. The same two ministries are responsible for the four training schools for young people who have been declared delinquent under the terms of the Young Offenders Act. The school program offered in these institutions is a combination of an academic syllabus for the appropriate grade, and vocational training of various types that is outlined by the Ministry of Education. For the most part, the teachers employed within these centres are required to have the same qualifications as teachers in the regular elementary and secondary schools of the province. In addition, the teaching staff is also generally responsible to and appraised by the appropriate Ministry of Education officials.

The Industrial Training Branch of the Ministry of Labour had the basic responsibility for the 125 programs outlined in the Apprenticeship and

Tradesmen Qualification Act of 1964. However, here again, the Ministry of Education not only certified certain teachers but also provided the actual centres and institutes in which the instruction was provided. The local and federal levels of government were also involved in this area, as the latter funnelled fiscal aid for such programs through the provinces, while the local authorities were very often called upon to carry out the actual administration of the programs. In 1973, the Industrial Training Branch of the Ministry of Labour was transferred to the Ministry of Colleges and Universities and, consequently, the latter assumed most of the responsibility for the program outlined in this act. However, ties between the Ministry of Labour and the Ministry of Education continue to exist in that credits in high school vocational and trades programs can be used to shorten the amount of time required for individuals to obtain their trade papers. Moreover, personnel teaching these courses at the high school level are generally required, in addition to holding their trade qualifications, to be certified by the Ministry of Education.

Other provincial ministries also maintain an active relationship with the Ministry of Education. The link with the Ministry of Natural Resources can be traced back several years. At one time, a senior official of the Ministry of Education served as a member of the Advisory Council of the Ontario Forest Ranger School. While this situation does not exist today, other connections between the two ministries are still maintained. For example, various natural Resource Centres, and the facilities offered therein operated by the Ministry of National Resources, are often used as alternative learning sites for elementary and secondary school students. Moreover, at the local level, school boards throughout the province make arrangements with conservation authorities to use sites under the jurisdiction of the parent ministries for regular outdoor education programs. The curriculum of such a program is generally established by the Ministry of Education and, while the teacher is usually the classroom teacher, very often the conservation authority will provide additional instructional help.

The provincial Secretary for Social Development, whose office has ties with various advisory committees, has a more indirect tie with the Ministry of Education. An excellent example of this is provided by one such operating committee—the Ontario Advisory Council on Multiculturalism. Not only does the council have a representative from the Ministry of Education on it, one could easily surmise that its recommendations might very well have far reaching effects on the elementary and secondary school programs.

Finally, it might be pointed out that there is a great deal of cross-pollination among the various provincial ministries and the Ministry of Education in the area of curriculum development. For example, a curriculum consultant from the Ministry of Education attempting to create a new high school curriculum in environmental sciences might very well invite representatives from the Ministry of the Environment to participate in the endeavour. It should also be pointed out that there is a flow in the opposite direction when another ministry engages in similar types of endeavours that might benefit from Ministry of Education representation.

One final provincial responsibility deserves special comment. Although universities have had a long history of academic autonomy and generally have enjoyed relative financial freedom from provincial governments from whom they hold their charters, nevertheless the influx of students during the decade after the late 1950s made it impossible for universities to maintain any semblance of fiscal autonomy. Provincial governments also felt the pressure of increasing enrolments and encouraged universities to expand their facilities and, in some provinces, new universities were founded. Moneys for new buildings, increased library holdings, more faculty members, support services including computer hardware and software for research purposes, and additional support staff could not be realized from student fees, private funding sources, or the now inadequate grants from the provinces. Consequently, the provinces, in conjunction with the federal government, were compelled to increase their funding base. In some provinces, the responsibility for university aid was lodged in the Department or Ministry of Education. In Ontario, a new ministry, the Ministry of Colleges and Universities, with its own minister and bureaucracy, was created in 1964. To maintain some independence between the universities and the government, two bodies were established. The first of these was the Council of Ontario Universities, consisting of the chief executive officers of each university together with their academic colleagues, which became an advocate for university causes. This group develops policies, conducts specialized studies, and makes recommendations to appropriate bodies. A second body, the Ontario Council on University Affairs was a creation of the government and, having a broad base of representation from across the province, has the right to make recommendations to the government concerning the financial support to be given to universities year by year.

The Ministry of Colleges and Universities also has responsibility for the Colleges of Applied Arts and Technology (CAAT), a network of colleges responsible for delivering non-degree programs of study in technological, trade, and commercial subjects, including the training and education of nurses who have the option of attending a CAAT or of entering a school or faculty of nursing at a university. The board of regents acts as a buffer between the governments and the colleges, having overall responsibility for curricula and instructors' salaries.

It should be noted that the provinces have different delivery systems for such programs and courses. In Quebec, for example, the collèges d'enseignement général et professional (CEGEPs) offer general and vocational education as an integral part of the post-secondary system. One must graduate from a CEGEP as a condition of entry to a Quebec university.

In summary, it is quite clear that the provincial departments and ministries of education play the decisive role in the educational process. However, as has been indicated, the ministry does not act completely independently. Its activities are related not only to other government departments at the provincial level, but also to both local and federal authorities. It is to the latter level of government that this discussion now turns.

FEDERAL INVOLVEMENT

Although section 93 of the Constitution Act of 1867 gave the provinces exclusive constitutional and legislative jurisdiction over education, Ottawa has argued that, of necessity, it has a role to play in educational issues that transcend provincial boundaries, and that such jurisdiction is founded in the "peace, order, and good government" clause of the B.N.A. Act. The federal government conceded that section 93 of the British North America Act, which states that "In and for each province, the Legislature may exclusively make laws in relation to education," gave the provinces jurisdiction over purely educational matters within their boundaries. However, the federal government claimed responsibility for those educational matters not solely concerning one province. Addressing the Canadian Teachers' Federation in 1967, Robert Stanbury, M.P., outlined Ottawa's position as follows:

> If there are national needs and objectives that require concerted educational policy in two, several, or all provinces, no provincial legislature is by itself competent in the matter, and judicial interpretation on other comparable aspects of the distribution of powers under the British North America Act makes it clear that parliament is competent, under the "peace, order, and good government clause." No Canadian federal government could fail to be sensitive to the need for full provincial freedom in education. No government should break faith with this vital element in the compact of Confederation. But no government either can draw back from its responsibilities for individual opportunity, economic development, and national unity, where they touch on the ever-widening sphere of education.[11]

In looking at education as a national enterprise affecting the country as a whole and because "there has been almost no authoritative definition by the courts about what education (as expressed in the Act) means," the federal government has itself attempted to delineate the extent of its meaning.[12]

One such attempt was provided at a federal-provincial conference in 1966. There, Prime Minister Pearson provided an indication of the federal government's viewpoint concerning jurisdiction in educational matters when he stated in his address to the provincial premiers that "Education is, under our constitution, a matter of provincial jurisdiction. The federal government does not dispute this or wish in any way to do so. At the same time education is obviously a matter of profound importance to the economics and social growth of the country as a whole."[13] This was a warning that the federal government was prepared to become more involved in what may be regarded as a broader view of education.

More recent signs indicate that the federal government's resolve in this area has not diminished. Federal politicians speak of the need for national criteria, minimum standards, and centralized authority in the educational field, and suggest that this can best be accomplished at the federal level.[14]

Needless to say, not every province welcomed the federal government's projected move into the field. In fact, the province of Quebec was so concerned with growing federal involvement even before the prime minister's speech that it had established a Royal Commission to look into the situation. Despite such opposition, however, the federal government has stuck steadfastly to its claim that, section 93 notwithstanding, it does have a role to play in the field of education.

The federal government, in fact, has argued over an extended period of time that it has not only a right but actually a duty to become active in the area of technical and trades training. It claims that, because such training relates more directly to the labour market than to general education, it could affect the level of employment, which in turn would affect the economy of the entire nation. Although the federal government had been contributing financial support on a co-operative basis to the provinces as early as 1913 with an agricultural training program, its influence became more marked with the passing in 1919 of the Technical Education Act and in 1961 of the Technical and Vocational Education Act. The latter provided the legislative foundation for the spread of comprehensive schools throughout Canada.

The argument for federal participation in education was clearly enunciated by Mr. Pearson in 1966 when he stated:

> The federal government believes that the training and retraining of adults for participation in the labour force are well within the scope of federal jurisdiction. They are manifestations of the federal government's responsibility for national economic development.... They are measures designed to ensure the maximum possibility of effective participation in production. They are measures to reduce unemployment; to increase the productivity and earnings of Canadian workers; and to maintain and improve the competitive position of Canada in relation to other countries.[15]

Subsequently, in the same year, Ottawa's participation in education again increased with the passing of the Adult Occupational Training Act resulting in, *inter alia*, a Training in Industry Program in 1967 and a Training on the Job Program in 1971. Again in co-operation with the provinces, the federal government has instituted standard examinations for those in certain trades so that they can work in any province.

Perhaps the Canadian experience may be encapsulated in the federal Vocational Rehabilitation for Disabled Persons Act. Under the act, the provinces, excluding Quebec, which has its own scheme, provide training for disabled persons through community colleges or trade schools or purchase appropriate programs from the private sector with the federal government funding fifty percent of the costs.

Ottawa is also involved in the educational programs of specific categories of Canadians. The rationale for such involvement has been based upon the argument that such education is of a special rather than a general nature, and hence does not fall under the mandate of section 93 of the Constitution Act. The actual participation on the part of the federal government takes the form of either the provision of the service itself or payments directly to institutions providing the educational service within the localities. The special groups receiving such federal attention and falling into this category include Native peoples, federal employees, veterans of military service, inmates of penitentiaries and members of the armed forces.[16]

The Department of Indian and Northern Affairs, co-operating with the departments of education of the Yukon and Northwest Territories, have direct control over the education of registered Indian and Innuit children. The government owns and operates some 170 schools on Indian reserves, and has the same general responsibilities as a provincial department of education in matters of curriculum and supervision of teachers. About 180 Native bands look after their own schools.

The Department of National Defence has established, and administers, a number of schools for children of armed forces personnel in military establishments overseas and in Canada, although the preference at home is for the children to attend existing schools. The department is also heavily involved in various forms of adult education. The Canadian Forces Training System, as its name implies, provides for officer classification and the training of recruits, tradespeople, and specialists. The department directly finances and controls three military colleges for the training of cadets and commissioned officers, and provides other forms of academic educational programs and technological and trades training for military personnel and their dependents.

Through the Public Services Commission, federal public servants may take refresher and upgrading courses and second-language training, thus opening for themselves career advancement opportunities. The Department of Veterans' Affairs pays allowances and tuition fees for the postsecondary education of children of those whose deaths resulted from military duties. The Department of the Solicitor General has educational programs, academic and vocational, for those in federal penitentiaries. In some cases, credit for the successful completion of such courses or programs is recognized by the province in which the penitentiary is located and, in rare cases, university degrees have been bestowed.

Because the courts had decided, as early as 1932, that communications, in particular the transmission and reception of broadcasting, were under federal jurisdiction, the federal government has argued that educational broadcasting, both radio and television, fall under its jurisdiction. Ottawa's power to actually allocate broadcasting licences has enabled it to become fairly well entrenched in the area, and partially explains the lack of strong provincial opposition. Moreover, in order to minimize any opposition, Ottawa worked out agreements with the provinces, whereby a great deal of educational programming authority was shared. However, the federal Department of the Secretary of State, the Canadian Radio-Television Commission, and the Canadian Broadcasting Corporation all retained considerable control in this particular aspect of the educational process.

The federal government has not only sponsored international conferences on education jointly with the provinces in Canada, but has also sent representatives purporting to speak for the Canadian educational community to similar gatherings in other nations of the world. Generally speaking, the provinces have not always looked upon this federal position positively. However, this has not placed a dampener upon Ottawa's action in this particular field.

Ottawa has also claimed certain rights in the postsecondary educational field. D.V. Smiley argues that "in the past two decades, successive federal governments have accepted the general viewpoint of the Royal Commission on the Arts, Letters, and Sciences, that universities, as distinct from elementary and high schools, were national institutions, and thus in some sense, partially Ottawa's responsibility."[17] While this argument is probably valid, it should also be pointed out that the fiscal reason for the federal government's move into this area is no less valid. When, in 1956-66, the fifteen chartered universities of one province required over 150 million dollars for operating purposes, the feeling arose that only the federal government could handle the costs in this field, and thus federal intervention was not only permitted but actually welcomed. Perhaps the best summary of federal involvement in this area was provided by the Association of Universities and Colleges of Canada in one of their briefs prepared for the Secretary of State. It read as follows:

> Our universities have grown rapidly during the past 25 years, and this growth has, in no small measure, been due to the encouragement and financial support of the Government of Canada.... Direct federal per capita grants made possible the expansion of the universities between 1951 and 1967 and hastened their recovery from the doldrums of the war and post-war period. Since then, financing has continued through the federal-provincial fiscal transfers in support of post-secondary education. The large and rapidly increasing demand for student places was supported and made possible for many who otherwise might not have benefitted from higher education, by the Canada Student Loans Plan and scholarship programs.... The concomitant capital construction in universities gained momentum through funds from the Canada Council, the Department of National Health and Welfare, and other departments and agencies, while various forms of federal assistance provided for the acquisition of important and costly equipment.... Universities must be free to deal directly with all those whom they serve. This is necessary if they are to maintain the flexibility and diversity expected of them.... Consequently, the universities wish to deal directly with the federal government...in dealing with matters which concern them.[18]

From 1963, the Department of the Secretary of State has been responsible for advising the government on postsecondary matters and, from 1967, for administering those parts of the Federal-Provincial Fiscal Arrangements Act that pertain to these matters. This act expired in March 1977, and was replaced by the Established Programs Financing (LPF) arrangements covering tertiary education, hospital insurance, and medicare. Since the mid-1970s, Secretary of State responsibility has expanded to include the development, implementation, and evaluation of all federal policies and programs. Clearly, such activities entail much "to-ing and fro-ing" with the provinces, the university community, and other interested and concerned parties. Additionally, the department has the responsibility of guaranteeing loans made by authorized lending institutions to students holding certificates of elegibility issued by all the provinces except Quebec, which has its own student financial support program.

At the provincial-federal conference of October 1966, Prime Minister Pearson staked out yet another federal claim in the educational field, as he differentiated between pure research and the teaching learning process. The former, it was claimed, was not implied in the clause giving sole jurisdiction over education to the provinces. Mr. Pearson summarized his views on this as follows:

> In our view, research, as the means by which we extend the frontier of knowledge, is today one of the most important factors in the economic and social growth of any modern political society. The restriction of federal aid to research to subject matters that are within federal legislative jurisdiction would frustrate the purposes of the scientific spirit.[19]

An indication of how far Ottawa moved into this area was provided in the speech from the throne opening the second session of the twenty-ninth Parliament of Canada in 1974. It indicated that the federal government felt a definite need to do the following: reorganize the councils that handle federal grants to universities because of the councils' tremendous expansion; strengthen the newly created federal Ministry of Sciences, which was to formulate a national science policy; and reorganize the powerful Science Council. A brief description of the resulting organization may be the best vehicle to indicate the number of federal agencies that became involved in this aspect of education.

> Federal grants to universities are going to be handled by special councils which do nothing else, under an umbrella co-ordinating committee. The granting functions of the National Research Council will be separated from the laboratories and called the Natural Sciences and Engineering Research Council. Grants for social sciences and humanities research will no longer be given out by the Canada Council, but by another new council-to-be called the Social Sciences and Humanities Research Council. The health sciences will continue to be handled by the Medical Research Council

which remains unchanged. In addition, the university granting functions of the Defence Research Board will be taken over by the new granting councils. To "ensure effective collaboration" among the three councils, an inter-council co-ordinating committee chaired by the deputy minister and reporting to the minister of science will be created. The committee is to advise on the allocation of funds among the councils, to co-ordinate and advise on council programs, as well as those of individual federal government departments in support of university research.[20]

The 1986 budget speech, which allocated 70 million dollars to the Social Sciences and Humanities Research Council, makes it quite obvious that, since 1946, when Ottawa first established the National Research Council, successive federal governments have not only maintained their right to support research, but actually expanded it a great deal.[21]

The federal government has also entered the educational field by proposing a subtle distinction between education and culture. Addressing the premiers of every province, then Prime Minister Pearson outlined national responsibility in this area as follows:

> The culture of Canadians, as of the citizens of any country, depends on many factors apart from the educational system. The federal government has long been active in the field of culture through the National Gallery, the Canada Council, the Canadian Broadcasting Corporation, the National Film Board, and other agencies.... Education is one of a number of formative processes through which culture emerges. But culture, as such, should be of interest to every level of government and the monopoly of none.[22]

By making such a statement, the prime minister was obviously opening the door to federal activity in a number of areas that at the very least would be considered quasi-educational. One such door that Ottawa opened was that of support for "official" language minorities. Based primarily upon the argument that the federal government had an obligation to preserve both of the official Canadian languages as a matter of cultural protection, from 1969 onward, it has inaugurated a program of federal grants-in-aid to encourage local boards to offer special classes in the official language spoken by the minority of local inhabitants. Because federal government action based upon this cultural distinction has never gone to the extreme limits that the 1951 federal Royal Commission on the Arts, Letters, and Sciences urged it to, the few educational areas that Ottawa has entered on this basis have seldom been contested by the provinces.

SUMMARY

Figure 2 attempts to show the intergovernmental responsibilities, involvements, relationships, and common interests in education.

FIGURE 2.
FEDERAL, PROVINCIAL, AND LOCAL RESPONSIBILITIES AND INVOLVEMENT IN EDUCATION

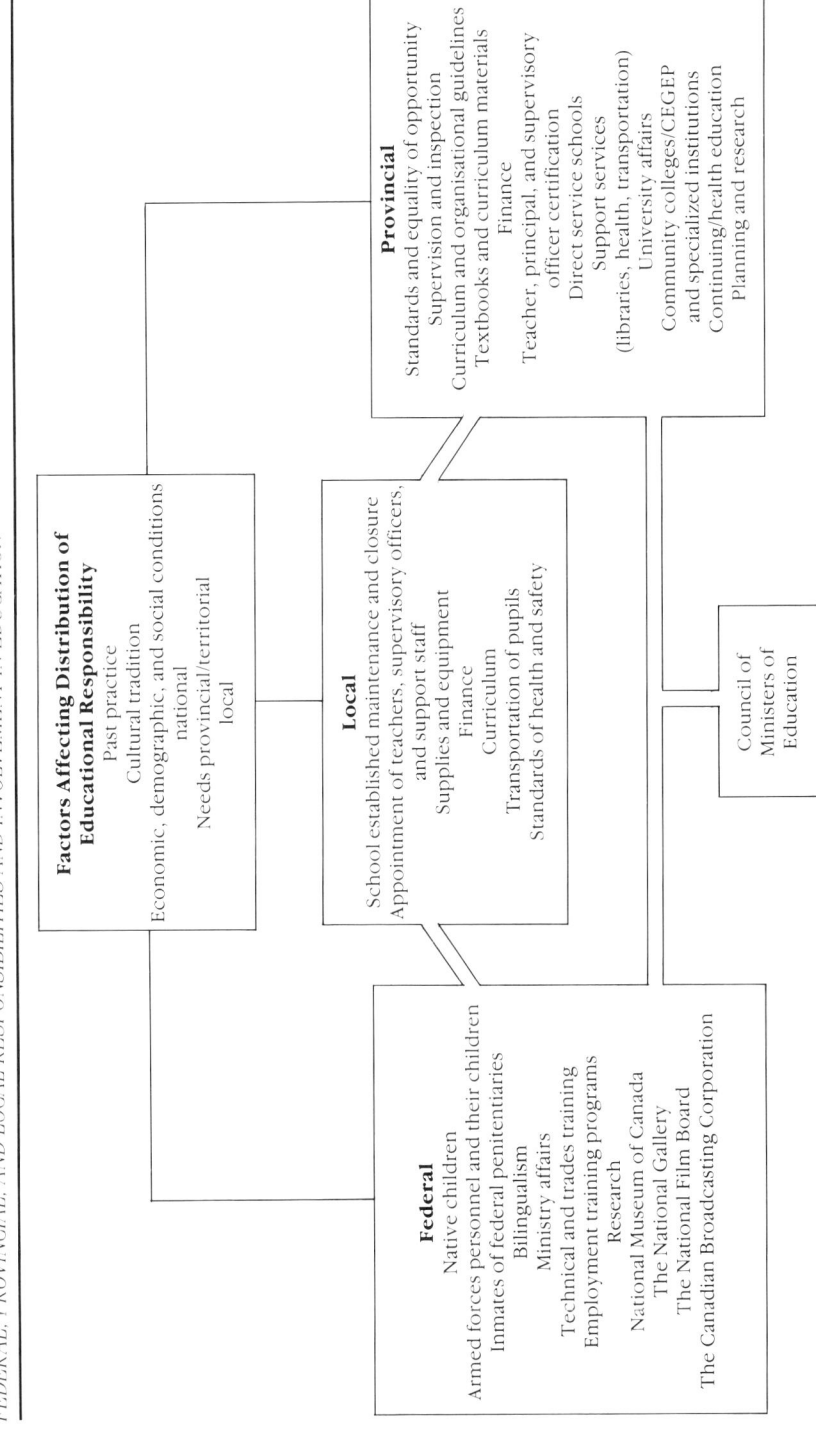

Factors Affecting Distribution of Educational Responsibility
Past practice
Cultural tradition
Economic, demographic, and social conditions
national
Needs provincial/territorial
local

Provincial
Standards and equality of opportunity
Supervision and inspection
Curriculum and organisational guidelines
Textbooks and curriculum materials
Finance
Teacher, principal, and supervisory officer certification
Direct service schools
Support services (libraries, health, transportation)
University affairs
Community colleges/CEGEP and specialized institutions
Continuing/health education
Planning and research

Local
School established maintenance and closure
Appointment of teachers, supervisory officers, and support staff
Supplies and equipment
Finance
Curriculum
Transportation of pupils
Standards of health and safety

Federal
Native children
Armed forces personnel and their children
Inmates of federal penitentiaries
Bilingualism
Ministry affairs
Technical and trades training
Employment training programs
Research
National Museum of Canada
The National Gallery
The National Film Board
The Canadian Broadcasting Corporation

Council of Ministers of Education

GOVERNMENT CONTROL OF EDUCATION   555

One may infer from the statements in sections 91, 92, and 93 of the Constitution Act, 1867, that the fathers of Confederation did not foresee the increasing centrality of the educational enterprise resulting from the changing economic and social conditions of the future. If they had, one could speculate that they might have assigned education to the federal government's domain, provided that it took into account past practice, cultural traditions, and the needs of the individual provinces. However, with Confederation, the prime responsibility for education was allocated to the provinces, with the local boards of education as their creatures. Over the years, it has become clear that the federal government's intrusion into the provinces' seemingly exclusive mandate has become more acceptable, albeit grudgingly in some cases, if for no other reason than that the senior government had greater financial ability to mount and support programs of national as well as of provincial interest.

Constitutional mandates tend to be fixed, or, at the very least, difficult to alter. In order to implement them, however, co-operation and shared involvement among the constituents who exist within the "corridors of power" is necessary. One group from which such co-operation may evolve is the Council of Ministers of Education in Canada. Although it has no statutory power, it does provide a forum for discussion and debate. Formally established in 1967 as a more permanent operation than the standing committee of ministers of education that was founded in 1960, the ministers, along with their senior officers, consult and act together on a wide range of educational issues that are of common concern including those matters that involve the federal government. However, while this group may debate and formulate issues that they perceive to be of common concern, since education is constitutionally a provincial responsibility, their recommendations and discussions are obviously not binding. Only through co-operation will any of their suggestions be implemented.

The purpose of this paper has been to outline the complexities of education in Canada in terms of constitutional realities and political processes. Although the sections dealing with education in the Constitution Act, 1867, may seem to be restrictive, nevertheless political acumen, while respecting the act's terms, has made education a viable intergovernmental enterprise.

NOTES

1. R.H. Leach, *American Federalism* (New York: W.W. Norton, 1970), 83.
2. A. Corry and J.E. Hodgetts, *Democratic Government and Politics* (Toronto: University of Toronto Press, 1965), 556.
3. I. Cheffin, *The Constitutional Process in Canada* (Toronto: McGraw-Hill, 1969), 39.
4. The Constitution Act, 1867, s. 93(1).
5. Government of Ontario, Education Act, 1983, s. 209(1).
6. J.F. Cramer and G.S. Browne, *Contemporary Education: A Comparative Study of National System* (New York: Harcourt, Brace, 1956), 55.
7. Ontario Committee on Taxation, *Report of the Ontario Committee on Taxation*, Vol. 11 (Toronto: University of Toronto Press, 1968), 13.
8. R.S. Harris, *Quiet Evolution* (Toronto: University of Toronto Press, 1968), 13.
9. Ibid. For an insightful look at sources and instruments of power, see J.K. Galbraith, *The History of Power* (Boston: Houghton Mifflin, 1983), passim.
10. Ontario Education Act, 1983, s. 256(2).
11. Robert Stanbury, "The Federal Role in Education," *Queen's Quarterly* LXXIV (1967), 368.
12. D.V. Smiley, *Canada in Question: Federalism in the Seventies* (Toronto: McGraw-Hill Ryerson, 1972), 31.
13. Stanbury, "The Federal Role in Education," 365.
14. Greta Chambers, "Liberals Covet Role in Education," *Windsor Star* (26 May 1984).
15. Stanbury, "The Federal Role in Education."
16. A.N. Brady, in *Canadian Federalism: Myth or Reality*, edited by J.P. Meekison, 3rd ed. (Toronto: Methuen, 1977).
17. Smiley, *Canada in Question*, 33.
18. Association of Universities and Colleges of Canada, "National Involvement Requires Federal Presence," *University Affairs*, (April 1975), 2.
19. Stanbury, "The Federal Role in Education," 366.
20. A. Gill, "The Federal Scence," *Urban Affairs* (April 1974), 5.
21. Christian Pouyez, *Social Science Federation of Canada Newsletter* (Ottawa, 4 March 1986).
22. Stanbury, "The Federal Role in Education."

THE FINANCING OF CANADIAN EDUCATION

LAWRENCE M. BEZEAU

Identifying issues in education finance is not difficult. Choosing a few issues from the many does present some problems, but with common-sense criteria for selection, the field can be narrowed considerably. The issues should be national in scope and current but should have relevance for the future. In addition, they should not be purely technical but should have important value and policy components. These criteria have been used to select two major issues for discussion in this article.

The first issue is that of public financial support for private schools. This has been an on-gain off-again issue since the voucher and performance contracting experiments of the late 1960s and early 1970s in the United States. In the face of formidable constitutional barriers, the American states have largely abandoned efforts to finance private schools. The Canadian provinces, on the other hand, have moved strongly in this direction with more than half the provinces now providing substantial financial support for private schools. This support has been hotly contested in every province that has implemented it and even more so in provinces now contemplating implementation.

The second issue is that of dependency in the Canadian population, that is, the extent to which certain age groups do not produce goods and services but must depend on the productive age group to produce for them. Changes in the numbers of persons in the two dependent age groups (children and the aged) have important long-term implications for the willingness of the public to be taxed to support education. Special efforts will be necessary to ensure continued support.

PUBLIC FUNDING OF PRIVATE SCHOOLS

Private schools have existed in Canada since before Confederation but it is only in recent decades that the question of funding them with public money has arisen. Quebec, the first province to face the issue, opted for significant public subsidies and, since then, five other provinces have done the same. Funding private schools is an issue in these six provinces and in Ontario, which does not now fund private schools but which has it under consideration. In the other provinces there is pressure on governments from private school supporters for financial support from the public purse.

CANADIAN PROVISIONS

Private schools now exist in all Canadian provinces. Two provinces make no provision at all for funding them; two provide small amounts of money; and six provinces have statutory provisions for partial public funding.

New Brunswick and Ontario are alone in providing almost no funding for private schools. Nevertheless, many private schools benefit from property tax remission and from other relatively minor benefits in kind from the provinces. Nova Scotia and Prince Edward Island are close behind in providing minimal subsidies. They assist in the purchase of textbooks for students in private schools.

The Province of Newfoundland and Labrador is in a class by itself in that it has a statutory provision to fund private schools at the same level as the public schools where there is no public school in the area, but has never had occasion to use this legislation because of the pervasiveness of the public system.

Private schools in Manitoba that are deemed to be offering education equivalent in quality to that offered by the public school system receive a significant instructional grant as well as a credit for the purchase of instructional materials from the province.

British Columbia has provided funding to private schools since 1977. It funds two classes of schools, one that meets ministry regulations resembling those the public schools must meet and the other that meets less rigorous criteria. The former type is funded at a much higher level.

Saskatchewan provides substantial grants in respect of grades 9 to 12 to private schools that offer these grades and that meet ministry requirements regarding supervision, teacher qualifications, and courses of study. Ten percent grants are also available for investment in school buildings. Saskatchewan is the only province to offer capital grants to private schools.

Alberta has elaborate legislation establishing four categories of schools with different rights to funding. The most heavily-funded schools are those that resemble the public schools in matters of curriculum and teacher certification. A second heavily funded category includes schools that serve handicapped children in accordance with strict ministry standards. A third category of school offers instruction in a language other than English and is intended to supplement rather than replace public school instruction. These schools may receive some money from the Ministry of Cultural Affairs but receive none from the Ministry of Education. A fourth category of private school offers prescribed courses with teachers who may not meet provincial certification standards. These schools receive no public money.

Quebec has had more experience funding private schools than any other province. Its Private Education Act, which was passed in 1968, contained the first systematic arrangement in Canada for the public financial support of private schools. It provided very high levels of financial support as well as some control over tuition levels but not over student admission or expulsion. There is a three-category classification system of schools for grant purposes. The three categories are "declared to be of public interest," "recognized for the purposes of grants," and simply holding a permit to operate. The highest grants are paid to schools in the first category. Schools that only hold a permit to operate do not receive grants.

All provinces have compulsory attendance legislation that can be used to control private schools offering instruction to children within the age range of required attendance, normally seven to fifteen years inclusive. New Brunswick and Prince Edward Island exemplify this arrangement. Children can be excused from the public schools if they are deemed by the minister, in practice an official appointed directly or indirectly by the minister, to be "under efficient instruction elsewhere." Approved private schools are accepted as providing efficient instruction. If the provincial Ministry of Education is not satisfied with the instruction offered by a private school, its recourse is to compel the school-age children to return to the public schools.

ARGUMENTS IN SUPPORT

Perhaps the most frequent argument in support of private schools is the claimed right of parents to exercise choice in something as important to the family as educating children. Article 26(3) of the Universal Declaration of Human Rights, which was proclaimed by the General Assembly of the United Nations and signed by Canada, is frequently quoted in support of this argument. It simply requires that "Parents have a prior right to choose the kind of education that shall be given to their children."

When parents exercise their right to send their children to private schools they are usually required to pay tuition while they continue to pay taxes to support the public system. This gives rise to the double payment argument. When parents remove their children from the public system, they ease the burden on that system. They should not have to financially support a system they are not utilizing and especially not while they are paying tuition to private schools for their children's education.

A third argument for private schools centres on the disadvantages associated with the monopolistic provision of any good or service. When public schools have a monopoly on education, the lack of competition encourages the provision of the service in a manner more in line with bureaucratic imperatives than public preferences. Monopolies are also associated with inefficiency and feather-bedding.

A closely related argument is that private schools are closer to the market and are therefore better able to detect shifts in public preferences, to respond to these shifts, and therefore to act as a model for the public schools.

Certainly the private schools must satisfy the market or at least a small segment of it. The alternative is to lose clients to the publicly-funded system, a system that they will find much less expensive.

A final argument, which is especially relevant to Canada, is the non-discrimination argument with respect to religion. Five of the ten provinces have statutory arrangements for Roman Catholic denominational schools in some form within the publicly controlled and funded system. Four of these make no provision for any other denomination. Other Christian denominations and non-Christian religions assert that if funds are provided for the Roman Catholic schools, they should be provided for those of other denominations as well.

ARGUMENTS AGAINST

The most frequently cited argument in opposition to private schools is that of equality of educational opportunity. Correctly or incorrectly, private schools are seen as creating a two-tier social system with the better-off families, socially and economically, sending their children to elite private schools where they receive education of a quality and quantity not available to those forced to spend their formative years in public schools. The private school crowd receives a disproportionate share of the opportunities to succeed in life through ascription rather than merit.

The social cohesion argument is closely related to equality of opportunity. Students in the elite private schools may never have to mix with the masses. They will never learn to understand the point of view of the common person. Private and public school education may differ to the point where the two groups develop antagonistic and incompatible values. In the extreme case they may not be able to communicate with each other. The result will be increased class conflict and difficulty in forming a unified nation.

Ardent supporters of the public system have always had serious concerns about the ways in which private schools select their students, something public schools cannot do. There is certainly financial selection based on the ability and willingness of the parents to pay private school tuition, although those who send their children to private schools are frequently not very well-off. There may also be selection, both self-selection and school-imposed selection, based on religion or ideology in cases where the school espouses a certain position in this regard. Private schools may refuse to accept or may expel students who are academically inferior or who have behaviour problems. Public schools have somewhat more difficulty in expelling students and much more difficulty in refusing them admission in the first place.

A final argument centres around the use of voice versus exit in bringing about educational reform. Private schools are a form of exit for persons who are disaffected with the public system. The parents who choose the exit are likely to be those most concerned and informed about educational quality. When they leave the public system, their voices are lost to the cause of reform in the public system. According to this argument, parents must be encouraged or even compelled to support the public system to ensure that it has the benefit of informed public input.

CONCLUSION

Support for and opposition to the public funding of private schools has followed a common pattern in all provinces. Private schools, with the exception of a few elite ones, strongly support public funding as do parents who send their children to these schools, especially if this funding can be obtained without an increase in public control. On the other side of the question are arrayed those with a direct stake in the public system: teachers and their associations, public school boards, and public school administrators.

There are no right or wrong answers. Much depends on how the individual evaluates the arguments on both sides.

DEPENDENCY AND EDUCATION

The term *dependency* has a special and specific meaning. It refers to the fact that certain age groups within our population do not contribute to production and therefore depend on the productive age groups to provide for them. There are two such groups in our society—the young and the aged.

Young people are dependent while they are maturing and receiving an education. In modern industrialized countries such as Canada, education for many people continues after they have reached physical and mental maturity, in many cases, into their twenties. When they then join the labour force, they become more productive because of the education they have received. If they choose homemaking as an alternative to paid labour force participation, they may have superior child-rearing skills. Nevertheless, until young people become productive, they must depend on others to produce goods and services for them.

At the other end of the age span, people cease to be productive when they retire. Traditionally, Canadians have retired at age sixty-five, but, theoretically, retirement at any specified age can no longer be required because of provisions in the Constitution Act, 1982. Retirement at age sixty-five is still very common, but both early and late retirements are becoming more frequent each year. Generally, persons who retire cease to produce for themselves and must depend on the active labour force to provide for them. Although retired persons are not frequent clients of educational institutions, they do require a disproportionate share of health and social services expenditures.

Demographic changes in the population that cause variations in the size of the dependent population have an enormous impact on the demand for and the supply of education. Virtually all the population between the ages of six and sixteen will be found in schools, and a large proportion of the population aged five and sixteen to twenty will also be in school. This segment of the population must be supported materially by persons in the active labour force and must also be taught by members of the labour force. Fluctuations in the birth rate produce populations waves, hills or valleys, that move through school into the productive adult years and then into retirement.

The importance of this can be seen by considering just how many people are involved in education in one capacity or another. On any school day, 20 percent of Canada's population will be in elementary and secondary schools as students being taught by another 1.1 percent of the population. At the same time, 3.3 percent of the population will be involved in post-secondary education as students or teachers. Adding in support personnel for all levels brings the total to over 25 percent of the population, or about 6.4 million people—a truly massive enterprise.

DEPENDENCY RATIOS

Dependency ratios are used to express the extent to which, at any given time, the population consists of dependent persons. These ratios are based on purely demographic information. They do not reflect who is actually in the labour force and who is dependent. As a consequence, rather arbitrary ages have been chosen for the transitions from dependent to productive to dependent. The convention used here is the one employed by Statistics Canada, the source of most Canadian data on both population and education. The productive period starts when a person turns eighteen and ends when he or she turns sixty-five. The 0–17 dependency ratio is the number of persons in this lower age group divided by the number in the 18–64 group with the quotient usually expressed as a percent. The 65+ dependency ratio is calcualted in the same manner with this upper age group substituted for the 0–17 group. The sum of the two gives the overall or total dependency ratio. A dependency ratio expressed as a percent gives the number of persons in the dependent age group or groups per 100 persons in the 18–64 group. The three dependency ratios for Canada for the years 1951 to 2006 are shown in figure 1 with ratios for future years based on the population projections done by Statistics Canada. Some significant conclusions can be drawn from this figure.

CANADIAN TRENDS

The total dependency ratio in Canada appears to be more a function of the 0–17 ratio than the 65+ ratio, expecially in the earlier years. This is because the lower group is larger although the two groups are clearly converging in size and are expected to be equal in the year 2013. Both the 0–17 ratio and the total ratio peaked in 1963 and have been declining since then and will continue to decline. The increase in dependency until 1963 was the result of

FIGURE 1. ACTUAL AND PROJECTED DEPENDENCY RATIOS FOR CANADA, 1950–2010

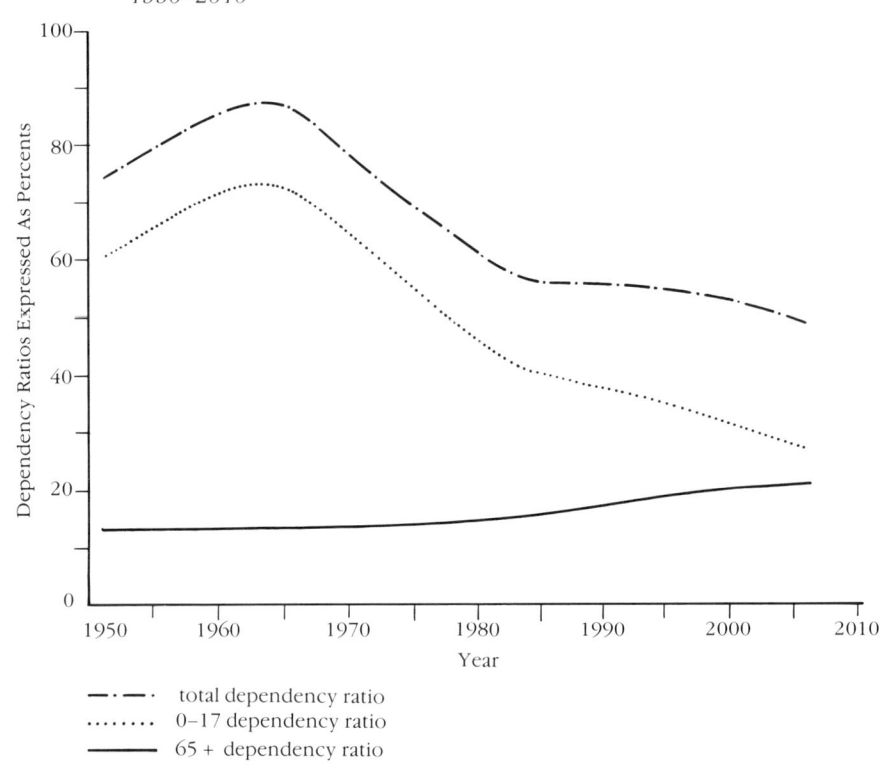

— · — · total dependency ratio
· · · · · · · 0–17 dependency ratio
———— 65 + dependency ratio

what is commonly known as the post-war baby boom although the fertility rate actually turned up from its Depression low in 1937 and continued to rise during and after World War II until it reached a peak in 1959. At the same time, the 65 + ratio shows a slow but steady increase that accelerates slightly toward the end of the century.

During periods of low dependency, society finds it easier to finance services for its dependent population. Each productive person has fewer "dependents" to support. We would expect, for example, that during periods of high 0–17 dependency, the emphasis would be on the quantity of schooling, just getting enough schools built and enough teachers trained to allow education to go forward. In times of low dependency the emphasis might be on quality, that is, on giving the best possible education to those few people who happen to be young enough to be students in elementary or secondary schools. During the two decades following World War II, Canada had difficulty building schools fast enough and training enough teachers quickly enough to educate the increasing number of students who appeared each year. When this bricks-and-mortar period came to an end and teacher shortages became surpluses, quality did improve but there have been complications.

Teacher quality improved as the provinces raised standards to the point where a university degree is now normally required of all newly licensed teachers. During the most difficult years of teacher shortages, high school graduates were recruited in June, given six weeks of teacher training during July and August, and put into a classroom in September. In 1952, seventy-eight percent of elementary and secondary school teachers in Canada did not have a university degree. This figure dropped to seventy-two percent in 1962, forty-nine percent in 1972, and by 1983 had reached twenty-one percent. Because of current certification requirements and the expected retirement of large numbers of teachers in the last decade of this century, teachers without degrees will be extremely rare by the year 2000. This prediction assumes, of course, that certification requirements will not be reduced in the face of anticipated teacher shortages.

COMMITMENT TO EDUCATION

Although the quality of education has increased in many respects, there are mounting concerns about society's commitment to education. The problem is apparent in figure 2. In 1970, when enrolment peaked at 5.9 million elementary and secondary students, Canada was spending nine percent of its gross national product on education. As can be seen from figure 2, this percentage was an historic high; it was also very high when compared to other countries of the world. The percentage of GNP spent on education is a measure of a country's commitment to its youth. Canada has been spending proportionately less on education in recent years even though lower dependency ratios make it relatively easy to spend more. It has been argued that this money is now being spent on the aged, but the 0–17 age group has been declining much more rapidly than the 65 + age group has been increasing.

Another factor to be considered is that young people have little real political power. They cannot vote and they cannot run for elected office. On the other hand, the 65 + age group is not only able to vote, it does so with very high percentage turnouts. Moreover, elected officials are not always young; young people, especially the very young, must depend on older persons to represent them politically.

Political theory predicts that decisions in democratic societies reflect the desires of the median voter. In Canada, the age of the median voter has been increasing, as it has in other industrialized countries. Experience in school board bond elections in the United States has underlined the importance of school officials obtaining the political support of persons who do not have a direct stake in the school system. The largest such group consists of persons whose children have completed their schooling, but it also includes the increasing number of adults who choose not to have children. At one time, the majority of local voters had children in the public school system, but in many jurisdictions this is no longer true.

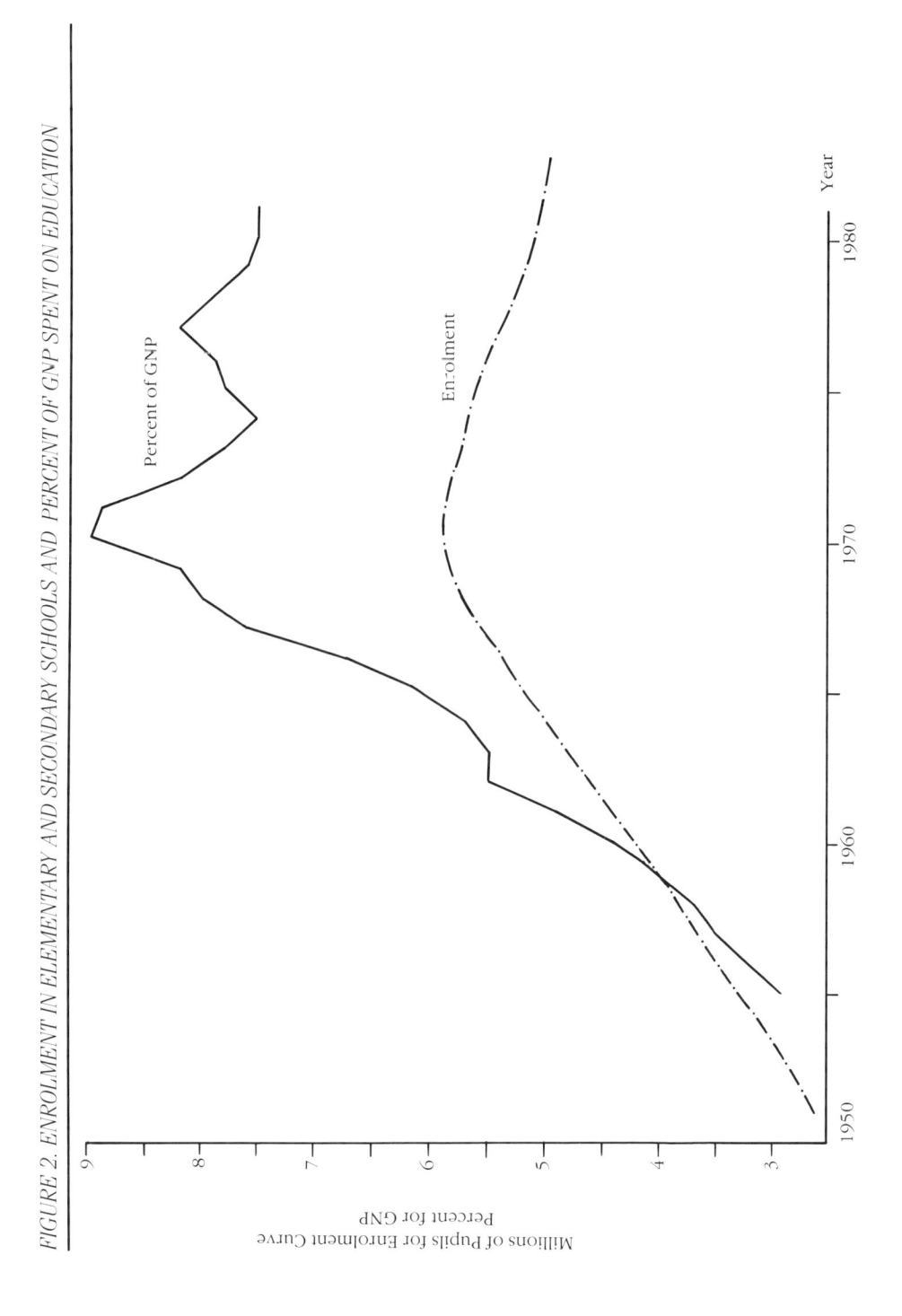

FIGURE 2. ENROLMENT IN ELEMENTARY AND SECONDARY SCHOOLS AND PERCENT OF GNP SPENT ON EDUCATION

566 EDUCATION IN THE FUTURE

CONCLUSION

How can those persons concerned about education ensure that schools benefit from the interest and support of citizens who no longer use them? One possible answer is to ensure that the school is a community resource available to citizens of all ages. This sounds good but it is not immediately obvious what the school can do for persons who cannot take advantage of the kinds of services it normally provides.

Many communities have tried to turn their schools into community centres available seven days a week during normal working hours and into the evening. Some have succeeded. School libraries have been combined with public libraries to serve the community. Day-care centres have been incorporated into school buildings. Community groups of all ages have been invited into the school facility. Some school districts have made a special effort to respond to the reduced geographic mobility of the elderly by recognizing that schools, due to their proximity compared to other public buildings, are often in a special position to provide services. Other districts have made a point of acquainting their pupils with the elderly in the community.

Future financial support for the education of Canadian young people will greatly depend on how successful educators can become in gaining community support. Much of this support will necessarily come from persons who do not have a direct interest in schooling as such. Can the school offer services that are needed and desired by these people? If schools are to do so, they may have to revert, in some ways, to the role they had in rural Canada earlier in the century.

REFERENCES

Bezeau, Lawrence M. "The Public Finance of Private Education in the Province of Quebec," *Canadian Journal of Education* 4, 2 (1979): 23–42.

Dumas, Jean. *Current Demographic Analysis: Report on the Demographic Situation in Canada 1983* (Ottawa: Statistics Canada, cat. 91-209E, 1985).

Education in Canada (Ottawa: Statistics Canada, cat. 81-229, various years to 1984).

Education Statistics for the Seventies (Ottawa: Statistics Canada, cat. 81-569, 1984).

George, M.V., and J. Perreault, *Population Projections for Canada, Provinces, and Territories, 1984–2006* (Ottawa: Statistics Canada, cat. 91-520, 1985).

Historical Compedium of Education Statistics from Confederation to 1975 (Ottawa: Statistics Canada, cat. 81-568, 1978).

Immigration and Population Statistics (Ottawa: Information Canada, 1974).

Intercensal Annual Estimates of Population by Sex and Age for Canada and the Provinces, 1976–1981 (Ottawa: Statistics Canada, cat. 91-518, 1983).

Perras, Lucien. "Summary of Legislation, Regulations, Policies for the Funding of Private Schools in Each of the Provinces of Canada Other than Ontario" (unpublished paper, Commission on Private Schools in Ontario, Toronto, 1985).

Population 1921–1971: Revised Annual Estimates of Population, by Sex and Age Group, Canada and the Provinces (Ottawa: Statistics Canada, cat. 91-512, 1973).

Postcensal Annual Estimates of Population by Marital Status, Age, Sex, and Components of Growth for Canada and the Provinces, June 1, 1982 and 1983, vol. 1, no. 1 (Ottawa: Statistics Canada, cat. 91-210, 1984).

Revised Annual Estimates of Population by Sex and Age for Canada and the Provinces, 1971–1976 (Ottawa: Statistics Canada, cat. 91 518, 1979).

Shapiro, Bernard J. *The Report of the Commission on Private Schools in Ontario* (Toronto: Commission on Private Schools in Ontario, 1985).

Survey of Elementary and Secondary Education (Ottawa: Dominion Bureau of Statistics, cat. 81-401 and 81-210, 1948 to 1963).

COMMUNITY COLLEGES IN CANADA: FUTURE ISSUES, FUTURE SOLUTIONS

JOHN D. DENNISON

INTRODUCTION

Community colleges, a relatively recent educational concept in Canada, have attained a certain degree of maturity after two decades of growth and evolution unprecedented in the history of postsecondary education in this nation. In 1964, there were only two institutions in Canada that resembled a multipurpose public college.[1] By 1985, community colleges of one kind or another had been established in nine of the ten provinces, and a new model of postsecondary education had been created.[2]

While each province adopted a community college design reflecting its particular educational, economic, and sociocultural imperatives, there are certain characteristics common to each system. As described by Campbell,[3] colleges were planned primarily to provide opportunities for advanced education to a segment of society that, for socio-economic, geographic, or academic reasons, had been denied such access in the past. The new colleges promoted a policy of "open" admissions, charged modest or no tuition fees, provided for part-time and evening study, and developed a comprehensive curricular structure that might include various combinations of university-equivalent, technical, paraprofessional, trades, upgrading, and continuing education programs.

The motivation for college development in each province was, in its own context, an example of the way in which an educational idea could be adapted and refined to meet the political and social goals of various provincial governments with quite different priorities. In Ontario, for example, the Colleges of Applied Arts and Technology were formed as a response to an economic plan that depended upon a much expanded role for a skilled workforce.[4] Quebec's colleges, on the other hand, were designed as instruments of educational and cultural reform that would change the status of the Francophone majority in a new political reality.[5] In Saskatchewan, colleges were created as a means of raising the quality of life in communities that needed to be retained as part of the essential fabric of prairie society.[6] In New Brunswick and Manitoba, occupational training and vocational upgrading were critical needs that only new and different institutions could fill. And in

Alberta and British Columbia, colleges were designed as alternatives to universities and as resources that would meet the wide and varied educational needs of their immediate communites.[7] As described later in this essay, in the "golden" years between 1965 and 1975, a period in which public support for tertiary education was strong and governments responded with generous funding, colleges flourished with fast-growing enrolments, new and exciting programs, and an optimism that appeared justified on all counts.[8]

The next decade, however, brought a complex range of frustrations into the new institutions. Economic difficulties, compounded by declining public confidence in education, caused governments to review their support for college systems. In turn, the institutions were forced to address increased demands for accountability, undertake program planning in which distinct priorities were essential, and experience increasing intervention by government into every aspect of their operation.[9]

As Canada's colleges enter their third decade it has become increasingly evident that, while they can be judged a success on a number of yardsticks, there are some dominant issues that must be resolved if the colleges are to meet the expectations that both they, and their critics and supporters at all levels, have set for them.

The four major issues discussed in the remainder of this essay have been selected with care. Each emerged during an exercise conducted by the author in which colleges and government agencies in all ten provinces were studied, and during which the activities of many institutions were analysed in an attempt to assess the effectiveness of their operations, the problems that confronted them, and the policy directions they might explore in the future.

The study suggested that, while there were many problems peculiar to the province or region in which the various colleges were located, there were also certain common issues that were characteristic of every provincial system and hence could be viewed as vital factors in the colleges' future success. The four most significant issues—relations with government, general education and the curriculum, quality and standards of performance, and labour relations—will each be discussed in turn.

RELATIONS WITH GOVERNMENT

While variety and diversity remain the outstanding characteristics of provincial college systems in Canada, relations with governments in every region and at every level have grown increasingly strained during the last five years. While much of the cause for the new degrees of tension may be attributed to economic realities, it also appears that governments perceive that several advantages may be gained by exercising greater control over curriculum, program development, and planning in individual colleges.

In their early years, most colleges in Canada enjoyed relative autonomy. The creation of governing boards for educational institutions that had previously operated under direct provincial control gave a new impetus to the planning process. Board members, administrators, and faculty encouraged the development of new programs, became entrepreneurial and competitive with respect to other institutions, and began to respond to many new educational needs within their communities.

In turn, community reaction was rapid and enthusiastic. Attracted by low tuition fees and liberal admission policies, students enrolled in numbers larger than anticipated.[10] In particular, mature learners, many of whom were women and primarily part-time students, took advantage of the wide range of educational offerings, both credit and non-credit, academic and occupational, in day and evening hours. In consequence, college budgets, buoyed by inflation, expanded at a rate that alarmed even the most generous of provincial governments.

It would be incorrect to imply that colleges in Canada have ever been as autonomous as the universities, despite delegation of power and responsibility by government to local boards. In most provinces, colleges have always been regarded as a part of a broader provincial plan in either economic, educational, or sociocultural terms. Even where direct government authority over planning had been delegated to a quasi-independent agency, its political interests have been protected.[11] In Quebec and Ontario, for example, La Direction générale d'enseignement collégial and the Council of Regents, respectively, have exercised a monitoring role. But, at the same time, most of the colleges were established in the euphoria of the late 1960s and early 1970s when decentralization of authority was politically fashionable, and when education enjoyed high public priority and government funding was relatively generous.

Popularity of college services, however, had a price, not all of which was financial. Unnecessary duplication of programs, conflicts among institutions over mandates, confusion regarding credit transfer, and unwelcome political pressure from local authorities convinced provincial governments that greater control of college activities was necessary. Further, generous salary settlements negotiated by college staffs, either at the provincial or local level, had followed the evolution of strong union organizations.[12] Inevitably, the trend towards greater centralization at the provincial level gathered strength.

This "new direction," which began as early as the late 1970s, has manifested itself in a number of ways. Program approval often rests within ministerial committees; the budgeting process has moved from "block" to "line-item" formats, while funding formulae have become more complex; multi-campus organization of college services are less encouraged, a practice sometimes justified by the proposed introduction of distance-education-based delivery systems;[13] greater priority has been placed upon programs of "economic" value, to the detriment of "personal development" activities,[14] and direct legislative intervention by government into collective bargaining has become increasingly common.[15] While all of the foregoing do not necessarily apply in every province, few college systems have escaped the thrust towards increased central control.

Provincial government intervention into the planning of college activities has usually been resisted and resented by faculty and other groups, who cherish their limited autonomy in the exercise of power and often draw invidious comparisons with universities, which they perceive as being relatively independent of direct government authority. The legitimacy of increased control over the college system, however, is a matter of debate that rests upon several arguments.

Community colleges have been, are, and will assuredly continue to be educational institutions whose role is to respect government policy whether the latter be economic (which has assumed a larger profile in most provinces) or of a less obvious political priority. Colleges will undoubtedly experience more explicit direction in their future planning. Financial deficits and the election of more conservative governments are factors that will combine to ensure this end. But there is another important side to the coin.

Colleges, unlike universities, are essentially regional or community institutions. They should continue to emphasize access, particularly for the less advantaged. Their programs should necessarily reflect a local orientation. Their governing boards, usually composed of community representatives, have a legitimate claim to some authority if their existence is to be worthwhile. College instructors do retain many characteristics of professionals, specifically in an educational context, and share an understandable concern for security of employment and for academic freedom.

Provincial governments can and must find ways to reconcile their own priorities with the significance of the history, development, and unique nature of community colleges. Control, exercised selectively and with sensitivity, must become the ideal if the colleges are to retain their commitment to innovation and responsiveness that has characterized their past.

Most of the foregoing applies to relations with provincial governments. However, the situation with respect to federal involvement in college programs has also created problems. The federal government funds education and training activities in colleges through a number of arrangements: Established Program Funding (EPF), which indirectly supports academic and technical studies; special programs such as Canadian Studies and second language education; and more direct assistance for vocational and trades training through appropriate legislation administered by the Department of Employment and Immigration. While particular problems of accountability continue to plague EPF,[16] more direct difficulties for colleges stem from the administration of vocational program funding.

While deflecting constitutional arguments by defining "training" as an activity that is legitimately under the aegis of the federal government, program priorities at the national level have been financed by a "training seat" purchase agreement with provincial authorities. A long series of legislative acts, beginning in 1913 with the Agricultural Training Act and continuing to 1983 with the introduction of the National Training Act, have ensured a constant flow of federal dollars to the colleges and institutes.[17]

In recent years, however, federal priorities have fluctuated with considerable speed, and the institutions have been frustrated in their planning exercise. Programs, such as adult basic skill development and lower level trades training, have been replaced by "high technology" as a federal priority. The impact of these changes upon the continuing utilization of certain personnel and capital resources in the college sector has been disastrous.

The most imminent need is for the development of long-term, financially workable, agreements between federal and provincial governments with respect to the funding of trades and vocational programs, if the institutions are to enjoy the stability to allow for effective planning. At the present time, the colleges are the unhappy victims of longstanding political disagreements between two levels of government.

GENERAL EDUCATION AND THE COLLEGE CURRICULUM

With respect to the curriculum in Canada's community colleges, the one issue that seldom fails to stimulate debate in all provinces is the matter of general education. There appears to be little agreement as to how general education should be defined, what might be its content, and what is its relationship to more specialized aspects of the curriculum. Ironically, the only apparent area of agreement is with respect to its value.

It is not difficult to argue the case for a curriculum that focusses upon an exploration of ethical values within an increasingly technically oriented society, or that emphasizes effective communication and logical reasoning in an age of dehumanizing technology. For, as Masuda notes in reference to the "New Industrial Age,"

> The current innovation in societal technology...is not concerned with the productivity of material goods, but with information productivity, and for this reason can be expected to bring about fundamental changes in human values, in trends of thought, and in the political and economic structures of society.[18]

No longer can postsecondary educational institutions assume the responsibility for merely preparing students with the practical skills of the workplace. The challenge for educators in the third millenium will be to fashion a curriculum that provides the bases for a lifetime of learning, for adjusting to technological change, which emphasizes quality of living rather than mere survival, and for multi-dimensional literacy. The heart of the curriculum of the future will be those experiences that will sustain the individual in a world of unprecedented change and complexity.

It is relatively easy to agree upon the values of general education. Its implementation is another, much more difficult task. What are the obstacles to general education in Canada's colleges?

In the rhetoric of the 1960s and early 1970s, when provincial college systems were unfolding, there was much reference to the need for a new, broader approach to curriculum in the "new" colleges. Quotes from the literature of college development in selected provinces include the following. In Ontario: "An adequate general education is the best basis on which to build and to rebuild the particular workskills which the future will require."[19] In Prince Edward Island: "All programs of studies should include the study of general education subjects and specific vocational subjects."[20] In Saskatchewan: "The colleges aim to provide opportunities to meet learning needs to perform all of life's roles in a satisfying way."[21] Finally, in British Columbia:

> Every field of education has its discursive and contemplative aspects as expressed in its historical, social, and aesthetic components. Within a college program they may be merged in ways that will enable students to comprehend their fields of study not merely as academic or technical but as powerful social and intellectual forces that are deeply and widely influential in human affairs.[22]

The Council of Regents in Ontario went so far as to require that one third of the curriculum of all programs in the Colleges of Applied Arts and Technology be composed of general studies. Despite such advice, a study in 1980 revealed a very different pattern: fourteen of nineteen responding colleges were deficient in the required proportion.[23]

Nor does the status of general education enjoy better health in most colleges across the nation. With one exception, Quebec, there is a haphazard, inconsistent approach to the inclusion of non-skill-specific courses in college technical programs in virtually all provinces.

The reasons for the lack of commitment to the rhetoric of the broad curriculum in most colleges are complex, but usually based on functional or financial considerations. The tradition of vocational preparation has long embodied the view that a highly skilled workforce results from a heavy emphasis upon specialized training. Many faculty and a majority of "task-oriented" students are neither convinced nor appreciative of education that lacks immediate relevancy. While others recognize the broader roles needed by those in the workplace, they argue that a generalized education is a personal responsibility that can and should be sought as an adjunct to employment.

Funding agencies, particularly governments, tend to measure their investment in terms of cost efficiency, job placement statistics, and by the relevance of the training function. Rarely is provision made to support non-specialized courses in budgetary planning.

Only in Quebec has general education been introduced on a systematic basis. The CEGEP were designed to incorporate a form of "cultural pluralism," an environment in which both traditional streams, pre-university and technical, would share a common core curriculum, which would comprise up to fifty percent of each program of study.[24]

A study, *Colleges in Quebec*,[25] reaffirmed the commitment to a "formation fondamentale" that included language and literature, philosophy and physical education, with a proposal to include additional courses in the Quebec economy and Quebec civilization. While the experience of the CEGEP remains the exception, in many other provinces the issue is far from being buried.

A PROPOSAL FOR THE FUTURE

In the prsent climate of concern over the need for a greater emphasis upon general education, several colleges have developed innovative strategies. Grant MacEwan Community College (1983) in Edmonton, for example, has recommended the introduction of a "functional course model" to include Genetic Learning Skills, Life as Learning, The Global Community, and Culture in the Value System. Other colleges require courses to be taken from elective "packages" as a means of adding breadth to highly specialized curricula.

Despite many valiant efforts, it appears that a course-focussed approach has enjoyed limited success. General education in many colleges is recognized in the form of one or two required classes in "technical writing," or "communication skills," a model that falls somewhat short of the ideal.

A more radical approach might be to shift responsibility for general education from a "content" to an "instructor" focus, in which all college teachers, irrespective of their subject area, would accept the responsibility for inculcating the goals of general education.

The concept on which this proposal is based is that every content area contains knowledge and ideas extending well beyond the relatively narrow scope of the stated curriculum and that, if studied further, will contribute to a broader education of the learners. Furthermore, an instructor who is fully committed to the concept will utilize this extended knowledge to develop critical judgment, creativity, affective and cognitive capabilities in her or his students well beyond mere acquisition of skills.

For example, communication skills, oral and written, are required in all subject areas. Technical reports, laboratory observations, artistic projects, and simulated job interviews are all examples of themes that fit this category. Broadly based moral and ethical issues, whether in the health sciences, industrial technology, business practices, or environmental studies, are effective and legitimate extensions of the acquisition of skill competencies in these areas. The challenges to economic and spiritual survival in an era of reduced or uncertain employment comprise relevant subject matter in any courses that prepare individuals for the workplace.

It must be recognized that this technique brings a new and different dimension to the roles of instructors in Canada's colleges. College teachers, particularly those in vocational-technical areas of the curriculum, often lack the background and rarely share the conviction that would enable them to participate effectively. Given that any effort by administration to impose the model would be unlikely to succeed, the probability of implementation must depend upon a logical and analytical examination of the proposal with the instructional staff. The latter task is an aspect of professional development, which has long suffered from a confusion or diffusion of objectives.

The issue of general education continues to challenge the imagination of dedicated college planners who, while recognizing the need, also face real and complex obstacles to its implementation. If colleges are to honour their commitment to provide an education that prepares students for survival in a complex and changing society, a realistic approach to curriculum reform must be found.

QUALITY AND STANDARDS OF PERFORMANCE

As "new" institutions, colleges in all provinces have long faced the task of establishing credibility with respect to the quality of their programs, the effectiveness of their graduates, and the competence of their instructional staff. The universities, regarded as the only "legitimate" tertiary institutions in Canada until the 1960s, slowly acknowledged the colleges, albeit with some reluctance. The colleges, in turn, were eager to earn recognition as institutions with a different mandate. Problems of identity, however, continue to confront the college systems in many provinces as they approach their third decade.

There are two areas in which the colleges must concentrate their efforts in a period when accountability is of major concern to taxpayers and governments. The first is in the matter of critical evaluation of each facet of their operation. The second area is in the upgrading and revitalization of their teaching staff, through professional development

EVALUATION

Although all levels in the college systems agree that a systematic and intensive evaluation of programs, administration, and instruction is essential, there is less agreement as to what should be its form, purpose, and eventual use. With regard to purpose, there are two primary goals: to document the performance of the colleges to government and society (i.e., accountability), and to form a basis for revitalizing their operations. The latter is the more desirable, but the first is more compelling during the current economic climate confronting education.[26]

Unfortunately, it is not easy to achieve both goals by using the same approach. Revitalization demands an honest and open assessment of current performance; in effect, a valid internal review that will identify both strengths and weaknesses. But to perform this task effectively would render the institution vulnerable to external criticism and perhaps more limited funding.

Another problem for evaluation lies in the fact that some colleges have no blueprint upon which to base the exercise, largely because they are unclear on just what their goals and objectives really are. Too often colleges have responded uncritically to public demand for new services or the availability of government funding, without determining whether such responses are consistent with their mandate or where their program priorities lie.

Finally, the issues of who should be responsible for conducting evaluation procedures and who should participate in the exercise have, for many colleges, never been decided. Government initiative in these matters, even through an intermediary agency, such as the Council of Regents in Ontario, is often regarded with suspicion as to its long-term intent. To conduct a comprehensive evaluation themselves would, for the institutions, demand a huge investment of time, resources, and energy.

The fact of the matter is, however, that a coherent system of evaluation, which will provide the institutions with clear directions for the future, must not remain undone. Priorities for the future must be set, there must be full confidence in current policies and practices, and students, government, and the public at large must be assured that colleges are performing effectively. Failure to complete this task would be to invite government intervention and funding limitations, which would eventually erode the essence of the community college concept.

Colleges in the 1990s will not be able to assume that external support will flow from a basis of trust alone. The claims that they have made with regard to job preparation for students, quality teaching, and efficient management must be documented, clearly and openly. Colleges do make a contribution to the economic and socio-cultural quality of life in their communities. But the rhetoric needs to be translated into reality.

PROFESSIONAL DEVELOPMENT

The second major aspect of quality, the performance of the instructional staff, introduces another concept, widely supported but often performed less well (i.e., the professional development of staff).

Colleges are, above all else, teaching institutions, whether the teaching be in academic, technological, trades, upgrading, or continuing education areas. If this claim is to be sustained, instructional faculty need to be competent in two primary respects; their ability to teach and the relevance of knowledge in their subject area. Both challenges demand to be addressed by sustained programs that fall under the aegis of professional development.

Quality programs in instructional upgrading may best be organized and conducted by instructors themselves. In every college there are outstanding teachers, with demonstrable competence in current instructional technologies, who have the potential to help their colleagues. Often, however, the incentive is lacking. Few colleges offer rewards, tangible or otherwise, for good teaching and/or leadership in the field. Faculty organizations rarely perceive the need to recognize quality instructors in their collective agreements. This is an issue in which the primary purpose of a community college has been subsumed under other admittedly more pressing demands.

The second aspect of professional development, relevance in the field of teaching, has also suffered from alternative pressures. Just as history instructors must constantly read and study, data processing and automobile mechanics instructors must be current in every new development in their field. This objective demands time and dedication, often involving visits to appropriate resource locations, reading and reflection, and, in a particular sense of the term, involvement in research projects. Few colleges provide the opportunity, incentive, or financial support for wide practice of these activities.

Although many budgets include an allocation for professional development, much of it is sacrificed during financial difficulties, or used to provide one or two sabbatical leaves. The future will require both an increased provision or protected funds for professional development activities and more appropriate applications of resources. College programs must prepare students who have the skills to display quality performance in their field of preparation. A goal such as this will require excellence in every dimension of their college experience, within which the quality of instruction will play no small part.

If community colleges are to continue to demand comparable recognition with universities by offering a different but equally demanding curriculum, they must not only seek excellence in their activities, but demonstrate both the commitment and the evidence that support their claims.

LABOUR RELATIONS

There are few issues in the community college sector in Canada that occupy as high a profile as the impact of collective agreements between teaching personnel and their employers, be the latter government or represented by governing boards. These contracts now include implications for almost every aspect of the operation of the institutions.[27]

Either directly or indirectly, the agreements influence such matters as evaluation procedures, particularly with respect to instructional skills. They have a profound impact upon the ways in which the colleges respond to changing program priorities. In their direct reference to working conditions, collective agreements influence the number of students who will be admitted to a program, the ways in which colleges provide services to communities beyond the major campus, and policies such as the use and deployment of part-time instructors to respond to society's changing needs.

Above all, the flexibility and responsiveness that colleges must display in meeting the evolving needs of students, the new demands for services from industry and expectations from all levels of government, are influenced by negotiated conditions for job security. Colleges are committed to change, and the extent of the commitment is often limited by legal constraints imposed through collective bargaining.

There is another reason to regard labour relations as an important issue. Particularly under conditions of financial uncertainty, bargaining can become a time-consuming and acrimonious process during which tensions among administration, teaching, and support staff rise to a high pitch. The consequences may produce a climate of distrust and fear that has the potential to permeate every aspect of the operation of the institution. Under such conditions, colleges are unable to plan effectively, to offer creative solutions to the educational problems of the community, and to preserve their commitment to a client-centred approach to society's needs.

The language of restraint, which has characterized governments' approach to education in the last few years, has included terms such as accountability, productivity, cost effectiveness, and program rationalization. Each term could be perceived as an ominous challenge to the job security of college personnel, and each holds implications for the direction that bargaining will follow.

It would be naive to believe that any dimension of the operation of a public community college in Canada today is unaffected by the particular agreement in place. Unionization has become an established practice in colleges, its presence is real, influential, and unlikely to decrease in the immediate future. In short, it is an issue that cannot either be ignored or underestimated.

THE STATUS OF LABOUR RELATIONS

As in so many other aspects of colleges' operations, collective bargaining has assumed different forms in every provincial system. The formats range from centralized, public sector structures, within which college instructors form one small unit, to local bargaining in which small faculty associations negotiate individual contracts with their governing boards.

With one exception, Alberta,[28] all college faculty organizations are free to bargain collectively under the labour code of their particular province. However, some groups, notably in Prince Edward Island and Saskatchewan, have chosen to bargain as professional associations.

Irrespective of the form and structure of bargaining, the motivation for teaching personnel is essentially the same. On one hand there is a need to preserve traditional privileges associated with "professional" status; on the other is the reality of an economic condition that threatens to place non-organized employees in a disadvantageous relationship with their organized colleagues.

Inevitably, the fundamental contradictions between *professionals*, who control many of the conditions governing their working lives, and *unionists*, with their acceptance of the confrontational relationship between labour and management, create problems for faculty that permeate every aspect of their activity. Further, the intervention of the Labour Relations Board, or its provincial equivalent, as an arbitrator on certain essential issues, can add other complications.

Faced with the need to retain their economic security and legal protection against the arbitrary action of management, most faculty groups have understandably chosen the "union" route—but there has been a price in confrontations and disputes, which have damaged the community college concept, limited the colleges' ability to respond to changing societal needs, and eroded their credibility as teaching institutions. The current economic climate in most provinces suggests that further deterioration in these areas will occur.

Obviously the solutions to these problems are extremely complex, but one first step seems to be essential. Governments must recognize both the legitimate needs of teaching faculty and the uniqueness of the community college concept as an educational organization different from universities and public schools and certainly quite unlike conventional departments of government. These differences must be translated into legislation that is designed specifically for the community college and that will form the basis for a unique collective bargaining framework.

CONCLUSION

Despite their impressive development during the past two decades, community colleges in Canada's ten provinces face an uncertain future. Growth, though often spectacular, has sometimes been uncritical and unco-ordinated. The demand to respond to a wide range of societal and governmental initiatives has often contributed to the creation of institutions unsure of their purpose and confused about their mandate.

As their second decade draws to an end, Canada's colleges are confronted with budgetary restraint and increasing demands for more accountability. While in many ways their performance has been impressive, these new institutions of postsecondary education continue to wrestle with a number of common issues that defy satisfactory solution.

This essay has addressed four of the more demanding of these issues. Those selected do not by any means represent the full extent of the challenges of the future, but they are all serious—and in need of urgent attention—if Canada's colleges are to retain the creativity and energy that have characterized their past. While the solutions suggested may not attract universal support, they are offered as an agenda for action that must not be delayed.

NOTES

1. Lethbridge Community College in Alberta and Lakehead College in Ontario.
2. Although Nova Scotia did not have a "community college," several institutions in that province perform similar functions.
3. Gordon Campbell, *Community Colleges in Canada* (Toronto: Ryerson Press, McGraw-Hill, 1971).
4. Read Ontario Ministry of Education, *Basic Documents: Colleges of Applied Arts and Technology* (Toronto: Queen's Printer, 1965).
5. Note Quebec Department of Education, *College Education and the General and Vocational Colleges* (Quebec: Queen's Printer, 1968).
6. Ron Faris, "Community College Development in Saskatchewan: A Unique Approach," *Canadian Forum* (Oct.-Nov. 1972): 60–61.
7. A good reference is Frank Beinder, *The Community College in British Columbia: The Emphasis is on Community* (Nanaimo, B.C.: Quadra Graphics, 1983).
8. Abram G. Konrad, ed., *Clientele and Community* (Toronto: Association of Canadian Community Colleges, 1974).
9. John D. Dennison, "The Canadian Community College in the 1980s: Strategies for Survival," *Canadian Journal of Education* 9, 2 (1984).
10. The full-time enrolment in colleges grew from 100 000 in 1970 to 270 000 in 1981. Statistics Canada, Report 81-222.
11. Several provinces have created, and later removed, intermediary agencies (e.g., the College Commission in Alberta and the College Councils in British Columbia).
12. Most college budgets involve proportions between 70 and 85 percent allocated to salaries.
13. An example is the Open Learning Institute in British Columbia.
14. Particularly in Saskatchewan.
15. A situation common to Ontario and Quebec.
16. D.C. Savage and R. Bellaire, "Universities and the Federal Government," in *Financing Canadian Universities: For Whom and By Whom* (Toronto: OISE Press, 1981).
17. B.M. Dwyer, "A Historical Perspective of Federal Policies for Adult Occupational Training and Their Impact on Post Secondary Education in British Columbia 1900–1983" (unpublished paper, University of British Columbia, 1983).
18. Y. Masuda, *The Information Society* (Tokyo: Institute for the Information Society, 1980), 5.
19. Ontario Ministry of Education, *Basic Documents*.
20. "Holland College: A College of Applied Arts and Technology" (unpublished paper, Charlottetown, 1 May 1969).
21. W.B. Whale and L.A. Riederer, "Colleges that Encourage Life-long Learning" in *Clientele and Community*.
22. Academic Record for Higher Education in British Columbia, *The Role of District and Regional Colleges in the British Columbia System of Higher Education* (Vancouver: The Academic Board, 1965).

23. Association of Colleges of Applied Arts and Technology, "Background Papers on Current Issues" (Toronto: ACAATO, 1980).

24. Quebec Department of Education, *College Education and the General and Vocational Colleges*.

25. Quebec Ministry of Education, *Colleges in Quebec: A New Phase* (Quebec: Ministry of Education, 1978).

26. W. Wyman and G. De Metra, "Who Controls Program Quality?" *College Canada* 5, 7 (Oct. 1980).

27. Special issue of *College Canada* on labour relations. See *College Canada* 6, 7 (Nov. 1981).

28. Alberta has legislation pertaining to the postsecondary education sector.

THE EMERGENCE OF DISTANCE EDUCATION FROM THE EDUCATIONAL MOSAIC

ALLAN W. HAYDUK

HISTORICAL ORIGINS

Scholastically-able people have often been denied access to education because of geographic isolation, financial difficulty, work and family responsibilities, physical disability, and so on. Throughout history, socially conscious educators and institutions have attempted to overcome such barriers. Plato's epistles to Dionysius, like Pliny the Elder's writings to Pliny the Younger, were essentially successful efforts to instruct via letter.

The development of reliable and inexpensive postal services in the early 1800s made two-way "correspondence" teaching a viable enterprise. For example, by 1840 Isaac Pitman, an Englishman, had reduced the principles of shorthand to fit onto postcards. The cards were mailed to students who used the shorthand instructions to transcribe Biblical passages. Translations were then returned to Pitman for correction. His sytem (the precursor to the modern day Sir Isaac Pitman Correspondence College) taught both biblical knowledge and a marketable commercial skill. No tuition fee was charged and "penny post" put the return communication expenses within reach of almost everyone.

Instruction has also been given via newspapers. For example, during the 1880s Thomas Foster of Scranton, Pennsylvania, concerned by miners' lack of fundamental mining safety knowledge, fostered a regular educational column in his daily newspaper, the *Mining Herald*. A strong demand encouraged him to systematize and extend the information into an individual-study correspondence course on mining and mining safety, which he did by 1891. His course was enthusiastically received. Miners who had had no way to obtain high quality technical training were subsequently able to study, to work more safely, and to advance their careers. Other successful courses in various technical fields soon followed. The collected courses eventually formed the curricular base of the International Correspondence School (ICS) of Scranton. ICS continues to be a major force in field-level technical training to this day.

In a more academic vein, the University of London began to grant external degrees in 1858. Oxford University established Wolsey Hall to house a successful correspondence teacher-training institute that prepared students for the Certified Teacher's Examinations. The University of Chicago formally accredited and incorporated correspondence courses in 1891. Fifteen years later, the University of Wisconsin established a separate extension division. During the same period, Queen's University in Kingston, Ontario, offered correspondence courses to teachers who wished to complete degree studies while working. In 1919, British Columbia became the first Canadian province to provide correspondence education at the public school level at the request of a lighthouse keeper off the west coast.

By 1963 more than twenty publicly funded Canadian agencies provided formally accredited correspondence instruction ranging from elementary education through degree programs. The majority were of high quality and were quite well accepted. In addition, several hundred private sector correspondence schools offered training in dozens of technical and vocational areas. Although active and productive, correspondence education in Canada in the early 1960s was essentially a peripheral educational endeavour. As such, it was not very different from correspondence education throughout the world.

The sweeping technological, social, and economic changes of the late 1960s produced new educational needs, markets, and methods. Most industrialized societies had become aware that life-long education was necessary if rapidly developing technological benefits were to be quickly and widely implemented. Rapid social and technological change seemed to imply that many citizens could expect two or three professional careers in one lifetime. It was simultaneously apparent that ongoing or serial vocational retraining was far too expensive to society if workers had to leave productive jobs (and substantial incomes) to attend centrally located classes. Many universities, colleges, and institutes attempted to meet the new educational needs by developing extension departments, outreach programs and night schools, but it was clear that only a small proportion of society could properly be served in that way. Traditional correspondence education seemed to hold some promise but it was, in general, too slow, too undeveloped, and too peripheral to react properly.

Coincident with the social changes and changing educational needs, the 1960s produced major developments in communications technology. Around the world, educators experimented with ways to use the new technology. In western Canada alone, experimental educational courses were delivered via some combination of print, telephone tutoring, telephone conferencing, radio broadcasting, radio sideband, television broadcasting, cable TV, audio tape, video tape, communications satellite transmission, two-way video satellite communications, computer-based instruction, computer-assisted instruction, and, in a few cases, computer-managed instruction. North Island College in British Columbia, which serves remote coastal communities, developed a ship-based learning centre and land-based mobile resource centres (like book-mobiles) all staffed by student-support personnel. Considerable research was also directed into identifying educational applications of telidon, personal computers, personal computer links with mainframe computers, and video disks.

Researchers learned early that technology and education were not always ideal partners. The best marriages between educational needs and technological capabilities seemed to occur at institutions that based their efforts on sound educational and communications theory. Particular emphasis came to be placed on instructional systems designs (typically cybernetic models), emergent theories of adult learning and development, and methods for individualizing instruction. The plethora of research that began in the 1960s and 1970s has continued to the present day.

Various emergent and experimental institutions have chosen vastly different technologies to accomplish similar goals. At other times they have used identical technologies but in different ways and/or in different combinations. The complex international mosaic of educational experience resulted in the identification of new kinds of administrative and instructional problems, new areas of research, and in the formation of several new theories and models of education quite different from either conventional correspondence education or conventional face-to-face education.

THE EMERGENCE OF "DISTANCE EDUCATION"

By 1975, the emerging technological mode of education had outgrown the title "correspondence education." Some traditional correspondence institutions continued to exist, of course, but they resembled the new technology-based institutions only superficially. Further, a potential for massive confusion developed rapidly because, to many minds, the use of the emerging educational technology was confounded with a number of new philosophical approaches to education that it attracted. The terms open learning, private study, independent study, free study, external study, outreach, and other quite distinct philosophical perspectives became increasingly confounded with the communications channels of the emerging technology. For example, Britain's "Open University," Iran's Free University, and Canada's Télé-université have similar technological delivery characteristics even though the educational concepts "Open," "Free," and "Tele" are worlds apart. A generic descriptor was needed to discriminate the technological from the philosophical aspects of the emerging educational technology. The title "distance education" found increasingly widespread acceptance. Continuing use of the title was assured in June 1982 when, following energetic debate, the powerful and prestigious International Council for Correspondence Education (ICCE) changed its name to the International Council for Distance Education (ICDE).

DEFINING DISTANCE EDUCATION

Not surprisingly, lively debate continues as to the exact semantic boundaries of "distance education." The literature, however, has begun to approach consensus on at least five central elements.[1] First, distance education teachers and learners are separated in space and, frequently, in time during the teaching/learning process. Second, the educational content of a given distance education course is carried by some technical medium, for example print or television. The use of educational technology in conventional programs is not distance education. Third, distance education students are provided with some form of two-way communication for purposes of clarification, feedback, motivational support, and so on. Typical feedback communications channels might include telephone calls, conference calls, two-way TV, or perhaps the mail. Fourth, distance education emanates from a formal educational organization rather than from an individual instructor. Perhaps this may best be seen by examining the typical organization of course development and delivery activities. A distance-delivered course is usually developed by a course development team. A team may consist of one to six subject matter experts who provide academically sound content, an instructional designer whose job it is to apply curriculum development and instructional knowledge to ensure pedagogically sound presentation of the academic content, a visual designer who applies knowledge of appropriate technical media (e.g., a TV producer or layout specialist or both), an editor who ensures proper continuity and expression of prose materials and assumes responsibility for legal and copyright issues, and a production manager responsible for the integration and performance of the team. Teams may be much larger or smaller depending on the needs of the specific institution or course.

Distance-education courses are highly visible, public offerings open to criticism (and adjustment) by professional colleagues. One result of team development coupled with high visibility seems to be less content idiosyncrasy and less individual academic prejudice in distance courses than in conventional courses. A danger is that, without constant vigilance, courses may become stereotyped and "middle-of-the-road" reviews of content.[3] By the time it is completed, a distance education course carries all the academic content judged appropriate by the institution. It is truly an institution-approved course.

Distance teaching requires different pedagogical and interpersonal skills from conventional teaching. Course development team members must be able to function comfortably in a team context where expertise must be shared and open to negotiated alteration. Further, there is no evidence that the ability to deliver lectures in conventional settings is of any benefit in preparing distance education courses. Keegan nicely captures the essence of what is required of "distance academics" for the development phase.

> When interviewing for distance education positions on the other hand, one seeks, firstly, competent academics; secondly, competent academics who can write; next, academics who have written or could write textbooks; finally, academics who can write distance education courses. Baath (1973: 65–89) has made the classic statement on the didactic construction of distance education courses and there is no need to repeat it here. Many of the skills listed by Baath are quite different from those of conventional teaching.[5]

In distance education, "course delivery" is a separate activity from "course development." A completed distance education course is typically "delivered" to students by a part-time "tutor" whose job is to provide interpersonal support, guidance, clarification, advice, and marking of assignments. The tutor is meant to be a warm, caring human contact. He or she assists in bridging the gap between relatively inflexible curricular material and individual student's characteristics. There is ample evidence from many sources that effectively trained and deployed tutors can enhance course completion rates and student success and satisfaction. Evidence gathered at Canada's Athabasca University shows that, when tutor listening and communication skills increase, student performance improves.[1] The 1982 ICDE conference produced more than a dozen papers describing different models in which tutors can be effectively deployed. We must await further comparative investigation before it will be possible to identify the best of these methods. Further, more research is needed before we can assess the importance of tutors relative to other student-support mechanisms such as study circles, regional study centres, teleconference study groups, local learner-support groups, peer tutoring, mobile learning centres, or intermittent workshops. It is becoming increasingly apparent that a large part of the student support load can be carried by a course-independent student-service department and/or a radically restructured university registry.

The above remarks were intended to clarify the fourth element of distance education, namely that distance education emanates from a formal educational organization rather than from an individual teacher. The content of distance instruction is carried by the materials, not by the tutor.

A fifth major element that can be derived from the above comments is that distance education is the most industrialized form of education. Peters describes it as:

> a method if imparting knowledge, skills and attitudes which is rationalized by the application of division of labour and organization principles as well as by the extensive use of technical media,

especially for the purpose of reproducing high quality teaching material which makes it possible to instruct great numbers of students... wherever they live.[5]

Keegan has aptly captured the impact of industrialization upon the didactic structure of distance education in contrast to conventional education.

In traditional education the teacher is present in the lecture room with students and his success often depends on the rapport he can build up with students: personality and even idiosyncracies may be central. In distance education a teacher prepares learning materials from which he himself may never teach. Another teacher may use the materials and evaluate students' work. The pedagogical structuring of the learning materials, instructional design and execution may be assigned to others. Personality needs to be played down, idiosyncracies eliminated. The teaching becomes institutionalised. Different skills are needed as even part of the content of what is taught may be contributed by others.[6]

The potential benefits of industrialization of education are many. Large-scale production offers substantial economies. Distance-education institutions should eventually be able to teach more courses to more people for less money than is possible in conventional settings. Private sector institutions that seem to be more lightly managed (e.g., ICS) already do so in some technical areas. Quality control standards may be more easily and consistently applied in distance education than in most educational settings. Instructional problems are public and visible, so staff motivation to improve instruction is high. Because of the systems approach, cumulative course improvement occurs with each revision cycle. That is, student, tutor, and collegial feedback is consistently incorporated into the redesign and redevelopment process producing progressively more effective and esthetically pleasing course offerings.

The industrial methodology suggests, and experience has proven, that distance education requires different administrative and management operations and skills than conventional institutions.[7] Not surprisingly, industrial style management may work best. Funding formulas and budget control are different in distance and conventional institutions.[8] The registrarial function in distance-education institutions is more complex because enrolment is non-synchronous and course work is not usually paced. For example, different students may enrol in a given course at different times (days, weeks, or months apart), proceed at different rates, and graduate at different times. Similarly, a given student may enrol in several courses, each with a different start date, work rate, and completion date. A sophisticated learner management system is required to monitor and record all student activity and to identify students who may be in special need of assistance before they get into serious trouble. Industrial production systems monitoring models appear to work well both for learner monitoring and management and for registrarial control. They also can work well in monitoring the amount and the success of personal contact between tutors and students that is so important to successful distance education.

EARLY SUCCESS

Tremendous worldwide consumer demand coupled with a political will to fund distance-education activity has produced enormous growth in the numbers of institutions involved in distance education during the last fifteen years. The 1982 Vancouver ICCE (now ICDE) conference drew more than 500 formal delegates from 55 countries. The 1985 Melbourne Conference saw an even greater response. At least 41 major accredited degree-granting, distance-education universities were established worlwide (excluding the USSR, South Africa, and the German Democratic Republic (DDR)) between 1969 and 1981. Distance education is nevertheless alive and well in the USSR, South Africa, and the DDR. Forty percent of all graduate and undergraduate university level enrolment (2.2 million in 1979) in the USSR is via distance teaching. The courses originate from over 114 different distance universities.[9] The DDR has developed a unique and highly successful style of university-level distance education in 30 of its 54 universities. Distance-education enrolment accounted for almost 30 percent of its total graduates between 1950 and 1975. The University of South Africa, which began to provide distance education exclusively in 1964, today is:

> a flourishing correspondence-based university with 56,000 students...and employing 1,000 full-time lecturers and 1,600 administrative personnel.... It appoints full time staff and like conventional universities, offers all its degrees of Bachelors, Masters and Doctoral levels in six faculties: Sciences, Law, Arts, Education, Economics and Management Sciences, and Theology.[10]

Although comprehensive formal documentation does not exist, it is apparent that both private sector and secondary distance-education institutions worldwide have grown at an even faster rate than the distance-teaching universities. Consistent with the world situation, student enrolment in all forms of distance education in Canada has grown geometrically between 1975 and 1985.

Canadian students wishing to pursue university studies at a distance have at least the following options open to them. Alberta's Athabasca University offers B.A., B. Admin., and B.G.S. degrees at a distance, providing a large range of courses that permit students to major in a variety of fields of study. The University of Waterloo offers the B.A. at a distance. The Télé-université of Quebec, Ryerson College in Toronto, and the Knowledge Network, Open Learning Institute, and North Island College in B.C. all offer high quality university courses that are, in most cases, transferable to other Canadian universities.

Distance education in Canada and worldwide has emerged quickly and made remarkable inroads into education in private and public sectors. Further technological developments and research projects are ongoing on all fronts. While the continued success of distance education is not guaranteed, it appears likely that proponents of distance education have some cause for optimism.

NOTES

1. D.J. Keegan, *On the Nature of Distance Education*, ZIFF Papiere 33 (Hagen: Zentrales Institute fur Fernstudienfoschung, 1980).

2. D. Keegan, "On Defining Distance Education," *Distance Education* 1, 1 (1980): 19–45.

3. Keegan, *On the Nature of Distance Education*, 16. Readers interested in an introduction to actual development techniques for effective distance education courses are well referred to J. Baath, *Correspondence Education in the Light of a Number of Contemporary Teaching Models* (Malmö, Sweden: Hermods, 1979; J. Baath and R. Flink, *Two-Way Communication in Correspondence Education* (Sweden: University of Lund, 1973); and B. Holmberg, *Distance Education: A Short Handbook* (Malmö: Hermods, 1974), *Distance Education: A Survey and Bibliography* (London: Kogan Page, 1977), "Aspects of Distance Education," *Comparative Education* 16, 2 (1980): 107-19.

4. V. Williams, "Research and Evaluation of Tutor Skills Training Project," *REDEAL Research Report No. 4*, Project REDEAL (Athabasca, Alta.: Athabasca University Press, 1980).

5. O. Peters, *Die Didaktische Struktur des Fernum Terrichts Untersuchungen zur Einer Industrialisierten Form des Lehrens und Lernes* (Weinheim: Beltz, 1973), translated by D.J. Keegan in *On the Nature of Distance Education*.

6. Keegan, "On Defining Distance Education."

7. W. Perry, *The Open University* (Milton Keynes/Open University, 1976); J.S. Daniel and W.A.S. Smith, "Opening Open Universities: the Canadian Experience," *Canadian Journal of Higher Education* 9, 2, (1979): 63–74.

8. B.L. Snowden and H.S. Daniel, "The Economics and Management of Small Post-Secondary Distance Education Systems," *Distance Education* 1, 1, (1980): 68–91; P. Guiton, "Resource Allocation in the Australian Two-Mode University" in *Learning at a Distance: A World Perspective*, edited by J. Daniel, M. Stroud, and J. Thompson (Edmonton: Athabasca University, 1982).

9. G. Rumble and K. Harry, *The Distance Teaching Universities* (London: Croom Helm, 1982).

10. Ibid., 17.

REFORMING POSTSECONDARY EDUCATION: POLICY INITIATIVES AND POPULAR SENTIMENTS[1]

D.W. LIVINGSTONE

The advanced capitalist economies are now facing an unprecedented surplus of highly educated people for available jobs. Two dimensions of this phenomenon can be distinguished: unemployment and underemployment.

Although employment growth has been sustained in some areas of specialization, the unemployment rates of postsecondary graduates increased markedly during the past decade.[2] Youth unemployment has been widely recognized as a serious problem, and is especially high among the least educated; but the unemployment rate in Canada among university graduates under twenty-five years of age has itself reached about ten percent in recent years.[3]

The ratio of youth to older adult unemployment is likely to diminish in the near future as the size of the youth cohort declines.[4] What is likely to happen to unemployment levels generally is an issue of extreme controversy. Some analysts foresee a secular trend toward massive unemployment as computer technologies continually replace industrial and office workers alike.[5] Others argue that there is no historical evidence that technological change has ever caused sustained and widespread structural unemployment in industrial capitalist societies, and that market mechanisms and complementary state economic policies are stimulating renewed economic growth and will substantially reduce unemployment rates.[6] What is clear, in Canada as elsewhere, is that current unemployment rates would be much higher without a reduction of the standard work week for full-time employees by about two hours per decade over the past century[7] and the rapid growth and acceptance of part-time employment since World War II.[8] It is probably fair to say that future unemployment rates, as well as the fundamental character of society, are becoming increasingly contingent on negotiations between employers and employees over the implementation of technological change and how many hours constitute a normal full-time work load.[9] In any case, during the past decade, long-term employment prospects have become very uncertain not only for the poorly educated but for growing numbers of highly educated job market entrants.

It has become even more apparent to most analysts that there are more people who are obtaining postsecondary educational certificates than there are commensurate jobs in the existing structure of the economy.[10] As Zsigmond notes:[11]

> Underemployment...is the issue today. A growing number of graduates are chasing an insufficient number of desirable positions. Blocked out of the top jobs, which are taken by those with specialized training or post-graduate degrees, many post-secondary graduates are applying for positions that in the past would have been filled by high school graduates.[11]

Moreover, the demand for postsecondary education has continued to grow.[12] In spite of very limited public funding for education during the economic slump of the past decade, universities and community colleges have found it very difficult to turn away the growing numbers of qualified applicants, thereby severely straining staff and physical resource capacities.[13] Regardless of the fact that the eighteen- to twenty-four-year-old age group, which has been the main "source population" for postsecondary institutions, has declined over the past few years, and may continue to do so for the next decade, demands for education are unlikely to diminish. It may well continue to grow as the children of the increasing numbers of parents with postsecondary education reach the eighteen- to twenty-four-year-old age group and older adults themselves participate more in recurrent education. Such increased demand is especially likely if the "credential inflation" to which Zsigmond refers continues to make it more difficult for less educated people to obtain even jobs with lower actual educational requirements.[14] In particular, youth cohorts of women and visible ethnic minorities have experienced very substantial cumulative growth in both educational expectations and attainments—from prior levels of virtual exclusion in some postsecondary fields—even while facing discriminatory credential inflation in an expanding job market over the past few decades.[15] These groups are especially unlikely to willingly reduce their educational demands in more generally restricted job markets.

While the required skill level of the future employed workforce is also an issue of considerable debate, it is reasonably well documented that the actual aggregate educational requirements of the existing job structure have not increased significantly over the past several decades.[16] In addition, the most thorough empirically-based projections of the job structure in Canada and other advanced capitalist societies indicate that most employment growth will be in low status manual jobs, which suggests a future prevalence of skill downgrading.[17] Thus, in the absence of major social policy reforms, there is little prospect that the underemployment of postsecondary graduates will diminish significantly in the near future.

If the burgeoning gap between the educational attainments of the population and the availability and commensurateness of jobs is to be reduced, substantial social policy reforms will indeed be needed. In the remainder of this paper we will examine the types of postsecondary educational reforms currently being considered by opinion leaders and policy makers, summarize the general sentiments of the public toward postsecondary education, and offer a brief critical analysis of the underlying social class forces that are likely to be involved in resolving the current crisis of postsecondary education.

POLICY INITIATIVES

Logically, there are two basic sorts of reforms that policy makers could recommend to resolve the current crisis of postsecondary education. On the one hand, they could propose fundamental economic reforms that would restructure the labour process to increase the discretionary control of lower level employees and/or redistribute highly qualified employment among more people on the basis of a shorter standard work time. Such reforms would be aimed at reducing underemployment and unemployment by more fully utilizing the available surplus of highly educated people.

Conversely, policy makers could propose restructuring of the postsecondary institutions to restrict access, reduce public funding rates, and adjust educational resource allocation more closely to the existing job structure. Such reforms would attempt to close the attainments/requirements gap by limiting the present surplus production of highly educated people.

In some respects, postsecondary institutions have been quite responsive to both student interests and labour force needs over the past decade. For example, the proportion of postsecondary students in Canada who are women has grown to more than half of the total undergraduate enrolment, and part-time enrolment has risen to nearly forty percent, while enrolment in business and commerce programs has nearly doubled as a proportion of total enrolment, and recent increases in engineering and computer science enrolments have been much greater than the overall university enrolment increases.[18] But the net effect of such adjustments has not appreciably reduced the surplus of highly educated people.

Calls for major reorganization of postsecondary education have increased in the past few years. The recent Commission on the Future Development of the Universities of Ontario (1984) is perhaps representative. The terms of reference of this commission emphasized: limiting resource allocations to the universities "to reflect the government's policy of fiscal restraint and prudent management of public funds"; reviewing mechanisms for determining accessibility "in the context of economic realities" and for adjusting levels of enrolment in response to changing labour market requirements; and rationalizing the structure of university programs through increased specialization, greater public accountability for operating grants, and consideration of new mechanisms of regulation for the entire university system.[19] Both these terms of reference and the predominately corporate business composition of the Commission predisposed it to encourage greater market determination of postsecondary education. A major thrust of the final report is to encourage restructuring of the university system through "institutional responses within a competitive context and stimulated by incentives in the financial system which reward excellence in education and research."[20]

The Royal Commission on the Economic Union and Development Prospects for Canada had considerably wider terms of reference and a somewhat broader composition, but the reliance in its social policy recommendations on market mechanisms is even more explicit. With regard to postsecondary education, the commission report states that "it is desirable to consider substantial changes in financing mechanisms in order to create a more competitive, dynamic, and diversified system."[21] To overcome what is characterized as very considerable inertia in postsecondary education, the commission recommends that the federal government give educational vouchers directly to students, that provincial governments be encouraged to deregulate free structures, and that students bear a greater proportion of education costs.[22]

In sum, most government commission policy initiatives to date dealing with the crisis of postsecondary education have focussed on the restructuring of educational institutions per se, with scant attention to economic reforms that could actually utilize the current surplus of highly qualified people.[23] Generally, more extensive competition between education and other public fiscal priorities, between institutions for students, and between students for available places are assumed by leading policy makers to be the best means to resolve the crisis. In the context of public fiscal restraint and strong continuing private demand for education, more direct market determination of the provision of postsecondary education would very likely entail relative reductions in the level of public educational funding, and even more restricted access for qualified students of economically disadvantaged backgrounds. Such a market model could thereby alleviate the surplus production of highly educated people that is at the core of the current crisis. But is there sufficient support in the general public to facilitate implementation of this educational policy initiative?

POPULAR SENTIMENTS

Over the past century, the North American public has been imbued with an enduring faith in the capacity of education to generate economic prosperity and to restore societal well-being in periods of crisis.[24] While the general level of public confidence in societal institutions may have been declining over most of the past decade,[25] faith in education has remained relatively high. In the United States, recent opinion polls have found that the overwhelming majority feel that developing the educational system remains very important for determining the country's strength, outranking both the industrial production system and military force.[26] Recent national opinion surveys have similarly found that the vast majority of Canadians believe that schools are extremely important for personal success, and that the public is now more likely to express confidence in the schools than in other major institutions such as the different levels of government, the courts, or even the church.[27]

With specific regard to postsecondary education, popular sentiments of support also appear to have remained strong and may well have increased during the recent years of fiscal restraint. Overwhelming majorities in virtually all recent North American surveys have expressed support for the principle of postsecondary access for all qualified applicants, as well as for increasing or maintaining rather than reducing real levels of government funding for postsecondary institutions.[28] The only regularly conducted Canadian survey of educational issues has found growing popular support in the past few years for increased postsecondary education funding in Ontario, both in absolute terms and as a relative priority among all areas of government expenditure. More specifically, with regard to the terms of reference of the Commission on the Future Development of the Universities of Ontario, the Ontario public is overwhelmingly opposed to decreasing the numbers of institutions, programs, or students enrolled in the university system.[29] Popular sentiments of support for postsecondary education access and funding may now be strongest in jurisdictions where governments have made the most concerted efforts to exercise fiscal restraint, notably British Columbia.[30]

Readings of public perceptions concerning the relationship between postsecondary education and employment remain relatively limited. However, the majority of the Ontario public has expressed the view that the job-skill requirements of most of the Canadian labour force have increased over the past generation,[31] and only a small minority believes that computer technology will generally reduce skill requirements over the next decade.[32] At the same time, there is a majority perception that most people currently do primarily routine work, coupled with a majority preference that most people should be able to exercise more discretionary judgment in their jobs.[33]

With such generally optimistic views of trends in job-skill requirements, it is not surprising that only a small minority of the Ontario public thinks that postsecondary graduates have been provided with higher levels of skill than required by available jobs.[34] More broadly, there is a growing majority sentiment that vocational training should be the main objective of public education,[35] and that even the universities should place more emphasis on job-related training in the future.[36]

Thus, the thrust of popular support for extending the provision of postsecondary education appears in sharp contrast both to existing surpluses of highly educated people for available jobs and to the direction of major proposed government policy initiatives.

PROSPECTS FOR POSTSECONDARY EDUCATION

Any technologically advanced society needs a technically knowledgeable labour force. Any hierarchically organized form of advanced industrial society needs both a general pool of manual labourers with the basic cognitive skills to follow abstract rules and perform operational detail tasks, and other groups of intellectual workers who attain sufficient general scientific knowledge in specialized fields to be able to plan the adaptation and redesign of various complex production systems.[37] What is distinctive about liberal democratic advanced capitalism's specific educational needs is that they are continually changing as the central production techniques are revolutionized in competitive pursuit of profits, while such needs must continue to be mediated through individual labour market transactions. If the class structure of paid work[38] is to be reproduced effectively, after first offering free educational access in response to popular demand and in order to provide basic technical skills, the schools must then attempt to restrict opportunities in terms of both the scope of the curricula and the numbers who are permitted to achieve their educational aspirations; moreover, the schooling process must both appear to remain independent from capitalist enterprises and avoid drastically upsetting popular educational aspirations. As Peter Meyer has expressed it, "The inherent contradiction confronting education in a capitalist society functioning under the guise of a democracy is the need to *appear* to promote equality while successfully producing the differentiated and unequal labour power demanded by corporations and other employers."[19]

As long as individual transactions in labour markets remain the major mediating mechanism, there are likely to be substantial discrepancies between the entry requirements of jobs and the educational qualifications of many applicants. Moreover, from the vantage points of both employers and individual prospective employees there is likely to be a general tendency in advanced capitalism toward qualifications exceeding requirements in aggregate terms. Capitalist employers have historically used reserve manual labour pools to discipline workers' demands; reserve pools of highly educated people have allowed the extension of this tactic to intellectual as well as manual labour.[40] At the same time, prospective employees are likely to continue to seek any form of schooling, most notably postsecondary programs, that might enhance their individual chances for attractive jobs.

Governments have historically played a pivotal role in both mediating among contending social groups' demands and generally ensuring the reproduction of capitalist social relations.[41] During the post-World War II expansion in all advanced capitalist societies, government intervention in the market economy increased greatly through fiscal and monetary management and the extension of social subsistence payments (unemployment compensation, transfer payments, health and education benefits) to the growing dependent population without gainful employment. But when profits generally declined again in the 1970s, the costs of legislated subsistence entitlements did not.[42]

Many employers now tend to regard the scale of some of these entitlements as major obstacles to economic growth;[43] they have also lobbied for the reassertion of property rights policies through such measures as tax incentives and deregulation of market activities.[44] In the context of this capital accumulation crisis and the attendant fiscal crisis for government, budgets for postsecondary education have come along with other social entitlements, under attack by business spokespersons. The presence of large numbers of overqualified employees and burgeoning reserve pools of educated labour is a major factor encouraging some corporate leaders to advocate more elitist educational models for postsecondary education, at the same time as they demand the allocation of greater fiscal priority to other more direct measures to stimulate sustained economic growth (e.g., deficit reduction, investment in infrastructure and applied research). Increasingly restrictive views of the public funding and accessibility of postsecondary education are becoming more evident in the public discourse of corporate spokespersons. For example, a special survey of corporate opinion leaders conducted for the Commission on the Future Development of the Universities of Ontario has found a strong consensus on the necessity for "rationalization" of the system, with particular emphasis on more rigorous entry examinations.[45] This growing corporate view finds one of its frankest Canadian expressions in recent statements of the chairman of Northern Telecom, Walter Light, who asserts:

> At a time when the country is in dire need of a technological, business and government elite, we are concerned with academic universality. We are in desperate need of the best brains to structure new industries and restructure old ones.... All minds are *not* created equal and all minds do *not* develop equally. We *must*, therefore, develop a university system that provides for, and develops, the intellectual elite, as well as the rest of us.[46]

Subordinate employees and other socially disadvantaged groups, such as the unemployed, mothers on social assistance programs, and chronic-care patients, have been compelled to mobilize in defence of social service entitlements.[47] Organized labour has been at the centre of many of these struggles. Labour leaders have been among the most consistent defenders of open access to postsecondary institutions. As the Ontario Federation of Labour has recently put it:

> The development of western society since the nineteenth century has seen the continued extension of public education simply because the economic and social well-being of the society required a more highly educated and skilled labour force. Given the accelerating pace of technological development, such an expansion of complete accessibility into the post-secondary system simply makes sense.... Furthermore, an open system would help to deal with the problem of large numbers of very capable working-class children who may not be motivated to participate in the post-secondary system immediately after leaving the secondary school

> system but who may become highly motivated to participate later in life. The gain in human resources for society as a whole and for the economy... would be enormous.[48]

Indeed, labour leaders are largely defending prospective education benefits for working-class people, as they have been relatively excluded to date from postsecondary institutions, especially universities.[49]

Professional and managerial employees' households have been major beneficiaries of postsecondary education. However, with the exception of faculty and staff associations of these institutions themselves, their associations have been notably more ambiguous with regard to the issue of postsecondary provisions, as well as most other social service entitlements.[50] Presumably, as the social groups whose positions are most dependent on their typically postsecondary educational credentials, professional and managerial employees are both concerned to maintain adequate educational channels to reproduce their groups, and also worried that more open access could devalue their own qualifications. Hence, such intermediate class groupings are often advocates of stricter standards to enhance educational quality while being less enthusiastic about fiscal rationalization of formal education at all levels.[51]

Overall, the limited available evidence suggests that the current political coherence of social class forces regarding restrictive postsecondary education reforms is quite limited.[52] Corporate executives may generally express more coherence and consistency in their opinions about enhancing the efficiency of education than other social class groupings, and corporate spokespersons increasingly advocate postsecondary rationalization.[53] But even executives as a group remain deeply divided over the prospect of actually reducing university programs; among smaller employers, as well as working-class, professional, and managerial groups, only tiny minorities now express support for reducing university programs.[54]

Nevertheless, protracted economic stagnation and diminishing discretionary tax revenues have compelled governments to make very hard choices among overall budget priorities, including relative and real dollar reductions in allocations to postsecondary education.[55] At least three levels of increasingly *contradictory* criteria are involved in the current administrative actions of the governments of advanced capitalist societies: basic legal principles including inviolable individual rights in private property as well as the "sacred trust" of social service entitlements; functions of facilitating economic growth through private market mechanisms as well as stabilizing the social order through corrective actions for individuals, groups, and environments damaged by market dynamics; and mediation of the declared interests of a diverse array of clients and reference groups.[56] Under present circumstances, the administrative actions of governments concerning postsecondary education are predictably contradictory, as the 1985 First Ministers' Conference in Halifax graphically illustrates. Given existing economic structures, both federal and provincial governments are compelled to devote more resources to directly stimulating the growth of capital (e.g., government debt servicing, tax incentives, stock market participation schemes, continued investments in infrastructure projects as well as research in "high tech" sectors, revised criteria to encourage wealthy or already highly educated immigrants). But in order to do this, they must reduce actual allocations to social services (of which postsecondary education, with its current surplus production of graduates, is among the most eligible), without, in light of the deep popular faith in the capacity of education, publicly declaring that they are doing so. Hence, the eagerness of each level of government to fix the blame on the other as the existence of actual postsecondary reductions becomes more evident.

More generally, the ideological resolution to this dilemma, which has been grasped most readily by both corporate and government leaders, is a reconstructed market liberalism that sees the sources of renewed economic growth in entrepreneurship, individual initiatives, and a winnowing out of the welfare state.[57] This ideology provides a convenient rationale for more direct corporate influence over the funding and redesign of educational programs to enhance their "economic relevance" and "efficiency." Currently emergent Canadian examples include Ontario's proposed Ministry of Skill Development, federal government research grant programs tied to matching private sector funds, and a growing variety of university institutes established through corporate funds. The critical ideological factor in fully implementing the market-determined models of postsecondary education in current government policy initiatives may well be the extent to which intermediate and working-class groups perceive an *equitable* meritocratic process of educational opportunity. An abstract perception of the current existence of equal educational opportunities for postsecondary education remains widely held[58] despite immense empirical evidence to the contrary.[59] So long as the belief persists, this "credibility value"[60] can serve to enable the rationalization of postsecondary education provisions and the restriction of access through increasingly high levels of qualification.

In the absence among subordinate groups of a sustained alternative strategy advocating the viability of economic and educational democracy based on *collective* rights rather than individualistic opportunity,[61] the immediate prospects for social change that can utilize the capacities of the current surplus of highly educated people appear dim. On the other hand, historically, it has been in just such periods of the frustration of rising expectations that the seeds of the most fundamental social transformations have often been sown.[62]

NOTES

1. I am grateful to Gail Buckland for typing this paper, and to Philip Corrigan for comments on an earlier version.
2. E.K. Abel, *Terminal Degrees: The Job Crisis in Higher Education* (New York: Praeger, 1984).
3. Statistics Canada, *Historical Labour Force Statistics—1983*, cat. no. 71-201 (Ottawa: Minister of Supply and Services, 1984).
4. D. Foot and J. Li, "The Demographic Determinants of Unemployment in Canada" (paper presented at the conference "Unemployment: Can It Be Reduced? An International Perspective," Centre for Industrial Relations, University of Toronto, 28–30 Nov. 1984).
5. C. Jenkins and B. Sherman, *The Collapse of Work* (London: Eyre Methuen, 1979); H. Menzies, *Women and the Chip* (Montreal: Institute for Research on Public Policy, 1980).
6. Royal Commission on the Economic Union and Development Prospects for Canada, *Report*, vol. 2 (Ottawa: Minister of Supply and Services, 1985).
7. C.F. Aw, "Standard Hours of Work: Trends, Determinants and Implications" (Ottawa: Labour Canada, Economics and Industrial Relations Research Branch, 1982).
8. Commission of Inquiry into Part-time Work, *Part-time Work in Canada* (Ottawa: Labour Canada, 1983).
9. A. Gorz, *Paths to Paradise: On the Liberation from Work* (London: Pluto Press, 1985).
10. W. Clarke and Z. Zsigmond, *Job Market Reality for Post-Secondary Graduates* (Ottawa: Minister of Supply and Services, 1981); R. Rumberger, *Overeducation in the U.S. Labor Market* (New York: Praeger, 1981).
11. Z. Zsigmond, "A Reply to the Critique of 'Job Market Reality for Post-secondary Graduates'," *Canadian Journal of Higher Education* 12, 1 (1982): 69.
12. Statistics Canada, *Education in Canada: A Statistical Review for 1983–84*, cat. no. 81-229 (Ottawa: Minister of Supply and Services, 1985).
13. E.g., M. Skoluik and N. Rowen, *Please, Sir, I Want Some More: Canadian Universities and Financial Constraint* (Toronto: OISE Press, 1985).
14. See Royal Commission on the Economic Union and Development Prospects for Canada, *Report*, vol. 2, 741–47.
15. E.g., R. Deem, *Women and Schooling* (London: Routledge and Kegan Paul, 1978); E. Herberg, "Education Through the Ethnic Looking Glass" (Ph.D. dissertation, University of Toronto, 1980).
16. Rumberger, *Overeducation in the U.S. Labor Market*; G.D. Squires, *Education and Jobs: The Imbalancing of the Social Machinery* (New Brunswick, N.J.: Transaction Books, 1979); K. Spenner, "Deciphering Prometheus: Temporal Change in the Skill Level of Work," *American Sociological Review* 48, 6 (Dec. 1983): 824–37; D.W. Livingstone, "Job Skills and Schooling: A Class Analysis of Entry Requirements and Underemployment," *Canadian Journal of Education* 11, 2 (1986).

17. E.B. Harvey and J. Blakely, "Education, Social Mobility and the Challenge of Technological Change" in *Transitions to Work*, edited by G. Mason (Winnipeg: Institute for Social and Economic Research, 1985): 46–65; H. Levin and R. Rumberger, *The Educational Implications of High Technology*, project report no. 83-A4 (Stanford: Stanford Institute for Research on Educational Finance and Governance, 1983).

18. Royal Commission on the Economic Union and Development Prospects for Canada, *Report*, vol. 2.

19. Commission on the Future Development of the Universities of Ontario, "Ontario Universities: Options and Futures" (Toronto: Ministry of Colleges and Universities, 1984), ii.

20. Ibid., 38.

21. Royal Commission on the Economic Union and Development Prospects for Canada, *Report*, vol. 2, 820.

22. Ibid., 821–22.

23. Cf. B.A. Scott, *Crisis Management in American Labor Market* (New York: Praeger, 1983).

24. E.g., Merle Curti, *The Social Ideas of American Educators* (Paterson, N.J.: Littlefield, Adams & Co., 1935); H.J. Perkinson, *The Imperfect Panacea: American Faith in Education, 1865–1965* (New York: Random House, 1968); A. Prentice, *The School Promoters* (Toronto: McClelland and Stewart, 1977); R. Carlton, "Educational Policies and the Labour Force: An Historical Perspective on the Ontario Case" in *The Sociology of Work: Papers in Honour of Oswald Hall*, edited by A. Wipper (Ottawa: Carleton University press, 1984), 41–70.

25. E.g, S. Lipset and D. Schneider, *The Confidence Gap: Business, Labor and Government in the Public Mind* (New York: Free Press, 1983); "Canadians losing respect for business, the church, Parliament, Gallup says," *Toronto Star*, 14 Jan. 1985, p. 2.

26. G.H. Gallup, "The 16th Annual Gallup Poll of the Public's Attitudes Towards the Public Schools," *Phi Delta Kappan* 66, 1 (Sept. 1984): 23–38.

27. G.E. Flower, *Speaking Out: The 1984 CEA Poll of Canadian Opinion on Education* (Toronto: CEA, 1984); *Toronto Star*, 14 Jan. 1985, p. 2. More extensive inventories of Canadian opinion surveys on educational issues may be found in D.W. Livingstone, D.J. Hart, and L. McLean, *Public Attitudes Toward Education in Ontario, 1982* (Toronto: OISE press, 1983); and D.W. Livingstone, D.J. Hart, and L.E. Davie, *Public Attitudes Toward Education in Ontario, 1984* (Toronto: OISE Press, 1985).

28. E.g., A.S. Hughes, *Public Attitudes Toward Post-secondary Education in the Maritime Provinces* (Halifax: Atlantic Institute of Education, 1979); Opinion Research Index, *Public Attitudes Towards Alberta Universities* (Calgary: Opinion Research Index, 1981); Sorecom, *Les Québécois face aux universités et aux universitaires du Québec?* (Montreal: CREPUQ/FAPUQ, 1982); Group Attitudes Corportion, *American Attitudes Toward Higher Education* (New York: Hill and Knowlton, 1982).

29. Livingstone, Hart, and Davie, *Public Attitudes Toward Education in Ontario, 1984*.

30. E.g., Provincial School Review Committee, *Let's Talk About Schools*, vol. 3, *Survey of the General Public and the Educational Professionals in British Columbia on the Provincial School System* (Victoria: Ministry of Education, 1985); M. Morissette, "Government cuts threaten B.C. universities, says public in faculty-sponsored poll," *CAUT Bulletin* 32, 7 (Nov. 1985), 1, 8.

31. D.W. Livingstone and D.J. Hart, *Public Attitudes Toward Education in Ontario, 1980*, (Toronto: OISE Press, 1981).

32. Livingstone, Hart, and McLean, *Public Attitudes Toward Education in Ontario, 1982*, 39-40.

33. Ibid., 39, 41.

34. Livingstone and Hart, *Public Attitudes Toward Education in Ontario, 1980*, 29.

35. E.g., Livingstone, Hart, and Davie, *Public Attitudes Toward Education in Ontario, 1984*, 30-40.

36. Livingstone and Hart, *Public Attitudes Toward Education in Ontario, 1980*, 30-31; cf. Group Attitudes Corportion, *American Attitudes Toward Higher Education*, 49-73.

37. For a provocative discussion of the historical origins and current character of this division, see especially A. Sohn-Rethel, *Intellectual and Manual Labour: A Critique of Epistemology* (London: Macmillan, 1978).

38. An explicit analysis of the class structure of paid work in relation to educational entry requirements may be found in Livingstone, "Job Skills and Schooling."

39. P. Meyer, "Caste, Class and Career Certification" in *Educating for Careers: Policy Issues in a Time of Change*, edited by T.F. Powers (University Park, Pa.: Pennsylvania State University Press, 1977), 92.

40. Livingstone, "Job Skills and Schooling."

41. P. Corrigan and D. Sayer, *The Great Arch: English State Formation as Cultural Revolution* (Oxford: Basil Blackwell, 1985); A. Epsing-Anderson et al., "Modes of Class Struggle and the Capitalist State," *Kapitalistate* 4-5 (Summer 1976), 186-220.

42. E.g., D. Wolfe, "The State and Economic Policy in Canada, 1968-1975" in *The Canadian State*, edited by L. Panitch (Toronto: University of Toronto Press, 1977), 251-88.

43. It should be noted here that, in contrast to the widespread assumption among employers and traditional economists of a simple negative relation between social transfer payments and economic growth, some recent detailed empirical research suggests a more complex *positive* relationship (R. Friedland and J. Sanders, "The Public Economy and Economic Growth in Western Market Economics," *American Sociological Review* 50, 4 (Aug. 1985): 421-37).

44. R. Piven and R. Cloward, *The New Class War* (New York: Pantheon, 1982).

45. A. Smith, "Business Executive Views About the Future of Ontario Universities," (paper for the Commission for the Future Development of the Universities of Ontario, 1984).

46. W. Light, "Brain Power—Our Neglected Resource," *University Affairs* (June-July 1984): 23-24.

47. Piven and Cloward, *The New Class War*.

48. Ontario Federation of Labour, "Presentation to the Commission on the Future Development of the Universities of Ontario" (Toronto, 18 Sept. 1984).

49. D.W. Livingstone, *Social Crisis and Schooling* (Toronto: Garamond Press, 1985). For recent critical analyses of the use of community colleges to "cool out" the educational aspirations of working-class youths, see F. Pincus, "The False Promises of Community Colleges: Class Conflict and Vocational Education," *Harvard Educational Review* 50, 3 (1980): 332–61, and D. Robinson, "Community Colleges and the Division Between Mental and Manual Labour," *Alternate Routes* 5 (1982): 133–66.

50. M. Oppenheimer, *White Collar Politics* (New York: Monthly Review Press, 1985).

51. E.g., H.V. Shapiro, "Class, Ideology and the Basic Skills Movement," *Interchange* 14, 2 (1983): 14–24.

52. A more detailed analysis of the interplay of social classes, with attention to their levels of consciousness and organized agencies for influencing educational practices, appears in Livingstone, *Social Crisis and Schooling*.

53. Livingstone, ibid.

54. Livingstone, Hart, and Davie, *Public Attitudes Toward Education in Ontario, 1984*, 17.

55. Organization for Economic Development and Co-operation, *Social Expenditure 1960–1990: Problems of Growth and Control* (Paris: OECD, 1985).

56. Cf. J. O'Connor, *Accumulation Crisis* (New York: Basil Blackwell, 1984); and C. Offe, *Disorganized Capitalism* (Cambridge, Mass.: MIT Press, 1985).

57. E.g., A. Hunter, "The Ideology of the New Right," in *Crisis in the Public Sector*, edited by K. Fox et al. (New York: Monthly Review Press, 1982), 309–32; and Livingstone, *Social Crisis and Schooling*.

58. Livingstone, Hart, and Davie, *Public Attitudes Toward Education in Ontario, 1984*, 18.

59. E.g., P. Anisef and N. Okihiro, *Losers and Winners: The Pursuit of Equality and Social Justice in Higher Education* (Toronto: Butterworths, 1982).

60. C. Karier, *Shaping the American Educational State: 1900 to the Present* (New York: Free Press, 1975), 138.

61. For general discussions of resources and prospects for economic democracy see, for example: S. Bowles, D. Gordon, and T. Weisskopf, *Beyond the Wasteland: A Democratic Alternative to Economic Decline* (Garden City, N.Y.: Anchor Books, 1984); and M. Carnoy and D. Shearer, *Economic Democracy* (White Plains, N.Y.: M.E. Sharpe, 1980). On democratic educational alternatives see, for example: S. Castles and W. Wustenberg, *The Education of the Future* (London: Pluto Press, 1979); and D.W. Livingstone, *Class, Ideologies and Educational Futures* (London and Philadelphia: Falmer Press, 1983).

62. G. Rudé, *Ideology and Popular Protest* (New York: Pantheon, 1980).

COUNSELLING AND COUNSELLOR EDUCATION IN THE FUTURE

HARVEY ZINGLE AND LAWRENCE DICK

Only twenty years ago, horizons seemed limitless. Counsellors prepared their clients not for unemployment but for considerable vocational change; not for stress but for positive use of leisure time. Counsellors attempted to encourage their clients to develop their human awareness.

The difference between the realities of the mid-1960s and the 1980s is little short of amazing. And the future is exceptionally unpredictable.[1] To attempt to evaluate the forces, isolate the trends, and discern the influences that will have an impact on our counsellor education programs fifteen to twenty years hence seems impossible. Counselling psychologists are at a crucial juncture in the development of "counselling" as a vocation. Decisions made in the near future regarding entrance requirements, core curriculum, practicum demands, licensing, and many other issues will set the course of counselling for years to come. The counselling profession has reached a turning point, a time when, internally, counsellors are somewhat uneasy and when, externally, pressure is being applied on them to grow and change. In fact, in many areas of counselling, *survival* of the profession is now the issue.[2]

What, then, are the crucial forces that will affect the future of counsellor education? This paper will examine six major forces that we believe will have the greatest impact on the process of counselling and the education of counsellors in the future: the "baby boom," the "new woman," technological change (here represented by computer technology), political/social disenchantment, the economy, and the increased tempo of life.

These social forces are creatures that every institution—educational or judicial, medical or religious—must confront. These forces cannot be ignored, or they will sweep us away in a tidal wave of chaotic change. Our universities, our departments, our counsellor education programs must confront these forces, examine them, and plan how best to absorb their pressures. By focussing on the effects of various trends and influences on these forces, outcomes may be more easily foreseen and, as a result, we may better prepare for them. While counsellors cannot always choose whether they play an *active* or *reactive* role, they should strive for an active role in planning and influencing, and not simply responding to, social trends.

CHANGING ADULT EXPERIENCES

Initially, for many institutions, particularly the school, the "baby boom" was an enormous wave of energy. Many of the trends of the 1960s and early 1970s in counsellor training may be attributed to this new wave of humanity. First, there was a powerful resurgence of career counselling as this generation faced decisions about what careers and training to pursue. This generation wanted more from a job than just a living. Money and security had to be balanced with interest and satisfaction. The children of the late 1940s and early 1950s got used to material possessions and the "good life." They found the dose of cynical reality provided by such events as the Vietnam war very hard to swallow. Awareness and sensitivity were important to this age group. Counselling programs reflected these concerns. Training for sensitivity became popular. Students were out communing rather than sitting in lecture halls. The openness and lack of structure in counsellor education decried by many to this day arose from this mass of special students.

The human force of the baby boom will exert great influence in the next twenty years. The numbers alone demand attention.[3] Career-change counselling is on the increase. Counselling for unemployment may well become a legitimate task. More courses will be needed on the stages of aging. Mid-life crisis is already a reality in our clinics. We are beginning to see a movement towards an awareness of the necessity of counselling for retirement, old age, and death.[4] Counselling programs must prepare students to work with groups sharing these specific concerns.

The general trend towards focussing on the difficulties of the "baby boomers" is unlikely to change in the near future. Indeed, it may increase as the strings of the institutions become theirs to pull.[5]

CHANGING SEX ROLES

Another social force is the "new" woman.[6] Women have become more confident, more oriented to the public sphere. They recognize their difference from men and are pleased with it.[7] This recognition of difference will influence the trends towards treating women as a separate entity. Women's studies will continue to gain in importance. Women's difficulties, aspirations, and concerns must be recognized, and students, both male and female, must be prepared to face new social situations.

A considerable influence on the new woman was the development of the pill. Now, the generation that has grown up with this contraceptive technology has a fundamental issue, a biological force. For women aged thirty to thirty-five, the biological clock is running out. The next twenty years will see an increasing trend towards women combining careers and motherhood. The male's parental role will change. Shared responsibility for housework and child care will become the norm. With these trends, counsellors must be prepared for the difficulties and needs of family members in this new family unit. Changing sex roles will have an impact on counselling in at least three major ways. Counsellors will find themselves: counselling men and women to cope with new role relationships; counselling youth relative to role possibilities; and counselling children because of the changing structure in the home resulting from new sex roles.

TECHNOLOGICAL CHANGES

We have chosen to focus on one major technological change—"the chip"—that must be reckoned with by all educators and, in particular, counsellor educators. We must prepare the practitioner to recognize the dangers and strengths of the new technology.

What trends exist in the field presently? Programs such as "Choices" are clearly established.[8] The influence of both government and private enterprise and the ability of computers to store information will fuel an explosion of vocational assistance through computers.[9] We will see interest analysis, aptitude testing, and ability measuring become computer-based fields. The client can sit in the family living room and work through a program of "job search," "job change," or "career decision."

Another trend in computer development that may rise to primacy is the Plato DCS—Dilemma Counselling System.[10] This computer program, now being tested on a number of campuses in the United States, leads clients through the labyrinth of psychological problem-solving. Obviously this trend is relatively new, yet the influences for its development are strong. The computer industry is healthy and growing, even in hard times, and Canada is a leader in program software production.

Counsellors must be prepared for changes stemming from the intrusion of computer technology into counselling. Do we want counsellors to be programmers or to be "people workers"?

> It is always a little humbling to hear yet another report of what machines can do better than man. Not just the repetitive assembly line job—they learned those years ago—but many of the functions of professionals: accounting, teaching, editing.... A recent Science Council of Canada report warns that Canada must keep producing more sophisticated machines. If other countries get too far ahead, many sectors of Canada's manufacturing industry could be rendered obsolete, leading to permanent unemployment for many Canadians, a decline in living standards and, for some, emigration.... Man cannot help but feel humbled by machines—so long as he judges himself and others primarily by performance criteria, by efficiency and productivity. But man is more than that.... "The world is in many ways a technological wasteland today, not because sciences and technology or the scientific method are bad, but *because they can tell us nothing about values or the meaning of life, or what it really is to be human.*"[11]

The implications for counsellor educators clearly lie in: preparing people to deal with technology (the retraining already mentioned earlier); the issue of values clarification; emphasizing the human element in the counsellor-client relationship; and learning to harness the technology (e.g., programs such as "Choices") in order to create time for counsellors to do what they do best: help people with their relationship skills.

DISENCHANTMENT

A mood of disenchantment appears to have developed over recent years. Governments are seen as incompetent. Big business is depicted as evil. The judicial system is unfair. The public is finding little security in major social institutions. Counsellors must offer some hope of security. Seeking help is becoming increasingly accepted. Self-help books are big sellers, and we have numerous "pop," yet credible, self-help psychologists. The counselling profession's biggest offering in the future may be assisting a rather disenchanted population in finding personal security within themselves and in their relations with other people rather than through external objects that can never really satiate the individual.[12]

Disenchantment has also created a move away from liberalism; there is clearly a political swing to the right. More significant, perhaps, for counsellor educators is the move towards a more traditional morality. While the population will seek out the counsellor, there will also be a return to the church as a place of solace and security. Counselling programs will experience an even greater influx of the clergy seeking training in dealing with questions of morality and values. The church as a community force may reappear and serve as a resource for people with personal and interpersonal difficulties. It may be easier for the faithful to discuss their difficulties with their clergy rather than with a stranger—a secular counsellor. This development will demand changes in the counselling curriculum. Values clarification and moral education will become necessary, rather than optional components.

THE SHRINKING DOLLAR

The problem of the shrinking dollar will not go away. However, increased demand for qualified counsellors will ensure money for their training. It must be kept in mind, though, that there will be fewer dollars to pay for counselling services—accountability will be foremost. Counsellors should be aware that, even if the public is moving towards acceptance of the profession, both this acceptance and funding will soon stop if disenchantment sets it.

While hard times will create more problems, and thus more people will be seeking counselling services, clients will be more selective and discerning.

People will know what they want and will expect results. This will force training centres to become more accountable for the product they produce. Over the next few years, if counsellor education institutions hope to survive, they will have to re-evaluate the kinds of people entering programs, the skills to be taught, and the practice given. As the public demands more, the practitioner will have to increase in competency. It is worth noting that the American Association of State Psychology Boards has recently contracted with Educational Testing Service to conduct a job analysis of licensed psychologists in the United States and Canada. The results obtained from such an analysis will subsequently be used in setting specifications for future licensing examinations. It becomes apparent that, if we make proper decisions, better counsellors with more training will be sought as more counsellors are needed: there will be an increasing demand on our counsellor education departments to educate more and more counsellors.

Given a troubled economy, how will clients pay for counselling services? Third-party billing will be standard practice fifteen years from now. We will know that counselling psychology has really arrived when employees are bargaining counselling plans into their collective agreements.

INCREASING LIFE TEMPO

Counsellor educators must get away from the idea that counsellors are mainly *therapists*. Rather, counsellors must be prepared to be teachers who instruct their clients how to live healthy lives.[13] Counsellors must espouse the philosophy of holistic treatment; they must focus on mind, body, and spirit, the *whole person*. Only by doing so, can they attack the problem of increasing life tempo not only from the reactive side (i.e., helping people to cope with life's stress) but also do something about slowing down the pace at which people live. Counsellors must teach people how to change their lifestyles.[14]

CONCLUSION

It is possible to isolate a few other general trends with implications for counsellor education. The new belief on the part of the public that counsellors have something to offer will, of necessity, create more specialization within counselling programs. The "jack-of-all-trades" approach to counsellor education will change. The practitioner will need to focus on specific areas to ensure competency. Research strategies will become more sophisticated and will offer support and direction to the field while appraising its success.

As the demand for credibility increases, the need for professional renewal programs will be ever-increasing. Thus, the future will see not only the expansion and specialization of university programs aimed at counsellor training, but the expansion of programs for the professional counsellor as well. As we have witnessed over the last two decades, trends and forces can change quickly and can have a major impact on society and the individual. Continuing education and professional renewal programs are crucial if counsellors are to keep abreast of these changes and the best methods for combatting the problems associated with them.

NOTES

1. H.G. Shane and R.A. Weaver, "Educational Developments Anticipating the 21st Century and the Future of Clinical Supervision," *Journal of Research and Development in Education* (1976): 990–98; A. Toffler, *Future Shock* (New York: Bantam, 1970).
2. J.F. Sunbury and J.R. Cochran, "Counsellor Education: If It Isn't Fresh, We're Out of Business," *Counsellor Education and Supervision* (1980): 132–38.
3. R. Mosher, "On Beating Dead Horses" in *The Present and Future of Counselling Psychology*, edited by J.M. Whitely and B.R. Fretz (Monterey, Calif.: Brooks/Cole Publishing, 1980).
4. T.J. Sweeney, "Trends That Will Influence Counsellor Preparation in the 1980s," *Counsellor Education and Supervision* (1979): 181–89.
5. M. Ferguson, *The Aquarian Conspiracy: Personal and Social Transformations in the 1980s* (Los Angeles: J.P. Tarcher, 1980).
6. A.S. Priutt, "Preparation of Student Development Specialists During the 1980s," *Counsellor Education and Supervision* (1979): 191–98; J.P. Leblanc, "Student Guidance and the Work Market of the 1980s," *Cognica* XIV, 3 (1982): 1–4.
7. C.G. Wrenn, "Observations on What Counselling Psychologists Will Be Doing During the Next 20 Years" in *The Present and Future of Counselling Psychology*.
8. B. Sloan and H. France, "Choices in B.C.: A Field Report," *Cognica* XIV, 3 (1982): 5–6.
9. Canada Employment and Immigration Commission, "L'Évolution du marché du travail dans les années 1980s" (Ottawa, July 1981).
10. M. Wagman, "Plato DCS: An Interactive Computer System for Personal Counselling," *Journal of Counselling Psychology* 21, 1 (1980): 16–30.
11. "Outperformed," *The Edmonton Journal*, 30 May 1982.
12. M.E. Hahn, "Counselling Psychology–2000 A.D." in *The Present and Future of Counselling Psychology*.
13. A.E. Ivy, "Counselling 2000: Time to Take Charge!" ibid.
14. C. Thoresen, "Reflections on Chronic Health, Self-Control and Human Ethology," ibid.

THE OWL, THE ROSE, AND THE BIG BANG: CURRICULUM OPTIONS FOR THE TWENTY-FIRST CENTURY

DAVID PRATT

MEANING AND CURRICULUM

There is an Eastern story of a certain Seeker after Truth. As a young man, he abandoned his wealthy family in Baghdad and left the city to wander wild and barren places in search of enlightenment. After some years of travel, he heard of a Holy Man who had helped many pilgrims in their quest. This Holy Man lived deep in the desert of An Nafūd, and could be reached only by the most determined. The Seeker after Truth, after many days of heat and thirst, reached the cave where the Holy Man lived. He poured out the story of his years of poverty and hardship in search of enlightenment. The Holy Man listened patiently and then said, "Walk five days toward the rising sun. You will come to a village. At the crossroads you will find what you are seeking." And the Holy Man retired to his cave. The Seeker after Truth followed the instructions, and coming on the fifth day to a small village at the edge of the desert, he eagerly made his way to the crossroads. But nothing was to be seen there but three small, mean shops. One sold wood of every kind. One sold wire of various strengths and calibre. And the third sold ivory in all shapes and sizes. The Seeker after Truth was overcome with anger and disappointment that he had been sent on this meaningless mission. He left the village and continued his solitary wanderings. It was many years later, when he was an old man, that he was resting one evening at an oasis in the Wadi Araba, when the sound came to him of the most beautiful and enchanting music he had ever heard. As he listened, it seemed that the music reconciled and resolved the meanings he had been seeking, harmonizing them in a way that could not be expressed in words. He rose and moved through the dusk toward the music, and found the musician sitting under a date palm. And in a moment of immense enlightenment, he saw that he was playing a sitar constructed of wood, and of wires, and of pieces of ivory.

The world of the curriculum planner is a world of meanings. I take it as axiomatic that the primary responsibility of the curriculum worker is to assist teachers and students with the recognition, construction, and integration of different kinds of meaning. In discussing curriculum options for the twenty-first century, I shall organize my remarks about three broad classes of meaning: public meaning, interpersonal meaning, and personal meaning. In the first of these domains, that of public meaning, Canadian schools discharge their responsibilities relatively effectively. Recent breakthroughs in instructional science give us the capability of working even more effectively in this area. That has been the great achievement of educational research in the last two decades. But it has not been matched by advances in the personal and interpersonal domains, which are being largely ignored by educators. I shall argue that this imbalance rests on a deficient concept of what it is to be a human being, and that this deficiency renders our schools increasingly anachronistic as we approach the twenty-first century.

THE OWL

PUBLIC MEANING

It has become a truism that the post-industrial society is an information society, a society in which information, its acquisition and use, are the primary routes to wealth and power. Conversely, those who lack information or the ability to acquire and use it will face in the next century lives of increasing poverty and powerlessness. I would like first to look at the challenges that confront us in this area, the area of knowledge and technical competence, which I refer to as the domain of public meaning. This domain embraces those areas of human experience that can be communicated and understood by people in common ways. "3 + 3 = 6," for example, means much the same to everybody; so does "Paris is the capital of France"; and so do most basic skills, whether of reading or using a typewriter. It is a characteristic of public meanings that they can be readily expressed in words or numbers. The conventional academic disciplines lie within this area of meaning, and it is the function of the disciplines to express areas of human experience in terms of public meanings. Such knowledge and skills are relatively straightforward to teach, to learn, and to evaluate, and schools traditionally spend most of their time and energy on such learnings.

A REVOLUTION IN INSTRUCTIONAL THEORY

In this area, the domain of basic knowledge and skills, a quantum leap has been made over the past ten or fifteen years. Twenty years ago, the curriculum field, by then about fifty years old, had virtually nothing to say to school practitioners that merited their attention. Faced with their failure to discover manipulable determinants of school achievement, many educational theorists sought comfort in sociological determinism. Aided by simplistic interpretations of such studies as the Coleman Report,[1] and by vaguely articulated notions of class, educators concluded that school achievement was fixed at birth by family background and social-economic status. Like many other myths in education, this one has taken a long time dying. As Enrico Fermi pointed out, the only way you can overcome opposition to a new idea is to wait for the opponents to die out.

The fact is that we are now aware of many variables that are under the control of the school and that can affect school achievement much more decisively than does social class. Indeed, a strong relationship between children's social class and success in school could now be taken as prima facie evidence of a malfunctioning school system.

The first major breakthrough was made with Benjamin Bloom's concept of mastery learning.[2] Bloom hypothesized that almost all students could learn most conventional learning very well if provided with certain conditions. In some ways, this was not a novel perception. Take driving a car—that requires a very high level of skills of observation, reaction, co-ordination, computation, and compensation. Yet almost everyone who attempts to learn to drive succeeds, and succeeds in doing so very well. This makes one suspect that when we say that certain students cannot learn well, we are commenting not on lack of student aptitude but on our own failure to find appropriate strategies of motivation and instruction. The conditions that Bloom identified as necessary for mastery learning included provision of cognitive prerequisites, high but realistic expectations, and rapid correction of error. Bloom's hypotheses were subsequently supported by thousands of experimental studies in almost all disciplines, age groups, and cultures.

No sooner had Bloom's concept of mastery learning taken hold than a second research theme—school and classroom effectiveness—began to yield results. Statewide testing in the United States made it possible to examine in detail and in naturalistic settings, while controlling for such factors as social class, those schools that were at the high and low extreme in terms of their production of student learning. As a consequence, researchers were able to identify the unique characteristics of effective and ineffective schools and classrooms. The characteristics that were typical of effective instructional settings included such factors as a positive, orderly atmosphere; a clear academic focus; high expectations; collegial planning of curriculum; active student involvement in learning; high student time-on-task; and appropriate difficulty of instruction.[3]

And then emerged a third type of research, meta-analysis, which triangulated and complemented the findings of mastery learning and school effectiveness. Meta-analysis is a statistical procedure that allows the integration of findings from many experiments into a single statistic representing the net effect of a particular treatment. In an integrative study using data from over 3000 experiments,[4] Walberg was able to show that such factors as socio-economic status, peer group influence, tracking, and class size had relatively little effect on achievement. Effects more than twice as great could be achieved by such practices as graded homework, peer tutoring, co-operative learning, and reinforcement. Many of these findings will not surprise practising teachers, but rather will reinforce their intuition. But some findings are more surprising. Research syntheses has shown clearly that acceleration—often frowned on by teachers and administrators—is highly effective in enhancing the achievement of faster learners.[5] It has also shown that retention in a grade—a practice that costs Canadian taxpayers several hundred million dollars a year—results in lowering the achievement and attitudes of most retained pupils significantly in the following year and for the rest of their school career.[6]

It is true that these findings have not yet penetrated very far into the schools, and that classroom learning in Canada today closely resembles that of twenty or even fifty years ago. But considerable progress is being made, often spearheaded by teachers' organizations rather than by faculties of education. One can be reasonably optimistic that research in instruction will gradually begin to inform instructional practice, with a consequent improvement in student learning.

MEANING AND BOREDOM

We are now in the happy position of knowing how to teach almost all students most of the things that teachers and parents have traditionally considered important. Does this mean that the curriculum issues for the next few decades amount to gradual implementation of research in cognitive learning? I think not. In fact, implementing the technology of instruction may actually distract us from the more significant and urgent agenda of curriculum planning. That agenda was proposed in 1860 by Herbert Spencer in his essay "What Knowledge Is of Most Worth?"[7] For evidence that we have not addressed that question, we need only to look so far as the surveys of Ontario students, conducted by Michael Fullan in the 1970s, which asked students to respond to the statement "Most of my classes are boring." Twenty-nine percent of elementary students and fifty percent of secondary students responded in the affirmative.[8] We are bored by what we find meaningless. And who would not find meaningless some of the knowledge taught in schools—the system of land tenure in New France; the solution of square roots by the formal method; the topography of Peru; the identification of predicate modifiers; the dates of birth and death of the major composers. This is a version of Trivial Pursuit. It is not the way to fill a mind; it is the way to fill a wastepaper basket.

I think we need a more creative approach to student boredom than to blame the victim. We are engaged in a dubious morality if we require students to commit their most precious resource, their time, to activities they find meaningless. In his recent memoir, Irving Layton writes that "people doing things to which they do not bring their whole selves—a job, a marriage, an affair, even a friendship—provides the real meaning of inauthenticity."[9] He is in good company. Pope John Paul II has written: "Non-fulfilment of a self in the performance of an act is a moral evil."

THE POLITICS OF CURRICULUM

Teaching and curriculum planning are intrinsically moral activities. One reason why our curriculum is out of step with our needs is that this moral activity has, in this country, become almost entirely a political activity. Not only are we not addressing the question of students' needs for the twenty-first century, we cannot properly address this question, given our present modes of curriculum decision-making in this country.

Curriculum change in Canada comes about largely by accretion, and through a process that is primarily political. Unfortunately, political solutions will not always solve non-political problems. (The citizens of Indiana learned this quite early when, in 1897, the General Assembly of Indiana passed a bill ruling that the value of pi was four. This ensured that all mathematical and engineering calculations in the state would be wrong.) But it is inevitable that, as new areas of intellectual activity develop, they build constituencies that press for their inclusion in the school curriculum. Those constituencies that use the political process most effectively will be most influential in affecting the curriculum. However, all areas currently represented in the school curriculum have constituencies of their own. They have teachers who have invested ego, time, energy, and training. This can be called "career justification bias." And they have graduates whose status or self-concept may rest in part on continuing recognition of the importance of their academic background—"initiation justification bias." Jurisdictions that choose to eliminate existing areas of the curriculum face a kind of wrath well known to newspapers that omit the horoscope or television networks that preempt the daily soap opera. Consequently, new curricula tend to be added, with existing curricula allowed to jostle for the diminishing proportion of student time and public resources. Eventually, established curricula will stage a comeback, as English has done recently in many provinces. One faculty of education in Ontario went even further in 1986, signalling its bold march into the future by reinstating Latin as a teaching option.

That this is a political process operating in a democracy does not make it a democratic process. Indeed, it can be seen as the reverse. Those who are close to educational decision-making in the provinces of Canada know how political, idiosyncratic, and often bizarre are the factors that influence curriculum decisions at the highest levels. But there are alternative models. Sweden and New Zealand have based major curriculum reforms on wide-ranging needs assessments and surveys of public opinion. The committees that draft curriculum documents in Canada are almost entirely composed of professional educators. Some of the committees working on curriculum for native students are an honourable exception to this rule. Usually, the clients of the schools, that is, students, parents, graduates, taxpayers, are treated as people whose opinions do not matter. Yet Gallup polls in Canada, as in the United States, show that the general public is interested in schools, concerned about the quality of schooling, supportive of educational efforts, and, at least when asked intelligent questions, manifestly sophisticated in its educational thinking.

WHAT IS SIGNIFICANT?

It is not my intention to abuse the Canadian educational system. On the basis of my experience in several English-speaking countries, I am convinced that we have in Canada the best educational system in the English-speaking world. So long as we compare ourselves with Britain and the United States (rather than Japan or the USSR), we can draw considerable comfort from the comparison. My purpose, however, is to talk about curriculum options for the twenty-first century, and, in this regard, I would say that Canadian schools are currently doing a commendable job of preparing their students for life in the 1960s—that is, for a world sufficiently rich and complacent that it can afford significant waste and inefficiency in its schooling. Student boredom is one symptom of this waste, resulting from a failure to determine and teach what is significant. And what *is* significant at this point in history, if not solving square roots by hand and learning about predicate modifiers?

It's the extinction of one animal species from the world every day that is significant. It's the destruction of eleven million hectares of forest each year. It's the native languages of Canada dying out at the rate of one a year. It's the ten thousand homeless families in Toronto. It's the one thousand girls in this country aged fifteen or younger who will have babies this year. It's the six thousand Canadians who will find existence so miserable or meaningless that they will take their own lives. It's the fact that, in the age of computer data banks, personal privacy has now ceased to exist. It's the fact that organized crime in North America is now virtually beyond the control of government. It's the routine use of torture in police stations, prisons, and military barracks in scores of countries around the world. It's the trade union official in El Salvador whose mutilated body is found by the roadside, her dead baby lying beside her with its fingernails torn out. It's the fact that half of the world's scientists are engaged in the development of weapons. It's the two billion dollars the world spends on armaments every day, which makes paupers of half the world and may make corpses of us all.

And then again, it's the vast outpouring of generosity toward the starving people of Ethiopia. It's the heroic work of organizations like OXFAM, Amnesty International, and CUSO. It's the retired clergyman in Ontario who said recently on his one hundredth birthday, "I feel as though I'd drunk fully from the cup of life, and all the sweetness is in the bottom of the cup." It's the flowering of the arts that we can see in many parts of Canada today. It's the moral stature of individuals like Mother Teresa, Alexander Solzhenitsyn, Jean Vanier, Martin Luther King, and Terry Fox.

TECHNICAL DEVELOPMENTS

If we are to develop a curriculum that is viable for students who will live most of their lives in the twenty-first century, then we must turn from tradition as a criterion of significance. Consider this question: What will be the significant events and discoveries of the next forty years? Pessimists tend to respond with such suggestions as world starvation or nuclear war. Optimists say world government or a cure for cancer. One of my more optimistic graduate students suggested that by the year 2000 a woman would be elected pope and Mrs. Thatcher would have defected to the Soviet Union. Some developments that might be anticipated over the next forty years are: controlled nuclear fusion; weather control; a science of parapsychological healing; organ and limb regeneration; successful brain transplants in humans; true artificial intelligence; and control of ageing.

The last of these is the most intriguing. Longevity cannot be much increased by control of disease, because the normal life span of the members of any species is determined genetically. Successive transplants of organs, including the brain, could extend life only in the same fashion as an Ottawa Valley woodsman proudly showing off his axe, who said to an acquaintance of mine, "I've had this axe since 1946; it's had two new heads and three new handles." The most interesting developments lie in the area of genetic engineering and recombinant DNA. Suppose the microbiologists discovered the exact structure of the molecules in the DNA that control ageing. They take this genetic material from a long-lived species such as a redwood fir tree, inject it into the nucleus of a newly fertilized human egg, and transplant the reconstructed egg into a human foster-mother. Nine months later, you are born human in all respects except for your life span, which is 700 years. (You might also be very tall.) Suppose this kind of development takes place thirty years from now. Scientists and technicians will not be the only people concerned. Legislators, lawyers, judges, editors, and clergy will also be involved. So will academics, for, as is well known, there is no crisis to which academics will not respond with a seminar. Most of these people are presently students in our schools. The understandings they will need are primarily philosophical and moral understandings, and now is the time for them to receive the necessary grounding. Valiant work is being done by values education and moral education specialists, but schools still pay little attention to a deliberate study of ethics, moral decision-making, logic, critical thinking, or other branches of philosophy. The consequences of such neglect are already apparent in the moral chaos that surrounds many recent medical advances. It is this chaos that has resulted in many valuable medical developments, such as chemotherapy, the respirator, and the venous drip, today being widely used not to save lives or alleviate suffering but to artifically prolong the dying process, and hence to add to the sum of pain and suffering in the world.

SIGNIFICANT LEARNINGS

It does not take enormous prescience to suggest some other areas that will become increasingly critical as we approach the year 2000. The major cause of death in Canada prior to the age of forty-five is traffic accidents. More than ninety percent of traffic accidents are caused by human error. Yet, in no Canadian province is driver education a credit subject in secondary school. A second major cause of death among the young is suicide. You will peruse Canadian curricula in vain for evidence that this tragic fact is taken seriously by educators. The most significant social role that the majority of our current students will play in the next century will be as parents. In the age of the single-parent family, many people are learning that parenting is a skill they will have to perform twice as well. We are a long way from recognizing parenting skills as core curriculum. Finally, take the most central, the most crucial task of the school, now and in the future—teaching people how to learn. Yet we do not even teach our students how to study, let alone how to learn. Some students will pick up such skills from parents or siblings. These students are mostly middle-class, and will be selected for advanced education. Working-class students, less likely to have parents able to provide models or advice on study skills, will tend to be discarded by the school. By deliberately withholding critical skills from their pupils (and ultimately we have to say it is deliberate), schools play into the hands of those Marxists who charge that the mission of the schools is to perpetuate class distinctions and class privileges.

Many teachers will immediately point out that they do indeed touch on some of the topics I have just mentioned. But, if there is one thing I am reasonably sure of after twenty years in the curriculum field, it is that "touching on" a subject is as good as useless. If we want to achieve something in education, we have to target it exactly, plan it systematically, and teach it wholeheartedly.

COGNITIVE REDUCTIONISM

In the area of information and technical competence, the domain of public meaning, we have a long way to go in this country in terms of developing a curriculum that is valuable (not relevant, or useful, but in the widest sense valuable), either in the present or the future. But there is a more basic reservation about a curriculum that concentrates exclusively on public meaning. The owl has for centuries been the symbol of wisdom. Its hunched posture and binocular eyes surrounded by radiating feathers gave it an air of studious and bemused intelligence. But is it owls that we want our schools to produce? Several years ago, the British philosopher Paul Hirst proposed that all areas of human experience were reducible to seven forms of knowledge, each consisting of a class of publicly testable propositions.[10] What was extraordinary was not Hirst's fantasy that an area like music could be reduced to publicly testable propositions, but the large following he achieved among curriculum specialists, particularly in Britain, where his seven forms of knowledge just happened to correspond to the academic organization of the British grammar schools. Hirst's philosophy can now be seen as a relic of logical positivism, purveyed to educators long after it had lost its credibility among most philosophers. I am not sure that this approach will even produce owls, in the sense that the owl is the symbol of wisdom, not merely of accumulated knowledge. There is more to wisdom than knowledge, and there is more to living than wisdom. The sole object of education is all too often construed as the mind—a mind conceptualized as distinct from the hand, the heart, the emotions, the will, the body, and the spirit.

It is some of these other areas of human experience I now want to explore. The domain of public meaning is important, indeed critical, for the future, but it is not sufficient. If people become happy by accumulating knowledge, then happiness could be purchased for the price of an encyclopedia. A central question educators must address is, what makes people happy?

THE ROSE

INTERPERSONAL MEANING

I suggest a simple answer: people make people happy. For most of us, our relationships with other people are the primary ingredient of our happiness and our unhappiness. "To be human," says Paulo Freire, "is to engage in relationships with others and with the world."[11] At this point, we enter the domain of interpersonal meaning. Unlike public meanings, which are accessible to everyone, interpersonal meanings are shared only among the parties to a relationship. A friendship, a family, a task force, a theatre company, a team, a community, are all replete with meanings that can be fully understood only by the participants.

ISOLATION

Such meanings cannot be taught like knowledge. But they can be facilitated. Schools can teach certain social skills and provide certain social experiences. Teachers in Canada generally take a commendable interest in the social experiences of their students. But not all children develop the capacity for rewarding human relationships. Some twenty percent remain isolates—these are the children you can spot in the schoolyard at recess who seem to ignore their peers and be ignored by them. Isolation is not a benign condition: it is probably the strongest single indication of future social and psychological problems. Almost all adult murderers, almost all adult sex offenders, were isolates as children. The vast majority of isolates grow up not criminal, but simply unhappy. Yet the condition is easily diagnosed, and can be considerably ameliorated by knowledgeable and skillful teachers. Essentially, we are talking about shyness, a condition that probably affects four million Canadians mildly, and four million severely. Philip Zimbardo describes shyness as the fastest-growing and most crippling social disease in North America.[12] Shy people fear social rejection, believe others are rejecting them, but constantly send out messages to others to keep away. Shy people are often intensely lonely, but are experts at rationalizing their loneliness, often in terms of "I don't need" kinds of statement. Many intelligent people are shy; the philosopher Immanuel Kant was such a person. It took him a long time before he finally plucked up courage to call on a lady to propose marriage, only to find that she had left the district twenty years before. Shyness is not unknown among teachers. Despite the social nature of teaching, teachers are often lonely people who lack deep relationships with their colleagues. Two questions might be asked of every teacher: whom do you nurture? And, who nurtures you? Many teachers who are themselves very nurturing of their pupils pay insufficient attention to their own needs for nurturance, affiliation, and friendship.

But how true is Francis Bacon's assertion of three hundred years ago: "It is a mere and miserable solitude to want true friends, without which the world is but a wilderness." A contemporary writer, Maurice Friedman, puts it this way: "Mutual confirmation is essential to becoming a self.... We do not exist as self-sufficient monads, ... we exist as persons who need to be confirmed in our uniqueness by persons essentially other than ourselves."[13] One recognizes here the influence of Martin Buber: "Spirit is not in the I, but between I and Thou."

Friends are not a luxury, but a necessity for human health. They are particularly necessary in times of stress, and, whatever the future holds, we can be sure it will bring its share of stress. Part of this stress is the burden of choice. There are no longer ready-made roles awaiting the young. Not in employment, and not in lifestyle. The life stages of the 1950s, viewed with the simplification of retrospect, appear to have consisted of two: childhood and marriage, separated by a short period of drive-in movies. People can now choose, with remarkably little social pressure, to live in nuclear or communal families, childbearing or childless marriage, heterosexual or monosexual unions, monogamous or polygamous relationships, and married or single lifestyles. These choices are themselves stressful, but additional stress is placed on relationships by the apparently long-term prospect of dwindling economic resources. As resources decline, competition intensifies; as competition increases, relationships deteriorate. The next century will be a hard time for those who cannot build supportive relationships.

CLASSROOM STRUCTURES

We need, therefore, to pay serious attention to the way in which our schools help students to construct interpersonal meanings. As a case study of our current approach to this issue, we might examine the seating pattern that prevails in most classrooms after about Grade 5. Many educators think of classroom layout as a relatively trivial and insignificant subject. I would maintain that it is neither trivial nor insignificant, but is highly revealing of teachers' beliefs about society and the world. In most classrooms you will find rows of desks all facing in the same direction, each isolated as far as possible from its neighbour. In such classrooms, what students learn best is the shape of the back of the head of the student sitting in front. The only legitimate social contact in such classrooms is that of the teacher with individual students, not a relationship of equality but of subordination. This social microcosm is a model of society of authority, fragmentation, isolation, focus, and task orientation—in a word, a masculine model. It does not reflect qualities of collaboration, diffusion, integration, process-orientation, and caring, which can be viewed as more feminine qualities. One of the obstacles faced by women seeking career advancement in education is that they work in institutions where not only are authority structures masculinized, but masculinization affects the very physical organization of space in the buildings where they work. In this model, in which people are objects rather than subjects and in which social interaction and co-operation are defined as disciplinary infractions, the model of society that we want to inculcate in the young?

I doubt very much that this mode of spatial organization reflects our own personal experience of learning. If we were to ask a random sample of adults to recall the three most significant learnings in their lives, I would predict that the great majority of these learnings would have been acquired in the context of some significant relationship. As it happens, we are now in a much stronger position than a decade ago to draw conclusions about the effects of different kinds of relationships in classrooms. This is largely because of the outstanding work on co-operative learning by such scholars as Robert Slavin at Princeton and Roger and David Johnson at the University of Minnesota. Their work is as important a breakthrough as mastery learning or meta-analysis. What it shows is that co-operative classroom structures have an enormously beneficial impact on learning. Syntheses of research show that introducing co-operative learning strategies improves student achievement by three-quarters of a standard deviation, the equivalent of raising the achievement of a student from the median to the seventy-fifth percentile. This increase in achievement is paralleled by increases in student attitudes towards learning, the teachers, the grading system, and one another. These results hold for all levels, subject areas, and types of learning task. Increases in achievement are supplemented by affective changes. Students who experience co-operative learning like the teachers more; regard the grading system as fairer; trust, communicate with, and share resources more with their peers; develop higher motivation and less fear of failure; become more divergent and risk-taking in their thinking; and are more inclined to believe that they are liked, supported, and accepted by other students.[14] To use only individualistic and competitive structures in the classroom can now be seen not only as socially dysfunctional but also as pedagogically unsound.

FUTURE NEEDS

In *Megatrends*, John Naisbitt claims that "we are shifting from a managerial society to an entrepreneurial society."[15] He points out that, in the United States, most of the new jobs created in the past decade have been in small businesses, the number of which is increasing exponentially. We might conclude from this that education for entrepreneurship should be considered core curriculum. But we do not need to conclude that this means fostering in schools competition and rugged individualism. The key qualities of the entrepreneur, in addition to creativity and drive, may well be the ability to co-operate, to listen, to trust, to delegate, to learn together, and to build small dynamic groups. Even for more conventional employment, social skills are at least as important as technical skills. The major reason for job termination, accounting for sixty-six percent of all firings, is a breakdown in human relations.[16] Attitudes and skills of co-operative work are probably the most relevant skills for employment, as for life itself.

We have to recognize that we are living through an age that militates against these principles. In some western countries, public callousness towards poor people and poor nations has not only become respectable, but an integral part of government policy. My own reading of history is that callousness, whether it appears in the form of conquest, persecution, colonialism, oppression, or patriarchy, rarely goes unpunished in the long run. Even in the short run the costs are high to the uncaring, as to the uncared-for. It is therefore reassuring to see indications of another kind of trend, represented by the publication of John Miller's recent book *The Compassionate Teacher*,[17] or by a new research-based method for selecting teachers in the mid-west of the United States entitled Project EMPATHY,[18] or by the emphasis on human relations and concern for humanity in the new Alberta social studies curriculum. We have another symbol to place beside the owl, and that is the rose. I have in mind the dictum of Baha'u'llah: "In the garden of your heart, plant but the rose of love."

THE BIG BANG

PERSONAL MEANING

The third kind of meaning, personal meaning, is the most difficult to describe, because personal meanings can be fully understood only by the individual who experiences them. They are not propositional, but essentially intuitive, what Polanyi calls "tacit knowing."[19] Our reaction to a work of art is to a great extent personal and incommunicable. As Kenneth Clark puts it, "It is extremely rare for anyone who is capable of the intense and dreamlike joy, which we call aesthetic emotion, to do more than utter cries of satisfaction." Our self-concept, our tastes, our physical being, our gender identity, cannot be fully understood by any other person. Most irreducibly subjective of all areas is the spiritual, the means by which we "transcend the limitations and conflicts of lived experience."[20] Such areas cannot be fully captured or communicated by words. As the Taoist saying has it, "The Way that can be spoken of is not the eternal Way." Despite this difficulty, some of the personal areas to which future-oriented curriculum planners might pay attention can be mentioned briefly.

PHYSICAL INTEGRITY

The coming decades are going to be stressful for most of us. If there is one thing we can be sure people will need, it is good physical health. Schools do not currently appear to be addressing this issue adequately. As long as curriculum thinks of people as disembodied intellects, it cannot do justice to the need for physical integrity. People's health and their sense of physical well-being are of the utmost importance to them. They are particularly important to adolescents, many of whom do not feel good about their physical appearance.[21] But this is an area of personal meaning and, as such, does not fit readily within the prevailing cognitive model of curriculum. There is no school of curriculum thought that recognizes the legitimacy of somatic objectives—outcomes having to do with the physiological status of students.

What is the consequence of this? From numerous studies we know that Canadian children are at their healthiest and fittest the day before they enter school. They deteriorate on almost every aspect of health and fitness until the day they leave—in their flexibility, body/fat ratio, aerobic fitness, eyesight, hearing, teeth, posture, and nutrition.[22] And how could it be otherwise? Cramped into standard and ill-fitting furniture, our children are surrounded with a hot, dry, ion-depleted, and chemically polluted atmosphere. We provide them with junk food from coin machines and school cafeterias. A national study conducted in 1973 by the Department of Health and Welfare showed that the overwhelming majority of Canadian teenagers are suffering from severe malnutrition.[23] And we systematically deprive them of exercise and sunshine at an age when the young of every species most require them. Whenever I visit a kindergarteen, I almost invariably see a group of children sitting on the floor around a teacher, and the teacher will say something like, "I like the way Jennifer is sitting up so straight and still. Wouldn't it be nice if all the rest of us could sit as straight and still as Jennifer?" Unfortunately, I have doubts as to whether it is appropriate for a five- or six-year-old to be sitting indoors, straight and still, at all.

THE ARTS

I would like to think that, in the twenty-first century, people will be able to achieve fulfillment more from being and doing than from getting and having. One of the implications of this would be much greater attention to the arts. At present, across North America, music and the visual arts receive less than five percent of curriculum time in schools.[24] Surveys show that most parents and teachers consider this about right. The arts simply do not seem to fit the prevailing norms of public meaning. In some ways the situation is better in elementary than in secondary schools, because many elementary school teachers, despite considerable difficulty, attempt to integrate the arts into their daily work. I was recently in a school where the popular principal was about to leave, and, in one of the Grade 4 classes I visited, each student had produced some work of art to give him. One child had written this poem: "Roses are red/Violets are blue/You're the best principal/We ever had." Another had painted a picture of a man standing in a field. The caption said, "This is a picture of Mr. Pritchard milking his cows. The cows have all gone to the barn. I can't draw cows."

In secondary schools, even mainstream arts like literature appear to be experiencing heavy doses of instrumentalism. In many secondary curricula, literature has been downgraded to nothing more than a mode of communication, to be analysed, understood, and emulated in students' own writing. This seems to me almost entirely to miss the point. People do not read novels or see plays or watch movies or go to poetry readings in order to study or perfect their communication skills. They engage in these activities as ends, not as means, because these are aesthetic and vicarious experiences. Two or more people who have read the same novel share not so much a body of knowledge as a body of vicarious experiences. Here is a passage from Gabriel García Márquez's remarkable novel *One Hundred Years of Solitude*:

> When it was opened by the giant, the chest gave off a glacial exhalation. Inside there was only an enormous, transparent block with infinite internal needles in which the light of the sunset was broken up into colored stars. Disconcerted, knowing that the children were waiting for an immediate explanation, José Arcadio Buendia ventured a murmur:
> "It's the largest diamond in the world."
> "No," the gypsy countered. "It's ice."
> José Arcadio Buendia... put his hand on the ice and held it there for several minutes as his heart filled with fear and jubilation at the contact with mystery.... With his hand on the cake, as if giving testimony on the holy scriptures, he exclaimed:
> "This is the great invention of our time."[25]

What results from contact with works such as this is not a body of knowledge but vicarious experiences realized by an access of imagination. And this is a crucial difference between private and public meaning. Public meaning is essentially cognitive; personal meaning is essentially experiential.

EXPERIENCES

Several years ago, Benjamin Bloom conducted a study of one hundred college students. The question he asked them was to recall a "peak learning experience" that took place during their formal education: any classroom experience that was totally absorbing, interesting, stimulating, memorable. From the one million hours of schooling undergone by his sample of students, he obtained reports of a total of only sixty such experiences.[26]

Here I think is an illustration of the extent to which schooling has become instrumental. Curriculum, it is assumed, must be a means to an end, and cannot be an end in itself. We cannot take a class to see a live Shakespeare production as an aesthetic experience, unless on their return they write an essay or a test to prove some accretion of knowledge. It has come to the point illustrated in a *New Yorker* cartoon. Two kindergarten children are looking at a rabbit on the teacher's desk, and one says to the other, "Don't touch the rabbit, or Teacher will make you write a report on it." In other words, nothing in schools is to be done for fun. People must not do things for fun. There is no reference to fun in any of the provincial curriculum guidelines.

But this is a perverted philosophy. All philosophies of life ultimately come down to personal fulfillment, for oneself or for others, in this life or in some other existence. An instrumental education is at variance with every philosophy. It makes everything an instrument, including people. A cognitively-oriented curriculum makes people objects; experience-oriented education makes people subjects. When we look back on our lives, what we see is not increments of knowledge, but key experiences like milestones along our path. Our personal identity is not cognitive, but experiential and historical.

THE BIG BANG

We are the products of experiences going back to our birth. But, for the historically enlightened, events before our birth are also part of our consciousness, determining the conditions within which we live and act. The study of history will take us back a few centuries, a few millenia at most, a tiny slice of the human experience on earth. To go back before the invention of writing we must turn to the work that anthropologists have done in cultures resembling those in which our forebears lived for hundreds of thousands of years. The work of anthropologists helps us to understand our roots back for two million years, and then we must rely on the ethologists, whose studies of animal behaviour provide the closest clues to the lives of our ancestors in the pre-human era. This takes us back some twenty million years, at which point we have to turn to the palaeontologists, and then to the geologists. The geologists' writ runs back to the formation of the earth. Beyond that, we are in the realm of cosmology and physics.

It is at this point that I part company with those who claim that modern science has deprived people of the sense of wonder, because the more I learn of the origin of the universe, the more my sense of wonder increases. It is astonishing to consider that our sun is one of more than one hundred billion such stars in the Milky Way galaxy, which is one of tens of billions of similar galaxies in the universe. These galaxies are speeding outwards through space at an enormous speed: in the case of our solar system, at thirty kilometres per second. run the film backwards in time, and the galaxies recede toward a central point. All the matter we can perceive in the universe and in our world was present at that point in a different form. Every human cell comes from that original source: every atom in our bodies was once part of a star. We are, literally, star children. As we go back further in time, temperature increases, matter has not yet condensed into galaxies. Further back still, and it is too hot for the existence of the heavy elements; only the lighter gases can exist. Further back, and it is too hot for the existence of atoms; the density of the universe is enormous. And further back, back to the first billionth of a second after the Big Bang, and the universe had infinite density: the entire observable universe "was compressed within a sphere of radius equal to one thousandth of a centimetre, the size of the point of a needle."[27] And before that, there was no matter at all, nor was there space or time, there was only energy. We are all products of that primal energy. I do not claim to understand this. I do not know whether it is, in any ordinary sense, understandable. If we wish to stay in school curriculum with what is readily understandable, we will avoid this area. One can only echo Einstein: "The most beautiful thing we can experience is the mysterious. It is the source of all art and science."[28] School curricula have profited from the doctrine of learning for mastery. I would like to see educators begin to pay attention to learning for mystery.

CHOICES

If curricula in the western world have a common characteristic, it is their restricted character. Narrow perceptions of mind and of human existence have led to narrow prescriptions for education. These prescriptions in turn limit the choices of the next generation. Those graduates of our schools whose social and personal capacities are underdeveloped are deprived of choices in significant areas. As we approch the twenty-first century, such deprivation becomes more damaging, more impoverishing, and more dangerous. And what is education if not the process of widening people's freedom of choice in all areas of their lives? Marilyn Ferguson, author of *The Aquarian Conspiracy*[29] was once asked what was the major thing adults could do for the young. She replied, to set the example of living a happy and joyful life. The agenda that the future sets for present-day curriculum planners is to find the means to develop in learners the public, personal, and interpersonal capacities that will enable them freely to choose lives that are happy and joyful.

NOTES

1. J.S. Coleman, *Equality of Educational Opportunity* (Washington: U.S. Office of Education, 1966).
2. B.S. Bloom, "Learning for Mastery," *UCLA Evaluation Comment* 1, 2 (1968): 1–12.
3. D.E. Mackenzie, "Research for School Improvement: An Appraisal of Some Recent Trends," *Educational Researcher* 12, 4 (1983): 5–17.
4. H.J. Walberg, "Improving the Productivity of America's Schools," *Educational Leadership* 42 (May 1984): 19–30.
5. J.A. Kulik and C.-L. Kulik, "Effects of Accelerated Instruction on Students," *Review of Educational Research* 54 (1984): 409–25.
6. C.T. Holmes and K.M. Matthews, "The Effects of Nonpromotion on Elementary and Junior High School Pupils: A Meta-analysis," *Review of Educational Research*, 54 (1984): 225–36.
7. H. Spencer, *Essays on Education* (London: Dent, 1911).
8. M. Fullan, *The Meaning of Educational Change* (Toronto: OISE Press, 1981).
9. I. Layton, *Waiting for the Messiah: A Memoir* (Toronto: McClelland and Stewart, 1985), 256.
10. P. Hirst, *Knowledge and the Curriculum* (London: Routledge and Keegan Paul, 1974).
11. P. Freire, *Education: The Practice of Freedom* (London: Writers and Readers Publishing Cooperative, 1976), 3.
12. P. Zimbardo, *Shyness* (New York: Harcourt Brace Jovanovich, 1977).
13. M. Friedman, *The Healing Dialogue in Psychotherapy* (New York: Jason Aronson, 1985), 14.
14. D.W. Johnson, "Student-Student Interaction: The Neglected Variable in Education," *Educational Research* (1981).
15. J. Naisbitt, *Megatrends: Ten New Directions Transforming Our Lives* (New York: Warner Books, 1984), 165.
16. K. Frost, "Why 4000 People Were Fired," *Administrative Management* 35, 2 (1974): 54–55.
17. J. Miller, *The Compassionate Teacher: How to Learn and Teach With Your Whole Self* (Englewood Cliffs, N.J.: Prentice-Hall, 1981).
18. V.W. Thayer, "Project EMPATHY: An Alternative Way to Hire Teachers," *North-Central Association Quarterly* 54, 2 (1978): 438–42.
19. M. Polanyi, *The Tacit Dimension* (New York: Doubleday, 1966).
20. A. Webster, "The Educative Process" (unpublished manuscript, Massey University, Palmerston North, New Zealand, n.d.).
21. A.J.C. King, A. Robertson, and W.K. Warren, *Canada Health Attitudes and Behaviours Survey: 9, 12 and 15 years olds, 1984–1985*, Summary Report by Queen's University Social Program Evaluation Group (Ottawa: National Health and Welfare Canada, 1986).
22. D.A. Bailey, "Exercise, Fitness and Physical Education for the Growing Child," *Canadian Journal of Public Health* 64 (Sept./Oct. 1973): 421–30.
23. Nutrition Canada, *Nutrition: A National Priority* (Ottawa: Information

Canada, 1973).

24. E.W. Eisner, *The Art of Educational Evaluation: A Personal View* (London: The Palmer Press, 1984), 122.

25. G. García Márquez, *One Hundred Years of Solitude*, translated by G. Rabassa (New York: Harper and Row, 1970), 25–26.

26. B.S. Bloom, *All Our Children Learning* (New York: McGraw-Hill, 1981).

27. J. Silk, *The Big Bang: The Creation and Evolution of the Universe* (New York: Freeman, 1980), 104.

28. A. Einstein, *The World as I See It* (1934).

29. M. Ferguson, *The Aquarian Conspiracy: Personal and Social Transformation in the 1980s* (Los Angeles: Tarcher, 1980).

CONTRIBUTORS

Michael A. Awender, Ph.D., is a professor of education and the chair of the graduate program in educational administration at the University of Windsor. His research and writing focus on the politics of education and organizational and administrative theory.

Bruce Bain, Ph.D., is a professor in the Department of Educational Psychology and an adjunct professor in the Department of Secondary Education at the University of Alberta. His research and writing revolve around issues of cross-cultural psychology, ethnic and minority group studies, comparative education, second language studies, and immigrant and ethnic counselling.

Lawrence Manning Bezeau, Ph.D., is an associate professor in the Faculty of Education at the University of New Brunswick specializing in educational administration. His research and writing interests lie in the areas of school law, education finance and planning, research methodology, and computer applications to social sciences research.

Daniel R. Birch, Ph.D., is a professor of education and vice-president (academic) at the University of British Columbia. His research and writing focus on teacher education and on social studies and cross-cultural understanding.

Stephen Thomas Carey, Ph.D., is a professor of psychology and educational psychology at Faculté St. Jean of the University of Alberta. His research and writing centre on information processing, and the impact of Canada's two official languages on society in general and education in particular.

Raymond T. Chodzinski, Ph.D., is an associate professor in the Faculty of Education at Brock University. His research and writing centre on counsellor skills and training, the vocational aspects of guidance and counselling, multiculturalism, and teacher education.

David Close, Ph.D., is an associate professor in the Department of Political Science at Memorial University of Newfoundland. His research and writing focus on political education and socialization and on Latin American politics.

Joseph E. Couture, Ph.D., is a professor in the Department of Psychology at Athabasca University. Dr. Couture's interests focus on Native philosophy and psychology of education, Native identity development, Native ways of learning, the psychology of consciousness development, interaction-communication variables between Indian Elders and non-Indians, and the psychology of shamanism.

Jim Cummins, Ph.D., is an associate professor at the Ontario Institute for Studies in Education and also serves as the director of the National Heritage Language Resource Unit. His research and writing focus on bilingual education, special education, and microcomputers and literacy development.

Brian Kenneth Davis, Ph.D., is an educational consultant in Toronto. His research and writing interests include the funding of private schools, effective lecturing, microteaching, and the general development of teaching skills.

Ivan DeFaveri, Ph.D., is an associate professor in the Department of Educational Foundations at the University of Alberta. His research and writing centre on moral education, tolerance, multiculturalism, and Native education.

John D. Dennison, Ed.D., is a professor of higher education at the University of British Columbia. His research and writing focus on the role, structure, and function of higher education in Canada with particular emphasis on the community colleges.

Laurence M. Dick, B.Ed., Mr. Dick is a graduate student in the Department of Educational Psychology at the University of Alberta. In the past, he has been a teacher, a counsellor, and a school administrator.

Larry Eberlein, Ph.D., is a professor in the Department of Educational Psychology at the University of Alberta. His research and writing are concerned with the implications of law and ethics in the fields of education and psychology.

Murray Elliott, Ph.D., is an associate professor teaching philosophy of education in the Department of Social and Educational Studies at the University of British Columbia. He is also the associate dean (teacher education). His research and writing interests centre on teacher education and moral and religious education.

Goldwin James Emerson, Ph.D., is an associate professor in the Department of Educational Policy Studies in the Faculty of Education at the University of Western Ontario. He is interested in the philosophy of pragmatism, John Dewey's concepts of education, student teachers' success in practice teaching, equality in education, censorship in schools, competition in schools, indoctrination versus education, and the creation versus evolution issue.

George William Fitzsimmons, Ph.D., is a professor in the Department of Educational Psychology at the University of Alberta. His research and writing interests are in career guidance, biofeedback, test development, standardization, and publication, and computerized scoring and reporting of test data.

Frederick Frank French, Ph.D., is an associate professor and the coordinator of the graduate program in school psychology at Mount Saint Vincent University. His research and writing focus on cognitive processing in children and adolescents, cognitive instructional models for use in schools, special educational administrative policies in Canada, and career development models as a part of the academic, personal/social, and career needs of youth.

John Friesen, Ph.D., is a professor in the Department of Counselling Psychology at the University of British Columbia. His research and writing focus on the family and the socialization of children, the interface between the school and family, career development, parenting, marriage preparation, and marriage and family therapy.

Robert Stephen Gall, Ph.D., is a professor in educational psychology at the University of Lethbridge. He is also an associate of the National Institute on Mental Retardation and co-ordinator of communications with the Alberta Education Response Centre Project. His interests are in rural special education, microcomputer applications to special education, microcomputer telecommunications in special education, and in right/equity issues in special needs education.

Michael Stephen Goodstadt, Ph.D., is the head of the Education Research Program of the Ontario Addiction Research Foundation. His research and writing are concerned with drug education, health promotion, epidemiology of drug use, attitude and behaviour influence, communications, and research methodologies.

William J. Hague, Ph.D., is a professor in the Department of Educational Psychology at the University of Alberta. His research and writing interests are in the psychology of religious and moral development and in counselling psychology.

Allan W. Hayduk, Ph.D., is the co-ordinator of psychology at Athabasca University. Dr. Hayduk's research and writing interests include conditioning in the human autonomic nervous system, techniques of stress management, affect control, anger management, teleconferencing, TV-based education, interactive TV, continuing education, and the application of several of the above to police settings.

Edward Stephen Herold, Ph.D., is a professor in family studies at the University of Guelph. His research and writing interests focus on the sexual and contraceptive behaviour of Canadian youth.

Edward H. Humphreys, Ed.D., is a Professor in the Department of Educational Administration at the Ontario Institute for Studies in Education. His major research and writing interest is in the use of student information in the management of individual student programs, schools, and school systems.

Steve Hunka, Ph.D., is a professor of educational psychology and the coordinator of the Division of Educational Research Services at the University of Alberta. His research and writing interests focus on computer applications for instruction, statistics, and research design, and the development of a CAI authoring system that will not require the author to use a programming language.

Janet Johnston, M.Ed., Janet Johnston is currently a Ph.D. student in the Department of Educational Psychology at the University of Alberta. Her research and writing focus on differences between learning disabled and average achievers in terms of learning and cognitive styles, on learning disabilities and reading comprehension, and on revising and expanding cognitive curricula for early intervention programs.

Nick Kach, Ed.D., is a professor in the Department of Educational Foundations at the University of Alberta. His interests focus on multiculturalism, the history of education and minority groups in Western Canada, prejudice and discrimination in Western Canada, the history of Catholic education, education and social policy, and Native education.

Gerard Martin Kysela, Ph.D., is a professor in the Department of Educational Psychology at the University of Alberta. Dr. Kysela's research and writing interests are in early intervention with families and younger children who exhibit exceptional conditions or handicaps, in policy development in the field of educating exceptional children, in early childhood intervention, and in transitional experiences for youth and young adults from secondary school to vocational life situations.

Hilary Margaret Lips, Ph.D., is associate professor in the Department of Psychology at the University of Winnipeg. Her research and writing interests focus on women in math and science, gender roles and power, and the psychology of pregnancy and early parenthood.

D.W. Livingstone, Ph.D., is a professor of sociology at the Ontario Institute for Studies in Education. His research and writing interests are in comparative political economy and education, ideologies and class consciousness, and alternative educational and social futures.

Romulo F. Magsino, Ph.D., is a professor in the Department of Educational Foundations at Memorial University of Newfoundland. Dr. Magsino's research and writing interests lie in the areas of multicultural education, the rights of students, parents, teachers and school boards, moral education, and teacher education.

Kofi Marfo, Ph.D., is an assistant professor in the Department of Educational Psychology at Memorial University of Newfoundland. His research and writing interests focus on cognitive education and learning strategies instruction, parent-child interaction processes, early intervention with mentally handicapped children, and special education and rehabilitation in developing countries.

Harry Marissen, M.Ed., is a secondary school teacher in Belleville, Ontario. His research and writing focus on multiculturalism.

Stewart J.H. McCann, Ph.D., is an assistant professor in the Department of Psychology at the University College of Cape Breton. His research and writing interests are in the interactions of student characteristics and teaching strategies; the effects of social, political, and economic threats on various aspects of society and education; individual differences and academic achievement; and worry, anxiety, sleep, and frightening dreams.

Erwin Miklos, Ph.D., is a professor in the Department of Educational Administration at the University of Alberta. His research and writing interests include preparation programs for educational administrators, conceptual bases of the study of educational administration, administrative and organizational theory in education, and teacher education.

John J. Mitchell, Ph.D., is a professor in the Department of Educational Psychology at the University of Alberta. His research and writing are in child psychology, adolescence, and the potential dangers of the nuclear arms race.

Robert F. Mulcahy, Ph.D., is a professor in the Department of Educational Psychology and director of the Cognitive Education Project at the University of Alberta. Dr. Mulcahy's research and writing interests focus on assessment and programming in cognitive strategies and cognitive style with exceptional children, and specific memory and reading comprehension strategies with the learning disabled.

A.S. Nease, M.A., is a professor of education at the University of Windsor. His research and writing interests are in comparative education (with a particular interest in the Soviet Union and the People's Republic of China), malpractice in education, and postsecondary administration.

Myrne Burdett Nevison, Ph.D., is a professor emeritus, and was previously the head, in the Department of Counselling Psychology at the University of British Columbia. Her research and writing interests centre on social issues and counselling.

Verner Richard Nyberg, Ed.D., is a professor in the Department of Educational Psychology at the University of Alberta. Dr. Nyberg's research and writing focus on the attitudes of students toward school subjects, achievement testing in the schools, and the evaluation of school programs.

G. Patrick O'Neill, Ph.D., is an associate professor in the Graduate Department of the College of Education at Brock University. His research and writing are in ethnic segregation, accountability, social mobility, gifted education, teacher education, teacher evaluation, textbook stereotypes, and postsecondary aspirations of high school seniors.

C. Paul Olson, M.A., is an associate professor in the Department of Sociology in Education at the Ontario Institute for Studies in Education. His research and writing interests are in the areas of inequality and social reproduction, the politics of bilingualism particularly in regard to the introduction of French immersion into the school system, and computer usage in the schools.

Robert S. Patterson, Ph.D., is the dean of education and a professor in the Department of Educational Foundations at the University of Alberta. His research and writing interests have been in the history of Canadian education in the twentieth century, the history of normal schools, progressive education in Canada, and teacher education.

Alan R. Pence, Ph.D., is an associate professor in the School of Child Care at the University of Victoria. He is interested in historical and ecological perspectives and research approaches to day care and working parents.

David Pratt, Ph.D., is a professor of education at Queen's University. He has also been a high school teacher in Ontario and in England. His research and writing interests are in curriculum planning, history teaching, selection and education of teachers, and technical and humanistic orientations to education.

Ronald G. Ragsdale, Ph.D., is an associate professor in the Department of Measurement, Evaluation, and Computer Applications at the Ontario Institute for Studies in Education. He is interested in the unstated assumptions of computer use and the side effects that result from computer applications.

Douglas William Ray, Ph.D., is a professor of educational policy studies in the Faculty of Education at the University of Western Ontario. His interests include human rights in education, multiculturalism, international understanding, international development, the development of human rights curriculum materials for elementary education, and international curriculum development projects.

Laurence Ernest Sackney, Ph.D., is a professor in the Department of Educational Administration at the University of Saskatchewan. His research and writing interests focus on teacher training and effectiveness, school improvement, system and school evaluation, and administrator development.

Ronald James Samuda, Ph.D., is a professor in the psychology and philosophy area in the Faculty of Education at Queen's University. His research and writing focus on the assessment and placement of ethnic minorities, occupational and educational aspirations of Canadian immigrants, issues in the streaming of culturally diverse students, multiculturalism and its implementation in teacher education, and methods and programs for teaching in a multicultural society.

Bernard J. Shapiro, Ed.D., is the director of the Ontario Institute for Studies in Education and deputy minister of education for the province of Ontario. Dr. Shapiro's research and writing focus on administration in higher education, the funding of private schools, the future of educational technology, teacher education, the future of Canadian universities, curriculum evaluation, credentialism in higher education, and educational finance.

David Charles Smith, Ph.D., is the dean of the Faculty of Education at McGill University. His research and writing interests centre on the teaching of history and the social sciences, peace education, and educational change and innovation.

Leonard L. Stewin, Ph.D., is a professor in the Department of Educational Psychology at the University of Alberta. His research and writing interests focus on the developmental aspects of concept formation information processing and its applications in learning, and the social psychology of the classroom.

Edmund V. Sullivan, Ph.D., is joint professor of applied psychology and history and philosophy in education at the Ontario Institute for Studies in Education. His research and writing focus on various religious and educational topics and issues.

Betty Mason Swindlehurst, Ph.D., is a psychologist in private practice in Edmonton consulting to a children's institution and psychiatric service. Dr. Swindlehurst's research and writing focus on child abuse and neglect, self-concept, children's rights, counsellor effectiveness, and legal issues involving children and parents.

Charles Samuel Ungerleider, Ed.D., is an associate professor in the Department of Social and Educational Studies at the University of British Columbia. His research and writing interests include the impact of family, schooling, and television on the socialization of children and youth, race relations and multicultural education, and teacher education.

Donald C. Wilson, Ph.D., is an associate professor in the Department of Social and Educational Studies at the University of British Columbia. His research and writing interests focus on the teaching of Canadian issues and curriculum development on Canadian public issues, transportation and communications, and the teaching of Canadian studies in American schools.

John Rowland Young, M.Ed., is an associate professor in the Department of Educational Foundations and the Department of Sociology at the University of Alberta. His interests are in social theory, multiculturalism, and the socio-historical analysis of Canadian education.

Agnes Yu, Ph.D., is the co-ordinator of the ESL Assessment Centre of the Edmonton Public School Board. Her research and writing are concerned with cross-cultural psychology, comparative education, second-language studies, immigrant and ethnic counselling, and ethnic and minority group studies.

Harvey W. Zingle, Ph.D., is a professor and the chair of the Department of Educational Psychology at the University of Alberta. His interests include self-concept and academic achievement of gifted students, counsellor effectiveness, the relationship between occupational stress and mental health, women's perceptions of social support relationships, interpersonal communication, marital adjustment and irrational ideas, research in counselling psychology, and developing understanding of self and others.

1 2 3 4 5   13 2050 91 90 89 88 87